The Bengal European Regiment

The Bengal European Regiment
An Elite Regiment of the Honourable East India Company 1756-1858

P. R. Innes

The Bengal European Regiment: an Elite Regiment of the Honourable East India Company 1756-1858
by P. R. Innes

Originally published in 1885 under the title
Royal Munster Fusiliers (101 and 104): The History of the Bengal European Regiment, Now the Royal Munster Fusiliers and How it Helped to Win India

Published by Leonaur Ltd

Text in this form copyright © 2007 Leonaur Ltd

ISBN: 978-1-84677-460-7 (hardcover)
ISBN: 978-1-84677-459-1 (softcover)

http://www.leonaur.com

Publisher's Note

The opinions expressed in this book are those of the author and are not necessarily those of the publisher.

Contents

Introduction	9
War Services of the Bengal European Regiment	11
The 'Black Hole'	15
War With the French	36
Plassey	53
The Northern Circars	71
Fighting the Dutch	92
Patna & Moghuls	104
Undwah Nálá	121
Massacre & Mutiny	144
The Battle of Buxar	166
Discontentment	183
Rohilla & Haidar Ali	207
The Second Maratha War	235
Gurkhas & Pindaries	265
Afghanistan	287
The First Sikh War	307
The Second Sikh War	333
The Second Burma War	361
The Indian Mutiny	377
Lucknow	416
Company to Crown	443
Appendices	453

Dedicated to

The Royal Munster Fusiliers

in glorious memory of their illustrious origin

The Bengal European Regiment

of whose honour, fame, and decorations
they are the inheritors and trusted guardians.

Introduction

I have placed on record the services of the Bengal European Regiment, in order that the inheritors of it's fame and trophies may for all time bear in grateful memory it's gallant exploits; which in so large a degree have conduced to the civilization, peace, and security of millions of Her Imperial Majesty's subjects.

The names of Clive, Warren Hastings, and Eyre Coote, are well known to history; those of Herbert Edwardes, Hodson, and Cavagnari, are household words; but there still remains a long list of heroes, both amongst the officers and rank-and-file, whose actions were as noble, and whose endurance was as great, though their valorous deeds have not been so prominently recorded. All their names it has been my endeavour to indelibly preserve.

In fulfilling this sacred trust, I owe my hearty thanks to all those who have afforded me their kindly aid; to the Secretary of State for India, who has courteously allowed me free access to the archives of his office; to Major John Henry Barnard, C.M.G., of the Royal Munster Fusiliers, who devoted much time and labour to research in the Adjutant-General's Office in Bengal; to my brother officers, who have furnished me with valuable information and details of personal experience, not otherwise obtainable: thus encouraging me to further and perpetuate this important record.

Lastly, I have been desirous to rescue from oblivion the glorious name of the Bengal European Regiment, the last remnant of which, in July, 1883, disappeared from the official army list.

P. R. Innes
Kensington
6th February, 1885

War Services of the Bengal European Regiment

1756
Capture of the Fort of Baj Baj
1757
Re-capture of Fort William, Calcutta
Capture of the Fort of Hugli
Battle of Chitpore
Capture of the Fort of Chandernagore from the French
Capture of the Fort of Kutwah
Battle of Plassey
1758
Battle of Condore (against the French)
Attack and capture of the French Camp
Occupation of Rajamundri
Capture of the French Position at Narsurpore
Storm and capture of the French Fortress of Musulipatam
1759
Relief of Patna
Defeat of the Dutch at Chandernagore
Battle of Bederra against the Dutch
1760
Defence of Patna
Battle of Seerpore
Defeat of the Emperor of Delhi at Belkoss
Relief of Patna
Battle of Beerpore

1761

Battle against Shah Alám and the French at Suan

1763

Battle of Manjee
Battle of Kutwah
Battle of Geriah
Capture of the fortified Position at Suti
Storm and capture of Undwah Nálá
Capture of Monghyr
Siege and capture of Patna

1764

Defence of Patna
Battle of Buxar
Assault of the Fort of Chunar
Storm of the Nawab Vazir's camp near Benares

1765

Capture of the Fortress of Allahabad
Capture of the Fort of Chunar
Action at Karrah
Battle of Kalpi

1774

Battle of Kutra

1781

Battle of Patuta
Capture of the Fort of Bidgeghur
Capture of the Fort of Karrungalli
Relief of Wandiwash
Assault of Chilambram
Battle of Porto Novo against Haidar Ali and the French
Second Relief of Wandiwash
Capture of the Fort of Tripassore
Battle of Pollilore
Battle of Sholinghur
Battle of Veracundalore
Relief of Vellore

1782

Battle of Arnee

1783
Siege of Cuddalore against the French
1794
Battle of Bœtura in Rohilcund
1804
Capture of the Fortress of Gwalior
Battle of Deig
Storm and capture of the Fortress of Deig
1804
Four assaults on the Fortress of Bhurtpore
1808
Expedition to the island of Macao
1810-1817
Operations in Java
1814
Nepal War
1817
Pindarie War
1826
Storm and capture of the Fortress of Bhurtpore
1838
Campaign in Afghanistan
1839
Storm and capture of Ghuznee
1840
Capture of the Fort of Pushoot
1845
Battle of Ferozshuhur
1846
Storm and capture of Sobraon
1848
Campaign in the Punjaub
Battle of Chillianwallah

1849
Battle of Goozerat

1852
Capture of Pegu
Relief of Pegu

1857
Battle of Budli-ka-Serai
Assault of the Eed Gar Serai
Battle of Subzi Mundi
Battle of Nujjufghur
Storm and capture of Delhi
Battle of Narnoul
Affair at Gungehri
Action at Puttiallee
Occupation of Mynpoorie

1858
Siege and capture of Lucknow
Action at Baree
Action at Sahadit

CHAPTER 1

The 'Black Hole'

Before commencing to place on record the origin and services of the Bengal European Regiment, which was the parent of the Royal Munster Fusiliers, we propose to give a passing glance at the political causes which led to its formation; causes altogether so widely different from those which preceded the enrolment of other regiments of the line, that it will be necessary to consider the position of affairs in. Bengal for some time prior to the enrolment of the Regiment.

The 1st and 2nd Bengal European Regiments, which now constitute the 1st and 2nd Battalions of the Royal Munster Fusiliers, were, until 1858 (when the European portion of the Indian army was brought under the immediate control of the Horse Guards), the only two British infantry regiments of any considerable standing attached to the Bengal Presidency in the service of the East India Company. Some additional European regiments, both cavalry and infantry, were raised by the East India Company for service immediately before, or in consequence of, the sepahi mutiny in India, 1857-58; but they were scarcely more than in process of organization when they were merged into the Royal Army.

In the early days of the East India Company, the officers in their service were appointed by the Court of Directors; their only requirements being good health, courage, and common sense. The pay of the officers was little more than nominal, prize-money was plentiful; and those officers who were fortunate enough to render services to the native chiefs were handsomely, and sometimes profusely, rewarded. Cadets so appointed were not promoted to ensigncies until they had educated themselves for their profession of the army; and in many instances they served as private soldiers in what was called the

Cadets' Company;[1] or carried their muskets in the ranks, attended all drills, and took their guards in common with the privates of the Regiment. Leave to Europe was not in any case permitted. A cadet took service for his life; and if he found it necessary, on account of ill health, or from any other cause, to absent himself from the country, he was deprived of his commission. All the servants of the Company, whether civil or military, were permitted to carry on trade on their own account; which, with the advantages they possessed over the native traders, ensured very handsome profits. Recruits were acquired by means of press-gangs, who were paid a handsome commission on the number of men engaged. These press-gangs were employed by the East India Company under the authority of the Crown. Men were usually pressed into the service when in a state of intoxication; and they were frequently kidnapped, forcibly conveyed on board ship, and embarked before they were aware of their fate. On arrival in India escape was impossible; the soldiers were at the complete mercy of their masters, whoever they might be for the time being; they were frequently harshly and even cruelly treated; and in cases of insubordination the culprits were placed in irons and made to work with the native convicts on the roads.

In later years enlistment for the Indian army has been conducted in precisely the same manner as for the British service. The East India Company's principal recruiting depôt was established at Parkhurst,[2] and no soldier was enlisted in India unless he could prove that he was of purely European extraction.

The establishment of English trade in Bengal, under the sanction of the Emperor of Delhie, and the patronage of the Nawab of Bengal, was secured in 1656, just one hundred years prior to the formation of the Bengal European Regiment, now the Royal Munster Fusiliers, upon whose colours are emblazoned the names of the many hard-fought battles and sieges, which they have inherited from their time-honoured ancestor.

It was in the year 1644 that Dr. Boughton obtained the sanction of

---

1. The cadets' company, or the Select Picket as it was usually called, was composed entirely of gentlemen cadets waiting for their ensign's commission. The Select Picket occupied the post of honour in the field, and was always posted on the right of the advanced guard.—East India Military Calendar, vol. 1, p. 44-45.

2. Ultimately the East India Company sold their recruiting depôt at Parkhurst to the English Government, and built barracks for their recruits at Warley.

the Emperor of Delhie for the removal of the restrictions on British trade, so serious an obstacle to its pursuit that its discontinuance in Bengal, and the breaking up of the factories, were contemplated. The circumstances which led to the cancellation of these restrictions are thoroughly authenticated, and savour so strongly of Eastern romance that we may be pardoned for detailing them.

In the year 1644, one of the daughters of the Emperor Shah Jehan met with a serious accident—her dress catching fire, and before the flames could be extinguished, she had sustained such serious injuries that the native doctors pronounced the Princess incurable. Shah Jehan, who had lately heard of the great skill of the English doctors, wrote to the British governor of Surat, begging him to send one of his surgeons to effect a cure. Now, on board the East India Company's ship *Hopewell* there was a doctor, Gabriel Boughton, who consented to try his skill on the Imperial patient. Boughton proceeded under a royal escort to the Emperor's camp, then in the Deccan, where he soon succeeded in restoring the Princess to health. The Emperor, overcome with gratitude, informed the doctor that he was prepared to grant him any favour he might ask. Boughton, influenced more by anxiety to serve his masters than to enrich himself begged that he might be empowered to establish an English factory for the East India Company on the banks of the river Hugli, and that the English should be allowed to trade without payment of any duty. His requests were granted, and Boughton was supplied with a firman to the Viceroy of Bengal, instructing him to treat the bearer with all honour, and to convey to him, or his assigns, land on which he was to be permitted to erect an English factory, and trade without payment of duty. On his arrival at Rajmahal, where Sultan Sujah (the Emperor's son), then Viceroy, was residing, Boughton's medical skill again did him good service, by effecting a cure on one of the favourite ladies in the Viceregal zenana, whose malady had baffled the native physicians; so that the goodwill and patronage of the Viceroy were secured, in addition to that of the Emperor.

Thus it was that a few years after the events just narrated, trade was firmly established with Bengal; and in 1652 a small force, consisting of an ensign and thirty men, was allowed to be employed by the East India Company, as a guard of honour; "which little band," says Colonel Broome in his Rise and Progress of the Bengal Army "may be looked upon as the nucleus of the present extensive army retained by the Company in the Bengal Presidency."

Thirty-four years after British merchants had established themselves at the town of Hugli, a dispute arose between the Nawab's representative and Mr. Job Charnock, the Company's agent at their factory, who in consequence was driven for a time from the country; and on his return moved the factory to a village on the left bank of the river, thirty-seven miles nearer to the sea. This village was called Chatanati, adjoining which was a place called Kalikata, and on the site of these villages now stands the capital of India.

In the year 1700, the viceroy of Bengal effected a loan from the East India Company, to enable him to dispute the succession of the Emperor; and in exchange for this accommodation the township of Calcutta and the adjacent lands, together with privileges which they had not hitherto enjoyed, were granted to the Company.

In 1707 Calcutta was formed into a presidency town, subordinate to Madras. Trade increased, and comparative security prevailed, notwithstanding that the Princes of India showed jealousy at the growing influence of the British, and placed restrictions on their commerce. Nor were the native rulers their only enemies, for the French, the Portuguese, the Danes, the Dutch, each with its rival East India Company, had in its turn to be dealt with. But of all the foreigners the French alone held large possessions, and exercised important influence in Bengal at the Viceregal Court.

It would be foreign to our purpose to trace the petty wars, the successes, and the disappointments of the next fifty years; and it will be sufficient to state that, as our trade and influence increased, our establishments had to be augmented in proportion: so that in the year 1756 the military force in Bengal consisted of four companies of European infantry and one of artillery, as well as some hundreds of native soldiers. In addition to these regular forces, there were two companies of Militia at the presidency which were composed of European and Armenian inhabitants, and officered principally by members of the civil service.

In 1756, Siraju 'd daulah succeeded his uncle, Ali Vardi Khan, as Viceroy of the provinces of Bengal, Behar, and Orissa; and it was during his short reign that events occurred which led to the formation of the Bengal European Regiment. Siraju 'd daulah was a Prince eminently unsuited to the position of Viceroy. As a child he had been petted and spoilt; as a man, Mills, in his History of India, describes him as "voluptuous; on his own pains and pleasures he set a value immense, on the pains and pleasures of other men no value at all. He was impatient, irascible, and headstrong."

Some authors have affirmed that, before his death, Ali Vardi Khan warned his nephew to be on his guard against the encroachments of the English, whose powerful navy he feared and whose influence he could not resist.

No sooner had Siraju 'd daulah ascended the throne, than the idea of driving the British from his territories gained power over him; and, to give his actions the semblance of justice, he sent a dispatch to the Government of Calcutta, couched in offensive and threatening language. He called on the Governor (Mr. Drake) forthwith to desist from repairing his fortifications or constructing any defences for his position; adding, that his neglect of these commands would be held as a *casus belli*, and the consequences must be on his own head. It was in vain that the Governor urged that he was repairing his fortifications solely with the view of resisting possible attacks from the French—as war between that country and England was considered imminent—and that the French fortifications at the neighbouring settlement of Chandanagore were in perfect repair, whereas those of Calcutta had been long neglected and were falling into decay. The Nawab was not to be pacified. On receipt of the Governor's reply, he ordered his troops to prepare for a campaign; and in a few days he left his capital, Murshedabad, at the head of an army 50,000 strong, and advanced on the English settlement of Calcutta. On June 1st, 1756, he attacked the English factory of Kassimbazar, which was situated within a few miles of Murshedabad, and garrisoned by some 50 men only, the defences being; altogether inefficient. Mr. Watts was the chief at this factory, and he had constantly represented to the Government at Calcutta that it was untenable. But reinforcements had been refused, and the commander had been informed that, if he could not hold his position with the troops at his disposal, he had better effect a retreat as best he could.

When the Nawab arrived before the factory, he summoned Mr. Watts into his presence, receiving him with anything but courtesy, and compelling him to sign an agreement, under severe conditions, that the new works at Calcutta should be forthwith demolished, and the servants of the Company, on duty at Kassimbazar, be given up. The factory was plundered, and the officers subjected to such indignities that Lieutenant Elliot, of the Company's service, commanding the troops, shot himself to escape from the hands of his torturers.

On the 9th of June, the Nawab proceeded on his march to Calcutta. On reaching the Dutch settlement of Chinsurah and the French settlement of Chandernagore, he endeavoured to induce the troops at those places to join him in his expedition against the British. He failed, however, in his attempts; so he levied a war-tax on the Dutch of £50,000, and on the French of a like amount; both being paid, partly in cash, and partly in munitions of war.

When the news of the capture of Kassimbazar reached Calcutta, the Council, feeling their insecurity, became seriously alarmed, and dreading lest the Nawab should be incensed against them, they had abandoned the repairs of the fortifications. To add to the confusion, the council were at variance amongst themselves, some strongly urging the necessity of placing the fort in temporary repair, others recommending that they should throw themselves on the mercy of the Nawab—to whom a dispatch, couched in submissive terms, was sent.

The letters were dispatched, but they either did not reach their destination or were unheeded, and the onward march of the Nawab's troops was unchecked; indeed, such was his impatience that his soldiers were not allowed sufficient time for rest or food, so that many died on the road from exposure and fatigue.

The position of affairs at Calcutta, although requiring courage, tact, and judgement, was by no means so desperate as to give ground for despair. It is true that the means of defence were poor, the soldiers, especially the militia, being indifferently armed, and many of the guns unmounted; but on the other hand, there were some 500 Europeans in the garrison,[3] trustworthy, and believed to be courageous. The walls of the fort, constructed of masonry, were four feet thick, and easily defensible by a few determined men against the rabble of which the Nawab's army was composed. Moreover, the north-west face of the fort was in communication with the river, the passage to which was covered by the guns placed on the two flank bastions, so that, should the fort be found untenable, and the enemy effect an entry, the defenders could easily retreat by the water-gate and get to the ships—seven or eight of which were at anchor within a convenient distance.

Unfortunately, Captain Minchin, the Commandant, lacked all the requirements essential for a commander. He neglected to make the best of his position. His conduct was not only unsoldierlike, but cowardly. Had he employed his time in strengthening his position, in place of throwing out works which he had not men to defend; and had he concentrated his force instead of scattering it abroad, he might have kept the enemy at bay until the monsoon (daily expected) had set in;

---

3. There were in the garrison the following Regular European troops: infantry, 145; artillery, 45.—Military Calendar, vol. 2, p. 81.

when the enemy, exposed to the constant rains, would be forced either to retreat or come to terms. But Captain Minchin did not possess sound judgement; neither had he the confidence of the soldiers who were serving under him.

On the 15th of June Siraju 'd daulah's army crossed the Hugli, and took up its position beyond the Maratha Ditch, which constituted the defences of the outskirts of the town; and on the 18th of June our outposts were attacked. Many of these were bravely defended: but the losses were heavy, and it was found impossible to furnish reinforcements. Retreat was inevitable; the outworks, which had been hastily constructed, were deserted, and in some instances the guns, which had been abandoned without having been previously spiked, were turned upon the fort; whilst the enemy, taking up a position behind the newly-formed trenches which had been thrown across the park, kept up an incessant fire on the ramparts, doing much execution amongst the defenders.[4]

On the evening of this the first day's attack, it was determined to send the. women and children, for security, on board the Company's ship *Dodaly* at anchor close at hand. Messrs. Manningham and Frankland, members of the council, were deputed to superintend the arrangements; but these men, who should from their position have set a bold example of self-denial and courage, so utterly failed that, reaching the ship with their charge, they steadily refused to return to their posts. Worse than all, after consulting with Captain Young, who commanded the vessel, they weighed anchor and dropped down the river; thus cutting off the principal means of retreat from the garrison, many of whom were defending their position, now threatened on all sides.

Next morning it was found that many of the ships, following the example of the *Dodaly* had deserted during the night; so that there was but scanty accommodation for the remainder of the women and children who had not been sent on board ship the previous evening. It was, therefore, deemed necessary that their safety should be at once secured; but by this time a panic had taken possession of many in the garrison. Mr. Drake, the Governor, Captain-Commandant Minchin, Captain Grant, and a large portion of the Militia, as well as some of the Regular troops, deserted their posts and fled on board the remaining vessels; which, in their turn, weighed anchor, and left the defenders to their fate. The number of the troops in garrison was now reduced to under 200 men. A council of war was called; and Mr. Holwell, though

---

4. For plan of Calcutta in 1756. see pages 40/41.

not the senior, was appointed acting Governor, and entrusted with the supreme command. A redistribution of the force was ordered; and the breaches hastily repaired with bales of cloth and cotton. The personal courage displayed by the gallant band who had elected to remain in the garrison formed a noble contrast to the cowardice of the deserters. The enemy, emboldened by their success, and by the knowledge that the strength of the defenders had been reduced by desertion, attacked the weakest parts of the fort in overwhelming numbers; so that the defenders, as soon as they had succeeded in repulsing an attack, had to rush at the top of their speed to render succour to their weaker comrades on the other side of the fort. Thus hour by hour their number was reduced; whilst the ranks of the attacking-party were being constantly reinforced. Still this courageous little band fought on until mid-day, when, to their surprise and relief, the enemy's fire suddenly ceased; and soon afterwards an officer from his ranks advanced, waving a flag of truce. A parley ensued; but it soon became apparent that the flag was simply a ruse on the part of the enemy to enable him to approach the defences; for, taking advantage of the cessation of fire, he attempted to seize the Eastern gate. In the meantime Mr. Holwell had hoisted a white flag, but all to no avail; the enemy pressing on with unabated energy.

One hope of effecting an honourable retreat remained—the Company's ship *St. George*, Captain Hague, having some days previously been sent up the river to assist in the defence of one of the outposts, called Perrin's Point. A boat was sent off from the fort to Captain Hague, with instructions to drop down to the river-gate, where the defenders would embark. But alas! fate was against them! The *St. George*, through the mistake of a nervous pilot, stuck in the mud, and the last hope of escape vanished. Resistance was now hopeless; the enemy pressed on; and at 5 o'clock all was over. The fort was captured, and Siraju'd daulah entered with his troops. The defenders, many of them badly wounded, were bound with ropes and brought before the Nawab. Amongst the prisoners was one lady, Mrs. Carey, who, when her husband (a commander of one of the ships) refused to leave his post in the fort, elected to share his fate rather than accompany the deserters. The Nawab received the prisoners courteously, and ordered them to be unloosed. He at the same time promised Mr. Holwell, "on the word of a soldier" that no harm should befall them. The prisoners were then handed over to a guard of native officers, who marched them off to one of the verandahs of the barracks. By this time the buildings in the vicinity of the fort were in flames; and the sultry air and hot smoke were becoming unbearable. About 8 p.m. a party of sepahis under native officers arrived, and ordered the prisoners to move into some place of security. Little dreaming of their destination, they readily complied; but before they had time to resist they found themselves forced into a small room annexed to the barracks, and which was called the Black Hole. It had been used as a prison for the European soldiers, and intended to hold. a few men only. It was but eighteen feet square, and had only two small barred windows. Into this room the prisoners, 146 in number, many of whom were badly wounded, were forcibly thrust. The door, which opened inwards, was, after some difficulty, closed upon them, and securely fastened on the outside.

Then followed one of those scenes of horror which we would gladly shut from our memory. The harrowing details of this terrible torture are described by Mr. Holwell, who was one of the sufferers, in a letter dated 28th of February, 1757, addressed to his friend, Mr. William Davis, in which he enters into the minutest details. Parching thirst, delirium; then madness, death, and putrefaction, rapidly succeeding each other, so that when the door was forced open in the morning after that terrible Sunday night, 23 ghastly figures were all that remained alive. Amongst the survivors was that noble woman, Mrs. Carey; her husband having succumbed to the torture on the previous evening, she was left alone indeed.

"Amongst those that perished on that fatal night, June 20th, 1756, were nearly all the military, including Captains Clayton, Buchanan, Witherington; Lieutenants Bishop, Hays, Blagg, Simpson and Bellamy; Ensigns Piccard, Scott, Hastings and Wedderburn; with Ensigns Coales and Dumbleton of the Militia, and 74 of the Regular and Militia force. The only commissioned Officer who survived was ensign Walcot. Mr. Patrick Moran, who subsequently received a commission, and rose to be a Captain in the service, and 13 men of the regulars and militia, only remained alive."[5]

Mr. Holwell, and Messrs. Court, Walcot, and Burdet, were heavily ironed, and placed under the charge of a man named Mir Modin, by whom they were treated with the greatest severity. The other prisoners were released, excepting Mrs. Carey, "who was too young and handsome."[6]

---

5. Captain Arthur Broome, Rise and Progress of the Bengal Army, p.69.
6. Wheeler's Early Records of British India.

The deserters who fled from the Calcutta Fort with Captain Minchin found themselves exposed to many dangers during their passage down the river Hugli. In passing the Forts of Tanná and Baj Baj they were exposed to a heavy fire, and 3 of their ships were driven on shore.

It was not until the 26th June that the fugitives reached Fulta, a Dutch shipping port situated at the mouth of the river. This town was selected as a rallying point, as it was near at hand when relief should arrive from Madras; and it was improbable that the Nawab would pursue them thus far over a difficult country. Furthermore, in the event of danger, they could at any time weigh anchor and drop further down the river; or, if necessary, put out to sea.

The military portion of the party at Fulta consisted of 4 officers and 100 regulars, as well as about 50 militiamen, who had been merchants and tradesmen in Calcutta. The names of the officers of the regulars were Captains Minchin and Grant, Lieutenants Smith and Wedderburn.

Day by day this force was augmented by accessions from the outposts; Ensign Carstairs and 25 men arriving from Balasore; Ensign Muir and 20 men from Jugdeah; and Lieutenant Cudmore and 24 men from Dacca. Then ultimately there were the brave survivors from the Black Hole, Ensign Walcot and Mr. Moran with 13 men, so that in a few weeks the force numbered some 450 Europeans.

The news of the capture of Kassimbazar, the settlement which was subdued by Siraju 'd daulah on June 4th, reached Madras on July 15th, when it was resolved at once to make arrangements for sending reinforcements to Calcutta, for it was thought not unlikely that the Nawab, flushed by his paltry victory at Kassimbazar, might possibly attempt the reduction of Calcutta itself.

Major Kilpatrick, of the East India Company's service, was selected for the command of the proposed expedition. He was an officer of much and varied experience, having taken a prominent part in the. capture of Arcot, 1751, and subsequent campaigns. The force placed under Kilpatrick's command consisted of 230 men, "chiefly Europeans." The Court of Directors had sent instructions to Madras, some months previous, that reinforcements were to be sent to Bengal, and Major Kilpatrick had been nominated for this command, with a seat in the Council at Calcutta; so that arrangements had already been made for an expedition to Bengal.

The force sailed from Madras in the troopship *Delaware* on the 20th of July, and reached Fulta on the 2nd of August, 1756.

It is to be regretted that the names of the officers who accompanied this expedition are unknown; but Mr. Archibald Keir, Surgeon of the *Delaware*, appears to have served also in a military capacity, being afterwards appointed a Lieutenant, and ultimately obtaining his company in the Indian Service. When Kilpatrick reached Fulta he learned for the first time that Calcutta had been captured and partially destroyed. Though his force had been so considerably augmented by the refugees, he did not feel himself strong enough to attempt its recapture and therefore determined to await instructions from Madras before taking further action.

It was on the 5th of August that the news of the loss of the fort of Calcutta, the terrible story of the Black Hole tragedy, and the flight of the defenders, reached Madras. The council was hastily summoned, and, notwithstanding that war between England and France was considered imminent in Europe, and all available troops would probably be required in Madras, it was determined to dispatch what was then considered an overwhelming force, to join Kilpatrick at Fulta, and to recapture our lost possessions.

Mr. Robert Clive, who had been a Writer in the service of the East India Company, had subsequently so distinguished himself, both as a soldier and a politician, that he was selected for the command of the second expedition. Clive had just returned to Madras from England, where King George II. had been pleased to reward him for his military services with a commission as Lieutenant-Colonel; so that he was in every way suited for the command to which the Madras Council appointed him.

It was not until the 16th October, 1756, that the expedition left the Roads of Madras.

The Military force consisted of 250 men of H.M. 39th Regiment, under Captain Grant, with whom were Captains Eyre Coote and Weller; also Lieutenants Waggoner, Corneille, and Carnac; and Ensigns Yorke, Donnellan, and Broadbridge. There were also five companies (570 men) of the Madras European Regiment; but of these only three reached their destination; some of the transports being disabled during the voyage, and obliged to bear off towards Vizianagram. The three companies of the Madras European Regiment were severally commanded by Captains F. Gaupp, Pye, and Fraser; and amongst the officers attached were Lieutenants R. Campbell, T. Rumbold, and Adnet; Ensigns R. L. Knox, L. Maclean, and H. Oswald. In addition to the infantry, there were 80 European artillerymen, under Lieutenant Jennings, and also 1500 Madras sepahis, under command of their own officers—whose names are unknown.

The naval force consisted of five of the King's ships of war: the *Kent* (64), the *Cumberland* (70), the *Tiger* (60), the *Salisbury* (50), the *Bridgwater* (20), under Admiral Watson; and there were also five Company's ships employed as transports.

The expedition, after several mishaps, joined Kilpatrick's force at Fulta, in December, 1756—the last ship arriving on the 20th of that month.

Colonel Clive's arrival at Fulta was hailed by the troops and fugitives with unbounded joy. They had been anxiously looking for relief for six weary months; succour had come at last. Clive., who was looked on as the very symbol of power,[7] in whose tact, skill, and. courage, all had confidence, had arrived amongst them; to restore them to their homes, to lead them to victory, and to retrieve the shaken honour of England. Clive's first care, on assuming the command of the land forces, was to mould into shape the material at his disposal.

Kilpatrick's force, hastily raised in Madras for service in Bengal, had consisted of 230 Europeans; who had suffered so severely from malarious fever that one-half had died, and of the other half not more than 20 or 30 were fit for duty. Then there was the remnant of the Bengal military force, which had been strengthened by a company of volunteers, formed from amongst the civilians and respectable inhabitants who had escaped from Calcutta and the out-factories. In addition, several sailors, belonging to ships which had arrived and were unable to discharge their cargoes, had offered themselves for service, and joined the military on shore.

Under Clive's orders, all these detachments were collected together on the 16th of December, in a camp pitched to the eastward of the town of Fulta; and a few days afterwards were formed, under Major Kilpatrick's supervision, into one regiment, which was then called the Bengal European Battalion.

Although the nucleus of the Bengal European Battalion had existed, in some shape or another, for eighty years previous,[8] it was not until December, 1756, that the different companies and detachments were enrolled as a regiment, and placed under one commander.

It is to be regretted that, in the confusion resulting from the loss of the British capital, the disorganization of the council, and the impossibility of sending regular dispatches to the Court of Directors, the military records about this time are in a very unsatisfactory condi-

---

7. Clive was known under the name of Sabat Khan, or, Daring in War.
8. Government Gazette. No. 1010. October 30th, 1868.

tion. Orders appear to have been issued without proper records having been preserved; and, indeed, some important measures, entailing changes in the military and civil systems, appear to have been carried out without proper sanction having been obtained or even solicited.

It appears quite clear from Colonel Clive's Diary, dispatched officially to the Court of Directors in February, 1757, that the Bengal European Regiment was organized by him on or immediately prior to the 22nd December, 1756; for he notes that, on that date, the grenadiers and the artillery companies from the Salisbury and Bridgwater, in which vessels they had arrived from Madras, "joined the battalion, which was in the camp." The battalion referred to must have been the Bengal European Battalion which he had just formed; for there was no other battalion in the camp or indeed with his army.

As Major Kilpatrick was the senior Company's Officer, and as his detachment had been merged into the Bengal European Battalion, it is highly probable (notwithstanding that he had been nominated to a seat in council) that he was the first Commanding Officer of the Regiment; but certain it is that it was under his supervision that it was organized.

The following is a nominal roll of some of the officers who first served with the Regiment, their names having been collected from various sources and authorities.

Rank	Name	Remarks
Captain	Dugald Campbell	Joined the force from Bulramguri in the sloop Dragon
	Mills	Escaped from Calcutta and made his way to Fulta.
	Dickson	
	John Meadows	Ditto
Lieutenant	Cudmore	Brought his European detachment from Dacca.
	Smith	Escaped from Calcutta and made his way to Fulta.
	Wedderburn	Ditto ditto.
	Le Beaume	Was sent with despatches from Fulta to Madras asking assistance. He returned with Clive's force.
Ensign	Walcot	Survived the Black Hole disaster and ultimately escaped to Fulta.
	Carstairs	Brought his European detachment in from Baleshwar.

27

Ensign	Muir	Brought his European detachment in from Jugdeah.
	Moran	A civilian who survived the Black Hole disaster, and obtained an ensign's commission in the battalion.
	Douglas	
	Sommers	
	Carr	
Surgeon	Nathanial Wilson	In medical charge.

In addition to those recorded in the foregoing nominal roll, it is probable that the officers with Major Kilpatrick's detachment from Madras also joined the battalion; but their names are, unfortunately, not known.

Captains Minchin and Grant were under arrest for having deserted their posts during the defence of Calcutta. Minchin was dismissed the service; but Grant was pardoned; having pleaded in his defence "that he had urged Mr. Drake (the Governor) to return the same evening that they fled from the fort to succour those left behind, and that there was truth in this assertion may be inferred from the fact of his having been readmitted to the service."[9]

Colonel Clive had been entrusted with despatches from the Madras Government for the Nawab Siraju 'd daulah. These, together with covering letters from himself and Admiral Watson, "which were full of threats,"[10] were forwarded unsealed to the care of Manakchand, now Governor of Calcutta; but he declined to forward these dispatches; they being couched in terms which he feared would cause the Nawab's resentment to rebound on himself.

Manakchand had not lost sight of the importance of defending the approaches to his capital. He first turned his attention to repairing the walls of Fort William, partially destroyed when it had been captured by the Nawab in the previous June. He had also repaired and strengthened the walls of the fort of Tanná; and commenced a new fort as an outpost, which he called Alighur. He also caused two large ships, laden with bricks and other heavy materials, to be kept in readiness, so that they might be sunk in the channel of the river if the British ships should attempt it's ascent. But it was to the fort of Baj Baj, on the left bank of the river Hugh, between the fort of Tanná and the port of Fulta, that Manakchand had devoted his special attention. Outworks

---

9. Broome's Rise and Progress of the Bengal Army.
10. Mill's History of India, Book 4., Chapter 3.

were constructed commanding the approaches, the defences strengthened, and it was garrisoned by some of his best troops.

Obviously Baj Baj would be the first point of Clive's attack; and, indeed, on its capture depended the primary success of his expedition.

In consultation with Admiral Watson and Captain Eyre Coote—who now commanded the detachment of the 39th Foot,—it was arranged that the royal troops should act as Marines on board the ships of war; the Bengal European Battalion, the three companies of the Madras European Battalion, and the Madras sepahis, together with the European artillery and 2 field-pieces with ammunition, to form the army for service on land.

Soon after Clive's arrival at Fulta, he was prostrated by a severe illness; probably the same malarious fever which had nearly annihilated Kilpatrick's detachment. On the 23rd December he wrote an official letter to Major Kilpatrick, making over to him the charge of the preparations for an immediate advance on the fort of Baj Baj.

A Council of War was held on board the Admiral's ship, when a general plan of action and order of march were arranged. The land troops were ordered to disembark with the 2 field-pieces at a village called Moyapore, from which point they were to march across country towards the Calcutta road, to the north-east of the fort, where the troops were to lie in ambush. The ships of war were, at the same time, to move up the river and take up their positions close to the fort, on which they were to open fire from their heavy guns. It was anticipated that the defenders would soon evacuate, in which case the fugitives would attempt to escape by the Calcutta road, near which it was planned the British troops would be lying in wait, to pounce upon them. This general plan of action was sanctioned by the Council of War, at which were present Admiral Watson, Colonel Clive, Major Kilpatrick, and Captain Eyre Coote. Clive recorded his disapproval of much that was sanctioned; but was out-voted. He was in favour of landing the guns and troops nearer to Baj Baj than Moyapore, as he feared a tedious and uncertain march over an unknown country would be attended with unnecessary fatigue and danger. He says in his dispatch dated January 8th, 1757: "You must know our march from Moidapore to Budge Budge was much against my inclinations."

It was on the 27th of December, 1756; just seven days after the arrival of the last ship from Madras, that the force, as just detailed, sailed up the river Hugli from Fulta, and next day anchored at the village of Moyapore.

The troops selected for service on shore landed the same evening; but, before giving an account of their midnight march, we will follow Manakchand's army.

Anticipating an immediate attack on his fort at Baj Baj, Manakchand assembled his troops, about 2000 men, and marched to its support, occupying on arrival the ground where our army had intended to lie in ambush.

Manakchand, who had dispatched his spies to watch and report on the movements of the British, had received information of their landing at Moyapore; and, hour by hour, these spies, hovering round our advancing troops, brought him information of our movements.

28th December, 1756: Kilpatrick, in immediate command,—although Clive accompanied the land force,—found his difficulties commenced as soon as he had landed his troops. He had hoped to procure cattle to drag his guns and ammunition, but the villagers, warned by Manakchand's spies, and fearing the resentment of the Nawab, had driven off their cattle into the jungle. Then Kilpatrick found himself surrounded by swamps and water-courses, whilst there was no road, and the guides pressed into his service soon proved their inability or unwillingness to assist him. The first difficulty was overcome by the soldiers volunteering to drag the guns, the second by trusting to the sagacity of the leaders; and thus the British force commenced its march; and Admiral Watson moved his ships further up the river, taking up his position during the night in close proximity to the fort of Baj Baj.

The country between Moyapore and Baj Baj was found to be a vast swamp, intersected by numerous ravines; the hardships and fatigues of the march are described as having been "very great." The guides in whom reliance had been placed purposely led the troops astray; and it was not until after sixteen hours' hard marching that they halted on the Calcutta road, to the north-east of the fort.

From the position which the British troops occupied, the ships could be seen at anchor; but the fort was hidden from their view by clusters of trees. Near the road was a deserted village, on the western side of which there was a hollow, formed by a large pond or lake, now dry. Into this hollow the main force, including the Bengal European Battalion, descended; the two guns having been placed on the north side of the deserted village A detachment of 200 sepahis was now sent from this position to reconnoitre in the direction of the fort, and to open communication with the ships. The reconnoitring party was:

.... followed by Captain Pye at the head of the grenadier company and the rest of the sepoys, with orders to possess himself of the suburbs of the town, and send an immediate report when he had effected it; but not attempt anything further. Captain Pye, finding the pillah abandoned, marched down the riverside and put himself under the orders of Captain Coote, who was landed with the king's troops. They had just struck a flag on one of the advanced batteries.[11]

It must not be forgotten that Clive was at this time in total ignorance of the presence of Manakchand, who had been previously informed of the British movements, and was now waiting in ambush to surprise our troops. Overcome by fatigue after their weary march, the British soldiers piled their arms in the bed of the dry pond, and retired to snatch a few hours' sleep amongst the ruins of the deserted village; the ordinary precaution of planting sentries for the protection of the guns and arms being neglected.

Clive has been justly censured for this neglect; but Malcolm, as an apology for him, urges that "having landed in Bengal only seven days, and being ill, he must have depended upon others for intelligence, and he justly complains of the want of it. The nature of the country is, however, such as to offer to almost any number the power of concealing themselves." But surely it need scarcely be observed that if the nature of the ground was such as is here described, the neglecting to take the ordinary precautions to guard against a surprise was all the more culpable! At any rate, no valid excuse can be urged for the officers in command, who were guilty of neglecting one of the first principles of warfare when in presence of an enemy.

It must, however, in justice be remarked, that although the story of the sentries not having been planted is accepted by all historians as authentic, Clive, in his own Diary, does not refer in any way to the subject, although he gives a very detailed account of the siege.

29th December, 1756: Scarcely an hour had elapsed when Manakchand, taking advantage of our neglect, dispatched his infantry to seize the British guns and arms. The former were captured without a blow from our sleeping gunners, and, indeed, might have been turned against us, had their captors understood how to bring them into action; neglecting to spike the guns, and having no draft cattle, Manakchand's soldiers did not attempt to remove them.

---

11. Clive's Diary.

A sharp matchlock fire was now opened from the jungle surrounding the hollow, which woke up the troops, who, pell-mell, hurried to secure their arms. It was a critical moment, but Clive's generalship never shone so brilliantly as when his position was all but lost. Notwithstanding that the enemy's fire was severe and incessant, the British infantry succeeded in gaining possession of their arms. Clive was now in their midst, and speedily formed them into platoons, despatching one from the centre and one from the left, to drive back the enemy. It was a moment of breathless anxiety; had the enemy resolutely charged down the sloping banks the result must have been disastrous; but, fortunately, they contented themselves with firing from the under-wood behind which they were concealed. Our centre platoon lost 8, and the left 3 men before they readied the bank; when, immediately rushing upon the enemy, they forced him to retreat towards the village. In the meantime, the Volunteer company, which it will be remembered was attached to the Bengal European Regiment, joined by our artillery, recaptured the two guns; and the artillery, rapidly loading with grape, opened fire on the retreating foe.

The tide was now turning in favour of the British when the hostile cavalry were observed advancing in great force, headed by Manakchand on his elephant. Clive, having succeeded in driving back their infantry, pushed forward under cover of his two guns, and threatened to engage the cavalry, who, timidly halting, awaited orders. Our artillery were now rendering splendid service, doing good execution amongst both the enemy's cavalry and infantry. Just at this time a bullet striking Manakchand's turban caused him suddenly to order a retreat in the direction of Calcutta, leaving the British in possession of the field. "This skirmish," says Clive in his Diary:

> .... in all lasted about half-an-hour, in which time Ensign Keir[12] with 9 private men were killed, and 8 wounded. The enemy's loss was computed at 200 of inferior note killed and wounded, 4 jemadars killed and 1 elephant, besides about 40 who perished in the confusion of passing a creek in the precipitance of their flight.

29th December, 1756: Whilst our troops were engaged in repelling

---

12. There must be an error in Clive's Diary. Ensign Keir was not killed on this occasion, for he was present with the Regiment on 28th February, 1757. It is probable he was wounded only, or that the name has been mistaken for Ensign Carr, who was killed.

Manakchand's army, Admiral Watson, in the Kent had out-sailed the other ships, and anchored in close proximity to the fort, on which he poured shot and shell from his big guns. At noon he had succeeded in silencing the enemy's cannonade and had effected a considerable breach. The whole British force on now marched down to the advanced battery near the river, which the enemy had abandoned in the morning; our troops drawing up in front of the fort, under cover of a high bank. At sunset 250 sailors, with 2 9-pounders, were landed from the Kent these guns being mounted on the enemy's advanced battery but this was not accomplished without loss, for, during the operation, some of the 39th Regiment were wounded.

Our troops being now utterly exhausted a bivouac was ordered: sentries being planted and every precaution taken to guard against surprise.

At 7 the next morning orders were issued for the storming of the gateway, under cover of the 2 9-pounders which had been landed from the Kent on the previous evening. The storming party consisted of the detachment of the 39th Foot, the grenadier company of the Bengal European Battalion, 100 seamen, and 200 sepahis.

At 8 o'clock, just before the troops moved forward to attack, a sailor named Strahan, who with a few of his comrades had been drinking freely in anticipation of hard work, conceived the idea of seeing what was going on inside the fort. Clambering through the breach Strahan found the walls deserted, and, shouting to his companions, proclaimed with cheers that he had captured the fort. His companions quickly followed, but soon found themselves hotly engaged with the enemy's rearguard, who were smoking over the fire before joining their comrades, who, having received the news of the defeat and flight of Manakchand's army, had evacuated the fort during the night. More of our sailors soon followed, and after a short skirmish it was proved that the drunken sailor, Strahan, was right when he proclaimed that he had taken the fort. But this capture was not accomplished without a sad loss; Captain Dugald Campbell of the Bengal European Regiment being unfortunately killed by accident as he was posting sentries over a captured magazine.[13]

In the fort 22 pieces of cannon and 33 barrels of gunpowder were

---

13 The widow of this officer, who had escaped with her husband from Bulramguri to Fulta, married Mr. Warren Hastings (afterwards Governor-General of India), who was serving at the battle of Baj Baj as a Volunteer with the Bengal European Regiment. Mrs. Hastings died at Kassimbazar. near Murshedabad, where she was buried.—Gleig's Memories of Warren. Hastings. Vol. 1., p. 49.

found. After disabling the guns, the batteries were demolished and the buildings inside the fort destroyed. On the evening of December 30th, 1756, the troops re-embarked, the sepahis taking the route along the banks of the river, and the artillery following in boats.

Manakchand and his troops were much surprised at the reception they had met with at the hands of the British, for it was fresh in their memory how they had captured the fort at Calcutta in the previous June, and how the British governor and military commander had deserted their posts. Their estimation of the courage and endurance of the British was at its lowest ebb and, in short, they despised their enemy, and had quite expected that he would a second time have fallen an easy prey. How great, then, was their dismay to find themselves not only beaten off the field by a mere handful of these men whom they despised, but their fort of Baj Baj also easily captured, and the victorious army, full of confidence, nearing the capital itself.

31st December, 1756: Manakchand was thoroughly cowed, and his fears were shared by his whole army, which, halting a few hours at Calcutta, and leaving 500 men only to guard Fort William, marched with all haste to join the Nawab at Murshedabad, and inform him of their disasters.

At 10 a.m. on the 31st the fleet sighted the Tanná Fort where the Kingfisher which had arrived on the previous day, was anchored. It was proved afterwards that the enemy at Tanná were so surprised at the sudden appearance of the Kingfisher just as they were preparing to sink their laden vessels in the channel of the river, that they desisted, and the vessels were found lying snugly under the guns of the Tanná Fort.

As our fleet approached random shots were fired by the enemy, but at 2 p.m. their guns were silenced and they abandoned both the fort of Tanná and Alighur, which were immediately occupied by our sailors.

Clive in his Diary says, "We found here 56 pieces of cannon, chiefly large, some shot, and a small quantity of powder."

On January 2nd at 5 a.m. the Bengal European Regiment and 3 companies of the Madras European Regiment landed near Alyghur where they joined the sepahis, who had marched along the banks of the Hugli; the united force proceeding with 2 field-pieces towards Turnam's Gardens, where some strong batteries had been erected by the enemy to impede our approach to Calcutta. As soon as our troops reached the Gardens the enemy retreated, leaving his guns in our possession.

At 10 a.m. our ships had arrived abreast of Fort William, the-land troops being still en route; but Admiral Watson of necessity commenced operations, for some of the ships were caught in the eddy whilst taking up their respective positions for action, and before they could right themselves the guns of the fort opened fire pretty warmly.

The ships soon came to anchor, and throwing some shots at the ramparts, drove the enemy from their batteries, through the Eastern Gate, before the arrival of our land troops. The boats of the squadron then landed a detachment of the 39th Foot, who, joining some of the infantry on shore, quickly occupied the fort. A large number of guns were captured, as well as shot, shell, grenades, &c.

Thus Fort William, after having been in the enemy's possession for upwards of six months, was recaptured on January 2nd. 1757, and British power so far re-established in Bengal.

General References—Chapter 1

Stuart's History of Bengal.
Hamilton's New Account of the East Indies.
The Seir Mutakherin. Calcutta Ed.
Grose, Voyage to the. East Indies.
Holwell's India Tracts.
1st Report, Select Committee, House of Commons.
Mill's British India.
Founders of the Indian Empire. Malleson.
History of the Bengal Army. Broome.
William's Bengal Infantry.
Clive's Dispatches and Correspondence. Malcolm.
East India Military Calendar.
Ive's Voyage and Historical Narrative.
Life of Lord Clive. Caraccoli.
Wheeler's Early Records of British India.
Proceedings of the Council, Bengal Presidency.
Gleig's Memoirs of Warren Hastings.
Orme's Military Transactions in Bengal.
&c, &c.

CHAPTER 2

War With the French

2nd January, 1757: The British residents found that sad havoc had been created amongst their property, which had fallen into the hands of Siraju 'd daulah when Calcutta had been captured by him in June, 1756. However pleasing the prospect of a return may have January 2nd, been to the fugitives, their joy was considerably abated when they found their houses burnt, property destroyed, and that they had not the wherewithal to re-establish themselves in comfort; nor was the government in a position to materially assist them. But the British army had regained a firm footing in the country by the recapture of Calcutta, and it soon became apparent that Manakchand's force had in its flight created such a panic by its description of the courage and strength of the British that, to ensure complete success, an immediate advance was advisable. Reliable information having at this time been obtained that a portion of the treasure which Siraju 'd daulah had captured at Calcutta had been conveyed to the town and fort of Hugli, situated on the river about 33 miles above Calcutta, a small force, consisting of 150 Europeans and 200 sepahis, was organized under Major Kilpatrick to reduce the fort; a 20-gun ship, with three smaller vessels, being told off to accompany the expedition.

Manakchand's retreating army had produced such an effect on the garrison at Hugli that they made but slight resistance, the town and fort being captured on the 10th of January; but the treasure—£15,000—fell far short of British anticipations.

It was during this expedition that intelligence reached Clive that War in Europe had been declared between the French and English. This news materially affected the aspect of affairs in Bengal, both from a political and a military point of view; for between the towns of Hugli and Calcutta there was the French settlement of Chandernagore, garrisoned by 300 French soldiers and a train of European artillery, as well as a considerable force of French sepahis. Should the French amalgamate with the Nawab's army it was to be feared that the latter would recover their confidence, and the united forces become formidable.

10th-31st January, Clive, under these circumstances, determined to treat with the Nawab, who, he anticipated, would now be willing to listen to his overtures; but in the meantime the news had reached the Nawab that our troops had captured and plundered his fort and town of Hugli. Siraju 'd daulah's fury knew no bounds. He would listen to no overtures; he would punish these impudent adventurers, and utterly exterminate them. With this intention he assembled his whole army, consisting of 18,000 horse and 15,000 foot, and 40 guns, and ordered an immediate advance on Calcutta. Clive had lost no time in strengthening his position. Some of his Europeans had been absent with the expedition sent to reduce Hugli; but he had with him the greater portion of the Bengal European Regiment and the detachment of the Madras Europeans, as well as a considerable number of Madras sepahis; all of whom he employed in the construction of a fortified encampment, with several entrenched outposts. With only so small a force at his disposal Clive deemed it advisable to concentrate his troops outside Calcutta, instead of having to defend its extensive walls. The position of the entrenched camp, which was about a mile to the north-east of Calcutta and half-a-mile from the river, was well chosen. To the eastward of the city was the Salt-Water Lake, which in those days extended further inland than at present; this lake stretching towards the sea formed an impassable barrier to a hostile army, and rendered it difficult for the Nawab to advance on Calcutta, except in sight of Clive's entrenchments.

On the 3rd of February, 1757, Admiral Watson was dining with Colonel Clive in his newly-formed camp when, during dinner, they were startled by seeing the advanced guard of the Nawab's army marching at about half-a-mile's distance in the direction of Calcutta. Watson hastened to his ship to prepare for action, and Clive ordered out a strong detachment with 2 field-pieces, at once opening fire on the enemy, who, nothing daunted, replied from 10 heavy guns, some of them 32-pounders. Darkness setting in, Clive ordered his troops to retire to the entrenchments, a few men having been killed and wounded.

The British force had lately been somewhat strengthened by the arrival of the Company's transport *Marlborough*, which had left Madras with Clive's army: but, being a heavy sailer, had fallen behind the other ships which had arrived at Fulta in December.

In addition to troops the *Marlborough* brought some field artillery, ammunition, and stores, which were much needed.

The Nawab, who commanded his army in person, took up an extended position on the plain to the south-east of- the city, having crossed the River Hugli on the 30th January, about 10 miles above the Hugli Fort.

From the French at Chandernagore, and from the Dutch at Chinsurah, he had demanded military assistance; but troops being refused, a war-tax was levied of £45,000 on the Dutch and £40.000 on the French; the Dutch, under threats, paying the amount demanded; the French compromising for £35,000 in cash and 250 chests of gunpowder.

Clive determined to attack the Nawab's army early on the morning of 4th February, having at his disposal upwards of 650 European infantry, 100 European artillery with 14 field-pieces, and about 600 Madras sepahis; besides Watson's sailors, available in case of need.

In Clive's letter to the Directors of the East India Company, dated 22nd February, 1757, he explains his reasons for making an immediate attack. These are given in his own words.

> Para. 4. I determined to attack him before daybreak, while two-thirds of his army were still encamped without the Moratta ditch, for when they had once passed and got into the streets of the town it would be too late to attempt it. Another pressing reason for the immediate execution of the enterprise, notwithstanding the smallness of my force, was the sudden distress we found ourselves in upon the approach of the Nawab's army, by the general desertion of the workmen, coolies, and servants, the breaking up of our market, and no provisions to be had but what we supplied from the fort by water, in which condition we could not have continued long, but must have retreated into the fort with disgrace.

Clive's general plan of action was as follows: starting from his entrenchments before daybreak, he intended to make a bold dash, under cover of darkness, upon the enemy's artillery, which was nearly all massed in one large park towards the rear of their army. Having spiked all the guns, he intended to push on rapidly to Amichand's house, situated inside the outer defences of the city at the eastern corner, D. It was in Amichand's house that Siraju 'd daulah had taken up his quarters; if, then, Clive could manage to seize the Nawab and carry him off prisoner to the fort, he could dictate his own terms and end the war.

Admiral Watson, who was in constant communication with Clive, sent 600 sailors armed with firelocks to the British camp on the evening of the 3rd, and they arrived at 2 a.m. on the morning of the 4th. The troops were then drawn up ready to start, the European infantry being all massed into one column, with half of the sepahis in front and half in the rear. The artillery, with 6 field-pieces, followed, the guns being dragged by the sailors and the ammunition carried by lascars.

4th February, the Nawab's army was encamped without method or order. Mir J'afar Khan—who was to figure so prominently in the future—was one of the Nawab's principal Generals, and he had, with a small division of cavalry, crossed the Mahratta Ditch close to Amichand's garden, D, and was, therefore, encamped within the outer defences of the city. Near at hand, and within the garden enclosure, was a compact corps of Moghul Horse, lately engaged as a special body-guard for the protection of the Nawab. The remainder of the army, with their camp followers and cattle, were spread over the plain between the outer defences of the city and the marshes which skirted the Salt-Water Lake. The enemy's park of guns lay to the south of the main road, which runs due east to Dum Dum.

At 3 a.m. the British column moved from their ground, taking the direction of the enemy's park of guns, but unexpectedly they soon came upon the outposts of the Nawab's army, who, after having fired a volley and discharged some rockets, hastily decamped.

But here a mishap occurred, which, owing to the darkness, threw our column into confusion. A rocket ignited the cartouch-box of one of the sepahis, which, exploding, communicated the fire to several others. This threw the native division into complete disorder, with the advantage, however, of separating the men, who—the fire extinguished—were rallied by the grenadier company, and the march was resumed. But the enemy had heard the firing at their outpost and were on the alert; so that the capture of the park of guns by a coup-de-main was impracticable: moreover, the getting the sepahis together after the accident had occupied so much time that the day began to break and a thick impenetrable fog now rose from the marshes. The British column was by this time near Amichand's garden, D, which was a few yards only to our right. Suddenly the Nawab's body-guard was heard charging down on the British right flank, but by this time the fog prevented the possibility of seeing even a yard's distance. Clive halted, faced his men towards the advancing cavalry, waited until he judged in the obscurity that they should be within a few yards, when

Sketch plan of the City of Calcutta and its surroundings in the year 1756-1757, showing the march of Colonel Clive's Army through the enemy's (Siraj-ud-daulah's) Camp on the 4 February 1757.

BATTLE OF
Cbit

Enemy's Camp.

Enemy's Camp.

The Enemy's Park of Arty.

Enemy's Camp.

Enemy's camp.

Enemy's camp.

Route taken by Colonel Clive's Army through the enemy's camp

Village of
Chitpur

A. The Fort.
B. Perring's Redoubt.
C. Batteries.
D. Omichand's House and Garden
E. Tank and Park.

British
Intrenched
Camp.

RIVER

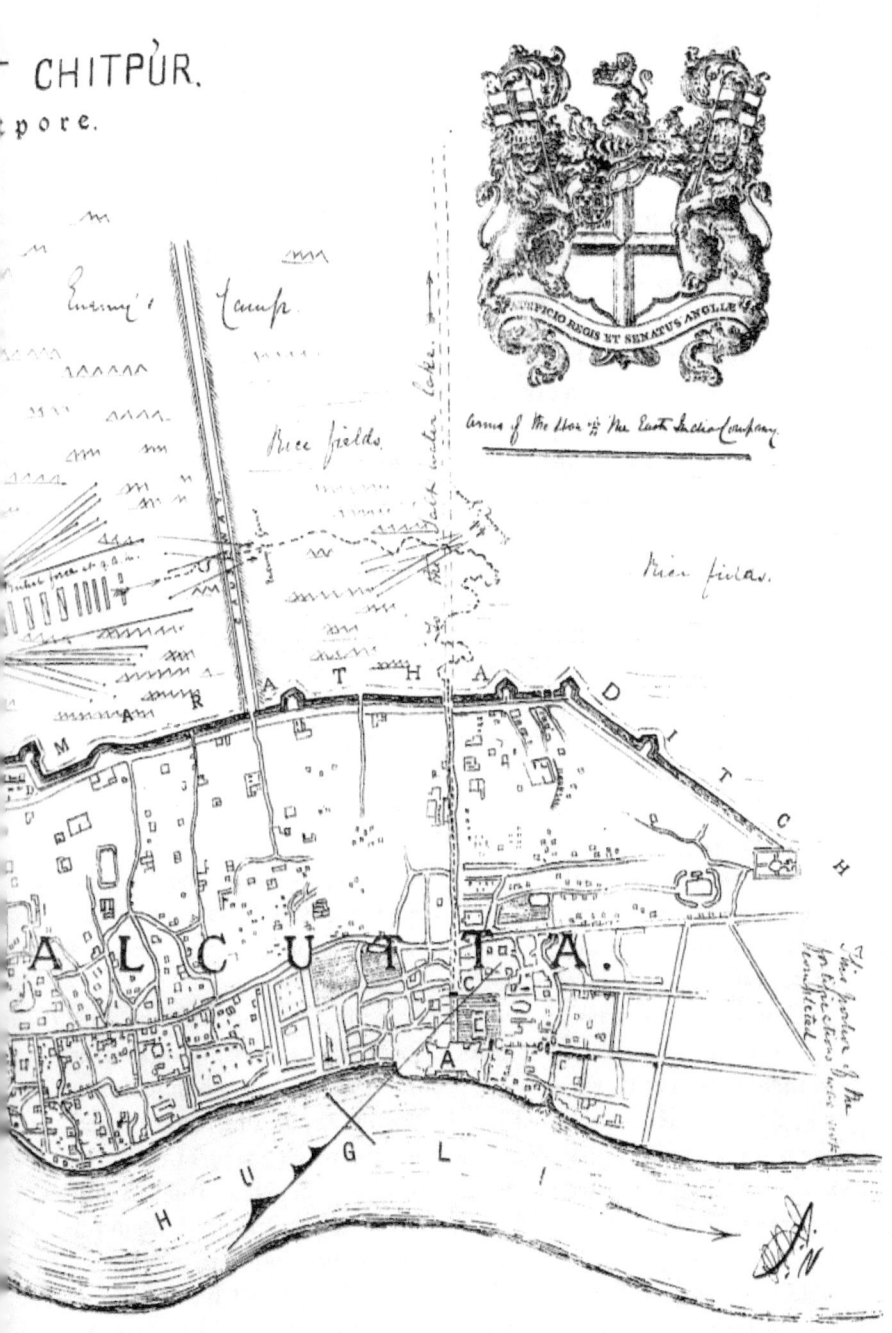

he fired a volley, creating havoc amongst them, emptying many of their saddles and sending them to the right-about.

4th February, the fog now grew thicker and thicker; the English column feeling its way, keeping up platoon firing right and left, and our light guns in the rear sustaining an oblique fire from each side of our advancing troops.

Clive felt that his position was one of great peril, but the thick fog told adversely on the enemy as well as on the British; for although the latter could not see in what direction they were moving, the former could not succeed in collecting their troops to oppose our onward march. Clive had missed the park of the enemy's artillery, and passed Amichand's garden without securing his prize; he was therefore obliged to change his plan of action. He now determined to march straight through the enemy's camp, knowing that by so doing his daring would overawe his foes; and further, he anticipated that by pushing forward he must reach the causeway dividing the Company's from the native territory, and would then be able to ascertain his exact position.

With this view our column moved on, followed by the field-guns, which kept up an oblique fire.

The causeway was reached at about 8 a.m., the fog still continuing as thick as ever; and here it was found that the enemy, taking advantage of the natural defence offered by the raised ground—on each side of which was a ditch—had thrown up a battery with two heavy guns, thus barricading the passage.

Clive had intended when he reached the causeway to have counter marched along the road running parallel with the Mahratta Ditch, which would have brought him right up to Amichand's garden, where he still hoped, under cover of the thick fog, to secure the Nawab; but on the head of our column taking ground to the right it was brought within the range of our own field-pieces, still firing obliquely from the rear.

The sepahis in advance first came within the range of our guns, which, causing dismay and confusion, forced them to hastily seek cover in the ditches beside the causeway; and for a time our whole column was thrown into complete disorder. The enemy at this time opened fire from their two guns which enfiladed the passage across the causeway, creating terrible havoc and killing several of our Europeans and sepahis. Clive now attempted to extend his troops, but anything like a regular movement in the fog and confusion was found to be impossible. Our commander's plan of action was again altered, his hope now resting in his being able to gain the main road leading-direct to the fort; but to accomplish this many difficulties had to be overcome, for, the fog now lifting, the smallness of our force became apparent, and our movements were impeded by squadrons of cavalry, who, taking advantage of our palpable discomfiture, threatened our advance.

Clive, having now re-formed his column, advanced rapidly across the causeway, passed the enemy's enfilading battery, and pushed on through the rice-fields in the direction of the main road to the fort.

Our movements were still hampered by the enemy's numerous cavalry; but as our infantry platoons regained their self-possession, a way was cleared for our guns over the difficult ground. As the fog cleared it was seen that the enemy had placed two additional guns in position to oppose our advance.

A determined charge was now made by the enemy's cavalry on our rear, our difficulties being enhanced by our own field-pieces having been disabled; one of these being gallantly recaptured by Ensign Yorke with a few Europeans, who rescued one of the disabled guns; and a charge of our troops to the front cleared a passage, so that the main road was at last gained. By following the road through Calcutta the fort was reached about noon, when it was found that our loss amounted to 27 European infantry, 12 sailors, and 18 sepahis killed; 70 European infantry, 12 sailors, and 35 sepahis wounded. Captains Pye and Bridges of the Madras service, and Mr. Belcher, private secretary to Colonel Clive, were killed. The same evening the troops returned to their fortified camp, boldly marching within a quarter of a mile of the enemy's position.

Thus ended the battle of Chitpore, which from a military point of view must be classed as a failure and a defeat, the more gloomy when we take into account that we had no means of supplying the places of our dead and wounded Europeans, whereas on the enemy an equal or much greater loss would have little or no effect. Dissatisfaction now showed itself amongst our troops, who blamed their commander for having sacrificed their comrades in a badly-concerted, rash attack. Had Clive, they argued, taken the road which runs parallel with the river and thus gained the Mahratta Ditch at Perrin's Point, he could have marched without obstruction under cover of the outer fortifications of the town, and so found himself at Amichand's garden. But they were not aware that Clive's plan of action included the seizing of the enemy's artillery—impossible had he taken the route by the river. Clive was on his mettle, and he never showed to such advantage as when he was surrounded by difficulties to most men insurmountable. He would not admit his defeat. What though he had been forced into a somewhat undignified retreat, why should he not turn his military mismanagement into a political success? He grasped the idea, and acted on it. Fortune was already smiling upon him, and he now learnt for the first time that the enemy were far more disheartened than the British.

Our guns, during our progress through their camp, had created terrible havoc amongst the enemy, their loss far exceeding anything Clive had imagined. They were dismayed and cowed; 22 "officers of distinction," 600 soldiers, and 500 horses having been killed, besides several elephants, camels, and a vast number of draught cattle. The Nawab also was terrified, having never before been so near the rage and tumult of battle, to which his temperament was averse. Whilst upbraiding his officers for their cowardice, he was himself only anxious to find an excuse for retiring from the presence of an enemy whom he had now learned to dread.

The next morning Siraju 'd daulah made proposals of peace, to which Clive replied that "he had marched through his camp with no other intention than to convince him of what the English troops were capable, who, he said, had cautiously hurt none excepting such as had opposed them, but that he was willing to renew the negotiations for peace."[1]

6th-9th February, the Nawab, to prove his sentiments of friendliness and sincere desire for peace, struck his camp and moved about 3 miles to the north-east, passing on his march the British entrenched camp without showing any hostile signs.

On the 9th of February the terms of a treaty were agreed to and ratified, under the oaths of the Nawab Siraju 'd daulah, Mir J'afar Khan, and Roi Dulab, the Nawab agreeing to restore the Company's factories, giving permission to the English to fortify Calcutta as they might choose, to coin gold and silver at their own mint, and hold their merchandise exempt from duty; the 38 villages granted to the British by the Embassy in 1717 to be restored; and in general all previous privileges, Imperial and Vice-regal, to be confirmed.[2]

Nor was this treaty the climax of Clive's success; for, on the 11th of February, when the Nawab commenced his return march to his Capital, he sent Amichand to Colonel Clive with a further treaty of alliance, offensive and defensive, against all enemies.

10th-15th February, Clive was naturally elated, for never in his

---

1. Orme, Book 7., p. 135.
2. Orme, Book 7., p. 136.

most sanguine hours had he anticipated such success; and this proposed treaty for an alliance, offensive and defensive, relieved him from a difficulty which had lately threatened to overwhelm him.

15th-18th February, News, as previously stated, had been received from England that war had been declared between Great Britain and France; thus Chandernagore with its garrison was at Clive's mercy, and, by his alliance with the Nawab, his anxiety lest the French and Siraju 'd daulah should foregather was dispelled.

This second treaty was signed as quickly as possible and returned to the Nawab, with an intimation from Clive that he desired to attack the French at Chandernagore, and asking the Nawab's sanction. Siraju 'd daulah hesitated; but trembling lest he should be again forced into hostilities with the British gave an evasive consent, at the same time asking that 20 English gunners might be permitted to serve in his artillery, and further that an English resident might be appointed to his Court.

Both these requests were readily acceded to, the gunners being sent and Mr. Watts appointed resident at Murshedabad. The Nawab now continued his march to his capital, and Clive determined to lose no time in prosecuting his plans for the reduction of Chandernagore.

Since the formation of the Bengal European Battalion in December, 1756, great changes had taken place in the materiel of the Regiment. Clive, on the recapture of Calcutta, had reinstated and formed into levies some of the old Bengal sepahis, who had fled from the settlement when it was captured by Siraju 'd daulah in June, 1756, and these new levies were now officered from the Bengal European Battalion. Again, some of the original officers of the battalion had disappeared, the records not showing what had become of them. Captain Dugald Campbell and Ensign Carr were killed in the action of Baj Baj, and Ensign Walcot had died from the effects of his sufferings in the Black Hole.

Captains Mills, Dickson, Meadows, and Grant; Lieutenants Cudmore, Smith, and Wedderburn; Ensigns Carstairs, Douglas, Somers, and Moran had become non-effective, although some of these rejoined the Regiment afterwards. Lieutenant John Fraser had been promoted to a company in the battalion in succession to Captain Campbell, deceased, and on the same day a commission as Lieutenant was granted to Ensign Carstairs, who-was appointed to do duty with the sepahi troops. Lieutenant Cudmore was promoted to Captain-Lieutenant, and Lieutenants Dyer and Keir, and Ensigns Prichard, Rider, and Delabare, and Adjutant Gibbons joined the battalion.

From a return signed by Commissary P. R. Peakes and laid before the council on 28th February, 1757, it appears that the battalion mustered on that date only 250 effective officers and men, including 38 artillery attached. The Volunteer company was reduced to 13 men, many who had served as Volunteers-having returned to their several callings when Calcutta was recaptured. The barracks which had been in Fort William were destroyed during the occupation of Siraju 'd daulah's troops, the-materials having been employed to construct a Mahomedan Mosque, which was, under the Nawab's orders, erected in the centre of the fort. The European troops, therefore, were quartered "in the Play-House, and dwelling-house of General Alsop, and the upper part of the horse stables," which had, under the orders of the council, been put into repair and adapted for the purpose.

The following is a nominal roll of the officers present with the Regiment on 28th February, 1757[3]:

Captain Grainger Muir	Lieutenant Keir
Captain Lebeaume	Ensign Prichard
Captain John Fraser	Ensign Rider
Captain-Lieutenant Carstairs	Ensign Delabare
Lieutenant Dyer	Adjutant William Gibbon

15th-28th February, Following Siraju 'd daulah's half-hearted permission for the British to attack the French, Clive now determined on sending an expedition against Chandernagore without further delay, and for this purpose crossed the Hugli with his whole available force on the 18th of February; but an unlooked-for difficulty arose.

The French, taking alarm at the British preparations, besought the Nawab "for his own safety" to render them his protection; pointing out that should he permit the English to destroy the French interests in Bengal, he would lose the alliance of the latter and the English would, then have him completely at their mercy. These representations had the desired effect. The Nawab had not previously seen matters in this light; so now warming up to the occasion, he wrote to Clive positively forbidding him to attack the French, evincing his earnestness and faith by sending to M. Renault, the French Governor at Chandernagore, a large sum of money to aid him in his preparations for defence, as well as a force of 1500 men, under command of Rajah Dulab Ram, to strengthen his garrison.

---

3. Broome says that Captain Christian Fischer, a Danish officer, joined the Bengal Battalion on 7th February, 1757, but though his name does not appear in the roll laid before the council on 28th February, he was present with the battalion at the Battle of Plassey, June, 1757.

Under these circumstances the Council at Calcutta, deeming it injudicious to act in direct disobedience of the Nawab's commands, waived the idea of sending an expedition against the French; and Clive was prepared to sign a treaty of neutrality. But at this stage another unforeseen difficulty presented itself. Admiral Watson positively refused to sign any treaty with the French, on the ground—to use his own words—"that no treaty can be binding with Chandernagore until it is ratified by Pondicherry. Calcutta is an independent, Chandernagore is a dependent settlement. If we sign a treaty, then, with Chandernagore we bind our own hands; we do not bind those of our rival." To this argument Colonel Malleson, in his Life of Clive, justly replies, "considering that the rival was the suppliant to have his hands bound, the objection, though doubtless sound in law, was more plausible than solid." The Admiral remained obdurate; and the treaty was held in abeyance.

During this delay intelligence had reached the Nawab that Delhie had been captured by Ahmud Shah Durani. This news filled the young Nawab with abject fear: for it was not improbable that the conqueror, flushed with his success, might attempt to obtain possession of the Bengal provinces. Siraju 'd daulah, therefore, wrote to Clive, urging him to march to his assistance; but in this communication no reference whatever was made to the French question.

15th-18th February, Simultaneously with the receipt of the Nawab's letter the Council in Calcutta learned that reinforcements which had left Bombay in the preceding October, had arrived at the mouth of the river Hugli, consisting of 2 strong companies of the Bombay European Regiment, under Captains Buchanan and Armstrong, with Captain-Lieutenant Egerton: Lieutenants Palmer, Moltimore and Walsh; and Ensign Robertson: and a detachment of artillery. The *Cumberland* 74, with a detachment of the 39th Foot, was also close at hand.

The English army, with these additions, was considered sufficiently strong to attack the French at Chandernagore, even though the Nawab should assist them with his troops. Our ships of war formed a very important part of the armament which Clive proposed to bring against the French; but the Admiral would not be influenced by Clive's arguments. He still determined that he would not move against the French without the express consent of the Nawab. Watson therefore wrote a threatening letter to the Nawab, accusing him of not having faithfully fulfilled the terms of the treaty, and telling him that if the conditions remained unfulfilled for ten days longer he "would kindle such a flame in the country as all the waters of the Ganges should not be able to extinguish."

The Nawab, much alarmed at the tone of Admiral Watson's letter, and hoping to allay his wrath, replied that he had faithfully observed that part of the treaty which provided for an offensive and defensive alliance, and further denied that he had in any way assisted the French; adding "if your enemy with an upright heart claims your protection you will give him life; but then you must be well satisfied of the innocence of his intention; if not, whatever you think right, that do."

25th-28th February, This letter the Admiral considered a sufficient authority to warrant his joining Clive in the expedition against Chandernagore; but the Nawab, on reflection, fearing that he had said too much in his letter, wrote to Watson next day, positively forbidding an attack on the French settlement. The Admiral, however, determined to act on the first letter, which he considered had given him the desired permission; so he now treated all further communications with contempt, and issued orders for his ships to prepare for action.

The French settlement of Chandernagore is situated on the banks of the river Hugli about thirty miles above Calcutta; the territory covering only a space of about two miles in length along the river bank and a mile-and-a-half inland; the Dutch settlement of Chinsurah adjoining to the north.

The French fort of Chandernagore, called Fort d'Orleans, was a square building situated about thirty yards from the river, with bastions at the corners, each mounting 10 32-pound guns. On the eastern side was a ravelin, abutting on the river and covering the approach to the water-gate; and on this ravelin 8 32-pounders were mounted. There were also heavy guns on the terraces surrounding the church which stood in the centre of the fort; many guns being also mounted on the walls behind the battlements.

1st-14th March, the French garrison consisted of 146[4] European infantry, 300 sepahis, and about 300 militia formed from amongst the European inhabitants of the town; and there were, in addition, a number of French sailors, drawn from the ships lying under the guns of the fort. The English force consisted of the Bengal European Regiment, the detachment of the Bombay and Madras European Regiments; these, after leaving sufficient men to garrison Calcutta and the outposts, amounting in all to about 700 European infantry. Besides, Clive had 150 European artillery and 1500 sepahis; but the most im-

---

4. Various authorities place the French garrison at a much higher figure,, but Malleson, who has examined the old records at Chandernagore, ascertained they only had 146 French infantry in the garrison.

portant part of the expedition was the ships of war. There were the *Kent* (64), the *Tiger* (60), and *Cumberland* (70), the detachments of the 39th Regiment still acting as Marines on board ship.

On the 7th March Clive commenced his advance, and on the 14th sighted Chandernagore.

The British approach was made from the westward, along the high road leading towards the north face of the fort. Here the French had thrown up a battery held by strong detachments ordered to dispute our advance. 14th-23rd March, Clive drove back the enemy's skirmishers, pushed on towards the French position, and gained possession of several houses offering admirable cover, and from which a continuous fire was kept up, compelling the French to spike those of their guns which they were unable to remove, and take refuge within their fort. Four of their outposts to the south of the fort were also withdrawn during the night, the guns being previously removed; and next day our troops occupied the town. The 16th and 17th were employed in landing our siege-train guns, which were got into position under a heavy cannonade from the fort; notwithstanding which, a battery on the banks of the river was occupied by our troops and 3 32-pounders placed in position. These latter guns were silenced on the following morning, and on the 21st the enemy's fire beat down a house near one of our batteries, in the ruins of which several of our men were temporarily imprisoned, but none mortally hurt. On the 22nd our battery was repaired and so strengthened that our 3 32-pounders were again brought to bear on the fort.

In the meantime, 23rd March, the ships of war were moving into their position, the *Tiger* (60) leading the advance, and as she passed the fort sweeping the ravelin with a broadside, and, taking up her position opposite the north-eastern bastion, pouring a heavy fire from her guns; and at the same time her sailors, mounting to the tops, discharged a constant musketry fire into the body of the fort. Next came the *Kent* (64), carrying Admiral Watson's flag, and appointed to the centre position; but just as she was about to drop anchor a deadly fire was brought to bear upon her deck, killing several of her sailors and disabling her Commander, who, stunned by his wound, could not give his directions with sufficient rapidity. The *Kent* in her confusion slipped her cable and was carried by the tide about fifty yards down the river to the position which should have been occupied by the *Cumberland*, and became exposed to a withering fire both from the south-east and south-west bastions of the fort.

The cannonade was now terrific—some 80 guns pouring forth their fire simultaneously; the broadsides of the *Kent* and *Tiger* being assisted by our batteries on shore, which ably assailed the two bastions of the fort with their cross fire. But the French guns were not to be easily silenced; and indeed it soon appeared that although the *Tiger*, which was pitted against the north-eastern bastion, held her own, she was getting badly mauled. The Admiral, nothing daunted, now brought the guns of his lower as well as those of his upper deck to bear against the bastions, and for a few moments succeeded in silencing several of their guns, but the French commander, rallying his men, concentrated the whole of his fire upon one particular part of the deck of the Kent; and at once the ship was on fire. The conflagration spread rapidly, and with it a panic ensued, during which some 80 men left their quarters and attempted to escape. It was an anxious moment, but Admiral Watson stood firm, surrounded by the flames, whilst his officers strove manfully to get the fire under. They were soon joined by some of the sailors who, recovering their self-possession, and finding that courage and exertion might still save their ship, rejoined their officers and set to work with a will which soon mastered the fire. The cannonade from the ships was now resumed in all its fury, the enemy on his side giving signs of exhaustion. One after another his guns had been dismounted, and his fire had perceptibly slackened; but for two hours more the battle raged, every minute giving greater promise of victory for the British. At 9 o'clock a white flag was seen floating on the walls of the fort, and the combat suddenly ceased. Admiral Watson was now requested to receive a deputation of the French on board his ship; but, fearful lest they should see the damage which had been done and the plight to which he was reduced, he deputed Captain Eyre Coote of the 39th to go ashore and receive the French proposals. But whilst the terms of surrender were being discussed several of the French officers and soldiers escaped from the fort and took the road towards Kassimbazar to join M. Law of Lawrieston, who, with a small body of French artillery and infantry, held the French factory at that place. After proceeding a few miles the fugitives reached Raja Dulab Ram's force, sent by the Nawab to assist the French; and under Dulab Ram's protection they succeeded in reaching their destination.

At 3 p.m. 23rd March, the English took formal possession of the French fort, and the British ensign displaced the Fleur-de-lis of France on the flag-staff battery.

Colonel Clive, in his letter to the Court of Directors, dated 30th

March, 1757, says, "You will observe that the surrender was made to Admiral Watson, but common report will be just in publishing how great a share the land forces had in this conquest. There were about 500 Europeans in the fort, 250 Seapoys, and 400 Topasses, Mustees, &c, bearing arms. Of the Europeans about 125 have given their parole of honour, 300 sick and well are prisoners, and the rest were either killed in the siege or made their escape." Besides these, Broome states that "there were nearly 50 ladies," and Ives mentions specially the case of M. Nicholas, who lost his all, as he had neglected to remove his goods from the town to the fort; a subscription was raised amongst his captors for his relief and he was presented with £1200, on receipt of which he, cried out with joy, "Good God! they are friends indeed!"

23rd, 24th March, the British loss was very severe—on board the *Kent* 3 officers and 37 men killed, 6 officers and 74 men wounded; on board the *Tiger* 1 officer and 14 men killed, and 5 officers and 40 men wounded. The *Kent*, soon afterwards condemned, had 6 shots in her masts and 142 in her hull; but the *Cumberland*, not having taken up her position on account of the *Kent* having slipped her anchor, took no part in the battle.

The loss of the land troops was trifling, not exceeding 30 or 40 in killed and wounded.

The English took £130,000 at Chandernagore.

The news of the French having lost their Settlement[5] reaching the Nawab the next day, he flew into a fit of ungovernable passion; publicly threatening to take the life of Mr. Watts, the English resident at his Court. He had daily sent letters both to Colonel Clive and Admiral Watson positively forbidding the attack on the French, but his letters and messages had not been even acknowledged.

Whilst the Nawab's passion was in a blaze a black cloud from the direction of Patna cooled his wrath against the British; a messenger arriving with the news that his dreaded enemy Ahmed Shah Durani was in full march against him. This news ultimately proved to be false; but it had the effect of reducing Siraju 'd daulah into a state of abject terror; and he now wrote both to Watson and Clive congratulating them on their victory over the French, and offering the Company the set-

---

5. On peace being established in 1763 Chandernagore was restored to the French; but when hostilities broke out in 1794 it was again seized by the English; restored by treaty in 1802, retaken the same year and held by the English till the peace in 1815; and finally made over to the French, 4th December, 1816.

tlement of Chandernagore on the same terms as it had been held by their vanquished foes: moreover, as a substantial proof of his sincerity, he sent £45,000, as a part of the compensation-money promised under his treaty as a peace-offering to the English residents of Calcutta for the destruction of their property in June, 1756.

GENERAL REFERENCES—CHAPTER 2

The Seir Mutakherin Calcutta Edition.
Grose's Voyage to the East Indies.
Holwell's India Tracts 3rd Edition.
First Report, Select Committee, House of Commons.
Mill's British India.
Malleson's Founders of the Indian Empire (Clive)
Broome's Rise and Progress of the Bengal Army.
Williams's Bengal Infantry.
Clive's Despatches and Correspondence.
Ive's Voyage and Historical Narrative
Caraccioli's Life of Lord Clive.
East India Military Calendar
Orme's Military Transactions in Bengal.
Proceedings of the Calcutta Council, 1757.
&c., &c.

CHAPTER 3

Plassey

1st-15th April, 1757: Immediately after the capture of Chandernagore Clive, having provided for the protection of his newly-acquired possession, withdrew the bulk of his army to Calcutta, and Admiral Watson took back his ships of war.

The early part of the campaign had in the past three months been brought to a successful issue; but still much had to be accomplished. There was now a temporary cessation of hostilities, and Clive turned his attention to his plans of future action. His first care was to protect himself against the machinations and intrigues of the Murshedabad Court. He had many opportunities of judging the real character of the young Nawab, whom he had insulted and defied with such impunity. Clive was firmly convinced that Siraju'd daulah was not to be trusted; that his friendliness had been the result of fear; and that he was only awaiting his opportunity to be avenged for the many humiliations to which he had been subjected at the hands of the British.

Clive appears at this time, 1st-15th April, to have determined to entwine a web around the young Nawab, against which the more he struggled the more entangled and weak he would become.

There is something pitiable in the position of this spoilt boy—born to the purple, petted in his childhood, his every wish anticipated, and his impulses uncontrolled; until Clive crossed his path—the strong, the determined, the wily Clive, pitted against this fractious boy, and bent on his destruction.

It will be remembered that the Nawab had dispatched a force of 1500 men under Raja Dulab Ram to assist the French at Chandernagore. This detachment had never reached its destination, as its commander had unwittingly been brought under the influence of Nandkumar, the Nawab's Governor of the town of Hugli, who had been bought over by the wealthy baboo, Amichand, in whose house Siraju 'd daulah had taken up his quarters when he invaded Calcutta in February. Amichand, who had amassed a large fortune in his dealings with the British before they had been driven from Calcutta, now tendered his services to the council, promising them his co-operation; which was held to be valuable, he having great influence at Murshedabad. Nandkumar, immediately prior to the capture of Chandernagore, had forwarded messages to Dulab Ram—who it will be remembered had been sent by the Nawab to the assistance of the French—assuring him that the French commander was on the point of surrendering to the English, and recommending him to await further orders from Murshedabad. Dulab Ram, believing in the integrity of Nandkumar, halted; the only benefit he conferred on his allies being assistance rendered to some of their fugitives Raja Dulab Ram was now returning with his 1500 men to Murshedabad when he received the Nawab's orders to halt at Plassey, a large village on the island of Kassimbazar, about 30 miles south of the Nawab's capital.

Such was the position immediately after the capture of Chandernagore; and had Clive obeyed the orders received from the Madras Government he would have returned with the main body of his troops to Madras—where his presence was urgently called for to direct the operations against the French in that presidency. But he felt he had to complete his great work in Bengal; and therefore determined at all hazards to remain, at any rate until after the approaching monsoon.

Instead, therefore, of leading his army back as directed, he prepared for further action; encamping his force to the north of the town of Hugli—as from this point he could either overawe or act hostilely against the Nawab.

Much as the Nawab had equivocated in the matter of the British attack on Chandernagore, he still treasured the idea that he would be able in case of need to make the French his allies, and pit them against the British; and it was therefore with dismay that he received a communication from Clive, requesting permission to attack the French at Kassimbazar, where M. Law commanded a small efficient force, lately augmented by 50 of the fugitives from Chandernagore.

The position was awkward; for if the Nawab consented to Clive's request he would lose the alliance of the French; whilst if he refused he would probably provoke the English, who might march upon his capital. There was a third course open to him, and he elected to adopt it. 10th-16th April he furnished M. Law with money, ammunition, and carriage, and dispatched him on an imaginary expedition, telling him he might expect shortly to be recalled, when the present difficulty had been surmounted. But M. Law replied, "Be assured, my Lord Nawab, this is the last time we shall see each other. Remember my words; we shall never meet again."[1] On the 16th April M. Law crossed the river and proceeded in the direction of Behar.

As soon as Clive heard of the Nawab's ruse he dispatched a party of the 39th Foot in pursuit; at the same time sending a small detachment of Europeans and sepahis to strengthen the English factory at Kassimbazar.

Soon after the departure of M. Law the Nawab became aware that the report of the threatened invasion of his provinces by Ahmed Shah Durani was false; he therefore plucked up his courage and determined to free himself from the thraldom imposed on him by the Calcutta Council.

Siraju 'd daulah was not only threatened from without, but he had, by his ungovernable temper and insolent bearing, alienated from himself even those whose interests might have induced them to support him on his throne.

The meshes which Clive had spread were being imperceptibly drawn closer round the Nawab; whilst the principal nobles of his own Court were assisting in the plots for his destruction. Siraju 'd daulah had not at this time, 1st-31st May, one friend, whilst he was surrounded by enemies at home and abroad; but of all these, Mir J'afar Khan—he who was most bound to him by strong ties of relationship, who had promised his predecessor on his deathbed that he would advise and protect the young Nawab—this man was the worst and basest.[2] He entered into a conspiracy with the British to secure himself the Viceregal throne, agreeing to pay to the East India Company £1,200,000; to the English inhabitants of Calcutta £1,600,000; and to the other inhabitants £325,000. In addition to these enormous sums he purchased the goodwill of the navy and army by promising them £500,000; and moreover he agreed to give the council and officers £600,000; lastly the commanders and members of council entered into a subsidiary agreement with him to receive an extra donation of £315,000.

These sums were duly apportioned so that each officer and ci-

---

1. Seir Mutakherin.
2. Mir J'afar Khan was married to the sister of Ali Verdi Khan (the late Nawab), and was consequently uncle to Siraju 'd daulah.

vilian should receive what, even now-a-days, would be considered a handsome fortune; Colonel Clive's share alone amounting to upwards of £200,000. During these negotiations and before the signing of the treaty, Mir J'afar Khan had stipulated that Amichand, the English agent, should remain in ignorance of the plot; but Amichand was far too cunning a schemer to be kept in the dark. He bided his time; and when all arrangements had matured he put in his claim for his share of the plunder, which he estimated at £300,000; telling Mr. Watts that unless his claim were admitted he would inform Siraju 'd daulah of the conspiracy and cause all concerned to be arrested.

This was a dilemma: but Clive and his council had no idea of allowing the Amichand difficulty to destroy the plot. It was, therefore, proposed that a false treaty should be prepared, in which the provision for Amichand should be inserted. This proposition was submitted to Admiral Watson, who sternly refused to be a party to such a disgraceful fraud; so Clive, with the consent of the council, forged Admiral Watson's signature to a sham treaty, which was shown to Amichand as the original document and accepted by him as genuine.

The plot matured; and under Clive's guidance relations between the British and the Nawab were strained to the utmost. It was pretended that Raja Dulab Ram's force, still at Plassey, caused umbrage to the Council at Calcutta; for although the Nawab had undoubted right to locate his troops in any part of his territories yet Plassey had always been considered a position the occupation of which indicated distrust. It was thence that an attack on the Nawab could be most easily effected; and, in fact, Clive secretly intended to make his attack on Murshedabad from that place. Now, not only Dulab Ram's force of 1500 men were located at Plassey, but the Nawab had ordered it to be considerably augmented.

On the 3rd of May a mysterious letter was received by the council, delivered by an unknown messenger, who represented himself as being in the service of Balaji Rao, the Mahratta Chief of Behar, proposing that the English should co-operate with him against Siraju 'd daulah. Now this proposal, had Clive believed it to be genuine, might have dovetailed in with his own views; but he was under the impression that he had discovered a plot. He thought that the letter had been instigated by the Nawab, in order that he might find out in what light the council would receive such a proposition. By Clive's advice the mysterious letter was forwarded to the Nawab, under cover of one from the council, in which it was pointed out how true and loyal were the intentions of the British. With these despatches was also sent a second letter from the council enquiring why the Nawab's army was kept at Plassey fully equipped for war; so injuring the trade and confidence which should exist between allies.

Now, in point of fact, the letter which had caused so much suspicion was genuine; Clive had over-reached himself; but the result was all that he could desire, for confidence was restored at Murshedebad, and the troops were withdrawn from Plassey.

The Nawab had been warned by M. Law, before he was sent away from Murshedabad, that he was surrounded by enemies and traitors, and he now began to realise the value of the warning. He became suspicious of all around him, removing Nandkumar from the Governorship of Hugh, whilst his relations with Mir J'afar were so hostile that the Nawab was preparing to attack him in his palace.

In the meantime Clive had sent instructions to Mr. Watts—British resident at the Nawab's Court, who had throughout been assisting in the plot—to be prepared to make his escape, and Mr. Watts had with this view secretly dispatched to Calcutta a great deal of valuable property from the English factory at Kassimbazar. Mir J'afar Khan now informed Mr. Watts that the time for his departure had arrived, sending at the same time a trusty servant to Clive to advise his immediate advance on the Nawab's capital.

On June 13th Mr. Watts with his assistants left Murshedabad; going out for their usual ride, they ordered supper to be prepared for their return, but when they had proceeded a few miles they put spurs to their horses and made for Clive's camp, which they reached in safety the next day.

Siraju 'd daulah heard of Mr. Watts's flight the following morning, when for the first time he fully realised his perilous position. He was overwhelmed with terror, and relinquished his intentions of punishing Mir J'afar, although now more than ever convinced of his perfidy. Regardless of his high position the Nawab sought the traitor in his palace, appearing before him as his suppliant. This visit resulted in an outward reconciliation, and Mir J'afar and his confederates, having sworn fidelity on the Koran, were restored to favour. The Nawab, now imagining himself secure, veered round to an attitude of defiance towards the English.

The time had arrived for Clive to throw off the mask; so, dismissing the Nawab's Ambassadors from his camp, he charged them with a despatch for their Prince, which said that. . . .

. . . . he had used every subterfuge to evade the accomplishment of the treaty of February, that he had in four months restored only one-fifth part of the effects which he had plundered from the English, that he had scarcely made peace before he had invited M. Bussy to come from the Deccan and assist him in extirpating them once more out of his dominions, that the party of French troops under M. Law were at this very time maintained at his expense within 100 miles of his capital. That he had on groundless suspicion insulted the English honour, at one time sending troops to examine their factory at Cossimbazar at another driving their vaqueel with disgrace out of his presence. That he had promised a sum of gold rupees then denied that promise and then sent Omichand from the city under pretence that it was he who had deceived the English Commanders in that business. At length seeing no other remedy their army was now marching on Muxadabad,[3] where they intended to refer their complaints to the decision of the principal officers of his Government namely Meer Jaffier, Roydoolab, the Seats[4] Meer Mudeen and Moonlall, to which arbitration it was hoped that he would acquiesce and spare the effusion of blood.[5]

The proposed arbiters were men bound to assist the English cause; bankers who were smarting under the extortions of the Nawab, or men of influence who had promised their support to the British plot. Clive now made final arrangements for his advance; all the troops which could be spared marching from Calcutta on the 12th of June, leaving only some sick Europeans and sepahis to guard the French prisoners, and a few artillerymen to protect the guns; Chandernagore was garrisoned principally by sailors and a few sepahis.

On the 13th of June the army, together with 150 sailors, marched; the English troops with the field-pieces, stores, and ammunition being towed up the river in 200 boats, and the sepahis marching along the right bank.

The ranks of the Bengal European Battalion had been considerably augmented by a great many of the French prisoners, released on condition of their taking service with the British. There were also many Dutch, some Germans, and other foreigners, who similarly joined the ranks of the Regiment. Some sailors of the *Kent*—their ship having been condemned—also enlisted for military service.

The English army on the 16th June reached the town of Pulti,

---

3. The old name of the city Murshedabad.
4. Bankers.
5. Orme, Vol. 2., Book 7., p. 164.2.

about 12 miles from the Nawab's fort of Kutwah. The Governor of this fort was believed to be in league with Mir J'afar Khan's party; but when Major Eyre Coote, with an imposing force, including a detachment of the Bengal European Regiment, summoned the garrison, the Governor refused to surrender.

Major Coote, first opening fire, despatched a body of Europeans who effected a passage across the river; when the enemy, firing some buildings adjoining the fort, took to flight.

The British troops immediately occupied the town and fort, and took possession of a very large supply of grain and a considerable quantity of military stores, as well as 14 pieces of artillery. The main army arriving the same evening encamped on the plain outside the deserted town; but the monsoon commenced with such violence the next day that the troops were forced to take refuge within the fort and town.

Clive was now within a few miles of the Plains of Plassey, where the fate of the British army—and indeed of British rule in Bengal—was to be decided. He had only received one communication from Mir J'afar since the army had marched from Chandernagore, though he had written to him every day. This one letter gave an account of Mir J'afar's reconciliation with the Nawab, and how he had sworn to assist him against the British; but he concluded by saying that the purport of his engagement with the English must be carried out.

16th-18th June; Clive's exploits, and his strokes of policy, have up to this time appeared as triumphs only; and we are hardly prepared to find our "heaven-born General" uncertain in his actions and doubtful of his policy. He had unhesitatingly pressed forward to accomplish his masterpiece of diplomacy; but now, when the moment had arrived for action, prudence and caution gained the ascendancy, and he hesitated. If Mir J'afar should be false to him, what would be his position? Separated from his base and deficient in reserves, his triumph or his fall depending on the whim of a man proved to be every inch a traitor. For the first time in his life Clive felt he must have recourse to a Council of War—the first and last he ever called. The council, which assembled next day, consisted of the following:

Lieutenant-Colonel Clive	in Chief Command.
Major James Kilpatrick	Second in Command, and Commanding Bengal European Regiment.
Major Eyre Coote	Commanding Detachment H.M. 39th Regiment

Captain George Gaupp	Commanding Detachment Madras European Regiment.
Captain Thomas Rumbold	Madras European Regiment.
Captain John Cudmore	Bengal Native Infantry.
Captain Alexander Grant	do. do.
Captain Andrew Armstrong	Commanding Bombay Detachment.
Captain Grainger Muir	Bengal European Battalion.
Captain Christian Fischer	do. do.
Captain Charles Palmer	Bombay European Regiment.
Captain Lebeaume	Bengal European Battalion.
Captain R. Waggoner	H.M. 39th Regiment.
Captain J. Corneille	do. do.
Captain Robert Campbell	Madras European Regiment.
Captain-Lieutenant Carstairs	Bengal European Battalion,
Captain W. Jennings	Commanding artillery.
Captain-Lieutenant Moltimore	Bombay European Regiment.
Captain-Lieutenant Barshaw	(service unknown).

Clive opened the proceedings with the following question:

"Whether under existing circumstances and without other assistance it would be prudent to cross the river and come to action at once with the Nawab, or whether they should fortify themselves at Kutwah and wait until the monsoon was over, when the Mahrattees, or some other country power might be induced to join them?"

Contrary to practice, Clive first gave his opinion: which was, to the surprise of the council, "against immediate action."

Major Eyre Coote next voted, for immediate action, arguing that hitherto they had met with nothing but success which had greatly elated the spirit of the troops, whereas delay would only serve to damp their ardour, that delay would further enable M. Law and his party to arrive which would not only strengthen the enemy and add vigour to their Councils but would serve to weaken the English force materially, owing to the number of Frenchmen in the ranks who had taken service after the capture of Chandernagore and who would undoubtedly desert to their countrymen on the first opportunity. That consequent on the numbers of the enemy and the great distance from Calcutta all supplies would be cut off and would reduce the Europeans in particular to great distress. Finally he suggested that if it was decided not to come to immediate action it would be advisable to return to Calcutta at once, although he fully admitted the disgrace this measure would entail on their arms, and the injury that must occur to the Company's interests from such a proceeding.[6]

With Clive 12 officers voted "against immediate action," amongst them were Captains Christian Fischer and Lebeaume; with Captain Eyre Coote 6 voted " for immediate action," amongst them were Captain Grainger Muir and Captain-Lieutenant Carstairs; all of these officers being of the Bengal European Regiment.

The resolution not to fight was carried by a majority of 12 against 7.

The decision of the Council of War by no means relieved Clive's anxieties; but, on the contrary, he. appears to have been much impressed with Major Eyre Coote's arguments. In the evening he left the camp unattended and bent his steps towards a clump of trees near at hand, where he could in solitude review the position and determine on his future course. He was a brave, determined soldier; but he possessed a large amount of prudence and caution; these qualities being so evenly balanced against his anxiety to consummate his schemes, that it required but one grain to turn the scale; and that grain Major Eyre Coote had thrown in. Clive determined to fight.

At this time, 17th June, Clive received a letter from Mir J'afar Khan saying that the Nawab had halted at Muncarra, a village six miles to the south of Kassimbazar, where he intended to entrench himself and await the event; and proposing that the English should surprise him, marching round by the eastern side of the Island. This counsel Clive thought savoured of treachery; for were he to follow the proffered advice he would be separating himself from his base, and thus afford the enemy an opportunity of overthrowing him by simple weight of men and guns. Any way the advice was bad, and not to be entertained. Clive replied that he should march to Plassey without delay, and would next morning advance six miles to Daudpore and should Mir J'afar not join him there, would make peace with the Nawab.

The messenger was dispatched with Clive's reply, and before sunrise the troops were en route. Nearly the whole of the 20th was spent in crossing the river, and it was evening before the whole force had landed on the opposite bank. The rain poured: in torrents, and the fatigue of the soldiers from wading through the mud and water was increased by having to protect their ammunition from the wet; but after a severe march they reached Plassey at 1 a.m. the, 23rd June, 1757.

---

6 Broome's Rise and Progress of the Bengal Army, p. 130; and Reference to Orme, Vol. 2., p. 70, 71.

23rd June, the troops now bivouacked under a grove of trees[7] 800 yards long and 300 broad, surrounded by a mud bank and a ditch June 23rd, which formed to some extent a ready-made entrenchment; sentries were posted and the weary soldiers were soon buried in sleep. But not so Clive, who knew no rest; for he soon discovered that the Nawab's army was close at hand, and in the stillness of the night he could distinctly hear in his front the sounds of drums and martial music.

Clive had under his command in the field 950 European infantry, 100 European artillery, with 8 6-pounders and 2 howitzers; 50 sailors: 2,100 sepahis and some lascars. The position of our troops in the grove faced north; on our left flank was the river Bhagirathi, on our right the open plain; in rear at a distance of about a mile was the village of Plassey; about three-quarters of a mile in front and resting on the river was a large mound surrounding a tank; beyond the latter being two redoubts, one forming part of the enemy's entrenchments, the other slightly in advance. Near the mango grove and on the banks of the river was a small hunting-lodge, which Clive occupied soon after the arrival of our troops.

The enemy's army consisted of 35,000 infantry and 15,000 cavalry. The cavalry were superior to the infantry in physique, well mounted, and, being chiefly enlisted in the north from amongst the Patan tribes, were born soldiers.

His artillery was still more efficient, with 53 guns, 32-, 24-, and 18-pounders; the whole directed by M. St. Frais, a Frenchman, who had with him a small body of French soldiers, mostly Artillerymen, working their own guns. M. St. Frais had no doubt materially assisted the Nawab's Generals with his advice as to the disposition of the troops and their general plan of action.

The position which the enemy occupied faced the grove about a mile-and-a-half to the north; their entrenchments running along their whole front, their right resting on the river Bhagirathi, their left extending far away on the plain; and behind the entrenchments was their camp.

Before daybreak Clive, from the roof of the hunting-lodge, watched the, movements of the enemy preparing for action. Many of their heavy guns were mounted on large wooden platform-stages raised about six feet from the ground, the ammunition as well as the gunners being mounted on the stages. These huge masses were moved along by 40 or 50 oxen; an elephant accompanied each stage, pushing it on

---

7. The last of these trees disappeared only a few years since.

with his head when the oxen gave in. Brigades of horse and foot, each with its proportion of artillery, extended over the plain in a curve until they nearly reached the village of Plassey. St. Frais and his Frenchmen, with 4 light guns, occupied the large mound to the north of the grove; supported by a body of 7000 foot and 5000 horse, with two heavy guns, all under command of Mir Mudin—the best and most faithful of the Nawab's Generals.

The enemy's main army was in three divisions; under Elijah Dulab Ram, Yar Luft Khan, and Mir J'afar; the last being on the extreme left. The right of the enemy's army rested on the redoubt which formed part of his entrenchments; and, circling round, completely out-flanked the British, who were, however, protected on their left by the river Bhagirathi.

It now appeared that the enemy's plan was to completely double up the British force, and to drive them by means of his heavy guns and cavalry into the river. But Clive had provided against this contingency; for, if unable to resist the masses and pushed by them from his ground, he could at any rate keep them in check whilst he gained his boats moored to the bank alongside the grove; and the rapid stream would soon convey him to the fort of Kutwah, where he could hold his own until he had communicated with Balaji Rao; who he knew would gladly join in an attack on the Nawab.

Clive formed his European troops into four battalions; the first, under Major Kilpatrick, was composed of the detachment of the Madras European Regiment; the second, under Major Grant, of the Bengal European Regiment; the third, under Major Eyre Coote, of the detachment of the 39th Foot; and the fourth, under Major Gaupp, of the detachment of the Bombay European Regiment. The four European Battalions Clive placed in the centre of his line, flanked on either side by 1000 sepahis; and his 6 guns between and slightly in advance of his European and native battalions.

All the forces were now in position, and the French fired the first shot, which killed one and wounded another of our grenadier company, posted on the right of the Bengal European Battalion. The example of the French was quickly followed by the whole of the enemy's artillery, which simultaneously commenced a heavy fire, which must have annihilated the British force had its aim been well directed. Our 2 howitzers replied to the French artillery, whilst our 6 light guns brought their fire to bear on the large stages carrying the enemy's heavy artillery. After the lapse of half-an-hour, during which we lost some 30 men, Clive ordered his troops to retire under cover of the grove. The enemy, elated at what they mistook for a retreat, made a general advance, and threatened to overwhelm the British; but fortunately, their guns being badly served, their shot for the most part flew over the grove. Clive had ordered his troops to lie behind the mudbanks, from which our guns were now doing good service, whilst our men were not exposed. At 11 a.m. Clive called his commanders round him, and informed them that it was his intention to act on the defensive during the day, and at night assault the enemy's camp. In the meantime our men were sheltered, and consequently were suffering no loss; whilst from behind the banks which enveloped the grove they continued to pour a well-directed fire on the enemy; creating some havoc amongst the masses, and ever and anon exploding their ammunition, which, packed close to the guns on the raised stages, caused much loss and confusion.

At 12 o'clock the rain, which had been holding off for some hours, began to fall in such torrents as is seldom seen, except in the early days of the monsoon; but Clive had remembered the old English adage to keep his powder dry; and this precaution being neglected by the enemy caused their fire to sensibly slacken and equalised the contest.

We must now record what was going on in the enemy's camp, where the Nawab had remained in his tent beyond the reach of our guns. He was surrounded by his attendants and flatterers, who were constantly assuring him that his troops were behaving nobly and gaining an easy victory; but he was ill at ease. About noon he learnt to his grief that Mir Mudin was mortally wounded; he was dearly loved by the Nawab, being the one man whom he felt he could really trust. Mir Mudin met his death in the following manner. Believing that the British guns must be silenced by the rain, he advanced at the head of a troop of cavalry towards the grove, but was received with a volley of grape, which mortally wounded him and caused his cavalry to retire in confusion, many being left with their general, killed .or wounded. Siraju'd daulah, terrified at this loss, sent for Mir J'afar Khan, to whom he told his grief and implored him to befriend him. In his terror and despair the Nawab took off his turban and casting it at Mir J'afar's feet, passionately exclaimed "Mir J'afar, that turban thou must defend!" But the traitor ,was unmoved, and, crossing his hands on his breast, swore eternal fidelity; but at the same time, feeling his helpless relative's crown within his grasp, he firmly resolved to seize and place it on his "recreant head."

Taking a respectful leave of his Prince he returned to his command, whence he wrote to Clive informing him of what had taken place, and urging him to push on, for the victory was in his hand. This letter did not reach its destination until after some hours, as the messenger could not approach the British Commander; so that Clive was left in doubt as to Mir J'afar's intentions.

St. Frais, notwithstanding that some of his supports wavered after the loss of their General Mir Mudin, fought manfully, holding his position with tenacity, although our howitzers had been dealing destruction amongst his men; but the Nawab's fire had by this time slackened all round, and the British were now able to confidently hold their own. Clive, who had not rested during the previous night, felt the necessity of refreshing himself for the contemplated night attack; so, giving orders to Kilpatrick to act on the defensive only, he handed over the command, directing that he was to be called if anything of importance should occur; and then, entering the hunting-box, soon fell sound asleep.

Shortly after Kilpatrick had taken command he noticed that St. Frais's supports were retiring, and he felt that if he made a bold dash on the French artillery he might drive him to flight and probably secure some of his guns. Hastily calling forward 250 European infantry with 2 light guns, he made a rapid dash towards St. Frais's position on the mound, and at the same time sent a messenger to Clive to tell him what he was doing. Clive was up and amongst them before they had advanced across the plain, and as soon as he saw that St. Frais had lost his supports he realised the importance of the movement, and heading the charge himself, sent Kilpatrick back to bring up the rest of the force, St. Frais, though terribly outnumbered, fought manfully; but finding himself deserted and betrayed by his supports he gradually gave way, disputing every inch of ground and deliberately limbering up his guns retired in perfect order. His position was captured and a well-directed fire opened on the retiring Frenchmen.

Some of the enemy now made a half-hearted advance towards the grove, but Mir J'afar's division held aloof. Clive, suspecting that the enemy contemplated a dash at his boats and baggage, despatched a party of sepahis to strengthen his river-guard, at the same time directing his fire on the advancing foe, which had its desired effect, but he was unable to account for the eccentric movements of Mir J'afar's division, still separated from the .rest of the enemy.

Although several of the Nawab's Generals were implicated in the plot against their Sovereign, their soldiers were in total ignorance of any treachery, and could not, therefore, understand how so small a British force could overwhelm so powerful an army as their own; so, declining to accept defeat, they brought up large bodies of cavalry—who had not hitherto taken an active part in the engagement—and who, having obtained dry powder from their entrenchment, poured a heavy fire on the mound which Clive had just captured from the French. Nothing daunted, Clive boldly advanced, posting a portion of his infantry and 3 guns at the smaller tank slightly in advance: and the rest of his troops, with 3 guns, he placed about 200 yards to his left. From this advanced position his light guns, at shorter distance and with surer aim, were now dealing destruction on the enemy; the oxen and cattle attached to their heavy guns being disabled and thrown into complete confusion.

It now for the first time struck Clive that Mir J'afar's division, apparently threatening his boats and baggage, must be hovering about to seize the first opportunity of communicating with him. This relieved the British commander from a great anxiety, and he was now enabled to reduce his guards over the baggage and bring them to the front, where they were much needed; for St. Frais, who had taken up a fresh position further off, was serving his guns well against our advancing troops. At this time it was noticed that Mir J'afar's division was being separated further from his main army; and Clive, now fully convinced that he had nothing to fear in that direction, resolved by a supreme effort to drive St. Frais and his artillery from their second position. This was the more important as they held the redoubt which formed part of the enemy's entrenchments.

Two Divisions of the British army were ordered to advance and attack the redoubt, one of them on the right and the other on the left; the main body being held in reserve, prepared to advance to the assistance of either of the divisions requiring support. The right storming-party gained an eminence commanding a portion of the enemy's entrenchments; whilst the left, charging the redoubt, succeeded in gaining a footing inside; when the right party, with cheers, rushing down the sloping ground, the two divisions uniting attacked the French, driving them from the redoubt at the point of the bayonet, and capturing all their guns.

In the meantime Siraju 'd daulah, yielding to the persuasions of his officers, mounted a camel, and, followed by 2000 horsemen, fled to Murshedabad.

Clive, who had by this time pushed forward his troops within the enemy's entrenchments, was complete master of the field and of their camp, and at five o'clock the enemy were in full flight towards Murshedabad. Mir J'afar's letter, which had been sent to Clive immediately after the interview with the Nawab, now reached its destination, and Clive sent a reply to the effect that he would receive Mir J'afar the next morning at Daudpore; whilst Major Eyre Coote was dispatched to take up and continue the pursuit of the enemy.

So ended the Battle of Plassey: and although Clive's success was mainly brought about by the treachery of Siraju 'd daulah's Generals, yet credit is none the less due to the soldiers of the British army, who fought in total ignorance of their commander's schemes.

The loss of the British was marvellously small; only 7 Europeans, including 2 artillery officers, and 16 native soldiers having been killed, and 13 European soldiers and 36 natives wounded.[8] The loss of the enemy, on the other hand, was comparatively enormous, his killed alone being computed at 500, whilst 3 elephants and vast numbers of cattle were left dead on the field; 53 pieces of cannon and the whole of the camp equipage falling into our hands.

"Plassey" was the first decoration emblazoned on the colours of The Bengal European Regiment; and it has been inherited by the Royal Munster Fusiliers.

The action decided, our soldiers saw before them the plain strewn with valuables of every description, all of which were theirs by right of conquest; but Clive, anxious to follow up his victory, offered the soldiers a donation of money to forego their prize and march at once to Daudpore, about ten miles on the road towards Murshedabad. The troops unhesitatingly acquiesced; and regardless of their fatigues started on their march with hearty cheers.

Next morning, 24th June, Mir J'afar, with his son Míran, was conducted to the British camp. His conscience told him how false he had been to his Sovereign—and how false he would have been to the British, if it had suited his purpose; but it was Clive's policy to let bygones be bygones, and to consummate his schemes, which had thus far succeeded almost beyond his expectations. On entering the British camp Mir J'afar, alighting from his elephant, was received by a guard of honour, the sound of whose presented arms startled and alarmed him. his hand impulsively seizing the hilt of his sword. But his anxiety was relieved as Clive, hastily advancing towards him, saluted him as Sovereign of Bengal, Behar, and Orissa.

---

8. Colonel Malleson gives this as the loss of the British; but the Historical Records of the Madras European Regiment place our loss at a much higher figure.

A conference then took place, at which it was arranged that Mir J'afar should proceed without delay to Murshedabad, and, if possible, prevent Siraju 'd daulah's escape. But the ex-Nawab, hearing of Mir J'afar's approach, expedited his flight; and on the night of the 24th June, 1757, disguising himself in a mean dress, and taking with him a casket of his most precious jewels, he escaped with his favourite wife Zutf-ul-nissa, who elected to share his fate. A boat manned by a picked crew was waiting at the ghât; and in four days the party reached Rajmahal, a distance of ninety miles. Here the ex-Nawab determined to rest: and having found a deserted garden on the banks of the river in which were some empty buildings, landed; and, after having cooked some food, retired for the night. In the morning the fugitives were discovered by a native Priest, whose ears Siraju 'd daulah had caused to be cut off some months previous, and who reported his discovery to a brother of Mir J'afar's, residing at Rajmahal. A party was at once sent to seize the fallen Nawab, who was treated with every indignity and conveyed back a prisoner to the presence of Mir J'afar Khan, before whom he prostrated himself and in abject terror pleaded for his life. Siraju 'd daulah was given over to the custody of Mir J'afar's son Míran, "a youth not seventeen, cruel and barbarous;" who caused his prisoner to be confined in a distant chamber—"one of the vilest in the Palace"—where this boy sent some of his menial servants to murder him. The intrusion of these men convinced Siraju 'd daulah that he was doomed, and his terror threw him into an agony of lamentation; but, finding his cries of no avail, he yielded to despair; imploring;a few minutes' respite to make his ablutions and to pray. A pot of water chancing to be near at hand was thrown over him by one of the servants, and he was then immediately stabbed; the other assassins advancing and hacking him to pieces.

Next morning his mangled corpse was paraded through the streets of Murshedabad on an elephant; after which it was placed in a plain stone coffin and buried beside the late Nawab Ali Verdi Khan.

On the 25th of June the British force marched to Maidapore, whence Mr. Watts was dispatched with an escort of sepahis to salute the Nawab Mir J'afar Khan, and arrange for the payment of the large sums due to the British under the Calcutta treaty: but it was found that the treasury did not in specie and jewels contain more than sufficient to pay one-third of the amount. Arrangements were consequently entered into with Raja Dulab Ram and the Bankers of Murshedabad, by which one half of the amount due—£1,100,000—was arranged for in jewels and cash, and bills for the other moiety extending over three years were accepted.

29th June, 1757; These preliminaries having been satisfactorily completed Clive entered the capital, taking up his residence at the Palace Murad 29th, Bagh; from whence he proceeded in state to the Nawab's Palace, where he was received in the public audience-hall by Míran and the principal officers of state. Mir J'afar was then led by Clive to the throne, on which with some apparent diffidence he took his seat, saluted by all present as their Sovereign, and immediately afterwards proclaimed throughout the city and provinces.

The time had now arrived to inform Amichand of the deception which had been practised on him; and, seeing how great a wrong had been done him, more charity might have been displayed in the manner in which he was undeceived. He was simply informed, when the two treaties were produced, that the one shown by the Council in Calcutta was a forgery and a sham, and that he was to receive nothing. The shock on discovering that he had been duped was so great that Amichand fell in a fainting fit to the ground; softening of the brain soon afterwards supervened, and he died two years after in a state of imbecility.

During the remainder of 1757, 1st July to 31st December, the Bengal European Regiment was for the most part divided into separate commands. A portion of the battalion accompanied Major Eyre Coote in his fruitless pursuit of M. Law and his French followers; who finally taking refuge in Oude, were protected by the Nawab of that country. The detachment, after an arduous and hazardous march through an unknown and hostile country, returned to Murshedabad on the 14th September, and was stationed at the factory of Kassimbazar; whilst the rest of the Regiment was ordered down country to Chandernagore and Calcutta, where it remained for several months in quarters.

GENERAL REFERENCES—CHAPTER 3

Orme's Military Transactions in Hindustan.
Proceedings of the Bengal Council, 1767.
Stuart's History of Bengal.
Mill's British India.
Williams's Bengal Infantry.
Caraccioli's Life of Lord Clive.
East India Military Calendar.

Broome's Rise and Progress of the Bengal Army.
Malleson's Founders of the Indian Empire. (Clive.)
First Report, Select Committee, House of Commons, 1773
Malleson's Decisive Battles in India.
Amber's Rise and Progress.
The Seir Mutakherin. Calcutta Edition.
&c, &c.

CHAPTER 4

The Northern Circars

The disgraceful treaty which the Calcutta Council had concluded with Mir J'afar Khan was now producing a plentiful crop of its inevitable fruit.

1st September, 1758; There was a general feeling amongst the officers of the army that now, possessed of ample means, they were independent of the service, and this feeling frequently resulted in insubordination; whilst the European soldiers, with their pockets full of money, plunged into every description of debauchery and excess, destroying their health and thinning their ranks to such an extent that had it not been for the timely arrival of a large body of recruits from England, the troops at Calcutta and Chandernagore would have soon become totally inefficient.

In this unsatisfactory state of affairs orders were received at Calcutta for the return of H.M. 39th Regiment to England; but, as liberty had been granted to the officers and men to enter the Company's service, nearly all the detachment volunteered for the Bengal European Regiment; and Colonel Clive, about this time, finding it inadvisable to send back the detachments of the Bombay and Madras European Regiments, at their own request incorporated these also with the Bengal European Regiment.

This amalgamation was carried into effect on September 1st, 1758; and on the 29th of January, 1759, the two Companies which had been sent to Bengal from Bombay in 1756, were struck off the strength of their Regiment at that Presidency.[1] Of the officers so transferred, Lieutenants Carnac and Yorke, and Ensigns Donellan[2] and Broadbrook, of H.M. 39th Regiment, received a step of rank in the Company's service.

---

1. Regimental Records, 1st Bombay European Fusiliers, 1759.

Major Kilpatrick, who had been so intimately associated with the Bengal European Regiment since its formation at Fulta in 1756, had died in the previous October, and Clive was now seeking a field officer of judgement and decision to command the Regiment. Just at this time Captain Govin reported his arrival in Calcutta, having been sent from Bombay to take command of the detachment of his Regiment lately absorbed into the Bengal Europeans. This officer was known to Clive as possessing "a high military reputation," and as he was considerably senior to all the other captains, Clive promoted him to the rank of Major, and appointed him to the command of the Regiment.[3]

In stating that Major Govin was nominated to the above command some explanation is necessary; for he was at the same time appointed second in command of the Bengal army.

In 1758 the number of troops employed in the Bengal Presidency was so small that the officer second in command of the army held also the command of the European Regiment, receiving at the same time reports from all other troops. The native infantry had but 2 European officers to each battalion; such officers, selected from the roll of the European Regiment, were simply struck off duty; as an instance of this we may quote the case of Ensign John Matthews, who was commanding the 1st Native Infantry—which afterwards bore his name, Matthews ka pultun—when he was promoted to a Lieutenancy in the Bengal European Regiment, vice Moltimore, killed in action.

Major Govin's promotion to a Majority was considered by the other captains in the Regiment as a grievance; and, smarting under what, they held to be an injustice, they made a strong and not over-respectful remonstrance to Colonel Clive; who, believing that the ill-feeling towards the new Commanding officer was the result of insubordination, refused to countenance their remonstrance. Captains Grant, Rumbold, Cudmore, Armstrong, Keir, Granger, Muir, Campbell, and Carstairs forwarded their commissions to Clive, and requested permis-

---

2. (Previous page) Donellan was executed at Warwick, in 1781, for the supposed murder of his brother-in-law, Sir Theodosius Boughton. He was condemned on the evidence of his mother-in-law, who, through remorse, on her deathbed, confessed that she had administered the poison herself which had deprived her son of life, and declared Mr. Donellan to have been innocent.—Williams, p. 62.

3. Major Govin was re-transferred to the Bombay Presidency in 1761, when he was appointed to the Command of the Bombay European Regiment.

sion, to resign the service, which request was complied with; Clive reporting the circumstances to the council in the following letter:

> The remonstrating captains have either wilfully or ignorantly misrepresented the nature of superseding. An officer cannot be said to be superseded unless one of inferior rank in the same corps be put over his head. Now I can safely aver that I never during the whole of my command, have done so by any officer except in the case of Captain-Lieutenant Wagoner to whom I refused giving a vacant company, as I did not think him deserving thereof. The incorporation of the troops having been determined on as a necessary measure the several officers of the three different establishments being now united were of course to take rank according to the date of their different commissions in the same manner as the officers of the different corps in Her Majesty's Service when they happen to meet. Now as Captain Govin had been ordered here by the Presidency of Bombay to take command of their detachment without their knowing that such incorporation was to take place, it is evident they could have no design of injuring the officers of this establishment, as has been injuriously represented; and therefore to have sent him back after having been so formally ordered here, would have been the highest indignity to the Council of Bombay, as well as to the gentleman himself; and, as he remained here, he had an undoubted right to take that rank which the seniority of the commission gave him. The truth of the matter is, that most of the gentlemen who have been so violent in their remonstrances were grown sufficiently rich in your service to be desirous of any pretence of quitting it. They will prove however no great loss, as no services can be expected from men who have so little spirit and gratitude as to resign their commissions at this critical time and on ill-grounded pretences.

Captains Muir, Carstairs, and Campbell having expressed their regret, their resignations were cancelled, and they were restored to the service, but not without loss of rank.

It is now necessary to turn our attention to events taking place in the Northern Circars. This country lies to the south of Bengal, and is now called the "Territory of the Nizam"; extending 470 miles along the sea-coast in the direction of Madras, and inland to a depth varying from 30 to 100 miles.

The country known as the Northern Circars was in 1758 completely controlled by the French, who, under their General, Count de Bussy, had in 1753 subdued the country; dictating his own terms to the Subahdar, and making the French practically the independent Governors of the Province. Bussy, at all times jealous of the English settlers, had expelled them from this territory.

In April, 1758, the French General, Count Lally, assumed command at Pondicherry, the chief seat of the French Government in India. Lally, contemplating war against Tanjore, directed Bussy, with all his available force in the Northern Circars, to join him without delay, and to make over the command of his province to the Marquis de Conflans—who was a man deficient in the qualities requisite for governing a country which had taxed all the energies of Bussy himself.

Count Lally was unsuccessful, and news soon reached the provinces of which Conflans had been appointed Governor that Lally had been compelled to make an inglorious retreat.

Anandraz Gajapati, the son of the Subahdar from whom the government had been wrested by the French, had for some time been heading a conspiracy for their overthrow, and he now felt that the time had arrived to act decisively. Haiderabad, the capital city, had been denuded of French troops, and certain measures which Conflans had dictated had rendered the French supervision irksome to the people. Anandraz, having assembled an army of 3000 men, on September 2nd, 1758, captured the French settlement of Vishakpatanam, took the French Chief prisoner, plundered the factory, and hauled down the French flag. Knowing that war existed between the French and English in Europe, and hoping to obtain assistance from the latter, he hoisted the British flag, and at once dispatched a messenger to the Council at Calcutta informing them what he had done. He pointed out that his countrymen were only anxious to rid themselves of the French control, and that with the assistance of a small English force he would drive the enemy from his country.

The council did not look with favour on Anandraz's proposals, but Clive at once saw the advantages to be derived by a British expedition to the Northern Circars, and determined to overcome all difficulties. Seeing that the state of affairs at Murshedabad was unsatisfactory, and Bengal threatened with an invasion by the son of the Emperor of Delhie, to denude the Presidency of European troops was attended with risk, but the importance of the undertaking, to Clive's mind, outweighed all objections. One thing was certain—Clive could not absent himself, and must therefore appoint some other officer to command the expedition whilst he watched affairs in Bengal.

Lieutenant-Colonel Forde, formerly of H.M. 39th Regiment,, had lately been sent from Madras to command the Company's troops in Bengal; and Clive, entertaining the highest opinion of his judgement, coolness, and capacity, entrusted to him the military command of the expedition; Mr. Johnstone being appointed by the council to act as political agent.

The troops with Forde comprised 5 companies of the Bengal European Regiment under Captain Adnet,[4] with Captains Christian Fischer, Martin, Yorke, and Moltimore, and Captain-Lieutenant Patrick Moran;[5] one company of European artillery, with 100 lascars, and 6 field-pieces, and 2000 sepahis.

This force embarked on the 12th October, reaching on the 20th the Port of Vishakpatanam, where it was augmented by Anandraz with 5000 followers—for the most part undrilled and unarmed—and 40 Europeans of different nationalities, with 4 field-pieces, under an adventurer named Bristol; these latter forming Anandraz's main strength.

It was anticipated that General Conflans would have resented the capture of Vishakpatanam before the arrival of our troops, but he was timidly awaiting reinforcements in the strong fortress of Mussulipatam with a force of 500 French soldiers, 6000 disciplined and well-armed sepahis, and a brigade of artillery, with 30 guns, and about 500 native cavalry.[6]

On the 15th October, Mr. Andrews, who had been dispatched from Madras to arrange terms, concluded the following treaty with Anandraz:

1.—The Raja to pay the extra expenses of the British army during the time it should be employed—£5000 a month—and pay the officers double batta—£600 a month—these sums being payable as soon as the Raja should be put in possession of the town of Rajamundri.

2.—The Raja to be possessed of all the inland territory belonging

---

4. Captain Adnet was one of those officers who had been lately transferred from the Madras to the Bengal European Regiment.
5. Captain Moran was one of the very few prisoners who had escaped the horrors of the Black Hole in 1756.
6. The troops under his (Conflans') command "were the most seasoned and the best disciplined of all those who served the French company in Southern India. They were the men before whom the famed Mahratta cavalry had been scattered, and who, but a short time before, had forced their way through the opposing hosts to relieve Bussey at Hydrabad."—Malleson's History of the French in India, page 531.

to the country powers, but the Company to retain all the sea-coast from Vizagapatam to Musulipatam, with the several towns and ports on that line.

3.—No treaty for the subsequent disposal or restitution. whether of the Raja's or the Company's possessions, to be-made without the consent of both parties.

4.—All plunder and prize to be equally divided.

After considerable difficulty carriage was provided, and Colonel Forde commenced his march; joining the Raja's force on December 1st, and on the 3rd coming within view of the French army, entrenched near the fort of Peddapore—a position well chosen and commanding the high road. On the 6th Forde took possession of an eminence called Chambol also commanding the high road, and here he awaited an attack, which on account of the enemy's superior strength he was hourly expecting. Having waited two days and the enemy not moving, Forde determined to force him into action next morning by threatening his rear. In the meantime a deserter from the Bengal European Battalion probably one of the French prisoners[7] who had joined the Regiment after the battle of Chandernagore persuaded Conflans that our army was composed mostly of untrained recruits; so, acting on this impression, Conflans sent a party of French soldiers with six light guns to seize a height which Forde had neglected to occupy, and which overlooked the British camp. Conflans intended to occupy this height under cover of the darkness on the night of the 8th December, and early on the following morning to open fire on the British camp.

Both the British and French Commanders had ordered the contemplated movements to take place on the same morning—each ignorant of the other's intention.

Colonel Forde had arranged with Anandraz that their united force should quietly quit their ground at 4 a.m., and move along the main road to Condore in rear of the enemy's camp. The result of these manoeuvres would be that, when the French fire should be opened at daybreak, 9th December, Conflans would find that the English camp had been struck and his enemy gone. Anandraz, thinking however that 9 o'clock would do for the march as well as the inconvenient hour of 4 a.m., had not moved off the ground when the enemy suddenly opened fire, which so accelerated his movements that they were turned into a

---

7. Many of the French prisoners taken at Chandernagore were serving in the ranks of the Bengal European Regiment during this campaign.

flight. Conflans, still believing that the British force consisted only of raw recruits, naturally concluded that they had run away and therefore determined to pursue them and gain what he anticipated would be an easy victory. The Raja, thoroughly alarmed, had dispatched several horsemen to beg Forde to return as the enemy were pursuing him; but Forde, who had marched as planned, was far on his road before the messengers overtook him. The fugitives, however, now not far behind, soon joined Forde, the united forces proceeding to Condore.

As soon as the British force had occupied Condore, the enemy appeared 1000 yards in their rear moving towards Forde's left flank. Orders were issued to prepare for immediate action. Forde placed the Raja's panic-stricken troops on his right and left flanks; next to them his native infantry; and in the centre the Bengal European Battalion, with whom were Bristol's artillery; the guns being placed on the right and left of the European battalion. The British now advanced to meet the enemy, who opening fire, Forde halted, his centre being covered by a field of corn which completely concealed the Europeans from view. The sepahis on either flank—for Anandraz's troops had by this time decamped and concealed themselves in a hollow—were in full sight of the enemy. Now the native regiments which accompanied the British force had, by Clive's order, been clothed in red; the French, seeing the red coats, were naturally under the impression that the European soldiers had been placed on the flanks and the sepahis— who usually wore white clothing—in the centre. Under this delusion, Conflans advanced his French Europeans towards our 2nd Native Battalion; Forde, who at once saw the enemy were at fault, rode up to the 2nd Native Battalion to encourage them, but when these found themselves out-flanked, and pitted against the French Europeans, they retired in the direction of Chambole.

The French, now thinking they had put the British Europeans to flight, advanced rapidly, obliquing to their right, but in so doing became somewhat scattered; Forde grasped the opportunity, and directing the Bengal European Battalion to change front, took the French in flank, pouring a heavy musketry fire on their disordered companies as they came up opposite to the British line. Nearly half the French grenadier company of the battalion of India fell under our first volley. Taken completely by surprise the French hurried back to regain the cover of their guns which they had left in rear. The Bengal European Battalion, elated with their success, now vigorously pursued the enemy, charging in echelon of companies, left in front. Captain Adnet, who commanded the Regiment, was leading, and Captain Yorke with No. 4 Company was acting in reserve, to afford immediate assistance to any of our companies needing succour.

The French rallied at their guns and opened a hot grape fire on our advancing troops, Adnet being mortally wounded and several of our men falling; but the advance was nowhere checked, the men rushing on the enemy's guns, 13 of which they captured, and again put the enemy to flight.

In the meantime the 1st Native Battalion had been taking a leading part in the fight; attacked by the French native infantry, who vastly outnumbered them; but our sepahis held their ground with tenacity.

The French sepahis, seeing their European comrades in full flight and their guns captured, also fled, and our 1st Native Battalion rejoined the British Europeans. The 2nd Native Battalion, who had early in the day fled towards Chambole, now returned to the field and joined the British army. Forde determined to rapidly follow up his success, and make a dash at the enemy's camp. With this view he attempted to induce Anandraz to send some of his cavalry ahead, but they were all concealed in the hollow and refused to expose themselves to danger; Forde, therefore, pushed on single-handed without his guns, which, on account of the muddy state of the roads, were left in rear; our troops now sighted the French, who, with the intention of protecting their camp, had placed in position some heavy guns, and with these disputed the British advance.

Forde halted for his guns, deployed his infantry, and took up a position from which he could, at a moment's notice, make a dash on his enemy; this movement had just been completed when our artillery appeared; and the British commander ordered the leading company of the Bengal European Regiment to advance and deliver a volley; when the enemy fled, leaving his camp and remaining guns in our possession. The British army now hotly pursued the French, who, throwing away their arms, fled or gave themselves up as prisoners of war.

The loss of the French was 6 officers and 80 men killed or mortally wounded, and 6 officers and 70 men made prisoners or wounded; all these belonging to the French European battalion of India; 32 brass cannon, 50 tumbrils and other carriages, 7 mortars, 3000 draught bullocks, and all the camp equipage fell into our hands. Of the British, Captain Adnet and 15 men of the Bengal European Regiment were killed, 4 officers and 30 men wounded, amongst the latter Mr. Johnson—political Officer—serving as a volunteer with the Grenadier

Company of the Bengal Europeans; and about 100 men of the Bengal native infantry were killed or wounded.

Captain-Lieutenant Oswald was promoted to a Company in the Bengal European Regiment, vice Captain Adnet killed, and Ensign John Nollikins was advanced to a Lieutenancy.

The Battle of Condore[8] is justly ranked by Colonel Malleson amongst "the Decisive Battles of India," for it was a battle between the English and French for supremacy in India.

The Hindus, the prehistoric owners of the Indian soil, are, and ever have been, a subservient race: mild, faithful, and obedient, but unfitted physically to govern or command. The Mahomedans had conquered the Hindus, and reigned over the land until the Portuguese, the Dutch, the Danes, the English, and the French appeared upon the scene as rivals. The Portuguese, the Dutch, and the Danes were few in number, and, although they at one time held considerable possessions in India, were soon eclipsed by the English and the French, who stood face to face, aspirants for the supreme power. These nations could not both govern India; the weaker must succumb absolutely. In Europe a peace would be a matter of treaty, but in India one of the rivals must retire, and the conqueror remain supreme. Condore was one of the test battles which declared victory to be in the ascendant for the British; on account of their superior generalship, and the coinage and perseverance of their troops.

For this ascendancy England is indebted, on this occasion, to Forde's generalship, and to the fortitude, endurance, and valour of the Bengal European Regiment—the only British Regiment employed on this campaign.

Colonel Forde's success was due to the masterly precision of his strategic movements. Forde intended that the French commander should fall into the trap of hurling his Europeans at our red-coated sepahis, whilst the Bengal Europeans were lying in wait to drop down on their hostile flank. Forde knew that his native battalion could not hold its own against the French Europeans, and that, retreating, it would be pursued by the French cavalry, thus leaving the Bengal Europeans to measure its strength against the French European battalion alone; that the former would be the victors he had no doubt, seeing that the French regiment would be taken at a complete disadvantage.

Condore formed only a part—an essential one it is true—of our brilliant successes in the Northern Circars; and, considered politically,

---

8. For remarks on the decoration Condore see Appendix A.

it marked the first step in the decline of French power in India as opposed to that of the British.

The cavalry under Anandraz were employed as scouts; and our 1st Battalion of Sepahis was dispatched in pursuit of the enemy, followed by the rest of the native infantry; Forde coming last with the Bengal European Regiment and Bristol's artillery. Our advanced force reached Rajamundri on the morning of 10th December and occupied the town; the French having vacated it on our approach.

Several pieces of artillery and a large quantity of ammunition, as well as many hundreds of bullocks, were found in the fort; these were reserved as prize—under the terms of the treaty with Anandraz. On the same day that our troops entered Rajamundri a party of the French fugitives were seen crossing the river with a quantity of stores, 4 field-pieces, and a howitzer, which they were landing on the opposite bank.

No time was lost in dispatching a party in pursuit of the fugitives. Under cover of the fort guns, lately captured from the enemy, boats were manned and sent across the river, on seeing which the French, completely demoralised, left their guns and stores on the bank an easy prey to the British.

11th December, Forde was now anxious to push on as quickly as possible to Mussulipatam—the principal fortress and town in the Northern Circars—where it was evident the French army would attempt to make a desperate resistance, and gain time for the arrival of reinforcements.

General Conflans had not waited the result of the battle of Condore. As soon as he found he had been outwitted by Forde he hurried from the field towards Rajamundri, protected by a body of French cavalry and artillery with 4 field-guns, and next morning, December 12th, he reached the fortress of Mussulipatam, instructing, en route, all his outpost commanders to follow him as quickly as possible.

Forde was unable to pursue, his treasure being completely exhausted. Six thousand pounds only had been brought in his treasure-chest from Bengal, as arrangements had been made with Anandraz that he should supply his proportion of the expenses of the campaign immediately after the capture of Rajamundri. Of the £6000, £2000 had already been lent by Forde to Anandraz for his current expenses. This chief's crafty policy became now apparent. Anandraz wished to drive the French from his territories, but being unequal to the task, he induced the English, under false pretences, to undertake the hazardous work, hoping afterwards to starve out the victors and derive the benefit of their conquests for himself.

Forde was waiting at Rajamundri for the funds which Anandraz had promised, and were now due under the treaty; but Anandraz sent messengers saying he was still tending his wounded and performing funeral services over his dead; so Forde, hoping against hope that the wily native would be shamed into fulfilling his part of the treaty, crossed the Godaveri.

Our commander was eager to follow up his victory before the French should have time to recover their defeat or obtain reinforcements from Pondicherry; but the Raja neither moved nor sent funds; so Forde, much to his disgust, was obliged on the 26th December to recross the river; upon which, Anandraz, thinking that Forde was returning to punish him for his perfidy, fled with his troops to the hills, where they concealed themselves.

The dilemma was serious; for the French had for some time been besieging Madras, bringing the credit of the British to a low ebb in the provinces, and Forde, without money, was unable to prosecute his war. He, therefore, left a small force to protect Rajamundri and marched to a place called Peddapore, about 10 miles from Condore, and there entrenched himself.

On hearing the state of affairs with Forde, Mr. Andrews, who had been sent from Madras to arrange terms with the Raja, came to Forde's assistance, lending him £2000, and then proceeding to Anandraz's hiding-place, which he reached on 15th January, 1759.

The Raja ignored the former treaty—which he said he had signed under a misapprehension—and Mr. Andrews was constrained to make a supplementary treaty by which Anandraz agreed "that whatever sums the Rajah should furnish should be considered as a loan, and that the revenues of all the districts south-west of Godaveri which might be reduced should be equally divided between the East India Company and the Rajah." This arrangement completed, Anandraz marched to join Forde's camp, having agreed to assist the British in their attack on Mussulipatam; at the same time paying on account £600, and giving bills for £6000 more, payable in 10 days. Preparations were now made for a general advance; Bristol, with his European artillerymen and a portion of the Rajah's troops, being left in command of the fort of Rajamundri, where a depot was formed for our stores, sick, and wounded.

Elur, a town nearly midway between Rajamundri and Mussulipatam, was reached on 6th February; the French soldiers who had garrisoned this place having been withdrawn by Conflans as he was retiring from Condore. Here Forde unwillingly halted for Anandraz, but the delay enabled him to detach a force to seize the French factory and town of Narsurpore, situated on an island in the Delta of the Godaveri.

On the approach of our troops the Narsurpore garrison of 100 French soldiers and 400 sepahis made their escape by water, and joined the French army of observation, under Du Rocher, composed of 200 Europeans and 2000 sepahis, encamped about 30 miles from Elur, and watching Forde's movements.

The British detachment captured several guns and a large quantity of stores at Narsurpore, after which it. returned to Elur, where it joined the headquarter camp of the British army.

On the 1st March Colonel Forde commenced his advance on Mussulipatam, Anandraz having by this time rejoined; the Zamindar of Narsurpore, a witness to our success, also joining Forde with 1500 men. On the 3rd the British army crossed the lake of Kolar, at this season little more than a swamp, and on the 6th arrived before the fortress of Mussulipatam, which stands on an inlet about 1½ miles from the sea. The south face of the fort, resting on this inlet, is upwards of 500 yards wide; rendering it practically unassailable. The three other faces of the fortress are surrounded by swamps, varying in depth from 3 to 18 feet. The shape of the fort was an irregular parallelogram, about 800 yards in length and 500 in breadth; and on the outline of the works were 11 bastions, connected by curtains, the whole surrounded by a broad wet-ditch. The town of Mussulipatam is about a mile-and-a-half from the fortress to the north-west, and connected with it by a causeway about 200 yards from the only gate leading into the fortress. This gate was defended by a ravelin and earthworks, further strengthened, by a wet-ditch all round. A range of sandhills extended on either side of the fortress for about a half-mile inland, and approached to within 800 yards of its walls, thus partially commanding the fortress, and affording good cover to an attacking army.

Colonel Forde with his main force occupied the sandhill on the-eastern face of the fort, on which he erected 3 batteries, one on the south-western angle which abutted on the sea, and near which our transports were at anchor with stores and ammunition; a second to the north, and a third in the centre, about 100 yards in rear of the other two. On the two flank batteries were mounted 24- and 18-pounders; and in the centre 13-, 10-, and 18-inch mortars. These works, commenced on the 7th, were not completed until the 25th of March. Whilst Forde was constructing his batteries he received

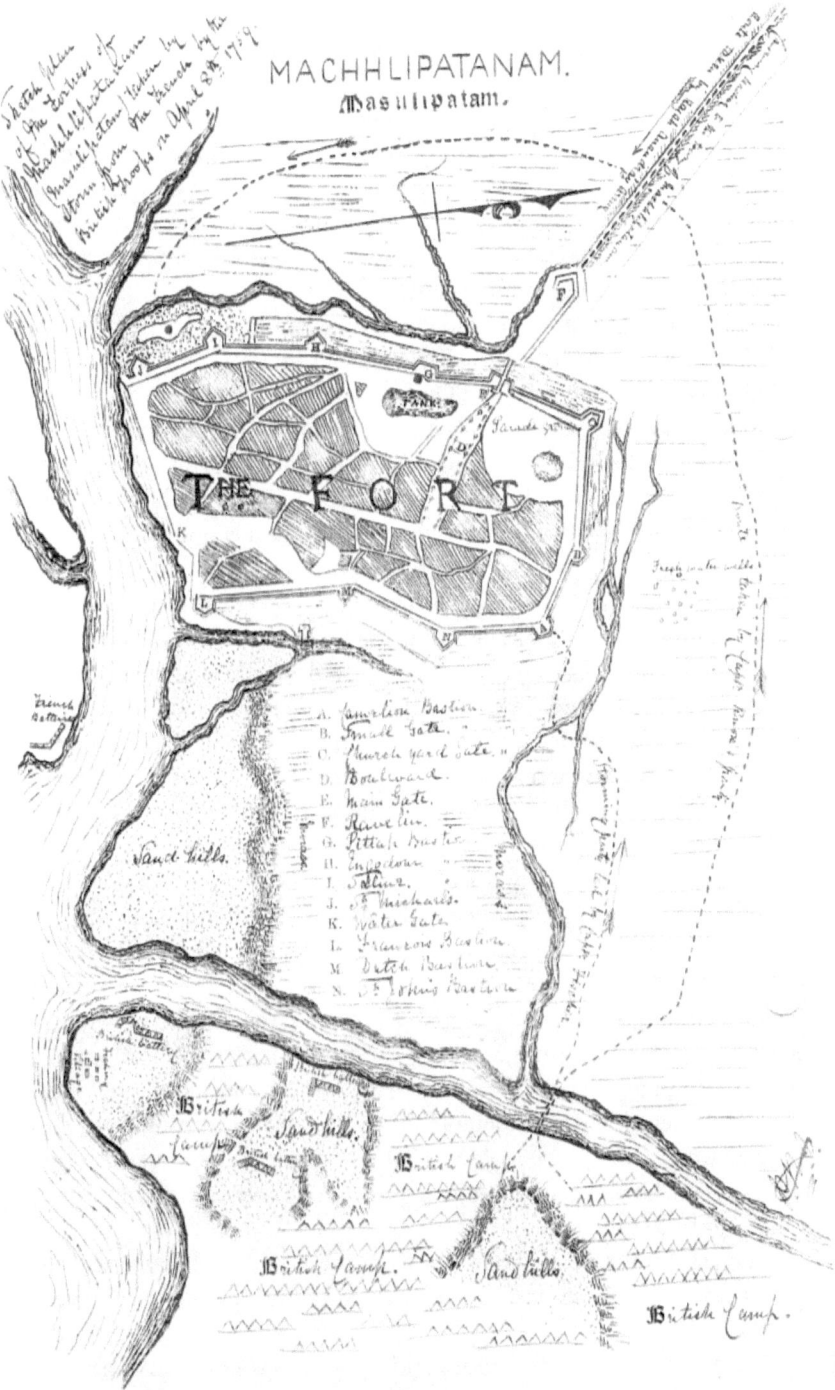

information that the French Army of Observation under Du Rocher was threatening Rajamundri,. where money and much-needed supplies had arrived.

It will be remembered that Rajamundri had been left under the charge of Bristol; who had found that with the small force at his disposal it would be injudicious to attempt a defence. He therefore sent off the sick and treasure—the former to, Vishakpatanam, and the latter to the Dutch factory at Kokanara—vacating Rajamundri, when it was immediately occupied by the French.

This movement, however judicious, involved not only the occupation by the enemy of Rajamundri, but the cutting of the British communication with their base; and Du Rocher now proceeded to threaten Anandraz's territories. This so alarmed our Ally that he refused to supply Forde with further funds; and, indeed, so frightened was he at the aspect of affairs that he actually left the British camp with all his followers and marched to protect his own dominions. But this was not all. Conflans, feeling perfectly secure in his fortified position, now only needed a powerful ally to attack the besiegers in rear, and therefore placed himself in communication with Salabut Jung, the Subahdar of the Deccan, asking assistance. Conflans's request was so readily acceded to that Salabut Jung immediately marched to the relief of the beleaguered French garrison with an army of 35,000 men, having previously sent his commands to the Raja Anandraz and to the Zamindar of Narsurpore to join him at once with all the troops at their disposal.

The beleaguering force was now in great peril, entirely due to the duplicity and want of courage of Anandraz. Had Forde been enabled to follow up his success immediately after the battle of Condore he would have, met with feeble resistance when he reached the fortress of Mussulipatam; but the delay had enabled Conflans to materially strengthen his position and collect his troops, so that he had now at his disposal a larger and stronger force than the besiegers. Notwithstanding these disadvantages the British kept up a continuous fire from their batteries, doing considerable injury to the fortifications; but the enemy were usually able to repair at night the damage of the day; our mortars, however, destroying and setting on five several important buildings in the fortress.

Such was the state of affairs when, on the 27th March, information was received that Salabut Jung had arrived within three days' journey of Mussulipatam.

But Forde's cup of difficulties and dangers was not yet full, for an incident now occurred which to a weaker mind would have probably proved fatal. Dissatisfaction had been showing itself amongst the troops, on account of their not having received their prize-money. It was perfectly true that the prize-money had been retained by Forde; and, moreover, the soldiers had a grievance, in that all the prize was, by usage, the sole property of the captors, whilst the Company had ruled that a moiety was to be reserved for the Government.

It was under these circumstances that the troops determined to make a stand for what they considered their just rights. Now Forde was not a communicative man, and had not made known to the soldiers the discouraging intelligence that he was hard pressed for money with which to supply their daily rations; that he and all the officers had given up their private money to buy food for the troops; and that, finally, the prize-money had been borrowed from the treasure-chest to supply the army with the necessaries of life. The dissatisfaction, however, broke into open mutiny; the Europeans of the force threatening to march away if their demands were not conceded.

Forde knew that the men had a grievance, and was prepared to acknowledge it; so, telling them to nominate a certain number of deputies to represent their grievances, he met them with much tact and judgement, and treated them with consideration and kindness. He made them acquainted for the first time with, the true position; and told them that money was on its way from Bengal, and that as soon as it should arrive the arrears of pay and prize-money should be distributed; at the same time assuring them that he would recommend to the Government that it should relinquish its moiety of the prize in consideration of the dangers, difficulties, and privations the troops had so loyally endured.

The men, more than satisfied, were delighted; and the siege was prosecuted with increased ardour.

28th March-1st April, 1759; But whilst Forde's master mind had been employed in overcoming what foreboded a serious disaster, he had dispatched Mr. Johnson to Anandraz—now en route to his own territories—to point out to him that he was exposing himself to great danger by separating himself from his alliance with the British. He could not, observed Forde, hope to escape from the clutches of both Salabut Jung and Du Rocher, but, returning to his allegiance and joining in the attack on Mussulipatam, he would, as soon as the fortress was reduced, have all the countenance and support of the British. Anandraz, more frightened at Forde's alternative than at the prospect of Du Rocher attacking his territories, returned; and under instructions received from Forde occupied the town of Mussulipatam, now entirely denuded of the enemy's troops.

Forde's next move was to place himself in communication with Salabut Jung, not with any hope of gaining him over, but simply to delay his march, so that he could deliver his assault before Salabut could arrive; and with this view he proposed that Salabut Jung should consent to receive a British envoy at his camp in order that he might be made acquainted with Forde's proposals. This Salabut accepted, informing Forde that he would remain at Baizwárá until the envoy arrived.

Forde was now determined to make his assault without delay; the more so, as he had just been informed that the ammunition for his heavy guns would not last more than two days.

The plan of attack was as follows:—During the whole of the 7th April Forde's batteries were to pour a continuous fire on the fortifications, in the hope that they would effect some breaches by which our troops could assault; he would then carry the fortress by storm. But, to mislead the enemy as to the real point of attack, and to prevent him from making repairs, our fire was to be directed equally against all the bastions. Anandraz's force was ordered to attack the entrenchments at the end of the causeway nearest to the fort, not in the hope that they would be able to storm the gate, but that they would employ the enemy in that direction.

Forde resolved to direct his main assault on the north-east bastion, A, and at the same time to make a demonstration against the south-west angle of the fort, J. For this latter purpose, Captain Knox was to be sent with a strong body of red-coated sepahis, who were, whilst making what was intended as a feint only, to effect an entrance if practicable. There was a deep swamp round this angle of the fort which was supposed to be impassable; but Forde had ascertained that at the ebb tide, due about midnight, a passage could be effected. If, therefore, Knox could pass the swamp unperceived he might find this part of the enemy's position unprotected, and effect an easy entrance. The portion of the British army to make the main attack—on which the success or failure of the enterprise depended—was formed into three divisions under Captain Callender[9] and consisted of 312 men of the Bengal European Regiment,

---

9. Captain Callender was an Officer of the Madras army who had been sent to the Northern Circars by the Madras Council with orders to assume military command should the Bengal troops succeed in driving the French from the Province. It appears that the Madras Government were fearful lest the Northern Circars should be annexed "by the gentlemen of Fort William" to the Bengal Presidency.

30 artillerymen, 30 sailors, and 700 sepahis; of the three divisions No I was composed of the grenadier company of the Bengal Europeans, and the grenadier companies of the sepahis battalions with some artillery, Captain Fischer commanding ; No. 2 Division consisted of the other 4 companies of the Bengal Europeans, and 50 sailors under Captain Yorke; No. 3 Division being formed from the remainder of the sepahis battalions, under Captain Maclean.

The various parties were all under arms at 10 p.m. on the 7th April, and as some extra time would be required by Captain Knox to effect this passage across the swamp, he was directed to start somewhat earlier than the storming party and to maintain absolute silence.

Colonel Forde ordered that the grand assault should be made at midnight, and each commander was to commence operations when he should hear the big gong of the French fortress strike twelve o'clock.

The main attacking party was drawn up in readiness to march, but was delayed on account of the incomprehensible absence of their Commander, Captain Callender, who was nowhere to be found ; and, consequently, Captain Fischer was appointed to command the main attack. All was now ready when, in the stillness of the night, the big gong tolled out the expected signal.

Captain Knox was now heard to open fire towards the south-west corner of the fort, opposite the bastions, I and J, and Anandraz, with his troops, immediately rushed along the causeway firing in all directions and making a terrible noise, which speedily attracted the attention of the garrison, many of whom rushed to defend the entrance gate, F.

The absence of Captain Callender caused some slight delay, so that the centre division was not quite up to time. They had struggled manfully through the mud and water, but their progress was more impeded than aided by their haste; for they heard the firing ahead whilst thirsting to take their share in the assault. Captain Fischer's, the centre, division first reached the breach, A, and charged up the. incline; Captain Yorke's on his right and Captain Maclean's on his left, both replying to the fire which was being poured on the centre party from the bastions, N and B.

8th April, 1759; Fischer's party had now gained a footing in the breach, Yorke's following close behind; and together they found themselves on the ramparts, when, turning sharply to their left, they charged and captured the St. John's bastion, N, thus leaving the way clear for Maclean's sepahis, who, quickly following, scaled the walls. Fischer, elated with his success, charged along the ramparts on the north face of the fortress, and, capturing the two bastions, B and C, pushed towards the ravelin beyond the second bastion, C, commanding the causeway where Anandraz was making his demonstration. Fischer, looking over the ramparts, saw a large body of French Europeans in the ravelin, which was separated from the fortress by the large heavily-ironed main gate; he seized the opportunity, and, without a moment's hesitation, ran along the rampart and dropping down close to the gate, E, closed and fastened it on the inside, thereby completely isolating the French soldiers, now uselessly employed in awaiting Anandraz's expected attack.

Fischer, now returning towards the Churchyard bastion, C, was to his amazement confronted by Captain Callender; who,.. without in any way accounting for his absence, claimed the command by virtue of his seniority. This was accorded, and the party moved on; but immediately afterwards Captain Callender was struck by a bullet which killed him on the spot, and Captain Fischer again assumed the command.

We will now turn to Captain Yorke's No. 2 Division, which, taking the direction of the south or river face of the fort, with the intention of sweeping along the ramparts on the east face; captured the St. John's and Dutch bastions, N and M, at the point of the bayonet. Captain Moran, accompanying Yorke's division, secured a light field-piece, near the Dutch bastion, M, which was now brought to bear with terrible effect on the enemy, crowding the ramparts in front. Yorke had not proceeded far when he, observing a body of French soldiers advancing towards him along a road below the ramparts, descended with a few of his men, and bravely seizing the French officer in command, told him the fortress had fallen and peremptorily ordered the party to surrender. They, obeying without resistance, were disarmed and sent under escort to the Camelion battery, A, which had been captured early in the assault. Yorke now continued to move along the lower road, where he had captured the French party, under considerable annoyance from one of the batteries above, from which a hot fire was poured on the British below. Yorke turned to attack them, when they gave a final volley of musketry and, immediately afterwards surrendering as prisoners of war, were disarmed and sent to join their fellow prisoners in the Camelion battery. Full of excitement at his success, Yorke pushed on to the Francois battery, L, at the south-east angle of the fort; but, as he approached, some of his men, passing near an "expense" magazine, raised a cry that there was a mine under their feet. The cry quickly attracted the attention of the whole party, who, calling out "a mine, a mine," fled in the opposite direction along the ramparts. Yorke was furious at seeing that the success of his last movement was placed in peril through this folly, which was rapidly developing into a panic, rushed with his officers after his men, and speedily overtaking some of those who had served with him in H.M. 39th, succeeded in persuading them that it was a false alarm. The party hereupon formed up and charged the bastion, L, Yorke leading, with a drummer on each side playing the grenadier march. But the delay had enabled the defenders to place a field-piece in position; and when the party were within a few yards of the bastion a charge of grape was poured on them, which killed the two drummer boys and several of our men, wounding many others, including Yorke, shot through both thighs. Yorke's party now retreated, carrying their wounded to the Camelion bastion.

Conflans during this time was at the magazine, protected by the grenadier company of the French European battalion; and made confusion more confounded by issuing contradictory orders, based on the exaggerated reports which were constantly reaching him. He appears to have completely lost his head, and given himself up to despair; and now receiving a report from his principal officers that all his batteries had been captured, sent an officer to Forde, who was giving his orders from the St. John's battery, offering to capitulate on honourable terms.

When this message was received Forde had just learnt that his ammunition was nearly expended, but he, nevertheless, replied that he would make no terms; the surrender must be absolute and at discretion, and if the garrison continued to offer resistance he would put them to the sword. The result was that Conflans surrendered the fortress unconditionally. The firing now ceased, and at daybreak the English collected their prisoners on the parade-ground, and placing them under a guard of 100 Europeans and 200 sepahis, with 2 field-pieces, the British flag was hoisted on the staff, and the fortress and town of Mussulipatam passed over, by conquest, on the morning of the 8th April. 1759, to the East India Company.[10]

---

10. Colonel Broome, in his Rise and Progress of the Bengal Army p. 241, says: When the whole attendant circumstances are considered—the numerical superiority of the enemy, the strength of the place, and the disadvantages under which the English force was labouring, as also the great importance of the conquest—few achievements on Indian record can be compared with this brilliant affair, which is surely deserving of commemoration. And it is to be hoped that the corps, still in existence, which were employed in that assault may, even at this late date, receive the distinction so justly due, and be permitted to emblazon the word Mussulipatam on their colours and appointments. These corps are the Royal Artillery, the 1st Bengal European Fusiliers, and the 1st Regiment of Bengal Native Infantry.

The British army took prisoners 91 European officers and civil servants of the French company; 409 European soldiers; and 2537 French sepahis. The French returns showed that 113 French European soldiers were killed, and that the British captured 120 pieces of heavy ordnance.

Of the Bengal European Regiment, Captain Moltimore and one Lieutenant—name unknown—were killed; Captain Yorke was severely wounded; and Captain Callender of the Madras Service—doing duty—was killed. The total loss of the British was 22 Europeans killed and 62 wounded; and of the sepahis, 50 killed and 150 wounded.

Lieutenant Thomas Robertson was promoted to a company, vice Moltimore, and Ensign John Matthews, and Francis Cozens to the two vacant Lieutenancies in the Regiment. Five Districts held to be amongst the most valuable possessions of France in the East Indies, with an annual revenue of £400,000, were wrenched from her and henceforward became possessions of the East India Company.

Salabut Jung, six days after the capture of Mussulipatam, signed a treaty conferring on the captors the whole Circar of Mussulipatam with eight districts, as well as the Circar of Nizampatanam and the districts of Kondavid and Wakalmannar. Ultimately the Emperor of Delhie, at the instance of Clive, granted the whole of the territory to Nizam Ali (the successor of Salabut Jung), since which time it has been known as "The Territory of the Nizam," but the right of the English to these districts has never been questioned.

Colonel Forde now gladly dispensed with the services of Anandraz and his troops; but it is only just to record that the soldiers of his army did the work appointed to them during the siege and capture of Mussulipatam satisfactorily, several of his soldiers being wounded in maintaining their position on the causeway which Forde had instructed them to hold.

It must not be forgotten that the success of this campaign was in a great measure due to Clive, who so truly estimated the value of the acquisition that he did not hesitate to accept the responsibility of overruling the decision of his council and undertaking the defence of the Bengal provinces with so few troops at his disposal. Clive also truly estimated the value of Colonel Forde's[10] soldier-like qualities, but had

---

10. On 14th October, 1764, Lord Clive addressed the Chairman of the Court of Directors, in the following words: Pray do not forget. Forde, who is a brave, meritorious, and honest Officer. He was offered a Jaghire by the Subah of the Deccan, but declined taking it upon terms contrary to the interest of the Company.

even Forde been pitted against a French commander of skill and courage, he would hardly have attempted the siege of Mussulipatam with the small force at his disposal, but he rightly calculated on the inefficiency of the French commander, whose only ability was shown in his capacity for securing his personal safety. Fully admitting Conflans's incompetence, still Colonel Forde, as Commander of the little besieging force in the Northern Circars, must ever rank as one of the first of English commanders.

After the capture of the fortress of Mussulipatam the British army in the Northern Circars was broken up, and the right wing of the Bengal European "Regiment returned to its own Presidency.

GENERAL REFERENCES—CHAPTER 4

Malleson's Decisive Battles of India.
Proceedings of the Bengal Council, 1758-59.
Mill's British India.
Malleson's History of the French in India.
Broome's History of the Bengal Army.
Williams's Bengal Infantry.
Amber's Rise and Progress of British Power in India.
East India Calendar.
&c., &c.

CHAPTER 5

Fighting the Dutch

During February, 1759, Clive received an earnest appeal from the Nawab Mir J'afar for British advice, assistance, and troops.

The Shah-zada—Shah Alám—who had rebelled against his father, Alám Ghir Sain, the Emperor of Hindustan, succeeded in collecting a numerous army; at the head of which he was marching with the avowed intention of invading the territories of the Nawab Mir J'afar. Shah Alám had offered Clive large rewards for the countenance and support of the British in his undertaking; but was informed that any attempt to set at defiance the authority of the Emperor, or any attack on the territories of our ally, Mir J'afar, would be resented by our Government. Copies of this correspondence were forwarded to the Nawab Mir J'afar, who was informed that we were preparing to march to his assistance; and to this end, Clive, with all his available force, left Calcutta on the 25th February. He took with him the five companies of the Bengal European Regiment left at Calcutta and Chandernagore when the right wing of the Regiment went to the war in the Northern Circars, 100 European artillery, and 2500 sepahis.

Calcutta and Chandernagore were now garrisoned by the sick and recruits of the Bengal European Regiment, a few gunners, some lately-raised sepahi levies and the Calcutta militia and volunteers

The British force, on reaching Murshedabad on the 8th of March, was joined by the Nawab's army, under Mir J'afar's eldest son, Míran, and on the 9th of April the united forces arrived before Patna, to find that Shah Alám, who had been vigorously assaulting that city, had raised the siege on hearing of the near approach of Clive's army.

Shah Alám had been reinforced by M. Law and his Frenchmen, but his army, composed of men of different nationalities and conflicting interests, had become so demoralised, that Shah Alám, was forced to take refuge within the territories of the Raja of Bundelkund.

Clive, having repaired the defences of Patna, injured during-the late siege, now cleared the country of the remnants of Shah Alám's rebel army, and brought into subjection several petty chiefs in arms against the Nawab; returning before the end of April to Patna. Here he left a detachment under Captain Cochrane, composed of one company of the Bengal European Battalion; a detail of artillery with two field-pieces; and five companies of sepahis; and, retracing his steps, reached Calcutta with his main force early in June.

In reward for these services Clive received something more than expressions of gratitude; Mir J'afar presenting him with the Zamindari of those districts south of Calcutta which had previously been rented to the East India Company, and the income of which was £30,000 per annum. These rents were afterwards a subject of contention between Clive and the East India Company.

Notwithstanding the many advantages that the Nawab Mir J'afar had derived from his alliance with the English, he would gladly have thrown off the restraint which their protection imposed on his actions.

He had been compelled to draw so heavily on his own resources, as well as on those of his friends, that the latter were being alienated from him; whilst the trade of his country was being seriously prejudiced by the superior advantages which he had been forced to grant to his Calcutta patrons; and his revenues had been mortgaged to enable him to meet the claims constantly falling due under his treaties with the council. Clive had forced Mir J'afar to feel that the patronage of the British was essential to his very existence; a state of thraldom from which the Nawab would gladly have emancipated himself. But how was this to be effected? The French had been rendered powerless by the loss of their possessions at Chandernagore; the Dutch had not at any time been sufficiently powerful to render material assistance, and much of their trade, by reason of the many concessions compelled by the British, had passed out of their hands.

June-July, 1759; But the Dutch, though effete in Bengal, were powerful abroad; and their agent at Chinsurah had applied to the Dutch Governor of Batavia—the capital of the Dutch colonies in the East—to prepare a powerful armament, which, he represented, if landed in Bengal would enable them to wrest the paramount power from the British, and place it in their own hands.

This scheme had been secretly submitted to the Nawab, and as far back as November, 1758, there had been an understanding that it should be carried into effect as soon as practicable. Then came the threatened invasion by Shah Alám, when Mir J'afar was compelled to seek the assistance of the British to enable him to protect his menaced provinces; but now, this difficulty; overcome, the Nawab re-opened negotiations with the Dutch.

Clive had long suspected that Mir J'afar had entertained hostile propositions from the Dutch, and he was confirmed in his suspicions when in August a Dutch vessel with a number of Malay soldiers arrived in the river Hugli. Clive at once informed the Nawab and solicited instructions; when the latter prohibited the landing of the troops, and desired the Dutch Governor at Chinsurah to co-operate with the English forces and prevent the landing of any foreign soldiers whatever.

To allay suspicion, the Dutch Governor informed the Nawab, that the vessel causing such needless alarm had been driven into the river by stress of weather whilst on her way to Nagapatanam, and that she was merely taking on board supplies before proceeding on her voyage.

Notwithstanding these plausible assurances, Clive remained on the alert. He posted troops in the Fort on the river, with instructions to board all suspicious craft, and, if necessary, detain them. A few days after, a Dutch boat containing 18 Malay soldiers was captured at Charnock's Battery. Under Clive's orders the prisoners were returned to their ships which soon put to sea; but Clive was now fully convinced, not only that the Dutch intended to land troops, but that the Nawab was playing into their hands.

In October, 1759, Mir J'afar came to Calcutta, avowedly to pay his respects to Clive; but in reality to be near at hand, as the Dutch Governor had informed him that he was now prepared to strike.

During the Nawab's visit to Calcutta seven Dutch war vessels filled with troops arrived at the mouth of the river Hugh. There could now be no doubt of their hostile designs. The Nawab assumed an air of injured dignity, declaring his intention of driving the whole of the Dutch from the country, and for this avowed purpose proceeding with his camp in the direction of the Dutch settlement of Chinsurah; but halting on his road at a place called Kojah Wuzeed's Garden, he summoned the Dutch agents to wait upon him and receive his orders. The conference does not appear to have been of a hostile nature, for on the agents going through the form of promising that the ships of war should be sent away as soon as the season permitted, the Nawab granted them some coveted privileges previously denied, thus clearly proving that he bore no enmity towards them. But the Dutch ships, in place of taking their departure, moved further up the river, and landed some of their troops; whilst at the same time reliable information reached Calcutta that the Dutch agents were enlisting sepahis at Chinsurah, Kassimbazar, and Patna, with the connivance of the Nawab.

It was now evident that Mir J'afar was in league with the invaders, whose schemes to overthrow the power of the British in Bengal were transparent to the far-sighted Clive, who at once correctly surmised that the Dutch with their powerful squadron would attempt to force a passage up the river Hugli, land their troops, and march towards Chinsurah; all which eventuated as he foresaw. But the Dutch force had no field-guns; they therefore arranged with their countrymen at Chinsurah to attempt to supply the deficiency by effecting a junction with their main army at a given point en route. It was not anticipated that any serious opposition could be offered by the English; for the Dutch Europeans far out-numbered their enemy,.and the Malay soldiers, who formed an important part of the Dutch expedition, were believed to be vastly superior in courage and physique to our Bengal sepahis. These schemes Clive had to counteract, without causing umbrage at the Murshedabad Court.

November, 1759; The force on board the Dutch vessels moving up the river consisted of 700 European infantry and 800 Malays, all well trained and fully-equipped soldiers. At Chinsurah the Dutch had 150 European infantry and artillery and a number of sepahis, who, in the event of a British disaster, would be quickly augmented by a part, or even the whole, of the Nawab's army.

The English available force at or near Calcutta consisted of 330 men, being a part of the left wing of the Bengal European Regiment, and 1200 sepahis.

But, notwithstanding this disparity in the forces of the belligerents, Clive had full confidence in himself and his resources. He immediately sent orders to the commanders at our outposts and factories to march at once towards Calcutta with every available European soldier; knowing well that though there was little chance of these reinforcements arriving before a blow had been struck; in the event of disaster or defeat, he would have some reserves to fall back upon. The Calcutta Militia, numbering some 300 men, mostly Eurasians, were hastily embodied; and finally about 50 Volunteers, half of whom were formed into a troop of cavalry, joined the English army. In addition to these precautions, a fast-sailing vessel was dispatched to inform Admiral Cornish, cruising on the Arracan coast, of the state of affairs in Bengal; and urging him to sail up the river Hugli with all dispatch. Clive's next move was to prevent a junction between the Dutch troops on board ship and those at Chinsurah, for, until their forces should meet, their main army was without field-guns. But here a difficulty presented itself; England was not at war with the Dutch in Europe, so that, until the invaders should make some hostile demonstration, Clive was not in a position to act offensively. This difficulty was, however, soon removed by the Dutch themselves; who not only advanced towards Calcutta in defiance of remonstrances, but early in November sent a threatening letter to the council, demanding that the British should forego their claim to the right of search, and that Dutch vessels should at all times be allowed free progress up the Hugli river. To this communication the council replied:—"That the British, in retaining the right of search, were acting under the orders of the Emperor, and the instructions received from the Viceroy, Mir J'afar; they, therefore, had no power to grant the requests of the Dutch, but proffered their services as mediators between the Dutch and the Emperor and Viceroy." The skilled effrontery of this reply was worthy of Clive, and it appears to have had the effect which he most desired; for the Dutch commander, irritated to a degree, without deigning a reply, immediately attacked and captured several small British vessels lying off the Port of Fulta, and, tearing down the British colours, transferred the guns and stores to the Dutch ships. Clive now reported the circumstances of the outrage to the Nawab, requesting that the insult might be avenged without any native interference whatever.

Just about this time Colonel Forde and Captain Knox arrived in Bengal from the campaign in the Northern Circars. Colonel Forde was at once appointed by Clive to command all the Company's forces in the Presidency, and Captain Knox to command the Fort of Tanná and Charnock's Battery, both on the river Hugli. Forde, on assuming command, immediately possessed himself of the Dutch position at Barnagore, and, rapidly crossing the river with a small body of troops, marched, under orders from Clive, direct to Chandernagore, to prevent a junction between the Dutch troops on board their ships and those at Chinsurah.

During these events there were three Company's armed ships lying near the mouth of the Hugli, and Clive had instructed their commanders to weigh anchor and proceed towards Calcutta to protect the town; but they were unable to comply, the Dutch squadron having sailed past them. The British ships, however, weighed anchor and approached the enemy.

On the 22nd of November the Dutch landed all their troops on the right bank of the river, with the evident intention of forming a junction with their fellow countrymen at Chinsurah.

Now, the Dutch invading army having separated itself from its base on board ship, Clive determined to attempt to destroy the Dutch vessels before their army could reach its destination on shore; seeing at a glance that if he could prevent its junction with the troops at Chinsurah he would have the whole Dutch armament at his mercy.

This was our commander's general plan of action, and, as the invading army was unacquainted with the country, Clive felt that he would probably be able to take them at a disadvantage; and crush them on their march.

Knox was at this time ordered to join Forde, who had with him the main body of the British force, and Clive at once turned his attention to the destruction of the Dutch fleet.

As soon as the Dutch troops had landed; their war ships dropped down the river, casting anchor at Melancholy Point. In so doing they passed close to our three India men, under command of Commodore Wilson, who made as if he intended to push past them and sail towards Calcutta, but the Dutch Commodore told Captain Wilson that if he persisted he would fire on the British ships.

Wilson cast anchor, referring for instructions to Clive, who told him to demand from the Dutch Commander instant restitution of the British ships captured at Fulta, as well as a full apology for the insult offered to the British flag; and, in the event of a refusal, Wilson was instructed to attack the enemy. The demand was made as ordered; but the Dutch commodore treated it with scorn; so, on the 24th November, Wilson weighed anchor and approached his enemy.

Wilson had under his command only three armed merchant ships—the *Duke of Dorset*, commanded by Captain Forrester; the *Calcutta*, by Captain Wilson; the *Hardwicke*, by Captain Sampson—these ships carrying amongst them 90 guns.

The Dutch Squadron consisted of seven ships of war. The *Vlissingen*, 36; the *Bleiswyk*, 36; the *Welgeleegen*, 36;. the *Prince of Orange*, 36; the *Elizabeth Dorothea*, 26; the *Waereld*, 26; and the *Mossel*, 16. Thus the Dutch Squadron was in strength double that of the English, both in number of ships and guns.

Captain Forrester led the British attack, bringing his ship alongside the *Vlissingen*.

It was Commodore Wilson's intention to have brought up his other two ships to assist Captain Forrester, but, the wind having suddenly veered round, they were unable to reach him. Nevertheless, Forrester engaged his enemy with vigour, pouring on him a furious cannonade, which after a couple of hours compelled the *Vlissingen* to strike. Just at this time the *Hardwicke* and the *Calcutta* managed to come up, attacking two of the enemy's vessels; but they, declining the challenge, cut their cables and ran; whilst a third, in her hurry to escape, went ashore. Soon afterwards the remaining Dutch ships weighed anchor and retired from the fight.

The *Bleiswyk* got as far as Kalpi, when she was captured by the British men-of-war *Royal George* and *Oxford*, which opportunely arrived and secured their prize whilst they were hastening to the protection of Calcutta.

The victory was in every way complete. The battle had been fought with courage, skill, and judgement, and is undoubtedly "worthy to be compared with the best achievements of the British Navy."[1]

The *Duke of Dorset* had ninety shots in her hull, but her loss in killed and wounded was considerably less than that of the enemy.

Clive had thus succeeded in destroying the naval base of the invading army whilst it was marching to join its compatriots at Chinsurah, who, it will be remembered, were to effect a junction and supply the much-needed field artillery.

To effect this object the Dutch commander at Chinsurah determined to attempt to drive the British under Forde out of Chandernagore before their reinforcements, which had left Calcutta, could arrive.

On the evening of the 23rd November the Dutch force left Chinsurah and, without opposition, occupied a portion of the city of Chandernagore; but, next morning, Forde, who had been nursing his wrath all night, advanced against his enemy; and it is a strange coincidence that the belligerents met at the same hour that Commodore Wilson was attacking the Dutch fleet off Point Desolation.

The numbers engaged at Chandernagore were about equal; but Forde had the great advantage of fighting on his own ground, and moreover his soldiers were used to hard knocks, whereas very few of the Chinsurah troops had been previously engaged. The enemy were

---

1. Malleson.

quickly driven out of Chandernagore—with the loss of those guns which would have been of such vital importance to the main army—and thrust back into their own territory, crippled and disheartened. The same evening Captain Knox arrived with 220 men of the Bengal European Regiment, bringing Forde's force up to 320 European infantry; 80 European artillerymen, with 4 field-pieces; and 800 sepahis; as well as the small troop of European Volunteer cavalry, well mounted and full of confidence.

There were close at hand 150 of the Nawab's cavalry, sent from Murshedabad avowedly to assist Forde, but in reality they were merely spies, with orders to allow the belligerents to decide the battle unaided, and then unite with the victors.

Forde now learnt that the Dutch main army, under a French Officer, Colonel Roussel, was expected to reach Chinsurah early the next morning, so he sent off an express to Clive telling him that if he were empowered to attack the Dutch main army whilst en route he believed he could utterly destroy them. This note was delivered to Clive late at night as he was playing cards with his friends. Without leaving the table he wrote on the back of Forde's letter, "Dear Forde.—Fight them immediately, I will send you the Order of Council to-morrow."

This reply reached Forde early on the morning of the 25th November, when he immediately occupied a position selected with great care on the previous day.

In front of this position was a deep, broad, irregular ravine, forming a natural strong defence; an arid plain stretching out in front, across which the Dutch army must pass. On the British right was the village of Biderra, which Forde at once occupied; his left resting on a grove of trees in which he concealed his artillery, supported by the Volunteer cavalry, who had been instructed to take advantage of any confusion occasioned by our artillery fire.

The enemy had no cavalry, and had found it impossible to move their heavy ship guns across country. In European infantry the Dutch vastly out-numbered the British; but they were deficient in every other branch.

At 10 a.m. December 25th, the enemy emerged upon the plain, when they saw the British infantry drawn up to oppose their advance. Full of confidence they rapidly pressed forward to the attack, under a smart musketry fire; but their progress was checked by the ravine and a halt was ordered, causing confusion, of which Forde took advantage by pouring a murderous shower of grape from the grove of trees. The Dutch stood their ground manfully for a time; then, seeking cover but finding none, they were mowed down by sections. During the hesitation our Infantry charged down on the enemy, struggling in the ravine, and, aided by the small body of Volunteer cavalry, put them to flight; the Nawab's cavalry now joining in the pursuit.

The route soon became so complete that only 14 of the enemy succeeded in reaching their destination. The battle, which is described as having been "short, bloody, and decisive," did not last an hour, the Dutch leaving 120 Europeans and 200 Malays killed, and 300 wounded, whilst Colonel Roussel, 14 officers, 350 Europeans and 200 Malays were made prisoners. The position of the British had been so judiciously selected that their loss was trifling; whereas the Dutch, in an unknown country, fell an easy prey to the victors.[1]

Immediately after the battle Forde occupied Chinsurah, meeting with only slight resistance.

We have here an illustration of what important events have frequently resulted from battles in which only a few hundred of our soldiers have been engaged. The battle of Biderra, taken in connection with the naval fight, is one of the most brilliant and important military combinations in Indian history, but is seldom referred to by English historians. The power of the East India Company was trembling in the balance when Forde on the 22nd of November left Calcutta with

---

1. The following is the account given by the Dutch East India Company, see Grose's Voyage to the East Indies, vol. 2., p. 376:—On the 25th, when the troops and other bands which on the 22nd before, were gone on shore, were, in their projected march, come near Chandernagore they were there met by the English; who according to their own account to the number of 1170 were posted very advantageously, and provided with a numerous artillery. No sooner were those troops come within cannon-shot but they were fired on by the English, and though all the people were extremely fatigued by a very long- march, which they were obliged to make for the space of three days; yet with much bravery they stood the fire of the English; and though unprovided with any artillery marched up with a full and steady pace to the enemy; but meeting on their way a broad deep ditch, which they were constrained to pass to avoid being destroyed by the artillery of the English, the troops in passing that ditch fell into some disorder; the English taking advantage of this circumstance, redoubled the fire of their artillery and musketry, and the disorder already arisen being thereby increased, caused the slaughter of a part of those troops, another part was made prisoners; and the rest were constrained to retire.

his handful of men to fight the Dutch army. The Nawab Mir J'afar had formed an alliance with our enemy, in the hope that their united forces might drive us from the country at a time when so large a proportion of our European army was employed in a foreign war. But Clive was equal to the occasion; his cool courage, great daring, and masterly strategy asserted the power of the British, and confirmed our supremacy in Bengal.

The Dutch—lately so subtle, so confident, and so overbearing—now appeared as humble suppliants. The Nawab, discovering that his schemes to be rid of the British yoke had failed, turned upon his crushed accomplices with vindictive hate, threatening them, now that they were smarting and prostrate, with utter annihilation; and doubtless he would have carried his threats into effect, had not Clive interceded in their favour.

Míran, who must have been close at hand watching the course of events, now appeared on the scene with 6000 horse, to drive the remnants of the Dutch from their possessions in Bengal. Clive, on learning this, proceeded at once to Chinsurah, and seeing he had nothing to gain by the extinction of the Dutch, whereas their presence in Bengal, as dependants on the English, might in the future be turned to account, arranged a peace for them with the Nawab, restored to them their factory at Chinsurah, and engaged that they should retain all their former privileges; at the same time taking care that their wings should be clipped, so that there should be no fear of their appearing in the field as our rivals. They were to be allowed to retain in their service only 125 European soldiers; and they agreed to pay £100,000 to the British as an indemnity for the expenses of the war.

The Dutch and English Governments in Europe subsequently appointed a mixed Commission to report on all the circumstances connected with these affairs; when it was recorded by the Commissioners that Clive's conduct throughout had been marked by a prudence, judgement, and generosity entitling him to unqualified commendation; and that the Dutch Naval Authorities were the unprovoked aggressors.

We must now, though unwillingly, part from Colonel Forde: who, though he had never held a Commission in the Bengal European Regiment, contributed so effectually to its honours and distinction. He was serving at Madras at the time Kilpatrick was selected for the command of the relieving force sent to Bengal; and Clive hoped to permanently secure Forde's services in the latter Presidency. The opportunity presented itself when Major Kilpatrick died: and Clive at once applied for and obtained Forde's services. He arrived in Bengal, 1758, with the rank of Lieutenant-Colonel; but the Court of Directors, for some unexplained reason, refused to confirm the selection. In the mean-time, however, Clive had appointed Forde to command the expedition against the French in the Northern Circars; and, although he learnt on his return that he had been dismissed the service under orders from England, he consented, at Clive's earnest solicitation, to undertake the direction of the military operations against the Dutch. Forde had fully demonstrated that he was a worthy successor to Clive, but the Court again declined to confirm his appointment, and he returned to England a disappointed and ill-used man. It was ten years after that the Court of Directors realised the value of Forde's services, when they attempted to make atonement by appointing him—with Messrs. Vansittart and Scrafton—to form a select committee to supervise affairs in Bengal; but the ship on which they were returning to India was supposed to have foundered at sea, for she was never again heard of. In the Bengal European Regiment Colonel Forde's name was a household word, and his memory was ever held in love, honour, and respect.

Clive, whose health was broken and constitution unpaired, now determined to seek in England the repose he so much needed; but, before leaving India, it was necessary that certain changes should be effected both in the civil and military departments.

The appointment of Colonel Forde not having been sanctioned, Major Caillaud of the Madras Service was nominated to the command of the Bengal army. This Officer had performed distinguished services in his own Presidency, where he had displayed marked ability; and his selection as Commander in Bengal gave universal satisfaction.

In the Civil department Mr. Holwell, the senior Member of Council, applied for leave to visit Europe to seek rest after the unparalleled hardships endured and services rendered during the past four years; and the services of the other members of council not being available, Mr. Vansittart—a Madras civilian— was appointed Governor of Bengal.

All these arrangements having been perfected, Clive felt himself at liberty to leave India; but, before doing so, he dictated the course of action to be adopted to oppose the advance of the Shazada Shah Alám, who had again appeared in the field.

In December Captain Fischer landed in Bengal with the right wing of the Bengal European Regiment, much reduced by the campaign in the Northern Circars; but in the previous October 200 recruits had joined the headquarters, and a number of Europeans, Dutch, French, and Germans, made prisoners at the battle of Biderra, were drafted to the Regiment, bringing it up to its full strength.

The force ordered to take the field against Shah Alám consisted of 300 of the Bengal European Regiment; 50 European artillerymen, with 6 field-pieces; and three sepahi battalions; under the personal command of Major Caillaud. The advance division marched from Calcutta on the 26th December under Captain Thomas Fenwick, with whom was Captain James Spier; both of these Officers having been transferred from the Madras army to the Bengal European Regiment.

Colonel Clive reached Murshedabad on January 6th, 1760, when it was arranged that a large native force under the Shazada Míran should join the British army and take the field against Shah Alám.

Clive now informed the Nawab Mir J'afar of his intended departure from India, the intelligence being received with much misgiving. Major Caillaud was introduced to the Nawab as Clive's successor.

It was, at the Nawab's request, arranged that 200 men of the Bengal European Regiment should be permanently quartered at Murshedabad for the protection of the native capital, and all necessary precautions having been taken Clive returned to Calcutta, whence he sailed for England on the 25th February, 1760.

General References—Chapter 5

Orme's Military Transactions in Bengal.
Malleson's Decisive Battles of India.
Amber's Rise and Progress of British Power in India.
Malleson's Founders of the Indian Empire (Clive).
Broome's Rise and Progress of the Bengal Army.
Williams's Bengal Infantry.
Philippart's East India Military Calendar.
Mill's British India.
Thornton's History of the British Empire in India.
Grose's Voyage to the East Indies.
&c, &c.

CHAPTER 6

Patna & Moghuls

Since the campaign in the previous year against the Shahzada Shah Alám a change of much importance had taken place at the Court of Delhie. The Emperor, Alám Gir Sani, had been put to death by his Prime Minister; and, at the instigation of the murderer, a puppet had been placed on the throne. Shah Alám, being the eldest son of Alám Gir Sani and the acknowledged heir to the throne, was now the Emperor of Hindustan, to whom all owed allegiance. But, although the pretext of Shah Alám being in rebellion against his father no longer existed, the right of the Emperor to interfere with the acts of his Viceroys was frequently ignored, or considered merely nominal; so, as Shah Alám had when he was Shahzada made war against the East India Company and their ally Mir J'afar, no change was now made in their attitude towards each other.

In consequence of the influence which Shah Alám was enabled to exercise now that he had become titular Emperor, he had been enabled to collect an army of considerable strength; at the head of which, towards the end of January, 1760, he threatened the city of Patna and our fortified factory near at hand.

Captain Cochrane, of the Bengal European Regiment, commanded the Company's troops at Patna, consisting of 100 Europeans under Ensign Winclebeck, with whom was another subaltern—name unknown; 70 European artillery, with 2 guns, under Lieutenant Buck; 5 companies of Regular sepahis; and 3 local companies,[1] under an ensign. Dr. Fullerton was the Surgeon to the detachment, and there was also a Mr. Barwell, serving as a Volunteer.

---

1. These local companies were frequently employed at our factories. They were composed of mercenaries of all nationalities. Their officers were sometimes attached for duty with the Regular troops.

Raja Ram Narian, the Governor of Patna, who had been of doubtful allegiance during the campaign in the previous year, was now a firm supporter of the English and Mir J'afar. Ram Narian had, under Captain Cochrane's orders, collected his troops from the district, and enlisted a considerable number of sepahis to act with the English detachment protecting the city and the Company's factory.

Raja Ram Narian held imperative orders, both from the Nawab Mir J'afar and Major Caillaud, the British Commander, not to risk a battle with the Emperor's troops, but await the arrival of the British force, rapidly advancing to his assistance.

Just about this time a considerable body of well-equipped cavalry, commanded by a distinguished Chief named Rehim Khan, joined Ram Narian's force. This acquisition made him numerically superior to the Emperor's force, and as there had been several skirmishes between the rival armies, which had usually resulted in victory to Ram Narian, he was sorely tempted to disobey orders by offering battle to the Emperor, and defeating him before the arrival of the British reinforcements.

Ram Narian had now under his command 40,000 men; and on the 9th of February, much against Captain Cochrane's advice, he moved out from his entrenchments and offered battle to the enemy. They, nothing loth, accepted the challenge, advancing from their camp and taking up their position in front of Ram Narian's troops drawn up in three lines; the English detachment under Cochrane being in reserve. The British commander had fully determined that the Company's troops should take no part in the action, unless it should be necessary to protect the Raja from injury or capture.

After a little skirmishing on both sides a body of the Emperor's troops made a gallant charge, breaking completely through the Raja's lines and creating much confusion amongst his platoons, some of which, thinking they had better secure their safety whilst there was yet time, deserted over to the Emperor's side.

Notwithstanding these defections the main body of Ram Narian's troops manfully re-formed, and now stoutly held their ground, materially assisted by the British in reserve with their two field-guns; but just when the scale seemed turning in the Raja's favour he found himself in considerable personal danger, many of his best officers having fallen around him, and he having received several slight wounds. Under these circumstances Ram Narian sent a message to Captain Cochrane, begging him to come to his assistance, he being hard pressed and unable to retreat.

Captain Cochrane held orders that he was under any circumstances to protect the Raja against personal injury; he therefore at once proceeded to obey the call with his two subalterns, Volunteer Barwell, and four companies of sepahis. This small party with much difficulty forced their way up to the Raja, who was bravely defending himself; but in doing so our loss was heavy indeed, for in repelling the repeated attacks of the enemy Captain Cochrane and his three subalterns were killed, and our sepahis, finding that their officers had fallen, broke and fled, quickly pursued by some of the Emperor's cavalry, who, charging amongst them as they were scattered over the field, cut them up piecemeal. A sergeant of the Bengal European Regiment now, seeing the perilous position of the Raja, placed himself at the head of 25 sepahis, and charging valiantly forward secured Ram Narian, whom he escorted to the European detachment, they having with great difficulty maintained their position in reserve, attacked by large bodies of cavalry on both flanks. The officer left in command of the reserve had also been killed, as well as Lieutenant Buck commanding the European artillery.

Dr. Fullerton, being now the only English Officer who had survived the battle, assumed command. Dr. Fullerton's name is known to history as a brave, gallant soldier, and his military prowess never shone with greater lustre than when he brought the remnant of the Ram Narian's defeated force into the city of Patna, not, however, without leaving one of his disabled guns in the hands of the enemy; but, before abandoning it, he had spiked it with his own hand.

The Emperor did not follow up his victory, or, beyond doubt. the city would have fallen into his hands. There is something most touching in the record of this great sacrifice of life of the Bengal European Regiment; 4 officers gave their lives in attempting to perform a simple act of duty; the officer commanding the sepahis infantry was also killed, as well as the only artillery officer with the force; none were left but that brave man Fullerton, who, when he saw all his comrades dead, manfully fulfilled the duty, to perform which these six officers had sacrificed their lives.

10th-18th February, 1760; Ram Narian, full of regret, now busied himself in improving the defences of the city, and knowing that Major Caillaud must be near at hand, finessed to gain time. He sent to the Emperor saying that he wished to enter into negotiations, but that at present his wounds prevented him from personally paying his respects.

On the 19th of February the joyful news reached Patna that Major Caillaud, with the British Force, was close at hand. In the meantime the Emperor, elated with his success in having, as he was pleased to think, subdued the British army, contented himself with making only a half-hearted attack on the city, which he discontinued as soon as he heard of the near approach of the British reinforcements.

Caillaud was anxious to offer battle at once, but Míran—commanding the Nawab's troops—urged delay; it was then arranged that our attack should be delivered early on the morning of the 22nd, and the British camp was advanced to within three miles of the enemy; but a second time Míran urged that his arrangements were not complete. Whilst our camp was being pitched on the newly-chosen ground, Caillaud with a small escort rode forward to reconnoitre, when, finding that the enemy was not on the alert, he seized two villages about a mile in advance of his position. In each of these villages he placed a company of his sepahis, and in the rear he posted a support of 400 men. The enemy, seeing this movement, made an advance, pushing forward some of their heavy artillery, supported by cavalry and infantry.

The British support of 400 men were now ordered to quickly join their comrades in the two villages, and a company of Europeans with two field-pieces added to their force. Major Caillaud at this time observed that the enemy had struck his camp, and was making a, general advance; a large body of his cavalry being seen moving towards the two villages. The British force took position in immediate front of its own camp, and between the two villages; the Bengal European Battalion in the centre, supported by 3 guns on either flank: these again being flanked by 2 battalions of sepahis, forming the right and left extremities of the line.

Míran had been instructed to place himself in rear of, and as a support to, the British force—his cavalry extended right and left; but in place of carrying out this arrangement—which he had previously agreed to—he massed his whole force in close column to the right and slightly in rear.

The Emperor's army was formed into three divisions, one of which now attacked the left of the British position and attempted to occupy the village of Seerpore; but Caillaud, turning his guns obliquely, poured a sharp fire on the advancing enemy, who hesitated. At this moment a troop of Shah Alám's cavalry circled round to the rear of the village, where they were unopposed, as Míran had, contrary to orders, massed all his troops to the right.

The remaining two divisions of the Emperor's army now attacked Míran's troops with such earnestness that the latter showed signs of discomfiture, inducing Caillaud, with some infantry and six field-pieces, to push forward towards the village on his right, to protect Míran and his frightened irregulars. The relieving force advanced steadily until they were about forty paces from the enemy's cavalry; when baiting and firing a volley, they effectually checked the ardour of the attacking force, and enabled Míran to rally his scattered troops.

Our infantry now fired a second volley, and, charging along the front of Míran's unsteady brigade, so successfully assailed the enemy that they fell into confusion; when our sepahis, rushing forward, engaged the enemy's infantry, who were driven back at the point of the bayonet, their cavalry following under volleys of our grape and musketry. Míran's cavalry, being now reassured, made a successful charge on the fugitives, completing the work which our sepahis had begun.

The Emperor's army broke and a general stampede ensued, their officers in vain attempting to rally the men.

In half-an-hour the field was cleared of the enemy, only the dead and wounded remaining to show where the battle of Seerpore had been fought.

The British now captured the enemy's camp—which had been deserted during their hurried flight—and here, to their surprise, our soldiers found and retook their own camp equipage and cattle, which had been looted by the enemy's cavalry, who had, early in the action, passed to the rear of the village of Seerpore.

The pursuit continued till nightfall, the Emperor with his fugitive troops having retired on the town of Behar, sixteen miles distant.

The casualties of the British were few; but the enemy lost two of their best commanders, as well as a large number of their troops. Míran was slightly wounded, and his uncle Mahomed Amir Khan was killed.

Major Caillaud was desirous of rapidly following up his success; but Míran, strongly opposing the measure, retired with his troops to Patna, where he celebrated his victory with much pomp and debauchery.

It was the 29th February before Míran consented to rejoin Major Caillaud, and it was the 2nd March before the British force reached Behar, when it was found that the Emperor's army had left that town on the 29th February and was now rapidly marching towards Bengal; thus the advantage which Caillaud had gained at Seerpore was hopelessly sacrificed by the wilful obstinacy of Míran.

Our army started in hot pursuit, Míran now realizing the fatal error he had committed. Shah Alám had got to our rear and was hastening to occupy districts which had promised him their support. After four days Caillaud, having taken advantage of a rapid stream which had checked Shah Alám's progress, came close to the enemy, and would have made a night attack had not Míran again proved obstinate.

6th March, 1760; The Emperor escaped a second time, and, taking a south-westerly direction, struck across the hills, still pursued by the British, Míran following.

Soon after Major Caillaud and Míran had left Murshedabad to relieve Patna—January 22nd, 1760—information was sent to Mir J'afar that Kuddum Hussain, the Nawab of Purneah—who owed allegiance to Mir J'afar—and several influential zemendars were in revolt, and had promised assistance to the Emperor, should he appear in their Provinces. Under these circumstances, fearing that the malcontents might attack the rear of Caillaud's army marching towards Patna, Mir J'afar proceeded towards Rajmahal, taking with him Captain Spier and the 250 men of the Bengal European Regiment stationed at Murshedabad for its protection. But no sooner had terms been arranged with Kuddum Hussain than Mir J'afar's attention was directed towards his Eastern frontier, where a large body of Maratha cavalry, under the notorious and dreaded chief Sheobut, had appeared with the avowed intention of assisting the Emperor if he should approach Mir J'afar's capital.

Sheobut exercised considerable influence in Bengal, so much so that on his approach the Council in Calcutta thought it necessary to embody the Militia and dismiss all armed natives not in the service of the Company.

Captain Fischer with 250 of the Bengal European Regiment, 4 light guns, and 300 sepahis, were sent to reinforce Spier, and Captain Yorke—who had by this time recovered from his wounds—was ordered to hold himself in readiness to take the field with 250 more of the Bengal European Regiment and 500 sepahis; this latter detachment being at the Presidency.

Captain Spier now had under his command 500 European infantry, 20 European artillery, with 6 light guns, and 500 sepahis.

On the 4th of April a junction was effected between Major Caillaud's, Captain Spier's, and Míran's forces at Mungulkote, the Nawab Mir J'afar still accompanying Spier's detachment.

The Emperor Shah Alám, who had been reinforced by the Maratha cavalry under Sheobut, was at this time at Maunkur. Captain

Fischer, with 200 men of the Bengal European Regiment, was ordered to march to Murshedabad to protect the capital, and Caillaud now moved in the direction of the Emperor's camp.

Caillaud was desirous of attacking Shah Alám in his new position, but Mir J'afar showed what then appeared an unaccountable disinclination to give his support, refusing to allow his troops to act on the offensive, and declining to accede to Caillaud's request for the loan of horses to mount some of his European infantry whom he wished to employ as cavalry. It now came to Major Caillaud's knowledge that the Nawab had secretly made overtures to the Emperor, and it was subsequently proved that before leaving Murshedabad he had proffered his allegiance to him, the British being left in ignorance of the negotiation.

Notwithstanding the altered circumstances Caillaud determined to attack the Emperor, with or without his allies; and on the morning of the 7th April he marched with his troops to the village of Belkoss, opposite to the Emperor's encampment.

The attack was led by the Bengal European Regiment, who, under cover of our Artillery, rushed into the stream; which they were rapidly fording, when the enemy, after firing a few shots, set fire to their camp and hastily withdrew; but the British, having no cavalry, were unable to follow. The Emperor and his Maratha allies having evaded pursuit, doubled round and returned towards Patna, which had been left under protection of Raja Ham Narian with only a few sepahis.

Knox, by this time near at hand, was sent by forced marches with his detachment of 200 Bengal Europeans, a complete battalion of sepahis, and a detail of artillery, with 2 light field-guns, to assist Ram Narian; whilst the remainder of the field-force under Caillaud—accompanied by the Nawab's troops— returned to Murshedabad, which they reached about the 25th of April.

Patna was now in imminent peril; for M. Law, with his corps of French Europeans—whose numbers had been augmented by April, our escaped prisoners and French deserters—had come to terms with the Emperor and marched to Patna, where he intended to await the arrival of his allies, and then carry the city before British reinforcements could arrive. But M. Law, after having been encamped close to the city for some days, marched towards Behar, where he formed junction with the Emperor; when the united forces returned to Patna and renewed the siege with vigour.

10th April, Dr. Fullerton, again the only English Officer in the garrison, undertook the general control of the defence; he had repaired old breaches and planted his guns in well-chosen positions; but the besiegers, led by the French Europeans and supported by the Emperor's and the Maratha troops, made such determined assaults that Ram Narian's soldiers, completely disheartened, wavered in their support. The walls of the city had been breached in several places, and the enemy succeeded at one time in planting the Emperor's colours on one of the bastions; when Fullerton and his gallant little band of sepahis rushed to the rescue, and, capturing the colours after a severe hand-to-hand tight, regained possession of the bastion. Just when help was so much needed a joyful cry was raised that relief was at hand. A cloud of dust and the glitter of the sun on bayonets was seen on the other side of the river; the shouts of the Europeans and the inspiring sound of the fife and drum were distinctly heard, reviving the spirits and hopes of the besieged, who, rushing to their deserted posts, defended them with renewed vigour.

Boats laden with refreshments were sent across the river to the relieving party; and Knox with the 200 men of the Bengal European Regiment, Maclean with his well-seasoned sepahis, and the European artillery with their field-guns, were heartily welcomed by the citizens: and Ram Narian's soldiers "gave up their apprehensions about an escalade and about an assault, and said openly that now the English were within their walls the enemy would not dare to come to attack again."[1]

Knox with his Europeans had marched from Burdwan to Patna—300 miles—in 13 days; but his men, being fresh and elated with their reception, at once marched through the city with their colours flying and drums beating.

The next day 26th April, Knox attacked the enemy's advanced position, surprising them whilst they were at their midday meal, driving them in confusion from their camp—which he captured, together with their guns, stores, and ammunition—and returning before sunset in triumph to the city, he was received by the citizens with acclamations of joy and relief. The next day the Imperial troops and the French Corps retired to the village of Gyah Manpore.

May, 1760; It is now necessary to refer to the movements of the native force under Kuddum Hussain, the Nawab of Purneah, who it will be remembered had in the previous month come to terms with the Nawab Mir J'afar Khan. The conditions of peace and promises of fidelity which Kuddum Hussain had made were all forgotten as soon

---

1. Words of a native historian, who was a witness to the scene described.

as Mir J'afar Khan with his European detachment was out of reach, and Kuddum Hussain—who all along had determined to link himself with the Emperor—now busied himself in extorting money from his people to enable him to raise an army. After a few weeks he had managed to collect a force said to consist of 6000 cavalry, 10,000 infantry, and 30 guns, with which he marched rapidly to join the Emperor's camp at Gyah Manpore. Major Caillaud started in pursuit; but Kuddum Hussain was well supplied with baggage, cattle, and elephants, so that the British were unable to overtake him. Under these circumstances Caillaud wrote to Knox at Patna, instructing him, if possible, to prevent a junction between Kuddum Hussain and the Emperor.

Captain Knox now learnt that Kuddum Hussain had reached Hajèepore, a town on the opposite side of the river Ganges; and having collected his force, which consisted of 200 of the Bengal European Regiment, a battalion of Maclean's sepahis, and 5 field-pieces, crossed the river on the 15th June.

Knox was accompanied by the brave Raja Shitab Roy, the commander of a choice body of cavalry, who had lately joined the British force.

As the enemy under Kuddum Hussain were within 10 miles, Knox, in consultation with Shitab Roy, arranged a night surprise, but the guide misled them; so, after a tedious march, they returned to their camp at daybreak. They had no time for rest, for the enemy appeared early in the morning, and Knox advanced to meet him, taking up a well-chosen position near the village of Beerpore, and leaving one company of sepahis to guard his camp and boats on the left bank of the river.

The enemy soon appeared in much greater force than Knox had anticipated, quite surrounding the British force, which in all did not exceed 800 men.

Knox formed his troops into a hollow square, receiving in this position several charges from the enemy's cavalry, who were, however, repeatedly driven back, our square being materially assisted by our Artillery; but such was the numerical superiority of Kuddum Hussain's force that these attacks were continued for six consecutive hours, exhausting the little band of heroes, who were at one time well-nigh overwhelmed. Captain Knox now sallied forth at the head of the grenadier company of the Bengal Europeans, who drove hack the enemy, enabling the sepahis maintaining the square to recover their position.

Kuddum Hussain, finding his attempts to break the British square futile, ultimately withdrew his army; leaving 400 men and 3 elephants dead on the field, and 8 heavy guns in our hands.

The loss of the British was comparatively small; a brave young Officer, Lieutenant McDowall, and 16 men of the Bengal European Regiment being killed, as well as many sepahis. Knox had now to learn that the company of sepahis left to protect his camp on the river bank had been overwhelmed and annihilated. The camp followers had rushed to the boats and pushed into the stream, leaving the sepahis a prey to the enemy, and carrying the news to the frightened inhabitants of the city that the British force had been completely exterminated. Captain Knox pursued the enemy for several miles, until, darkness supervening, he reluctantly gave up the chase, and, crossing the river, returned to Patna. When the inhabitants found that, in place of a defeat, the British had gained a glorious victory, their joy knew no bounds, a native historian recording that "from that day the English acquired a reputation for determination and invincibility that did them good service in many a subsequent action."

Knox, having replenished his camp, started next day, 17th June, to renew his pursuit of Kuddum Hussain, who had of necessity abandoned his plan of joining the Emperor, and was pushing towards Bettea.

On the 22nd June Major Caillaud and Míran arrived at Patna with their forces, so, Knox and his detachment having been recalled, Major Caillaud took up the chase.

On the 25th the enemy were sighted, their movements much hampered by their heavy baggage. Caillaud prepared for an attack, the enemy opening fire from his heavy guns, and doing some execution; nevertheless, the British advanced against Kuddum Hussain's position, behind some villages and a grove of trees, which he abandoned on the near approach of our troops. The enemy now finding himself opposed by a much larger force than on the previous occasion when he was driven from the field, fled, leaving in our possession a number of heavy guns and a great quantity of camp equipage.

During this action Míran displayed his usual disinclination to cooperate with his allies; nevertheless, Major Caillaud followed up his victory, in the hope of gaining possession of the large amount of treasure which Kuddum Hussain was carrying off.

On the 2nd of July the periodical rains commenced with unusual violence. The British army were forced to seek shelter from their watery fury, the camp being pitched in a grove of trees at the foot of the Nepaul Mountains.

During the night the lightning flashed incessantly, and the storm raged with constantly-increasing and alarming violence. Míran, fearing that his state tent, which had been pitched in an exposed position, might be blown down, moved into one sheltered by the trees, in which he was being shampooed by his body servant, whilst his court story-teller was lulling him to sleep. In a moment the Shahzada's tent was seen to be surrounded by a blue flame, a vivid flash of lightning illuminated the scene, and when the frightened attendants arrived three blackened corpses were found amidst the débris of the burning tent. So died Míran, respected by none and despised most by those who knew him best. He is justly described as having been tainted with all the vices of his cousin Siraju 'd daulah, without possessing one of his redeeming qualities.

This event increased rather than diminished Major Caillaud's difficulties, for it was the custom amongst the native armies in India on the death of their commander to disperse to their homes; and it was probable that Míran's soldiers, knowing that their late chief's interest had been more with Kuddum Hussain than the British, would either go to their villages or desert to the enemy.

Caillaud sought and obtained the influence of some of Míran's generals, but, the pay of the troops being several months in arrears, the soldiers became insubordinate and threatened to forcibly possess themselves of whatever they could secure, and desert to their homes. With much tact Major Caillaud succeeded in quelling the mutiny by promising to quickly obtain funds from Calcutta, on arrival of which the discontented troops should receive their arrears of pay; and it was ultimately arranged that he should command the united forces, pending orders from Murshedabad.

Under the circumstances it was deemed prudent to discontinue the pursuit of Kuddum Hussain; and Caillaud, therefore, retraced his steps, the army reaching Patna on July 29th, 1760.

The monsoon being now at its height the war was suspended. Caillaud quartered his troops in the city of Patna, and the Emperor occupied a position at Dandnuggur, about 30 miles to the west.

But affairs in Calcutta—of which we have of necessity for some time lost the thread—were in a very unsatisfactory state. Mr. Vansittart, the new Governor, had arrived from Madras to find that, although the payments under the notorious Mir J'afar treaty had temporarily enriched the Company's servants and citizens of Calcutta, the treaty had left all the country under the Murshedabad administration in a dissatisfied and impoverished condition.

In order to pay the instalments due under the treaty the Nawab had of necessity made such heavy demands on the resources of the wealthy nobles and bankers that their allegiance was shaken; whilst the cultivators of the soil, in many instances, were reduced to abject poverty. The pay of Mir J'afar's troops was much in arrears, inducing them to desert to the enemy; his treasury was exhausted, and his debt under the treaty had not been fully discharged. But affairs were not in a much better condition with the Calcutta Council, whose credit was at so low an ebb that they had been unable to raise money to pay their European army; indeed, at this time, the current expenses of the Government were only met by drawing so heavily on the Court of Directors in London that they were nearly driven into bankruptcy.

Under these circumstances, the Governor having sent for Major Caillaud to assist the council with his advice, he handed over his command to Captain Knox, the next senior officer, and proceeding to obey these orders, arrived at Calcutta on the 10th of September, where a Commission as Lieutenant-Colonel was awaiting him, this promotion having been awarded for his distinguished services in the field.

On the death of the Shahzada Míran, Mir J'afar had recognised his son-in-law, Mir Kassim Khan, as heir to the throne, and as such he was deputed by the Nawab to welcome the new Governor, and assist in the deliberations of the Calcutta Council. Mir Kassim, who is to figure so prominently in this history, being a master of intrigue and a shrewd politician, at. once conceived the idea of converting the trust which his Sovereign had reposed in him to his own advantage. On the 27th September Mir Kassim entered into a treaty with the Calcutta Council stipulating that he should be appointed Mir J'afar's Deputy at the Murshedabad Court, and as such should be endowed with almost absolute powers. This treat, concluded with what had become the usual provision for pecuniary payments to the contracting officials. The members of council were promised from £30,000 to £50,000 each, Colonel Caillaud[1] £20,000, and Captain Yorke £13,400.

On October 1st Mir Kassim returned to Murshedabad to pave the way for the approaching *coup d'état*. On the 3rd Mr. Vansittart, accompanied by Mr. Warren Hastings and Mr. Lushington, reached the capital, and Mir J'afar was made acquainted with the resolutions of the Calcutta Council. The interviews which took place between the Governor and the Nawab—15th, 16th, and 18th—bore no fruit; so the latter was informed that he would be allowed only two more days to

---

1. Colonel Caillaud voted against the treaty, and left India before those payments were stipulated for.

decide. Mir J'afar, terrified at the aspect of affairs and fearing that he might be assassinated at Murshedabad, retired to his palace on the opposite side of the river; and, as no communication had been received from him on the 19th, Colonel Caillaud was ordered to proceed with 200 men of the Bengal European Regiment to join the troops of Mir Kassim and surround the Nawab s palace.

The English soldiers occupied the centre square; and Mir J'afar was called on to formally resign in favour of Mir Kassim now appointed by the English Deputy-Nawab and successor to the throne. These overtures were refused by the Nawab; but Mr. Warren Hastings giving him to understand that resistance was useless, Mir J'afar declared that his life would be insecure if he were left in Mir Kassim's power. At length he consented to resign absolutely, the council guaranteeing his personal safety; and, this having been done, Mir J'afar the ex-Nawab, was conveyed under a strong escort to Calcutta, where some fitting houses were prepared for his reception and a liberal allowance was provided by Mir Kassim, who now reigned in his stead.

The newly-appointed Nawab had long since realised that the defects in Mir J'afar's government were primarily due to his obligations to the English. A system of dependence and thraldom had existed, which had completely paralysed the late Nawab's actions, and rendered him absolutely subservient to the Calcutta Council. Mir Kassim, therefore, determined to make bold stroke for freedom.

November-December, 1760; On assuming the Government the many court favourites, who had amassed fortunes to the detriment of the State Treasury, were made to disgorge their ill-gotten wealth: their estates were confiscated; and such sweeping reforms introduced that the Nawab was enabled very shortly after having assumed power to satisfy to a great extent the claims of the English, and to advance £25,000 to the Council to enable them to make a remittance to Madras, urgently-required, and £70,000 for the arrears due to the British troops at Patna.

With this latter amount Colonel Caillaud returned to Patna, accompanied by Major Carnac—previously appointed by the Court of Directors to command the Bengal army, Colonel Caillaud's services being required at Madras.

Before leaving Bengal Colonel Caillaud[1] made some changes in the organization of the Bengal European Regiment, now 1200 strong,

---

1. Colonel, afterwards Brigadier-General, Caillaud retired from the East India Company's Service on 17th March, 1775, when he resided at his seat in Oxfordshire, where he died at a very advanced age in 1810.

many of the soldiers being French, Dutch, and Germans who had purchased their freedom by consenting to serve in the ranks of the Regiment. With the approval of the council two troops of dragoons and one of hussars were raised; the troopers being taken from the Bengal European Regiment, which was now in consequence only 1000 strong, including two grenadier companies. The newly-raised cavalry were officered from the infantry, each troop of dragoons having 1 captain, 2 lieutenants, and 1 cornet, and the hussar troop, called The Body Guard, having 1 lieutenant and 1 cornet only. The experiment of mounting our infantry soldiers and employing them as cavalry did not prove a success, on account of the smallness of the underbred Bengal horses, which were not up to the weight, of the English troopers. A body of Moghul Horse, found to be far more efficient, was employed about this time with the English army, being engaged on the same system as those of the Irregular cavalry of the present day, but no European officers were attached to the native cavalry.

Soon after Major Carnac had assumed command a circumstance occurred which produced a complete change in the system of the Murshedabad army. Captain Martin White was sent with a detachment of the Bengal Europeans and some sepahis to suppress an insurrection in Bhirboom. The Raja of that district, at the head of an army of 20,000 infantry and 5000 cavalry, had taken up his position near the village of Kirwah, defying his Sovereign's power. Captain Yorke, with 200 Europeans and a body of the Nawab's troops, had proceeded from Murshedabad to join White, Mir Kassim accompanying Yorke's division. On ascertaining the enemy's position, Yorke instructed White to take a circuitous route and attack the enemy in rear, whilst Yorke would assail him in front as soon as he should hear the firing of White's party. This simple manoeuvre was executed with so much judgement and tact that the enemy, finding themselves simultaneously assailed both in front and rear, broke and fled; leaving their camp, guns, and stores in our possession. This victory over the Raja of Bhirboom had the effect of tranquillising the whole of his provinces as well as that of Burdwan; and is specially worthy of our attention, as it resulted in vast reforms being introduced by the Nawab into his army. Mir Kassim, who seldom ventured under fire, had been present during our attack on the Raja of Bhirboom's camp; and, much impressed with the great superiority of our tactics and troops over those of the native states, determined, on his return to his capital, to reorganize his army and, as far as possible, introduce amongst them the English system.

Major Carnac, now in chief command of our army at Patna, prepared to pursue with vigour the campaign against the Emperor Shah Alám, who had established his headquarters at the city of Behar, having with him M. Law's French corps. Carnac experienced many difficulties on account of the remnant of Míran's army clamouring for their arrears of pay. £90,000 had been sent by Mir Kassim, in addition to the £70,000 which Colonel Caillaud had distributed; but still the Nawab's troops were somewhat in arrears, and consequently refused to march. Major Carnac, therefore, determined to take action with his own troops only. When he was at his first camping-ground, however, the dissatisfied troops joined him, having, in secret council, elected to serve with the British in their campaign against the Emperor.

On 15th of January, 1761, the united forces arrived at Suan, 6 miles from Behar, on a stream formed by a branch of the Mahani river; and here Carnac found the Emperor's army drawn up on the opposite bank. Our artillery immediately opened fire, under cover of which the British crossed the river without opposition, the enemy retreating amongst the dykes and rough ground formed by the changing course of the stream. The Nawab's troops, as usual, remained in the rear, awaiting the turn of events.

Carnac now advanced, but the enemy continued to retire, although on three occasions they halted and took up fresh ground, finally electing to encamp on the open plain. The British army formed up for attack; the Bengal European Regiment being in the centre, flanked on either side by a battalion of native infantry; the artillery between the Europeans and sepahis. A third battalion of native infantry and a small body of cavalry were held in rear as a reserve. Our guns were now pushed slightly forward, and a general advance made: but, the enemy's cavalry attacking our line on both flanks, some confusion arose, making the result of the battle doubtful; when, most opportunely, a well-directed shot from one of our 12-pounders killed the Mahout and wounded the elephant on which the Emperor was riding, and directing the movements of his army. The animal, now freed from restraint, frightened, and wounded, rushed uncontrolled to the rear. The news that the Emperor had disappeared from the field soon spread, creating a panic amongst his troops; who, in the absence of their commander, were rushing about seeking orders, but finding none.

By this time the British force had been re-formed, and our artillery opened fire on the confused masses of the enemy, who began to give ground; and, our infantry charging, broke and fled from the field.

M. Law, with his French soldiers, endeavouring to check the flight of the Emperor's troops, took up a strong position to cover their retreat; drawing up his infantry in line with his six guns in front, from which he discharged grape on the advancing British; but, as the French were occupying an elevated position, the Bengal European Regiment managed to get below their fire; and, charging up the hill, captured the French guns.

The Bengal Europeans now advanced with shouldered arms towards the French officers, 13 or 14 of whom stood by their commander and colours on the rising ground, with some 50 French soldiers in their rear. The Frenchmen, wearied with the vagrant, profitless life they had been leading since we had captured their possessions at Chandernagore, seemed determined to sell their lives as dearly as possible; but, when they saw the English soldiers advancing with shouldered arms, they were amazed at the generosity of their conquerors. Major Carnac now, ordering his soldiers to halt, advanced towards the French officers: and, saluting, told them he did not wish to take their lives if they would surrender. M. Law replied that he and his comrades would submit only on the condition that they might retain their swords; but, this stipulation not agreed to, they would resist to the last. The terms were accepted; and M. Law with his officers giving themselves up as prisoners of war were placed on their parole. All our officers now advanced, cordially shaking hands with their prisoners, and the British troops were marched back to their camp, where the French officers were hospitably entertained by those of the English army.

The Emperor was soon enabled to collect his scattered troops, amongst whom there had been but slight loss; and proceeded at once towards Patna, which he knew had been left but poorly protected. But Major Carnac, intercepting him, forced him south towards those districts where for several months his troops had been encamped, and where he was not welcomed on his return. The British were now pressing on the Emperor's rear; he had but a scanty supply of provisions, his treasury was empty, and his troops deserting.

On the 2nd of February, 1761, the English army overtook the enemy, who attempted to make some show of resistance; but, on Carnac forming his force for attack, they all fled, not rallying until they had covered some twenty miles. The Emperor Shah Alám, feeling his case to be hopeless, sent an express intimating his readiness to come to terms, and proposing that he should visit Major Carnac in person. The meeting took place at the town of Gyah, when an agreement was entered into, under the stipulations of which Shah Alám's claim to be Emperor of Hindustan was to be acknowledged by the Company, and, for his maintenance, he was to receive from Raja Ram Narian Rs. 1000 a day. Hostilities having now ceased, the Emperor, with Carnac's permission, pitched his camp with that of the British Army, and the conditional treaty was sent to Calcutta for the consideration of the Council.

A detachment of 200 of the Bengal European Regiment, with some native infantry. artillery, and cavalry, was ordered to remain at Gyah under Captain Alexander Champion and watch events in Behar; but, shortly afterwards, Champion's detachment took the field against a chief named Ramghur Khan, who with his lawless troops had seized a fortress and was devastating the whole district. The British detachment, having defeated Ramghur Khan's army, drove them back amongst the jungles and low hills.

Major Carnac, with the main army and accompanied by the Emperor, returned to Patna, which he entered on 14th February, 1761.

The Emperor, on learning that the Calcutta Council would not accede to his request that he should he escorted to his capital by British troops and placed on his throne under British auspices, accepted the invitation of some powerful chiefs who offered to join him with their troops, advance on Delhie, and seize the capital in his name.

The Emperor, naturally anxious to occupy his throne, left Patna in June under the escort of these supporters; a British guard of honour accompanying him to the Bengal frontier.

GENERAL REFERENCES—CHAPTER 6

Colonel Broome's Rise and Progress of the Bengal Army
Williams's Bengal Infantry.
Philippart's East India Military Calendar.
Thornton's History of the British Empire.
Wilson's Edition of Mills's British India.
Malcolm's Dispatches and Correspondence of Clive.
Caraccioli's Life of Lord Clive.
&c, &c.

Chapter 7
Undwah Nálá

As soon as the Nawab Mir Kassim Khan had assumed the reins of government he introduced vast reforms into his military and civil departments. Three years after his accession to power he had discharged all state debts, and his revenues showed a surplus over expenditure. The many grasping favourites who had surrounded Mir J'afar's Court had been forced to disgorge their ill-gotten gains; and the Murshedabad army, formerly an expensive, ill-trained, badly-equipped rabble, had been remodelled into a serviceable force, vastly superior to the armies under any of the native rulers in India.

Mir Kassim, who had been a witness to the superiority in battle of troops trained by British officers over those of native commanders, determined to reform his army on the English system: and for this purpose engaged the services of some able adventurers, on whom he conferred military rank and titles.

Amongst the men so commissioned were two whose names are well-known in Indian history; Reinhard, the Alsatian, called Sombre or Sumru, and Markar, the Armenian. To these men was entrusted the remodelling of Mir Kassim's army; and it is admitted that they performed their military reforms with judgement and skill. Under their supervision a gun factory was established at Murshedabad, where guns, after English patterns, and quite as serviceable as any that could be brought against them, were cast; and the carriages, constructed with elevating screws and the latest improvements, were as highly finished as any in the country. At the same time agents were employed at the ports to purchase any serviceable European guns offered for sale.

Before the end of 1762 Mir Kassim had thus organized an army of 25,000 men; the sepahis equipped and drilled on the English system; a regiment of artillery with a siege-train and batteries of field-guns, the artillerymen being chiefly Europeans; and cavalry, composed of northern horsemen distinguished for their valour and skill in war.

The Nawab had proved himself an able governor, and worthy of the confidence which the council had placed in him when they elected him to the Subadarie; but, although truly anxious to remain at peace with the British, Mir Kassim felt that he was strong enough to maintain his independence. He well knew that the evils which had befallen his father-in-law, Mir J'afar, had been the result of his cringing, servile attitude towards the Calcutta Council; and he determined that he would not allow himself to fall into a like error. He removed his court from Murshedabad to Monghyr, in order that he might not be too closely watched by the Calcutta Council: improved the defences of his new capital, converting the city into a fortress of considerable strength, from whence he spoke with an authority and confidence widely different from the suppliant terms employed by Mir J'afar.

The reforms introduced by the Nawab Mir Kassim had substantially improved the wealth and trade of his country; but their effect was considerably marred by the Calcutta Council having passed a rule that no country goods were to be allowed down the river Hugli free of tax unless accompanied by an official English permit. The issuing of these passes or permits was assumed to be the private privilege and gain of certain high officials in the Company's service, who, in many instances, had sold their interest to outsiders; so that it soon became impossible for the Nawab's officials to discern who did and who did not legitimately hold these passes; for it was only necessary to put on board a cargo-boat a few men dressed as sepahis, and show the Company's flag, to hold the boat exempt from the inspection of the Nawab's customs-officers.

Mir Kassim felt that this enactment of the council was an infringement of his rights as Nawab; placing his subjects in an unfair position, and seriously affecting the trade and revenues of his country. It was under these circumstances that he represented the hardships of the case to the authorities at Calcutta, and urgently called for reform. Mr. Vansittart, the Governor, fully acknowledged and much regretted the evil; but he had not the support of his council; Mr. Warren Hastings being the only member who shared the opinions of the Governor that the enactment of which the Nawab complained was a disgrace to British legislation. Soon, however, the wrong became so apparent that the council were forced into countenancing the introduction of some measures tending to lessen the evil.

With this view, Mr. Vansittart, having obtained—what he believed to be—the full powers of his council, was deputed to visit the Nawab at Monghyr and arrange terms. The Governor knew full well that his colleagues would not ratify any agreement for sweeping reforms, which would deprive them of the pecuniary benefits accruing to them from the system, but he hoped, at any rate, to modify the evil.

The terms arrived at between the Nawab and Mr. Vansittart stopped far short of the former's requirements, but Mir Kassim reluctantly gave his consent to a trial, warning the Governor that, should the amended regulations fail to afford relief to his subjects, he would proclaim free trade throughout his provinces. The Calcutta Council, however, on being informed of the proposed terms, refused to give them even a trial; and the Nawab was informed that the negotiation had fallen through.

Mr. Ellis, an injudicious man of violent impulses, had lately been nominated to the Council; but, notwithstanding these defects, he was inadvisedly appointed at this time our Government agent at Patna, and thus brought into close communication with the Nawab at Monghyr.

It soon became apparent that the council were hastening the country into war. They knew that their predecessors had reaped rich harvests under the treaties which had placed the native rulers on their thrones, and they hoped to derive equal benefits for themselves, if they could find a puppet who would accept the throne and meet the wishes of the council by consenting to confirm the enactment for the continuation of the objectionable passes.

There was no difficulty in finding a candidate for the throne, should Mir Kassim be deposed. Mir J'afar, the ex-Nawab, forgetting his bitter experiences, allowed himself to be again put forward; but, before arrangements had been completed in Calcutta for his resumption of power, the storm had burst at Patna.

When Mr. Vansittart found that the council would not accept the terms he had arranged with the Nawab, he persuaded them, before taking active measures, to send a deputation to Mir Kassim asking him to modify his views, so that hostilities might be avoided. For this purpose, Messrs. Hay and Amyatt proceeded to Monghyr; but on arrival—14th May—they found Mir Kassim firmly resolved not to accept any compromise beyond that to which he had agreed with Vansittart; so that negotiations again failed.

But, whilst the English deputies were at Monghyr, the Nawab's agents at Patna reported that Mr. Ellis was preparing to seize that city, and the rumour was apparently confirmed by the arrival at Monghyr of a fleet of boats from Calcutta, containing munitions of war for the British troops at Patna. The Nawab ordered these boats to be detained, and Messrs. Hay and Amyatt, although treated with respect, to be placed under surveillance.

An envoy was now sent by Mir Kassim to the .Calcutta Council to represent the threatening attitude assumed by Mr. Ellis, and request that the English soldiers on duty at Patna might be sent to Monghyr, so that he might be assured of peaceable intentions.

The council declined to entertain the Nawab's request, and indeed treated it as an act of hostility, and directed their deputies to return to Calcutta forthwith. Mir Kassim, however, was bent on making one last effort to preserve peace. He charged Mr. Amyatt—before he had received the order of withdrawal—to proceed to Calcutta and represent to the council the painful position in which he was placed by the hostile attitude assumed by Mr. Ellis, and the undisguised preparations which he was making for war. Mr. Amyatt, following the course suggested by the Nawab, started on his return journey to Calcutta; but he was assassinated near Murshedabad, and his escort either shared his fate or were taken prisoners.

Mr. Ellis, learning that the Nawab Mir Kassim was strengthening his garrison inside the city of Patna, and that it was most improbable that peace would be preserved, determined to take the initiative. Early on the morning of the 25th June Ellis ordered the Company's troops, consisting of 4 companies of the Bengal European Regiment and 2500 sepahis, to forcibly take possession of the city. The soldiers marched from the fortified factory on the bank of the Ganges, and, scaling-ladders being in readiness, there was no difficulty in ascending the undefended walls and opening the city gates from the inside; when the English, having gained an entrance, marched through the main streets of the city in two columns.

The Nawab's soldiers on guard over the gates, not anticipating any hostile movement, were completely taken aback; and, hastily firing a few shots, some sought shelter in the back streets, whilst others fled into the open country. Mir Mehdie Khan, the Governor of the city, at once rode off towards Monghyr to report to the Nawab what had occurred. A large building in the city, called Chetul Situn, used as a hospital for our Europeans, was taken possession of by a party of the Nawab's soldiers who deemed it safe from attack, as it contained our sick.

The Nawab's troops also held the Citadel, the gates of which had been closed on the first alarm, the occupants afterwards refusing to surrender.

Captain Peter Carstairs, of the Bengal European Regiment, commanded all the Company's troops at Patna, but his actions were controlled by the senior civilian. Carstairs, who had previously done good service, held the reputation of being an able Commander: but on this occasion, and during all the later operations, his actions were neither soldier-like nor judicious; for, as soon as the city had been occupied by the British, he, together with his officers, returned to the factory to breakfast, leaving his-soldiers to create havoc in the town and plunder the shops and houses at their discretion.

Mehdie Khan, hurrying on with his report towards Monghyr,.. reached Futwah, where he met the advanced guard of the Nawab's relieving troops under Markar, who, hearing of the state of affairs at Patna, and that the Citadel was still holding out, pushed forward so rapidly that his advanced guard reached the eastern gate of the city in a few hours. Here the English had placed some artillery and 2 field-pieces to protect the gate, which had not been closed, so Markar's men, effecting an entrance almost unopposed, overpowered the British artillerymen, who, spiking their guns, hastily retired.

By this time Markar's main army had arrived, and quickly poured into the city, the English troops—scattered in all directions, eager to loot—being only too glad to seek shelter within the walls of the factory outside, where their officers had preceded them immediately after they had occupied the city.

Markar possessed considerable military experience, having distinguished himself during the wars in Holland, where he had learnt the importance of following up a victory with vigour. Immediately after he had recaptured the city, Markar reinforced the Nawab's troops holding out at the citadel and hospital, and then pushing on to the English fortified factory outside, surrounded it with his European troops and kept up a continuous fire on the building's occupied by the English.

Affairs inside the factory in a few days became desperate: there was no hope of relief, provisions were scanty, and as the English fleet of boats had been detained at Munger, there was but a small supply of ammunition. An attempt to effect a retreat on the neighbouring factory at Bankipore had proved futile, and the garrison came to the unwelcome conclusion that their present position was altogether untenable, and that their only chance of escape was by crossing the river Ganges at night in the boats kept close at hand for the use of the factory. The garrison escaped on the evening of the 29th June; and having landed on the left bank of the river, marched hastily in the direction of Chupra, from whence they hoped to reach the territories of the Nawab of Oude, that Prince being at this time on friendly terms with the Company.

Immediately the Nawab heard from his Governor, Mehdie Khan, of the capture of Patna by the British, and its subsequent occupation by Markar, he dispatched a second brigade under Sumru with orders that should the English attempt to escape in a westerly direction he was to cut off their retreat. The position of the English was not improved by their having crossed the river, for they were poorly supplied with ammunition and provisions, and the river, swelled by the periodical rains, overflowed its banks, making the country a vast swamp.

Sumru, with his brigade, had pushed along the high road so rapidly that he had nearly reached Buxar when, hearing of the escape of the English from Patna, he crossed the river Ganges near Arrah; barring the progress of the fugitives in front, whilst Markar, with his Brigade, was pressing on their rear. The English, however, managed on July 1st to reach the village of Manji, where they sighted Sumru's division. Had Clive been in command, he might—indeed, he would—have triumphed; it was just the kind of hopeless position that placed Clive on his mettle, but Carstairs was a very different stamp of man, and lately he had clearly demonstrated that he was not to be trusted on a great emergency. Had Carstairs made a bold dash at Sumru's division in front, he might have forced him back and gained the town of Chupra; or, had he on the previous day turned on his pursuers, he might have beaten them back and retaken the city of Patna, left by Markar poorly protected; but he had hesitated to take either course, and ultimately allowed the enemy, pressing on him in front and rear, to take the initiative. Carstairs seized a position near the village of Manji, where he placed his four companies of the Bengal Europeans on some rising ground, supported on his flanks and rear by his sepahis battalions, who made some gallant charges, headed by Carstairs[1] and seven or eight of his European officers all of whom were soon shot down; when several of the French soldiers who. had taken service in the Bengal European Regiment, looking on the battle as lost, deserted over to their compatriots under Sumru and Markar. Further resistance was now considered hopeless; and the British who had survived

---

1. Captain Carstairs was probably severely wounded at the Battle of Manji, as he died on the road before the prisoners reached Patna.—Military Calendar, vol. 2., p. 74.

the enemy's onslaught were made prisoners[2]. Many of the sepahis, believing that the power of the British was on the wane, agreed to take service with the Nawab; and those who refused were stripped of their regimentals and sent to their homes. The English—civilians, officers, and soldiers—were marched back to Patna, and confined in the Chetul Situn, where they were placed under a strong guard and kept close prisoners.

Early in July, 1763, alarming rumours flew about in the Calcutta bazaar that a fatal disaster had befallen the British arms at Patna. No reliable intelligence had been received by the council, but on the 7th a letter reached the Governor from Mir Kassim, full of reproaches and sarcasms, saying, that Mr. Ellis had "in consequence of his inward friendship favoured me in this fray and slaughter, with all the muskets and cannon of his army, and is himself relieved of his burden." This letter was believed to imply that war had not only been precipitated at Patna, but that Mir Kassim's troops had gained possession of all the British arms and munitions of war; and, next day, reliable information was received that Kassimbazar, but weakly garrisoned, was invested by the Nawab's troops.

It was now evident that we were on the eve of a great war; and preparations to act on the offensive were quickly undertaken.

At this time the Bengal European Battalion consisted of two grenadier and ten battalion companies—each having 55 rank and file; but only a few of these were available for active service, Four companies, as already mentioned, were at Patna under Captain Carstairs; three at Jessalore under Captain Champion; two at Amboa under Captain Knox; leaving only three companies at or near Calcutta under their several captains.

In addition, there was attached to the Bengal European Battalion a company of French rangers, commanded by Lieutenant Claude Martine.[3] These had deserted in a body from the French army and taken service with the English after the siege of Pondicherry, and, as a precaution, were sent by the Madras Government for service in Bengal.

In addition to the Bengal Europeans there were, quartered in Fort William,[4] H.M. 84th Regiment, lately arrived, only about 400 strong,

---

2. Many years afterwards a quantity of the Company's muskets, issued in 1761, were discovered buried near the place where the battle of Manji was fought. It is probable that the European soldiers buried their arms before they were made prisoners.
3. It was this Officer who built the Martinieres at Lucknow and Calcutta.
4. This was the new fort (also called Fort William) which was situated on the esplanade to the south-west of Calcutta, just completed about 1781

Copy of Muster-Roll of the Four Companies of the Honourable Company's Bengal European Regiment present at Patna, 30th April, 1763.

	Officers Commissioned				Officers Staff			Cadets	Sergeants		Drums		Effective Rank and File			Total Non-commissioned Officers and Privates.
	Captains.	Capt.-Lieuts.	Lieutenants.	Ensigns.	Adjutants.	Qtr.-Mstrs.	Surgeons.		Fit for Duty.	Sick.	Fit for Duty.	Sick.	Fit for Duty.	Sick.	Total.	
Captain Carstairs' Company......	1	...	1	2	...	...	1	1	3	1	3	...	43	5	48	55
Captain Joecher's Company......	1	...	1	2	1	...	...	1	4	...	3	...	42	6	48	55
Captain Perry's Company.........	1	...	1	1	...	1	...	...	4	...	3	...	45	3	48	55
Captain Somer's Company	1	...	1	2	...	...	...	...	4	...	3	...	42	6	48	55
Total..............	4	—	4	7	1	1	1	1	15	1	12	—	172	20	192	220

(Signed) PETER CARSTAIRS,
Captain in the Company's Infantry.

the company's European cavalry, and two companies of European artillery with 10 field-guns; making a total of only 850 Europeans available for service in the field, and about 1500 sepahis.

For the protection of Chandernagore and Calcutta, 80 sick Europeans, a few artillerymen, and a company of invalids, with a detachment of native infantry, were all the Regular troops which could be spared; but the militia and volunteers were embodied and placed on garrison duty.

Notwithstanding that every exertion was made to prepare the army quickly for the field, it was not until the 5th July that Major Adams—lately appointed to the chief command of the Bengal army—crossed the river Hugli.

A treaty had been previously concluded between the Calcutta Council and Mir J'afar Khan—the Nawab-elect—and under the articles of which he was proclaimed a second time Nawab of Bengal,. Behar, and Orissa; all privileges previously granted to the English were confirmed—including the obnoxious pass-notes; it was agreed that the expenses of the coming war should be borne by the Native Government; and Mir Kassim Khan was proclaimed a rebel.

On the 17th July Mir J'afar Khan joined Major Adams's army with such of his followers and soldiers as he had been able to collect.

The first action of the campaign was fought by Lieutenant William Glenn, commanding some sergeants of the Bengal European Battalion, a detail of artillery with six guns, and the 2nd Burdwan Battalion. He had under escort £20,000 in specie, as well as supplies of cattle and grain for the headquarter army.

This slender force reached the river Adji on the 17th July, 1763 when it was attacked by an army of 17,000 men, cavalry and infantry, but fortunately without artillery. Glenn chose his position on some rising ground, intersected by ravines, which he rightly conjectured would prove a difficulty to the attacking cavalry. His treasure and cattle he placed in his rear. Here Glenn awaited the enemy, who made a determined advance, hoping by sheer weight to crush the weaker force, but the English artillerymen served their guns so effectively that the masses of the enemy, who again and again came to the charge, were successfully repelled; every onset was received with a deadly discharge of grape and musketry; but, as the enemy fell, the gaps in their ranks were repaired by their reserves. Three times the guns[1] and treasure

---

1. The two field-guns which were three times recaptured by the native infantry were presented by the East India Company to the 2nd Burdwan Battalion, afterwards the 8th Regiment N.I.—Broome.

were captured by the enemy, and as often wrenched from their grasp by the determined charges of our sepahis, nobly led by the sergeants of the Bengal European Regiment, all of whom were killed whilst assisting in the recapture of their convoy.

After four hours' hard fighting, the enemy drew off, leaving in the ravines many of their dead and mortally wounded. Glenn, with his gallant little band, was now complete master of the position, having preserved his treasure and commissariat intact. He then followed up his success by marching on the Fort of Kutwah, which he captured the same evening, the enemy showing but slight resistance. Here Glenn found a vast store of grain and a , large number of cattle, which he added to his convoy; and, crossing the Bhagirathi river the next day, joined the headquarter army under Major Adams, which was encamped on the left bank, with a strong body of the enemy's cavalry waiting to oppose his forward march.

On the 19th Major Adams moved forward with the view of giving battle to the troops disputing his advance towards Plassey and Murshedabad. The enemy was commanded by one of the ablest of the ex-Nawab's Generals, Mohamed Taki Khan, who had, on the previous day, been reinforced by the troops defeated by Glenn; but, whether from jealousy or fear, these held aloof, declining to take part in the coming action. Mohamed Taki Khan, renowned in Mir Kassim's army for his conspicuous gallantry, now advanced to meet the British without the aid of his allies. He had under his command a body of cavalry held to be the flower of the ex-Nawab's newly-organized army, the troopers, Afghans, Rohillas, and Persians, all noted for their horsemanship and skill in the use of their weapons. The English Cavalry on their small horses, unable to hold their ground, were forced back on our main army by Mohamed Taki Khan; seeing which, the enemy made a general advance as if to follow up their success. Mohamed Taki Khan now rode forward amongst his men, encouraging them to make a grand effort to drive the British, once and for all, from their country; reminding them that the English were not invincible; how they had been defeated at the battle of Manji by Mir Kassim Khan's troops, and urging them to stake their lives on the issue. Excited and encouraged by the address of their commander, the troopers rushed forward with cheers and shouts to drive their enemies from the field, but, as they advanced they met with a check; our artillery for the first time opening fire and creating much havoc in their ranks. The British infantry came steadily to the front, under cover of their guns, receiving repeated charges from the cavalry on the points of their bayonets. The mastery was now desperately contested; our cavalry, vastly out-numbered and over-matched, seeming paralysed, when the enemy successively renewed their charges with much vigour. It was an anxious moment, for it appeared that the tide had turned against the British, and that they could not hold their ground; but, just when all seemed lost, Mohamed Taki Khan's horse was struck by a shot which also grazed the rider's foot: but, nothing daunted, he mounted a fresh horse and rode to the front, encouraging his men to wheel round and outflank the British line. Seeing the danger, Adams rested his right flank on a rivulet behind the banks of which he had, with judgement, placed a company of sepahis in ambush, who had been directed to keep close and reserve their fire.

Mohamed Taki Khan, still bent on turning our right flank, but baulked in his purpose by Adams's movement, dashed into the stream, followed by a chosen band of his cavalry; but, as they were ascending the bank, a red line rose from the ambuscade and poured a deadly fire right into their faces. Mohamed Taki Khan was the first to fall, with a bullet through his brain; and the leading troopers perished beside their commander.

The whole body of the cavalry now, disheartened by the loss of the man in whom they placed so much reliance, gave way; but in re-crossing the rivulet they had to run the gauntlet of the fire of our troops, and those who escaped, joining their comrades in rear, galloped off, leaving Adams in command of the road; so that, pursuing, he soon came upon the enemy's camp abandoned in their flight, containing a large quantity of grain, some artillery, and cattle.

In this action, called the battle of Kutwah, Lieutenant Smith of the Bengal European Regiment was killed.

That night the British army under Adams bivouacked near the Nawab's hunting-box, on the field of Plassey, where Clive, just six years before, had watched Siraju 'd daulah's stupendous army circling round the mango grove which sheltered the brave little force under his command; and that night, when Adams's sentries were planted round the British camp, they were told that "Clive" was their parole and "Plassey" their countersign.

The enemy, still opposing our onward march, took up a position about 2 miles south of Murshedabad, their front covered by a large tank called Motijhil; whilst Adams, to secure a base for future operations, improved the defences of the fort of Kutwah, which he converted into a depôt for his wounded men, surplus provisions, and ammunition. Here a detachment of sepahis was left for the protection of the fort.

On the 23rd July Adams again attacked the enemy in their Motijhil entrenchments, but they, making only a show of resistance, retired on their main defences at Suti, about 37 miles to the north of the city Murshedabad, which was now occupied by our troops. The Governor of the city escaped to Suti, but the inhabitants for the most part welcomed the English. Mir Kassim's reign had not been popular amongst the Hindus, of whom he had always been suspicious, and towards whom he had shown great severity; foremost amongst the sufferers being the wealthy family of Seths—the great bankers—several of whom he had imprisoned in order that he might confiscate their property. The nobles, Mahomedan as well as Hindus, had been mulcted of their fortunes; and now that the capital had been removed to Monghyr the business of Murshedabad was seriously injured; all these causes tendered to make Mir Kassim's reign unpopular with the citizens of the old capital, who felt that they could hardly change for the worse. Under these circumstances the Nawab Mir J'afar's return to power was hailed with every demonstration of joy, and his triumphal entry into the city on 24th July, 1763, when he was formally placed in the Musnud by the English commander, was celebrated with much rejoicing.

Although some divisions of Mir Kassim's army had been sent in advance to oppose our forward march, it was at Suti that the ex-Nawab had instructed his generals to make a determined stand. For this purpose large reinforcements, including the two brigades under Sumru and Markar, with 16 field-pieces manned by European artillerymen, and a large body of northern cavalry under Assad' Ullah, had been pushed forward. On the 26th the British force under Adams advanced along the high road towards Suti. Captain Knox, with his two companies, joined the Regiment from Amboa on this day; and Captain Robert Campbell, also of the Bengal European Regiment, being placed in command at Kassimbazar, where our wounded Europeans and a detachment of sepahis were left for the protection of the Company's factory. Captain Knox was appointed Quartermaster-General, and Captain Champion, who had joined the headquarters of the Regiment from Jellasore, was nominated Major of Brigade; and Lieutenant Glenn was rewarded for his distinguished gallantry by being placed on Major Adams's personal staff as aide-de-camp.

The British force now comprised H.M. 84th Regiment and the

Bengal European Regiment—with Claude Martine's French company—just over 1000 European infantry; 150 European cavalry; 120 artillerymen; and 4000 sepahis.

The enemy's force consisted of about 20,000 infantry, amongst whom were Sumru's and Markar's trained brigades; 12,000 cavalry; a large body of European artillery; and an effective Rocket Corps.

On the 1st August Adams crossed the river Bansli, over which he had found it necessary to throw a bridge; his army now deploying on the plains of Geriah, the rivers Bansli and Bhagarathi forming an angle in his rear.

On the morning of the 2nd the enemy was seen advancing; but as his position at Suti was known to be very strongly entrenched, and as it completely barred the road, Adams had not anticipated that Mir Kassim's General would offer him battle, and that he did so was probably due to his desire to take advantage of what he deemed to be the dangerous position in which Adams had placed his army. The enemy, with his powerful Northern cavalry, vastly out-numbering the whole English force, hoped, by a crushing charge to break through the British line; and, forcing it back, whilst broken, right and left into the rivers in its rear, to utterly exterminate it, and thus end the campaign.

Adams was fully aware of the danger of his unwillingly-chosen position; but, the enemy having taken the initiative, the choice had not rested with him. He found himself threatened by a powerful body of cavalry in front, whilst in his rear there were two rapid streams which, in the event of disaster, would form an effectual barrier to his retreat; moreover, he knew there was no reliance to be placed on his European cavalry when opposed to that of the enemy, mounted on northern horses, superior in every way to the poor type of animal procurable in Bengal.

It appeared for some time doubtful if the enemy were really in earnest, but, as they were now advancing in battle array, Adams prepared for action, forming his European infantry into one battalion, the Bengal Europeans representing the right, and the 84th the left wing. On each flank of his European infantry he placed two field-pieces, beyond which his sepahis, flanked again by artillery. The British line now stretched completely across the plain, the right and left resting on the rivers Bansli and Bhagarathi. The rear of the British line at the angle formed by the two rivers was the reserve, consisting of the European cavalry, one battalion of sepahis, and two field-pieces with a few artillerymen.

Adams now advanced his line, keeping his flanks close to the rivers, and the engagement commenced with a heavy cannonade from each side.

It was soon seen that the formation of the enemy's troops resembled our own, Sumru's and Markar's trained brigades being in the centre, flanked by their European artillery in great force, whilst their native infantry, in masses, was on their right and left. Their numerous divisions of cavalry did not appear to have any appointed positions, but, spread about, were apparently awaiting an opportunity to attack any part of the British line showing weakness. Amongst the enemy's cavalry were seen the picked troopers who had fought at the battle of Kutwah, under Mohamed Taki Khan.

The two lines approached, each showing a determined front; but the accurate fire of our European infantry at first caused the centre brigades of the enemy's line to give ground, and it appeared for a moment as if we were going to gain an easy victory.

To enable them to recover themselves, Mir Kassim's General sent a body of his cavalry to charge the British left, occupied by Captain Sibbert's battalion, which was, after a struggle, forced back; and, although the sepahis fought nobly to hold their ground, they were hurled into the stream, where most of those who had escaped the sword were drowned.

During this cavalry charge the enemy, temporarily relieved, re-formed, and were now returning our musketry fire along their whole line.

As soon as Adams saw that Sibbert's battalion had given ground he brought up his reserves, which, though they succeeded in forcing back a portion of the cavalry, were too late to save Captain Sibbert's battalion from disaster.

The British line was now fairly broken on its left, and the enemy's cavalry, pouring through the gap to our rear, boldly charged and captured the two guns on the left of the 84th, the Rocket Corps at the same time concentrating their rocket-fire on that regiment.

By this time our reserves had worked their two guns with such judgement and effect that the large bodies of the enemy's cavalry threatening our line in front had been forced to retire; and the Bengal European Regiment, relieved, were enabled to come to the support of the 84th, by engaging the Rocket Corps. The 84th also relieved from pressure in their front, at once gallantly faced about, and, charging the native cavalry in their rear, recaptured the two guns which had been temporarily lost. Just at this time the commander of the attacking cavalry was severely wounded and left the field, accompanied by many of his troopers, who, smarting under our continuous fire, sought shelter in retreat; and a fresh body of cavalry, sent to reinforce those who had given way, hesitated on seeing the advance-party hurrying towards them and bearing their wounded commander.

Adams grasped the opportunity, and rapidly re-forming the British line, closed it on its centre: when, placing himself at the head of his troops, he made a determined advance. The two lines met, and for a time the result seemed doubtful; but our European infantry proved too strong for Sumru's Brigade, who were ultimately driven back at the point of the bayonet.

2nd August, 1763; The right and left of the enemy's line, consisting principally of Irregular infantry, quickly followed the example of the trained brigades, flying in all directions; and the cavalry, who had up to this time so fully maintained their reputation for gallantry, fled, Sumru's and Markar's men alone preserving order in their retreat.

Adams pressed on in hot pursuit, driving the enemy through and beyond their fortified position at Suti, which they attempted only feebly to defend. Their camp, containing 17 pieces of cannon, a vast amount of stores and ammunition, and on the river 150 boats laden with munitions of war, was captured.

The loss of the enemy was very great, but not so heavy in proportion as that of the British. Of Captain Sibbert's battalion few men escaped; our Europeans also had suffered heavily. That brave young Officer, Glenn, was killed, also Lieutenant Walter Furlong, of the Bengal European Battalion. Captain Knox, who had signally distinguished himself during the action was promoted to a Majority, Lieutenant Francis Couzens being promoted to a company, vice Knox.

The Battle of Geriah is worthy of prominent notice in tins history of our early conquests in Bengal, illustrating in the clearest manner how unvarying is the success of good generalship versus force only.

Mir Kassim laid no claim to generalship, lacking every requisite—even that of personal courage. The ex-Nawab was a good legislator, but he was avowedly no soldier.

The British force at the battle of Geriah numbered under 5500 men; the enemy, according to Broome, had 40,000 men. Malleson computes the number at 28,000 "of good stamp." Mir Kassim's general had the choice of position, his cavalry was as 120 to 1, his artillery was numerically superior; either Sumru or Markar might have led

Mir Kassim's army, but the native commanders would not serve under an alien; for, though foreigners were employed to educate the native army, they were not trusted with the supreme command.

Adams, having opened the road and driven the enemy beyond their fortified position at Suti, returned to Geriah, where he pitched his camp; collecting the wounded, both of his own and Mir Kassim's army, all being sent to the Murshedabad hospital.

Having re-formed his army Adams advanced one march on the 4th of August, when he found that the enemy, anything but cowed, had retired to Oodwah Nullah (Undwah Nálá), a fortified position on a low range of hills, where Mir Kassim had instructed his commanders to bar the road effectively against the British advance, and, although the fortune of war had been against him in the open field, he was confident that an action at Undwah Nálá would be to him a crowning victory.

To. this end Mir Kassim's engineers, taking advantage of a deep gorge, cleft out of the rocks by a mountain torrent, formed a position which, naturally strong, was now aided by powerful and scientifically-planned fortifications. Its capture was deemed impracticable, even when held by a small army only, but, as the defenders vastly out-numbered the force moving forward to its .assault, no fear was entertained by Mir Kassim of the result.

Immense sums had been expended on the defences, extending completely across the gorge, flanked by the Rajmahal mountains on the right and the river Ganges on the left, and completely commanding the high road leading from Murshedabad to Monghyr and Patna.

A commander, however determined, would hardly attempt to force the road without having previously reduced the works by which it was commanded, for it was defended at every point by scientifically-placed batteries; and even, could the passage be effected, Adams was not the man to leave the enemy undisturbed in his rear. The batteries and fortifications of Undwah Nálá were of enormous strength; whilst spreading out for miles in front was a deep morass bordered by an artificial wet ditch 60 feet wide and 12 deep. Behind this ditch was a wall 18 feet high and 7 feet thick, over which were ramparts on an average 60 feet high and 10 feet thick. The left of the entrenchments abutted on the river, close to which was the only road, running in a south-westerly direction for about a mile, with batteries, erected on the scarped rocks.

The right of the fortifications abutted on a steep hill, the precipices and ravines being strongly fortified and garrisoned. Behind these new fortifications the old line of works extended, through the centre of which the high road passed. These old works were still used for auxiliary defence, having been formerly built as an adjunct to the natural strength of the position increased by the steep banks of the mountain stream flowing along the rear, and across which there was a stone bridge, also strongly defended. The enemy's camp was pitched on an open space between the old and new defences.

As soon as Mir Kassim heard that his army had been driven from from their advanced camp at Suti and were retiring on the fortifications at Undwah Nálá, he sent from Monghyr large reinforcements, amongst which was an additional brigade, drilled and equipped on the English system, commanded by an Armenian, named Aratoon. The army of defence now amounted to 40,000 men, including three Regular brigades, commanded by Sumru, Markar, and Aratoon, as well as a large body of European artillery.

On the 11th August the British army arrived within four miles of the enemy's position, when the appalling strength of the fortifications was realised; but Adams did not despond, though he felt acutely the responsibility of his position, and the difficulties of the task which he must accomplish.

He pitched his camp on the southern border of the morass, parallel to that of the enemy. Our heavy guns were now landed from the boats, fascines and gabions, E, were constructed along the face of the river, and batteries, E, erected opposite to what was held to be the best point of attack. As our men, during the construction of these works, were constantly harassed by the enemy's cavalry, entrenchments were thrown up extending along the entire front of the British position.

On the 4th September our works had been advanced along the banks of the Ganges to within three hundred yards of the enemy's fortifications; but it was found that our siege guns made only small impression on the massive works in their front. The only result of our cannonade, which had now been maintained without intermission for several days, was one very imperfect breach effected near the river-gate, B.

The position of affairs in the British camp was anything but promising; for Adams could not advance his batteries any nearer to the fortifications, and at the distance at which his guns were placed he could not effect a practicable breach. He was unable to move his infantry across the morass—which he believed; at this season was quite impassable, and, altogether, the prospect of carrying the enemy's fortifications appeared far distant, if not altogether impracticable.

Adams had retired to his tent intending to form some decided plan of action, when one of those unforeseen events occurred which so repeatedly in our early Indian history mark the turning-point in British undertakings. Just at this time, a strange-looking European appeared before Adams's tent, and having forced himself into his presence, stated that he had deserted from the British service in the hope of obtaining advancement in Mir Kassim's army, but, his expectations not having being realised, he had left the enemy's camp on the previous evening. Creeping past their guards, he had just succeeded in making his escape, and he now presented himself before the British commander a suppliant for mercy, but prepared to give valuable information for his absolution. He had ascertained, whilst in the enemy's service, that there was a ford through the morass, by using which a body of soldiers could safely reach the extreme right of the fortifications, where, at a point described, the enemy's outpost, D, could be reached and overpowered by a few determined men. Near this outpost an attack could be made on the rampart, A, capping the hill which overlooked and partially commanded the enemy's main position. As the deserter's pardon depended on his truthfulness and the feasibility of the scheme, his conditions were accepted, he undertaking to successfully pilot a body of our men across the morass up to the enemy's defences; his absolution and return to the ranks of his Regiment being his reward.

Little did Adams think, when he retired almost in despair to his tent, that a light would break upon him which would enable him to map out a plan of action promising such glorious results. If he could gain possession of the conical hill, A, and at the same time effect an entry at breach, B, near the water-gate, the enemy finding themselves unexpectedly assailed on both flanks at once would probably be dismayed: and in their disorder Adams was confident that he could gain such an advantage as would place the enemy at his mercy. So assured was he now of the success of his scheme that he determined to attempt its execution that very night. A code of signals by lights was very carefully arranged to meet every contingency. Should the commander of the storming-party succeed in gaining the height, A, under cover of the darkness, a lighted torch was to be raised high in the air; on seeing which, a vigorous attack was to be made on the breach, B, near the water-gate, which, even though unsuccessful, would draw the attention of the enemy from the storming-party,. whilst effecting

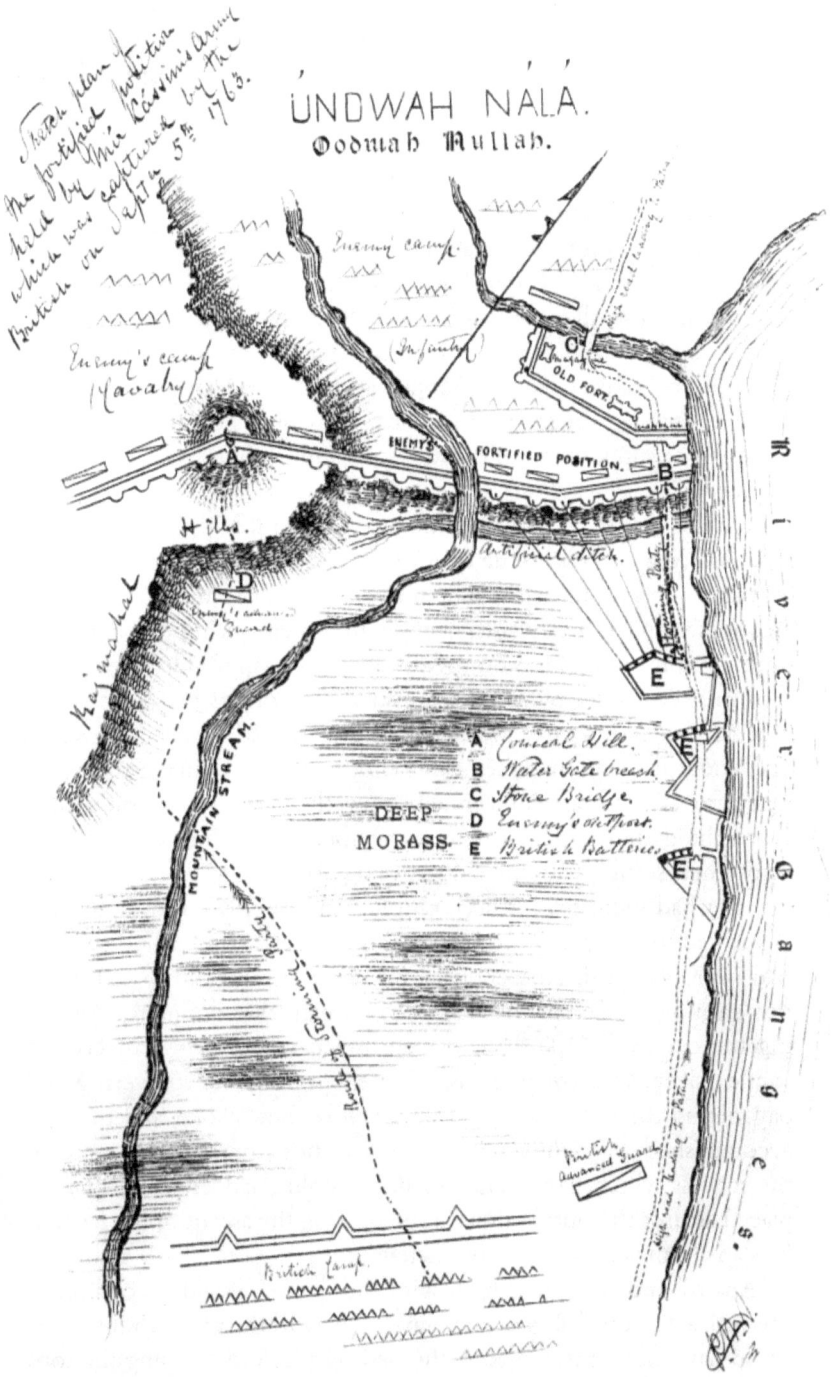

its entry. Should the breach be successfully carried, a junction was to be effected between the two storming-parties, in rear of the enemy's foremost batteries; and, this done, the main difficulties of the attack would be overcome.

Captain Irving, of the Bengal European Regiment, was appointed to command the storming-party fording the morass; under him were the Grenadier Companies of the 84th and Bengal European Regiment, and two complete battalions of sepahis. The rest of the attacking force was put under Captain Moran. The reserve was under Major Carnac, and a small force was left to protect the standing camp.

5th September, 1763; The assaulting parties left the British camp three hours before daybreak; Moran, at the same time, with the main force, occupying the trenches, E, near the water-gate. Carnac was in readiness to support any of the attacking force where assistance might be needed.

Irving's task in crossing the morass was far more difficult than had been anticipated. It was true that the ford was not impracticable, but it was intricate and uncertain. The men had to wade through the water, frequently up to their waists, necessitating their having to carry their ammunition and muskets on their heads; the scaling ladders being carried in like manner by camp followers. Strict orders had been issued that the storming-party were to move along as silently as possible, and under no circumstances was a shot to be fired during their passage across the morass. After much labour the wading-party succeeded in reaching the rising ground at the foot of the hill, when Irving dispatched some of his men in advance in the direction which the deserter had indicated as the position of the enemy's outpost, D. The British advanced-party found all as still as death; and, as no sentries had been planted by the enemy, our men cautiously advanced without creating any alarm. They now discovered that the men composing the enemy's outpost-guard were rolled up in their blankets and sound asleep. Our soldiers rushed at them, soon overpowering and bayoneting them, In most instances, before they awoke, and this was accomplished so silently that Irving was not immediately aware of the success which had been gained; the scaling ladders were quickly placed against the outer ramparts, but during the ascent of the leading files an alarm was raised by the defenders.

Adams' anticipation that all with the enemy would be confusion was realised to the full. A dozen brave men, with their wits about them, could have easily thrown back the besiegers before reaching the tops of the ladders; but the enemy were so unprepared for an attack at this point, and so confused by the darkness, that they ran about hither and thither in the wildest perplexity, looking for orders which no one was at hand to give. Amidst the general confusion the European grenadiers gained the rampart; and, almost unopposed, drove the terrified enemy before them. A vigorous assault was now made on the stockade at the summit of the hill, which was captured; the sepahis at the same time streaming into the batteries as they ascended the walls on the scaling ladders, all of which had been successfully placed without difficulty.

Whilst these events were taking place, Captain Moran with his division concealed in the trenches was watching anxiously for the signal from Irving that he had succeeded in attaining the summit of the opposite hill, A, and to his satisfaction he now perceived the burning torch exultingly waved above the stockade.

Moran, as ordered by Major Adams, had made a feint with part of his troops in the direction of the breach, B, with the object of attracting the enemy's attention and increasing their confusion; but, on seeing the signal that Irving's party had succeeded Moran's delusive attack was at once converted into a vigorous assault.

Our advanced batteries, E, now opened a violent fire on the breach, under cover of which Moran advanced to the attack; the ditch was crossed with some difficulty, but our soldiers were so completely concealed by the smoke of the enemy's guns that his advance was unperceived; and, indeed, from his having retreated to the trenches and silently awaited the signal to attack, the enemy assumed that the storming of the breach had been deemed impracticable and abandoned.

Moran's party now boldly pushed on: and although the breach, B, admitted of but one man passing in at a time, a few soon gained a footing inside the battery, before the enemy attempted to oppose them.

A detachment was now sent to open the gates from the inside; and the main body of the English army, flushed with their success, rushed upon the defenders, forcing them along the ramparts in the direction of Irving's party, now, as previously arranged, pushing their way along the ramparts from the right to meet the main storming-party advancing from the left. The defenders, thus finding themselves between two fires, fled in the direction of their inner works, hotly pursued by the victors, who drove the terrified masses before them towards the bridge, C, in rear of the enemy's camp.

The day broke upon a sickening scene. A strong guard had been placed by the enemy in rear of the bridge, with strict orders that should any of the defenders desert their posts and attempt to escape, they were to be shot down or driven back to the batteries in front. These orders were so sternly carried out, that a ghastly heap of dead and wounded soon rendered escape by the bridge impossible, and the flying masses were precipitated over the parapets down the deep gorge into the rapid stream below. It is computed that 15,000 of the enemy perished during that eventful night; by far the greater proportion having fallen through their disorganized and precipitate flight; the trained brigades again escaping early in the fight in good order.

As soon as victory was assured the British ceased their fire, and all unnecessary slaughter was forbidden; a vast number of the enemy taken prisoners were simply disarmed and released.

The whole of the enemy's camp, a great quantity of ammunition, a large supply of stores, a vast number of horses and cattle, as well as upwards of 100 guns, were captured.

The fugitives, some of whom escaped by the numerous passes and ravines, fled as far as Monghyr without attempting to rally at the fortified town of Rajmahal, which could easily have been defended. They found Mir Kassim in his palace, and informed him of the disaster which had befallen his army.

The successful assault by the British at Undwah Nálá has been justly classed by Colonel Malleson amongst the "Decisive Battles of India." The success of this great undertaking was mainly due to the military skill of its commander. The soldiers, European and native, all had their separate tasks mapped out, and in each instance those tasks were valiantly and faithfully performed Amongst the defenders were three brigades, equal in number to our whole force, well equipped and in every way formidable, commanded by Europeans, and disciplined and drilled on the English system; whilst their artillery, far outnumbering our own, was principally manned by European gunners.

The capture of the Fortress of Undwah Nálá was a feat of strength and valour seldom, if ever, surpassed; and stands on record as a signal proof of what stupendous successes can be attained by troops led by a General who is a, master his profession, commanding the confidence, respect, and love of his subordinates. Such a man was Major John Adams.

GENERAL REFERENCES—CHAPTER 7

Secret Proceedings of the Bengal Council.
The Seir Mutakherin. Calcutta Edition.

Founders of the Indian Empire. Malleson.
Broome's Rise and Progress of the Bengal Army.
Williams's Bengal Infantry.
Thornton's History of India.
Mill's British India.
Malcolm's Dispatches and Correspondence of Lord Clive.
Military Calendar.
&c, &c.

CHAPTER 8
Massacre & Mutiny

September 1763. The ex-Nawab Mir Kassim, when information reached him of the capture of his stronghold of Undwah Nálá, and the complete defeat and dispersion of his army by the British under Major Adams, was at first incredulous; but when the remnant of his vanquished army—too demoralised to attempt a rally behind the walls of the fortified city of Rajmahal, too precipitate in their flight to attempt the defence of the numerous mountain passes through which they had hurried—verified the news of the disaster, Mir Kassim's rage and despair knew no bounds.

Appearing to discard the idea that his fortress had been captured in fair fight, he became suspicious of his officers, one of whom was mysteriously murdered, it was believed under Mir Kassim's orders. The ex-Nawab became daily more irascible and cruel, visions of revenge and murder rising before him. He had in his power at Patna some hundreds of English prisoners captured at the battle of Manji; the sick Europeans left in the hospital at the Chetul Situn; the Raja Ram Narian, Governor of Patna who had shown partiality to, and been protected by, the hated English, and many of the family of the Seths, the wealthy bankers; making, in all, a fine crop on which to feed his cupidity and revenge. With these thoughts in his mind, he wrote on September 9th to Major Adams, saying:

> Although I have in no respect intended any breach of public faith, yet Mr. Ellis, regarding not treaties or engagements, in violation of public faith, proceeded against me with treachery and night assaults. All my people then believed that no peace or terms now remained with the English, and that wherever they could be found it was their duty to kill them. With this opinion it was that the Aumils of Murshedabad killed Mr. Amyatt, but it

was by no means agreeable to me that that gentleman should be killed. On this account I write if you are resolved on your own authority to proceed in this business know for a certainty, that I will cut off the heads of Mr. Ellis and the rest of your chiefs and send them to you. Exult not upon the success which you have gained merely by treachery and night assaults, in two or three places over a few jemindars sent by me by the will of God you shall see in what manner this shall be revenged and retaliated.

Adams's reply was forwarded at once; he wrote as follows:

I received your letter, and understand the contents. The English having always had in view the articles of the treaty endeavoured by pacific measures to reconcile all differences with you, till the perfidious murder of Mr. Amyatt compelled them contrary to their inclinations to declare war against you. You say it was not your intention to murder Mr. Amyatt why then did you not punish the aggressors with the utmost severity. There are three months elapsed and nothing done. We have now, by the assistance of Providence brought your affairs to a very low ebb. It is true you have Mr. Ellis and many other gentlemen in your power; if a hair of their heads is hurt you shall have no title to mercy from the English and you may depend upon the utmost fury of their resentment and that they will pursue you to the utmost extremity of the earth; and should we unfortunately not lay hold of you the vengeance of the Almighty cannot fail overtaking you if you perpetrate so horrid an act as the murder of the gentlemen in your custody.[1]

Adams halted only one day at Undwah Nálá and on the 6tn of September marched to Rajmahal, where he established a temporary hospital, next day resuming his march towards Monghyr, which he reached with the main body of his army on the 1st October, having previously sent a division in advance to throw up entrenchments, erect batteries, and prepare for the siege of the town and fort.

As soon as Major Adams arrived at Monghyr a heavy cannonade was opened from his batteries, a breach effected, and an assault ordered; but the governor of the fort, deeming resistance useless, next morning surrendered unconditionally.

Two thousand men were made prisoners, and Adams's army took

---

1. Vansittart's Narrative, vol. 3.

possession of the fortress and the town; immediately after which the breaches were repaired and the defences strengthened. Mir Kassim had left Monghyr as soon as he found that the English were advancing on his capital; and, retiring to Patna, fanned his wrath against the conquerors into a flame. When he found that his Fortress of Monghyr also had fallen, he prepared at once to carry into effect the threats contained in his letter to Major Adams. The wholesale murders which he contemplated were so repulsive in their details that he experienced difficulty in finding anyone to undertake their execution; but at last Sumru the Alsatian, volunteered to do the cruel work.

The English prisoners— mostly soldiers of the Bengal European Regiment—had been previously removed from the Chetul Situn to a large house or palace, the residence of one Hadji Ahmed; and to this place Sumru proceeded on the 5th of October with 200 of his trained brigade whom he had selected to do his bloody work. There was even a refinement of cruelty in this assassin's method of carrying out the Nawab's inhuman orders; he informed the prisoners that he had planned an entertainment to enliven their captivity, and that their knives and forks were essential at the feast, "in order to entertain them in the English manner." This ruse was played to disarm the prisoners so that they could make no resistance. Sumru then secreted a body of armed men in the outer square of the palace; and, as soon as all was ready, he summoned Messrs. Ellis, Hay, and Lushington, into his presence; when, the prisoners, accompanied by five or six of their companions in captivity, appearing before him, were ruthlessly attacked, their bodies hacked to pieces, and thrown into a well.

The massacre was now ordered to be carried out wholesale, in the larger square; but it is said that Sumru's soldiers were so disgusted with the part they had taken that they told their captain he might do his murderous work himself; for that they had undertaken to fight as soldiers, and not act as assassins. They were, however, soon brought to reason by their commander, who ordered the ringleaders to be shot on the spot; after which his instructions were obeyed and the slaughter completed.

The rest of the prisoners—including, it is said, Mrs. Ellis and her child—collected in the larger square, were shot down and then hacked to pieces, their bodies being thrown into a large well in the centre of the building. When one of the prisoners named Gulston was found still alive, the men employed in clearing away the bodies would have saved him, but he declined their proffers of assistance, and was thrown into the well alive. There still remained a few European soldiers, probably some of the sick in hospital at the Chetul Situn, who were murdered under the Mir Kassim's orders on October 11th. Altogether, between 150 and 200 prisoners were put to death, most of them soldiers of the Bengal European Regiment. A native contemporary tells us that the prisoners, "without losing courage, marched up to the murderers, and with empty bottles, stones, and brickbats, fought them to the last man, until they were all killed."[1]

Dr. Fullerton and four sergeants were the only Europeans who escaped. Fullerton had been professionally useful to Mir Kassim, who said he considered him "as an acquaintance and a friend." He was therefore allowed to go to a Dutch factory near at hand, from which he escaped, and on October 25th joined Major Adams' army. The 4 Sergeants, Davis, Douglas, Speedy, and another, name unknown, had been sent to Purneah, to which place the ex-Nawab sent orders that they were to be assassinated; but the Governor, who entertained a high opinion of the soldiers, delayed compliance, entreating Mir Kassim to recall his mandate; adding that "if he was still determined on it, it would be a difficult matter, as the men were beloved by all his people, to find one that would undertake the task." The ex-Nawab, on receipt of this letter, flew into a violent passion; directing a reply to be sent to the Governor to tell him that if he had not spirit himself to put his command in force, he was to send the soldiers immediately to Patna, where ample justice should be done for the crimes which their countrymen had committed. The Governor then sent, for the sergeants and, telling them that he was now compelled to send them under escort to Patna, said that he hoped the Nawab's rage would cool before they arrived. They were sent off next day in a native boat under charge of a jemadar and twelve burkendazes; but, as soon as they reached the river Ganges, two of the sergeants clambered on to the roof of the boat, where they found the jemadar and four of his men asleep, with their faces covered. The sergeants approached stealthily, gathered the tulwars and matchlocks of the guard, and one of the soldiers, taking hold of the captain of the boat, pushed him overboard. The two sergeants were now joined by their comrades from below, but the noise had awakened

---

1. Hadji Ahmed's palace was soon afterwards razed to the ground and the site consecrated as a Christian cemetery. "A monument has been erected at Patna near the house where the sanguinary deed was committed. It is surrounded by an enclosure which forms the English burying-ground. The column is in good style, but has neither an inscription or any device explanatory of the purpose for which it was erected".—Military Calendar, vol. 2 page 81.

the jemadar and his men asleep on deck; who, seeing the Europeans now armed, fell on their knees and begged for mercy. Pardon was granted on condition that the guard would submit and deliver up the remaining arms to the sergeants. The native captain, who was found hanging on to the rudder, implored to be taken on board, which was done on his undertaking to pilot the boat safely past Patna and land the fugitives at the British camp, which was known to be between Monghyr and Patna. The camp was reached in safety the next morning, when the sergeants reported themselves to Major Adams, who ordered them to rejoin the Bengal European Regiment.

A sketch of the career of these sergeants, which has been fortunately preserved, will be found full of interest.

Sergeant Davis, a native of Edinburgh, enlisted in the Company's Service in 1761, and served in Captain Somers's Company, Bengal European Regiment, where he was soon selected by his captain for promotion to sergeant. He was present with the force under Carstairs at Manji, returned to Patna after the defeat at that place, and, for some reason unknown, was sent a prisoner by Mir Kassim to Purneah. On his rejoining the Regiment after his escape he was posted to one of the grenadier companies, with which he served during the whole war. On the Bengal army being remodelled by Lord Clive in 1765, Sergeant Davis's regiment was attached to the 1st Brigade at Monghyr under Colonel Sir Robert Fletcher, where in 1766 the insubordination and resignation of the officers took place. Sir R. Fletcher sent for Sergeant Davis and offered him a commission, but he refused it, declaring "that as the officers could not live upon their pay which was the cause of their quitting the service, it was impossible that he could do so." He was, however, afterwards appointed a Quartermaster, and subsequently obtained an Ensign's Commission, and died a Captain in 1788.

Sergeant Douglas having rejoined the Bengal European Regiment whilst it was encamped with the army under Major Adams near Patna, was present at the memorable storm and capture of that fortified position, together with the subsequent operations of the army, and in 1766 was appointed Sergeant-Major and employed on revenue duty at Morad-bagh. In 1773 he was sent with Captain T. Edwards's battalion to clear the district round Rungpore of the Sanassies, a clan of marauding; robbers, when the detachment with which he was serving was overpowered, and Douglas, who rendered valuable service in attempting to reform the broken Sepahi force, was killed.

The narrative of Sergeant Speedy's career is specially valuable, as he is the only man whose name has been recorded as having joined the ranks of the Bengal European Regiment when it was raised at Fulta by Clive in December, 1756.

Speedy was an Irishman, and in common with so many of his countrymen has reflected honour and credit on the Bengal European Regiment. In 1748[1] he enlisted in the East India Company's Service, was sent to Madras and took part in several battles against the French. On the 20th July, 1756, Speedy's company composed part of the detachment sent to Bengal under Major Kilpatrick to the succour of the fugitives from Calcutta after the capture of Fort William by the Nawab Siraju'd daulah. Speedy was one of the few soldiers who survived the terrible malarious fever, which carried off nearly three-fourths of the men of the detachment; and was, on Clive's arrival at Fulta, transferred to the Grenadier company of the Bengal European Regiment, which was then in course of formation. Sergeant Speedy served with the Regiment at the Battle of Baj Baj, Recapture of Calcutta, Battle of Chitpore, Capture of Chandernagore, Capture of Kutwah, Battle of Plassey, Battle of Condore, Capture of Mussulipatam, and Battle of Biderra. In 1760 Sergeant Speedy was appointed Sergeant-Major of a sepahi battalion, with which he appears to have been present at the disastrous Battle of Manji, when he was made prisoner, conveyed to Patna, and then sent by Mir Kassim to Purneah. His escape in the native boat in which he was being conveyed to his contemplated execution at Patna has been fully detailed, and how he joined Major Adams's advancing army. Sergeant Speedy was now re-posted to the Bengal European Regiment, with which he served until the year 1767, when he died, after having led as eventful a life as perhaps any recorded in history.

The following is a nominal roll of the officers of the Bengal European Regiment, either killed at the battle of Manji, or murdered by the infamous Sumru at Patna.

---

1. During the commencement of the Spanish, or Ten Years' War, Speedy enlisted in the 32nd Foot, and was present at the Battles of Dettingen, Fontenay, and Lafeldt, losing in the last engagement two fingers of his left hand. In 1748 he received his discharge from His Majesty's service and, fond of adventure, immediately enlisted under the East India Company. Captain Williams, the Author of The Historical Account of the bonsai Native Infantry, who died in 1805, knew Sergeant Speedy, and obtained from him the above particulars.

Captain Peter Carstairs	Ensign John Greentree
Captain Charles E. Joecher	Ensign Robert Roberts
Captain Ambrose Perry	Ensign Duncan Macleod
Captain Henry Somers	Ensign William Crawford
Lieutenant John Downie	Ensign William Hincles
Lieutenant Richard Holland	Ensign Isaac Humphries
Lieutenant Maurice Roach	Ensign John R. Roach
Lieutenant George Alston	Ensign John Perry
Lieutenant Sir William Hope	Ensign Walter Mackay

Dr. Anderson in Medical charge

Two of these lieutenants and two ensigns were attached to sepahi regiments.

1st-28th October; Whilst the Patna massacres were being perpetrated, Adams was pursuing his onward march towards that city. The ex-Nawab, on the approach of the British army, retired, taking up a position about 20 miles distant; where he pitched his camp, having with him Sumru's division and a brigade of his northern horsemen. Mir Kassim had sent his family and a large amount of treasure, which he had taken with him when he fled from Monghyr, to his stronghold at Rotas; intending to follow and make his last stand at that place, should the British succeed in capturing Patna.

Patna was a fortified city of considerable strength, the batteries of which formed an irregular parallelogram; the north face stretching about a mile-and-a-half along the bank of the Ganges, the south being about a mile inland. In the north-east corner, and abutting on the river, was the kella or citadel, protected by fortifications all round. Beyond the north-west corner, and also abutting on the river, was the English factory, protected by defensible stone walls.

There were three main entrances to the city; the principal gate being in the centre of the south face, with one on the east side close to the citadel, and another to the west in the direction of the English factory.

On the 28th October Adams encamped on the east side of the city. His many anxieties and the calls on his unfailing energy during the campaign had so completely undermined his strength and health that he retained his command with difficulty, but he felt that until Patna should be captured, the murder of the British prisoners avenged, and Mir Kassim made prisoner or driven out of the country, his mission was unfulfilled. The north-east angle of the fort, where the citadel was situated, was selected as the point for the intended assault. Near at hand was a village, the buildings in and about which would afford cover for his working parties. A battery was thrown up opposite this angle of the fort, which was connected by trenches with the village; the right of the battery resting on the river; so that the besiegers were enabled to land their stores and provisions from boats in place of employing land carriage. This arrangement was the more necessary as Mir Kassim's cavalry was scouring the country, with the object of cutting off our supplies and thwarting our operations. Opposite the centre of the east face a second battery was thrown up, on which Adams mounted his heaviest guns, thus bringing his diverging fire to bear on the south-east as well as the north-east angles of the fortifications. On the 31st October the enemy made a determined sally, stealing along under the banks of the river to the rear of our batteries, and making a vigorous attack on our position. Our sepahis, taken by surprise whilst working in the trenches, at first gave ground, but, soon rallying, seized their arms and defended their position until Captain Knox arrived with reinforcements; when the enemy were driven back, the English following them up to the eastern gate, and inflicting on them considerable loss; but the sally had so far succeeded that one of our heavy guns was spiked and our expense magazine exploded.

During the next few days repeated sallies were made from the city, but our working-parties in the trenches having been strengthened by two grenadier companies of the Bengal European Regiment and H.M. 84th combined, the enemy found their assaults foiled, and abandoned their attempts.

By the 5th November two practicable breaches had been effected; one near the eastern gate and one towards the south-east. The fortifications, constructed of solid masonry, had been protected on the outside by loose earth piled against the walls to a height of upwards of twenty feet; flanking towers had been built at intervals; and finally a wet ditch, 50 or 60 feet wide and 7 to 10 in depth, surrounded the whole fortifications.

On the 6th November Major Adams delivered his attack in two columns; the first under Captain Champion, the second under Major Irving. Captain Moran accompanied Champion's column, in command of a small party of the 84th Regiment and one of the grenadier companies of the European Regiment; with 5 companies of sepahis attached.

Major Irving's column consisted of two companies of the Bengal Europeans, and some sepahi grenadier companies.

The Reserve was placed under Major Carnac.

Captain Champion's attack on the breach near the eastern gate was conducted with good fortune as well as skill; for he managed to ford the ditch unperceived, and, quickly placing his ladders, his party were ascending before an alarm was created; when a heavy fire of grape was opened, but the enemy's range was laid so high that the escaladers were rather assisted by the; smoke than hindered by the shot, and were soon enabled to gain ;a firm footing on the ramparts. Major Irving's party was not altogether so fortunate; for, finding that he was unable to ford the ditch without wasting time, Irving changed his tactics, and keeping as close as possible to the walls followed the first column, which had succeeded in passing through the breach; and thus both columns obtained a footing within the fortifications. Irving, with his grenadiers, now gained possession of the tower on the south face, from which a heavy fire had been brought on the besiegers: Champion at the same time clearing the ramparts towards the west.

Major Adams had planned that, when the two columns should effect an entry by the breaches, they were to seize the eastern gate on the inside, which was to be then thrown open, and the main column of his army admitted; but, as has been shown, this plan had only partially succeeded, and Irving now turned his attention to carrying out Adams's orders. Placing a party of his men in the battery which he had captured, he proceeded with the remainder of his column to seize the eastern gate. Captain Champion also, as soon as he had cleared the ramparts, made his way towards the eastern gate, where the two columns met. But here an unforeseen obstacle presented itself; the inside of the gate being found to be defended by an entrenched masonry wall of great strength, and beyond this a courtyard, which could only be approached by passing through a narrow defile. This courtyard was defended by the enemy in great strength, who poured a concentrated fire on our storming-parties, which mortally wounded Major Irving, whilst Champion also received a severe wound and was placed *hors de combat*. Lieutenant Nicoll of the native infantry, the next senior officer, now assumed command of the column, ably assisted by Lieutenant Crown of the Bengal European Regiment, who, without a moment's hesitation, charged the wicket which held the narrow defile. There was only room for two men to pass abreast, but, notwithstanding this difficulty, charge after charge was made, the passage forced, and the storming-party entered, obtaining complete possession of the court-yard and the eastern gate, which was now thrown open. Captain Scotland was the first to enter the gate with a portion of the European grenadiers, by virtue of seniority taking command;

but soon afterwards his jawbone was shattered by a musket-ball, and the command again devolved on Lieutenant Nicoll, who ordered a general advance.

The enemy took up their position at a place called the Burra Mulah, where they elected to make a determined stand. Whilst the besiegers were preparing to attack it was reported to Nicoll that they had expended all their ammunition, the enemy bringing at the same time their artillery fire to bear with great effect. Nicoll quickly got his men under cover, where they remained until the sergeants had collected ammunition from the pouches of the dead and wounded. The British detachment was now formed up, and made a very gallant charge on the Burra Mulah; which, after a severe struggle, was captured at the point of the bayonet, the enemy flying towards the southern gateway. The capture of the city was complete; and Major Adams, collecting all his troops together, issued very stringent orders against plundering; guards being told off and the city garrisoned by the captors. Major Shirlock commanded the Citadel, with orders to imprison all stragglers; and the peaceful inhabitants were invited to return to their several callings, when, they were informed, they would be protected from injury. The British loss was considerable, several men as well as officers having fallen; and, Major Irving dying of his wounds on the 10th November, Captain Champion succeeded to the vacant majority.

The enemy also suffered severely; 300 being found dead within the fortifications.

November-December, 1763; Mir Kassim, hearing of the capture of his last stronghold, and being convinced that further resistance was useless, now placed himself under the protection of Shuja' u'd daulah, the Nawab of Oude, towards whose territories he proceeded, under escort of Sumru's brigade and a body-guard of Northern horsemen.

A British detachment was sent in pursuit, but having pushed forward as far as the Karamnassa river—the boundary of the Bengal Province—and failed to overtake the fugitives, it returned to Patna.

Major Adams's task fulfilled and his health completely broken—he handed over his command to Major Yorke and proceeded to Calcutta, *en route* to his native land: but nature was exhausted, and he died at the Presidency on the 16th January, 1764; universally regretted and specially beloved by all ranks of the Bengal European Regiment, which he had commanded with so much courage, ability, and success.

In memory of Major John Adams, it must be said that no more

daring, more competent, or more honourable soldier can be found amongst the long list of England's great warriors, who have distinguished themselves in all climes and countries.

Mir Kassim Khan, the ex-Nawab of Bengal, having obtained promises of protection from Shuja' u'd daulah, the Nawab Vazir of Oude, crossed the Karamnassa river on the 5th December, 1763, and proceeded to Allahabad, accompanied by his European artillery, his trained brigades, Northern cavalry, and levies subsequently enlisted; amounting in all to 30,000 men.

The three brigades under Sumru, Markar, and Aratoon had escaped almost unscathed from the battles of Geriah, Suti, and Undwah Nálá It will have been noticed that Sumru had drilled his brigades, not only in the art of fighting, but in that of retiring in order after defeat, teaching them that security in retreat can only be attained by maintaining strict obedience to orders, and unity of action; he never allowed himself to be tempted into engaging with his enemy, until he had provided for safe retreat in the event of disaster.

Mir Kassim had no occasion to appeal to the Nawab Vazir of Oude for pecuniary assistance—his treasure having reached his Fort at Rotas in safety from the pursuit of the British detachment: he had therefore sufficient money for his current expenses, and experienced no difficulty in obtaining promises of a resting-place in the Oude territory, where he could mature his plans for future action.

Shah Alám, the Emperor of Delhi, having failed in obtaining possession of his capital, was also the guest of Shuja' u'd daulah, who rejoiced at being the patron and host of so exalted a personage. Shah Alám, although a fugitive and accompanied by only a few trusty followers, was nevertheless acknowledged by the mass of the people throughout India as representing the authority of the great Mogul, who, though an exile from his capital, was none the less Emperor of India.

The Nawab Vazir now found himself placed in a difficult alternative; having promised his patronage to Mir Kassim, the ex-Nawab; and also sent a dress of honour to the Nawab Mir J'afar congratulating him on his success. The Nawab Vazir had intended to watch the course of events before determining whether he would accept the alliance of Mir J'afar, or of Mir Kassim; and now that the former was securely seated on his throne, he rather inclined towards him; but he determined to visit Mir Kassim in his camp before deciding on his future conduct.

Shah Alám also was interested in these complications, for, though possessing influence, he needed support; and it was therefore arranged that he should accompany the Nawab Vazir on his visit to Allahabad.

On arrival at his destination the Nawab Vazir proceeded with an escort of 10,000 cavalry to pay his guest a complimentary visit. On entering Mir Kassim's camp, he was received by a guard-of-honour, composed of such a body of soldiers as he had never seen or conceived, well-armed, uniformly-dressed, equipped and drilled on the English system; the artillery for the most part manned by Europeans, and the cavalry in every way superior to those composing his own escort. Shuja' u'd daulah at once realized that he had found a valuable ally in Mir Kassim, and left his camp resolved to give him the preference over Mir J'afar. The Emperor of Delhi, also, much impressed with the appearance of Mir Kassim and his troops, determined to seek the alliance of the ex-Nawab.

Just at this time, and when negotiations for a Triple Alliance were proceeding, the Raja of Bundelkhund, a vassal of the Nawab Vazir of Oude, openly declared his independence; and, collecting an army, was extending his conquests into the territories of the Emperor of Delhie, as well as those of the Nawab of Oude. This state of affairs called for immediate action and rendered a campaign in Bengal difficult, if not impossible. Mir Kassim offered the services of a division of his troops, with which he-undertook to bring the rebel Raja to reason and punish him for his audacity; the condition being that, if he should succeed, both the Emperor and the Nawab Vazir would support his cause against the British. A treaty to the foregoing effect was signed:, and Mir Kassim proceeded, accompanied by his trained brigades, to fulfil his mission.

Sumru, at the head of his brigade, gained an easy victory over the Irregular regiments of the Raja of Bundelkhund, who was speedily reduced to submission, and Mir Kassim returned to Allahabad, where he was received with honour both by the Emperor and the Nawab Vazir, who declared their readiness to assist him in his schemes if he would agree to pay all the expenses of the proposed war, and divide equally all treasure that might be captured, either from Mir J'afar or the British. March, 1764; These terms having been agreed upon, Mir Kassim further promised that when he should be seated on the throne of Bengal he would fully acknowledge Shah Alám as his Suzerain.

Whilst the Emperor, the Nawab Vazir, and Mir Kassim are organizing their armies for the invasion of Bengal, our attention must be directed to events occurring on the other side of the Karamnassa river.

Major Knox had been constrained by wounds and ill-health to hand over the command of the army to Captain Jennings of the artillery, as *locum tenens* for Major Carnac, who was ordered from Burdwan to command the troops in the field.

Great changes had taken place in the composition of the Bengal European Regiment since its formation in 1756. It had taken a leading part in eighteen important battles and sieges, in some of which the casualties had been great. In addition, 4 complete companies and 17 officers had been massacred in 1763 at or near Patna.

These casualties had during the past seven years been partly made up by reinforcements from H.M. 39th Regiment and the Bombay and Madras European Regiments. In October, 1763, orders had been sent to Bengal for H.M. 84th Regiment to return to England, as it was ordered that its soldiers should be paid off and discharged; at the same time the Bengal Government were informed that both the officers and men of this Regiment could, if they so desired, take service under the East India Company in preference to returning home. With few exceptions the remnant of the 84th Regiment, including the following Officers,[1] volunteered for the Bengal European Regiment:

Lieutenant Thomas Goddard	Ensign A. F. Achmuty
Lieutenant Charles Fielding	Ensign Thomas Roper
Lieutenant John Nelson	Ensign Christian Kundson
Lieutenant Douglas Hill	Ensign James Skinner
Lieutenant John Cummings	Ensign Jacob Carnac
	Ensign J. G. Robinson

All these Officers received a step of rank; those previously in the service also getting promotion.

On account of the increase of the native army, several commissions were granted to sergeants in the Bengal European Regiment and artillery; amongst these being Sergeant Davis, one of the four who escaped with the boat in which they were being-conveyed from Purneah to Patna in the October of the previous year.

It would have been far more conducive to the discipline of the Bengal European Regiment had the Council in Calcutta been content to fill vacancies from the above sources only; but it will be remembered that, after the capture of Chandernagore, many of the French prisoners took service in the Regiment; and, again, after the

---

1. The Officers of H.M. 84th who volunteered for service in the Bengal European Regiment were granted half-pay for life.

Battle of Biderra, a large number of Dutch and other foreign prisoners obtained their freedom on condition of taking military service under the Company; and, finally Captain Martine's French company was attached to the Regiment, as well as two other French companies sent from Madras for service in Bengal. These latter companies were known to be of doubtful reputation, having manifested bad faith whilst on service with the Madras troops at Manilla. These numerous enlistments resulted in two-thirds of the Bengal European Regiment being composed of foreign mercenaries, many of whom had taken service simply to obtain their release from prison. Such men, not bound to the English by ties of nationality, were prepared to seize any opportunity to transfer their allegiance, if they thought that by so doing they could improve their condition.

This was not a happy state of things, more especially as it soon became evident that many foreigners in Mir Kassim's army were in constant communication with their countrymen in the Company's service, to whom they represented themselves as enjoying comparatively higher rank and larger emoluments. Nor were these communications imparted to the foreigners only, but they were translated for the information of the British soldiers, some of whom were dazzled by the descriptions, and talked freely amongst themselves of the liberal treatment the European soldiers received at the hands of the native Princes.

At the same time Mir Kassim's emissaries in the British camp were tampering with our sepahis, and holding out the temptation of increased pay and commands to any who would transfer their allegiance from the British to the native armies.

In consequence of these intrigues a feeling of discontent, which assumed alarming proportions, was spreading amongst our troops, and a single spark might at any moment set the whole fabric into a blaze.

Before the troops entered on the late campaign against Mir Kassim in June, 1763, Mir J'afar had promised them that if they should secure to him the throne, and refrain from sacking or injuring the inhabitants of his cities, he would pay them a sum of money as a reward for their services, and in lieu of prize; and this promise was endorsed by the Calcutta Council; and, under sanction, communicated to the men of the army. On the capture of Murshedabad, Monghyr, and Patna, in consequence of these promises, no prize was declared. At Undwah Nálá it is true that a large quantity of horses, stores, and cattle, which were captured, were sold at Rajmahal, and the proceeds paid to the troops, but Undwah Nálá was not a town, and treasure captured where there were no inhabitants to suffer was, under the agreement with Mir J'afar, allowed to be lawful prize. Mir J'afar's proposals had been accepted by the soldiers of the army, who had abstained from plunder, and their part of the conditions of the agreement had been thus conscientiously fulfilled. The first payment under the agreement was promised to the troops as soon as the campaign against Mir Kassim should be victorious, and our army reach the boundary of the Company's territories at the Karamnassa river. It was now two months since these conditions had been fulfilled; but the promised donation in lieu of prize had not been paid. Mir J'afar acknowledged the debt, but the Calcutta Council—who had now the sole control of his finances—turned a deaf ear to the demands of the soldiers. On the 30th January Captain Jennings ordered a general parade, at which the assembled troops refused to obey the word of command. On the commander demanding an explanation he was informed by the ringleader, named Straw, that the soldiers had lost all trust in the integrity of the Calcutta Council; for, though they had faithfully performed their duties throughout a campaign of extraordinary severity, they had been deceived and defrauded; and they were resolved not to serve the Company until the promises made to them should be redeemed.

Captain Jennings knew that although no grievances could justify the insubordination of the troops, yet that undoubtedly they had been defrauded by the council, which he strongly suspected would still evade payment unless heavy pressure was put upon them.

The next day the following General Order was issued by Captain Jennings at Patna.

> It is with the utmost concern that the commanding officer sees any discontent arising amongst the troops he has the honour to command he shall always esteem it a happiness in himself to see them righted in every respect as far as he can with justice, allow, or they with prudence demand. As they have hitherto showed themselves brave and good soldiers, he hopes that they will not now be guilty of any rash action that may in any way sully their former good behaviour. In respect to the prize-money he gives his word of honour the payment shall be made as soon as it arrives; and in case any other complaints happen if they were made in a proper manner as becometh a soldier, he will endeavour to give them all the satisfaction that lies in his power.

3rd February, 1764; This order temporarily pacified the men, who returned to their duty; but the spirit of insubordination was still strong amongst them; and, three days after, Captain Jennings deemed it necessary to detach the grenadier companies, who had taken a lead in the demonstration to the Karamnassa, together with a portion of the artillery and two sepahi battalions. Immediately after the demonstration on parade Captain Jennings communicated to the Calcutta Council the mutinous state of the troops; and urged the necessity of meeting the just demands of the soldiers without delay.

4th-10th February; But the troops were determined to obtain something more than bare promises. The minds of the English soldiers had been poisoned by their intercourse with their foreign comrades, who, still outnumbering them in the Bengal European Regiment,[1] were bent on mischief. The malcontents elected as their leader the man Straw, upon whom they conferred the rank of Major; and after a few days, as the promised payments had not been made, the private soldiers and many of the sepahis, in open mutiny, turned out on parade with loaded arms and fixed bayonets, the European artillery with their 6 field-pieces being prepared for action on the flanks of the European Regiment.

The officers soon appeared on parade, when Captain Jennings, seizing Straw by the collar, attempted to force him towards the quarter-guard; but the troops, charging forward, rescued the man whose orders alone were obeyed. Captain Jennings endeavoured to pacify the men; who declared that, as they saw no prospect of obtaining the promised money by fair means, they were resolved to march to Calcutta and force the council to comply with their just demands; but in the first instance they should proceed to the Karamnassa river, and join the grenadier companies, who, they said, were prepared to support them.

---

1. It is necessary that some further explanation should be given of how it came about that at this time—1764—the ranks of the Bengal European Regiment contained so many foreigners. It will be remembered that many French, Dutch, and German prisoners, taken at Chandernagore and Biderra, were allowed their freedom on their acceptance of military service under the Company. In addition, the French fortress of Pondicherry, in Madras, surrendered to the British in January, 1761. In the garrison of Pondicherry when it surrendered there were quartered the French Regiment of Lorraine, Lally's Irish Regiment, and the French East India Company's European Corps called the French Battalion of India. The men of these regiments offered to serve the British, many of them being sent to Bengal and drafted to the Bengal European Regiment, at this time employed on the campaign against Mir Kassim Khan.

The mutineers, including nearly all the privates of the Bengal European Regiment, the European cavalry, a considerable portion of the Bengal artillery, the Moghul Horse, and many sepahis, left the British camp. On their march towards the boundary of the Company's territory they were seen by the Nawab Mir J'afar; who, alarmed at their decided action, offered the men £10,000 in part payment, if they would return peaceably to their duty; but, disdaining all offers of reconciliation, they proceeded on their way.

Captain Jennings now ordered the officers, with several of the most influential non-commissioned officers, to follow the mutineers, and to persuade them to return to their duty; whilst he rode quickly to the Karamnassa and ordered the grenadier companies and the sepahi battalions quartered there to march to the headquarter camp by a side road.

The officers, partially successful, brought back to camp about 100 European soldiers and the 6 guns which had fallen in rear.

Lieutenant Claude Martine did good service on this occasion, as well as Ensign Allen—who had been a Sergeant in the 84th, and was now Adjutant of the Bengal European Regiment. Martine, although he failed to bring back his men, obtained valuable information which he communicated to Jennings. One of his Frenchmen had privately told him that it was the French soldiers who were the instigators of the mutiny; their object being not so much to obtain their prize-money as to desert and take service with Mir Kassim's army, where so many of their compatriots were serving; they subsequently intended, in conjunction with Sumru's brigades, to gain possession of the whole country; and they had deputed the informant to offer Martine the supreme command of the proposed rebel army. This information gave our officers a handle on which to work on the feelings of the British soldiers, who had been kept in ignorance of the ultimate intentions of the Frenchmen. The English soldiers were now informed that they had been deceived and led into a rebellion, from a participation in which they would find it extremely difficult to extricate themselves. Captain Morgan and Ensign Davis went a second time to the rebel camp, armed with the information gathered from Martine, and they persuaded about 80 more of the men to return—amongst them, Straw, the rebel Major; and at the same time the officers of the sepahi regiments collected about 300 repentant sepahis, who returned to our camp.

The mutineers now elected as their commander a Sergeant named Delamare, who had formerly been promised a commission by Major

Adams; but, probably on account of misconduct on the Sergeant's part, the promise was unfulfilled. Although a Sergeant in the 84th, Delamare was of French extraction and spoke French with fluency. The march of the mutineers was continued across the Karamnassa river into the Oude territory; but before they left the British side 70 more of our European soldiers returned to camp; there remaining now only 157 men of the Bengal European Regiment in the rebel camp, and these nearly all foreigners.

Of the native deserters about 100 men, chiefly belonging to the Moghul Horse, followed the rebels, all of whom proceeded to Allahabad; and there joining Mir Kassim's army were drafted either into his artillery or into one of Sumru's trained brigades.

On the day after the mutinous troops had marched from camp Captain Jennings received £10,000 from the Nawab Mir J'afar; and, having borrowed all the money he could obtain from other sources, issued an order directing a first distribution of prize-money to the troops on the following scale:

	Rs.	
Sergeants of Infantry, Corporals and Bombardiers of Artillery	80	each
Corporals of Infantry and Gunners of Artillery	60	,,
Private Soldiers and Drummers	40	,,
Havaldars	12	,,
Naiks	9	,,
Sepahis	6	,,

But this order, although it put an end to the mutiny amongst the Europeans, had a contrary effect upon the sepahis; who deemed that their services had not been sufficiently appreciated by the award of less than one-sixth of a European soldier's share. Under these circumstances, the native regiments, in a body, refused their prize-money, insisting on a fairer distribution.

The next day, February 13th, the Bengal European Regiment and artillery were ordered under arms to protect the magazine and guns; and steps were taken to prevent communication between the Europeans and the sepahis; but this latter precaution was unnecessary, as the English soldiers were only eager to prove that their penitence was sincere. Two of the sepahi Regiments marched off towards the Karamnassa river; but on a sepahi's share being increased to Rs. 20, the deserters, as well as the discontented sepahi regiments who had remained in camp, expressed their regret for their misconduct, and were permitted to return to their duty. Captain Jennings, deeming it judicious to keep his troops employed after their insubordinate conduct, ordered a march to Sahsaram; and again, a few days afterwards, moved his camp to Hariganj on the Soane river.

On the 6th of March Jennings handed over command of the field force to Major Carnac; who, it will be remembered, had. been ordered from Burdwan to assume command in succession to Major Adams.

Major Carnac, as soon as he had taken the command, ordered a general parade; addressing the troops specially with reference to their late misconduct, which he reprobated in the strongest terms. He then informed them that the enemy was already in the field, so that they would soon have an opportunity of recovering the confidence and esteem of their officers. This address was received by the troops with wild enthusiasm; the British soldiers having now fully realised that they had been made tools of by the foreigners, who had all along kept them in ignorance of their real designs; and they were anxious to meet them in the field as enemies, and be even with them for their perfidy.

The British army was now numerically equal to any that had hitherto taken the field in Bengal. The Bengal European Regiment was reinforced on the 17th March by a complete English company, which joined from Calcutta, under Captain Kinlock, bringing the Regiment up to a strength of nearly 800 men, and the more efficient for having got rid of the French element, which had always been a source of difficulty and danger. There still remained in its ranks some 80 or 100 Germans; but the British and the German soldiers had always fraternised; and now, as they had been equally duped by the French, there was more than ever a bond of union between them.

Carnac had, besides the Bengal European Regiment, 2 companies of the Bombay European Regiment, and 1 of marines; 70 European and 400 native cavalry, as well as 7 complete battalions of sepahis; making in all between 6000 and 7000 soldiers; in addition was Mir J'afar's army, numbering 12,000, and bringing the total force under Carnac up to 19,000 men.

These latter troops had accompanied the British force throughout the advance from Murshedabad to the final capture of Patna, but Major Adams had seldom employed them actively against the enemy; they had been of assistance in guarding the camp and conveying stores, but he had always felt more at ease when they were on separate command.

Nothing could be more promising than the hope now entertained for a successful campaign against the armies of the Emperor, the Nawab Vazir, and Mir Kassim. Our troops, wearied with inactivity, were longing to be again employed on active service, and anxious to efface the memory of their insubordination, of which they had become heartily ashamed; they were, moreover, numerically strong, and, moreover, large reinforcements were on the road from Calcutta.

Major Champion, recovered from his wound received at the storm of Patna, joined the army as second in command under Major Carnac.

Unfortunately, at this time, some irritation manifested itself amongst the troops, from its commander having ordered his tent to be pitched with Mir J'afar's army instead of with his own. He had further ordered all reports to be made, in the first instance, to his second in command, who was instructed only to refer to the "Commander-in-Chief when there is anything extraordinary."

This order caused dissatisfaction in the British camp; and the promise of a speedy advance not having been fulfilled, the soldiers began to throw doubts on their commander's capacity,, some even hinting at his being deficient in personal courage.

In the meantime the enemy's allied armies had reached Benares on the 7th March, and thrown a bridge of boats across the Ganges; but, when about half of their army had crossed, the bridge was broken by the stream. Here was a grand opportunity for Carnac to attack the broken enemy, and the result must have been the destruction of half their army, and the probable demoralisation of the rest; but Carnac, to the annoyance of his troops, declined to move. The bridge was repaired; and the whole of the enemy's army crossed, and continued its march unmolested.

The discontent of the European soldiers at the palpable want of good generalship displayed by their commander was assuming a serious aspect; when Carnac, on the 12th, ordered the British camp to be struck, and on the 17th reached Buxar, where he halted.

Arrangements were now made to collect provisions, and entrenchments were ordered to be thrown up; but these measures were not efficiently carried out. In the meantime, the Council in Calcutta having learnt that the Nawab was advancing towards the British territory, urged on Major Carnac the absolute necessity of bestirring himself, and he was peremptorily directed to cross the Karamnassa river.

These orders were received on the 23rd, and an officer was at once sent forward to make arrangements for throwing a bridge across the river. Carnac reported to the council the measures which he was adopting, and that he was collecting provisions to enable him to advance. On the 3rd of April another communication was received from the council which said:

> We have paid due regard to the reasons which you urge in your letter for having continued to act so long on the defensive; but we must say that they do not carry the same weight with us.

A Council of War was now called, at which Carnac presided; and urged that he had been unable to collect sufficient provisions to warrant him in making an advance. This council decided that without provisions the army could not act in the field; and that, if there were no provisions to be had at or near Buxar, the army had better be marched back to Patna, where provisions were plentiful. But at the same time some of the commanders of regiments expressed an opinion that a little forethought might have prevented the unfortunate position in which they now found themselves.

The army broke camp on the 4th of April and commenced its retreat towards Patna, leaving Buxar unprotected. On the 13th Dinapore was reached, when Carnac ordered a halt, and announced his intention of preventing the enemy from crossing the river Soane. Five days were lost in making preparations and issuing orders; when it was discovered that all was too late, for the enemy had secured the passage of the river by dispatching a strong advanced guard of cavalry, which, doubling round, now held the east bank of the river, and very nearly succeeded in capturing Carnac, whose head-quarter camp, was as usual, pitched at a distance from the main army. The European cavalry under Captain Hay was quickly dispatched to keep the enemy in check, and, having engaged them, to hastily retire towards a grove of trees, amongst which a strong body of infantry was to be held in ambuscade. The European cavalry, on reaching the grove, were ordered to file off to the right and left; when the infantry were to advance from their place of concealment and suddenly open fire on the pursuing enemy, who, it was anticipated, would by the unexpected movements be thrown into confusion, when the British cavalry, having wheeled about, would return to the charge. Hay carried out his part of the programme with precision, the enemy's cavalry being engaged and decoyed up to the grove; but in the meantime Major Carnac had countermanded the infantry ambuscade, without informing Hay, who was in consequence left in the lurch, and only succeeded in getting out of his difficulty with heavy loss.

GENERAL REFERENCES—CHAPTER 8

Broome's Rise and Progress of the Bengal Army.
Malleson's Decisive Battles of India.
Williams's Bengal Infantry.
The Military Calendar.
The Seir Mutakherin.
Proceedings of the Bengal Council.
Thornton's History of India.
Stuart's History of Bengal.
&c, &c.

CHAPTER 9

The Battle of Buxar

15th-23rd April, 1764; The Nawab Vazir Shuja 'u'd daulah, who had been nominated to the chief command of the enemy's allied army, was moving towards Patna with all practicable speed. He had correctly gauged the incapacity of his English rival, and now made a bold stroke to out-general him; which, but for the merest accident, would have placed the British army completely in his power. Shuja 'u'd daulah dispatched two of his divisions by rapid marches, and a circuitous route, to seize Patna before the retreating British army could reach their destination; but this scheme was frustrated by a fortunate accident. A sepahi regiment and a detachment of artillery with 3 guns were escorting a convoy of provisions from Patna to the British camp: when information reached the officer commanding that the enemy were advancing to meet him. He at once occupied a strong position close at hand; a dry tank with mud embankments forming a ready-made entrenchment, and concealing him from view; and here the British detachment took up its position, hastily cutting embrasures for the guns. The enemy, in ignorance of what was awaiting them, advanced along the road; when they unexpectedly found themselves opposed by a force of unknown strength; and, believing that they had fallen into an ambuscade, and that their plans for seizing Patna by a surprise had been anticipated, abandoned their project and retreated on their main army.

Carnac was thus, by a stroke of good fortune, enabled to continue his retreat without serious opposition; but his soldiers, unaccustomed to retire before an enemy, had lost heart, and their march was in consequence conducted in an irregular, sulky manner; the enemy's cavalry hovering around, and no order of battle having been arranged in the event of their being unexpectedly forced into action. Fortunately, the

British army reached Patna without disaster, and took up its position, previously selected and prepared by Mir J'afar, who had been deputed by Major Carnac to arrange for the defence of the city. The positions were well selected, and serviceable entrenchments made protected by a deep ditch. Mir J'afar placed his own troops along the outside of the east and part of the south faces of the fort; his left flank resting on the river Ganges. Carnac's army was placed along the west; its right resting on the river, and its left extending round as far as Mir J'afar's right, which it joined near the centre of the south face. It will be seen that the British and the Murshedabad troops under Mir J'afar thus completely enveloped the fortified city, the walls being in rear of the beleaguered army, which was covered by the heavy guns on the walls and bastions; the river Ganges extending along the whole of the north face of the city.

Our Europeans were encamped outside the west face and south-west angle of the fortress, their left resting on a mound occupied by one of our sepahi battalions. The south-west angle was considered the most likely point of attack, and Mir J'afar, therefore, had thoughtfully taken the precaution of clearing away a village and all the trees in front, so that the enemy might find no cover during his advance.

In front of the position held by the Europeans the entrenchments were only partially completed, but the ground occupied was commanded by the south-west bastion of the fortress, the guns on which were worked by a British detachment sent by Carnac into the city to assist our army encamped without the walls.

The enemy arrived before Patna on the 24th April; taking up his position to the west and south of the city, nearly opposite to and parallel with the British entrenchments.

The Emperor Shah Alám with his Irregular troops threatened those of Mir J'afar; whilst Mir Kassim's trained brigades and artillery with 16 field-guns took up a position in front of the right wing of the British army; Mir Kassim with the rest of his force being in reserve near Bankipore, about a mile from Patna.

The enemy's allied force was computed at 35,000 men, and in addition a mob of 5000 fanatics, all perfectly naked, armed with tulwars, their bodies besmeared with paint and ashes, and their long hair streaming down their backs.

24th April-2nd May; The rival armies remained inactive for upwards of a week; when the enemy having received authentic information that British reinforcements[1] were near at hand, the Nawab Vazir gave orders for an immediate attack.

At this time the British force consisted of the Bengal European Regiment, 2 companies of the Bombay European Regiment,[2] 2 troops of European cavalry, and 7 battalions of sepahis, besides which there was the Moghul Horse, and Mir J'afar's native army; amounting in all to about 19,000 men.

3rd May; The Nawab Vazir's plan of attack was to concentrate his main strength against the Europeans; to strike terror amongst them by hurling at them the trained brigades; and finally to overwhelm them by making constantly repeated charges with his cavalry and infantry; whilst a portion of his Irregular troops-would be employed in keeping Mir J'afar in check, so that he could not come to the assistance of the Europeans during the onslaught.

It must be borne in mind that the Bengal European Regiment and the 2 companies of the Bombay Europeans held the ground under the south-western corner bastion; on their right and left were sepahi battalions; whilst our field-guns were placed at intervals along the whole line.

The mound on the left of the Europeans was held by a sepahi battalion against the combined attacks of Shuja' u'd daulah's Rohilla Horse, 3000 strong, and the contingent of his ally the Raja of Benares.

A general cannonade was now opened, the British firing from the walls of the city as well as from their entrenchments, and the enemy from their numerous field batteries. The Nawab Vazir led the attack, and Sumru, with his three trained brigades, charged across the open plain towards the position held by the Bengal European Regiment, but soon found himself exposed to a heavy cross-fire from the batteries above and the guns and musketry below, which broke his ranks, and whilst his officers were exerting themselves to rally their men, a well-directed volley caused them to again break, and this time seek shelter in a ravine about 800 yards in front of our entrenchments. Upon this ravine, a heavy fire was opened from one of the bastions of the fort; but the shot intended for the fugitives went far beyond them, causing dismay amongst Mir Kassim's reserve in rear, who had deemed themselves safe and beyond range.

---

1. These reinforcements consisted of 200 marines, under Captain Maurice Wemyss, and two midshipmen lately commissioned as marine officers. The marines joined the British force six days after the battle of Patna.
2. These 2 companies of the Bombay European Regiment under Captain Pemble were incorporated with the Bengal European Regiment on August 24th, 1765.

The battle still raged fiercely towards the south-west corner, defended by the Bengal European Battalion and the Bombay Europeans. The Nawab Vazir, who, commanding in person, now pushed forward his whole division, and brought his artillery close up to the entrenchments; but the English fire was too much for him, obliging him after two hours' fighting to withdraw with heavy loss. During this time he had sent several messages to Mir Kassim Khan to come to his assistance; but Mir Kassim Khan, always more useful in the council than in the field, paid no heed to the Nawab Vazir's messages. At last, enraged at Mir Kassim's cowardice, the Nawab Vazir sent a special messenger to him, asking him why he was "lagging behind, whilst," said he, "I am warmly engaged with your enemies? Advance as I do and engage the enemy on your side as I do on mine." But Mir Kassim, ensconced with the reserves behind his entrenchments, vouchsafed no reply.

As a next chance, the Nawab Vazir ordered the 5000 fanatics to charge the Europeans. With screams and yells they rushed forward, presenting to our soldiers a pitiful appearance, evidently drunk with bhang or they would not have rushed on certain death; they fell by hundreds under a deadly fire poured on them from our fortifications and entrenchments; when, screaming and terrified, those poor wretches who had not been killed or wounded fled to the rear.

Some gallant charges were now made by the Rohilla Horse, but they were ultimately driven back with heavy loss; when, about three o'clock the Nawab Vazir, undismayed by Mir Kassim's cowardice, collected his whole available force, and made a spirited charge along the entire face of the British position. The Europeans, who received these repeated onslaughts at the point of the bayonet, were now completely exhausted, and for a moment the enemy gained a footing inside the earth-works, where they succeeded in capturing and carrying away three of the drummer-boys of the Bengal European Regiment. This so exasperated the Europeans that they sprang from the entrenchments, dashed forward, broke through their assailants, and re-took the drummer-boys, whom they brought back in triumph amidst loud shouts and great rejoicing.

The enemy, now disheartened, smarting under our fire, and foiled at all points, were compelled to accept their defeat; but a final and gallant charge was made by a large body of cavalry under their brave Commander Sheik Din Mahomed, who was killed in the advance, when his cavalry, disheartened, fled from the field, bearing with them the body of their valiant leader.

Never had a commander a finer opportunity than now presented itself to Carnac of converting a gallant defence into a crowning victory. One of his officers made a dash with his sepahis at one of the enemy's batteries of artillery, which, being provided with bullock-draught only, might have been captured; and another officer was in the act, with a few of his men, of seizing two of the enemy's field-guns, when Carnac commanded both to desist and return under cover of the entrenchments. Thus, by reason of the incapacity of their commander, our troops were under the. necessity of allowing their defeated enemy to retire from before them in full possession of his guns, ammunition, and stores. The Battle of Patna was now over; and, although a few days after the European reinforcements arrived, Major Carnac still remained inactive.

Captain John Nollikins of the Bengal European Regiment—who had been transferred from the 39th Regiment—was severely wounded in this action.

On the 30th May the allied forces of the enemy broke camp and retired on the strong fort of Buxar, the works of which Major Carnac had considerably improved when he contemplated its defence during his occupation in March.

It is unnecessary to dwell upon the Calcutta Council's repeated failures to induce Major Carnac to advance against the enemy; suffice it to say that a welcome order was received from the Court of Directors, announcing the removal of Major Carnac from their service,[1] and on the 28th June he handed over the command to Major Champion as locum tenens. Although this order of the Court's was not issued in consequence of Carnac's blunders whilst in command, it was none the less acceptable to the council, who gladly hailed the opportunity of placing a more efficient officer in command of the army in the field.

Major Hector Munro, late of H.M. 89th Regiment, was appointed to succeed Major Carnac. Munro was on the eve of his departure from Madras to England early in the year, with the remnant of his Regiment, when intelligence was received of the death of Major Adams. The offer of the command of the Bengal army was at that time made to Major Munro; in the mean time, however, Carnac had been appointed, but on that officer's removal the offer was renewed, and accepted by Munro. The remnant of the 89th and. some of the 90th Regiment, .amounting to a little over 100 men, volunteered to ac-

---

1. Major Carnac was removed for having opposed Mr.Vansittart, but he was ultimately restored to the service, in which he rose to the rank of Major-General.

company Major Munro to Bengal, and, the Bengal Government having accepted their services, they were transferred to the Company's service, ultimately joining the Bengal European Regiment.

On the 18th August Major Munro assumed command of the field force then at Patna. He was in every way the very opposite to his predecessor; brave, almost rash in his daring; a strict disciplinarian, but though despising unnecessary pomp, rigidly insisting on military etiquette and the strictest obedience to orders.

One of Munro's early acts was to publish a code of regulations, with which all officers were instructed to make themselves thoroughly acquainted. This code enjoined strict attention to many essential points of military duty, which, during Major Carnac's time, had been allowed to fall into disuse. For the first time a concise system of manoeuvres was introduced, in which officers commanding regiments were instructed to exercise their men at daily parades. No difficulty was experienced in introducing these reforms amongst the European troops; but the case was different with the sepahi regiments, unused to the strict discipline enjoined, and they resented it as an innovation. The European officers attached to the sepahi battalions struggled in vain to induce their men to submit to the additional parades and drills enjoined; but information soon reached Major Munro that the discontent had spread into open mutiny, the sepahis threatening to desert sooner than submit; and on the 24th August Major Munro issued a General Order warning the sepahis of the inevitable consequences of their insubordination, "which, if continued, must end in their just punishment."

The mutinous spirit amongst the sepahi regiments, however, was in no way suppressed; and on the 8th September one of the battalions stationed at Manji revolted, seizing and imprisoning their European officers and sergeants, and setting all authority at defiance. Next day the prisoners were released, but the sepahis refused to obey orders.

With an enemy in force close at hand Major Munro's position was one of difficulty and danger; but he was quite equal to the occasion. He immediately dispatched a detachment of the Bengal European Regiment and a sepahi battalion not contaminated by the mutiny with instructions to attack, disarm, and march the mutinous regiment to Chupra, when they would receive further orders. Captain Wemyss, commanding this detachment, found the mutineers bivouacked in a grove, which owing to the heavy rains was completely surrounded by water, when, taken by surprise, the mutineers surrendered and were disarmed, and immediately marched to Chupra, arriving on September 13th. Major Munro was on parade to receive them, supported by the 2 grenadier companies of the Bengal European Regiment, a company of European artillery, and a battalion of sepahis.

Munro called on the commanding officer of the mutinous regiment to select 50 of the ringleaders; from whom 24 were picked out and arraigned before a drum-head court-martial, which sentenced them to be blown away from guns. The proceedings were confirmed at once, and the sentence ordered to be carried into execution on the spot; when four of the condemned prisoners were immediately seized and tied to the guns, but four native grenadiers, amongst the prisoners awaiting execution, claimed, the right, "as they held the post of honour in the field," to be executed first. The request was granted, the battalion men being unfastened; and the grenadiers executed in their stead.

The scene which followed was trying in the extreme. The gallantry of the grenadier prisoners caused a violent reaction in their favour amongst those native troops who had hitherto been uncontaminated; and who now told Munro that they would not allow the executions to be proceeded with. It was an anxious moment for the prisoners, and perhaps more so for the commanding officer; but, without any hesitation, Munro ordered the European artillery to load with grape and prepare for action, the European infantry being moved round to support the guns. The European officers with the sepahi battalions were ordered to stand aside, and the sepahis commanded to ground their arms. Instinctively they obeyed, and were marched from their arms, which were taken possession of by the Europeans. Sixteen more of the prisoners were then blown from the guns, the remaining four being marched to Moniah, where they met their fate in presence of the two sepahi battalions at that station. The drill parades were recommenced, and the sepahis exercised in the new manoeuvres.

13th-30th September, 1764; Major Munro, by these severe though necessary measures, having brought his native troops into a complete state of obedience, turned his attention to his preparations for the capture of the fortress of Buxar, now the headquarters of the allied enemy. The force which Munro selected to form his main army for active service consisted of the 2 grenadier and 6 battalion companies of the Bengal European Regiment; the 2 companies of the Bombay Europeans; the marines; some details of the King's Regiments who had not volunteered for the Company's service—about 200 men under Captain Wemyss—2 companies of European artillery; and a troop of European cavalry; making a total of about 1000 Europeans. In addition to these there were 8 battalions of sepahis and 1000 Moghul Horse, lately remodelled. Major Champion, of the Bengal European Regiment, was sent in command of a detachment to cross the river Ganges, and rejoin the main army as soon as it should arrive at the river Soane.

The defence of Behar was provided for by 300 of the Bengal European Regiment, 1 company of European artillery; some native cavalry and infantry being sent to guard the frontier of that province.

Munro, with his army, reached Kalvaghat, on the east bank of the Soane, on the 10th October, to find the opposite bank, occupied by the enemy. This precaution on the part of the Nawab Vazir might have caused difficulty to the advancing army, had not Munro provided a counter-move in having sent Champion to make his way on the morning of the 10th along the west bank of the river. Champion had left Chupra on the 6th October, reaching the mouth of the Soane river on the 9th; and next morning had advanced, under cover of a dense fog, close upon the enemy, entrenched with the intention of disputing the ford.

Champion formed his detachment in line, and advanced stealthily close up to the entrenchments, when he suddenly opened a brisk fire, which was feebly replied to; and the enemy, surprised by the attack of a force of unknown strength, hastily withdrew in the direction of Arrah. The main force under Munro then crossed the river unopposed, and halted about half-a-mile from its west bank. The forward march was resumed on the 12th October, when Munro formed his army into three divisions; the first under Major Champion, the second under Major Pemble, and the third under Major Sibbert; Champion's division forming the advance-guard. When Champion reached Arrah he found the town deserted; so he pushed on to the Bonas Nálá, on the other side of which he perceived about 4000 or 5000 of the enemy's cavalry prepared to dispute his passage across the bridge. Champion ordered his cavalry to advance, the European dragoons leading; when the enemy, after only a slight show of resistance, fled towards a village about a mile distant, pursued by the British cavalry. It, however, soon became apparent that the latter had been led into an ambuscade, for the village was held by a large body of the enemy's troops, who, concealed behind the buildings and trees, received our cavalry with an unexpected fire. Taken completely by surprise, our men wheeled about and in their turn were pursued by the enemy's cavalry now largely reinforced. Our Moghul Horse broke and fled in confusion, the English dragoons holding better together; but many were sabred and shot down. As soon as Champion saw the turn which affairs had taken, he threw forward his infantry towards some broken ground, thus giving cover and support to his cavalry, who, with difficulty found their way across the Nálá, with a loss of 4 sergeants, 12 European troopers, and about 40 of the Moghul Horse killed or wounded.

In the meantime some important events had occurred in the camp of Shuja' u'd daulah, the Nawab Vazir. The Emperor Shah Alám still remained under the protection of the Nawab Vazir, who continued to exercise the supreme command of the Allied Armies, but the Emperor fully realised that he was little more than a State prisoner, and was quite prepared, should opportunity offer, to free himself from a position of dependence and restraint. Mir Kassim had sunk immeasurably in the estimation of his Commander-in-Chief since his hasty retreat, and refusal to join in the attack on the British entrenchments at Patna. Every one now seemed to raise his hand against Mir Kassim. Sumru, when accused of cowardice by the Nawab Vazir, declared that no order had been sent to him by Mir Kassim to re-advance, or he would readily have done so.

Now, Mir Kassim felt that, though courage in presence of an enemy was not his strong point, he would have made plausible excuses were he a free agent, but unfortunately he could not afford to quarrel with Sumru. He had no funds with which to meet the arrears due to his troops, who were clamorous for payment; and, still worse, there was the treaty made with the Nawab Vazir—when the triple alliance was entered into—under which Mir Kassim had agreed to pay £11,000 a month towards the expenses of the war from the day the Allied Armies should cross the river Ganges.

Mir Kassim knew that his ability to pay the large amounts required from him was contingent on his regaining his throne; his treasure collected at his Fort of Rotas was all expended, but he felt secure in the friendship of his Allies, so long as his trained brigades and European artillery remained faithful to him. His reliance on all these soon vanished, for he had been outwitted and betrayed; Sumru, Markar, Aratoon, with their soldiers, and his European artillery, with their officers—all false—had been bought over by his Ally the Nawab Vazir.

This was the final blow; disgraced, deserted, insulted, and deceived, Mir Kassim looked around in vain for advice and consolation; he had no friend but one solitary servant, who was faithful to him in his reverses and dangers as he had participated in his prosperity and triumphs. The Nawab Vazir, finding that Mir Kassim was powerless and completely at his mercy, ordered him to be robbed of the few valuables that remained to him; and mounted on a lame elephant, he was ejected, October 22nd, from the camp. Mir Kassim—the ex-Nawab of Bengal, Behar, and Orissa—eventually died at Delhie in extreme poverty, June 6th, 1777: a native historian assuring us that his last shawl was sold to pay for his winding-sheet.

But now to return to the British army, which without further mishap arrived before the fortress of Buxar ,on the 22nd October, where Munro found the Nawab Vazir occupying an entrenched position on the plain to the east of the fortress, outside which the enemy's whole army was drawn up in battle array.

The two forces remained watching each other for upwards of an hour; when the enemy retired within his entrenchments.

Munro now seized and occupied a village about a thousand yards in advance of the left of his line, and threw a strong picket forward to occupy a grove of trees about the same distance in front of his right, his camp facing that of the enemy; double sentries being posted all round, and communication maintained with his two advanced posts.

These arrangements complete, Munro called a Council of War, which recommended that the troops should be allowed a rest during the 23rd, and that an assault should be made on the enemy's entrenchments on the 24th, on the following plan:—

Lieutenant Nicoll, of the native infantry, who had been employed by Major Carnac in the preceding month of March to survey the ground now occupied by the enemy, was ordered to conduct a detachment proceeding along the bed of the Torah Nálá and endeavour to turn the enemy's right flank; the British army at the same time making a vigorous attack along the whole of the enemy's front. It was anticipated that by this manoeuvre the enemy would probably be thrown into confusion, during which it was hoped our troops would be enabled to effect an entrance into their camp. It had also been ordered that, with the view of keeping the enemy in ignorance of our real intentions, sham batteries should be at once commenced opposite the left of their entrenchments; so that the enemy might fall into the error of supposing that we intended to proceed by regular approaches.

Our heavy baggage was, as a precaution, sent on board our boats-close at hand, by the river's bank.

Major Champion commanded the working-party, which, early on the morning of the 23rd October, advanced with a company of pioneers and a covering detachment of sepahis, to throw up the dummy batteries; but he had hardly reached his ground, when, just as day was breaking, he saw the enemy in great force leaving their entrenchments and forming up for action. It appeared evident to Champion that the Nawab Vazir was preparing to attack the British camp, and no time was to be lost in communicating his suspicions to Major Munro; so Champion rode forward alone to take note of the enemy's movements, having previously sent a messenger to warn the British commander of the probable advance of the enemy. Major Munro, already on the alert, beat to arms, forming up his troops outside his camp to meet the enemy's attack. It is necessary that the exact nature of the ground between the rival armies should be now clearly defined.

To the left front of the British camp was the village, to the right front the grove of trees; both these positions having been occupied by our troops on the previous day.

Between the village on our left front and the British camp-there was an extensive morass, through which was a ford, difficult to find without the assistance of an experienced guide. To the right of the grove was another village; but between the village on the left and the grove on the right the space was open and clear.

About three miles intervened between the rival camps, which faced each other. It has been recorded that when Munro assumed command of the army he instituted a course of manoeuvres, which he ordered commanding officers to practise on parade, so that when their soldiers should be in presence of an enemy they would take up their allotted positions without delay or confusion.

When, therefore, the army took the field on the morning of the 23rd October, every man knew his appointed position, which he occupied without confusion.

The advanced pickets were now called in; that in the village on our left-front joining the main army, whilst that which had occupied the grove on our right-front was ordered to join the Moghul Horse, and take up its position in a village in rear of our left wing, charged with the protection of the camp and baggage. The British army advanced to the front of their camp in two divisions, one in immediate rear of the other, about a hundred yards apart, and the reserve in the centre between these two lines.

The front line was formed of two battalion companies of the Bengal European Regiment and two companies of the Bombay European

Regiment, these being formed into one battalion, commanded by Captain Macpherson; the detachments of the Royal troops and marines under Captain Wemyss; four battalions of sepahis, and the greater portion of the artillery. The Europeans were in the centre of this line, the artillery at intervals between the battalions. The rear line, under Major Pemble, was formed of the remainder of the Bengal European Regiment, four battalions of sepahis, and some artillery, the same order being observed as in the front line.

The reserve, under Captain Hay, was formed of the two grenadier companies of the Bengal European Regiment and some cavalry.

The front line was in two divisions or wings, the right commanded by Major Champion, the left by Major Sibbert.

Lieutenant Vertue commanded the detachment guarding the camp and baggage.

It is also necessary to say something of the enemy's position.

The Nawab Vazir, who had proved himself a gallant soldier and an able General, was still in chief command of the enemy's army. The Emperor Shah Alám remained in his tent behind the Torah Nálá. The ex-Nawab Mir Kassim, ejected from the camp, was a wanderer, his trained brigades being now in the service of the Nawab Vazir.

The ground occupied by the enemy was well selected; indeed his position was formidable. His left rested on the river Ganges, where were the town and fortress of Buxar, occupied by several native battalions.

The Nawab Vazir's Regiments were mostly commanded by European officers, and supported by numerous bodies of cavalry. In the centre were the trained brigades under Sumru, consisting of 8 battalions, and 8 field-pieces, the latter manned by Europeans: the whole strengthened by a reserve of 6000 men.

The Raja of Benares commanded the enemy's right wing, composed principally of Rohilla Horse, supported by 5000 Durani cavalry, known to be experienced soldiers, who had distinguished themselves in many a hard-fought battle.

The enemy's Allied army numbered in all between 40,000 and 50,000, whereas the British had but 7080 men.

The enemy were the first to advance, and their guns—of greater calibre than the British—took effect before the English field-pieces could reply; Munro, therefore, ordered a general advance; but, on nearing the morass, was obliged to detach the left wing in order to take ground to his right. This necessary movement in the face of his enemy might have been attended with serious results, had not his troops been practised on parade in the manoeuvres by which in war he was enabled to effect his purpose. Notwithstanding that the fire from the enemy's heavy batteries was trying, the British army steadily advanced; and, having cleared the morass, the original order of battle was resumed. Our artillery, from its position in front, was now firing with effect amongst the dense masses of the enemy.

A determined charge was at this time made upon the British left by the Durani Horse, who attempted to force a passage between our two advancing lines, and thus crush our reserve in the centre; but, as soon as their intention became apparent, Munro ordered his reserve to take ground to their left and face outwards, whilst half a battalion in the front line wheeled back and half a battalion in the rear wheeled forward, so that the whole interval on the left of our army was closed up, rapidly formed into three sides of an oblong square, and was thus enabled to prevent the cavalry from effecting their purpose.

The result of this manoeuvre, which Major Munro had caused to be frequently practised on the line of march and on parade, illustrated the advantages derived from a frequent exercise in the code of movements he had ordered for his troops, but which the sepahis had so stubbornly resisted.

Foiled in their attempts to break through the British lines, the Durani cavalry beat a retreat, hastened by our fire; but, having passed to our rear, they now charged our rear-guard, consisting of the Moghul Horse and a detachment of sepahis under Lieutenant Vertue.

The Moghul Horse gave way before the Durani cavalry; when our infantry, now unsupported, moved towards the main army in admirable order, and as steadily as if on parade, but all our baggage fell into the enemy's hands, and our camp was left unprotected.

Flushed with their success, the Durani cavalry now made a desperate charge on our rear line; which, rapidly facing about, prepared to receive them. Our guns, however, were so well served, that the enemy's cavalry sheered off; but soon afterwards a second charge was delivered by a squadron of picked men under a distinguished chieftain. A desperate struggle ensued, several of the men of the Bengal European Regiment being sabred in the ranks; but the British line remained firm and unbroken. The charge was again renewed with increased vigour, but the leader, in making a vigorous dash at the English line, was received on the bayonet of one of our Europeans, who at the same moment discharging his musket, the chief fell a lifeless corpse amongst his gallant followers. This last effort proving a failure, the Durani cavalry, disappointed and disheartened at the loss of their leader, retreated, leaving a large proportion of their men on the field.

In the meantime the British front line had not been unemployed. A battery of heavy guns had been brought up by the enemy, and posted in the village to our extreme right. This battery, firing obliquely on our advancing divisions, rendered it impossible to preserve our line, and at the same time Sumru's brigade kept up a continuous fire; whilst the enemy's cavalry made repeated and determined charges on our right wing, where some wavering was now perceptible.

Major Munro, observing this unsteadiness, ordered a sepahi battalion on the right of our line to storm the battery in the village. After some hesitation the battalion advanced under Lieutenant Nicoll, and having made a slight détour to the right, suddenly wheeled round, and, gallantly charging the position, drove back the enemy at the point of the bayonet, carried the village, and captured the battery. Supports were immediately sent forward from the rear line, by this this time completely relieved from the attacks of the enemy's cavalry.

Nicoll now pushed his success so far as to attempt to gain possession of the enemy's guns posted in the grove of trees to his left; but they were found to be strongly supported, and his efforts failed. In retreating he was hardly pressed; the native cavalry charging both his flanks, and dealing destruction amongst his sepahis.

The chief interest was now centred in the fight for the possession of the grove. Major Munro directed Champion, at the head of the remainder of the right wing of the front line, to advance to the support of our retreating sepahis, who had been foiled in their attempt to seize the grove, and were now in full flight. With Major Champion's detachment were the two companies of the Bengal European Regiment; the Royal Company under Captain Wemyss; two sepahi battalions, with a company of artillery and 4 field-pieces, forming his support.

Orders were issued that our infantry during the coming charge were to reserve their fire and trust solely to their bayonets. As Champion advanced the enemy's cavalry drew off, and Nicoll's sepahis, rallying, took their place on the right of the advancing line. Major Champion's advance was watched with breathless interest as he dashed forward, and, pushing right through the grove, forced the enemy back at the point of the bayonet; and then pouring on them a well-directed volley, sent them flying from the field, leaving their guns, 27, in our possession.

But the trial of strength was not yet over, for the Nujeebs, who had been protecting the guns, escaping early in the fight, had taken the direction of Sumru's trained brigades, which they joined; when the united force, forming a new alignment, advanced to retrieve the fortunes of the day by retaking the position.

Such was the aspect of affairs, when Shuja Kuli Khan, one of the Nawab Vazir's commanders supporting Sumru's brigades, imagining that Champion's volley, which he had heard, implied the flight of the English from the grove: and thinking his services were no longer required in support, without communicating his intentions left his position in reserve, and advanced his troops to attack the British left wing. Leading his cavalry in person, he circled round the morass, instructing his infantry to advance by the ford. His cavalry made some gallant charges, which were repelled by our square; whilst his infantry, scattered in its attempts to struggle through the morass, suffered severely from our grape-fire, which effectually kept them in check. Charge after charge was made by the brave Shuja Kuli Khan, but a grape-shot striking him in the forehead, he fell from his horse mortally wounded. The cavalry, discouraged at the loss of their leader, were, whilst endeavouring to recover his body, thrown into some confusion; and, abandoning their attempt to break the English square, retired towards the fortress.

Shuja Kuli Khan fell ignorant of the injury which his want of judgement entailed on his master's cause. Sumru's brigades, deprived of their support, hesitated, and watched the result of Shuja Kuli Khan's bold attack on our left; but as soon as the failure of his cavalry and the discomfiture of his infantry was seen, Sumru retired his brigades—in good order, it is true—but his retreat was accepted by the enemy as a signal for a general flight. Major Champion's force now held the grove and village to our right; whilst the left wing, relieved from the attacks of Shuja Kuli Khan's cavalry, were free to act on the offensive.

The result of the Battle of Buxar was no longer doubtful; and as Major Munro rode along the front of his victorious army he was received with hearty cheers and congratulations. The English army was ordered to be broken into column, the left wing pursuing the enemy towards the Torah river, whilst the right wing advanced on the enemy's entrenchments.

A final effort was still made by the Nawab Vazir; who, collecting some of his troops, attempted to retrieve the battle. He might have succeeded, at any rate, in checking the precipitate flight of his army, had not Bene Bahadur, entrusted with the protection of the camp and fortress—in ignorance of Shuja Kali Khan's failure and fate—deeming success secured, allowed his troops to-dismount and wander about at their ease. Suddenly the right wing of the British army appeared in their midst, when, taken by surprise, and hurriedly mounting under our musketry fire, they made but a feeble attempt at resistance, and fled in the direction of the troops which the Nawab Vazir was attempting to re-form. Their flying cavalry effectually frustrated all the enemy's endeavours to rally, and, thoroughly demoralised, they were now in full flight towards the ford over the Torah river.

But a strange scene was being enacted in the enemy's camp; where the Durani Horse—notorious plunderers—as soon as they found that the battle was decided against them, determined to appropriate to themselves whatever they could lay their hands on. Regardless of personal safety, they fell upon the Nawab Vazir's baggage, helping themselves to his valuables; whilst the British troops, deeming the captured camp and baggage to be their lawful prize, resented the cupidity of the Durani Horse; the result being that the whole camp presented a scene of bloodshed and confusion beyond description, the cavalry cutting down all who attempted to thwart them in their purpose, and the British bayoneting and shooting the plunderers indiscriminately.

In the meantime the Nawab Vazir gave up as hopeless the attempt to rally his followers, and, accompanied by a strong party of chosen horsemen, crossed the Torah river with some of his most portable treasures; and, as soon as he ascertained that his trained brigades had followed him, ordered the bridge of boats to be destroyed, thus completely cutting off the retreat of his infantry and camp followers.

A fearful scene of carnage ensued, and a general rush was made towards the stream; elephants, camels, bullocks, horses, men, women, and children, all pressing forward to gain the opposite bank of the river, were precipitated into the stream; indeed, so great was the indiscriminate rush that the weaker fell under the strong, so that, at last, a mole three hundred yards long was formed by the dead and dying, across which the remnants of the fugitives made their escape.

The Nawab Vazir had been so confident of victory that no arrangements had been made for the removal of his baggage and treasure, or that of his army so that, notwithstanding the multiform plunder during the day of the battle, the English prize-agents succeeding in collecting booty to the value of £12,000 sterling. One hundred and seventy-two guns[1] were captured by the British.

At the Battle of Buxar the Bengal European Regiment had Lieutenant Thompson severely wounded, 37 men killed, and 58 wounded; the total loss of the British army amounting to 9 European officers and 838 rank and file, killed and wounded.

Upwards of 2000 of the enemy lay dead on the field of battle or in the camp, and considerably more than that number were wounded; these calculations not including the masses who perished in attempting to escape. Amongst the slain were found several of the French deserters; in addition to these three Frenchmen were made prisoners; one of whom purchased his ransom by bringing in with him seven of the enemy's guns, whilst the other two were tried by Drum-head Court Martial, and hanged by the provost-sergeant in presence of the whole Regiment.

The Battle of Buxar brought to a conclusion a series of important actions, fought, in all instances, against vastly superior numbers, the later engagements against soldiers equally well trained and equipped as our own.

British authority had now been established and maintained throughout the East India Company's territories; and although there had been instances of crime, mutiny, and desertion, the achievements of the troops must be admitted to form a group of successes unsurpassed in history, and effected by a display of courage and endurance never exceeded by the army of any nation in the world.

The decoration, Buxar, was ordered to be emblazoned on the colours of the Bengal European Regiment; a device inherited by the Royal Munster Fusiliers.

General References—Chapter 9

Malleson's Decisive Battles of India.
Broome's Rise and Progress of the Bengal Army.
Williams's Bengal Infantry.
The Seir Mutakherin.
Historical Records, Bombay European Regiment,
Proceedings of the Bengal Council.
Thornton's History of India. &c, &c.

---

1. (See foot of previous page)
Captured on the field   113 guns.
Brought in by an European deserter   7   ,,
Mounted on the works   52   ,,
                       Total 172   ,,

CHAPTER 10

Discontentment

The night succeeding the Battle of Buxar was passed by the troops on the field; and the three following days were employed in burying the dead and attending to the wounded, many of whom—the dhooley bearers having absconded during the fight—were left unattended on the ground where they fell; and, worse still, the Medical Department was so numerically weak that several days elapsed before requisite operations were performed, or all the wounds dressed. It is, however, specially recorded that the officers did all in their power to alleviate the pain and distress of the sufferers, by visiting them constantly and administering "rice and water to the unfortunates."

On the 27th October the Bengal European Regiment accompanied the main army on its advance towards Benares; the fortress and town of Buxar being left under the protection of the wounded Europeans and 4 companies of sepahis.

Major Munro, fully alive to the importance of securing the goodwill of the inhabitants of the country through which he was passing, issued stringent orders against plundering on the line of march and firing buildings or villages; these orders being held by the native soldiers and camp-followers to be an infringement of their just privileges, much discontent was openly expressed.

On the 5th November a native non-commissioned officer detected in plundering was brought before Major Munro, and immediately arraigned before a Drum-head Court Martial, by which he was sentenced to be hanged in presence of the whole army. The sentence was carried into execution the same afternoon; after which all insubordination and pilfering ceased, and the country was, for the first time in the history of Bengal, exempted from the terrors and miseries which had invariably accompanied an invading army in India.

The 6th and 7th November were occupied in constructing a bridge across the Goomtee river, and on the 8th the army encamped under the walls of the city of Benares.

The wealth of Benares was said to be equal to that of Delhie itself, and the temptation to pillage was great; but Munro protected the city from plunder by publicly making it known that any soldier or camp-follower found in the city without permission should be severely punished; and any person detected in plundering would "be immediately hanged," and, to ensure the enforcement of these orders, a strong European guard was constantly quartered in the city.

The day after the arrival of the British army at Benares the inhabitants paid £40,000 to the troops in lieu of booty; the sum being divided as prize in the usual proportions.

Whilst the army was encamped on the plain outside the city the two grenadier companies of the Bengal European Regiment formed part of a force under Major Pemble detached from the main army to lay siege to the fortress of Chunar. Mahomed Bahadur Khan, the Governor of Chunar, notwithstanding that the British occupied the country, still acknowledged the authority of the Nawab Vazir of Oude; but, hearing that the Emperor commanded obedience to the British, he attempted to persuade his garrison to submit to their authority, which so incensed his followers that they turned him out of the fort and appointed his lieutenant to the command.

The Fort of Chunar is picturesquely situated on an isolated rock, which forms the termination of the Rajmahal range of mountains where they abut on the river Ganges. The fortress, about 200 feet above the river and standing on its right bank, overhangs the town of Chunarghar, which is to its rear.

The defences, naturally as well as artificially formidable, follow the summit of the rocks on which the fortress is built; and, although there were several batteries of considerable strength in which guns of heavy calibre were mounted, the defence of the garrison depended much on the facility for rolling down on the assailants masses of rock and stones, great quantities of which were always accumulated within the walls.

The main army at Benares, under Major Munro, had lately been reinforced by two companies of the Bengal European Regiment, one company of the Select Picket and two battalions of sepahis; which augmentation had enabled him to detach the two grenadier companies of the Bengal Europeans to Chunar, and these he now increased by the company of cadets, three battalions of sepahis, one company of pioneers, 50 artillerymen with 9 guns, and a detachment of lascars.

The cadets forming the Select Picket were anxious for an opportunity to distinguish themselves, the commissioned officers in the Company's service being chiefly selected from amongst the cadets of the Select Picket, foremost in discipline and efficiency.

The division under Major Pemble crossed the river Ganges on the evening of the 26th November, and, passing quietly under the walls of the fortress at night, pitched camp on the morning of the 27th on the plain to the south-west of the enemy's position, whilst Major Munro moved the headquarter camp to Sultanpore, a town opposite to the fortress of Chunar, the river Ganges intervening.

Major Pemble threw up two batteries, one opposite to the south-west angle of the fortress, the other on the east side, but the work of breaching was very slow; and it was not until, on the 2nd of December, a breach at the south-west angle of the fortress was reported practicable, and orders were issued for an assault early the next morning.

The grenadier companies of the Bengal European Regiment and the company of cadets, with a sepahi battalion, formed the storming-party; whilst the rest of the force remained on the plain below awaiting orders. Major Pemble, unwilling to unnecessarily expose his Europeans, adopted the unusual course of sending the sepahis to the front to storm the breach. Before daybreak the army left camp, the advance party reaching the base of the hill without any obstruction: but as soon as the sepahi battalion commenced the ascent a heavy musketry fire was opened on it from above. The sepahis at first advanced up the hill with great coolness but their progress was soon impeded by large masses of stones hurled down upon them from the walls. These stones, bounding over the rocks in uncertain directions, struck many of the men in their course, some being killed, whilst others, bruised and wounded, were precipitated down the hill. The retreat of the storming party now became general; the sepahis, rushing headlong down the incline, carried away first the Select Picket, and then the European grenadier companies, all being rolled up in a confused mass below, and exposed to much danger by reason of the stones and bullets now falling thickly amongst them. As soon as the disabled troops had been extricated from their perilous position, Major Pemble temporarily withdrew from the attack, but on the night of December 4th the assault was resumed, with the order of advance reversed; the European grenadiers taking the lead, followed by the Select Picket, and last of all the sepahis. The grenadiers, under cover of the darkness, soon reached the crest of the hill, but, on nearing the breach, it was discovered that the enemy had employed the interval between the assaults in repairing it and building up the face of the rock, now scarped for several feet, so that the breach was no longer practicable.

After several unsuccessful attempts to ascend the rock the troops were withdrawn, and, as Major Munro had reason to anticipate, an immediate attack from the Nawab Vazir, orders were issued for Pemble's detachment to recross the river immediately and join army headquarters at Sultanpore, which orders were carried out next day, December 5th, when the following General Order was issued by Major Munro:

> The Commander-in-Chief is fully convinced, from the report Major Pemble has made him, the two assaults made on the Chunar Fort miscarrying was owing to no misbehaviour of the troops, but to the steepness of the ascent He is much obliged to the officers for their gallant behaviour, and desires the men may be assured he shall always regard them in the same manner as if their endeavour had been attended with success.

Fearing that the Nawab Vazir might attack Benares during his absence, Munro broke up his camp on the 6th December, and returned to that city.

The policy pursued by the Emperor of Delhie now calls for our attention. As soon as the Battle of Buxar had decided the fate of his patron the Nawab Vazir, the Emperor wrote to Major Munro congratulating him on his success, and requesting that he might be permitted to join the British camp.

Major Munro had no authority from the Calcutta Council to treat with the Emperor; and, although showing him every courtesy, he declined to extend his protection; but the Emperor insisted on following the British camp, close in rear of which he pitched his tents. Major Munro soon afterwards received the authority of the council to treat with the Emperor and give him protection, pending negotiations.

In the meantime the Nawab Vazir, convinced of the superior power of the British, sought a reconciliation, but an unexpected difficulty presented itself; Major Munro firmly stipulating that, before any basis of arrangement could be considered, Mir Kassim and Sumru must be handed over to be dealt with in such manner as the British Government should deem right. The first of these conditions was impossible of fulfilment, for Mir Kassim was out of reach; and, as to the second, the Nawab Vazir would have complied—having lately discovered that Sumru[1] had been treating with another master—but the laws of native hospitality would not allow him to surrender a man in his actual service; he, therefore, speciously proposed that the English commander should send to him two or three British officers, acquainted with Sumru's appearance, and the Nawab Vazir would then cause Sumru to be murdered in their presence. Needless to say, the proposition did not meet with Munro's views, and negotiations suddenly ceased; but the Nawab Vazir, still anxious to come to terms, offered to pay £25,000 for the expenses of the war and £25,000 for the troops, and in addition a douceur of £8000 to Munro if he would use his influence with the council to induce them to accept the terms. But Major Munro was not to be bribed, Mir Kassim and Sumru must be delivered over for judgement before even the preliminaries of a treaty could be considered; so the Nawab Vazir, collecting his scattered forces, formed an alliance with the Marathas, amongst them Mulhar Rao Holka, and prepared to oppose the advance of the English.

Again the British army was to lose its Commander. Major Munro, sadly needing rest, and having nobly accomplished his work, asked to be relieved of his command that he might visit England. Just at this time, Major Carnac—who, it will be remembered, was deprived of his command early in the late war—had returned from England. The loss of his commission had been in no way connected with his misdirection during his former tenure of office; and the Court of Directors, with whom he had made his peace, had promoted him to the rank of Colonel; and he was now ordered to relieve Munro, with the rank of Brigadier-General.

General Carnac, although the army was again preparing to take the field against the Nawab Vazir, delayed his departure from the Presidency; two months elapsing before he had completed his arrangements, and during the interval important events had occurred at headquarters.

Pending Carnac's arrival Major Sir Robert Fletcher, of the Ben-

---

1. Sumru ultimately retired with the remnant of his trained Brigade to his estate at Sirdhana, awarded to him by the Marathas for services rendered. He died in 1781, leaving immense wealth to his widow, the Begum Sumru. Sumru's granddaughter married Mr. Dyce, an Officer in the Begum's service; the issue of this marriage being Dyce Sombre, who married (1840) the daughter of Lord St. Vincent.

gal European Regiment, by seniority assumed command of the army. This officer had rejoined the Regiment on October 24th, the day after the Battle of Buxar, with 300 recruits.

The Head-quarter army had lately been considerably reinforced both from Patna and Calcutta; the Emperor also joining his small force to that of the British.

The Nawab Vazir, who still had with him the trained brigades under Sumru, was hovering about in the vicinity of Benares; but, after his Buxar experience, he did not seem inclined to hazard another engagement, contenting himself with perpetually harassing the British and intercepting their communications.

On the 14th January, having obtained information that the Nawab Vazir's camp was at Seerpore, Fletcher ordered a night attack, but his information being defective and the guns hindered by a river—which it was found impossible to cross without appliances not at hand—the night attack was countermanded.

Our army now encamped; but as the enemy's cavalry caused much annoyance Fletcher changed his plan of action. A Light Brigade was formed consisting of 8 companies of the Bengal European Regiment, made up to a full strength of 100 men each, 60 European cavalry, 1 company of artillery with 6 field-guns, and 8 battalions of sepahis; 7 days provisions being carried on camels with the brigade. The rest of the Head-quarter army under Captain Sibbert was ordered to cover the city of Benares, and keep open communication with the advanced force.

The enemy, having failed against the British in open fight, now fell back upon strategy. Their commander, realising the intended British attack on his camp, ordered only a feeble resistance to be at first offered. It was believed that the assailants, having gained an easy victory, would occupy the Nawab Vazir's camp and then break up for loot; when the enemy's cavalry would be held in readiness to swoop down on the plunderers, recapture the camp, and destroy the broken British army.

The English commander, fully alive to the enemy's stratagem, now caused all the native officers of the sepahi regiments "to swear their men on the Alkoran that they would neither plunder nor leave their platoons without orders."

On the 18th January Fletcher delivered his attack on the enemy's camp, which after a feeble resistance was occupied by our troops, who were quickly embattled to meet the stratagem.

A steady artillery and musketry fire convinced the enemy that our troops had not fallen into the trap; so, after a spiritless charge, they retired to consult; when it was arranged amongst them that a more vigorous attempt to recapture their camp should be made later on; but Fletcher at once advancing engaged the Nawab Vazir's army, which now fairly broke and fled, pursued and utterly dispersed by our cavalry.

Two days after the British army encamped at Joanpore; when it was ascertained that the Nawab Vazir had partially succeeded in reforming his broken army, with which he was retiring towards Karrah, the headquarters of the Marathas, Fletcher, therefore, pushed forward to Allahabad, before which fortress he arrived early in February.

With the view of reducing the fortress of Allahabad—which is of considerable strength and commands the confluence of the Jumna and Ganges rivers—some siege guns had been ordered to be sent by boats from Benares to join the Head-quarter army. Batteries were now erected, and the heavy guns having been placed in position, a vigorous cannonade was commenced; which, after a few hours, destroyed a portion of one of the main walls, and on the 11th February, Ali Beg Khan, the, Governor, deeming resistance useless, surrendered the town and fortress of Allahabad to the British commander; stipulating that the Nawab Vazir's troops should retire unmolested, taking with them all private property; but the guns, stores, ammunition, and treasure fell to the captors.

The British were now in possession of all the principal strongholds of the Nawab Vazir of Oude, who, with the small remnant of his broken army, was wandering about the district powerless and ignored by his Allies; the whole country submitting to the British as their conquerors, and to the Emperor Shah Alám as their Sovereign.

In the meantime Major Sibbert, who, it will be remembered, was left in command of our troops at Benares, finding that the enemy had retired and that he could spare some soldiers from his headquarters, organised a small force to attempt a second time the reduction of the fortress of Chunar.

Batteries were again erected, some practicable breaches effected, and the storming-party formed; but before the attack was delivered the commander of the fortress, who had on the two previous occasions so successfully defended his position, offered to capitulate. Having no provisions, without money, his troops mutinous and refusing to fight, the Nawab Vazir having fled, there was no one to whom he could apply for aid; and on handing over the keys of the fortress he said, "I have endeavoured to act like a soldier; but, deserted by my Prince, and with a mutinous garrison, what could I do?"

On the 13th February Brigadier-General Carnac assumed command of the army; but the war was now over, and there being no enemy in the field he proceeded to annex the whole of Oude; and taking up his headquarters in the palace of the fugitive Prince, employed himself in arranging the collection of the revenues and receiving the submission of the native chiefs.

On March 1st, 1765, the headquarters of the British army, with which was the Bengal European Regiment, were concentrated at Allahabad. Although there was no force in the country of sufficient strength to endanger the supremacy of the British, the whole country between the Ganges and the Jumna was exposed to constant raids from the Maratha Armies; which, unopposed, were carrying on their depredations up to the very walls of the fortress of Allahabad, and, setting all authority at defiance, burning the villages and collecting the revenue on their own account.

On the 3rd of May the British troops had an engagement with the Maratha army near the village of Karrah, when the enemy were forced back on their headquarter camp at Kalpi. On this occasion the Nawab Vazir was present with the enemy, but on their defeat he went off towards the Rohilla country, without having paid a sum of £50,000 promised to the Maratha chiefs for the services of their troops.

Sir Robert Fletcher, who had been appointed by General Carnac to command the troops in the field, being anxious to capture the Nawab Vazir, ordered a Light Brigade to pursue him; but the Nawab Vazir with only a small number of well-mounted followers eluded the grasp of the British; so our troops returned to their camp on the banks of the Jumna. On the 15th of May Fletcher again took the field against the Marathas, intending to attack the enemy in his stronghold at Kalpi, and drive him to a distance from what had now become British territory, and thus put an end to the annoyance caused to our peaceful .subjects by the incursions of these marauders.

On the 21st of May the British army, with which was still the Bengal European Regiment, attacked the enemy's outposts, which were carried; their main body retiring on their fortified position at Kalpi. A further forward movement was made by our army, when the Marathas appeared on the plain in great force, offering battle. By a judicious manoeuvre our cavalry and infantry encircled the enemy, whilst our artillery concentrated its fire on his position with such effect that, with their front and both flanks threatened, they were forced back into a morass and ground intersected by deep ravines, which completely crippled the movements of the Maratha army, formed mostly of cavalry. Still circling round, our infantry and artillery advanced; our grape and musketry fire doing terrible execution, and preventing the enemy from massing his troops, which in their scattered condition were charged by the Bengal European Regiment with such effect that they were driven at the point of the bayonet from every position they attempted to hold.

For some hours the action, which was of a desultory nature, was hotly contested; when at length the enemy gave ground, and their retreat soon became a disorderly flight. All the objects for which the expedition had been undertaken having been fully accomplished, and the Doab completely cleared of the Marathas, who retreated towards Gwalior, our army next day commenced its return march to Allahabad; 400 of the Bengal Europeans with 8 field-guns forming the advance.

The approaching rainy season now rendered it necessary that the troops should move under cover; and on arrival at Allahabad the army was divided into three columns; one being quartered at that fortress, one sent to Joanpore, and one to Benares.

The Bengal European battalion had suffered severe casualties in the field and from continued exposure during this, the hottest, season of the year; a great number of the rank and file as well as the Officers having succumbed; amongst the latter being Captains Henry Spelman, Thomas Bonaker and Ross.

Two subjects of interest must now be noticed, viz., the death of the Nawab Mir J'afar Khan and the submission of the Nawab Vazir Shuja u'd daulah.

Mir J'afar Khan had accompanied Major Carnac to Calcutta in June, 1764, when he handed over command of the army in the field to Major Hector Munro. The council desired the presence of the Nawab at Calcutta to assist them out of their financial difficulties; their treasury being exhausted, and their main hope of relief depending on the power of the Nawab to pay the large amounts due under the treaty which had placed him a second time on his throne. Amongst these amounts in arrears was £50,000 a month payable for the British army during the war. In the mean time Mir J'afar's revenues had been considerably reduced by three of his richest provinces—Burdwan, Midnapore, and Chittagong—having been coded to the English. Iniquitous treaties and illicit trade had impoverished the revenues of the council, and the Nawab's territories were again well-nigh reduced to the same exhausted condition as when Mir J'afar resigned the Subadarie.

The Nawab, harassed by the demands of the council, supplanted in his authority, worn out in his constitution, and sick at heart, retired to his capital in December, 1764; and in the following January he died.

Under the Nawab Mir J'afar's will £50,000 was bequeathed to Lord Clive for his own use; but Clive, feeling that the new covenants precluded him from accepting the legacy, instituted a fund for the relief of officers and men of the Bengal army who might be forced to retire from the service, either on account of wounds or disease, before they were entitled to pensions or relief from the Government.

This bequest, known as Lord Clive's Fund, proved a sterling boon to the Bengal army, which enjoyed its benefits for nearly a hundred years. In 1859 the capital sum was claimed by Lord Clive's heirs on the plea that, the British possessions in India having been transferred from the East India Company to the Crown of England, the Bengal army had ceased to exist. The claim was held to be valid in law, and the amount of the fund, £50,000, was made payable to the claimants.

The Nawab Mir J'afar Khan was succeeded by his son Nujm 'd daulah, who was, by the orders of the council, reduced to a mere cypher. The provinces of Bengal, Behar, and Orissa were placed under the government of a deputy Nawab, whose appointment was subject to the approval of the council. The revenues were collected by the Calcutta Council, who undertook to provide for the defence of the country; the government of these rich provinces thus virtually passing into the hands of the East India Company.

The Nawab Vazir Shuja u'd daulah, who, after the skirmish at Karrah had ceased his alliance with the Marathas, soon found that his Rohilla subjects, whose assistance he had sought, showed coldness in his cause.

Sumru—the arch traitor—had transferred his allegiance and that of his trained brigades to the Jaths; and the Emperor had, as already stated, placed himself under the protection of the British.

The Nawab Vazir, deserted by his allies, alone, and powerless, determined to follow the example of the Emperor and submit unconditionally to the English commander.

On 4th May he wrote to General Carnac, informing him that all the disturbances which had taken place were contrary to his inclinations. He now saw things in their proper light, and was desirous of delivering himself into the hands of the British.

In reply, General Carnac informed him that he might with perfect confidence come to the British Camp "as to his own house," and if he should prove that his attachment to the English was sincere he would receive every consideration at their hands.

The Nawab Vazir entered our camp on the 26th May, when he was received with much ceremony, and informed—under instructions from the council—that there was every prospect of his dominions being restored to him on easy terms.

Lord Clive's second administration commenced on May 3rd, 1765. His previous services in India had been acknowledged by his Sovereign and Parliament; and he had been promoted to the rank of Major-General, nominated a Companion of the Bath, and created a Peer of Ireland under the title of Baron Clive of Plassey.

The Court of Directors, not placing implicit confidence in the judgement of their Council at Calcutta, had appointed a Select Committee, with almost unlimited power, to supervise its proceedings. Of this Committee Lord Clive, as Governor and Commander-in-Chief, was nominated President. His duties included the remodelling the army, and correcting the abuses existing both in the civil and military services. Clive had in former years largely benefited from the very system which he had now undertaken to expose and eradicate. The vast responsibility and the certainty of the universal dissatisfaction which his proceedings must entail would have made most men hesitate before accepting a trust which must transform his friends into enemies, and evoke results, the effects of which would probably involve him in life-long disputes and difficulties.

Clive's responsibilities at this crisis were of a nature to call forth all the energies and forethought of that great Commander; the Emperor of Hindustan, Shah Alám, stood a suppliant before him; Shuja u'd daulah, the ex-Nawab Vazir of Oude, was seeking mercy; and beside him stood Bulwant Sing, the ex-Raja of the rich province of Benares, who had been deposed by our commander after the Battle of Buxar.

Lord Clive determined to adopt a lenient policy towards his suppliants, thinking that our later conquests—however glorious from a military point—had increased the responsibilities of the council beyond all reason, and weakened their power to govern or control. Under these circumstances he resolved that the territories of the East India Company should be confined strictly within its own limits; beyond which native Princes should be placed in authority, they signing treaties with us and each other, offensive and defensive; thus converting our late enemies into friends and allies.

The Select Committee ordered that the Nawab Vazir should be forthwith restored to his Government in Oude; and that henceforward he should be relieved from his suzerainty to the Emperor of Delhie—ascending his throne as King of Oude.

The Government of the East India Company consented to acknowledge Shah Alám as Emperor of Hindustan, and for the maintenance of his dignity ceded to him the rich provinces known as the Douab, situated between the rivers Ganges and Jumna; and, further, they agreed that, until he should be enabled to possess himself of his throne at Delhie, they would protect these provinces by retaining a garrison of Company's troops at the fortress of Allahabad. In consideration of these conditions the Emperor, on his part, confirmed the British in their possession of Bengal, Behar, and Orissa, with authority to collect and apply all the revenues.

Lord Clive restored Bulwant Sing, the ex-Raja of Benares, to his former position; and treaties offensive and defensive were concluded between all parties.

Although the fortress of Chunar was within the province of Benares it was ordered to be garrisoned by Company's troops.

We must now treat of the reforms which Clive introduced into the army.

It had always, since the earliest days of the East India Company, been a recognised privilege that, if the officers of the army should render special services to native Princes, they should be allowed to receive presents in proportion. Further—although not perhaps strictly recognised—it was well known by the authorities, that the officers in the service participated in profits accruing from trading transactions. The net military pay of the officers of the army was insignificantly small; for, even admitting that the actual necessaries of life were inexpensive, all articles of European manufacture were proportionately the reverse. The privilege of being allowed to accept presents from native chiefs, and to participate in profits from trade, was occasionally abused, and by none more so than those highest in power; but, rightly or wrongly, these privileges were viewed by the officers of the army in the light of compensation for insufficient pay; and any interference with these established usages was likely to produce ill-feeling and resentment.

Now the pay proper per month, half batta, full batta, and double batta, of the officers of the European infantry of different grades, calculated in English money had been as follows:

Rank.	Pay proper in Garrison or at the Presidency.			Half batta in cantonments.			Field batta within the Company's territories or in cantonments beyond them.			Double batta on service beyond the Company's territories.		
	£	s.	d.	£	s.	d.	£	s.	d.	£	s.	d.
Colonel	31	0	0	38	15	0	77	10	0	155	0	0
Lieut.-Colonel	24	16	0	31	0	0	62	0	0	124	0	0
Major	18	12	0	23	5	0	46	10	0	93	0	0
Captain	12	8	0	9	6	0	18	12	0	37	4	0
Capt.-Lieut.	6	4	0	9	6	0	18	12	0	37	4	0
Lieutenant	6	4	0	6	4	0	12	8	0	24	16	0
Ensign	5	0	0	4	13	0	9	6	0	18	12	0
Cadet	...	...		3	2	0	6	4	0	12	8	0

Surgeons were paid as captains, assistant-surgeons as lieutenants.

In addition to these sums colonels commanding brigades were entitled to £4 per diem on account of "table allowances."

Officers were supplied with tents—according to rank—these being carried on the line of march free of cost.

It is now necessary that some explanation should be given regarding batta, which formed so large an item in the officers' allowances. Batta was originally granted as a donation intended to compensate officers for extra expenses when at a distance from the presidency town.

"Field and double batta" had been granted to officers of the Bengal army under special conditions and circumstances—a boon which had not been granted in the other presidencies—and Clive was, under orders from the Court of Directors, about to place all the armies on an equal footing as regards batta.

There were these two reforms to be introduced, both trenching on what was held by the officers to be their rightful privileges, and both materially effecting their emoluments; and it was Clive's aim, as far as possible, in carrying out the orders of the court, to provide against unnecessary loss of emoluments, and to secure, as far as possible, the goodwill, at any rate, of the senior officers.

With this view Clive established what now-a-days would be called "A Joint Stock Trading Association." As all private trade by the Company's servants was to be prohibited, he intended that the proposed "Association," superintended by the Government, should supply funds to compensate the senior officers of the army and others for the loss of privileges hitherto enjoyed.

The nominal capital of Clive's "Trading Association" was fixed at £320,000, upon which, says its proposer—"the most moderate may expect to make 50 per cent, clear of all charges, others 75 per cent, and the most sanguine 100 per cent."

The meaning of this was that, at the most moderate computation there would be a net profit on the transactions of the Association of at least £160,000 per annum; this profit to be divided amongst the shareholders in lieu of the profits hitherto derived from their private trade.

Reference has previously been made to the "permits" or "distues" which led to the war against Mir Kassim; and which brought the largest profits, specially in trading in salt; and as under the new regulations all permits would be withdrawn from private hands, it was from a tax on salt, principally, that Clive intended to pay his dividends; and by the new arrangement the natives of the country would be supplied with the commodity some fifteen per cent cheaper than heretofore.

The capital of the "Association" was divided into 35 full shares, corresponding with the interests of the holders, and it was estimated that each share would yield a profit of £5000 per annum.

The shares were allotted as follows:

	Shares
The Governor	5
Second in Council and Commander-in-Chief, each.	3
10 other Members of Council and Colonels of Brigades, each.	2
1 Chaplain, 14 Senior Merchants, and 3 Lieutenant-Colonels, each.	2 thirds
13 Factors, 4 Majors, 6 Surgeons, 1 Secretary to Government, 1 Sub-Accountant, 1 Assistant, each.	1 third

Having thus assured the interests of the senior officers of the army, Clive, on the 3rd August, 1765, issued the following Order:

> A General Court of Proprietors having resolved that certain covenants should be executed by all officers in their service, the Governor and Council having received the strictest injunctions from the Court of Directors to put the resolution of the said

General Court in execution immediately in obedience to these commands, it is hereby ordered that the said covenants be immediately executed.

No serious opposition was at first raised to the terms of the new covenants; copies were sent to the different stations, which were duly executed, and returned to headquarters without comment.

In August Clive turned his attention to the re-organisation of the Bengal army. The Bengal European Battalion—at this time upwards of 1600 strong—was ordered to be formed into three Regiments; or, as it would now be designated, the Regiment was ordered to be broken into three battalions. To enable Clive to carry out this change effectively, several officers, specially selected for commands, and a large number of recruits, had been sent by the Court of Directors for service in Bengal.

The command of the 1st European Regiment was conferred on Brigadier-General Carnac; the second on Lieutenant-Colonel Knox;[1] the third on Lieutenant-Colonel Sir Robert Barker.

Majors Sir Robert Fletcher, Peach, and Chapman were promoted to Lieutenant-Colonelcies; and Majors Chapman and Sibbert, and Captain Hugh Grant, were appointed to the three Regimental Majorities.

Each regiment of European infantry was officered as follows:

1 Colonel	18 Ensigns
1 Lieutenant-Colonel	1 Surgeon
1 Major	3 Surgeon-Mates
6 Captains	1 Adjutant
1 Captain-Lieutenant	1 Quartermaster
9 Lieutenants	

and consisted of 731 rank and file. The whole of the Bengal army was divided at the same time into three brigades, each brigade consisting of—

1 Battalion of European Infantry	1 Company of Artillery
	1 Russalah of Cavalry
7 Battalions of Sepahis	

The first division or brigade of the army was stationed at Monghyr, supplying detachments for Calcutta and Murshedabad; the second at Allahabad, its special duties being the protection of the Emperor's

---

1. Lieutenant-Colonel Knox having died before the Second European Regiment was organized, Lieutenant-Colonel Richard Smith was appointed to its command.

provinces in the Douab; and the third at Bankipore. The second and third brigades supplied detachments for Lucknow, Jaunpore, Chunar, Benares, Midnapore, and Chittagong. The colonels of the European battalions commanded the brigades of which they formed part. Brigadier-General Carnac, therefore, commanded the first; Colonel Richard Smith the second; and Colonel Sir Robert Barker the third; but as General Carnac's extra duties required his frequent presence at the Presidency, the charge of his Brigade devolved on the next senior Officer,. Lieutenant-Colonel Sir Robert Fletcher.

The number of European soldiers available to bring the battalions up to the assigned strength fell far short of their requirements; the first and second Battalions being tolerably strong, but the third very weak, and composed mostly of recruits. On the 24th August the following order, under which the Bombay troops serving in Bengal were incorporated into the latter army, was published:

> His Lordship has directed that all the officers and private men both artillery and infantry of the Bombay detachment, are to be immediately incorporated into this establishment, and such of their officers who can obtain permission from Brigadier-General Carnac Commanding Officer of the army shall be received as youngest of the rank they now possess.

Under this Order the two companies of the Bombay European Regiment under Captain Pemble were incorporated with the Bengal European Regiment. By the above regulations the army was placed on a more efficient footing, each brigade forming a force complete in all its branches, and capable of encountering any native army that could be brought against it.

To maintain the strength of the European army in Bengal, the Select Committee requested the Court of Directors to supply 500 European recruits annually.

But the time had now arrived for Clive to carry out the orders of the Court of Directors and cancel the payment of the "double batta" to the troops. It has been already explained that double batta was originally intended to cover extra expenses entailed on officers of the army, whilst on service, or stationed, at a distance from the Presidency town.

It was after the Battle of Plassey that the newly-appointed Nawab, Mir J'afar Khan, in the fullness of his gratitude to the army which had so materially assisted him to his throne, promised them double batta as long as they might be employed in his service.

When Mir Kassim had succeeded Mir J'afar in the Soubadarie, he provided for the continuance of the double batta; and to ensure its regular payment by the Company, Mir Kassim assigned to them the rich provinces of Midnapore, Burdwan', and Chittagong. Thus the double batta had been regularly paid to the army for seven consecutive years, and was considered by the officers as property in which they had a vested interest, the more so as the funds from which payment was made had been provided for in perpetuity out of the revenues of the above ceded districts.

Now, the Court of Directors had turned their serious attention to the subject of curtailing expense under this head, and on several occasions had sent peremptory orders to the council for the discontinuance of double batta payments. On the last occasion on which the orders of the Court on this subject had been received the troops had just gained an important victory at Buxar; and the council rightly judging that it would be an impolitic measure, just at that time, to deprive the troops of the greater part of their allowances, the consideration of the batta question had been again deferred.

Clive had now arrived in Bengal with reiterated orders on the subject, and although he had informed the Court that he disapproved of their order, he felt that the execution of their positive instructions could not be longer delayed.

In September a Government notification was published, stating that on January 1st, 1766, the issue of double batta to the troops would be discontinued, an exception being made in the case of the 2nd Brigade, stationed at Allahabad, "on account of the high price of provisions at that station, and the expenses of procuring the necessary European articles at so great a distance from the Presidency."

No opposition to Clive's orders was apparent for some weeks; but a feeling of discontent had pervaded the minds of a large proportion of the junior officers of the army.

The field officers who had been promised shares in the "Trading Association" felt themselves compensated for any loss of allowances, and they for the most part discouraged discontent amongst their juniors; but as the effects of the order began to tell on the monthly pay, and as communications between the malcontents became more frequent, feelings of a sense of their wrongs were openly expressed.

Committees were secretly appointed in the several brigades to ascertain the feelings of individual sufferers, and it soon became apparent that the dissatisfaction was general; it being universally felt that the order was a cruel attempt to rob the juniors of their just rights, and that the seniors had been bought over by the Governor with shares in his "Joint Stock Association", in order that they might assist the Government in depriving the juniors of the batta to which they deemed themselves justly entitled.

The malcontents determined in the first instance that an appeal should be made to the council for redress; but, should this not be accorded, that a "union" of the captains and subalterns should be organised, all binding themselves to resign their commissions on a given day.

Funds were largely subscribed, and an oath administered; the confederates swearing that they would protect "at the sacrifice of their. lives" any of the members who might be condemned to death for mutiny. It was arranged that the general resignation of commissions was to take place on June 1st, 1766; after which it was considered that, as those who had resigned the service would no longer be bound by the army regulations, they would be at liberty to lawfully render assistance to any of the confederates under arrest or sentence of a Court Martial.

A portion of the 2nd Brigade, with which was the 2nd European Regiment, at first quartered at Allahabad, had lately been sent to Karrah to take the field against a Maratha army assembling near that place with the intention of disturbing the provinces lately ceded to the Emperor. Under these circumstances the officers of this brigade, being on active service, felt that they could not with honour join the defection, but they said that after the campaign "they would not continue to hold their commissions to the prejudice of those officers who should resign."

Having thus justified themselves to their comrades for taking independent action, they sent a petition to Lord Clive—at this time at Murshedabad—pointing out their grievances in respectful language, and praying for redress; this petition being signed by 6 captains, 3 lieutenant-captains, 12 lieutenants, and 20 ensigns.

Clive replied that, as the memorial had not been sent through the authorised channel, it could not be acknowledged officially; but he told the petitioners that, as the order of the Court of Directors was peremptory, the council had no power to grant their petition.

Some other memorials of a like nature had been received by the Government, but still no suspicion existed of the extent to which disaffection had spread.

On the 25th April Colonel Sir Robert Fletcher informed Lord Clive that the officers of the 1st Brigade were bent on making a supreme effort to recover their batta; and that they had forwarded to him their commissions, and refused to draw their pay for the month of May; at the same time expressing their willingness to serve as volunteers until the decision of the Government should be made known. It soon became apparent that the movement was universal. A letter found its way into Lord Clive's-possession, which was written by an officer at Karrah, signed "Full batta," from which it appeared that 150 officers had entered into an agreement to resign their commissions on a given day.

Just as these alarming reports of the mutinous feelings amongst the officers of the army reached Clive he became aware that the Marathas were not only threatening the districts under the government of the Emperor, but had also avowed their intention, of invading the Company's territories in Bengal.

Under the recent army re-organisation one of the newly-formed brigades would have been sufficient to protect the country against any such invasions; but should the army be deprived of its officers the case would be serious, the more so, as it was not impossible that in the height of their resentment they might even attempt to suborn their men.

Clive, quite aware of the gravity of the situation, ordered a Special Committee, composed of himself as Chairman, and General Carnac and Mr. Sykes as members, to advise on the question of what was called "the Mutiny of the Officers of the Bengal army."

The committee resolved to make no concessions, but to repress the disorder with a strong hand; to discover the ringleaders of the mutiny, and punish them severely, but to deal out mercy to the penitents judiciously. Clive fully admitted that the aspect of affairs was something more than serious; with an enemy day by day approaching nearer, and looking with an hungry eye on the fertile provinces of Bengal; and the officers of the army, who should be guarding these provinces, unreliable.

Under orders of the Special Committee the following measures were adopted. A dispatch was sent to the Madras Government requesting that they would at once send as many captains and subalterns as could be spared; the urgency of the case being explained, and every encouragement held out to officers who would volunteer for service in Bengal. A resolution was also passed that any officer resigning his commission should be debarred from ever again holding any appointment whatever in the Company's service; and copies of these resolutions were sent to commanding officers with instructions to communicate them to their subordinates.

It has been stated that Clive was at this time at Murshedabad taking measures with Nujm u'd daulah, the young Nawab, for the government of bis provinces under the new arrangements concluded with the Emperor. Now, as there was a large force at Murshedabad, Clive rightly supposed that the officers quartered there had joined the defection. With these men Clive undertook to deal personally, and sending for the officers singly, he placed before them the enormity of their offence, urging them to pause before committing the serious crime of mutiny. After some hesitation the two senior captains declared their intention of cancelling their resignations, their example being followed by all the juniors except two lieutenants.[1]

This course which had succeeded so well at Murshedabad was tried with equal success at the Presidency; most of the malcontents returning to their duty.

Clive's hands now strengthened, he proceeded to Monghyr, where the disaffection was at its height. The troops at this station were commanded by Sir Robert Fletcher, who had pursued a course of deception which tended to mislead and embarrass the Government; for, whilst openly condemning the conduct of the officers under his command, he had secretly encouraged them in their disaffection.

Previous to his departure from Murshedabad to Monghyr, Clive had wisely deputed Major Champion of the 1st Bengal European Regiment to endeavour to bring the officers at Monghyr to reason; but his attempts had not been attended with much success. It was discovered that the officers at Monghyr had communicated with their comrades at Madras, explaining the nature of their grievances, and attempting to dissuade them from taking service in Bengal.

Immediate measures were now adopted by the committee to prevent any letters of a seditious nature leaving Calcutta.

In the meantime several officers of the Madras army had accepted the offers of the Bengal Government, and some of these had already arrived in Calcutta and proceeded to stations up country.

Instructions were now sent to officers commanding brigades to accept all resignations tendered, and to dispatch those so resigning to Calcutta.

But affairs at Allahabad had taken a more serious turn. As soon as Major Smith, commanding, discovered that his officers were implicated, he placed several under arrest; and, turning out his sepahis,

---

1. These two officers afterwards expressed contrition, and were restored to the service with loss of rank.

ordered them to shoot any of the prisoners who might, attempt to escape; and by this bold measure he brought the disaffected officers to reason; Major Smith sending the six ringleaders to Patna to be tried by Court Martial, and releasing the rest on their making promises of good behaviour.

On the 15th May Lord Clive arrived at Monghyr; the disaffected officers not being present, as Fletcher had on the previous day ordered them out of cantonments.

A detachment of sepahis under a trustworthy officer was now sent to the officers' encampment with orders for them to proceed forthwith to Calcutta. The effect of this order was startling; for there was no time allowed for preparations of any kind; and those not provided with the means of transit were obliged to proceed on foot, sad and disgraced.

On the 20th May Lord Clive reached Bankipore, where was quartered the 2nd Brigade under Sir Robert Barker, who, when his officers handed him their commissions, had simply declined to receive them; the officers still maintaining a determined attitude; but continued performing their duties with regularity. Simultaneously with Clive's arrival at Bankipore, came the intelligence of the fate of the malcontents at Monghyr, causing symptoms of hesitation on the part of the Bankipore officers, which terminated in absolute submission.

It only remains for us to state the measures adopted by Lord Clive to punish the offenders. Repentance was now the order of the day; and the majority of those who had been sent in disgrace to Calcutta petitioned to be allowed to cancel their resignations, and return to the service. These petitions were ultimately granted; but not until the offenders had waited in uncertainty and anxiety for several months, during which time those officers who had taken service in Bengal from Bombay and Madras had been promoted over their heads; Clive being thus enabled to mete out punishment according to the demerits in each case.

Several of the ringleaders were ultimately dismissed the service by sentence of Court Martial; amongst them Colonel Sir Robert Fletcher,[1] found "guilty of mutiny and having excited sedition, and after coming to the knowledge of a mutiny having delayed to give information thereof to his commanding officer." he was cashiered.

On the 22nd September a General Order was published by the au-

---

1. Sir Robert Fletcher was ultimately restored to the service by the Court of Directors, by whom he was appointed Commander-in-Chief of Madras, where he took a loading part in the opposition to Lord Pigot.

thority of the Court of Directors, granting an amnesty to all concerned in the mutiny, and to prevent the possibility of a recurrence every officer was required to sign a "Covenant,"[2] under which he engaged to serve the Company for a period of three years, undertaking that he would not "then or at any other time quit the said Service without giving twelve months' previous notice in writing of such intention."

The means which Clive adopted to suppress the mutiny in the Bengal army, proved him to be pre-eminently a leader of men; whilst the officers were guilty of defection and insubordination he was fearless, uncompromising, and even severe: but as soon as signs of contrition were perceptible—tempering justice with mercy, and throwing to the winds all feelings of revenge—he again stood forward as the soldiers' champion and friend.

The Bengal European Regiment had now served the East India Company for ten years; and it will be interesting at this period to refer to a work published at the Cape of Good Hope in 1814, by Mr. George Francois Grand, called *Narrative of the Life of a Gentleman Long Resident in India*. Mr. Grand joined the Bengal European Regiment as a cadet immediately after the events just recorded, and his experiences can hardly fail to be of interest to those serving in the Regiment in after years. He says:

> After bearing a soldier's musket on the line of march, constantly attending the mock sieges and battles which took place in our fixed encampment on the borders of the river, the colonel was pleased to accede to the wishes expressed to him on my behalf by Lord Clive, and I suddenly found myself rewarded for the activity and diligence which I had displayed in unremitting attention to my duty, by being nominated to act as Ensign. We returned soon after to cantonments, where I had the gratification of seeing myself confirmed by a Commission of Ensign, signed by his Lordship on the 4th September (1766). This early act of approbation actuated my zeal, and for three years that I served in the European Regiment under the celebrated martinet, the late Colonel Gilbert Ironside, I can equally vouch my constant perseverance in the readiest observance to my superiors acquired me new friends and the esteem of the Commanding Officer

---

2. This "Covenant" was to be signed by civil as well as military employees, hence the term "Covenanted Servants," in contradiction to local servants, who were not required to sign.

of the Brigade—Colonel Charles Chapman—in whose family I lived, and acted as assistant-secretary to his staff establishment. The army, at my entrance into the service, consisted of three brigades. Each brigade consisted of one European Regiment, 6 battalions of sepoys, and a proportion of artillery, with 100 black horse; and the highest rank enjoyed for such a command was that of colonel. Besides these, there were in different cities of the three Provinces Militia Sepoys, under the name of Pergunnah. These served for the purpose of guarding the treasuries.

In the month of September, 1766, I was on orders to proceed up the country with a detachment of recruits for the 3 brigades under the command of the late Colonel James Hannay (then Captain Hannay), who as well as myself had recently arrived from Europe. Arrived at Bankipore, then the cantonment of the 2nd Brigade, I was introduced by him to the late General Richard Smith, then the Colonel thereof. This brigade took the field soon after repairing to the banks of the Carumnassah, and was there stationed at hand to assist our Ally, the Nawab Vizier Shujah ul Dowlah, had the Afghan Prince Abdulah Khan put his threats into execution of invading the former's dominions. Our cantonments in 1767 took fire, and such was the rapidity with which the thatched bungalows burnt that scarcely an officer had one moment to save anything of his equipment. The Government, with that liberality consistent to men vested to such a trust, required upon honour a statement from each officer of his loss, and every one was reimbursed accordingly to the stated amount. This accident gave rise to the question of barracks both at Dinapore and Berhampore, and the grand scale on which these were formed entailed such an expense on the Honourable Company and sunk such a capital as to have caused them to regret that the double full batta had been struck off by Lord Clive instead of being continued in the field, and the full batta preserved in the Company's provinces conditionally that each officer found his own quarters.[1]

---

1. It will add to the interest attached to these extracts to state that George Francois Grand subsequently married at Chandernagore the beautiful Mdlle. Nöel Catherine Werlèe, the daughter of M. Werlèe, Capitaine du Port and Chevalier de Saint Louis. This lady, the victim of a heartless trick which compromised her beyond all redress, was in consequence divorced from her husband in 1779; two of the judges (continued on next page)

GENERAL REFERENCES—CHAPTER 10

Broome's Rise and Progress of the Bengal Army.
Proceedings of the "Select" Committee.
Royal Military Calendar.
Williams's Bengal Infantry.
The Seir Mutakherin.
Proceedings of the Bengal Council.
Founders of the Indian Empire. Malleson.
Thornton's History of India.
&c, &c.

---

entering a protest against the verdict. After an eventful and not altogether reputable life, she married on the 10th September, 1802, the Prince Talleyrand de Perigord, Foreign Minister of France, and for good or evil exercised considerable influence at the Emperor-Napoleon's Court.

CHAPTER 11

Rohilla & Haidar Ali

Lord Clive's estimate of the profits likely to be derived from the working of his "Trading Association" was found not to be over-sanguine, and the scheme had proved so remunerative that the senior officers of the army were satisfied, and Clive was enabled to carry out the orders of the Directors for the reduction of the batta; but when the Court had before them the details of the Trading Association they condemned it absolutely, and insisted on its abolition. This order placed Clive in a serious dilemma, from which he might have extricated himself by abandoning the scheme; but he had entered with the field officers of the Bengal army and others into certain obligations which he felt bound to fulfil. Under those circumstances, he sanctioned the continuance of the Trading Association for another year, when he hoped the directors would have consented to a general increase of military pay.

The amelioration of the distress caused to the junior officers by the loss of their batta allowance now engaged Clive's attention, and he arranged that the stringent rules regarding private trade should in their case be temporarily modified.

On the 29th January, 1767, Lord Clive left India for the last time, accompanied by his friend General Carnac; Mr. Verelst succeeding as Governor of Bengal.

At this time Delhie, the capital of Hindustan, was in the hands of the Afghans; but, the puppet-king having lately died, the Emperor Shah Alám again showed a natural anxiety to gain possession of his throne. With this view he dispatched one of his ministers to Calcutta, in the hope of inducing the council to assist him in his schemes. Though the Emperor's proposals did not altogether find favour in Calcutta, the British Government did not oppose his wishes; and Shah Alám therefore determined, with the assistance promised by the Marathas and other powerful chiefs, to attempt to possess himself of his capital and throne; the King of Oude, for purposes of his own, encouraging him and advancing him large sums of money.

In the month of May, 1771, the Emperor marched from Allahabad with an army of 16,000 men, and on the 25th of the following December made his public entry into his capital. Hardly had he occupied his throne when his Maratha allies obliged him to take the field against the Rohillas: their object being plunder, whilst the Emperor hoped to annex the Rohilla country.

The Rohillas were a warlike tribe of Northmen, who originally migrated from Roh, a district situated amongst the Afghan mountains. The Rohillas were constantly employed on military services in India, and composed for many years the chief part of the Moghul armies. In reward for their services they had obtained large and valuable possessions in the rich country lying between the Upper Ganges and the Himalayah mountains. The Rohillas, being unable to compete with the army of the Emperor and the Marathas combined, their chief Zabita Khan was defeated; and, flying across the Ganges, was pursued, his troops dispersed, and Rohilkund, in consequence, placed in peril. The Rohillas had possessed an army of 80,000 men; but their chiefs of the different tribes refusing to amalgamate, their united strength was never available. Their rich country extended on the east as far as the confines of Oude, and had always been watched by the king of that country with a covetous eye. The Marathas held all the country to their south, the Rohillas had just been driven from their western provinces; and, with a disjointed and crippled army, they found themselves powerless against the forces by which they were surrounded.

It was under these circumstances that the Rohillas sought the protection of the King of Oude; and, knowing his majesty's dread of the incursions of the Marathas, proposed to enter into a treaty with him, offensive and defensive; and after several months of deliberations a treaty on these lines was signed on May 17th, 1772. Under its articles Shuja u'd daulah, the King of Oude, engaged to expel the Marathas from the Rohilla country, for which accommodation the Rohillas agreed to pay the king £40,000.

Notwithstanding this treaty the Marathas continued, unopposed, to devastate the Rohilla country; whilst the King of Oude had returned to his capital so terrified at the encroachments of the Marathas that he wrote to the Calcutta Council urging them to send European troops for his protection, as he was fearful that the Rohillas and the Marathas combining would invade the Oude provinces.

Under the treaty between Lord Clive and the King of Oude when the latter was restored to his throne—1765—it was stipulated that the British should aid the king with troops if his country should be seriously threatened; and the council now feeling bound to comply with the king's request, Sir Robert Barker, with a portion of his brigade, including the Second Bengal European Regiment, some sepahi battalions, and artillery, was ordered to take the field and prevent the Marathas from menacing the King of Oude.

The combined armies of the King and the East India Company entered Rohilkund, taking up a position which acted as a check to the incursions of the Marathas; but, notwithstanding these-precautions, a Maratha army crossed the Ganges, over-ran the Rohilla country, and destroyed the cities of Moradabad and Sumbul. Sir Robert Barker's orders were to protect the provinces of Oude, but on no account to act on the offensive. The Marathas, finding themselves unopposed by the British, laid waste the Rohilla country; but fortunately in May, 1773, they were recalled by their Government for the protection of their own provinces, threatened from without.

The departure of the Marathas was a source of joy both to the King of Oude and the Rohillas; but no sooner was the former relieved from fear of invasion than he applied to the Council to-assist him to exterminate the Rohillas.

Mr. Warren Hastings had been appointed Governor-General early in the previous year; and had lately received peremptory instructions from the Court of Directors to reduce his military expenditure. The King of Oude offered high terms for the services of the British soldiers, and to accept his offer appeared to the Governor-General a simple way of complying with the orders of the Court. To use Warren Hastings's own words:

> A saving of near one-third of our military expenses would be effected during the period of such service the stipulation of 40 lacks (£400,000) would afford an ample supply to our treasury; the Vizir would be freed from a troublesome neighbourhood and his dominions be much more defensible.

The offer of the King of Oude was accepted by Mr. Warren Hastings, on the part of the council, at a meeting arranged between both parties at Benares.

On this occasion another subject of vast importance occupied the attention of the contracting parties. After the Maratha army had placed Shah Alám on his throne at Delhie, they compelled the Emperor to give them in reward for their services the districts of Korrah and Allahabad. It will be remembered that Clive had handed over these districts to the Emperor, when resettling the country in 1766. This transfer to the Marathas did not meet with the approval of the council; they ruling that, as the Emperor had permanently absented himself from the provinces, he had forfeited his claim to the Government, as well as to the 26 lacs (£260,000) annually, which under treaty he had received from the council.

The Governor-General did not desire to retain possession of the Korrah and Allahabad districts, but the King of Oude had always coveted these possessions and now offered to pay 50 lacs—£500,000—for them. This bargain was struck by the Governor-General at the Benares conference; and, having obtained a treaty signed by the King officially recording these transactions, Hastings returned to Calcutta, and Shuja u'd daulah visited his newly-acquired provinces. In doing so he took the opportunity—in the absence of the Maratha army—to possess himself of some forts and strongholds still held by small detachments of the Marathas.

It was not until November that the King was prepared to carry into effect the plans which he had arranged with Hastings for the reduction of the Rohillas; and he now applied to the council for the use of the Company's troops to effect his purpose.

The King's application caused some embarrassment, for Warren Hastings had not given his colleagues to understand very clearly what had been arranged at the Benares conference; but in January Colonel Champion, the Commander-in-Chief, received orders to advance with a brigade, including the 2nd Bengal European Regiment, form a junction with the King's troops, and place himself under the orders of that Prince.

On the 24th February Colonel Champion's force arrived within the Oude territories, and on the 17th April crossed the border into the Rohilla country.

There was no doubt as to the king's intentions; for when the Rohilla Chief Hafiz Kehmut expressed an earnest desire to come to terms, Shuja' u'd daulah put forward a claim of no less than two crores of rupees—£2,000,000—and declared that unless that amount were at once paid, the Allied Armies would proceed to war.

Hafiz Kehmut was admitted by all to be a brave, dauntless Commander; and had been appointed Chief of his tribe after the death of Nujeeb u'd daulah, and judiciously governed the provinces nearest to Oude.

The demand of the king for so large an amount was rejected with scorn, the Rohilla Chief feeling that the terms of the treaty under which the money was demanded had not been fulfilled by the King; and that, under any circumstances, the amount claimed was vastly in excess of what could be justly due.

The Rohilla army, under Hafiz Kehmut, took up a strong position at Kutra, near the Babul river; and determined to maintain their ground to the last extremity.

The English troops pushed forward, but Champion soon found that he would receive no support from the King's troops, which were rather a source of danger than succour to the English; for having arrived at Gurrah—the ground which had been occupied by the British the previous day—the King declined to combine His scheme was now evident; to leave the English soldiers to do the fighting; and, should they succeed in overpowering the enemy, his troops would then advance and appropriate the plunder.

The King even declined to assist Champion with the loan of some particular cannon, which he thought might prove of service, and the Oude cavalry, much needed, were nowhere to be seen.

The following is Colonel Champion's description of the engagement, fought on the 23rd April:

> Hafiz and his army consisting of about 40,000 men showed great bravery and resolution, annoying us with their artillery and rockets. They made repeated attempts to charge, but our guns being so much better served than theirs, kept so constant and galling a fire, that they could not advance, and where they were closest was the greatest slaughter. They gave proof of a good share of military knowledge, by showing inclinations to force both our flanks at the same time, and endeavouring to call off our attentions by a brisk fire on our centre. It is impossible to describe a more obstinate firmness of resolution than the enemy displayed. Numerous were their gallant men who advanced and often pitched their colours between both armies in order to encourage their men to follow them; and it was not until they saw our whole army advancing briskly to charge them after a severe cannonade of two hours and twenty minutes and

a smart fire of musketry for some minutes on both flanks that they fairly turned their backs. Of the enemy above 2000 fell in the field, and amongst them many Sirdars. But what renders the victory most decisive is the death of Hafiz Kehmut, who was killed whilst bravely rallying his people to battle. One of his sons was also killed, one taken prisoner, and a third returned from flight to-day and is in the hands of Suja-ed-dowla[1]

The battle decided and the enemy put to flight, Champion issued strict orders that his troops were not to plunder or fire the villages; but the King's army pushed forward, and, under sanction of their Generals, plundered and laid waste the country, "while the Company's troops in regular order of their ranks most justly observed—we have the honour of the day and these banditti the profit."[2]

Rohilkund now lay at the mercy of the King of Oude; and "never were the rights of conquest more savagely abused." Most of the chiefs who survived the battle surrendered at discretion; those few still resisting were, together with their families, subjected to imprisonment and brutal treatment. The plunder of the country which passed into the hands of the King was estimated at a million-and-a-half sterling.

One of the Rohilla Chiefs, named Fyzulla Khan, escaped to his Fort at Patir-Ghur, with many of his followers; but his towns were sacked, and his encampment burnt. In July the Company's and the King's troops approached Fyzulla Khan's Fortress, but this Chief was so confident of his strength that he set the Allied Armies at defiance. The King of Oude now evinced a strong-disposition to come to terms with the chief and end the war. He proposed to make Fyzulla Khan the head Zamindar of the whole Rohilla country, and to allow him £60,000 per annum for his expenses; but these, even as well as more favourable terms, were rejected by the Rohilla Chieftain.

By this time the Oude troops were aiding the British, and under instructions from the King, the armies prepared to advance by regular approaches; but the Company's soldiers—Europeans as well as sepahis—were disgusted with their Oude allies, and signs of discontent were openly expressed.

---

1. Sergeant Littellus Burrell, who had formerly served in Captain Rawstone's Company, Bengal European Regiment, greatly distinguished himself in this action. This Non-Commissioned Officer was promoted to an Ensigncy in 1779, and ultimately attained the rank of Major-General; becoming one of the most distinguished Officers in the Company's army.
2. Colonel Champion's letter to Warren Hastings, 24th April, 1774.

£10,000, promised by the King to the Company's troops in lieu of plunder, were not forthcoming; and the troops had not received their monthly pay, provided for in the treaty.

Under these circumstances Shuja u'd daulah was more than ever anxious to come to terms with Fyzulla Khan; to whom he offered a district with an annual revenue of £147,500 if he would on his part surrender to the King one-half of his effects; which terms were accepted; and the first Rohilla War came to an end.[3] The difficulties which Colonel Champion had to contend with are feelingly set forth in his correspondence with the Governor-General; and all credit is due for the masterly moderation displayed in the discharge of duties which, if mismanaged, would have been as ruinous to his military reputation as they were adverse to his feelings as an Officer.

Colonel Champion's services had been entirely with the Bengal European Regiment, of which for many years he had been Adjutant; he was always held by his comrades in respect and affection, and few men have done more to maintain the honour of the Bengal European Regiment.

In the early part of 1775 Shuja u'd daulah, the King of Oude died, and was succeeded by his son Asoff u'd daulah.

For some unexplained reason the Calcutta Council ruled that by the death of the King of Oude all former treaties became extinct; a fresh treaty being arranged with Asoff u'd daulah on the 21st May, under the provisions of which his succession to the throne was sanctioned, and his possession of the districts of Korrah and Allahabad confirmed; he, on his part, agreeing, in addition to some heavy money payments, to make over to the Company the Zamindary of the Raja Chete Sing—successor to his father, Bulwant Sing, whose territories had been restored by Lord Clive in the previous year—this territory yielding a revenue of £221,000.

It will be seen that by the transfer of the districts of Benares to the

---

3. An incident illustrating the customs of the army in India at this period may here be noticed:
On the 15th April, 1775, William Dibbens and Mathew Stevens of the Bengal European Regiment had been sentenced to death by Court-Martial. The preparations for the execution completed, the prisoners were informed that they were to cast lots on the drum-head with dice, "and that he upon whom the favourable lot fell would be remanded back to his quarters, and the punishment remitted, but that the other would be executed on the spot."
Dibbens threw the higher number, and Stevens was immediately shot.

Company the Raja Chete Sing had become their feudatory; and, as such, was bound to supply money and troops to his Suzerain in time of war. This transfer of his allegiance by no means met with the approval of the Raja, who had hitherto paid his tribute to the King of Oude; and, since he had become a vassal of the British, had punctually met their financial claims.

In the year 1778 the Government of Bengal was again sorely pressed for money; a costly war in the Carnatic, and large remittances to be sent to England, making it absolutely necessary that funds should be forthcoming from some source or another; and Benares seemed the most likely field from which they could be obtained.

Under these circumstances the Governor-General in Council demanded from Raja Chete Sing a lump sum of £50,000, in addition to his yearly tribute. This demand was called "extraordinary," but it was repeated in 1779; the sum being a second time paid with a remonstrance, and a hope expressed that no further "extraordinary" demands would be asked for. But next year the demand was again renewed, when the Rajah pleaded poverty, asked for time, and evaded payment; on which Hastings made a peremptory addition of £10,000, in compensation for the delay, and sent troops to Benares to exact payment.

Thus squeezed and frightened, Chete Sing paid the money, but the Government was bent on pressing for more; obviously intending to fix a quarrel on Chete Sing, and make him pay largely for his reconciliation.

The Raja was now ordered to keep a body of cavalry for the service of the British; he protested his inability to fulfil this demand, but his remonstrance was met with threats, and so great was his fear that he offered £200,000 to propitiate the council; but Hastings replied that nothing under half-a-million sterling would purchase his pardon; and at the same time announced his intention of visiting the Raja in person at his capital.

Soon afterwards Warren Hastings visited Benares, the interview convincing the Raja that his destruction was contemplated. Taking off his turban and placing it in the lap of the Governor-General, he swore submission and fidelity, but to no avail; he was arrested on the spot and placed in confinement in his own capital; two companies of sepahis being told off to mount guard and prevent his escape. This was too much for the Raja's subjects, who thronged the city in tumultuous crowds; they were well-armed, and determined to resent the insult passed on them and their Raja. The officer commanding the guard over the Raja ordered out most of his sepahis to quell the riot in the city, when a fight ensued in the narrow streets, the officer and his men defending themselves bravely, but being at length overwhelmed, shot-down, and hacked to pieces, amidst the yells and execrations of the infuriated crowds.

The Raja, taking advantage of the confusion, improvised a rope with the turbans of his attendants, who lowered him from the window of his prison; and, reaching a boat near at hand, he escaped to the south side of the Ganges.

Protected by his subjects at a village close by, the Raja at once issued orders for the assembling of his troops, his people flocking to his standard by thousands; the whole country was in a commotion, and the entire population in arms.

In the meantime the building in which the Governor-General had taken up his quarters, with an escort of some sepahis, was beleaguered, but the Raja, still frightened, refrained from making the Governor-General prisoner; indeed, he sent humble apologies for his conduct, and liberal offers if the Governor-General would restore him to favour. But affairs had assumed too serious an aspect to be arranged by compromise; Hastings—calm, dignified and firm—did not deign to send a reply, and instructions written on strips of paper, concealed in the ears of the messengers, were conveyed to Chunar, ordering immediate relief to be sent. The messengers having reached the fortress in safety, Major Popham started in command of a detachment with which were the two flank companies of the 2nd Bengal European Regiment.

17th August, 1781; In the meantime an officer of the Governor-General's escort, crossing the Ganges with a few of his men, made an ill-judged attack on the Raja's army, which, suddenly falling on the sepahis, killed the officer in command and nearly all his men who had accompanied him on his rash expedition.

Chete Sing now assumed an attitude of defiance, but still shrank from the responsibility of seizing the Governor-General.

The news of the defeat and slaughter of the party of sepahis was magnified into the defeat of the British army and spread like fire; the people of the Allahabad and Korrah districts, as well as of Oude itself, rising against their King, who was supposed to favour the British cause, refusing to pay their taxes, and putting the Revenue officers to flight.

But the British army was fast assembling. Whatever the faults of Hastings, he was beloved by the army, and specially so by the men of the Bengal European Regiment, who remembered that he had served in their ranks and shared with them the dangers and triumphs of their early wars; and the European soldiers of the Regiment volunteered to a man to avenge the insult passed on their Governor-General and friend.

Captain Hill was sent in advance to attack the Raja's army—an undisciplined, badly-armed force of several thousand men—entrenched near the village of Patuta. Hill at once assaulted the position, which he carried without difficulty and with only slight loss. 20th September; The enemy, however, soon rallied, and again entrenched themselves at the town of Suttufpore, where they were a second time defeated and now completely dispersed; the Raja, with a few of his cavalry, escaping in the direction of his Fort of Bridge-ghur. Mr. Warren Hastings, having been released, proceeded to Chunar. Major Popham, in chief command of the British force, quickly followed the Raja; but the latter, well-mounted and lightly escorted, pressed on, eluding the grasp of his pursuers.

The British troops, following, soon arrived at Bridge-ghur, and completely surrounded the fort, which, standing on a hill, possessed great natural strength. Popham intended to capture Chete Sing in his stronghold; but the Raja had, in the interval, escaped, and taken the direction of Bundlekand, where he had placed himself under the protection of some friendly chiefs. The wife and mother of the Raja, left in the fort—which contained a considerable amount of specie—expressed their intention of holding out; but after a few days' siege they offered to capitulate on condition of being allowed to-retain their treasure. The orders of the Governor-General were applied for; when he refused sanction to the proposed terms, and Popham was ordered to continue the siege and capture the fort. At this time the Governor-General wrote to Major Popham a letter, the misunderstanding of which gave rise to much discussion and ill-feeling. The following is an extract from the letter:

> With respect to the booty, that is rather your consideration than mine. I should be sorry that your officers and soldiers lost any part of the reward to which they are so well entitled, but I cannot make any objection, as you must be the best judge.

Having obtained what he believed to be the Governor-General's sanction to appropriate the booty as prize for his troops, Major Popham renewed the siege; and after 14 days, the garrison surrendering unconditionally, the large amount of treasure captured was declared lawful prize, and immediately divided according to custom "on the drum-head."

The Governor-General, however, subsequently denied that his letter, quoted above, conveyed his sanction to the division of the booty amongst the troops, threatening to force the army to disgorge, and warning them that if they refused he would "propose whether the law may not compel them."[4] It docs not appear, however, that any means were taken to enforce the repayment of the prize.

In whatever light we may view the conduct of the Governor-General in having deposed the Raja of Benares, the ultimate benefits, both to the inhabitants and the Government of India, must be admitted. A Police Force—which Warren Hastings says "was after his own heart"—was established, and security of property ensured; and in a letter dated January 21st, 1782, he says:

> I lost the Zamendary with a rent of 22 lacs, I recovered it with a rent of 40. The Company possessed only its stipulated rent from Chete Sing. It is now as much a member of the Government as the Zemendarry of Burdwan.

In August, 1778, two European battalions of artillery were ordered to be raised, the gunners to be selected by lot from the Bengal European Regiments: at the same time the grenadier companies were reduced to half their strength, the Light Companies being increased in proportion, and on the 26th September, 1779, the three Regiments of Bengal Europeans were each formed into two battalions; the total strength of European infantry in Bengal being at this time about 3000.

War against Haidar Ali in the Carnatic

Our attention must now revert to the state of affairs in the Madras Presidency.

In September, 1780, a fast-sailing vessel arrived at Calcutta from Madras with dispatches from Mr. Whitehill, the Governor of that presidency, setting forth the painful position in which the Madras Council were placed, and imploring that succour might be sent from Bengal.

The presidency town of Madras—indeed the whole of Southern India—was at the mercy of their old enemy Haidar Ali, who with the assistance of his French allies had out-generalled the British troops;

The following is an extract from General Orders, 1st October, 1779, publishing a complete List of the reorganized Regiments of Bengal European Infantry.

FIRST REGIMENT OF INFANTRY.

BRIGADIER-GENERAL—GILES STIBBERT.

1st Battalion.	2nd Battalion.
LIEUTENANT-COLONEL.	LIEUTENANT-COLONEL.
Fred. Upton	William Blair
MAJOR.	MAJOR.
Alexander Hannay	John Webber
CAPTAINS.	CAPTAINS.
George Renny	Silvester Ramsay
Edward Curfey	James Dunn
Thomas Harding	Robert Davis
James Moore	Thomas Bolton
Charles White	Samuel Farmer
John Grant	Henry Harvey
Richard French	Solomon Earle
Robert Baillie	William Hyde
John Worship	James Denhy
Edward Keard	
LIEUTENANTS.	LIEUTENANTS.
John Collins	Ralph Broome
Robert McMurdock	William Kilpatrick
Alexander Thomson	James Collins
Thomas Birrell	Archibald Ferguson
Charles Stewart	Cozens Framlingham
David Ochterlony	Andrew Smith
John Reid	William McCullock
John White	Edward Summers
Alexander Grant	James Erskine
Edward Swift Broughton	Randolph Ransford
Philip Colebrooke	Robert Colebrooke
John Stewart	Thomas Hawkins
Henry Monk	Edward Clayton
Robert Weatherstone	John Patterson
John Gearie	John Smith
William Carden	John Ralph
Lewis Morley	Sutton Donellan
Fredk. Davey	
Fredk. McCaskell	
Fredk. Elwood	

FIRST REGIMENT OF INFANTRY—continued.

1st Battalion.
Ensigns.
John Arnott
Robert Burrows
T. W. Payne
John Mougah

2nd Battalion.
Ensigns.
— Villiers
Henry Wye
John Jarratt
John Abercrombie
J. Walter

SECOND REGIMENT OF INFANTRY.

Colonel—James Morgan.

1st Battalion.
Lieutenant-Colonel.
Thomas Goddard

Major.
John Stainforth

Captains.
John Erskine
George Wright
James Buchanan
Charles Maitland
Lewis Smith
Turner Carnac
Robert Dennis
Samuel Hunt
John Cowe

Lieutenants.
William Alston
Thomas Gladwin
Fredk. Winwood
Samuel Jones
Archibald Scott
Thomas Phipps
Henry Chalcroft
Henry Saunders
John Gowen
Thomas Williamson
David Birrell
J. Dubois
Thomas Bateman

2nd Battalion.
Lieutenant-Colonel.
John Tottingham

Major.
Jacob Carnac

Captains.
Henry Wray
Christopher Gough
William Lane
Stephen Downes
Patrick Hay
Robert Limond
Sir Patrick Balfour
Charles Forbes

Lieutenants.
Thomas Edwards
Robert Gillespie
Henry White
Richard Forbes
William Moore
Whitwell Butler
James Gold
Jeremiah Symes
Robert Harrison
Michael Heffernan
Patrick Fallon
Thomas McFie
Francis Rudledge

SECOND REGIMENT OF INFANTRY—continued.

1st Battalion.

LIEUTENANTS—continued.

William Moore
William Addie
James Powell
James McCleod
John Home

ENSIGNS.

James McKenzie
James Hutchinson
William Hastings

2nd Battalion.

LIEUTENANTS—continued.

Edward Jackson
Edward Burnett
Francis Kinlock
Francis Britzcke
Philip D'Auvergne

ENSIGNS.

James Hutchinson
James Hamond
John Malcolm
John Crow
John Wilson

THIRD REGIMENT OF INFANTRY.

COLONEL GILBERT IRONSIDE.

1st Battalion.

LIEUTENANT-COLONEL.
Fredk. Nevill Parker

MAJOR.
Christopher Kundson

CAPTAINS.
John Cockerell
Edward Clarke
James Dickson
John Bateman
George Mends
Robert Maxwell
Charles Livingston
William Black
John Dodds
George Martine

LIEUTENANTS.
Godfrey Baker
Thomas Hoggan
James Goldfrap
Henry de Castro
James Underwood
John Norf

2nd Battalion.

LIEUTENANT-COLONEL.
Arthur Ahmuty

MAJOR.
Charles Ironside

CAPTAINS.
Thomas Nicholls
Robert Roberts
Walter Bourke
James Smith
Thomas Hall
John Campbell
Richard Scott
William Ogilvie
John Stacey

LIEUTENANTS.
Samuel Watson
Patrick Douglass
John Mawbey
George Wood
James Sinclair
Colin Monteath
John Darby

THIRD REGIMENT OF INFANTRY—continued.

1st Battalion.

LIEUTENANTS—continued.

Charles Hamilton
Gabriel Martindall
William Davis
Lewis Mordaunt
William McNamara
Joseph Edgar
William Keasburry
James Edwards
S. Bridgeman
George Balfour
H. Foster
Thomas Creighton

ENSIGNS.

George Shaw
Thomas Smith
Robert Bowie
Alexander Fotherington
George Robertson

2nd Battalion.

LIEUTENANTS—continued.

Frederick Griffiths
William Lally
George Lally
Thomas Shaw
John Dickinson
Thomas Williamson
John Jackson
James Barker
Henry Reid
Lewis Thomas
Henry Mercer

ENSIGNS.

George Adams
J. Dring
Edward Hall
Joseph Earley

the resources of the country were well-nigh exhausted, provisions scarce, and the treasury empty.

Before detailing the measures which were adopted in Bengal to relieve the pressing necessities of the sister presidency, we must give a hurried glance at the circumstances which led to this state of affairs.

Haidar Ali, on the death of the Raja of Mysore in 1766, being hereditary Prime Minister, or Peshwar, assumed the reins of Government. From that time there had followed a succession of wars with the British, plainly manifesting that, although Haidar Ali had been induced to sign treaties of peace with the East India Company, he had proved himself of a very different calibre from the class of native Generals against whom the British had hitherto contended. It is true that Haidar Ali had sometimes met with reverses at the hands of his enemy; yet, in May, 1768, at the battle of Mangalore, he had compelled the British force of 240 European soldiers and 1200 sepahis to hurriedly escape in their boats, leaving their sick and wounded prisoners in Haidar's hands; then he had, in the following November, surprised Colonel Wood, in chief command of the British army in the field, capturing from him his heavy guns and baggage. Again Haidar Ali had completely out-generalled Sir Hector Munro—the hero of Buxar—and having induced him, by a clever manoeuvre, to divide his forces, attacked the weaker portion under Colonel Baillie, and, after a desperate fight, in which the British army lost nearly half their numbers, compelled the remainder to lay down their arms. Twice Haidar had the Presidency town of Madras at his mercy; on the second occasion when it was completely denuded of troops; but he unaccountably declined to make a decisive dash. Arcot had fallen into his hands; Ambore with its garrison had surrendered to him; and although it is true the Forts of Velore, Parmakol, and Wandiwash, still held out, they were all, as well as other of our garrisons, vigorously besieged by divisions of Haidar's army; whilst the Madras Government had no troops with which to rain the sieges.

Haidar still unaccountably abstained from attacking Madras; and, whilst he hesitated, he heard that General Sir Eyre Coote had arrived from Calcutta with the first division of the Bengal troops.

When the news of the alarming position of affairs in Madras had reached Bengal, Warren Hastings strained every nerve to supply the entreated succour. Money had to be raised, for the Government was much embarrassed by the heavy expenses incurred by the war against the Marathas; but he determined that the defence of the British possessions in Madras should he undertaken in no half-hearted spirit; and that every available soldier should be sent on this duty.

In the early part of September the Calcutta Council passed a resolution that "2 companies of European artillery, with 3 battalions of lascars, and 4 field-pieces, and 1 Battalion of European Infantry from the 1st Brigade," were to embark immediately for Madras. The European Battalion selected for this service was the 2nd Battalion of the 1st Bengal European Regiment. Reinforcements, consisting of one company of European artillery with 16 field-pieces, six battalions of sepahis, and the corps of Foreign Rangers, were ordered to march by the coast route to Madras.

Haidar Ali's army, commanded by him in person, consisted at this time of 80,000 men, including his best cavalry; and amongst his infantry were numbers of those men whose descendants may be seen to this day in the Mysore and Madras districts, running without any apparent effort their ten miles an hour for many hours consecutively. He had also a complete corps of Frenchmen, ably commanded; whilst his artillery was second to none in India.

The Governor-General appointed General Sir Eyre Coote to the independent command of all Military operations; and to avoid any misunderstanding on the part of the Madras authorities, he suspended Mr. Whitehill, the Governor of Madras.

General Coote, with 350 of the Bengal European Regiment, landed in Madras on the 5th November, and they were immediately posted to the 1st or Right Division of the army under Major-General Hector Munro.

Coote found the presidency of Madras in so exhausted a condition that he could not take the field until after an unwelcome delay of more than two months; and it was not until the middle of January, 1781, that the British army marched from Madras, General Stewart being left with a small force in command of Fort St. George and the Mount.

On the 21st Karumgalli was taken by storm, with a British loss of 170; the enemy, however, suffering much more severely.

The Commander-in-Chief, Sir Eyre Coote, in thanking the army for its cool, determined bearing, says that it now has "an ample and opportune supply of provisions, a post of the first consequence, and will prove of essential advantage to our future operations."

Next day the siege of Wandiwash[5] was raised. This fortress had been closely beleaguered by Haidar Ali's army since the beginning of December, 1780.

Coote now hastened in a southern direction towards Pondicherry, encamping on the 5th on the Red Hills, where he destroyed large quantities of provisions and Military stores which were being landed from the French squadron, under Chevalier d'Ornes, anchored off the coast.

Haidar had previously entered into an alliance with the French at Pondicherry, and told them that he would follow Coote by forced marches and bring reinforcements before the English General could deliver his attack; and he, as good as his word, at once massed his troops, and pushed in the direction of that, town, but in doing so he had been obliged to raise the siege of Vellore.

D'Ornes's squadron of French war-vessels was unopposed; for Admiral Hughes, commanding the British ships at Madras, had only a few light vessels, too weak to engage the French fleet.

Haidar Ali, as soon as he heard of the arrival of D'Ornes's squadron,

---

5. The garrison of Wandiwash consisted of natives only, commanded by Lieutenant Flint, with whom was Ensign Moore. These officers with their handful of troops had gallantly repulsed every assault of the enemy, made several sorties, spiked some of the enemy's guns and partly destroyed their works. The siege having been raised by Coote's force, the British army encamped on the same ground where twenty years previously the siege of Wandiwash had been raised and a memorable Battle fought.

at once decided to separate Coote from his base; whilst the French ships would blockade the coast, and thus starve out the British army. But, to enable him to execute his plans he must seize and hold a strong position near the village of Chelambram; and, succeeding in this, he could effectually sever Coote from Madras, and prevent his collecting supplies from the interior.

Haidar, marching with great rapidity, made as if he would seize Cuddalore from Coote's grasp; and Coote fell into the trap, moving his army further to the south to cover Cuddalore; Haidar thus gaining his coveted position without firing a shot.

Coote had been completely outwitted, and seemed now at his enemy's mercy; severed from his base and with but a scanty supply of provisions, and he saw that, these exhausted, he must either attack Haidar in his advantageous position or starve.

But, by a stroke of great good fortune for Coote, the Chevalier d'Ornes determined to act independently of the land forces; he would neither be dictated to by the French commander at Cuddalore, nor listen to the advice of Haidar Ali. D'Ornes positively refused to land any of his troops; and, disregarding the earnest entreaties of the French commander and his allies, he, on the 15th of February, weighed anchor and bore away, leaving the coast clear.

Supplies were immediately dispatched from Madras by sea, Coote being thus saved by their timely arrival from a great disaster.

Although Coote was now secured from actual want, he was still unable to attack his enemy's stronghold, from which Haidar watched the British camp. Five months passed and still there were no signs of any movement.

At last, on the 16th June, Coote suddenly crossed the river Vellore. Haidar Ali was absent from his headquarters at this time, having gone with a flying brigade to plunder some neighbouring towns.

On the 19th of June the Commander-in-Chief, having received information that Haidar had converted a mosque at Chelambram into a store for provisions and ammunition, determined to take it by assault, though strongly fortified and garrisoned by 3000 of Haidar's troops. A gun was run up close to the outer gateway, which was quickly blown in and captured; but, on arriving at the main street which led to the mosque, it was found that the houses on both sides were loopholed and filled with troops, who poured on the assailants such a continuous fire that they retired under cover, when our artillery at once bravely pushed forward their two 12-pounders, forcing the enemy to call for quarter. It soon, however, became apparent that the English troops had expended all their ammunition; on which the enemy, having been opportunely reinforced, made a successful onslaught on their assailants, who were ultimately driven back, but not before they had inflicted terrible loss on their enemy and carried away a large quantity of grain captured from their magazine.

Haidar's soldiers, during the fight, succeeded in capturing one of the British guns, but not before all the gunners had fallen.

General Coote, now recrossing the Vellore river, encamped close to the village Porto Novo, on the sea-coast, and here he was making arrangements to renew the attack on the mosque, and retrieve lost prestige, when Haidar, hearing of the repulse of the British, hastily returned to his headquarters, to exterminate his enemy before he could recover from his recent defeat, Haidar accordingly broke camp, and, making a rapid movement towards the north-east, placed himself between the English and Cuddalore.

Coote was completely taken by surprise; indeed, he was unaware that Haidar had changed his position until he found he was fortifying himself within three miles of the British camp.

On July 1st Coote moved from Porto Novo nearer to Haidar's position, which now completely barred the Cuddalore road, and was immensely strong; his left resting on sandhills near the sea shore, his front and right spreading far inland, and occupying three villages; the ground being intersected by deep ravines, amongst which his artillery was placed, embrasures having been cut in the rising banks.

Haidar was still a formidable enemy, but he had led a hard life, the latter years of which had been spent in combating a foe, who had strained his energies to the utmost; and now, prematurely old and unable to lead his troops in person, he was constrained to sit cross-legged on a raised platform erected in the centre of his camp, from which, surrounded by his officers, he directed the movements of his troops.

He had in his camp at this time 25 battalions of Regular infantry, between 40,000 and 50,000 horse, above 100,000 Matchlock-men, Peons, Polygars, and 47 guns, besides a corps of 400 Frenchmen.

The British force, on the other hand, consisted only of 2070 Europeans and 6400 sepahis, with 55 field-pieces.

On the morning of July 1st Sir Eyre Coote, under the advice of a Council of War, moved out of camp to engage his enemy. His baggage he placed for its better protection on the beach, close into which Admiral Hughes had anchored his ships, so as to afford the land troops his co-operation and support; and it is probable that had the British army been forced to retreat Coote would have sought shelter under cover of the guns of the British fleet.

Up to 7 a.m. Sir Eyre Coote does not appear to have fixed on the details of his attack; but preparatory to issuing orders for his advance he separated his army into two lines or divisions.

The first consisted of H.M. 73rd (71st), the Bengal and Madras European Regiments, 1 troop of European cavalry, 2 Regiments of sepahis and 30 guns under General Sir Hector Munro. The second line or division was commanded by General James Stuart[6].

Sir Eyre Coote and his staff having carefully reconnoitred the enemy's position, found that Haidar's left was the most assailable point, by a road which intersected the sand-hills. He at once dispatched General Stuart, with the 2nd Division, instructing him to move under cover of the sand-hills along the sea-shore to the enemy's extreme left; and, having seized the road, to push forward by it and turn the enemy's left flank.

The first Division under Munro would at the same time employ the enemy in front; and should Stuart, succeed in turning the enemy's left the assault in front would be carried into the very heart of the enemy's camp.

Coote had judged correctly; for Haidar had devoted his principal attention to strengthening his front and right, deeming that the sand-hills and the sea on his left would form a natural protection against attack.

Till 10 o'clock the enemy's artillery had kept up a continuous fire which had not been replied to, as Coote was anxious to reserve his ammunition for his assault in front; but now, as he advanced, his guns for the first time opened their fire.

The plain in front was covered with hordes of the enemy's cavalry, who made repeated and desperate charges on the first Division as it slowly advanced in line. After a lapse of a couple of hours intelligence was received by the Commander-in-Chief that the second Division was gaining ground satisfactorily on the enemy's left, and thereupon Coote pushed the first Division forward with all his strength.

General Stuart had marched his division, under cover of the sandhills on his left and the English ships on his right, so that he succeeded in gaining the neck of the road which passed between the sand-hills before his movement was perceived by the enemy.

Haidar Ali now dispatched a strong body of his cavalry under a

---

6. Sir Eyre Coote's dispatch to the Calcutta Council. July 3rd, 1781.

chosen leader to assist his infantry in opposing Stuart's advance. Twice the second Division was hurled back towards the sea-shore returning to the attack with renewed vigour, and the third time its efforts were crowned with success.

Mir Sahib, the able General whom Haidar had chosen to command his cavalry opposed to Stuart, was struck by a round shot from one of our ships, and not only was he killed, but his troops suffered severely from our naval guns. A panic now ensued amongst the enemy, and Stuart, taking advantage of their confusion, threw himself forward with such decision that the left wing of Haidar's army was turned and forced back on his centre and right.

As soon as the English General found that Stuart had succeeded he charged to his front, and although obstinately opposed by the enemy's infantry, their cavalry on each flank, as well as their artillery on the heights above, he succeeded in driving back several battalions of the enemy's infantry, who now sought cover behind their entrenchments. Munro's division, following up their success, captured the entrenchments; and before midnight the two divisions of the British army united, and the enemy were in full flight.

Haidar Ali could not be brought to believe that his strong position had been captured, and he consequently refused to quit his post; until at last, crying aloud that if he only had the strength to lead his troops in person he would yet retrieve the day, he was seized by his attendants who bore him from the field.

The enemy's strong entrenchments at Porto Novo were taken: and the British troops pursued Haidar Ali's broken army until two o'clock the next morning. The enemy's camp, stores, and equipage were also captured, but they succeeded in carrying off their guns and standards.

The loss of the British in the Battle of Porto Novo was 587 killed and wounded; of whom 17 were officers and 50 European rank and file. "The lowest estimate of Haidar Ali's loss was 10,000 men, the dense masses of cavalry and infantry and the immense extent of Irregulars scattered in all directions causing an almost certain effect at every shot."

After the battle Sir Eyre Coote returned thanks to the troops for their gallantry, using the following words in his dispatch—"every individual of this little army seemed to feel the critical situation of our national concerns; our falling interests required uncommon exertions for their support; and to the honour of this array every nerve was exerted to the very extent of possibility."

Two days after the Battle of Porto Novo Sir Eyre Coote moved his army to the north-west, to the relief of Wandiwash, which was again beleaguered by a strong detachment of Haidar's army under Tippoo Sahib, who having failed to take the fortress by storm, retired before the British force, which on the 20th of July encamped on the plain of Wandiwash; Coote immediately reporting to the Government, "Wandiwash is safe, being the third time in my life I have had the honour to relieve it."

After the relief of Wandiwash Coote advanced to Punamalli, where he prepared for an attack on the strong fortress of Tripassore, 30 miles to the west of Madras; a position considered to be the keystone of the adjoining country, in which grain and other supplies could be obtained. The fortress of Tripassore had lately been much strengthened, both in its defences and its garrison, which now numbered 1500 men. The British army encamped before the fortress on the 19th of August, when batteries were erected, and on the 22nd, a practicable breach having been effected, and orders were given to storm, the garrison surrendered at discretion.

Haidar's army having retired from Tripassore, encamped at Pollilore, on the ground rendered memorable by Baillie's defeat—September 10th, 1780—when the British detachment was almost annihilated.

On August 26th Coote arrived at Parambacum; and on the morning of the 27th found the enemy drawn up in front of their encampment at Pollilore.

Coote immediately prepared for action, sending forward his first—Munro's—division, with which was the Bengal European Battalion under Major MacGowan; the second division, under General Stuart, forming at right angles to the leading division. Munro charged the enemy's batteries in front, but a heavy cannonade on both flanks forced Coote to bring up his whole right, and form line on the leading division. It was now seen for the first time that the enemy was strongly entrenched, and the broken ground rendered an advance in line extremely difficult; but as the British approached, Haidar's army withdrew, taking with them their guns and equipage.

The British army immediately occupied the entrenchments, and before night the enemy fell back still further; but this success had not been gained without severe loss; 600 of the English force being either killed or wounded, amongst them the gallant General Stuart, who lost his leg.

A camp was formed at Pollilore with the object of providing cover and provisions during the remainder of the monsoon; but on the 29th August it was found necessary to again change ground, and on the

21st September the small fort of Paloor was captured, containing sufficient grain for a few days' consumption.

The British army now moved rapidly in the direction of Vellore, Haidar barring the road at the pass of Sholingur.[7] The British arrived in front of the enemy's position on the 27th September, the latter opening fire from 70 guns; but the pass, notwithstanding the rocky and broken nature of the ground, was successfully earned at the point of the bayonet. During the action a specially-gallant charge was made by the 1st Division against the enemy's cavalry, who attacked them simultaneously in front and rear; the British rear rank, facing about, forced the cavalry to retire with heavy loss. Again Haidar contrived to retire with his guns; but 3 cavalry standards were captured and 1 gun retaken, our loss being only 100 killed and wounded.

The British army now continued its advance to the relief of Vellore, where our troops in that Garrison were beleaguered, and short of provisions.

Coote personally led a flying brigade, with the flank companies of the Bengal European Regiment, 5 battalions of sepahis, 3 guns, and a squadron of cavalry, to collect supplies for the relief of Vellore; and after a rapid march of 80 miles he surprised a large detachment of the enemy's army, capturing from them their camp, provisions, and baggage.

On the 23rd October the flying brigade encamped near the pass of Veracundalore, where it was unexpectedly attacked in the early morning by nearly the whole of Haidar's army, under his personal command. The brigade, unable to hold its ground in the face of so powerful an army, was forced to retreat, and whilst entering the pass one of the British guns was taken by a strong body of the enemy's horse from a battalion of sepahis under Colonel Walker, the attached sepahis being routed. "The flank companies of the Bengal European Regiment under Captain Moore, at this critical moment wheeled back to enable the flying sepoys to pass to the rear, and after pouring in a volley on the enemy, who were dragging off the captured gun in triumph, rushed forward, recovered the gun, and drove the Mysorean Horse and foot back at the point of the bayonet with great slaughter. In the meantime Walker's battalion had rallied in the rear, and advancing boldly to the support of the Europeans the entry to the pass "[8]

---

7. The decoration Sholingur was worn on the colours of the Madras European Regiment.
8. Historic Records, Madras European Regiment.

During this action the English detachment lost 317 men; but the enemy admitted a loss of upwards of 3000.

The following order was issued by Sir Eyre Coote immediately after the affair:

> The brave and seasonable exertion of the company of Bengal grenadiers, under the command of Captain Moore is worthy of the highest applause and should be ever held in remembrance as a proof of the merit of the Company in particular and honourable to the corps they belong to.

Although this affair at Veracundalore deprived the flying brigade of its camp and baggage, it had the effect of causing Haidar Ali to raise the siege of Vellore just as its garrison was reduced to one day's supply. On the 3rd of November Coote, having collected a supply of grain to relieve the distress of the garrison, advanced by rapid marches on Vellore, but on his approach Haidar's beleaguering army struck camp and retired across the river, when the much-needed provisions were safely delivered to the starving garrison.

Next day Coote, having relieved Vellore, commenced his march towards Madras, but, as he was crossing a morass, he was attacked by Haidar's army, one column pressing on his rear, and one in front. The advanced-guard of our army, composed of the Grenadiers of H.M. 73rd and the Bengal and Madras Europeans, charged the enemy in front, and then afforded cover to the main body of our troops, who, extricating themselves from the swamp, formed up on firm ground, and drove the enemy before them, on whom they inflicted considerable loss, darkness alone preventing us from following up our success.

In March, 1782, a French fleet arrived off Pondicherry with 3000 French soldiers; these troops, disembarking al Porto Novo, marched, under M. de Bussy, to Cuddalore, at this time garrisoned by a small body of our sepahis, who surrendered to the French. A junction was now formed between the French and Haidar Ali's forces, who held a strong position covering Pondicherry. Supplies for the united Armies of the enemy being obtained from the Arnee district, Sir Eyre Coote made a rapid advance towards the fortress of that name, arriving under its walls on June 1st; and on the following day Haidar's whole army suddenly appeared, having made a forced march of 43 miles. A battle ensued, during which the Grenadiers of H.M. 73rd and the Bengal and Madras Europeans, engaged Lally's French corps, capturing from them one gun and eleven tumbrils. The enemy was repulsed with considerable loss, and Sir Eyre Coote, the next day, issued the following General Order:

> The Commander-in-Chief returns his most sincere thanks to the army for their animated and steady conduct yesterday. Such was the eminently spirited behaviour of the whole, that he has it not in his power to point out the superior merit of any one corps.

The war against Haidar Ali was now continued with varying success. The enemy's Irregular cavalry had so scoured the country that all the crops were destroyed and the villages burnt: our troops being unable, in consequence, to produce proper provisions, or even the bare necessaries of life. The state of the Madras presidency in 1782-83 is described by an eye-witness as having been appalling. The country bereft of the control of the British, lawless marauders carrying on their depredations without check, the finances at the lowest ebb, and the pay of the Madras army many months in arrears—all were waiting for money and supplies from Bengal; whilst a terrible famine made dreadful havoc amongst the people, depopulating a large part of the Carnatic. The streets of Madras were covered with starved "wretches, many of whom were dead, and others were dying; the vultures, the pariah dogs, jackals, and crows often seen eating the bodies before life was extinct."

About this time a fleet arrived from Bengal, laden with grain, so urgently required by the starving inhabitants; but it was, unfortunately, wrecked on the Madras coast, the ships being caught at night in a monsoon gale, and dashed upon the shore. It is estimated that upwards of 10,000 of the inhabitants of the town of Madras perished from starvation.

On the 1st of July Sir Eyre Coote moved to Wandiwash, where he met Haidar Ali; and terms of peace were in course of arrangement, when Haidar suddenly broke off negotiations and withdrew his vakeels—the British army returning to Madras.

Soon afterwards Sir Eyre Coote was forced, by ill-health, to hand over command of the army to General James Stuart—who had resumed his military duties—Coote proceeding to Bengal to arrange with the Governor-General for the means of continuing the war.[9]

---

9. Sir Eyre Coote returned to Madras in 1783, (continued on next page) but the General died two days after landing. His body was conveyed to England and interred on the 14th September, 1784, at the church of Rockburne, in Hampshire. His loss caused unfeigned sorrow to the whole army, especially to the Bengal European Battalion.

During his absence Haidar Ali died; his son, Tippoo Sahib, succeeding to the command of his army, now in full march to the eastward.

During the early part of 1783 the British army, under Stuart, marched towards Wandiwash, and offered battle to Tippoo's army, but they refused to fight, when the following General Order was published to the army:

> It is supposed that the enemy, who would not stand to fight, will endeavour in a cowardly manner to annoy the army in the next march; perhaps they may throw some distant cannon-shot and rockets as usual. The General will give five pagodahs for every rocket-boy taken by the flanking parties.

On the 21st April Stuart commenced his march towards Cuddalore, opposite which—June 4th—he took up a strong position—his right resting on the sea and his left on the adjoining hills. A few days afterwards the Marquis de Bussy took up position to the south, facing the British.

The French army consisted of 3000 European infantry, 3500 caffres and sepahis, with 2000 cavalry and 3000 infantry of Tippoo's army.

The English army had 1660 Europeans, 8000 sepahis, and 1000 native cavalry.

The first assault on the enemy's position was delivered on the 12th June, on which occasion a strong detachment of our army was sent to drive the French from a fortified hill commanding our left flank; and if this attack should succeed, its commander was to hoist a black flag, on seeing which Colonel (afterwards Lord) Cathcart with a battalion formed of the grenadier companies of all the European infantry regiments[10] was to advance and carry the grand battery held by the French. The advanced party succeeded and the flag was shown; when the grenadier battalion advanced, but the ditch was found to be full of water and strongly stockaded, so that it was impossible to carry the battery, and the grenadiers were repulsed with heavy loss. General Stuart now ordered them to attempt to turn the enemy's flank by getting to the rear of the French entrenchments; but the whole ground being laid under water, they, after wading some hours through the mud, were ultimately driven back under a severe artillery fire

Maddened with their repeated failures the grenadiers, having been joined by the line battalions, made a desperate charge, gained

---

10. H.M. 73rd, 78th, 101st, Hanoverian Corps, Bengal and Madras European Battalions.

the enemy's ramparts, and swept along the entire front; but the British troops, unable to hold all the ground which they had captured, were forced back on the French grand battery, which they retained—this battery commanding the whole range of the French works. The battle had now lasted all day, and towards evening both sides lay on their arms, prepared to renew the fight on the next morning. The enemy, however, retired during the night, seeking the protection of the walls of Cuddalore, and leaving in our hands 17 guns and 50 prisoners. Our loss during the day was 1030 men, almost every officer of the leading division being either killed or wounded: and it is estimated that the French loss was fully equal to that of the British.

On the 14th June a French squadron arrived on the coast, and Admiral Hughes with 17 British ships dropped down to prevent the French from landing reinforcements; but a squall coming on, the Squadrons were separated, and on the 20th the French Admiral succeeded in landing 1700, and on the 24th 2400, French soldiers from the Fleet.

During the night of the 25th June the French, reinforced, June 25th made a determined sortie on the English position, their whole force advancing on our trenches; but they were repulsed with heavy loss, Colonel Damas and 100 French soldiers being made prisoners.[11]

But provisions were scarce, and there was no food for the cattle, the army being in consequence unable to change its ground, or move its heavy guns. Everything wore a gloomy aspect when, to the joy of all, a flag of truce was unexpectedly raised by the enemy, who announced that a French ship had just arrived bringing the welcome news that peace between Great Britain and France had been concluded; so that the war against the French was at an end.

Against Tippoo Sahib the war languished, and ultimately he sued for peace, which was obtained on the sacrifice of half the dominions which Haidar Ali had gained, and a payment of upwards of £3,000,000 sterling.

In 1784 the 1st Bengal European Battalion returned to its own presidency, having left more than half its Officers and men in graves on the many battle-fields where it had been engaged during the four years it had served in the Carnatic War.

The Regiment on its return to Bengal was quartered at Ghyretty, where on the 25th January, 1785, it was inspected by the Governor-

---

11. Amongst the prisoners taken on this occasion was a young French Sergeant named Bernadotte, who afterwards became a Marshal of France, and ultimately swayed the sceptre of Sweden, where his descendants still reign.

General, Mr. Warren Hastings, who spoke feelingly of the "small remains" returned from the war, and he expressed his mixed sentiments of gratitude for their valuable services and regret for their heavy losses. In a General Order of that same date His Excellency affirms that to "the aid rendered by the Bengal troops, the Company's possessions and interests under the presidency of Fort St. George owe their present existence."

Gold, silver, and bronze medals[12] were granted to all the officers and men who served during the Carnatic war; and the pay of all the non-commissioned officers and men was, as a special mark of appreciation of their services, permanently raised two rupees a day.

GENERAL REFERENCES—CHAPTER 11

Malleson's Decisive Battles of India.
Historical Records, Madras European Regiment.
East India Military Calendar.
Wilks's Sketches of the South of India.
Proceedings of the Bengal Council.
Broome's Rise and Progress of the Bengal Army.
Williams's Bengal Infantry.
Army Dispatches. &c, &c.

---

12. The late Colonel R. S. Wilson gives the following description of the medal granted under the orders of the Governor-General in Council—22nd January, 1785—for service during the Carnatic War. On one side is an inscription in Persian of which the following is a translation:
The courage and exertions of those valiant men by whom the name of Englishmen has been celebrated and exalted from Hindustan to the Deccan, having been established throughout the world, this has been granted by the Government of Calcutta in commemoration of the excellent services of the brave. In the year of the Hegira 1199; year of Christ 1784.
On the obverse, the figure of Britannia seated apparently on military trophies and extending her right hand holding a wreath of laurel towards a fort on which the British Colours are flying.

CHAPTER 12

The Second Maratha War

In the year 1794, whilst the Commander-in-Chief, Sir Robert Abercrombie, K.C.B.—who in the previous year had succeeded Lord Cornwallis in the command of the Bengal army—was on his tour of inspection, disturbances occurred in Rohilkund which rendered necessary the interference of the Calcutta Council, who instructed Sir Robert Abercrombie to prepare for action.

It will be remembered that at the conclusion of the first Rohilla War in 1774 the British troops, under Colonel Champion, were withdrawn from before the fort of Patirghur, which had been successfully defended against the united forces of the Company and the King of Oude, by Fyzulla Khan, who forced Shuja u'd daulah to conclude a treaty with him, under the provisions of which Fyzulla Khan obtained the valuable district of Rampore with an income of £40,000 per annum, and gained his independence.

Thus the first Rohilla War came to an end; and for ten years the territory of Rampore was governed with so much judgement and "paternal solicitude that the inhabitants led a life of peace, prosperity, and security to which they had previously been but little accustomed."

In 1793 the Nawab Fyzulla Khan died; when a dispute arose amongst his children as to which should succeed to the Zamindary. The rivals raised large armies, and the fertile country of Rampore, which had prospered under years of good rule, was disorganized and laid waste.

The King of Oude, Asoff u'd daulah, under his treaty with the British, called for their co-operation and assistance; for although the district of Rampore under its late ruler had maintained its independence of Oude, the present disturbed state of the country called for the interference of its legitimate suzerain.

Sir Robert Abercrombie, fortunately near at hand on his tour of inspection, hastily collected a force of about 10,000 men, amongst which was the 2nd Bengal European Regiment; and at the head of this army he entered the Rampore district, proceeding in the direction of the city of Bareilly.

When the rival armies in the Rohilla country found that the British Government had undertaken to settle their disputes, they made common cause together. Their different armies were amalgamated, and placed under the command of their most experienced General, Gulam Muhamed, their forces mustering in all 25,000 men, amongst whom were some 4,000 cavalry, second to none in India.

On the 26th of October the rival armies sighted each other near the village of Bœtura[1] on the plains of Rohilkund, not far distant from Kutra, where the celebrated battle against the Rohillas had been fought on St. George's Day, 1774, when the 2nd Bengal European Regiment were engaged.

General Abercrombie, with his staff, in the early morning rode some miles in advance of his army to reconnoitre the enemy's position. He found them already in battle array, and preparing for action. Hastily returning to his headquarters, he changed the arrangement of his army, which he now formed into one line, his reserves being placed on the right.

Notwithstanding the extent of ground covered by the British line it was out-flanked on the right by the enemy, who threatened the 2nd Bengal European Regiment, now under Major John Macdonald,[2] and the two sepahis battalions on its flanks.

The engagement opened with a heavy cannonade from both armies; but the enemy's cavalry, in overpowering numbers, threatened our cavalry brigade, now formed on our extreme right.

Just at this time, from some misunderstanding—which has never been accounted for—the officer commanding our cavalry gave the word "Wheel inwards by quarter ranks;" when, obeying the order, the utmost confusion was occasioned, increased by a determined charge of the enemy's cavalry, who taking advantage of the disorder, attempted to turn the British right flank.

Our cavalry broke headlong amongst the native battalion on the right of the British line, and, penetrating clean through them, poured upon the 2nd Bengal European Regiment.

The officers commanding the infantry regiments had no choice

---

1. Bœtura was subsequently called "Fatehgunj," or the *Town of the War.*
2. Afterwards Lieutenant-General Sir John Macdonald, K.C.B.

other than to protect their men; and treating our cavalry as enemies vigorously defended themselves against this unlooked-for assault. At the same time the enemy's cavalry became intermixed with our own, and such a scene of confusion ensued as has seldom, if ever, been witnessed on any field of battle.[3] The cavalry, British as well as Rohilla, were ultimately beaten off, but not until a great number of the officers and men of the 2nd Bengal European Regiment, as well as of the native battalions, had been killed or wounded.

In the meantime, seeing the confusion which this *contretemps* had occasioned, the enemy made a most gallant and daring charge; "it is utterly impossible it could have been surpassed."

Gulam Muhamed had formed his regiments into a succession of massive wedges, about 50 deep; and thus they moved forwards until they were within 500 yards of the British, when they spread out, vastly out-flanking our line.

The enemy appeared to despise our musketry fire, but upon every discharge of artillery they threw themselves forward on their faces, rising immediately afterwards, and continuing then-advance until they neared the British line; when they made a desperate rush, so that all the troops were completely intermingled. The Rohillas were armed with spears, matchlocks, and tulwars;. the last of which they used so effectually that for many years afterwards the attack of the enemy on this occasion was talked of as "The Highland Charge." It now became a hand-to-hand fight —the bayonet *versus* the tulwar—the Rohillas were experienced swordsmen and the British were taken at a disadvantage by reason of their cavalry having so seriously disturbed the equanimity of the men and created such havoc in their ranks. At length, however, the bayonet prevailed; the Rohillas gradually gave ground and ultimately took to flight, when they were hotly pursued by the British and driven across the Dugura river.

Thus ended the battle of Bœtura: the enemy, having displayed marked bravery, felt the superiority of our disciplined armies, and sued for peace.

The loss on both sides was very great. Lieutenants Jollie and Rob-

---

3. The officer commanding the British cavalry on this occasion, when he discovered the fatal error which he had committed, fled from the field during the action, and succeeded in crossing the Ganges before his absence was discovered. He ultimately effected his escape, entered the French service, and was afterwards employed in the commissariat of Napoleon's army.— *East India Military Calendar,* Vol. 3. p. 300.

ertson of the Bengal European Regiment were only severely wounded; but a monument on the right of the road from Rampore to Bareilly marks where the action of Bœtura was fought, recording the names of fourteen British officers who fell there.

This monument is a large obelisk of red sandstone slabs; it stands in a small, but shady enclosure which is entered by a Roman archway. At its base on the side facing the road is engraved the following inscription:

Erected
By order of the Governor-General in Council,
In Memory of
Colonel George Burrington,
Major Thomas Bolton, Captain Norman Macleod,
Captain John Mambey, Captain John Mordaunt,
Lieutenant Andrew Cummings, Lieutenant Edmund Wells,
Lieutenant John Plumer, Lieutenant Joseph Richardson,
Lieutenant William Hinksman, Lieutenant Y. Q. M. Birch,
Lieutenant William Odell, Lieutenant Edward Baker,
Lieutenant-Fireworker James Telfer,
and the European and native non-commissioned officers
and privates who fell, near this spot
in action against the Rohillas.
October 26th, a.d. 1794

Ahmed Ali, the grandson of Fyzulla Khan, being direct successor, was granted an estate which produced a revenue of £100,000; but the rest of the rich provinces of Rohilkund passed into the possession of the East India Company, and have always since been under the rule of the British.

The following is an extract from General Orders, dated Headquarters, Banks of Bedourah river, 26th October, 1794:

> The Commander-in-Chief has much pleasure in expressing his satisfaction at the good conduct of the officers, and the bravery of the troops in the action of yesterdays against an enemy of such determined courage and of such superior force. The gallantry which the whole line displayed does not leave the Commander-in-Chief room to distinguish any particular corps or individuals, and he only laments the great loss which was experienced in excellent officers and brave soldiers. The Commander-in-Chief requests that the army at large, will ac-

cept his acknowledgements and thanks and to rest satisfied that he shall represent their important services to the Governor-General in Council.

In 1797 the 1st Bengal European Regiment, then under command of Lieutenant-Colonel Edward Clarke, and stationed at Cawnpore, formed part of the force under Sir John Shore which dethroned Vazir Ali and placed Sydaat Ali on the throne of Oude; and the following year, 1798, the Regiment again took the field under Sir J. Craig against Zeeman Shah who had threatened an invasion of our provinces from Lahore.[4]

Since the Bengal European Regiment had been raised by Clive at Fulta in 1756, it had been so frequently remodelled and its constitution altered, that a review of the different changes becomes necessary.

On August 5th, 1765, the Bengal European Regiment was formed into three battalions or Regiments, as they were then called, numbered the 1st, 2nd, and 3rd Bengal European Regiments.

Each Regiment was constituted of the following strength:—

1 Colonel, Commanding the Brigade
1 Lieutenant-Colonel, Commanding the Regiment

1 Major	36 Sergeants
6 Captains	36 Corporals
1 Captain-lieutenant	27 Drummers
9 Lieutenants	630 Privates
18 Ensigns	

and consisted of 9 companies—2 of which were grenadiers. Each company had 1 field-officer or captain, 1 lieutenant, 2 ensigns, 4 sergeants, 4 corporals, 3 drummers, and 70 privates. All the field-officers commanded companies except the colonel commanding the brigade.

The staff of a regiment consisted of:—

1 Adjutant	1 Drill-Sergeant
1 Quartermaster	1 Drum-Major
1 Surgeon	1 Fife-Major
3 Surgeon's Mates	9 Pay-Sergeants
1 Sergeant-Major	9 Camp-Colourmen
1 Quartermaster-Sergeant	

On September 26th, 1779, the following General Order, materially effecting the organization of the European Regiments, was issued:

---

4. East India Calendar.

Resolved, that the 3 regiments of European infantry under this presidency be reformed, and the following establishment and regulations do take place in lieu of those now in force. The European infantry to be formed into 3 regiments, each regiment to be formed into two battalions, and each battalion into 9 companies—

1 of Grenadiers   7 Battalion Companies
1 of Light Infantry

The Grenadier and Light companies each to consist of

1 Captain	4 Corporals
3 Lieutenants	2 Drummers
4 Sergeants	60 Privates

The Battalion companies of—

1 Captain,	3 Corporals
2 Lieutenants	1 Drummer
1 Ensign	1 Fifer
3 Sergeants	50 Privates

The staff of each battalion to be as follows—

1 Adjutant	1 Surgeon
1 Quartermaster	2 Assistant-Surgeons

The battalions numbered 550 rank and file and the total strength of the Company's European infantry in Bengal was 3,300

On the 26th December, 1780, it was ordered that:

The three regiments of Europeans be formed immediately each into one battalion, consisting of 10 companies, viz., 1 grenadier, 1 light infantry, and 8 battalion companies, to be composed as follows:

1 Grenadier Company to consist of	1 Captain	5 Corporals
	3 Lieutenants	2 Drummers
	5 Sergeants	2 Fifers
		80 Privates

1 Light Infantry Company to be of the same strength

1 Battalion Company to consist of	1 Captain	4 Corporals
	1 Lieutenant	1 Drummer
	2 Ensigns	1 Fifer
	4 Sergeants,	70 Privates

And in January, 1781, the two battalions of the 2nd and 3rd European Regiments were doubled up, but the 1st Bengal European

Regiment temporarily retained its two battalions; the 1st Battalion, then quartered at Fort William, was formed into five companies; and the 2nd Battalion, on service in the Carnatic under Sir Eyre Coote, formed the remaining five companies of the Regiment.

During the early part of 1785 the composition of the European Regiments was completely changed. The word *Battalion* was substituted for *Regiment*, and the Bengal European infantry was formed into six battalions, called 1st European Battalion, 2nd European Battalion, &c.

On May 4th, 1796, the following General Order was issued:—

The battalions on the present establishment to be formed into 3 Regiments of 10 companies each—the 1st and 5th Battalions to form the 1st Regiment—the 2nd and 6th the 2nd Regiment—the 3rd and 4th the 3rd Regiment. The Regiments to consist of 1 Grenadier, 1 Light and 8 Battalion Companies.

In 1797 it became the custom to call all Regiments after their commanding officer, a usage prevailing in the Irregular cavalry to the present day.

The 1st Bengal European Regiment was at this time commanded by Lieutenant-Colonel Edward Clarke, and was therefore called Clarke's Regiment, or *Clark ka Gora*, under which name it was entered in the army list and known by the natives in India whilst the rule of the East India Company lasted.

During this decade many General Orders were issued assimilating the dress of the European troops in the East India Company's service to that of the Royal army; round hat, white linen waistcoats and breeches, cocked hats and pigtails, being strictly enjoined in conformity with the dress worn by the British troops at home.

In 1798 the non-commissioned officers and men of the 3rd European Regiment were drafted into the 1st and 2nd, which were each ordered to be made up to the following strength—

1 Colonel	10 Ensigns
2 Lieutenant-Colonels	48 Sergeants
2 Majors	60 Corporals
7 Captains	26 Drummers and Fifers
1 Captain-Lieutenant	1140 Privates
25 Lieutenants	

In 1803[5] the 2nd European Regiment was reduced; its officers being transferred to the newly-formed "Marine Battalion," and its non-

---
5. East India Register.

[From the Official Directory, 1796.]

FIRST BENGAL EUROPEAN REGIMENT,
Stationed at CAWNPORE.

RANK.	NAMES.	RANK.	NAMES.
Colonel	—	Lieutenant	John Anderson.
Lieut.-Colonel	Edward Clarke.	,,	William Prior.
,,	James M. Vibert.	,,	L. B. Morris.
Major	Richard Grueber.	,,	Gregory Hickman.
,,	John Hilliard.	,,	T. H. Welsh.
Captain	John Gillanders.	,,	William Richards.
,,	Richard Walker.	,,	William M. Watson.
,,	George Hardyman.	,,	John Morse.
,,	John Darby.	,,	Thomas Whittaker.
,,	James Collins.	,,	John Sheepland.
,,	George Ball.	Ensign	C. Baldock.
,,	James Lawtie.	,,	James Dalrymple.
Captain-Lieut.	Peter Burrows.	,,	E. P. Wilson.
Lieutenant	Benjamin Cuthbert.	,,	John Robertson.
,,	Thomas Long.	,,	Edward Clarke.
,,	Alexander Morrison.	,,	Edward Cartwright.
,,	James Hodgson.	,,	C. M. Roberts.
,,	Thomas Hickman.	,,	George Maxwell.
,,	B. L. Grenier.	,,	—
,,	D. V. Kevin.	Surgeon	Thomas Phillips.
,,	John Leslie.	Asst.-Surgeon	—
,,	Edward Allison.	,,	—
,,	Joseph Fletcher.	Adjutant	Lieut. G. Hickman.
,,	John Carig.	Quartermaster	Lieut. A. Morrison.

Facings, Buff.   Lace, Silver.

SECOND REGIMENT EUROPEAN INFANTRY,

Stationed at FORT WILLIAM.

RANK.	NAMES.	RANK.	NAMES.
Colonel	Edward Rawstorne.	Lieutenant	Charles Greig.
Lieut.-Colonel	R. E. Roberts.	,,	John Gillespie.
,,	George Mence.	,,	S. Denny.
Major	Henry Vincent.	,,	Edward Parry.
,,	Thomas Edwards.	,,	M. Macnamara.
Captain	W. Kirkpatrick.	,,	Andrew Fraser.
,,	J. Hutchinson.	,,	W. E. Leadbeater.
,,	John Wood.	,,	J. Carruthers.
,,	Joseph Channing.	,,	Anthony Greene.
,,	W. B. Davies.	,,	W. H. Hough.
,,	A. Grant.	,,	John Slessor.
,,	Robert Haldane.	,,	Robert Swinton.
Captain-Lieut.	Joseph Wade.	Ensign	C. Simson.
Lieutenant	A. Davis.	,,	T. Wilson.
,,	C. Gladwin.	,,	T. S. Knox.
,,	G. Robinson.	Surgeon	Adam Freer.
,,	T. Whinyates.	Asst.-Surgeon	James Robertson.
,,	J. O. Rock.	Adjutant	Lieut. M. Macnamara
,,	John Barrow.	Quartermaster	Lieut. Leadbeater.
,,	P. Baldwin.		

Facings, White.   Lace, Silver.

THIRD REGIMENT EUROPEAN INFANTRY,
Stationed at BERHAMPORE.

RANK.	NAMES.	RANK.	NAMES.
Colonel	Edward Ellerker.	Lieutenant	Ulysses Brown.
Lieut.-Colonel	Thomas Nicholls.	,,	Patrick Scott.
,,	W. Duncan.	,,	Thomas Cowley.
Major	E. Sandford.	,,	John Barnes.
,,	Sir Jno. Murray, Bt.	,,	John McGrath.
Captain	William Scott.	,,	A. Saumarez.
,,	Peter Murray.	,,	D. Robinson.
,,	Thomas Clayton.	,,	J. P. Auberry.
,,	John Clarkson.	,,	J. W. Pleydell.
,,	William Preston.	,,	H. Griffiths.
,,	Richard Forbes.	Ensign	Francis Shaw.
,,	T. G. Williamson.	,,	Samuel Bate.
Captain-Lieut.	John Arnold.	,,	Hastings Dare.
Lieutenant	John Mouggah.	,,	C. Darke.
,,	James Radcliffe.	,,	William Casement.
,,	D. T. Richardson.	,,	Thomas Lowry.
,,	Hiram Cox.	,,	C. L. Showers.
,,	T. Shuldham.	,,	W. W. Kitchin.
,,	John Towers.	Surgeon	Thomas Bainbridge.
,,	S. W. Nangrave.	Asst.-Surgeon	—
,,	H. R. Patton.	,,	—
,,	John Ashworth.	Adjutant	Lieut. D. Robinson.
,,	J. O'Halloran.	Quartermaster	Lieut. S. W. Nangrave
,,	P. Tolfrey.		

Facings, Yellow.   Lace, Silver.

commissioned officers and men being incorporated with the 1st European Regiment or the artillery; thus, in 1803, the Bengal European Regiment returned to its original formation and name.

During the early part of 1803 the Marquis Wellesley, Governor-General, turned his attention to permanently destroying the power of the French and their allies the Marathas in Central India.

General Lake, the Commander-in-Chief, received instructions from the Governor-General in Council to undertake the subjugation of a powerful force—French and Asiatic—with which Scindia had obtained possession of the fortress of Agra and the fortified city of Delhie—the capital of Hindustan—where our ally, Shah Alám, the Emperor, was held prisoner.

These hostile troops had been originally organised by a Savoyard Officer named De Boigne, and after his withdrawal a Frenchman, M. Perron, succeeded to the command.

M. Perron had not only obtained considerable influence with Scindia, but had been rewarded for his services with a large-territory on the banks of the Jumna, where he sought to establish an Indo-French state on our most vulnerable frontier. It was under these circumstances that Marquis Wellesley instructed General Lake to undertake "the effectual demolition of the French state erected by M. Perron on the banks of the Jumna as the primary object of the campaign."

There was a second and not less important object to be attained by General Lake. Marquis Wellesley felt the time had arrived for firmly establishing a permanent peace throughout the central provinces of India; and this object could only be attained by reducing the iniquitous rule of the Marathas, and with a strong hand giving to the people of India the blessings of security of property, hitherto almost unknown.

General Lake advanced from Cawnpore at the head of a powerful army; and on the 29th August entered the territory, reducing on the 4th September the strong fortress of Alighur.

Leaving a detachment at this fortress, Lake pushed on to Delhie, meeting on the way a messenger from M. Perron, announcing that he had retired from the Maratha service; and soliciting a safe passage for himself and family through the Company's territories to Lucknow.

This request was granted and Lake pushed on to Delhie, which he reached on September 9th, and on the 11th fought the celebrated battle of Delhie, ending in the complete defeat of the French and Maratha armies, who suffered heavy loss.

Three days after the battle the whole of the French officers surrendered as prisoners; and on the 13th September the British army marched into the city of Delhie, releasing the blind Emperor Shah Alám from his prison and placing him on the throne of his ancestors.

General Lake proceeded, in command of a strong force, in pursuit of Holkar's army. Agra was reduced—18th October—176 guns and a vast amount of treasure being captured. The battle of Laswarie was fought on 1st November, and the Maratha army completely routed, with the loss of its guns, camp, and treasure.

On the 8th of November the commander-in-chief's army returned to Agra, and on the 30th the following reinforcement joined headquarters—the flank companies of the Bengal European Regiment, under Captain Thomas Waguelen, and the flank companies of three other British Regiments; the whole being formed into what was known as "The Flank Battalion" and placed under command of Major McLeod.

The "Flank Battalion" formed part of a column under Colonel H. White[6] sent by the commander-in-chief on December 21st to reduce the Fort of Gwalior, defended by a powerful Maratha army.

This fortress was known as the Gibraltar of the East; as from its natural strength it was held by the native powers to be impregnable.

Colonel White, feeling that if he could succeed in capturing Gwalior all subordinate forts would speedily surrender, determined to concentrate his whole strength on this his first point of attack.

From spies it was ascertained that the enemy defending the fortress believed that, should the British attempt to enter the town of Gwalior, the guns from the upper fortifications overhanging the lower works would render the assault of no avail. This was also the opinion of the commander-in-chief, who had instructed Colonel White to commence operations by securing the upper works of the fortress, and thus make his way down to the town, which, deprived of its covering batteries, must succumb; but Colonel White, having previously made several successful sieges against hill forts, elected to act on his own responsibility, and to make a night assault on the town before securing the fortress above.

The main fortifications, which surround the citadel, stand on a very steep hill, about a mile-and-a-half in length by about 300 yards across in the broadest part; and its greatest height towards the north is about 350 feet.

---

6. Colonel H. White had commanded the 2nd battalion of the Bengal European Regiment in 1801.

The night assault on the town was made on the 3rd of February, the walls were scaled, and a firm hold of the town obtained. Colonel White immediately reported his success to the commander-in-chief, and asked for reinforcements, which were immediately dispatched. White in the meantime had erected breaching batteries within the town, and a practicable breach in the upper fortifications was effected; but before the main assault was made the fortress surrendered, and was occupied by our troops on the 4th February.

White's surmise that all the smaller strongholds would now surrender was fully justified; for the important Forts, Gohud and Doudpore, soon tendering their submission, the Maratha army retreated from every part of the conquered provinces.

The following copy of a General Order, issued on the 10th of February, 1804, will prove how fully the commander-in-chief appreciated these important services:

> The Commander-in-Chief has great satisfaction in publishing his high sense of the distinguished services of the detachment employed in the reduction of the fortress of Gwalior, under Lieutenant-Colonel White, throughout the whole of this arduous and important service, which claims his Excellency's best thanks and warmest approbation. The Commander-in-Chief derives great pleasure from Lieutenant-Colonel White's report of the spirited and meritorious conduct of Major McLeod and the whole of the officers and men under his command. His Excellency desires Lieutenant-Colonel White to signify to Major McLeod and officers and men of the European flank companies, his Excellency's cordial thanks and approbation of the spirit and zeal which they manifested on the occasion, and of the cheerfulness and alacrity with which they submitted to severe labour and fatigue.

BATTLE OF DEIG

During the early months of 1804 several actions were fought by the British troops against Scindia and his allies.

In October a field-force, consisting of H.M. 76th Regiment the Bengal European Regiment—under Lieutenant-Colonel Burnet—together with 6 native battalions and some Irregular horse, under command of Major-General Fraser, marched to subdue the strong fortress of Deig, defended by Holkar's powerful army.

On the 12th of November General Fraser's force encamped at the

DEIG.

Sketch plan of the Battle of Deig fought on 13th November 1804 and of the Capture of Deig on December 24th 1804.

- British Infy
- Enemy's Infy
- British Cavalry
- Enemy's Cavalry

A Shah Bourj
B Gopalghur
C British Camp Novr 1804
D Deep Morass
E Artificial Tank
F The Citadel
G Fortified Village
H Mound occupied by Enemy's Infy & Guns
I Grove occupied Decr 15th
J British position during the Seige
K Enemy's counter battery
L British batteries erected Decr 20th
M British battery erected Decr 22nd

village of Goverdown, C, about a mile-and-a-half from the fortress of Deig, and separated from it by a deep, un-fordable morass.

Early on the morning of the 13th it was seen that the enemy in strong force was preparing for action, having selected a position between the morass, D, and a large deep artificial tank, E.

The enemy's cavalry was drawn up in two large compact divisions to the south of the tank, evidently intending to take the British in flank and rear should an attempt be made to advance round the morass. General Eraser now pushed forward his Irregular horse, with four light guns, to watch and keep in check the enemy's cavalry, whilst he brought his infantry round the southern end of the morass, D; when emerging on the plain to the south of the fort, he found himself confronted by large masses of the enemy's artillery and infantry, opposing his advance.

Behind and under cover of a village, G, Fraser placed his infantry in two lines, one immediately in rear of the other, H.M. 76th occupying the centre of the first line, with a sepahis battalion on each flank, and the Bengal European Regiment the centre of the second line, also supported by a sepahis battalion in the same manner.

The action commenced with a heavy cannonade from the enemy, their field-guns being ranged in lines immediately in front of their infantry divisions.

It was now found that the village, G, in front of our two infantry lines was strongly held by the enemy; whose infantry, concealed amongst the loop-holed houses, were causing us much annoyance. H.M. 76th with the Sepahi Battalions in our front line advanced, and soon succeeded in driving the enemy from their cover on to their main army on the plain beyond. The Bengal European battalion having joined the 76th made a gallant charge on the enemy's artillery, which had been supporting their infantry in the village, G, and was at this time pouring its grape-shot and shell on our advancing troops.

To our right at the head of the morass, D, and under cover of a mound, H, a large body of the hostile troops had taken their position, intending to attack our right flank, whilst their cavalry at the head of the tank would attack our left.

Two sepahis battalions with four guns were sent to keep the enemy occupying the head of the morass in check whilst the Bengal European Regiment and H.M. 76th attacked the enemy's leading batteries, which they carried, capturing their guns, and driving their supporting Infantry back on their second line.

General Fraser now advanced, and, reforming his infantry, headed a charge on the enemy's second line of guns and Infantry; but our troops had only advanced a few paces when he was struck by a round shot which carried off his right leg. Our army was thus at this critical moment deprived of the example and skill of this distinguished General, in whom his soldiers placed such well-deserved confidence.[7] Colonel Monson now assumed command of the army.

The second line of the enemy's guns was also captured after a severe fight; their Infantry being driven from line to line for a distance of nearly two miles under the walls of their fortress behind which they took refuge.

Our infantry now having no enemy within its grasp, and being severely handled by the heavy guns on the walls of the fortress, retired to support our sepahi battalions employed in keeping the enemy in check at the head of the morass, D, and support was sorely needed; for it was seen that a squadron of the enemy's horse, having escaped the vigilance of our Irregular cavalry, had recaptured, the first range of the enemy's guns taken by the 76th and the Bengal European Regiment during their advance from the village, G.

The British Regiments now took the guns a second time, driving the cavalry back on their base; but this success was not achieved without loss; the gallant British commander being cut down as he headed the charge.

The Bengal European Regiment now arrived to the succour of our sepahi battalions at the head of the morass, who had gallantly maintained their position, keeping in check vastly superior numbers of the enemy who brought their 12- and 18-pounders against our light field-guns.

On the arrival of the British reinforcements the sepahis, hard pressed by the enemy, re-formed, and with the aid of their European comrades charged forward, capturing the mound, H, and driving the enemy into the morass, D, with such precipitancy that his guns were abandoned, and secured by our victorious troops. Great numbers of the enemy, including two of the leading generals of Holkar's army, perished in the morass, the remnant seeking cover in the fortress.

Our third Brigade, which had been left in camp to protect our equipage and baggage, seeing that the enemy were retiring within the walls of their fortress, had marched round the morass and now joined our troops in the field; and our Irregular cavalry also, having been relieved

---

7. General Fraser survived only a few days, he dying in the British camp before Deig.

from their duty of keeping the enemy's horse in check, joined our infantry, assisting them in clearing the field and villages of stragglers, and collecting the captured guns, which were sent under escort to our camp. Our army now bivouacked on the field of battle, strong pickets being placed on the several mounds on the plain to the south of the fortress.

Although the battle of Deig lasted but a few hours, the loss of the enemy is stated to have been 2000 killed, including those drowned in the morass. Eighty-seven guns were captured by the British, as well as a large amount of ammunition found in tumbrils abandoned on the field.

Considering the numbers of the small British force our loss was great, 651 officers and men being killed or wounded; amongst the latter the following Officers of the Bengal European Regiment, Lieutenants A. Maxton, J. Chatfield, T. Bryant and T. Merriman.

In giving an account of the battle of Deig, Thorn, in his *Memoir of Lord Lake's Campaigns in India*, remarks:

> The conduct of the First European Regiment under Lieutenant-Colonel Burnet was in every way worthy of British troops. Their example had the happiest effect and was emulated by all the native troops.

GUZERAT

The decoration, *Guzerat*, was in 1830 placed on the colours of the Bengal European Regiment as a reward for its services in the province of Guzerat—Bombay Presidency—in 1803-4; but neither history, the General Orders, nor the records show that the Regiment took any part in that campaign.[8]

SIEGE OF THE FORTRESS OF DEIG

During the last days of November and the early part of December the British were encamped on the plain to the south of the fortress of Deig, until the camp was moved to the west, J, in close proximity to the fortress.

On the 1st December General Lake, having received the orders of the supreme Government to reduce the fortresses within the Burtpore territory, moved his headquarters towards Deig; instructions having been sent to Colonel Don to march from Agra with a battering-train and a large convoy of stores, and join the British camp before Deig with all practicable speed. On the 15th December General Lake,

---

8. See Appendix A, Decorations.

having assumed command of the British force before Deig, and Colonel Don having arrived with the heavy siege-train, preparations were made for the attack; Colonel Don, with his division, taking possession of a grove of trees, I, in front of our camp, J, which had been chosen as a position from which to commence our approaches.

Our pioneers worked with such industry that a trench 300 yards long, with batteries at intervals, had been completed before sunrise on the 16th; and on the 17th the foremost breaching-battery, within 750 yards of the main or King's Redoubt, A (*Shah-bourj*) was in a forward state; this redoubt being considered the most assailable point.

South of the *Shah-bourj*, and at a distance of about half-a-mile, was a mud fort, B, of considerable strength, called Gopal Ghur, which was occupied by the enemy's matchlock-men, causing considerable annoyance and injury to our working parties.

Our advanced battery mounted six 18-pounders and four 12-pounders; but although a constant fire had been poured on the *Shah-bourj* for several days only a slight impression had been made, and the breaches effected during the day were usually repaired by the enemy during the night.

Another battery, L, now erected nearer to the redoubt, was completed during the night of the 20th, when three of our 18-pounders opened an enfilading fire on the *Shah-bourj*.

The enemy in the meantime had erected counter-batteries, K, judiciously placed under close cover of some rising ground near the walls of the fortress; a position which could not be reached by our guns.

A cross fire from the enemy's batteries, K, necessitated our erecting additional earthworks on the plain, M, from which our-guns soon told with effect.

On the 23rd December a practicable breach had been effected in the *Shah-bourj* redoubt, A, and the commander-in-chief ordered an attack at half-past 11 o'clock on that night.

Three columns were ordered to be formed. The centre or main storming-party, under Lieutenant Colonel Macrae, consisted of the flank companies of the Bengal European Regiment, H.M. 22nd and 76th, with one complete battalion of sepahis. The right supporting column, under Captain Kelly, was formed of 4 battalion companies of the Bengal European Regiment and 5 companies of sepahis. This column was ordered to storm the enemy's outworks to the north and west of the *Shah-bourj*, and, having carried them, to follow the main storming-party through the breach.

The left column, composed of 4 battalion companies of the Bengal European Regiment and 5 companies of sepahis, commanded by Major Radcliffe, was ordered to assault the enemy's outworks to the south and east, and, having carried them, to follow the centre storming-party.

The remainder of the British force formed a reserve, and was stationed on the plain.

The three columns, in position before midnight, advanced simultaneously soon afterwards.

The centre of Macrae's column found the plain under the breach so covered with the *débris* of the broken walls that their progress in the darkness was seriously impeded, their movements also being hampered by the continued random fire from the batteries above and all around them. The right or Kelly's and the left or Radcliffe's columns, diverging, first came into action, springing into the enemy's outworks which they soon succeeded in capturing, forcing the enemy to seek cover within the fortress, and securing the guns, which they spiked.

In the meantime Macrae's column having with great difficulty crossed the plain formed up for the attack under cover of the walls of the fortress; and the order to storm the breach having been given by Macrae a rush was made up the incline and the leading files, scrambling over the masses of broken masonry, gained the breach, when a desperate fight for its possession ensued. The first few men who forced their way through the breach were sabred by the enemy, but the rest of the column quickly following and favoured by the darkness flocked through the breach, and charging forward carried the southwest bastion of the *Shah-bourj*. The enemy's artillerymen showed great courage and determination, fighting with their tulwars against the bayonets of our soldiers; until at last, overpowered, they lay in mangled heaps around their guns.

Kelly's and Radcliffe's columns now joined Macrae in the captured bastion; and, having re-formed, the main walls of the fortress, south and west, were attacked, most of .the bastions being carried at the point of the bayonet.

The British columns now formed up inside the walls and steadily advanced towards the Citadel; but under cover of the darkness some of Holkar's troops got round the British line, making a bold attempt to recapture their guns and turn them round on their enemy; but fortunately just at this time the clouds broke and the moon shone out with great brilliancy, enabling the British line to return to the captured bastions, which were a second time wrenched from the

THE BENGAL EUROPEAN REGIMENT.
"CLARK KA GORA."

RANK.	NAMES.	Rank in the Regiment.	Rank in the Army.	REMARKS.
Colonel	Robt. Rayne	8 Jan., '01	...	On Furlo.
Lieut-Colonel	William Scott	21 April, '00	1 June, '98	
Major	Law Rawstone	10 Aug., '01		
,,	George Wilton	...	...	Invalid, Tannah Establishment.
Captain	J. Cunningham	29 May, '00	7 Jan., '96	
,,	Samuel Kelly	do.	do.	
,,	T. H. Waguelen	10 Aug., '01	do.	
,,	W. G. Palmer	22 Aug., '01	do.	
,,	George Downie	22 Oct., '01	do.	
,,	Peter Littlejohn	...	8 Jan., '98	
,,	John Anderson	...	do.	
Captain-Lieut.	Thos. Ramsay	...	Captn., do.	
Lieutenant	H. Blankenhagen	23 April, '97		
,,	T. D. Broughton	30 Oct. ...		
,,	James Smith	9 Aug., '98		
,,	Geo. Hammond	—		
,,	John Stewart	28 Oct., '99		
,,	George Moore	do.		
,,	Anth. Maxtone	do.		
,,	John Chatfield	do.		
,,	Edm. Morris	do.		
,,	John R. Smith	8 Feb., '00		
,,	Wm. Hy. Wood	29 May ...		
,,	Jem Bryant	do.		
,,	Alex. Hamilton	do.		
,,	Richd. Higgott	4 Sept.	...	Ramghur Battn.
,,	James Merriman	13 Jan., '01		
,,	William Home	10 Aug. ...		
,,	Edm. B. Higgins	8 April, '02		
,,	James Auroil	22 Oct. ...		
,,	Foster Walker			
,,	Saml. Corbett			
,,	Alex. Brown			
Ensign	Thomas Watson	10 Aug., '02	...	Doing duty.
,,	Chance	...	...	Joined immediately after publication.
Adjutant	Thomas Ramsay.			
Quarter master	John Chatfield.			
Surgeon	John Lamb.			
Assist.- Surgeon	—			

grasp of the enemy, and the guns spiked. The reserve was now employed in removing from the enemy's outworks and the *Shah-bourj* the captured guns, which were placed in safety on the plain outside; whilst the storming-Columns again advanced towards the gates of the citadel; which they were preparing to assault, when it was found that, under the apprehension of capture, Holkar's troops had been escaping from the fortress by the outer gates on the north and east, and having gained the open country were hurrying off in the direction of Bhurtpore.

When day broke on the morning of the 24th of December, 1804, the British were in full possession of the town and fortress of Deig.

Our loss amounted to 43 killed and 184 wounded: amongst the latter being Lieutenant Merriman of the Bengal European Regiment, who, although wounded in the action of the 13th November, was in command of a company during this siege, and was thus again placed *hors de combat*.

The British captured 100 guns, large quantities of ammunition and grain, and £20,000 in specie.

The fortress of Deig, now garrisoned by our troops, was repaired, the guns remounted, and the fortifications and outworks improved and strengthened; and on the 28th December General Lake commenced his advance on the fortress of Bhurtpore.

Assault of Bhurtpore

The Raja of Bhurtpore, lately our sworn ally, had been guilty of every kind of double-dealing. After the battle of Delhie a treaty had been arranged between the British and the Raja granting to the latter the possession of territory with the view of confirming him in his supposed attachment to the Company; but notwithstanding the obligations into which he had entered, it was soon discovered that he was carrying on a clandestine correspondence with our enemy Holkar, with the object of arranging an alliance to extinguish the British power in that part of India.

At the battle of Deig the Raja of Bhurtpore had assisted Holkar with his troops; indeed the garrison of that fortress had been composed principally of Bhurtpore troops. From this time all duplicity was abandoned, and the Raja and Holkar were avowedly allies.

Under these circumstances the siege of the fortress of Bhurtpore was a necessity, it being the only means by which the remnant of Holkar's power could be effectually extinguished.

On New Year's Day, 1805, the British army neared Bhurtpore, having been augmented by H.M. 75th Regiment.

> On the 2nd January our camp was pitched within a couple of miles to the west of the fortress. Trenches were at once commenced, to facilitate the construction of which a grove of trees was occupied, about half-way between our camp and the fortress. In front of this grove were two breaching batteries, on one of which six 18-pounders, and on the other four 8-in. and four 5½-in. mortars were placed.[9] These batteries, both completed on January 7th the 7th, constantly threw shells into the town with great effect, causing the enemy to reply from the whole line of their ramparts.

> On the 9th of January, a practical breach having been effected,. an attack was ordered for that night, and three storming-columns were formed; the left consisting of 150 of the Bengal European Regiment under Lieutenant-Colonel Ryan; the right of two companies of H.M. 75th under Major Hawkes; and the centre on main column of the flank companies of the Bengal European Regiment, H.M. 22nd, 75th, and 76th Regiments under Colonel Maitland—about 500 European soldiers; a sepahi battalion accompanying each column.

> The left or Ryan's column had orders to force the main gateway of the fortress, followed by the right or Hawke's column, both to push on to the town in the heart of the fortress, 1805 whilst the main column under Maitland should attack the breach. At 8 p.m. the three columns advanced under a random fire of shot and grape from the fortress and outworks, which, although it was quite dark, did great execution. The ground was much broken by water-courses and ravines, causing the columns to be intermixed, and resulting in great confusion.

> The general had anticipated that the enemy, in the darkness, would be taken by surprise; but, remembering Deig, they were on the alert. The flank companies of the 22nd crossed the wet ditch successfully, although the water in some parts was breast-high, and some of their men, led by Lieutenant Manser, ascended close under the breach; they were, however, unable to complete the ascent without support.

---

9. During the construction of these batteries, Captain-Lieutenant Thomas Ramsay was wounded in the trenches and incapacitated from resuming his duties until the 20th of the following month.

The remainder of the storming-column had become separated in the darkness, and, though heavy firing was heard right and left in the entrenchments below, it was found impossible to attract their attention. The officer commanding the small party at the breach placed two of his officers and some of his men amongst the *débris* underneath, and descended the counterscarp, intending to collect his men below and pilot them to the breach; but he found the columns so intermixed that, although they had succeeded in clearing the outworks of the enemy and taking the guns, he was unable to collect his men.

The left column in the meantime had made its way up to the main gate, capturing the works and guns outside; but they could not follow up the advantage gained, as the ditch in their front was unfordable.

The small party concealed at the breach was soon discovered by the enemy, who attacked them in overwhelming numbers, killing; both the commissioned officers and many of the men; when, no supports arriving, the survivors were forced to retire. Colonel Maitland now arrived at the breach, followed by a number of his men, and the assault was again attempted; but by this time the enemy, expecting that an attempt would be made to storm the breach, had retired three of their guns, with which they enfiladed the breach on the inside. Colonel Maitland charged at the head of his men, and succeeded in gaining a footing inside, when he and his men were killed by the enfilading fire. Several of the officers and men fell in attempting to carry the breach, but ultimately the storming-party was ordered to descend the walls.

Had Colonel Maitland collected together sufficient of his column before he made the first ascent it is probable that he would have carried the breach; but he discovered his mistake when it was too late, and gave his life in palliation of his error.

The three columns were now ordered back to camp; our loss on the occasion amounting to 43 Europeans and 42 sepahis killed, 206 Europeans and 165 sepahis wounded; amongst these latter being Lieutenants Wood, Hamilton, and Brown, of the Bengal European Regiment.

The distress of this mortifying failure was increased by the melancholy fate of many of our wounded men; who, being unavoidably left behind, were barbarously mutilated by the enemy. On the following day, the defenders having repaired the breaches, it was determined to direct our fire on the right bastions of the fortress; and for this purpose General Lake ordered additional batteries to be constructed, on which 2 24-pounders, 10 18-pounders, and 8 mortars were mounted.

On the 16th January all of these guns opened a furious cannonade with good effect, our mortars specially doing great execution, and dismounting several of the enemy's guns; but although our siege artillery fired incessantly from all our works it was not until the 21st January that a practicable breach had been effected.

As the enemy, on account of our day and night fire, had not been able to repair or stockade the breach, they withdrew their guns from the embrasures, placing them in such a position right and left of the breach that should our storming-parties reach the summit a heavy enfilading fire would be brought upon them before they could gain a footing. It was this plan that had served their purpose so well during the first assault.

But General Lake determined that the second attack should not be delivered until our engineers had ascertained which part of the ditch could be most easily forded.

This information three troopers of our native cavalry volunteered to obtain from the enemy themselves; so, discarding their uniforms and donning the ordinary dress of the natives of the district, they mounted their horses and galloped across the plain in the direction of the fortress. It had been previously arranged that a detachment of our sepahis should give colour to the artifice by chasing and firing blank cartridges at the supposed fugitives, to give the enemy the impression that they were deserters making their escape from the British camp.

Arrived under the walls of the fortress they surveyed the breach and ascertained the best means of ascent; then, calling to the soldiers on the walls of the fortress to point out where the ditch was most easily fordable, they said they were seeking the protection of Holkar's army, which they wished to join; when, having obtained the required information they put spurs to their horses and returned to our camp.

To enable the storming-parties to cross the ditch without wading through the mud and water, three broad ladders were constructed, covered with strong laths, and fitted with elevating-screws and levers, so that they could be raised or depressed at will.

All being now ready, the storming-party, under Colonel Macrae, was selected as follows—130 men of the 75th, 150 men of the 76th, 100 of the Bengal European Regiment, and 50 flankers-of the 22nd; this column was entrusted with storming the breach, and should it succeed, the remaining Europeans and three sepahi battalions were to follow their comrades and support, the escaladers.

At night on the 21st the storming-party moved into the advanced trenches; and our cavalry with two batteries of field-Artillery were sent in rear of our camp to keep the enemy's horse in check.

At 3 p.m., 22nd, the storming-party moved out of the trenches under cover of our guns. The portable bridges were carried by picked men, who had been previously exercised in the mode of using them: the 75th and 76th keeping up the fire upon the batteries above, whilst the Bengal Europeans and the 22nd fixed the bridges. The advanced-party, reaching the ditch, were mortified to find that they had been outwitted; for the enemy, having rightly conjectured the object of the trick which had been put upon them, had so dammed up the ditch below the ford, that a quantity of water was collected in it, so that the portable bridges were too short for the span, and were in consequence quite useless.

One of the tallest of the grenadiers, who sprang into the water, proved that it was upwards of 8 feet deep; and some parties were then told off to swim the ditch; and Lieutenant Morris of the Bengal European Regiment, accompanied by Lieutenant Brown with 12 of the grenadiers of the Regiment, volunteered to lead the swimming-party. The gallantry of Sergeant Allen, of the grenadier company, on this occasion, should ever be remembered by the Regiment with pride. The swimmers all plunged into the water, and, led by their gallant Commander, Morris, reached the further bank of the ditch; and they even succeeded in mounting up to the breach, but here Lieutenant Morris and several of his men were wounded, and the enemy having made a rush upon them before they had gained a firm footing inside the walls, they were all hurled down the ascent.

To carry the breach on this occasion being now found impossible, the storming-party was ordered to return to the trenches disappointed but not disheartened. Our loss on this the second assault was again very severe; for, during the unavoidable delay-on the brink of the ditch, and during the retreat, the enemy poured a grape and musketry fire with such murderous effect on our troops that 18 officers and 573 rank and file were either killed or wounded; amongst the latter being Lieutenant Morris and Ensign Watson of the Bengal European Regiment.

On the 6th February the British camp was moved opposite to the north-east face of the fortress, and preparations made for the next assault. Our troops were at this time employed day and night in constructing vastly-extended outworks, with fascines and gabions, and additional batteries connected by chain-posts and trenches round our new ground, extending to our foremost batteries.

The officers and men of the Bengal European Regiment were conspicuous for their exertions in the trenches; the commander-in-chief, who personally supervised the siege-works, frequently expressing his warm thanks for the unremitting activity of the men in the performance of their arduous duties; and it was on one of these occasions that some of the men of the Regiment, apologising to their chief for their dirty appearance, and urging as an excuse that they had not found time to change their shirts for several weeks, General Lake remarked approvingly that their dirty shirts were an honour to the wearers, showing that they had willingly sacrificed comfort to their duty; and his Excellency used frequently to address the Regiment as his own "Dirty Shirts"—a name which has been cherished with pride by the Bengal Regiment ever since those days in the trenches before Bhurtpore; and to this day some of the handsome plate on the mess-table of the Royal Munster Fusiliers will be seen to have been presented by "an old Dirty Shirt."

On the 10th of February the British army was reinforced by a column from the Bombay Presidency, consisting of H.M. 86th, 65th and about 800 cavalry.

The engineers were employed in constructing a number of wicker boats, covered with leather, and a portable raft, about 100 feet long, and 16 broad, placed on casks to serve as pontoons; and trenches had been made reaching to within a short distance of the ditch under the walls of the fortress. Our new batteries mounted 16 additional heavy guns, and a large mine had been dug with which it was intended to blow up the counterscarp; the *débris* of which it was hoped would form a sloping bank up to a new breach which had been made immediately above it.

On the night of the 20th of February, 1805, all was ready for the third assault. The main-storming party, under Colonel Don, being formed by the Bengal European Regiment, H.M. 22nd,, 75th, and 76th Foot, supported by 3 battalions of sepahis. The left column, consisting of H.M. 86th and 1 sepahi battalion, was appointed to storm the enemy's trenches outside the batteries, and the right column, consisting of 300 men of H.M. 65th and two battalions of Bombay sepahis, was told off to attack and force the main entrance gate. During the evening, taking advantage of the absence of our working-parties from the neck of our approach, which abutted on the ditch, the enemy made a sally and demolished a part of our works. The storming-party, at 5 a.m. first reached the approach, when, finding the enemy in possession, a fight ensued, which resulted in our regaining our trenches, but in doing so several of our men were killed and wounded. A detachment of H.M. 22nd

Regiment was then sent forward, who assisted the Bengal European Regiment in driving off the assailants, many of whom were bayoneted, and the rest fled.

The storming-party proceeded on their way through the approach, but as they neared the ditch an alarm was raised that the enemy had placed a slow match in the mine; thus causing a check in the advance. The flank companies of H.M. 22nd and a sepahi Regiment with two 6-pounders kept up a fire of grape on the walls and bastions, whilst the storming-party now attempted the assault. The ditch was found to be impassable on foot, and in the darkness and confusion consequent on the alarm the pontoons could not be found, but notwithstanding this a number of the storming-party managed to cross, and seeing that the bastion on the right presented a rough appearance on its face they at once made an attempt to ascend it. The grenadiers of H.M. 22nd and the sepahis of the 12th Regiment Native Infantry behaved with conspicuous gallantry on this occasion; the colours of the native regiment having been planted on the bastion; but there was not sufficient support to hold the position, and Lieutenant Moore of the Bengal European Regiment was mortally wounded.

At this time some of the enemy's mines which they had constructed close to the breach with the intention of blowing up the besiegers should they succeed in entering, were accidentally sprung, and the aperture was considerably enlarged, so there was still hope of the assault succeeding; but the loss of the British had been very severe, the ramparts above and the whole counter-scarp below being strewn with our killed and wounded. Colonel Don, commanding the storming-party, judging that further attempts would result in irredeemable loss, retired with his whole party to the trenches; leaving 49 Europeans and 113 sepahis dead, and having 176 Europeans and 556 sepahis wounded during this, the third, assault.

The next morning a general parade was ordered, at which the commander-in-chief pointed out that the failure on the previous day was mainly due to the needless alarm in the trenches; and he called for volunteers for an immediate assault. The troops volunteered to a man; so the fourth assault was ordered for 4 p.m. on that day.

Orders were immediately given for all our heavy guns to be brought to bear on the right bastion, in the expectation that in its tottering condition, the whole structure might be brought down by the cannonade; and although in this Lake was disappointed, the fourth assault was nevertheless organised.

The storming-party on this occasion consisted of the whole of the European force, supported by the several battalions of sepahis; the command being conferred on Colonel Monson.

The commander-in-chief received hearty cheers from the men as they advanced to the assault, and it appeared as if on this occasion there could be no failure. The advanced-party made for the ruined bastion, but to their disappointment it was found to be so steep that the soldiers could not effect an ascent. The assailants now attempted to form steps with their bayonets, which they drove into the crevices of the stone wall; and many of the men ascended to a considerable height, but they were dislodged by various missiles hurled on them by the defenders from above. Separate parties were now hurriedly formed and placed under selected officers to storm any breaches that could be found promising a fair chance of success; but the enemy had by this time gained confidence from our repeated failures, and threw down on our soldiers large masses of masonry, flaming bales of cotton, pots filled with gunpowder and other combustibles, which, bursting in the air amongst our men, caused terrible loss of life. After a couple of hours fruitlessly occupied in attempting to ascend the bastion the troops were again withdrawn to camp, with a loss of 69 Europeans and 56 sepahis killed, and 410 Europeans and 452 sepahis wounded.

In this, the fourth, assault Captain Ramsay,[10] Lieutenant Hamilton, and Ensign Chance of the Bengal European Regiment were wounded.

In our attempts to carry the fortress of Bhurtpore the British army had up to date 103 officers and 3100 rank and file either killed or wounded.

Many of the British battery guns were by this time blown at the vent; the men were suffering from want of proper provisions, and our ammunition was nearly exhausted. Under these circumstances the siege was temporarily converted into a blockade, and detachments were sent off to collect supplies.

The absolute necessity of carrying the fortress by storm was still felt by all; and convoys arrived daily at camp with provisions, guns, ammunition, fascines, etc., and preparations were made for erecting fresh batteries; the old guns as soon as they were repaired being placed in position.

The garrison, although it had resisted four of our determined assaults, was by no means confident of ultimate success, and indeed

---

10. Captain Ramsay commanded the Light Company of the Bengal European Regiment during this assault, and was severely wounded in the face by a musket-ball.

trustworthy information had reached our camp that the Raja's troops were deserting in large numbers, whilst others clamoured for peace.

At this time intelligence having reached their camp that General Lake had been raised to the Peerage, the Bhurtpore Raja availed himself of the circumstance to send his congratulations to his Lordship, saying that as he was now desirous of arranging terms of peace he was prepared to visit our camp in person.

Negotiations for peace were opened on March 10th; but as delays and prevarications ensued, Lord Lake on the 8th of April changed ground .to the south-east of the fortress, and made preparations for a renewal of hostilities.

Holkar, the ally of the Bhurtpore Raja, had previously deserted the fortress with his followers; who, in attempting to escape, were roughly handled by our detachments of cavalry sent in pursuit.

On April 9th the Raja sent his vakeel saying he was at last prepared to conclude terms of peace ; and, negotiations having been re-opened, the preliminaries were signed on April 10th; the son of the Raja being sent to the British camp as a hostage for the due performance of the terms of the treaty.

It was arranged that the fortress of Deig should remain in British possession until our Government should be assured of the Raja's fidelity; when it would be returned to the native Government. The Raja agreed, on his part, never to enter into alliance with any of the enemies of the British, nor to entertain any European in his service; also to pay twenty lacs—£200,000—for the expenses of the war; and, finally, that his son should remain as a hostage until the terms of the treaty should be fulfilled.

The British camp before Bhurtpore was, in consequence of this treaty, broken up on the 21st April, 1805; and "The Bengal European Regiment" went into quarters at Futty Ghur.

Holkar, after his retreat from Bhurtpore, had succeeded in collecting some troops, and marched in a northerly direction in search of plunder or conquest; and, the country being well stocked with adventurers, he soon found himself at the head of a numerous rabble of untrained troops, with 60 pieces of cannon, with which he marched towards the Punjab. Lord Lake, fearing that the Seiks might be induced to join the *Maratha chieftain*, assembled a flying column, consisting of H.M. 8th and 25th Dragoons, two regiments of native cavalry, H.M. 22nd Foot, and the Bengal European Regiment, with two sepahi battalions; and, on the 25th October, started in pursuit. About midway between the rivers Sutlej and Bias a portion of our cavalry sighted Holkar's rearguard, pressing forward through the very heart of the Punjab, where they were closely pursued by Lord Lake's flying column.

Arrived at Umritzur Holkar found that the Seik chiefs in council unanimously determined to deny him all aid and countenance; and with the object of getting rid of both the armies Runjit Sing—the Maharajah of the Punjab—offered to interpose in the character of a mediator.

In the meantime Lord Cornwallis, the Governor-General—who had during his tenure of power endeavoured to bring the turbulent tribes of Central India into subjection, and thus bestow the blessings of security of property on all peace-loving inhabitants—had died in Bengal and was replaced by Sir George Barlow, who, to Lord Lake's mortification, directed him to restore to Holkar, the territories which had at such a sacrifice of life and money been wrenched from his grasp; thus practically destroying all hopes of permanent peace, and instituting a reign of terror and disorder.[11]

A treaty was arranged in accordance with Sir George Barlow's orders, under the terms of which Holkar was reinstated in his dominions; and on the 9th of January, 1806, the flying brigade commenced its return march to Delhie, which it reached on the 15th of February.

In February, 1807, Lord Lake embarked for England; dying on the 21st of February in the following year. He was beloved by the Bengal European Regiment. The anniversary of his death was for many years observed with solemnity, and his memory was at all times held dear by those officers who had had the glorious privilege of serving under him in the field.

GENERAL REFERENCES—CHAPTER 12

History of the Bengal Army. Broome.
General Orders and Dispatches.
Williams's *Bengal Infantry.*
East India Military Calendar.
Mills's *British India.*
Thorn's *Memories of Lord Lake. Campaigns in India.*
The Seir Mutakherin. &c, &c.

---

11. Thornton, in his *British Empire in India* Vol. 4., p. 172, says "What we have gained by our arms we have lost by our diplomacy, our soldiers and seamen having poured out their blood in the purchase of conquests, to be calmly yielded up by the liberality or incompetence of our statesmen."

Chapter 13
Gurkhas & Pindaries

In June, 1808, Lord Minto, then Governor-General of India, ordered an expedition to be prepared for the defence of the Portuguese settlement at Macao, in order to meet any attack that might be made by the French, with whom England and Portugal were at war in Europe. Major Thomas M. Weguelen, of the Bengal European Regiment, was promoted to the local rank of Colonel, and placed in command of the expedition, which consisted of 200 men of the Bengal European Regiment, a like number of the 30th Foot, 100 European artillery, with eight 18- and four 12-pounder guns, two 8-inch mortars, and two field-pieces, as well as 650 sepahis.

The expedition above detailed sailed from Bengal in August, 1808, and anchored in the Macao Roads on the 20th October.. The duties which now devolved on Colonel Weguelen were of a Political as well as a Military character, and required the utmost tact and delicacy. The alarm of the Chinese Government at the close proximity of a British force created complications which culminated in feelings of enmity on the part of the Chinese inhabitants, manifesting itself in repeated affrays and assaults; so that it became necessary to strictly confine all the troops to their quarters. Trade was brought to a standstill, and every endeavour at explanation was rejected, the only reply being, "Put your troops on board ship and then we will hear you."

To watch the proceedings of the British expedition and to guard against surprise, a Chinese force disembarked at the extremity of the island, occupying a joss-house, where they ultimately made preparations for war. It now became necessary for Weguelen to determine on some decided course of action, the adoption of which would prevent hostilities, re-open trade, restore confidence, and re-establish our commercial relations with China.

Under these threatening circumstances Colonel Weguelen judiciously determined to re-embark his troops, carefully avoiding any cause for alarm to the peaceable inhabitants of Macao; and this measure having been successfully accomplished the expedition returned to Bengal, where it landed in the middle of February, 1809.

The soldier-like demeanour of the men who formed this expedition is beyond all praise; confined to their quarters, on short provisions, and surrounded by a hostile population, they maintained that strict discipline which is as essential in peace as in war.

The Governor-General in Council as well as the commander-in-chief expressed the highest satisfaction, and tendered the thanks of the Government for "the great prudence, discretion, vigilance, and activity manifested" by Colonel Weguelen and the soldiers under his command. The detachment of the Bengal European Regiment returned to their headquarters at Dinapore, when Major Weguelen was appointed to the command of the Regiment.

In the year 1810 events in Europe had placed the colonial possessions of the Dutch in Java, and in the Molucca Islands, in the hands of the French—at this time England's most inveterate foes. Lord Minto, the Governor-General of India, accordingly inaugurated a vigorous policy, under which he directed the complete conquest of these Settlements. This proposition had been submitted for the approval of the English Cabinet; but pending the receipt of instructions from home, Lord Minto ordered that a small force should be organized at Madras to seize on the Island of Amboyna—one of the group of the Molucca Islands—and thus at once secure a position which, if necessary, would form a basis for the future operations of an invading army. The troops employed on this service consisted of 404 men only, 130 of whom were selected from the Madras European regiment, together with a detachment of Madras artillery and three of His Majesty's ships of war. A landing was effected without opposition, and after only a slight resistance the enemy—believing that he was opposed by an overwhelming British force—capitulated, and Fort Victoria was surrendered on the 19th of February, 1810, to the British.

Immediately after the conquest of Amboyna the Dutch settlements depending on this Island were taken possession of by His Majesty's ship *Cornwallis*, and thus the British obtained a firm footing in close proximity to the enemy's possessions.

The objects for which the Madras detachment had been organized having been obtained, Lord Minto ordered that it should be relieved by Bengal troops, who, it was intended, should permanently garrison the Islands.

It was under these circumstances that in September, 1810 September orders were issued for a strong detachment of the Bengal European Regiment—then quartered at Dinapore—to hold itself in readiness to embark for Amboyna.

The detachment consisted of one flank company and three battalion companies, making in all 368 officers and men; the whole under the command of Major Kelly.

The detachment sailed for its destination in October, 1810; very severe storms being encountered during the voyage, and the transports sustaining considerable injuries.

On its arrival Major Kelly, who had been promoted to a Lieutenant-Colonelcy, assumed command of all the forces on the Island by virtue of his seniority.

The headquarters of the Regiment and six companies had been ordered to remain at Dinapore.

A second detachment of the Regiment, under Captain Sir Thomas Ramsay, Bart., sailed in the Company's ship *Mentor*, for Amboyna in January, 1811.

This detachment suffered greatly from malarious fever, which was raging throughout the Islands; Lieutenant-Colonel Kelly being amongst the Officers who succumbed to the disease (December, 1811), when the command devolved upon Captain Sir Thomas Ramsay.

Although the climate of Amboyna was anything but salubrious the scenery is described as being very beautiful, exhibiting mountains thickly wooded, and valleys teeming with luxuriant verdure; numerous villages and hamlets being dotted about, surrounded with an abundance of rich cultivation.

The bay is entered between two high hills, which diminish in height as they approach the town. This bay stretches about seven leagues into the Island, separating it nearly into two parts; and on the north shore Fort Victoria is situated. Whilst quartered at Fort Victoria the duties which devolved on the officers of the Regiment required much tact, judgement, courage, and vigilance: the elements of discord amongst the native population of the islands causing frequent disturbances. The Malays, who formed a large proportion of the inhabitants, were universally noted for their perfidy and cruelty; whilst the Chinese were distinguished for their dishonesty and lack of principle. Finally the slaves,

Extract from "The East India Register," August 12th, 1812.
THE BENGAL EUROPEAN REGIMENT.

RANK.	NAMES.	Regl. Rank.	Army Rank.	REMARKS.
Colonel	John Haynes	22 May, 1810	4 June, 1811	On Furlo'
Lieut.-Col.	Robert Haldane	27 Jan., 1804		
,,	Samuel Kelly	4 Sept., 1811		
Major	Th. M. Weguelen	5 Nov., 1808	...	Dy. Comg. General
,,	Peter Littlejohn	4 Sept., 1811	25 July, 1810	Comg. Hill Rangers
Captain	Sir Thos. Ramsay, Bart.	27 Mar., 1804	M. do.	Amboyna.
,,	H. Blankenhagen	21 Sept., 1804	27 Mar., 1804	Comg. Amboyna Corps
,,	T. D. Broughton	20 Oct., 1805	29 Dec., 1804	On Furlough
,,	John Stuart	3 Mar., 1808	20 Oct., 1805	
,,	Edm. Morris	15 Dec., 1808	20 April, 1808	Amboyna
,,	W. H. Wood	4 Sept., 1811	15 Dec., 1808	
,,	James Bryant	22 June, 1812	4 Sept., 1811	Brig. Maj. Dinapore
Capt.-Lieut.	Richard Higgott	do.	...	Ramghur Battn.
Lieutenant	William Home	10 Aug., 1800		
,,	James Annoe	22 Oct., 1802		
,,	Foster Walker	13 July, 1803	...	Amboyna
,,	Alex. Brown	do.	...	Act. Maj. Brigade, Dinapore
,,	T. Kirchoffner	30 May, 1804		
,,	Thos. Watson	30 June, 1804		
,,	Chas. C. Smith	30 Sept., 1804		
,,	Charles Smith	do.	...	Isle of Banda
,,	George Bolton	do.		
,,	P. S. Van Swinden	30 Sept., 1804	...	Maj. Brig. Amboyna
,,	Saml. Watson	24 Oct., 1804		
,,	Edw. Fitzgerald	20 Nov., 1804	...	Amboyna
,,	Robt. McKerrell	8 May, 1805	...	Isle of Banda
,,	Robt. Ledlie	18 Aug., 1805	...	Amboyna
,,	John Fulton	12 Sept., 1805	...	Adjt. Amboyna Corps
,,	Wm. Burroughs	22 Nov., 1805	...	Amboyna
,,	Metcalf S. Hogg	11 Sept., 1807	...	Actg. Adj. 1 and 2 M. Presdcy. Divn.
,,	Joseph Orchard	8 Mar., 1808		
,,	John Irwin	15 Dec., 1808		
,,	Hen. P. Carlton	26 Dec., 1808	...	Fort Adj., Amboyna
,,	Francis Crisley	4 Sept., 1811		
,,	John Cockburn	22 Jan., 1812	...	Amboyna
Ensign	James Harrison	22 Aug., 1807	...	Amboyna
,,	George Wray	30 Oct., 1808	...	Amboyna
,,	David Ruddell	31 Mar., 1808	...	Ramghur Battn.
,,	Ben. Ashe	do.		
,,	Alex. Irvine	1 Sept., 1808		
,,	Thos. J. Godney	24 Sept., 1808		
,,	James Marshall	10 Nov., 1808		
,,	Wm. Davison	15 Feb., 1809		
Adjutant	Foster Walker	26 Feb., 1809		
Quartermstr.	James Annoe			
Surgeon	George Rankin	...	...	Amboyna
Assistant do.	Patk. Halkit	...	...	do.
do.	John Eckford	...	...	do.

Facings, Buff; Emby., Silver.

the number of whom was enormous, had been subjected to a constant system of cruelty; so that, maddened by their wrongs and sufferings, they were always anxiously watching for some opportunity to free themselves from the bondage and hardships to which they had been subjected. Under these circumstances, and taking into consideration that young officers of the Regiment were unavoidably placed in command of detachments on the different islands and outposts, where they were unable to hold frequent communication with their superiors, it argues well for the discipline of the Regiment and the intelligence of the officers that there is not any instance on record of the conduct of any of the officers or men whilst on these detached commands having called for anything but approbation from their superiors.

It was whilst on one of these detached commands that Captain Blankenhagen, of the Bengal European Regiment, lost his life. This officer had been appointed to the command of the *Amboyna Corps* which had been raised by him from amongst the Malays and other inhabitants of the island. Captain Blankenhagen had proceeded with some of his men to the island of Ceram with the view of bringing into submission one of the refractory chiefs. An attack on the enemy's stronghold was unsuccessful, and this gallant officer was killed at the head of his regiment.

The principal possessions still remaining to the Dutch were situated in the Island of Java; and a qualified approval of Lord Minto's policy for the subjugation of these possessions having been received from England, the Governor-General gave orders-for the dispatch of a force to capture Batavia and the principal fortifications on the Island of Java. The army was placed under the command of Sir Samuel Auchmuty, and consisted of 12,000 men, of which number nearly one-half were Europeans. On the 4th of August, 1811, the expedition, with which was Lord Minto in person, arrived in the Batavia Roads; and after a series of successes, attended unfortunately with much sacrifice of life, the conquest of the settlement was achieved. The views of the home authorities extended no further than the expulsion of the Dutch and the capture of their fortifications, after which it was ordered that we should vacate the island; but Lord Minto was of opinion that such a termination to the expedition would be ill-judged and mischievous. The captured forts were therefore garrisoned by British troops, and order was maintained by a properly-organized Government.

It was under these circumstances that on the 27th of February 1812, the headquarters of the Bengal European Regiment, under command of Lieutenant-Colonel Eales, embarked at Calcutta in the transports *Indiana, Good Hope,* and *Mussafer,* to join their comrades at Amboyna. The Regiment remained in the Molucca Islands and at Macassar in the Isle of Celebes until early in April, 1817, when the Spice Islands were delivered over to the Dutch authorities,[1] and the Regiment returned to Bengal, when it was again quartered at Dinapore.

THE NEPAUL WAR AND EXPEDITIONS AGAINST THE PINDARIES
1814-1818

The Earl of Moira, who succeeded Lord Minto as Governor-General, having landed in Calcutta in October, 1814, commenced his Government by instituting a wise and high-minded policy His predecessor had represented in strong terms the necessity of curbing the aggressive policy of the Gurkhas; and a treaty had been concluded with the authorities at Nepaul, under the stipulations of which they were bound to respect the rights of the Company; but the conduct of the Nepaulese had compelled our Government to declare the treaty dissolved.

The encroachments of the Gurkhas extended into almost all the Company's territories which abutted on those of Nepaul; and thus necessitated the institution of active measures, not only for the repression of these aggressions, but for the protection of those native rulers who owed allegiance to the British Government.

Lord Minto, with the view of avoiding a war which the Government could ill afford, had made more than reasonable concessions. Without seeking any atonement for the insults which had been inflicted on the Company he had simply demanded that the Gurkha Government should withdraw from the territories they had wrongfully appropriated; but his just demands were rejected with scorn, and the enemy prepared for war.

Lord Moira now assembled a considerable force to maintain the authority of the Company, the chief command being assigned to Colonel David Ochterlony; whilst a force under Major-General J.

---

1. Thornton, in his *History of the British Empire in India,* Vol. 4, p. 348, remarks "the blood and treasure expended in the capture of the Dutch settlements were ultimately thrown away. By the arrangements consequent on the general pacification of Europe these settlements were restored—an additional illustration of that levity and disregard to consequences which seem to be inherent in British diplomacy. The maintenance of Java and its dependencies was necessary to the safety and integrity of our Eastern Empire, and they ought never to have been surrendered."

Sullivan Wood penetrated into the Gurkha country, by the route of Rutswild, to prevent the transfer of the war to the westward.[2] A detachment of the Bengal European Regiment formed part of General Wood's Division,[3] but it does not appear to have come into actual contact with the enemy.

In 1816 the Nepaul War was brought to a conclusion by the ratification of a treaty, under the conditions of which the rights of the Company were to be respected in the future, and the territories which had been wrongfully annexed were restored to the British.

But a war of far greater importance than that which had to be maintained against the Gurkhas threatened the early Administration of Lord Moira—who had since his assumption of office been created Marquis of Hastings. A war of extermination against the Pindaries formed one important feature in Lord Moira's Administration, and at an early period of his government he had directed the attention of the Court of Directors to this subject, and solicited their instructions. The Pindaries had now become the pest of society; and it was necessary not only to punish and destroy them, but to overawe those powerful native states under whose protection they carried on their depredations. The Pindaries were a clan of freebooters; but, although their condition was one of constant war against their neighbours, they did not claim to be soldiers. They supported themselves by plunder and murder; their victims in most cases being the unoffending cultivators of the soil. They congregated in the native states. where they formed themselves into different bands, composed of the outcasts of society, perpetrators of crimes, and escaped felons; any ruffian who could possess himself of a horse and sword being welcomed into their ranks. Their means of existence depended upon the amount of their spoliation; and whenever their treasury was exhausted an excursion against a wealthy village or group of villages was planned; their councils being held in secret, their movements were rapid both in attack and retreat, and their sole object being plunder, they obtained it in the most expeditious manner, darting on their victims with velocity, and where they met with determined opposition, flying with precipitancy.

The cruelties to which the unoffending villagers were thus subjected by these marauders were unsurpassed in their disregard for suffering.

---

2. *East India N. S. Journal* 1835.
3. *East India Military Calendar,* Vol. 1., p. 382.

The banditti on their appearance in a village demanded instant information of the position of treasure supposed to be concealed, and any hesitation ensured the immediate application of some horrible torture; the soles of the feet being seared with red-hot irons, or a bag of hot ashes tied over the face of the victim, who was then severely beaten on the back, forcing him to inhale the heated ashes; time was not allowed to the women and children to remove their bangles from their arms and feet, their limbs being frequently chopped off. Nor was the committal of these atrocities by the Pindaries confined to the men only; for in their excursions they were usually accompanied by their women, who are said to have surpassed the men in rapacity and crime.

A few hours sufficed for the work of murder and theft, when the villages were fired and the robbers retired with their spoil to their homes. This accomplished, the native Government—almost invariably Maratha—under whose protection the Pindaries lived, had first to be satisfied; in some instances one-fourth of the booty being surrendered to them, in others a heavy heriot being demanded.

All external claims having been discharged, the spoil was divided according to an acknowledged scale. The women then held a fair which was conducted with dancing, singing, and debauchery; attracting purchasers to their mart from far and near. Not satisfied with plundering the villages in the native states, the Pindaries had now grown more reckless, and had made incursions within the territories of the Company. Under these circumstances it became incumbent on the Indian Government to adopt decided measures of reprisal and punishment.

It was not to be disguised that this undertaking was one of considerable magnitude, seeing that, although the Pindaries were in themselves despicable and in every way unworthy to be classified as foes, they were openly encouraged by many of the influential native rulers, who unblushingly derived a considerable portion of their revenues from their plunder.

Holkar had bestowed upon Gurdi Khan—one of the Pindarie Chiefs—a golden flag, the possession of which entitled the bearer to high rank amongst the Marathas. Kurreem Khan, at this time the Chief of the Pindaries, on the occasion of receiving a visit of ceremony from Scindia, prepared a throne for his guest erected on a pedestal composed of Rs. 125,000, which he tendered to his patron as a gift of honour. A campaign, therefore, against the Pindaries necessitated a series of concomitant wars against many of the powerful Maratha states, and it was accordingly ordered by the Calcutta Council that they should be undertaken on a scale of magnitude and efficiency commensurate with the important services on which it was intended that our forces should be employed.

The *Grand army,* for the complete subjection of the Pindaries and their patrons, was assembled immediately after the rainy season in 1817, and was divided into two commands, that of *Bengal* and *The Deccan*; the former army consisting of 12, and the latter of 24 brigades, numbering in all close on 100,000 men.

The Grenadiers and Light Companies of the Bengal European Regiment again formed part of the *European Flank Battalion,* with six Companies of H.M. 17th, 24th, and 59th. This battalion, formed entirely of flankers, was said by an eye-witness to have been "a magnificent Corps;" and as it was composed of picked men from the different British regiments serving in Bengal the emulation was very great.

The Flank Battalion of the *Army of Bengal* was in the 2nd Infantry Brigade, commanded by Colonel George Dick; and this brigade marched in October, 1817, to Secundra, and in November was joined by the Marquis of Hastings, who assumed the chief command.

The army of the Peishwar showed open hostility to the British; but a treaty was entered into with Scindia and some other influential Maratha chiefs, under which their active co-operation against the Pindaries was promised. Although the British Government were well aware that these treaties were entered into by the chiefs only to be violated should the occasion arise, yet, in the face of the powerful army which we had assembled, it was calculated that in all probability their fulfilment would be a matter not of choice but of necessity.

This so-called "Pindarie War" was in reality the assertion of the Company's Government to paramount superiority over all others in India. Up to this period the powerful Maratha chiefs had controlled the destinies of Central India, but a change was now effected; for after a few months, during which several important victories had been gained, the Peishwar was our prisoner; Scindia was, of necessity, our ally; the Raja of Nagpore—who had opposed us—was a fugitive; and the Pindaries, who were not even worthy to be called our enemies, were driven from their possessions; and those who declined to follow an honest mode of life were forced into the jungles, where they met with a miserable termination to their worthless and baneful existence. The Pindarie War not only cleared the country of what was a disgrace to all civilized governments, but, more than this, it firmly established the supremacy of the Government of the East India Company

BENGAL EUROPEAN REGIMENT.
28th February, 1821.

RANK.	NAMES.	Rank in the Regiment.	Rank in the Army.	REMARKS.
Colonel	John Hayes	28 May, 1810	M. G. 4 June, '11	On Furlough.
Lieut.-Col.	Udny Yule, C.B.	4 April, 1814		
,,	Edw. P. Wilson	4 June, 1818		
Major	T. D. Broughton	4 Mar., 1816	4 June, 1814	
	John Lewis Stuart	1 June, 1818	...	Agent for building public boats
Captain	Wm. H. Wood	8 Sept., 1811	15 Dec., '808	Benares Levy.
,,	Jeremiah Bryant	22 Jan., '12	5 Sept., '11	Judge Adv.-Genl.
,,	James Auriol	6 March, '14	31 Aug., 13	
,,	Foster Walker	13 Aug., '15	6 March, '14	
,,	Alex. Brown	24 March, '16	13 Aug., '15	
,,	Thos. Kirchoffer	8 July	8 Jan., '16	
,,	Thos. Watson	1 June, '18	do.	
,,	Chas. C. Smith	1 August	8 Jan., '17	
,,	George Bolton	1 Jan., '19	1 do., '18	
Lieutenants	Robt. Ledlie	18 Aug., '05	Capt., do.	
,,	Wm. Burroughs	22 Nov.	do.	Barrack Master 6th or Allahabad Div.
,,	Metcalfe S. Hogg	11 April, '07	do.	
,,	Joseph Orchard	3 March, '08		
,,	John Irwin	15 Dec.		
,,	Hen. P. Carleton	26 do.		
,,	Francis Crossley	5 Sept., '11		
,,	James Harrison	10 March, '12		
,,	George Wray	2 July, '13	...	On Furlough
,,	David Ruddell	31 August	...	Asst. Hindû Stanni Prof. Coll. Fort William
,,	Ben. Ashe	6 March, '14	...	A.D.C. to Gen. Ashe
,,	Thos. J. Goding	1 July		
,,	Jas. Marshall	16 December		
,,	Wm. Davison	do.		
,,	Hen. W. Bennett	13 Aug., '15		
,,	Thos. H. Coles	4 March, '16	...	On Furlo'.
,,	Wm. H. Howard	28 July		
,,	J. A. Thompson	1 August, '18		
,,	W. G. Beachamp	do.		
,,	Chas. T. Foster	10 October		
,,	David Birrell	20 October		
,,	George Warren	30 April, '20		
Ensigns	—	—		
Adjutant	H. P. Carleton			
Quartermstr.	M. C. Hogg			
Surgeon	John Stephens			
Assistant do.	Wm. Duff			
,,				
,,				

Facings, Pompadour.   Lace, Silver.
*** The Regimentals of the Infantry, Red.

throughout India. Although *the Flank Battalion*, of which the grenadiers and the Light Companies of the Bengal European Regiment formed a part, were not called on to engage in more than guerilla warfare, the services rendered were important and formed a link in the chain of conquests resulting in a term of peace, security, and prosperity in India, which remained unbroken for many years.

A the conclusion of the war in 1818 *the Flank Battalion* marched to Allahabad, where it was broken up, and the companies of the Bengal European Regiment joined their headquarters at Berhampore.

In the year 1824 an important change was ordered in the constitution of the Regiment which was then separated into two Regiments.

The officers of the Bengal European Regiment were divided equally between the two Regiments, but no full colonels were appointed; the senior lieutenant-colonel being termed "lieutenant-colonel commandant." A complete staff was nominated to each regiment, which was composed of five companies only, each company consisting of 6 sergeants, 7 corporals, and 100 private soldiers. Both Regiments wore the same facings and lace, viz., sky-blue and silver.

The Bengal European Regiment was quartered at Ghazeepore when the orders for its reorganization were effected; and the 2nd Regiment was, on its re-formation, ordered to Dinapore, where it remained until 1825, when it proceeded to Arracan to guard our new frontiers, as defined after the Burmese War of 1824.

Siege and Capture of Bhurtpore

The Maratha, or, as it was called, the "Pindarie" War had the desired effect of firmly establishing the supremacy of the East India Company over the whole of the country south of the Sutlej. Peace and prosperity, such as had not hitherto been known, had been ensured to the inhabitants of Hindustan; and millions of subjects were praising the just and decided policy of Lord Hastings, which had ensured to them the previously-unknown blessings of security in land, home, and person.

Budher Sing, the Raja of Bhurtpore, died in 1823, leaving no direct issue. He was succeeded by his brother, Buldeo Sing, who acknowledged his allegiance to the Company by soliciting from them the Khelat of Investure.

At this time General Sir David Ochtolony—whose name has ever been associated with all that is honourable and just—the British

FIRST EUROPEAN REGIMENT.

"Plassey," "Rohilcund," "Mysore," "Deig."

January 1st, 1825.

RANK.	NAMES.	Rank in the Regiment.	Rank in the Army.	REMARKS.
Lieut.-Colonel Commandant	Edw. P. Wilson...	1 May, '24	L. C. 1 June, '18	
Lieut.-Colonel	Thos. Garner ...	14 July, '21		
Major	Jeremiah Bryant	11 July,' 23	...	Judge Adv.-General
Captain	Alex. Brown......	24 Mar., '16	13 Aug., '15	
,,	Chas. C. Smith...	1 Aug., '18	8 Jan., '17	
,,	Robt. Ledlie......	11 June, '22	1 Jan., '19	
,,	Joseph Orchard	1 Jan., '24	27 Mar., '21	
,,	Hen. P. Carleton	1 May	24 May	On Furlough
Lieutenant	David Ruddell ...	31 Aug., '13	Captain, 4 Sept., '22	Assistant Hindostanee Prof. Coll. Fort William
,,	Wm. Davison ...	16 Sept., '14	Captain, 16 Sept., '23	
,,	W. H. Howard ...	28 July, '16		
,,	George Warren ...	30 Apr., '20		
,,	Charles Wilson...	18 Jan., '22		
,,	G. A. C. Stewart	11 June		
,,	Alex. C. Scott ...	11 July, '23		
,,	Francis Beaty ...	do.		
,,	James Matthie ...	1 Jan., '24		
,,	Charles Jorden...	27 May, '24		
Ensign	Henry Candy ...	11 July, '23		
,,	—	—		
,,	—	—		
,,	—	—		
,,	—	—		
Adjutant.........				
Quartermaster				
Surgeon				

Facings, Sky-Blue.   Lace, Silver.

*** The Regimentals of the Infantry, Red.

SECOND EUROPEAN REGIMENT.

"Plassey," "Rohilcund," "Mysore," "Deig."

January 1st, 1825.

RANK.	NAMES.	Rank in the Regiment.	Rank in the Army.	REMARKS.
Lieut.-Colonel Commandant	Wm. H. Perkins	1 May, '24	L.-C. 8 June, '19	On Furlough
Lieut.-Colonel	Wm. H. Wood...	do.	...	On Furlough
Major	James Auriol	do.		
Captains	Thomas Watson	1 June, '18	8 Jan., '16	First Adjutant. Fort William
,,	George Bolton	8 Jan. '19	1 Jan., '18	
,,	Wm. Burroughs	11 July, '23	1 Jan., '19	Barrack Mastr., 6th or Allahabad Divsn.
,,	John Irwin	1 May, '24	29 Mar., '21	
,,	James Harrison	do.	28 Feb., '22	
Lieutenants	James Marshall	16 Dec., '14	Captain. 30 Apr., '23	
,,	H. Wm. Bennett	13 Aug., '15		
,,	J. A. Thompson	1 Aug., '18		
,,	David Birrell	20 Oct.		
,,	John S. Pitts	7 Oct., '21		
,,	John P. Ripley	7 May, '22		
,,	Wm. Shortreed	2 July	1 May, '23	
,,	Thos. Lysart	11 July, '23		
,,	Edw. Rushworth	do.		
,,	Robt. Crofton	1 May, '24		
Ensigns	—	—	—	
,,	—	—	—	
,,	—	—	—	
,,	—	—	—	
,,	—	—	—	
Adjutant	J. Marshall	17 June, '24		
Quartermaster	J. P. Ripley	do.		
Surgeon	—	—		

Facings, Sky-Blue.   Lace, Silver.

Resident at Malwa and Rajpootana, represented to Lord Amherst, the Governor-General, that one Durjun Sal had claimed the throne of Bhurtpore, but that on impartial inquiry the man had failed to vindicate his claim, which rested solely on his bare assertion that the late Raja had acknowledged him as his heir and nominated him as his successor.

Buldeo Sing was, therefore, formally placed on the Musnud, under the authority of the East India Company; and, at his request, his infant son was acknowledged by our Government heir to the throne.

On the 20th January, 1825, Buldeo Sing died, and this infant son, in accordance with the ruling of the Calcutta Council, succeeded his father.

Durjun Sal again claimed the throne, and, although his letters were couched in specious language, he by his acts set at defiance the authority of his suzerain, the East India Company; and, having gained over a large number of the Bhurtpore troops by promises of reward, attacked and seized the feebly-defended fortress of Bhurtpore, murdered the uncle of the young Raja, took the boy prisoner, and occupied the throne in defiance of all remonstrances.

As soon as it came to the knowledge of Sir David Ochtolony that the authority of the British had been outraged, he at once ordered all available troops to move towards Bhurtpore, and issuing a proclamation to the inhabitants of the country, called upon them in the name of his Government to rise and vindicate the rights of their youthful Sovereign, assuring them that in so-doing they should have the support of the Calcutta Council.

Lord Amherst declined to sanction or maintain the Resident's policy; it was in vain that Ochtolony urged that if decisive measures were not adopted to uphold British authority the rebellion of Durjun Sal would probably be productive of an extensive and costly war; he was instructed to immediately countermand the march of our troops and reverse his policy, allowing the people of Bhurtpore to fight for the succession and settle the dispute amongst themselves.

Never was an official placed in a more perplexing or humiliating position, but General Ochtolony acted with promptitude on the instructions received from the Governor-General, and, in his letter of the 15th April, 1825, he said, "I lose no time in communicating his Lordship's sentiments as freely as I should if they had conveyed an approbation of my measures;" but, at the same time, he forewarned the Government in strong terms what must be the inevitable result of their weak, short-sighted policy, urging upon them that "every moment's delay was submission to disgrace," and, with this caution, he tendered his resignation; but saying, at the same time, that he should be guilty of falsehood if he acknowledged any conviction of the incorrectness or impropriety of his actions, for he was fully convinced that his policy, had it been followed, would have speedily brought matters to an amicable and an honourable issue.[4]

Sir David Ochtolony died at Meerut shortly after his resignation; when the Government of India paid tribute to his memory by issuing a notification in which it was set forth that "the diplomatic qualifications of Sir David Ochtolony were not less conspicuous than his military talents."

In the month of June following it became apparent that the time had arrived when the Government of India must of necessity interfere in Bhurtpore affairs, or lose the little respect which remained to it. Large bodies of mercenary troops, many of whom came from our own districts, crowds of Marathas, and descendants of the Pindaries, attracted by the cry of war and the hope of plunder, had collected together. Madhoo Sing, the brother of the usurper, had seized the fortress of Deig and attempted to possess himself of Bhurtpore. The troops, who depended solely on plunder for their sustenance, were not only devastating the Bhurtpore and neighbouring districts, but threatening to carry their depredations into the territory of the Company itself. The danger of a general war now became apparent, for there was every probability that those turbulent Princes who had been brought to subjection by Lord Hastings in 1817 would take advantage of the apathy of the present Government, and attempt to regain their former possessions.

Still the Calcutta Council were undecided, whilst the Governor-General stood timidly aloof. A man was wanted to lead, and fortunately such a man was at hand. Sir Charles Metcalfe penned an able Minute on the state of affairs at Bhurtpore, which turned the scale and reversed Lord Amhurst's non-interference policy. The Governor-General having the fairness to acknowledge that his opinions "had undergone some change" and that "a system of non-interference would be exposed to signal failure."

Thus it was that the boasted impregnability of the fortress of Bhurtpore was to be again tested, and our army to be allowed an opportunity of completing the task which it had failed to accomplish in 1804.

---

4. Letter to Secretary to Government, 25th April, 1825

A proclamation was now issued, denouncing the pretensions of the usurper Durjun Sal, and setting forth that the infant Raja, whose succession had been sanctioned by the Company, should by their authority and under their protection be firmly seated on his throne. Sir Charles Metcalfe was appointed by the Government to carry into effect the purport of this proclamation, and should it be necessary he was empowered "to resort to the measures of force."

Lord Combermere, the Commander-in-Chief, assumed the command of the field force; and the Bengal European Regiment was ordered to be immediately held in readiness to march towards Bhurtpore.

The order for the Regiment to proceed on active service was hailed by the men with delight, not only on account of a natural desire to complete the reduction of the fortress of Bhurtpore, which had withstood our four successive assaults in 1805, but cholera[5] and a virulent malarious fever had within the past few months reduced the Regiment in strength and spirits, making welcome the prospect of a change to a more healthy climate and vigorous life.

There still remained with the 1st Bengal European Regiment some of the officers and rank and file who had been present during the unsuccessful attempts to capture Bhurtpore in 1805. There had been no lack of courage on that memorable occasion, but there had been failure; "Deig" was inscribed on the Regimental colour, but "Bhurtpore" was remembered by its absence. Major Alexander Brown was one of those who swam the ditch with the grenadiers on 22nd January, 1805; this officer was still with the Regiment—a tall, handsome man, of courage unsurpassed; to the young officers he was specially kind, ever ready to help them in their difficulties and assist them with his advice. There was also present with the Regiment a man named Allan, known as "Tinker Allan." Private Allan was a regimental character; he was upwards of six feet high, and always took the right of the grenadier company, and no feat was too daring for him to attempt. Captain Morris,

---

5. In the burial ground at Ghazeepore may still be seen sad mementos of this visitation of cholera, in the long rows of graves of the men of the Bengal European Regiment. On one of these the following epitaph to the memory of a deceased soldier may be seen:
I'm billeted here by death,
And here I must remain;
When the last trumpet sounds,
I'll rise and march again.
Erected by his Comrades.

who had commanded the grenadiers at the siege of Bhurtpore, had been shot in the neck and his leg broken whilst leading the escaladers across the ditch; it was Allan who rescued his wounded officer, and it may fairly be said that he saved his life. Allan was not a drunkard, but he was a wild, reckless fellow, frequently in trouble, but ever ready to make atonement for his errors. On one occasion he had been tried by a Court-Martial and sentenced to be flogged. The proceedings of the Court were as usual read on parade, and Allan began to strip to receive the lash, when Colonel Roberts,[6] then commanding the Regiment, called him to the front and thus addressed him:

> Private Allan, you have proved yourself on many occasions to be a brave and gallant soldier, and your deeds are well known in the Regiment. I will not submit you to the disgrace of the lash. I will remit your punishment, and I hope that the mercy which I have now shown you, will induce you to be as good a soldier in quarters as you have been in the field.

Allan was ordered to take his place in the ranks, and his release was hailed with joy by his comrades.

It was with a full measure of applause that the order to join the army before Bhurtpore was received by the 1st Bengal European Regiment, and five days sufficed for collecting the necessary carriage, when amidst hearty cheers the Regiment commenced its march. On arrival at Shekoabad orders from the commander-in-chief were received directing that the Regiment should push on as quickly as possible, for the day of attack was at hand. The march was resumed immediately and a distance of 14 additional miles was accomplished, the Regiment reaching Etimadpore before daybreak the next morning. A halt was then ordered for breakfast, and without pitching camp the Regiment continued its march a further distance of 15 miles, when of necessity it halted a few hours to obtain service ammunition and exchange condemned arms. At 4 p.m. the same day, January 6th, the men were drawn up on parade in heavy marching order, and the word of command having been given, the Regiment commenced its final march of 36 miles, which was to bring our soldiers face to face with their old enemy, who, just 20 years previously, had foiled and defeated them.

Before dawn the signs of exhaustion were apparent and it seemed

---

6. This was the father of Lieutenant-General Sir F. S. Roberts, Bart., V.C., G.C.B., C.I.E., of Afghanistan celebrity; now Commander-in-Chief, Madras.

as if the men would be unable to complete their task; a halt appeared inevitable, when a deep boom was heard in the distance, the roar of the cannon becoming louder and louder, and the flight of the shells becoming visible as the men with a hearty cheer and refreshed vigour pushed along the road. Extra liquor was served, and at daylight on the morning of the 7th the "Dirty Shirts," having again proved their title to their *sobriquet,* arrived on the plain before Bhurtpore.

The Regiment had in 18 hours marched 60 miles, during the last 36 of which the men had carried 60 rounds of ball ammunition in pouch.

In consideration of these extraordinary exertions and the fatigue which the Regiment had undergone, the commander-in-chief ordered that it should be allowed three days' entire rest, during which time it was excused from all duties.

After this repose, the Bengal European Regiment was appointed to the 2nd Division of Infantry, commanded by Major-General Nicolls; the position of their camp being to the west of the town of Bhurtpore.

Preparations for the grand assault were now nearly completed. Lord Combermere had transmitted to Durjun Sal a proposal for the withdrawal of the women and children from the fortress, and a safe conduct was promised through the British camp, but the proposal was treated with contempt; notwithstanding which, it was humanely repeated; a second time it was rejected.

The 18th of January was fixed as the day for the grand assault. The commander-in-chief's plan of action was to drive a mine capable of containing an unusually heavy charge, right under the *Futteh Bourj,* the name by which the main battery of the fortress was known. Previous to the attack a strong party of cavalry had been sent round to prevent the enemy from cutting the *dam* of the lake (Motee Jheel), and it may be remembered that it was owing to the enemy having succeeded in cutting this *dam* during the first siege of Bhurtpore, that so many difficulties were encountered, and so many lives sacrificed in endeavouring to cross the ditch.

During the early part of January two or three mines had been pushed towards the fortress; some of which had been counter-mined by the enemy, and some had been exploded with the view of distracting the enemy's attention from the main work. The British had now 130 heavy guns in position. The Bengal European Regiment had been told off to work in the trenches which were connected with the right battery.

On the 17th January orders were issued by the commander-in-chief for the grand assault; and on the following morning, the preparations having been completed, the troops commenced to occupy the trenches, so as to be in readiness for the contemplated attack; the springing of the mine under the *Futteh Bourj* being the signal for a general advance.

H.M. 14th Regiment were appointed to lead the centre storming-party against the main breach; four Companies of the Bengal European Regiment leading the right attack, and H.M. 59th the left.

One company of the Bengal European Regiment, under Lieutenant-Colonel Cartwright, joined the reserve in the trenches.

The morning of the 18th June, 1826, was bright and clear. The enemy having learnt that the British troops had all taken position during the night, and finding that our trenches were packed with our soldiers, anticipated an immediate attack; the *Futteh Bourj* was crowded with the enemy's artillery and infantry, who by signs and gestures were seen to bid defiance to the besiegers, who were silently awaiting the signal. Exactly at 8 o'clock a low rumbling sound was heard; there was no smoke yet, but the large bastion was noticed to silently disconnect itself right and left from the fortress, and for a few seconds it seemed to oscillate with its human load; who now for the first time suspected they were over a gigantic mine. The rumbling sound was soon succeeded by a roar; when, in the midst of flames and blinding smoke, the huge mass of the *Futteh Bourj* rose for a second towards the cloudless sky, and then split and crumbled into a million fragments, which were scattered far and wide.

It was now seen that the mine had been very much overcharged, and the destruction dealt around had not been confined to the enemy only, for several of our main assaulting-party were killed and three of the officers wounded.

The stunning effect of the explosion of this surcharged mine caused a temporary cheek in the British advance; but, as the dust and smoke passed off in a dense cloud, the stormers were all seen steadily advancing towards the breaches, unchecked by the heavy fire from those bastions which had escaped injury from the explosion; H.M. 14th Regiment conspicuously displaying the black or "No Quarter" flag, on account of one of their comrades having been captured by the enemy in the early part of the siege, and barbarously murdered.

The four companies of the Bengal European Regiment leading the right attack having to make their way across 200 yards of the plain, several of the men fell before reaching the ditch; on nearing which an order was received for Nos. 1 and 2 Companies to attack and force the Jungeena or Main Grate; the former under Captain William Davison, and the latter or No. 2 Company under Lieutenant George Warren.

These companies, carrying escalading ladders, kept close under the walls of the fort, from which a constant fire was sustained, fortunately passing over the heads of the escalading party.

On reaching the gate the ladders were quickly placed, but the fortifications being strongly defended, it at first appeared doubtful if our men could overtop the walls; but, scrambling, struggling, and shouldering one another, the summit was reached, but so obstinate was the, resistance, that our loss was very severe; Lieutenant Candy being mortally wounded, and several of our men killed and wounded.

The cool courage of the two Officers, Davison and Warren, who led the storm of the Jungeena Gate, is beyond all praise; they having been the first to ascend the ladders, and bear the brunt of the assault.

An entrance having been effected, a desperate struggle ensued; when, the enemy having recoiled, a rapid and determined charge was made on a four-gun Battery, which covered the approach of the main entrance into the fortress; the guns were soon captured, most of the enemy being bayoneted at their posts. In the assault on this battery Lieutenant Warren was attacked by one of the defenders, who, feigning death, suddenly sprang up and desperately wounded this officer before he had time to defend himself; but his life was saved by Corporal Quin of his Regiment, who arrived just in time to strike the fellow to the ground.

The Jungeena Gate was now opened by our men from the inside, and the British troops were rapidly entering; but such was the desperate nature of the attack and defence that all three officers of the escalading party of the Bengal European Regiment had fallen during the assault.

In the meantime the right assault under Lieutenant-Colonel Wilson with the two remaining companies of the Bengal European Regiment had carried their breach in gallant style, and, clearing the bastions and ramparts of the fortress towards the Jungeena Gate, joined their comrades, the united companies now pushing forward towards the Citadel.

By this time the left as well as the right escalading columns had succeeded in carrying all the breaches; and the enemy, being convinced that further resistance was useless, fled through those gates of the fortress of which they still held possession; and at 4 p.m. the fortress of Bhurtpore surrendered unconditionally.

Durjun Sal with his wife and sons and 160 chosen followers attempted to force their way through our cavalry, but were captured and brought prisoners into our camp; when the Raja was sent first to the fortress of Agra and afterwards to Allahabad to await the orders of Government, as to his ultimate disposal.

Thus were the pretensions of the fortress of Bhurtpore impregnability annihilated; and thus was the power of the British, which had been shaken by the indecision of Lord Amherst and his Council, re-established by the courage, self-sacrifice, skill, and determination of the army under Lord Combermere.

The fortress of Bhurtpore was now levelled with the ground, and all its defences which had survived the siege were destroyed; but the ever-memorable name of Bhurtpore—which had cost the Bengal European Regiment, during the five assaults in which it had been engaged, the lives of so many of its officers and men—was now added to the decorations borne by the Regiment, and the memory of this glorious siege is recorded on the colours of the Royal Munster Fusiliers.

The companies of the Bengal European Regiment actively engaged in the final storm and capture of Bhurtpore lost in killed, 1 lieutenant, 1 sergeant, and 9 rank and file; in wounded, 1 captain, 1 lieutenant, 2 sergeants, and 38 rank and file.

The following is a list of officers of the Bengal European Regiment killed and wounded during the siege and capture of Bhurtpore, January 18th, 1826:—

Captain William Davison, severely wounded.
Lieutenant Henry Candy, killed.
Lieutenant George Warren, severely wounded.

In the fortress and outworks 133 guns and 300 "wall pieces" were captured, and the loss of the enemy, as reported to the commander-in-chief, was 4,000 men; the number of wounded was not known.

The following forts, some of great strength, surrendered on the approach of the British army:—

Brana, Weir, Kombeir, and Kama; and the expeditions against these garrisons having returned to Bhurtpore, the British army remained encamped for. about six weeks, during which time the terms of a treaty were being arranged under the stipulations of which the young Raja was now reinstated on his throne.

The army before Bhurtpore broke up early in April, when the 1st Bengal European Regiment proceeded to Agra; the 2nd Regiment joining them on their return from Cheduba, Arracan, before the close of the year.

On the 1st January, 1830, the two Regiments were again joined into one, which was designated as heretofore "The Bengal European Regiment;" but the officers continued in two separate cadres for promotion. In 1831 the Regiment moved from Agra to Dinapore, and in 1835 it proceeded to Meerat.

On September 1st, 1838, the organisation of the Regiment was again altered, the following establishment being sanctioned:—

1 Colonel	1 Schoolmaster-Sergeant
2 Lieutenant-Colonels	1 Drum-Major
2 Majors	1 Fife-Major
10 Captains	1 Drill-Sergeant
16 Lieutenants	40 Sergeants
8 Ensigns	1 Drill-Corporal
2 Surgeons	40 Corporals
2 Assistant-Surgeons	20 Drummers
1 Sergeant-Major	650 Privates
1 Quartermaster-sergeant	

General References—Chapter 13

Major W. Thorn's *Conquest of Java*.
Thornton's *British Empire in India*.
Raffles's *History of Java*.
Crawford's *Indian Archipelago*.
East India Military Calendar, 1820.
Broome's *Bengal Army*.
Historical Records, Madras European Regiment.
Creighton's *Narrative of the Siege and Capture of Bhurtpore, 1825-20*.
General Orders and Dispatches. &c, &c.

CHAPTER 14

Afghanistan

Lord Minto, during his administration as Governor-General, 1817, had turned his attention to the necessity of watching carefully the north-west frontier of India; and with this view he dispatched Mr. Montstuart Elphinstone to Cabul on a political mission, which resulted in the conclusion of a treaty with the Amir Shah Shujah-ul-Mulk; under the provisions of which that Prince engaged to resist the attempts of any foreign power to pass through any portion of the Afghan territory with hostile intentions towards the East India Company.

After the ratification of this treaty, dissensions arose in Afghanistan, terminating in the dethronement and flight of Shah Shujah-ul-Mulk, who sought and obtained the protection of the Indian Government.

Dost Mohamed ultimately succeeded to the Afghan throne; but under this Prince's rule the above-referred-to treaty was set at naught. Russian intrigue was so rife in Persia and Afghanistan that Lord Auckland—then Governor-General of India—following Lord Minto's policy, dispatched—September, 1837—Captain Alexander Burnes on a mission to Cabul to report on the relations existing between the Amir and the Russian and Afghan Courts. Captain Burnes, on his arrival at Cabul, soon satisfied himself that the Amir, Dost Mahomed, was completely under Russian influence; he further discovered that a Russian agent, named Vickovich, had been deputed to Cabul by his Government with promises of a large annual subsidy in exchange for Dost Mohamed's interest and services on Russian behalf. These overtures had been accepted by the Amir, who, dazzled by the prospect of such substantial assistance, had thrown himself completely into the arms of Russia.

Under these circumstances Captain Burnes returned to India, and, in his report—December 23rd, 1837—to the Governor-General, he says,

"I am satisfied that much more vigorous proceedings than the Government might wish to contemplate are necessary to counteract Russian or Persian intrigue in this quarter than have been hitherto exhibited."

It now became apparent to Lord Auckland's Government that Russia was endeavouring to work her way stealthily and surely towards the frontier of India; and that if active measures should not be adopted to check her progress the result must inevitably be dangerous and disturbing to the peace of India; the interests of Russia in Afghanistan appearing to be rising in the same proportion as those of England appeared to be declining.

The primary question to be decided by Lord Auckland's Government was, whether they should allow the country on their north-west frontier to be governed by an intriguing enemy, or whether they should restore Shah Shuja-ul-Mulk, who had sought the protection of the British, to his throne, and thus secure the goodwill of a powerful ally.

The Government of India elected to support the interests of Shah Shuja-ul-Mulk; and for this purpose a triple alliance was formed between the East India Company of the first part; the Maharaja Runjeet Sing of the second; and Shah Shuja-ul-Mulk of the third; the East India Company undertaking to supply troops and money; the Maharaja agreeing to supply a Contingent of 6000, and an "army of Observation" of 15,000 men, on the condition that Shah Shuja-ul-Mulk would agree to acknowledge the right of Runjeet Sing to the Afghan territory which he had annexed; and lastly Shah Shuja agreeing to protect the interests of the East India Company, and strengthen the advancing army, by employing such Afghan troops as should desire to further the cause of their dethroned Prince.

This treaty was confirmed and ratified at Lahore in June, 1838; and on the 1st of October following a proclamation, setting forth the views of the Indian Government, was promulgated, in which it was stated that:

> His Majesty Shah Shuja-ul-Mulk will enter Afghanistan surrounded by his own troops, and will be supported against foreign interference, and factious opposition by a British army. The Governor-General confidently hopes that the Shah will be speedily replaced on his throne by his own subjects and adherents and when once he shall be secured in power and the independence and integrity of Afghanistan established the British army will be withdrawn.

"The army of the Indus" was formed on a scale commensurate with the important objects which it was required to attain.

The Bengal portion of the army consisted of a siege-train, European Horse and Foot artillery, British and Native Light Cavalry, and five brigades of infantry; the fourth brigade being composed of the Bengal European Regiment (under command of Lieutenant-Colonel Joseph Orchard, OB.) and two native regiments. Bombay supplied an army consisting of artillery, cavalry, and infantry, and the "Poona Auxiliary Force."

Shah Shuja-ul-Mulk's contingent was composed of a troop of native horse artillery, two regiments of cavalry, and five of infantry.

In addition to the above the Maharaja Runjeet Sing supplied an "army of Observation" of 15,000 Seiks and a moveable contingent of 6000 under General Ventura, a French officer in the Punjaub service.

The following is a numerical summary of the troops employed in the "army of the Indus":

	Men
The Bengal portion of the army consisted of	9500
The Bengal Reserve division	4250
The Bombay portion of the army consisted of	5600
The Scind force, which formed the Reserve to the Bombay portion of the army	3000
Shah Shuja-ul-Mulk's contingent	6000
The Shazada's division, commanded by Timur, the son of Shah Shuja-ul-Mulk	4800
The Seik contingent	6000
The Seik army of observation	15,000
Total	54,150

The advance towards Afghanistan was made in five columns separated from each other by one day's march; the 4th Brigade, commanded by Major-General Duncan, in which was the Bengal European Regiment, being the last to leave Ferozpóre.

On the 29th of December, 1838, the army reached Bahawalpore, 229 miles from Ferozpóre and just half-way between that station and Bhakkar; which town is situated close to the river Indus, and was reached on the 24th of January, 1839. Much difficulty had been experienced en route by reason of the mortality amongst the camels and draft cattle; no less than 28,000 camels accompanying the force.

Shah Shujah's army had in the meantime reached Bhakkar, and had crossed the Indus in boats about seven miles higher up the stream.

Affairs at Haidarábad in Scinde, being found in an unsatisfactory condition, the Commander-in-Chief in India, General Sir H. Fane, ordered a detachment of 5000 men of the Bengal army to join that of Bombay, which was under the command of General Sir J. Keane.

The 4th Infantry Brigade, together with some cavalry, artillery, and sappers, was ordered to remain at Bhakkar; and this brigade—in which was the Bengal European Regiment—was employed in the construction of the bridge of boats by which the invading army was to cross the river Indus; and further, the brigade was instructed to take possession of the small fortress of Bhakkar, stated to have been originally built by Alexander the Great when he invaded India in B.C. 327.

Though in a very dilapidated condition the fortress of Bhakkar would, if repaired and garrisoned, have possessed considerable strength. The castellated building is picturesquely situated on an island in the middle of the river Indus, and was at this time within the territory of the Amir of Khyrpore; who consented, under treaty 23rd January, 1839, to hand it over to the British Commander. The fort was accordingly taken possession of on the 29th of January, and the English flag raised upon its ramparts

The Command-in-Chief of the "army of the Indus" was now assumed by Lieutenant-General Sir John Keane, and the infantry of the Bengal column was denominated the 1st Infantry Division, and placed under Major-General Sir W. Cotton.

On the 15th of February the headquarters of the 1st Infantry Division were established on the right bank of the Indus, and on the 19th it reached Shikarpore. At Shikarpore the 1st Infantry Division joined Shah Shuja's contingent; the advanced force numbering over 15,000 men.

The invading army was now nearing the enemy's country; and Dadur, a small town in the gorge of the Bolan Pass, 146 miles distant from Shikarpore, was reached on the 10th March; but this progress had been made with difficulty, for a desert 26½ miles in extent had to be crossed, and the troops and cattle had suffered terribly from want of drinkable water. The suffering from the heat was very great, the thermometer reaching 98° in the shade. Provisions also were scarce, and non-combatants were placed on half rations.

The column entered the Bolan Pass on the 16th of March, 1839; but notwithstanding that the temperature was now considerably lower, and good water plentiful, the passage through the pass is described by an officer[1] of the Bengal European Regiment, who was present

---
1. General George Warren.

during the march, as having the-appearance of an army "retreating under every disaster; public stores and private property lying about scattered and abandoned in every direction."

The mountains on either side of the pass are irregular and barren, occasional green patches of cultivation which surround the villages affording an agreeable contrast to the rugged and desolate appearance of the rocks.

The distance between the hills which enclose the pass varies considerably; in some places the valley being three to four miles broad, but in others constricted to less than a hundred feet; the huge rocks rising perpendicularly on either side. Fortunately the passage of the troops was unopposed, and the Force on the 26th of March reached Quetta, where the temperature was now very considerably reduced; causing as much suffering amongst the troops from the cold as they had previously sustained from the excessive heat. Much of the baggage, amongst which were the blankets, had been abandoned in the pass, so that the men's night-covering was insufficient. The thermometer now ranged from 30° at 4 a.m., to 60° at 3 p.m. Fruit-trees were in full blossom around, and the snow covered the mountain peaks on either side of Quetta, which is 5637 feet above the level of the sea.

On the 6th of April General Sir John Keane established his headquarters at Quetta, and immediately issued orders for a general advance to Kandahar.

The march between Quetta and Kandahar was one of privations and terrible suffering; insufficient food and the absence of water causing much sacrifice of life, and the miseries endured by the troops and cattle passes all description. The horses, numbers of which fell exhausted on the road, were goaded with lances from behind in the hope that they might be enabled to struggle on to a longed-for stream ahead. Captain Havelock in his narrative says: "Horses, already half-starved for want of grain and good grass, were throughout the day panting in all the agonies of thirst, and in the evening a few drops of water could not be obtained even to mix with the medicines of the sick in our hospital."

Under these circumstances the greatest difficulties were experienced in transporting the heavy guns; the draft-cattle, being starved and exhausted, were quite unequal to the task; and indeed the nature of the ground was such, that through a large portion of the defile the siege-train had to be dragged up and lowered down by manual labour.

The road over the Kojuck Heights rises steadily for a distance of upwards of a mile; and it was there that the Bengal European Regiment was employed in transporting the heavy guns and ammunition; the Officers of the Regiment working with their men for four consecutive days at the drag ropes, from sunrise to sunset.

The headquarters of the army reached Kandahar on the 26th of April, 1839; but the 4th Brigade and heavy guns did not arrive until the 30th, when a halt, so much needed to recruit the energies of the army, was ordered.

The Bengal column had marched 1005 miles, under circumstances of the greatest difficulty and privation; the troops having endured tortures from the scarcity of water;[2] and on the arrival of the army at Kandahar they had all been on half rations for 28 days. The sufferings to which the troops had been exposed are but inadequately recorded. Nature was well-nigh exhausted; there "was no time for the luxurious ablutions which, under the sun of Central Asia, preserve the health and restore strength, no time to waste a single drop of the precious fluid on any bodily comfort, or for any purpose but for preparing food or slaking—a raging thirst."[3] The draft-cattle, as well as the horses, had perished in great numbers, and food both for man and beast was still insufficient.

On the 8th of May Shah Shuja-ul-Mulk was installed at Kandahar by Lieutenant-General Keane, as Amir of Afghanistan;[4] and consequently Dost Mahomed was to be treated in the light of an usurper.

On May 10th, 1839, the army commenced its march towards Ghuznee, but the draft-cattle were so deficient in numbers and strength that it was found impossible under the circumstances to carry sufficient provisions, or to advance the siege-train. To meet these difficulties the troops were again placed on half rations, and the heavy guns were ordered to remain at Kandahar.

---

2. Major Hough (Campaign in Afghanistan) gives the following graphic description of the army reaching a river on the line of march. "The moment the horses saw the water they made a sudden rush into the river as if mad; both men and horses drank till they nearly burst themselves. Officers declared that their tongues cleaved to the roofs of their mouths; the water was very brackish, which induced them to drink the more. The river was three feet deep and more in some places, and was five or six miles off the proper road. Many dogs and other animals died. No officer present ever witnessed such a scene of distress."
3. Thornton's Hist. British Empire. Vol. 6., p. 174.
4. Shah Shuja-ul-Mulk was about 60 years of age when he was re-seated on his throne. He had lived under the protection of the East India Company for 24 years.

"East India Register," January, 1840.

THE BENGAL EUROPEAN REGIMENT.
(Right Wing.)

"Plassey," "Buxar," "Guzerett," "Deig," "Bhurtpore."

Station   Arrived

RANK.	NAMES.	Rank in the Regiment.	Rank in the Army.	REMARKS.
Colonel	Wm. Dunlop	11 Feb., '39	22 Jan., '34	Qrmr. Genl.
Lt.-Col.	J. Orchard, C.B.	27 July, '36		
Major	George Warren	25 Feb., '37	L.-C. 23 July, '39	
Captain	Francis Beaty	2 July, '33		
,,	James Matthie	8 Sept., '35	...	Asst.G.G.Agent N. W. Frontier
,,	Charles Jorden	16 Dec., '36		
,,	Thos. Box	27 July, '36		
,,	A. Wm. Taylor	25 Feb., '37	*	
Lieut.	Charles Clark	15 Jan., '29	...	On Furlo.
,,	John G. Gerrard	15 Dec., '30		
,,	Wm. Broadfoot	2 July, '33	*	
,,	Wm. Jas. Parker	8 Sept., '35		
,,	Jno. W. Bennett	16 Dec., '35	...	Sylhet Light Infantry
,,	H. T. Combe	27 July, '36		
,,	F. S. Macmullen	18 Dec., '37		
,,	F. Shuttleworth	20 July, '38		
Ensigns	R.W.H.Fanshawe	12 July, '38	12 June, '37	
,,	James Pattullo	,,	,,	
,,	Robt. H. Hicks	,,	26 July, '37	
,,	E. W. Salusbury	1 Sept.	11 Dec., '37	
,,	Geo. O. Jacob	,,	,,	
,,	John Lambert	,,	,,	
,,	E. J. Boileau	,,	,,	
,,	Tho. W. Gordon	,,	14 Jan., '38	

* With Shah Shujah's Army.

Facings, Sky-Blue.

THE BENGAL EUROPEAN REGIMENT.
(*Left Wing.*)
"Plassey," "Buxar," "Guzeratt," "Deig."

Station   Arrived

RANK.	NAMES.	Rank in the Regiment.	Rank in the Army.	REMARKS.
Colonel	Philip Le Fevre	18 Dec., '34	18 June, '31	On Furlo'
Lieut.-Colonel	Ab. Roberts, C.B.	28 Sept., '34		
Major	J. A. Thompson	27 Sept., '37		
Captain	David Birrell	26 April, '27		
,,	John P. Ripley	19 June, '31		
,,	Wm. Shortreed	15 Nov., '36	14 Feb., '35	
,	Thos. Lysart	27 Sept., '37	3 June	Hydrabad
	Alister Stewart	5 Mar., '38		
Lieutenant	Wm. Edm. Hay	9 May, '25	Captain, 19 July, '37	Brig. Major, Agra
	Jas. Rath. Pond	11 May, '32		
	Fran. Harrison	2 May, '33		
	Bernd. Kendall	13 Mar., '35		
	Douglas Seaton	29 July, 35		
,,	Edward Magnay	15 Nov., '36		
,,	John Fagan	3 Mar., '38		
,,	W. K. Haslewood	10 Aug., '38		

Adjutant to the Regiment,   —
Intr. & Qr. Mr.   do.   J. G. Gerrard.
Surgeon   do.   H. Guthrie, M.D.
Asst. do.   do.   Alex. Gibbon.

Facings, Sky-Blue.

The march towards Ghuznee did not commence under propitious circumstances, but there was now no deficiency in water, the men were cheerful under their privations, and though the columns were surrounded by pilferers, which kept the troops constantly on the alert, nothing worthy of notice occurred until the army, on the 21st July, 1839, arrived in the vicinity of Ghuznee, distant 290 miles from Kandahar and 90 from Cabul.

A careful reconnaissance showed that the fortress of Ghuznee had been much under-rated, and it was ascertained by inspecting the works that they possessed great strength. Captain Thompson, the Chief-Engineer with the army, gives the following description of the fortress of Ghuznee:

> We were very much surprised to find a high rampart in good repair built on a scarped mound about thirty-five feet high, flanked by numerous towers and surrounded by a fausse braye and a wet ditch. The irregular figure of the enceinte gave a good flanking-fire whilst the height of the citadel covered the interior from the commanding fire of the hills rendering it nugatory. In addition to this the towers at the angles had been enlarged. Screen walls had been built before the gates, the ditch cleared out, and filled with water (stated to be unfordable) and an outwork built on the right bank of the river, so as to command the bed of it. We had no battering-train, and to attack Ghuznee in form a much larger train would be required than the army ever possessed.

The Citadel, in itself a fort of considerable strength, is situated at the top of the hill upon which the city and its fortifications are-built.

The British force fit for duty amounted to about 8000 men, in addition to which was Shah Shuja's Contingent of about 4000; and our artillery consisted of 40 guns, of which 18 were light field-pieces.

To await the arrival of our siege-train was out of the question, as it was known that one of Dost Mahomed's Generals had been sent from Cabul with a considerable force to act against the besiegers, in concert with the commander of the Ghuznee garrison. This hostile force could not now be more than one or two marches distant; and it was a matter of importance that action should be taken before reinforcements could arrive. It was under these circumstances that the commander-in-chief made up his mind to carry the fortress by a *coup-de-main* and for this purpose he determined on the following plan of action. A double charge of powder would be placed by an explosion party against the Cabul Gate of the city, and this charge was to be fired at a given signal; the attention of the defenders having been previously diverted in the opposite direction by a false attack.

On the explosion taking place the storming-party were to enter and possess themselves of the fortress; this plan being elaborated in a General Order dated Ghuznee, 22nd July, 1839.

The storming-party was placed under the command of Brigadier-General Sale, C.B., and the advance was ordered to consist of the Light Companies of H.M. 2nd, 17th, and the Bengal European Regiments, and a flank Company of H.M. 13th Light Infantry.

The main column consisted of the Bengal European Regiment under Colonel Orchard, H.M. 2nd and the remainder of the 13th Light Infantry formed as skirmishers on the flanks.

H.M. 17th Regiment was ordered to form "the support and to follow the storming party into the works."

Finally a detachment of native infantry was directed to "quit camp and move round the gardens on the south of the town where they will establish themselves; and about 3 a.m. open a fire upon the place for the purpose of distracting the attention of the garrison."

Immediately after the explosion at the Cabul Gate "the chief-engineer finding the opening practicable will have 'the advance' sounded for the column to rush on. When the head of the column has passed the gateway a signal must be made for the artillery to turn their fire from the walls of the town on the Citadel."

At midnight—23rd July, 1839—the British army was astir, but their allotted positions were taken up in absolute silence. The night was stormy, and the wind so boisterous that the movements of the troops were not discovered by the enemy; and within the fortress no sound was heard, all being so still that it was for some time suspected that the place had been evacuated.

The detachment of native infantry which had taken up its position in the gardens to the south of the town were heard to open fire in the distance, but they failed to attract much notice from the garrison.

The engineers, who formed the explosion-party, had silently advanced, carrying with them bags containing 300 lbs. of powder.[5]

The explosion-party had not advanced more than a few hundred

---

5. A charge of from 60 to 120 lbs. of powder is said to be usually ample for blowing in a gate, but the commander-in-chief gave special orders for a full double charge to be used.

yards when their movements were observed by the enemy's sentries, who immediately gave the alarm, and in a few minutes a great number of blue-lights were burned on the tops of the walls of the fortress. It now became apparent to the explosion-party that the enemy did not suspect that they had any design on the gate, for the blue-lights, instead of being thrown into the sortie passages below, were held high in the air so that while lighting up the country around they afforded no guidance to the besieged, who appeared to be in ignorance that an immediate attack on their fortress was contemplated.

The enemy were not kept long in doubt, for the explosion-party hastened forward under a severe fire from the ramparts, and placing the bags of powder in position, and laying the fuse, they retired under whatever cover they could find. A moment's silence followed; when the chain of fire, taking its serpent-like course, was seen to run along the ground, and on reaching the charge an explosion followed which blew the gate and some of the surrounding buildings to atoms.

There was no longer any doubt as to the intentions of the besiegers, and the silence which had been enjoined on the troops was now broken by a succession of hearty cheers; our artillery at the same time opening fire, and the Afghans hastening to their allotted positions on the ramparts.

The commander-in-chief now gave the order for the party forming the advance to push forward and secure the entrance to the fortress. The light companies made a dash for the ruins of the gate, but their progress was opposed by a strong force of the enemy, who advanced outside the sortie and contested the passage. A galling musketry and grape-fire was poured on the "advance party" as they charged, and their ranks were thinned before they reached the outer works; but after a desperate resistance the enemy were driven back amongst the ruins of the gate. But the passage was still hotly contested; the light companies again and again charging the masses, and at each charge obtaining some slight advantage: until the enemy fairly gave way, and the advance-party with a cheer and a rush, was scrambling over the ruins.

The enemy were driven back but not dismayed; and now rapidly forming into two parties they made a desperate onslaught on both flanks of the advance, so that it appeared for some minutes doubtful if any of the men composing the light companies would be left to hold the ground. But at this critical moment our storming-party arrived in support, and the enemy were bayoneted in such numbers that our troops was much impeded by the heaps of dead and débris round the ruined gate.

But this advantage had not been secured without terrible loss on our side; the wounded of the light company of the Bengal European Regiment, including its three Officers, Lieutenants Broadfoot, Magnay, and Haslewood, as well as thirty of the rank and file. It was here that Brigadier-General Sale, who commanded the storming-party received a severe cut in the face; after which he had a desperate hand-to-hand encounter with his enemy as they rolled together on the ground, both fighting for their lives; until the General, although much exhausted from loss of blood, succeeded in wrenching his enemy's sword from his grasp, and with it cleft the Afghan's head in two.

The main opposition at the gateway having been now overcome, the bugles sounded the advance; and, as had been previously ordered, H.M. 13th and 17th Regiments took the road to their right which led round to the Citadel.

Our guns had for some hours been directed on the walls of the Citadel, which was at the top of the hill on which the fortress of Ghuznee was built; and it was hoped, by the time an entrance into the fortress had been effected, a practicable breach would have been made on the walls of the Citadel, so that the 13th and 17th Regiments might carry it by storm. Inside the Cabul gate was a large square about 150 yards across and commanded by houses on three sides, whilst on the fourth side was the Citadel, which was immediately opposite to the captured gateway. As soon as the storming-party had reached this square some of the enemy rushed towards the Citadel, whilst others took possession of the houses; from which they continued to pour a galling fire on our advancing troops.

The route taken by the Bengal European Regiment was through narrow streets, the houses on each side as well as those in the square being filled with the Afghans, who sent a raking fire on the Regiment as it advanced; and, in addition to this fire, the streets were occupied by the enemy, who stoutly contested the passage of our troops. Two hours were occupied in thus fighting our way through the streets of the town towards the Kandahar gate; on each side of which were outworks only approachable through a narrow passage, from above which a constant fire was kept up by the enemy. In these outworks there was an expense magazine, which fortunately had exploded, and made the capture of the position comparatively easy.

The Bengal European Regiment now turned off to the left, passing along a street which led back towards the ruins of the Cabul gate;

when suddenly the colours of the 13th and 17th Regiments were seen flying on the walls of the Citadel above, and the enemy rushing down the slope only eager to effect their escape. The Bengal European Regiment was still employed in forcing its passage along the street, when Major Warren, the second in command of the Regiment, was struck in three places and fell to the ground severely wounded.

The scene in the centre square at this time is described as having been one of horror and confusion:

> Horses, many wounded, were running about in all directions, fighting with each other, kicking and biting, and running quite furious at anyone they saw; so dangerous had these animals become that the men were obliged to be ordered to shoot the horses in self-defence as they endangered the lives of all, and particularly of the wounded men while being carried out in dhoolies.

The Afghans became thoroughly demoralised, and abandoning their guns fled in all directions; throwing themselves from the walls into the depth below where many of them perished; many others refusing quarter and rushing on the bayonets of our soldiers, eager to die whilst fighting the battle of the faith, rather than crave for mercy at the hand of the Infidel.

Hyder Khan, the Governor of Ghuznee, received a bayonet-thrust through the waistband of his dress, and would have lost his life had he not surrendered to Captain A. W. Taylor of the Bengal European Regiment, who happened to be near at hand in the mêlée.

The loss of the enemy will never be known; but the bodies of upwards of 500 Afghans were found within the walls of the fortress, and 1500 were taken prisoners.

The Bengal European Regiment suffered very severely in wounded; but it is remarkable that throughout the British army the number of killed in the siege was very small in proportion to the wounded. The Bengal European Regiment had only 1 rank and file killed; whilst amongst the wounded there were Lieutenant Colonel Joseph Orchard, C.B., commanding the Regiment, Major Warren, Captains Hay and Tayler, Lieutenants Broadfoot, Haslewood, and Fagan, and Magnay, and Ensign Jacob; with 51 rank and file. Of these Officers, Major Warren and Lieutenant Haslewood were in considerable danger.

Major Warren was wounded in three places; the upper part of his left wrist being carried away by a shot, a second striking his left breast and passing round the surface of his chest, and a third entering the upper part of his right arm, in which he had received a severe wound at the capture of Bhurtpore, 1826.[6]

Lieutenant Haslewood was cut down soon after the advance-party had got into the fortress; and, although he succeeded in shooting the first man who attacked him, he was immediately afterwards surrounded by the enemy, who inflicted five sabre wounds of great severity, the first on the head which felled him to the ground; and whilst in a half-conscious state the Afghans hacked him with their tulwars, cutting through his right scapula, another wound crossing this, and in addition his right thigh was severed at the joint; at this critical moment a private soldier in Lieutenant Haslewood's company, named Kelly, coming up just as the Afghan was about giving Haslewood his coup-de-grace, rushed to his officer's rescue and ran his assailant completely through the body with his bayonet. From the serious nature of Lieutenant Haslewood's injuries, the surgeons did not think that he would recover the use of his arm or leg; but he was more fortunate than was anticipated, and under the skilful treatment which he received he was, after a long convalescence, again fit for duty.[7]

And now is a fitting time to refer to the valuable services rendered to the Bengal European Regiment by their indefatigable Surgeon, Dr. G. Paton; who, though suffering from a painful illness, was ever at his post, rendering, by his scientific experiments, inestimable benefits to both the officers and men, who suffered as much from diseases peculiar to the country as from the ravages of war.

After the storm was over, and quiet had been in some degree restored, the General Commanding-in-Chief conducted his Majesty Shah Shuja round the fortress and Citadel; and the Amir expressed his astonishment at our having captured in a few hours the fortress which had heretofore held the reputation of being impregnable.

The Governor, Hyder Khan, was brought before His Majesty, who, at the intercession of the English Commander, spared his life; he being ordered to be kept a prisoner of war, for which purpose he was sent to the headquarter camp and placed under the charge of Sir Alexander Burnes.

---

6. Major Warren was afterwards appointed by Lord Auckland, Town-Major of Fort William, as a special reward for his services on this occasion.
7. Lieutenant Haslewood was rewarded for his services by Lord Auckland, who placed him on his personal staff. Lieutenant Haslewood was, however, afterwards invalided on account of his wounds.

A few days' rest was now allowed to the troops; the wounded being placed in the depôt hospital at Ghuznee, and the convalescents, with such of the sick and wounded as could be moved without risk, being ordered to accompany the army on, its forward march.

On the 30th of July, 1839, the British force continued to march towards Cabul; Dost Mahomed[8] flying from that city on the approach of the army, and on the 7th August the Amir Shah Shuja made his public entry into his capital.

The inhabitants of Cabul seemed marvellously indifferent to the changes which had taken place. The city was filled with immense crowds, but they made no demonstration; there was no shouting or sounds of joy; the nobles rose as the king appeared and made their salaam, but as soon as His Majesty had passed they reseated themselves, and the crowds dispersed to their usual avocations.

On the 3rd September, 1839, the Shahzada Timur marched into Cabul with his army. On the 17th of September, H.M. Shah Shujah held a grand durbar at the Bala Hissar, for the purpose of conferring upon certain Officers of the British army, who had been selected to receive the distinction, the Order of the Duranee Empire. The following Officers of the Bengal European Regiment received the Order.

Brigadier-General Roberts, C.B., who had commanded the Amir's force during the campaign, was created a Member of the 2nd Class. Lieutenant-Colonel .Joseph Orchard, C.B., and Major Warren were created Members of the 3rd Class. A Brevet Lieutenant-Colonelcy was also conferred on Major Warren. W. O., 13th December, 1839.

A medal was ordered to be struck and presented to all those officers and soldiers who had been engaged at the capture of Ghuznee. Subsequently the names "Afghanistan" and "Ghuznee" were ordered to be inscribed on the colours of all the Regiments who had served during the campaign; these being inherited by the Royal Minister Fusiliers.

---

8. It having been ascertained that the ex-Amir Dost Mahomed had fled in the direction of Bameen, a force was dispatched in pursuit under the direction Hajee Khan Kakur; Captain Arthur William Tayler and Lieutenant William Broadfoot, both of the Bengal European Regiment, serving with this detachment. Hajee Khan Kakur, who had received many favours from Dost Mahomed, now defeated the object for which the expedition had been organised and connived at the Dost's escape; the detachment returning to Cabul without the ex-Amir; who, however, subsequently surrendered himself a prisoner of war, and claimed the protection of the British after the battle of Purwan, 3rd November, 1840.

Orders were now issued by H.E. the Commander-in-Chief, 9th October, 1839, for the breaking up of "the army of the Indus," the purposes for which it had been assembled having been fully attained. The ex-Amir, Dost Mahomed, had been dethroned and was a fugitive; and our ally, Shah Shujah, had been replaced upon his throne, after an absence from his capital of thirty years. The army had marched 1527 miles, under circumstances of great hardship and privation; it had occupied Kandahar, stormed and captured the strong fortress of Ghuznee, and it was now in undisputed possession of the capital city of the Afghan Kingdom.

The death of the Maharaja Runjeet Sing on the 27th June, 1839, was not generally known in the army at the time of its occurrence as fears had been entertained that in the event of the Maharaja's demise his successor might withdraw his army of observation from Peshawar; the consequences of which would have been very serious and probably might have imperilled the safety of our army on its return to India. Satisfactory arrangements were however made with the Punjab Government, and the policy of the late Maharaja was adopted by his successor.

On the breaking-up of the army of the Indus three of its brigades remained in Afghanistan; one at Kandahar; one at Cabul; and the third at Jellalabad. The fourth Brigade of the army of the Indus, in which was the Bengal European Regiment, was directed to form part of the "army of occupation," and proceed to Jellalabad; but, as a General Order had been published—29th July, 1839—ordering the embodiment of the 2nd European Regiment, volunteers from the 1st European Regiment were called for to form the nucleus of 2nd Regiment. Eighty-two men were selected and proceeded to Hazarebagh with the invalids and time-expired men of the Regiment, under command of Lieutenant-Colonel Warren, who by this time had sufficiently recovered from his wounds to undertake the duty.

Although many of the officers of the old 2nd European Regiment[9]—which had been joined with the 1st in 1830—were still serving with the latter Regiment all the officers of the newly-formed Regiment were taken from the general list of the army. 1839. The promotion of the officers of the right and left wings of the European Regiment, which had continued since the amalgamation of the 1st and 2nd Regiments, was so involved that it was found impossible

---

9. White facings were prescribed for this Regiment on its reorganisation, as worn by the old 2nd European Regiment in the last century.

to separate them without causing great injustice. Under the orders regulating the promotion of the officers of the two wings, no wing officer could receive substantive promotion until his parallel officer in the other wing had been promoted. Under the working of this order a captain has commanded the Regiment whilst a major has been present and on duty.[10]

The detachment of the Bengal European Regiment under Colonel Warren marched from Cabul on the 15th October 1839. with the second column of the returning army, under command of Major-General Thackwell.

Subsequent political and military events proved that it would have been well had Lord Auckland elected to withdraw his army from Afghanistan immediately after the occupation of Cabul, whilst the British army was crowned with all the honours of victory; but such was not the policy of the Government of India, who, though bound by the terms of the Governor-General's "Proclamation," were unwilling to relinquish the power obtained over the Afghan country. In vain His Majesty Shah Shujah, urged the withdrawal of the British troops; his request was refused on the ground that he was not yet secured in power, the Government of India reserving to itself the right of determining when the time of withdrawal should arrive.

The people of Afghanistan were justly alarmed at the decision of the British Government; they hinted at a violation of faith, and pointed to the Governor-General's "Proclamation," promising them independence; the hostile feeling increased; powerful Chiefs assembled armies and assumed a threatening attitude, claiming their independence and openly taunting the King with being the puppet of a foreign power.

The Bengal European Regiment had scarcely taken up its quarters in the garrison of Jellalabad when one of these discontented Afghan chiefs named Syad Husain, at the head of a considerable force, took up his position in the fort of Pushoot, about fifty miles from Jellalabad, and assumed a defiant attitude. Lieutenant-Colonel Orchard, C.B., commanding the Bengal European Regiment, was ordered to proceed with a company of his regiment under the command of Captain Thomas Box, and a small native force with three guns, to dislodge the rebel chief.

On the 18th January, 1840, the British detachment arrived in the vicinity of the fort. The march to Pushoot had been performed under

---

10. It was said that no one outside the Regiment understood the working of this Government Order, and very few of those affected by it could explain its effects.

very trying and harassing circumstances, a constant downpour of rain saturating the roads and drenching the troops; the cold being intense, and violent storms rendering progress difficult. On taking up position our field-guns opened fire on the walls of the Fort, no difficulty being anticipated in reducing its inmates to subjection. A practicable breach was soon effected and Captain Box, with his company of the Bengal European Regiment, together with some sepahis, forming the storming-party, effected an entrance; but it soon became apparent that the breach had been made in the outer works only, and that the inner fortifications could not be carried without scaling ladders or blasting operations.

At this time, by some mistake, one of our buglers sounded the "Advance," which indicated to the outer force that we had succeeded in making our way into the fort. On hearing; the signal the rest of the besiegers pushed forward, and thus the outer works became dangerously crowded, and our troops exposed to a heavy fire from the walls of the fort. An attempt was now made, to blow in the inner gate, but the powder was damp and refused to ignite; but still, notwithstanding that the explosion-party were exposed to considerable danger, a second attempt was made to blow open the gate; but again the powder failed.

The troops had been exposed during these operations to a heavy cross fire for several hours, the rain at the same time pouring down in torrents; and, as Colonel Orchard considered that no further progress could be made, he ordered his troops to retire to their camp. The officers and soldiers had manifested the greatest gallantry and resolution under difficult and disheartening circumstances; our loss was considerable, Lieutenant Hicks, of the Bengal European Regiment, being mortally wounded; 19 men were killed and 48 wounded. It is, however, satisfactory to be able to record that the determination and valour of the troops engaged convinced the enemy that prolonged resistance would be useless; and they evacuated the fort during the night of the 19th January, taking with them all their valuables; and, with the exception of a small store of grain and gunpowder, the fort had been completely cleared. Colonel Orchard occupied the fort, and remained with his troops at Pushoot until the 16th of February, when they returned to Jellalabad.

In November, 1840, the 1st Bengal European Regiment returned to India, and during its homeward march it learned with satisfaction that, under .instructions received from the Court of Directors, it had been rewarded by being formed into Light Infantry, and was henceforth to be designated the "1st Bengal European Light Infantry."

On its arrival in India the Regiment went into quarters at Kurnaul, a new station built on a scale of grandeur hitherto unknown in India. Kurnaul had been selected as a suitable site for a cantonment, and barracks had been erected for the accommodation of a strong frontier force, but the situation of the station was soon found to be unhealthy, on account of its close: proximity to the irrigation canals, which, from their having been constructed at a higher level than that of the cantonment, produced a destructive epidemic of fever amongst the troops. The station was in consequence abandoned, and most of the Regiments were removed to Umballa, which henceforth was the principal frontier station.

Notwithstanding that some compensation was granted by the Government, sad losses fell upon the officers of the regiments, stationed at Kurnaul, as they all had expended very large sums on the erection of houses, &c.

It is beyond our province to more than glance at the horrors and misfortunes which befell so many officers and soldiers of the army of occupation soon after the 1st European Light Infantry returned to India.

The cold-blooded murder of the Amir Shah Shujah, assassinated, near the Bala Hissar by order of the usurper Zeman Khan, was perpetrated in the following manner. Shah Shujah had started in his palanquin to join his army, encamped near at hand, when the son of Zeman Khan accompanied by his followers fired a volley into the palanquin, which killed its occupant as well as several of the bearers. The body of the Amir was thrown into a ditch and hacked by the murderers with their tulwars.

On the 2nd of November Sir Alexander Burnes and his staff were attacked and murdered in the Residency at Cabul;[11] these atrocities being followed by the assassination of the British resident, Sir William McNaughten, and his assistant. Captain Trevor; by the imprison-

---

11. Amongst the Staff Officers who fell on this occasion was Lieutenant William Broadfoot of the Bengal European Regiment. Thornton, in his. History of the British Empire, Vol. 6., p. 258, says that Lieutenant Broadfoot was "an officer whom all reports unite in eulogizing, and whose life was dearly paid for by his assailants, six of whom met destruction from his hand before it was paralysed by death." Two days afterwards near Char-ee-kar fell another promising young Officer of the Bengal European Regiment, Ensign Ed.W. Salusbury, who had been specially selected for service with the Amir Shall Shujah's contingent. Ensign Salusbury, who was desperately wounded at Lughman whilst fighting bravely against overwhelming numbers near the military post of Char-ee-kar, died of his wounds the same night.

ment of Lady Sale and all those who accompanied the British in their disastrous retreat from Cabul. The city of Cabul and the fortress of Ghuznee were wrenched from the hands of the British; and finally the British Brigade under General Elphinstone was annihilated in attempting to force its way from Cabul to Jellalabad.

But ultimately the honour of our arms was fully vindicated, and the death of so many of our countrymen avenged, by the gallant and victorious march of General Pollock from Jellalabad,[12] and of General Nott from Kandahar. Ghuznee was recaptured, Cabul was reoccupied, Lady Sale and all the English prisoners were released, and the British "army of occupation" vacated Afghanistan with honour.

In June, 1842, an army of Reserve was ordered to be formed at Ferozpóre, under the immediate command of His Excellency the Commander-in-Chief in India; with orders, in case of need, to act as a relieving force to the army of occupation on its return march from Afghanistan. Lieutenant-Colonel Orchard, C.B., was appointed a Brigadier to command the 1st or Light Brigade of the army of Reserve, in which was his Regiment, the 1st Bengal European Light Infantry; and, after the arrival of General Pollock's victorious army within British territory, the army of Reserve was broken up, and the 1st European Light Infantry was ordered to Subathoo, a station situated on the summit of the range of hills between the plains of India and the sanatorium of Simla. Subathoo will ever be remembered as one of the most beautiful spots in the Himalayas. It may fairly be said that—after nearly a hundred years of almost constant warfare, constant exposure to extremes of climate, constant scenes of bloodshed and privation—here was a haven of rest and peace, surrounded by God's most glorious and most pleasing works; the valleys teeming with verdure, the hills covered with evergreen pines and silver oaks, and the old half-ruined Fort, that had in former years stood many a siege, with its background of eternal snow.

Early in February, 1845, the author of this work, a boy just eighteen years of age, toiled up the Subathoo hill to join his regiment; the scene above, but faintly described, suddenly burst upon him as he emerged from the gorge overhanging the grassy plateau which forms the Regimental Parade forcibly striking his imagination by its glorious aspect, the vision of which can never be erased from his memory.

---

12. Captain John G. Gerrard of the Bengal European Regiment served in the defence of Jellalabad against Akbar Khan. 7th April. 1842 (severely wounded); he also served with General Pollock's force on its victorious march.

CHAPTER 15

The First Sikh War

In the early part of the year 1845 the 1st Bengal 1845 European Regiment (Light Infantry) was, in point of physique, discipline and smartness, second to none in the British service. Amongst its rank and file there were many service-scarred, grey-haired soldiers, who had passed twenty years in its ranks: men whose lead the younger soldiers were prepared to follow, and whose example they would emulate. An officer,[1] whose opinion commands respect, speaks of the appearance of the Regiment at this time as "glorious!" He says, "I saw it stand on parade at Subathoo in 1845 close on a thousand strong, and after the battles of the Sutlej Campaign it mustered on parade at Lahore two hundred and fifty. The rest were killed and wounded."

At this time the Regiment was commanded by that grand old Officer, Lieut.-Col. Joseph Orchard, C.B., a rigid disciplinarian, but a kind-hearted, just man; essentially the young soldiers' friend, whom he was ever ready to assist with his advice and kindly aid. Colonel Orchard had joined the Bengal European Regiment early in the century; his experience and services extending back to some of the greatest victories in Indian history.

It was during the middle of 1845 that Colonel Orchard took leave of absence to England, and was succeeded in the command of the Regiment by Lieutenant-Colonel David Birrell.

There was at this time another officer present with the Bengal European Light Infantry of whom notice cannot be omitted— Lieutenant Herbert Benjamin Edwardes—a man who commanded the respect of his brother officers, and whose genial, kindly nature endeared him to all; in education and talents he was superior to most of his comrades, and in sound, clear judgement, and common sense

1. Field Marshal Lord Napier of Magdala, G.C.B., G.C.S.I.

was far beyond his years. In 1845 this young unknown subaltern published, under the pseudonym of "Brahmine Bull," a series of political papers, which immediately attracted the attention not only of the Indian Government officials, but of those in power in England. These letters were believed to be from the pen of a man of high standing and much Indian experience, but when it was surmised that the author was a young subaltern doing duty with his Regiment at Subathoo all officials were sceptical. The Commander-in-Chief, Sir Hugh Gough, called the young man into his presence, and the Governor-General, Sir Henry Hardinge, interviewed him; when it became known that young Edwardes was, both as a writer and as a soldier, the rising man of the day. As a temporary measure Edwardes was appointed an extra aide-de-camp to the Commander-in-Chief; and a few years afterwards his exploits of coolness, courage, and sound judgement caused all England to ring with respect, admiration, and praise.

But though all seemed in the early months of 1845 so like a permanent peace in India, there was a storm gathering not far distant which was shortly to burst upon us with a fury unparalleled in our Indian history; but before recording the events connected with the coming Seik War, it will be necessary to glance at the circumstances that brought about an invasion, to encounter and repel which called forth all our energies and resources.

It may be fairly stated that the Sutlej War was quite unprovoked on the part of the Indian Government; the invasion was made by the Seiks in defiance of treaties and at a time of profound repose, and it was incumbent on the British in their own self-defence to exert all their influence and strength to drive the invaders from their soil.

The Seik Campaign, although in no way a religious war, was brought about by reason of the Punjaubees having so intermixed their religious spirit and tenets with their Military system that their army became the usurper of their civil government; and it was to free themselves from a Military despotism that the Government of the Punjaub encouraged the Seik army to confront the British, in the hope that it might in some way be relieved from the intolerable bondage in which it was held, and against which it found itself by any other means unable to combat.

The Seik religion varies materially from all other forms of worship in India. Its founder was one Nanuk, a Guru,[2] born in the year A.D. 1468. At the early age of eleven he became a teacher of men, and

---

2. Fakir or Priest.

soon afterwards had several disciples, to whom he taught his doctrines. Nanuk had studied the writings of the Mahomedan and Hindu fathers, but they had failed to convey his conception of the Deity. He loathed the sensual symbolism of the Hindus, and the ostentatious worship of the Mahomedans was repellent to him. He was desirous of finding a God of simplicity and truth, all-merciful, abhorring war, and a lover of goodwill and peace. He wrote many holy effusions on the unity and attributes of God, and these poems are still held in supreme reverence by the Punjaubees. Nanuk was believed by his followers to have seen God, who had nominated him to be His teacher, and enjoined on him the three simple lessons of (1) the worship of the name of God, (2) of charity to all men, and lastly of ablution. Notwithstanding his great mission and the favours which were supposed to have been conferred on him,. Nanuk returned to his home, a disappointed man, and died—1539 —feeling that human nature could never aspire to a realization of the knowledge of God, which he sought in vain to obtain.

Nanuk's successors compiled from the writings and traditional sayings of the Guru's the Khalsa Bible, called the "Grunth;" under the authority of which they gained temporal as well as spiritual power, and even aspired to the throne.

The Guru who forms the connecting link between the past history of the Punjab and the invasion by the Seiks of our Indian possessions was named Hur Govind—1675—under whom the religion of the Seiks for the first time was employed as an adjunct to military power. At the head of his troops Hur Govind defeated those of the Emperor of Hindustan; thus gaining prestige and power otherwise unattainable. He placed his military organization strictly on a religious basis; and, taking advantage of his priestly office, taught his followers that bravery in battle was an incomparable virtue, whereas cowardice carried with it condemnation and spiritual death. Hur Govind, finding in time that superstition gained ground amongst his people, simplified the dogmas of his faith, forbidding all effigies whatever of the Deity, and all caste differences; "for," said he, "God is one, and in his presence all men are equal."

Such was the religious organization which was engrafted into the Seik military system, with the object of creating an army capable of reducing to subjection any force against which it might be pitted, and during his reign of nearly 30 years Hur Govind succeeded in spreading his tenets amongst the whole Seik nation, who gladly accepted the faith, by embracing which its votaries became Khalsas, or "the pure ones;" and thus he inaugurated a powerful military system, and imbued its soldiers with a religious enthusiasm inspiring them with the belief that they were the chosen people of God, and that they must invariably be invincible in war.

Although during the following century the Government of the Punjaub was subdivided into independent districts the military training and enthusiasm of the Khalsas progressed, and in the year 1780 a Prince was born to them, named Runjit Sing, called the Lion of the Punjab, who by his tact and skill tranquillized conflicting interests and amalgamated the feudal clans, so that when he was seated on the Khalsa throne he ruled over a kingdom more powerful than the Marathas, and more influential than that of the Emperor of Delhie.

It will be in the memory of our readers how, in 1804, Lord Lake, at the head of his flying column—with which was the Bengal European Regiment—pursued his enemy Jeswant Roa Holkar to the very gates of Lahore, when the Maharaja Runjit Sing mediated between the British and the Marathas, and, refusing to give Holkar an asylum, forced him to put his seal on the compact acknowledging the supremacy of the British over the whole of the Maratha Empire.

The Maharaja Runjit Sing, holding the memory and actions of his predecessor Hur Govind in supreme-veneration, determined to perfect the great work which he had inaugurated. The Seiks had by this time become essentially a military nation, their religion and education prepared them for the arts of war; they were men of magnificent physique, obedient, enduring, brave, and unfettered by caste prejudices: but they, in common with all the Eastern nations, failed in the great requisite of capable commanders. To supply this deficiency Runjit Sing sought and obtained the services of Generals Allard, Avitabile, Court, and Ventura; all men of established ability, who had gained their reputation under the great Napoleon. These Generals, on the downfall of the Empire—being unemployed—accepted Runjit Sing's offer of service, and were appointed to high military commands in the Khalsa army; and by them the French system of drill was introduced, the Seik regiments completely remodelled and exercised in military movements on the European system.

It has been stated in the last chapter that Maharajah Runjit Sing died—27th June, 1839—during the time that the British were employed in the Afghan War. Runjit's death was followed by rapid changes in the Government of the Punjab; within a very few years several successors to the throne having been murdered, the Fort and City of

Lahore besieged and captured with all the horrors of rapine, pillage, and murder, terminating in the boy Dulip Sing—the son of Runjit Sing by his favorite wife, the Rani Jinda Kaur—being proclaimed by the Khalsa Maharajah of the Punjab.

Scenes of murder, intrigue, and bloodshed were still rife; the boy Dulip Sing was closely guarded, and the Rani appointed Regent; with her brother, Jowahir Sing, and her paramour, Lal Sing, forming a triumvirate of which Jowahir Sing was Prime Minister; but a rebellion soon following, Jowahir Sing was arraigned before an army Council and ordered to be shot, the sentence being carried into effect in the compulsory presence of the Regent and the young Maharaja.

There was no longer any doubt that the Khalsas intended to assert their power to control their Sovereign and their Government; and it was now fully realized that the Gurus had created a military despotism which paralysed and eclipsed all the functions of their Government.

Lal Sing, who was in constant communication with the Rani-Regent, admitted into their confidence Tej Sing, the Chief of the Khalsa army, which was the actual ruler of the country.

But matters were rapidly approaching to a crisis; the treasury was exhausted and the army clamorous for their arrears of pay to supply which the thought of conquest arose before the minds of the soldiers. Why should they not demonstrate their power and replenish their treasure-chest by the invasion of British India, capturing the rich cities of Delhie and Calcutta, and bringing all Hindustan under their sway?

In vain the Rani and many of the influential Sirdars pointed out to the Khalsa troops the perilous nature of their undertaking. But the Seik army sought excitement, pillage, and conquest. The edict was sent forth; war was proclaimed against the East India Company; and the Khalsa army, 70,000 strong, with upwards of 100 guns, marched to invade India.

The knowledge that this violent proceeding must ultimately end in defeat and disaster, induced the French Generals in the Seik service to obtain leave of absence to Europe before the invasion of India had been finally determined on. These officers had, by their influence, and in the general confusion, amassed large fortunes, which they had from time to time transmitted to France through British agencies; and now, crossing the frontier into the Company's territories, their retreat was secured.

There remained still with the Seiks several European officers of inferior rank; but when the army was deprived of the services of such men as Avitabile and Ventura, insubordination quickly appeared in its ranks, and it soon retrograded into the state from which it had been raised by Runjit Sing, at such great expense and with so much judgement.

Tej Sing and Lal Sing were now on the horns of a dilemma. They had both secretly encouraged the Seik army to make war on the British, as this course appeared to them the easiest way of ridding the country of what had become a source of so much danger; but now the whole army called on these Sirdars to join the troops and lead them to victory. Lal Sing was no soldier; he loved the society of the Rani far more than joining in what he felt must ultimately prove a hopeless struggle, Tej Sing, on the contrary, every inch a soldier, readily consented to lead the Khalsa troops; they looking to him with confidence and reliance to subdue the British in open fight.

One other personage here claims special notice. Golab Sing, the Raja of Jamu, had been solicited to accept the Prime Ministership of the Punjaub Government, but he preferred the comparative peace of his own country. He however possessed considerable power at the Lahore Court, and he now demanded of them their reasons for ignoring the treaties of friendship which had existed between their Government and the East India Company; and asked what cause of offence the latter had given.

No reply was made to his demand; and Golab Sing, for his own safety, dissembled by promising to raise an army of 40,000 men, and declaring his readiness to assist the Khalsa; but at the same time he made specious excuses for delay, determining to cautiously await the course of events before committing himself to action.

Lord Ellenborough, before his recall—1844—had foreseen the gathering storm in the direction of our north-west frontier, and intended to form a vast entrenched camp; for which purpose he had already massed troops at Umballa, and increased the British force at Ferozpóre; but on his sudden recall this policy was abandoned. Sir Henry Hardinge, his successor, did not anticipate that the Seiks would prove dangerous neighbours; he accordingly substituted a policy of peace, and no step was taken or contemplated which could give umbrage to the Seiks.

On December 11th, the Khalsa army crossed the Sutlej, and invaded the British territory; the suddenness of their movements causing something approaching to consternation; the more so as, under the Governor-General's orders, preparations for defence had been abandoned, and we were in no way ready to repel an invasion, although

Sir Hugh Gough, the Commander-in-Chief, had warned his troops to be on the look-out for a sudden move; but his actions had been so hampered by Government orders that he could not make any active preparations until the Seik thunderbolt had been launched.

The Seik army crossed the river Sutlej, and having made two marches, strongly entrenched itself around the village of Ferozeshah before reliable information reached the Government of the unprovoked invasion. Fortunately the Governor-General was at this time in the North-Western Provinces. The crisis demanded the full energy and power of all departments. The Commander-in-Chief could issue orders to mass his troops, but this was not all—the troops must be fed, and enormous quantities of carriage must be instantly forthcoming.

As soon as it became known that the Khalsa army had crossed the Sutlej and taken up its position, as above described, within British territory, the Governor-General no longer placed any restrictions on the actions of the Commander-in-Chief; but published a manifesto, declaring that the responsibility of the war rested with the Seiks alone; that their unprovoked aggression should be severely punished; and British authority preserved over all the countries which had been living under its protection: and, further, that as the Seiks had, by their unprovoked aggression, broken the treaties which had existed between the two nations since 1809, the Seik possessions on the left bank of the Sutlej should be confiscated and annexed to those of the East India Company.

As Lieutenant-Colonel Orchard, C.B., was now on leave of absence, the command of the 1st European Light Infantry devolved on Major David Birrell.

At 9 p.m. on the 10th December, 1845, whilst the officers of the Regiment were at mess, an orderly from army headquarters galloped in hot haste up to the door of the mess-house, and delivered a dispatch to the commanding officer, directing the 1st European Light Infantry immediately to prepare for active service, marching as soon as arrangements could be completed. Not a moment was to be lost. The officers proceeded forthwith to the barracks, aroused their men, and ordered them to prepare for their march at once; and at 10 o'clock the next morning the Regiment was in full march to Kalka a distance of 19 miles across the hills.

Lieutenant Williamson of the Regiment was left in charge of the station and depôt, and Ensign Hamilton, who was on the sick-list, was also left at Subathoo with the regimental hospital, which contained

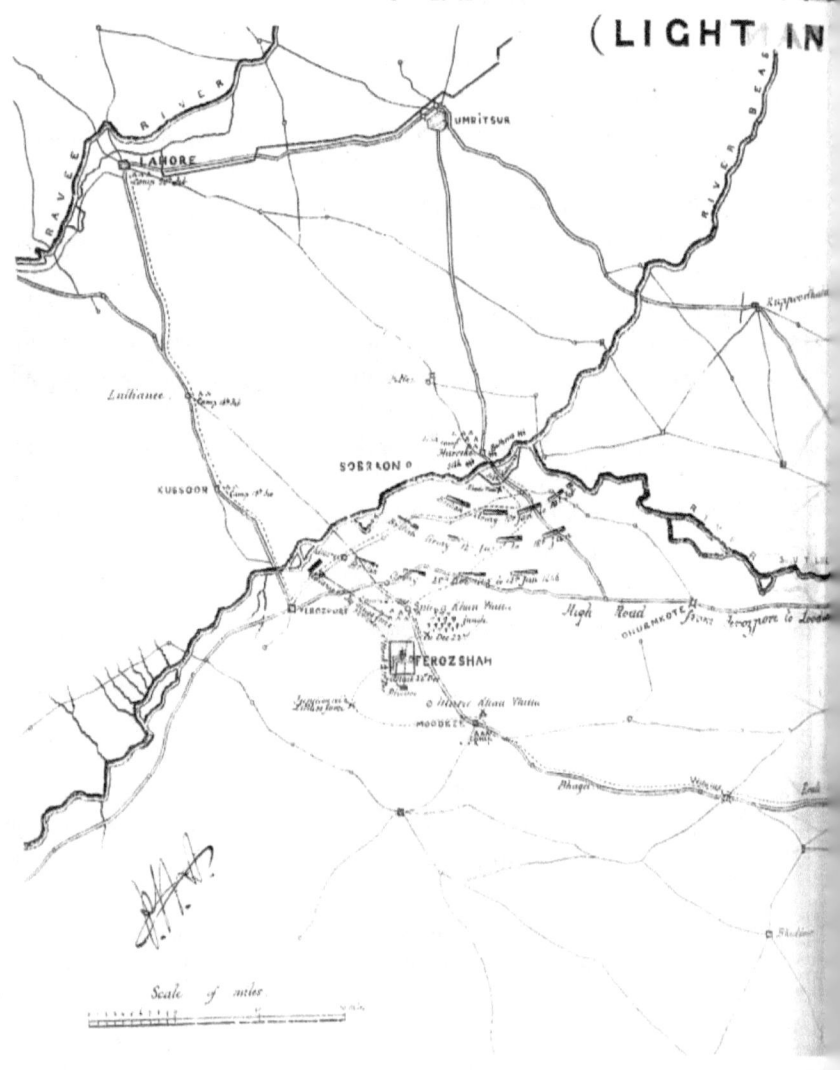

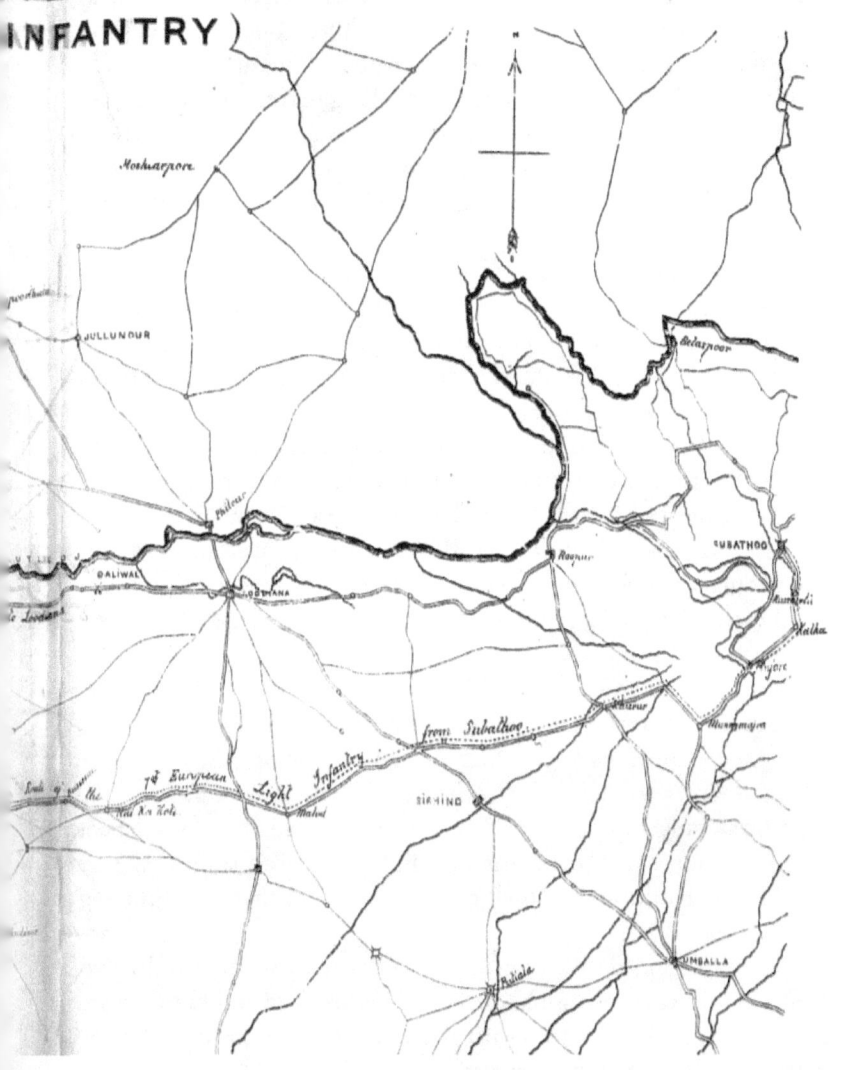

about 60 men. The soldiers of the Regiment were full of excitement and in the highest spirits at the prospect of the coming campaign.

On our arrival at Kussowlie—a military station about ten miles from Subathoo, where was quartered H.M. 29th—we learnt that that regiment had also marched on the same morning, and it was understood that the two regiments were to serve in the same division in the coming campaign.

We found the commissariat arrangements perfect; for on our arrival at the foot of the hills our camp was already pitched, food abundant, and every reasonable comfort prepared for the men.

On the 12th December H.M. 29th Regiment, which had been ordered to halt for our arrival at Munnymarjera, was joined by the 1st European Light Infantry; and the two regiments then advanced together towards Mudki in charge of some heavy artillery for the army. Our regiments made double marches daily; leaving ground at about 2 a.m., halting for breakfast at about 7 a.m., and after a rest of about a couple of hours marching to the new ground, which was usually reached about 2 p.m.; thus covering from 25 to 40 miles daily.

On approaching Wudni, a fortified town of some importance, much excitement was caused by the receipt of an order from the commander-in-chief to the effect that, as the inhabitants of that place had refused provisions to the British force on its forward march a few days previous, H.M. 29th and the 1st European Light Infantry were to reduce the fort to submission. But when we arrived near Wudni a countermanding dispatch arrived, informing us that as the rival armies faced each other, and an immediate action was anticipated, we were to push on to the front with all practicable speed.

Disappointed as were the soldiers at not being allowed to try their strength on the fort of Wudni, they still gave many hearty cheers as they passed under its walls, their excitement being vastly increased when, as they advanced, they heard the distant heavy artillery. This sound was, indeed, a proclamation that the war had now commenced; and fears were entertained that we might arrive too late to take our share in the battle, which in all probability was at that very time raging; in front.

Louder and nearer the constant roar of artillery became as the regiments with eagerness pushed on; but all became still and calm towards the middle of the day, and we naturally concluded from the kill that a great battle had been won or lost.

In the afternoon we received the welcome intelligence that the

"East India Register," May 24th, 1845.

FIRST EUROPEAN REGIMENT (LIGHT INFANTRY).
(Right Wing.)

"PLASSEY," "BUXAR," "GUZERAT," "DEIG," "BHURTPORE," "AFGHANISTAN," "GHUZNEE."

Station, Subathoo. Arrived, April, 1844.

Season of Appoint.	RANK AND NAMES.	Rank in the Regiment.	Rank in the Army.	REMARKS.
	COLONEL.			
1798	Sir J. Bryant, Knt., C. B.	27 June. 1835	M. G. 23 Nov., 1841	On Furlough
	LIEUT.-COLONEL.			
1805	J. Orchard, C. B. ...	27 July, '36 ...		
1818	George Warren	6 Aug., '43 ...	23 July, '39 ...	Town Major Presidency
	MAJOR.			
	—	—		
	CAPTAINS.			
1820	James Matthie	8 Sept., '35 ...	M. 22 Nov.,'43	Depy. Commy. Assam
1822	Thomas Box	27 July, '36 ...		
1825	Charles Clark	10 Nov., '43 ...	13 Feb., 41 ...	
—	John G. Gerrard ...	22 Nov., '43 ...	1 July	Sub. Asst. Commy. General
	LIEUTENANTS.			
1828	Jno. W. Bennett ...	16 Dec., '35 ...	C. 25 Dec., '43	
1829	H. T. Combe	27 July, '36 ...	C. 23 July, '44	
1835	F. Shuttleworth	20 July, '38 ...		
1837	R. W. H. Fanshawe	3 Oct., '40 ...		
,,	James Pattullo	do.		
,,	Robt. H. Hicks	2 Nov., '41 ...		
1838	Geo. O. Jacob	16 July, '42 ...		
,,	John Lambert	do.		
1840	Geo. G. Dennis	1 Nov.		
1839	Edm. D. Byng	6 Aug., '43 ...		
1840	Southwell Greville...	4 Nov.		
,,	H. B. Edwardes......	10 do.		
1841	Alex. Hume	22 do.		
1842	J. Williamson	25 Dec.		
,,	E. Cunliffe	23 July, '44 ...		
,,	Thos. Staples	1 Nov.		
	ENSIGNS.			
1841	H. E. Smith	4 Nov., '43 ...	26 Aug., '41 ...	
	F. W. A. Hamilton	10 Nov.	6 July, '42 ...	
	F. O. Salusbury	8 Dec.	9 June, '43 ...	
	P. Moxon	8 Dec.	do.	
	C. O'B. Palmer	12 Dec.	do.	
	G. H. Davidson	23 Jan., '44 ...	do.	
	M. H. Coombe	8 Oct., '44	30 Dec., '43 ...	
	P. R. Innes	2 Nov., '44 ...	30 Dec., '43 ...	
	C. R. Wriford	29 Jan., '45 ...	1 Jan., '44 ...	
	Edw. Brown	14 March, '45	29 Dec.	

Regimentals, Scarlet. Lace, Gold.

FIRST EUROPEAN REGIMENT (LIGHT INFANTRY).
(Left Wing.)

Season of Appoint.	Rank and Names.	Rank in the Regiment.	Rank in the Army.	Remarks.
	COLONEL.		M. G.	
1800	George Hunter, C. B. ...	27 Jan., '41	23 Nov., '41	Comg. Field Force, Sukkur
	LIEUTENANT-COLONEL.			
	—			
	MAJOR.			
1817	David Birrell	10 Nov., '43	23 Nov., '41	
	CAPTAINS.			
1818	John Ripley	19 June, '31	M. 23 Dec. '42	On Furlough
1819	Wm. Shortreed............	15 Nov., '36	14 Feb., '35	
,,	Thos. Lysart...............	27 Sept., '37	3 June	
1823	Alister Stewart	5 March, '38		
1827	Jas. Ruth. Pond	1 Nov., '44	22 May, '43	
	LIEUTENANTS.			
1828	Fran. Harrison............	2 May, 33 ...	C. 4 Dec. '43	On Furlough
,,	Bernd. Kendall	13 Mar., '35	C. 1 Jan., '44	
,,	Douglas Seaton	29 July, '36	C. 1 April	
,,	Edward Magnay	15 Nov.,' 36	C. 31 Aug.	
1835	John Fagan	9 March, 38		
1836	W. K. Haslewood	10 Aug., '38	...	do.
	ADJUTANT TO THE REGIMENT.			
	D. Seaton	7 March, '45		
	INTR. AND QUARTER-MASTER.			
	—			
	SURGEON.			
	W. L. McGregor, M.D.	7 Feb., '43 ...		
	ASST. DO.			
	—			

Facings, Sky-Blue.

victory of Mudki had been gained by our troops; and later on we were assured that our exertions to reach headquarters were, notwithstanding the excitement of the battle, fully recognised both by the Governor-General and the Commander-in-Chief; elephants being sent twenty-seven miles on the road to bring in the footsore men; and a string of camels laden with fresh water for the relief of the thirsty troops on their arid march.

Towards dusk the day after the battle of Mudki had been fought, we neared the British camp, the Governor-General sending out his band to welcome us and play us into camp; but it was late at night before we reached our ground. The baggage and tents of the Regiment were far behind, and the Quartermaster-General had not yet marked out the position where the newly-arrived Regiments were to pitch their tents. The men were much fatigued with their forced marches, but were all excitement to learn the details of the battle fought on the previous day; and they were therefore allowed to visit their friends who had been engaged in the action, and from whom they learnt the details of the "Battle of Mudki."

The commander of the Khalsa army, entrenched around the village of Ferozeshah, about ten miles distant from our camp, rightly calculating that the British soldiers would be exhausted by their severe marches, concluded also that they would be easily overwhelmed by a small determined body of chosen Seik troops, and had therefore detached only one division of his army, consisting of 10,000 cavalry, 2000 infantry, and 22 guns, to attack the British force; and the report that the enemy was close upon him reached Gough on the 18th of December. Sir Henry Hardinge, the Governor-General, had in the meantime placed his services at the disposal of the Commander-in-Chief, and had been appointed second in command of the army of the Sutlej. Our soldiers were preparing their dinners when the alarm of the advancing enemy was given, and the bugles and trumpets at once sounded the "Assembly," the troops hastening to the front as the enemy's videttes appeared in sight. Our regiments quickly deployed into line; our field artillery taking post in the centre, and the cavalry on either flank. The main body of our army was formed hastily in rear of the above advance, and again in rear of them was a small reserve. The enemy's artillery commenced the action with a heavy fire, and their numerous cavalry at once visibly out-flanked our line, Gough did not hesitate—he never did—but he gave the order to our dragoons to speedily advance; and, diverting the attention of the enemy by their brilliant charge, he brought the main body of his infantry into line, and threw them at the Seiks. After some severe fighting, the Khalsa army retired in order, foiled in their expectation to take the British at disadvantage and disperse them with their cavalry; and their plan of action having thus failed they retired regularly, disputing every inch of ground; and, resisting doggedly, they readied their camp at Ferozeshah under cover of the darkness.

The British troops had gained a victory; but they discovered that they had no mean enemy to contend with. The English infantry was numerically superior to that of the enemy in this battle; but the 3rd Dragoons and our native cavalry had been pitted against the Khalsa Horsemen, outnumbering us as twenty to one; notwithstanding which odds, the British dragoons had ridden through and through the enemy, the superior weight of our men and horses carrying everything before them; whilst, on the other hand, the Khalsa artillery and Infantry had fought bravely and well. We had still to try our strength against the whole Seik army, having only as yet had a brush with one of their divisions. On the night of battle it was found that we had indeed captured 17 out of the enemy's 22 guns, but the field of Mudki was covered with the dead and wounded, amongst them being 872 of our soldiers; so that the results of the battle could not be considered altogether satisfactory. Some of our best officers had fallen; killed or wounded. Amongst the former was General Sir Robert Sale, whose name is so honourably connected with the Afghan War; and amongst the latter Lieutenant Herbert Edwardes, of the Bengal European Regiment, who was serving on the Commander-in-Chief's Staff!

This was the news that awaited the 1st European Light Infantry as we reached our ground on the night of the 19th December. The position for our camp was now marked out; and the baggage having arrived the tents were soon pitched, and the men, worn out by long marches and excitement, hurried to their beds, but not to sleep, for we were soon reminded that we were in the presence of an enemy—a patrol coming round with orders that we were to remain under arms all night.

The next day, 20th December, was one of comparative rest, but in the morning we changed our ground, taking post with the 29th Foot, in the Second division of the army.

In the evening, at dinner, private written orders were placed in the hands of captains commanding companies, instructing them to proceed silently with their officers to the tents of their men at 1 a.m. the next day, as the whole Regiment was to be on parade an hour after the time named. An attack was to be made on the enemy's position. As soon as the servants had left the mess-tent, the officers talked freely amongst themselves of the engagement which was to be fought on the following morning; one of them only, Captain Thomas Box—"Jerry" Box, as he was familiarly called—showing a total absence of any excitement or emotion. Box had proved himself in many a fight a fearless soldier, and was beloved by his men; but on this night he was in low spirits, and being questioned as to the cause he simply said, "I feel I shall get a shot right slap in the face." This remark caused some merriment; for all knew Captain Box to be constitutionally brave, and none of us believed in presentiment.

We separated for the night, and after a few hours' sleep, the officers—who were forbidden to give any order to their servants to wake them—were seen moving noiselessly amongst their men, and enjoining silence as they accoutred and prepared for parade. Each man was instructed to fill his can with water, and a piece of bread and ready-cooked meat were served out to be carried in the haversacks; and sixty rounds of ball ammunition were issued to every man.

At 2 a.m. on the 21st December the Regiment was on parade, and before 3 o'clock the whole army was in position.

The march commenced over the field of Mudki, which was still strewn with the dead: many of ours having been frightfully mutilated since the battle.

The sun, although it was the cold season, was in the middle of the day intensely hot. It being the object of the commander-in-chief that a junction of his army with the Ferozpóre division, under Sir John Littler, should if possible be effected, the two forces met at 2 p.m., about five miles to the south-west of the enemy's position at Ferozeshah, after much marching and counter-marching through the thick *jhow* jungle and over rough ground, very fatiguing to the soldiers. The troops now took up their respective positions; but for some unaccountable reason the principal attack was ordered to be made on the west face of the Seik entrenchments fronting towards Ferozpóre; although it ought to have been known that this was the strongest part of their defences. The entrenchments were in the form of a parallelogram, including within its enceinte the village of Ferozeshah; and being about a mile in length and half-a-mile in width, the east side facing the open country.

The force of the enemy within the entrenchments has never been accurately ascertained; it having been given by different authorities at numbers varying from 30,000 to 70,000 men.

Our force in the field consisted of infantry: seven British Regiments (H.M. 9th, 29th, 31st, 50th, 62nd, 80th, and the 1st Bengal European Light Infantry); cavalry: H.M. 3rd Light Dragoons, four regiments of native and two of Irregular cavalry; artillery: seven troops of horse and four companies of foot, with 42 6-pounders, 24 9-pounders, and 2 siege-guns; in all 68 guns and about 17,000 men.

Major-General Sir Harry Smith commanded the 1st Infantry, or "Reserve Division;" Major-General W. R. Gilbert the second; Brigadier Wallace the third; and Major-General Sir John Littler the fourth or "Ferozpóre Division." The 1st Bengal European Light Infantry, H.M. 29th and 80th Regiments being in the second or General Gilbert's division. At 3 p.m. the troops were in position for attack: General Littler's division on the extreme left, Brigadier Wallace's in the centre, and General Gilbert's on the right. Sir Harry Smith's division and the cavalry in reserve forming a second line.

Sir Hugh Gough assumed the command of the left and Sir Henry Hardinge of the right wing of the army.

The left of the British line, being ordered to lend the attack, first advanced, whilst the centre and right awaited their turn. At this time videttes of the enemy's cavalry coming sometimes within fifty yards of our line, the Rifle Company of the 1st Bengal European Regiment was sent to the front to skirmish and drive them back, which they did in good style.

Our field artillery now opened fire from some batteries on the right, and some on the left, of General Gilbert's division; the enemy at once replying from all their batteries on the west and south faces of their entrenchment.

The sound of a sharp musketry-fire to our left soon told us that Littler's division were nearing the enemy; when our division (Gilbert's) formed up to advance. At this time an officer arrived from the direction of Littler's division reporting that the left attack had failed, and that our troops were retiring. The enemy were naturally triumphant, and their shouts could be heard above the roar of the artillery; when the order was given for Gilbert's division to advance rapidly. Major Birrell warned our men to reserve their fire until they sighted the enemy; a wise precaution. Birrell, who commanded the 1st European Light Infantry, rode in the centre; Captain Box, the second in command, on the right; and Captain Douglas Seaton on the left; Ensigns F. O. Salusbury and P. Moxon carrying the colours.

As our line approached the enemy's entrenchments, the fire from their batteries increased in violence, the round-shot and grape tearing through our ranks and leaving considerable gaps; and such was the violence of the fire that branches from the trees fell upon us as we advanced, the splintered trunks being scattered around us. Here the fated Captain Thomas Box received the shot he had foretold, which struck him "right slap in the face;" a bullet passed through his head, and he fell from his horse a lifeless corpse. During this advance Captain Kendall, commanding No. 6, and Captain Clark, commanding No. 1 Company, both fell mortally wounded; and Ensign Salusbury, his right arm deeply lacerated by a grape-shot, denuding the bone throughout its length, fell under the Queen's Colour, which was immediately taken by Ensign P. R. Innes, just as the orders were given to bring down our bayonets and charge home. We were in a few minutes right under the enemy's batteries; but the air was so filled with fire and smoke that it seemed to be as dark as night.

The Seiks had thrown along the edge of their dry ditch stumps and branches of trees, over which our men fell in multitudinous confusion, and as they struggled to regain their footing at the bottom of the ditch their language was anything but choice.

The sloping bank below the plateau upon which the Seik batteries were mounted was about ten feet high, measuring from the bottom of the ditch. Surmounting this in a few seconds our men were amongst the guns, and a desperate hand-to-hand fight ensued for their possession, in which the Seik Artillerymen were bayoneted to a man; revealing immediately behind the plateau, and about six feet below, the Khalsa infantry drawn up in line, and behind them their tents formed into camp-streets.

During the fight for the mastery of the guns the Seik infantry had reserved their fire, the British soldiers and the Khalsa artillerymen being so completely intermingled that the Seik infantry fire would have been as fatal to their friends as to their foes; but now that their gunners were laid low the British infantry stood under a galling fire for a few seconds, while they formed in line on the brink of the eminence, and prepared to dash down on the Seik infantry below. Most of the front rank of the enemy now dropped on one knee as if preparing to receive cavalry; and no charge of cavalry could have been more effective than that of our Regiment, as with a cheer they rushed down the incline upon the Khalsa infantry below; who first fired a volley, then, either throwing down their muskets or using them as shields, drew their tulwars and rushed forward to engage in a hand-to-hand fight with our men. The battle now raged with fury along the whole line; compact bands of the enemy again and again dashing at our colours, and more than once grasping the staves; but the colour-sergeants, closing up around them, formed an impenetrable wall, through which even the valour and number of the Seiks could not break. Soon the space below the plateau contained a mingled heap of dead and wounded men; but the Khalsa infantry had given way, and seeking cover amongst their tents, kept up a severe dropping fire upon our troops in front. But hard work still remained, most of the batteries along the face of the western entrenchments being still held by the Seiks; so wheeling round on its left, the Bengal European Regiment joined H.M. 9th Foot, already inside the entrenchments, attacked the Seik batteries in flank, and rushing transversely along the defences forced the enemy back in broken masses, whilst their guns on the ramparts were captured and spiked.[3]

Orders were now issued for our regiment to charge along the centre camp-street of the Seiks, and secure the village of Ferozeshah. The soldiers, encouraged by their success, gallantly carried out these orders; but they had not proceeded more than two hundred yards when there was heard beneath their feet a frightful roar; the ground heaved and the men in the vicinity were blown away amongst the tents, the air being filled with fire, and a dense smoke arising, which, as it cleared away, exposed to view a horrible and appalling scene, numbers of our men having fallen frightfully burnt and mutilated, and in some instances their pouches ignited, causing terrible wounds, agony, and loss of life. The Regiment was now scattered in every direction, about 150 men only joining the colours after the explosion, which was followed by that of smaller mines, adding to the confusion, but comparatively harmless. Our line was at length re-formed, and advanced towards the village, but we returned to the central street on finding that it was already in the possession of our troops. General Sir Harry Smith, having brought up his Reserve division, had carried some of the batteries on the south face of the entrenchments and penetrated into the very heart of the enemy's camp. After the great explosion numbers of the men of our regiment, detached and scattered by the convulsion and disorder, were collected by Captain D. Seaton; forming a party which fell in with Sir Harry Smith's division just after it had entered the camp, and accompanied it into the village.

---

3. Before the troops left Mudki, every fifth man of the Bengal European Light Infantry had been supplied with a bundle of spikes and a small hammer—a very necessary precaution

Our men now parched with thirst sought water from a well near at hand, but under a galling fire from the enemy concealed amongst the tents. Across a camp-street facing this well a barricade had been formed of half-burnt tents and débris, and behind this barricade a group of Seiks brought their fire to bear direct upon the well, where several of our men had fallen; others, nevertheless, pressing forward and seizing the tin pots from their wounded comrades, preferring the immediate prospect of death to the fearful torture of thirst.

Lieutenant Greville was now the senior Officer present with the colours, and therefore assumed command; forming his men into two divisions, and placing the colours in the centre, he gallantly led the charge against the barricade. During our advance the enemy's fire had almost ceased, but as we approached the barricade a volley was suddenly poured upon us, which forced our whole party back upon the well. There was but a moment's pause; the men were re-forming for a second charge, when it was realised that the Regimental colour had disappeared. Without waiting for orders Ensign P. R. Innes returned alone to the barricade, in front of which lay Ensign Philip Moxon's body, quite dead; he having fallen upon the Colour, which was saturated with his blood.[4] The Colour was hastily recovered and brought back in safety; the soldiers of the Regiment hailing its restoration with shouts of joy. "The recovery of the Colour by Ensign Innes was most important, as otherwise it must have fallen into the hands of the Seiks."[5]

Greville now, having formed his men, gallantly led them to a second charge, clearing the street, and this time capturing the barricade. Amidst the excitement which had prevailed during these operations, it had not been perceived that it had suddenly become almost dark; but our men still charged on, clearing the burning tents of every lurking enemy; but the darkness increasing the "Assembly" was sounded, and our men collected together, when it was discovered, to our dismay, that the Queen's Colour—which after Moxon's death had been handed to Colour-Sergeant Higgens was nowhere to be seen.

Just then an aide-de-camp came up with orders from the General for all the scattered detachments in the enemy's camp-to collect on the plain outside. Every bugler, both in and outside the entrenchments, sounded his regimental call, making the previous confusion worse confounded.

---

4. On the colour, which now hangs on the walls of Winchester Cathedral, the blood-stains of this gallant young officer may still be seen.
5. Extract from a letter from the officer commanding.

Lieutenant Greville, still commanding, now ordered his men to recross the entrenchments which had been captured a few hours previous with so much sacrifice of life; and in the darkness the-party groped their way towards the direction in which they thought they could distinguish their regimental call frequently repeated; and, after a full hour's search, the main portion of the 1st European Light Infantry was found rapidly collecting its scattered men, and forming up for further action. It was now discovered, to the satisfaction of all, that the Queen's colour which had been entrusted to Colour-Sergeant Higgens was at the Quarter Guard; he, having heard his regimental call, had, accompanied by some stragglers, reached the Regiment and deposited his charge in safety.

The Seik entrenchments on the east side were still held by the Khalsa army; who, as soon as they discovered that the British had evacuated the conquered position, reoccupied their entire camp, with the exception of the village, which was still partially held by our troops. The night was bitterly cold, a keen wind blowing over the plain, and the field being strewn with the wounded, who lay upon the damp sand. Piteous were their cries for water, warmth, and help. But there was no water, no warmth; and what help could their comrades afford who needed so much themselves? Some covering had, however, been secured in the enemy's camp, and this was gladly made over for the wounded men. Gilbert's division, which was at this time somewhat separated from the rest of the army, bivouacked to the south of the enemy's camp. Between two and three o'clock on the morning of the 22nd, it was found that Sir Harry Smith's Reserve division, who had been forced from the entrenchments, had retreated to a village—Misree Khan Walla—some two miles to the south-east of Ferozeshah.

Both Sir Hugh Gough and Sir Henry Hardinge, who were now with Gilbert's division, were indefatigable in their attentions to the wants of the wounded soldiers, going about with a cheering word for all. But they were not so confident as they appeared to be, for they must have felt that the prospect just then was gloomy indeed. The enemy, under cover of the darkness, had recaptured his entire position; and, Sir Harry Smith's reserve, having been forced from the village of Ferozeshah, the Seiks were in undisputed possession of their first ground, after a large and almost fruitless loss of life on our side.

In the early morning, the Seiks brought one of their heaviest guns to bear on Gilbert's division; the enemy serving this gun with such deadly effect that the soldiers were ordered to lie down, the shot and grape sweeping over them, but still doing fearful damage to the cattle and horses, and passing into the divisions of our army on the plain beyond.

Sir Henry Hardinge, who commanded our wing of the British force, called upon the Bengal European Light Infantry and H.M. 80th Foot, at this time close at hand, to "go and stop that gun."

These regiments were anxious to be on the move, having been painfully cramped by the cold sand; and now, eagerly springing to their feet, were rapidly formed in line, and advanced at the double, H.M. 80th Foot leading, and the 1st Bengal Light Infantry in support. The big gun, said to be an 80-pounder, was protected by a strong force of Khalsa infantry, who, finding themselves attacked by a force of unknown strength, threw forward their supports, who at once opened a sharp musketry fire.

It was exciting to watch the two lines of fire steadily approach each other in the dark; whilst the monster gun in front poured forth double charges of grape and shot. As the British infantry neared their enemy, there was a forward rush, a hand-to-hand struggle, and the big gun was spiked.[6] There was, of course, no attempt made to remove the gun, or those which had been captured at the same time in a battery close by; but they were all spiked, and our troops returned to their former position.

Soon afterwards the day began to dawn, and there was now no doubt how seriously our strength had been reduced. At daybreak, the European portion of the British force was assembled opposite to the southern face of the enemy's camp, and in the bright clear morning it was visible that, although the guns on the enemy's works had been captured, and many of them spiked, on the previous evening, the Khalsa infantry had again occupied the entrenchments, bidding defiance to our troops as they formed in line preparatory to making their final charge; the Commander-in-Chief leading the right, and Hardinge the left wing of our army. The "Advance" was now sounded, and the charge was delivered with a gallantry never surpassed on any field; the Seik entrenchments being again captured at the point of the bayonet, and the enemy driven completely through his camp into the jungles to the north. The east-face of the entrenchments, which had been obstinately held by the enemy on the previous day, was now also captured, as well as the village, from which the Reserve division had been forced to retire during the night.

---

6. "The gun was captured by as brave a charge as there is on record."—Commander-in-Chief's Dispatch.

The British troops were now drawn up in line to the north of the captured camp; and as the commanders rode along the front of their victorious army, they were loudly cheered.

Many of the officers and soldiers had rejoined the ranks, tattered, torn, exhausted, and more or less bleeding, but in the best of spirits, and joining in many a joke at their own dishevelled plight.

Scarcely, however, had this cheering ceased, when our cavalry videttes, who had been sent in front to watch the enemy's retreat, hastily returned, reporting that they had been confronted and driven back by a Reserve Seik army, coming from the direction of Ferozpóre to the succour of the Khalsa troops.

The statements of the videttes were soon verified; for a dense cloud of dust, which showed the position of the approaching enemy, rose from amongst the jungle towards the direction indicated by our scouts. Nearer and nearer it came; and we soon found ourselves in the presence of a new army, who were taking up position in our front, either with the intention of covering the retreat of Lal Sing's defeated force, or, probably, to attempt to regain possession of the Seik camp.

This second army, which out-numbered the British force then' confronting it in the field, was under the command of Tej Sing, who had been watching the Ferozpóre Garrison with the intention of preventing it from forming a junction with the Commander-in-Chief's force marching from Mudki to Ferozeshah. Tej Sing had allowed Littler's division to escape him, and pass along the road unopposed, and he now hastened apparently to retrieve his error, and bring assistance to Lal Sing's retreating army.

Rapidly the position of the British army was changed; but it soon became evident that our artillery as well as our infantry ammunition was nearly expended. The centre of our force, in which was Gilbert's division, now faced to the west, in front of our fresh enemy; the right and left divisions, being at the same time thrown back, faced north and south; so that our army was formed into a large hollow square, with the view of preventing the recapture of the Seik camp. The Khalsa artillery now, unlimbering, opened a heavy fire on our square, our light field-guns being completely over-matched; and indeed, after we had fired a few rounds only, our ammunition was found to be completely exhausted.

At this time a staff-officer rode up to the Regiment, reporting that our artillery had no more ammunition. Lieutenant J.. Lambert, moving forward, called out, "We don't want artillery; we'll take those guns directly, if they will let us at them." In response there was a hearty cheer, but the Regiment was not permitted to advance.

The enemy's fire was now doing terrible execution amongst our troops, and the men were consequently ordered to lie down on their faces, in order to avoid the storm of round-shot; but the enemy had got our range, and in some instances whole sections of our men were riven by the hostile artillery.

Nos, 4 and 5 Companies of the 1st European Light Infantry suffered at this time most severely, some shots killing several men in No. 6, whilst three men in No. 5 Company, lying next each other, were killed; two of them by the concussion of an 18-pound shot which fell amongst them, scattering to atoms the centre man. The position was well-nigh unbearable. The troops, inactive, were simply waiting death, and an order was now issued for our army to retire to the plain beyond; whilst some of the infantry, supported by cavalry and horse artillery—the latter having left their guns under charge of infantry—attempted to keep the enemy in check. The Khalsa troops were of course fresh, whilst the British were sinking from sheer exhaustion; having had no food except the scanty supply which they had brought with them in their haversacks from Mudki. The Khalsa artillery was well provided with ammunition, the British guns were silent. No wonder, then, that the force which Gough had sent to keep Tej Sing's army in chock was driven back with heavy loss.

The European infantry were now threatened on their right flank by hordes of cavalry, who emerged from the jungles skirting the plain.

Orders were again given by the Commander-in-Chief to change front; and the movements, performed in presence of the enemy's cavalry, were executed with creditable steadiness.

We, by this last movement, faced to the north in echelon of Regiments, formed into squares four deep, and prepared to receive cavalry, though without any ammunition in pouch. It was about 2 p.m., and the enemy's cavalry were not more than a hundred yards to our front, moving forward as if preparing to charge; but, whilst they hesitated, a rush of horsemen was suddenly heard to our rear. The 3rd Dragoons, terribly reduced in numbers but not in courage, were coming to our succour at full gallop, supported by two regiments of native cavalry. Colonel White, commanding the dragoons, was joined by General Gilbert as they dashed past us into the midst of the enemy, when a hand-to-hand fight ensued. But the Seik cavalry did not recover the first shock of the charge; they being stationary, whilst our dragoons came down upon them with their full force and weight. The enemy made a struggle to maintain his ground, but gradually gave way; when the strange spectacle presented itself of hundreds of dismounted men fighting single combats on the ground, whilst their riderless horses were manoeuvring in front of our squares.

No sooner had the enemy's cavalry been broken and forced back into the jungle, than we learnt to our surprise, that Tej Sing, with his whole force, was in full retreat; leaving us complete masters of the field.

Thus ended the two days' battle of Ferozeshah; in which we had captured and retained the enemy's fortified camp, with 73 of their guns. But our victory had been dearly purchased. Indeed, one-seventh of the British army had fallen, 2415 being the aggregate of our killed and wounded; amongst the former being 37 officers and 694 men. The loss of the enemy will never be known; but the entrenchments, indeed the whole field of battle, was strewn with their dead.

The Bengal European Light Infantry lost 51 killed and 164 wounded, including the following 8 Officers:

Captain Thomas Box (killed).
Ensign Philip Moxon (killed).
Captain Charles Clark (mortally wounded).
Lieutenant Bernard Kendall (mortally wounded).
Lieutenant R. W. H. Fanshawe (slightly wounded).
Lieutenant Beatson—Interpreter and Quartermaster—(severely wounded).
Ensign Frederick O. Salusbury (severely wounded).
Ensign C. R. Wriford (slightly wounded).

The suddenness of Sirdar Tej Sing's unexpected retreat filled the British with conjecture and surprise; for they reflected that he could hardly have been ignorant that his enemies were well-nigh exhausted, their ammunition expended, and the captured camp within his grasp. Tej Sing's hasty retirement from the field may have been the result of an honest desire to cover Lal Sing's retreat; or he may have wished to leave the British masters of the field in order that they might, later on inflict a heavier blow on the unruly Khalsa. Be this as it may, the Seik army had been driven from its strongly-entrenched position at Ferozeshah, and it had lost 92[7] of its guns; but it had not been finally vanquished. The Khalsa army

---

7. Nineteen guns were captured at the Battle of Mudki, and 73 at Ferozeshah.

was now in full retreat to a position on the river Sutlej; from which all additional strength, all the strategy and skill of the British Commanders, would be required to dislodge them.

During the afternoon of the 22nd of December, the men of our regiment were employed in collecting our wounded, who were temporarily housed in the village of Ferozeshah, where large quantities of bedding had been found. But up to this time these wounded had been sadly neglected; and Dr. W. L. McGregor, the Surgeon of the 1st Bengal European Light Infantry, is loud in his condemnation of the medical arrangements. He says:

> During the night of the 21st many a poor wounded European soldier found his way to the rear in search of medical aid; but the arrangements for affording it were very incomplete excepting through the efforts of the Regimental Surgeons who did everything in their power with the means at their command. As for the field hospital it had no existence, so confidently had the opinion been entertained that the Seiks would not offer resistance, that it was deemed unnecessary to make any arrangements for a field hospital. There were no medical stores or surgical instruments on the field, except those attached to Regiment hospitals and the hurry of the movements prevented any sufficient supply from being obtained without great delay.[2]

From the severity of Ensign F. O. Salusbury's wound, before described, combined with exposure and exhaustion, the acute sufferings of that Officer may be easily conceived. But a graver danger awaited him, for his life was saved during the night of the 21st by one of the men of his regiment, who ran to his assistance just as one of the enemy, close at hand, was in the act of shooting him; and the soldier, drawing the Ensign's pistol from his belt, shot the assailant dead before he could effect his murderous purpose.

Lieutenant Beatson was found to have been shot in the abdomen, the ball having carried a portion of his woollen clothing deep into the wound; and these officers, with as many of our wounded soldiers as could be collected, were tended during the night by Surgeon McGregor and his assistants, who were conspicuous by their zeal and careful attention.

But there were two—Captain Box and Ensign Moxon—beyond the reach of our surgeon's skill. The happy, genial Thomas Box—the

---

2. McGregor's History of the Seiks, Vol. 2, p. 115.

life of the mess-table, the man who had no enemy, who never spoke an unkind word—was gone from us, causing to all unfeigned sorrow, even during those scenes of excitement and privation; and Ensign Philip Moxon, whose death we have described, carrying the symbol of his Regiment's honour, which he so well sustained, leaving the impress of his heart's blood on his trust as lasting testimony of his brave and dauntless spirit. They both died the death which a soldier may justly prize. They both deserve to have their deeds emblazoned in gold on the annals of their Regiment, that their successors may honour and revere the names of Captain Thomas Box and Ensign Philip Moxon.

Night now supervened. The wants of the wounded were supplied; ample provisions and covering brought from the captured camp; fires were soon blazing round; and cattle, rudely slaughtered and cooked, were eagerly devoured by the half-starved groups. At this time the camels, laden with our canteen stores, arrived; and as we sat at night around the blazing fires, talking over the adventures of the previous days, it would hardly be supposed by a strange visitor that we had so lately been engaged in the bloody work of war.

Chapter 16

The Second Sikh War

Immediately after his defeat at Ferozeshah, Lal Sing hastened to Lahore with the news of the disaster; and during his absence Tej Sing assumed the sole command of the Seik army in the field. He at once applied to the Lahore Durbar for additional troops, having in view the promises of assistance which had been offered by Golab Sing, the Raja of Jamu. But, after the defeats which had been sustained by the Khalsa army, Golab Sing was more than ever doubtful of the advisability of espousing the Seik cause; moreover, he shrewdly suspected that the commanders of the Seik army had been playing a double game, and he was unwilling to expose his soldiers to the risk of being sacrificed in order to further the interests of the Lahore Durbar. Under these circumstances, Golab Sing determined to watch the course of events, and not at present commit himself to any decided course of action.

Under Tej Sing's orders, the Khalsa army hastily recrossed the Sutlej, near the village of Sobraon, and encamped within the territories of the Punjab, on the right bank of the river below its junction with the Bias.

The enemy's plan of defence, suggested by their European engineer officers, was well designed, although in its execution, the details were somewhat defective, from the works having been, apportioned for execution amongst the different commanders of Seik regiments; this arrangement naturally resulting in a want of uniformity, and in some instances in weak construction.

An admirably-designed pontoon-bridge was thrown across the river; the end on the left or south bank being defended by earthworks, which the enemy intended to strengthen and extend day by day, as time and opportunity might be afforded.

The Seik commander had constructed another bridge of boats about twenty miles further down the river, which was guarded by a strong force of cavalry.

The British commander-in-chief, as we need hardly state, felt himself unable to immediately follow up the advantages which he had gained at Mudki and Ferozeshah; and, consequently, he determined to await the arrival of the Meerut force ordered to the front under Sir John Gray, and of our heavy guns, escorted by the 9th and 16th Lancers, and H.M. 10th and 53rd Foot; for, although this delay enabled the enemy to strengthen their entrenchments on the Sutlej, it was deemed prudent not to risk another general engagement until these reinforcements should have arrived.

On the 28th of December the British camp was advanced about ten miles nearer to the enemy's position, Sobraon; the left of our army now resting on the village of Altari, and circling round from that point in an easterly direction; and on the 12th of January, 1846, a further forward movement of about eight miles was made.

The British army was now gradually closing on its enemy; but it must be borne in mind that the Seik bridge of boats constructed across the river always afforded them a means of escape.

During the time that Sir Hugh Gough was awaiting the arrival of his reinforcements under Sir John Grey, he dispatched the 1st Division of the army, under Sir Harry Smith, with orders to. reduce the fort of Dhurrumkote; to cover the march of the: Meerut force; and afford relief to our station of Lodiana; which was threatened by a Seik army of considerable strength, advancing from Phillour, under the command of a well-known Seik General, Runjour Sing.

The alarm occasioned in the neighbouring Hill, and other British stations, when it became known that Lodiana was threatened, amounted to a panic. The object of the enemy's general was, not only to possess himself of Lodiana, but to swoop down by a rapid movement upon one of our native detachments, which was escorting some of our siege-guns along the high road to his south; and had Runjour Sing succeeded in his purpose, nothing would have been easier than for him to detach small parties of his troops to plunder our stations, which had been almost denuded of military protection—the sick in hospital, and a small guard of soldiers only, having been left to protect the wives and families of those employed in the field. At Subathoo—where was the depot of the 1st European Light Infantry—as well as at Simla,. Kussowlie, and Umbala, the greatest consternation prevailed Lieutenant

Williamson, who it will be remembered was left in charge of the depôt at Subathoo, with the women, children, and sick of our regiment, having but scanty means of defence at his disposal, sought and obtained the advice of General Tapp, residing in retirement near Subathoo, who had served with the Bengal European Regiment as far back as 1803; and under this experienced Officer's advice, wise precautions were adopted for the safety of the station and troops. Fortunately, the success of Sir Harry Smith's division at Aliwal, where he gained a signal victory over Runjour Sing's army on the 28th of January, dissipated the fears of the unprotected stations, and confidence was again restored.

On the 18th January a further forward move was made by the British army in the direction of Sobraon, which was now completely invested, both the right and the left of our army resting near the banks of the Sutlej; so that the enemy's position, which was at the bend of the river, was, so to speak, within the grip of the British army.

The news of Sir Harry Smith's victory at Aliwal reached the Headquarter camp on the same day on which it was fought (28th January, 1846). No difficulty had been experienced in reducing the fort of Dhurrumkote; and although the enemy had captured Smith's camp equipage and baggage at Budiwal, he, by the rapidity of his movements, had saved the station of Lodiana, and then completely defeated his enemy in open fight at Aliwal. The news of this victory was hailed by the Headquarter army with great joy, for it relieved the anxiety of those officers and soldiers whose families were left at their regimental depôts. A Royal salute was fired on the early morning of the 29th, announcing the victory of Aliwal; but the Seiks, now entrenched only a short distance in front of our camp, either in defiance—or possibly because they wished to keep their troops in ignorance of our having gained a victory over Runjour Sing—imitated our example, not only by firing a Royal salute, but by their bands turning out in front of their entrenchments, and playing our National Anthem.

During the time that we had been awaiting the arrival of our heavy guns, the enemy had been daily strengthening his position, until it now formed an extensive semi-circle around the *tête-du-pont* on the south bank of the river. Their entrenchments had been gradually extended; now forming a succession of earthworks enveloped in outer batteries of enormous strength. Those on the left and centre faces of their position were the strongest and most massive; but, though those on the right face were not constructed in so scientific a manner, they were strengthened by masked batteries on the right bank of the river.

The commander-in-chief gives the following description of the enemy's position at Sobraon. He says:

> The enemy's works had been repeatedly reconnoitred during the time of my headquarters at Nihalkee (Akhberwala) by myself, my departmental staff and my engineers and artillery officers. Our observations, coupled with the reports of spies, convinced us that there had devolved on us the arduous task of attacking in a position covered with formidable entrenchments no fewer than 30,000 men the best of the Khalsa troops with 70 pieces of cannon united by a good bridge to a reserve on the opposite bank on which the enemy had a considerable camp and some artillery commanding and flanking the field works on our side.

In the early days of February, the division of the army which had been detached, under Sir Harry Smith, to operate against the Seik force under Runjour Sing, had rejoined the headquarter camp; and the siege guns, with the Meerut force under Sir John Grey, had arrived; so that, on the 9th of February, Sir Hugh Gough was enabled to form his plan for the attack of the enemy's position.

As has already been stated, the right face of the enemy's works was considered the most vulnerable; because, although it was flanked by a battery on the north bank of the river, there were but few guns on this face of the entrenchments; and consequently it was determined to make their right the first point of our attack.

The commander-in-chief in his despatch thus describes his disposition of the British force:

> On the margin of the Sutledge on our left two brigades of Major-General Dick's division under his personal command stood ready to commence the assault against the enemy's extreme right. The 7th Brigade, in which was the 10th Foot reinforced by the 53rd Foot and led by Brigadier Stacey was to head the attack supported at 200 yards distance by the 6th Brigade under Brigadier the Hon. T. Ashburnham which was to move forward from the entrenched village of Rhodawala leaving if necessary a regiment for its defence. In the centre Major-General Gilbert's division was deployed for support or attack, its right resting on the village of Little Sobraon.

This plan of operations having been arranged, it was decided that the attack on the enemy's entrenchments should take place on the following morning (10th February, 1846); and secret orders were accordingly issued to commanding officers. During the 9th of February three Officers joined the 1st European Light Infantry, *viz*:—Lieutenant-Colonel Orchard, C.B., and Ensigns Hamilton and G. C. Lambert. Colonel Orchard had cancelled his leave of absence to take command of the Regiment in the field, but, to the universal regret of our officers and men, an unforeseen difficulty presented itself: Colonel Orchard, being senior to some of the brigadiers in command, and the arrangements for all the brigades for the next day's attack having been completed, Orchard was promoted to the rank of brigadier, and appointed to act as second in command of the 7th Brigade.

Ensign Hamilton, who had been left with the depôt, had now so far recovered, that his earnest request to be allowed to join his regiment in the field was granted, and he had hastened, at considerable risk, to join headquarters. Ensign George C. Lambert, a young Officer who had just been gazetted to the Regiment, had hastened up the country, eager to take his share in the campaign; his brother, Lieutenant J. Lambert, was one of the most gallant Officers in the Regiment, and the young Ensign met with a hearty reception for his brother's sake.

Experience had taught most of us that we had no light before us on the morrow. When we separated after our mess-dinner, before the battle of Ferozeshah on the 20th of December, 1845, many of the officers were strangers to the realities of war; but before we separated after mess, on the 9th of February, 1846, a ceremony was performed, at the commanding officer's request, which savoured more of serious reality than it would have done on the previous occasion, when all, with the exception of Captain Thomas Box, were light-hearted and merry. Addressing the officers of the Regiment, Colonel Birrel reminded them of the many absentees who had fallen since the commencement of the campaign; and he enjoined on all officers present to shake hands, so that, should there have been ill-feeling on the part of any, it might end for ever. He reminded us that we had a perilous undertaking before us on the next day; and that, to a certainty, we should not all meet again at the next mess-dinner. There was a solemnity in Colonel Birrell's address, and the ceremony enjoined had the effect of cementing old friendships, and in some cases healing ill-feeling which might otherwise have existed for years, perhaps till death. All the officers present solemnly shook hands and retired to their tents, but not to sleep; for there were letters to be written home, many of them the last. It was not till past midnight that all the lights in the camp were extinguished; and two hours afterwards we were forming on parade, and taking up position with our separate brigades and divisions. The enemy was evidently not aware of our intended attack. There was dead silence in his camp as we noiselessly approached under cover of a dense fog, which prevented our seeing more than a few yards ahead, and rendered the taking up our allotted positions a matter of some difficulty.

Gilbert's division—in which were the 1st European Light Infantry—faced the north, right opposite to the centre, the strongest part of the enemy's entrenchments.

The rising sun rapidly dispelled the fog—which suddenly rose in a dense cloud—when a magnificent picture presented itself.

Our artillery was now seen in position awaiting orders to open fire, and the plain was covered with our troops; the fortified village of Rhodawala on our left being filled with our infantry. As the fog cleared, our mortars and siege-guns opened a simultaneous fire, and the enemy appeared now for the first time to realize their danger.

The Seik drums beat the alarm; their bugles and trumpets sounded to arms; and in a few minutes the whole of the enemy's batteries were manned, and their guns pouring shot and shell in the direction of our troops.

Gilbert's division was ensconced under cover of the banks of the dry bed of a small river, which partially encircled the outer works of the enemy's position. The action was commenced by an artillery duel, which lasted about two hours; when Gough was informed that our ammunition was nearly expended. Immediate orders were now given for the two brigades on our extreme left[1] to carry the right entrenchments of the enemy.

From the dry bed of the river we had a splendid view of the advance, and the effect of the attack. The Bengal Horse artillery—than which there were no finer or more efficient artillery in the world—came forward at full gallop; and, suddenly halting and unlimbering their guns at a distance of only three hundred yards from the enemy, opened a regular and rapid fire. As the infantry advanced to the attack this fire was slackened, and as the final charge was made it ceased. The Infantry charge was at first decided and effective; the entrenchments being carried at the point of the bayonet without a musket-shot having been fired, and the enemy forced back on its inner works. Now, for the first time, our commander's plan of action seemed to dawn upon the

---

1. Under Major-General Dick.

Seiks, and they hastened to redeem their want of foresight; rapidly concentrating their whole strength in their weaker right defences; and, utterly disregarding feints which had been made towards their centre and left, their troops rushed towards their right, bringing with them many of their field-guns, which they rapidly placed in position to cover their advancing infantry. They apparently felt that if they could regain possession of their entrenchments on their right, we could not with our whole strength carry the more formidable fortifications on their centre and left. The first British division wavered, under the overwhelming force which was bearing down upon it; and amidst the shouts of the enemy, now redoubling their efforts, Dick's division began gradually to lose ground, nobly disputing every inch, but evidently unable to hold the batteries which they had captured, and which were quickly wrenched from their grasp and re-occupied by the enemy.

The 2nd Brigade of our left division now charged forward in support, and Ashburnham's reserves pushed gallantly to the front; but it was of no avail; our 1st Division, as well as the reserve, vastly outnumbered and over-matched, being all forced back.

The first part of Sir Hugh Gough's programme having failed, there was but one course left; the feint attacks of our centre and right must at once be converted into real assaults. The demonstration which Gilbert's division had made on the enemy's centre had the effect of drawing the fire from his strongest batteries on it; this being part of Gough's plan. He wanted the attention of the enemy to be diverted from their right; so he arranged that Gilbert's (the centre) division should be protected from the fire which it must necessarily attract, by taking advantage of the cover afforded by the dry bed of the nulla; but now it was called upon to make a real attack upon the batteries from which it had just attracted the enemy's heaviest fire. Relieved from the pressure on their right, the enemy had swarmed to their centre and left batteries just as the order arrived for Gilbert's division to assault, and Sir Hugh Gough, who was watching the movement, was heard to exclaim: "Good God! they will be annihilated."

The fire from the enemy's heavy guns in their centre batteries, their *zamburucks*,[2] and musketry, was terrific; and the air, charged with sulphur, was stifling, and so heated that it was almost unbearable. Now on rushed the Bengal European Regiment, with a determination which promised to carry everything before it; soon reaching the ditch which formed the outer defence, and springing into it, they found

---

2. 1lb. swivel guns.

themselves confronted by the massive walls which in the distance had appeared less formidable, for they now found these works too high to escalade without ladders. To retire was again to encounter the storm of fire through which they had just passed, to remain in their present position was annihilation; therefore, the Regiment, mortified and chagrined, was forced again to seek shelter under cover of the bank of the dry river which it had left but a short time before. During our advance several officers and men had fallen; Captain Shuttleworth being shot dead, and Ensigns Hamilton, Davidson, and Innes struck down, as well as many of our soldiers killed and wounded.

As our regiment was retiring the enemy sent out their dismounted cavalry to cut up those who had fallen; and these men barbarously murdered many of our wounded who might otherwise have found their way to our camp in safety.

On reaching the dry bed of the river it was found that Brigadier McLaren, commanding our brigade, was mortally wounded, and Colonel Birrell, the next in seniority, assumed command of the brigade; the command of the 1st European Light Infantry devolving on our Adjutant, Brevet-Captain Douglas Seaton, who, rapidly forming up the Regiment and instructing his officers to rush at the embrasures and spike the enemy's guns, led them to their second charge. Having taken ground to its left the line now boldly advanced; but it was a second time hurled back. A third time the Bengal Europeans, having inclined further to the left, charged with a hearty cheer and a determination which no fire could check; dashing forward without halt or hesitation this time, notwithstanding that the ranks were thinned at every step. The embrasures were now reached, the foremost men having been propped up on the shoulders of their comrades; shouts of joy rang through the ranks as the little parties who had gained a footing found their numbers inside the batteries increasing; and a rush was made at the enemy's heavy guns, which were now captured and spiked.

The glad news soon reached us that, as the mass of the Seik army had been withdrawn from the weaker entrenchments on the right, to unable them to repel our repeated attacks on centre and on left, the 1st Division and its reserves under Ashburnham had successfully renewed their attack on the enemy's right, driven them from their entrenchments and recaptured their guns. From our right also came the welcome intelligence that the enemy's batteries' had at last been carried at the point of the bayonet; so that how the whole semicircle of the enemy's outer batteries was in our possession. The Bengal

European Light Infantry, as well as our other troops, now faced the inside of the enemy's works, which were found to be a succession of entrenchments concentrating on their *tête-du-pont*.

From our right-centre and left our troops pushed forward, dislodging the enemy step by step towards their bridge. "No Seik offered to submit, no disciple of Govind asked for quarter. Everywhere they showed a front to the victors and stalked slowly and sullenly away, whilst many rushed singly forth to meet assured death."[3]

This was no time for mercy or clemency; the soldiers of the British army had just passed over the dead bodies of their comrades, many of whom had been ruthlessly and barbarously hacked to pieces by the Seiks; our men thirsted for revenge, and a terrible revenge they wreaked upon their enemy.

Step by step the Khalsa army was forced back in the direction of their bridge, the pressure on which became so great that the-sides broke away. Nature also seemed to conspire against the Seiks, for since the morning the river Sutlej had suddenly and unexpectedly risen some seven feet, so that the ford was not now passable; and, worse than all, the centre boat of the bridge—which it was said had been loaded with powder, so that it might if necessary be exploded to prevent pursuit—had been removed.[4] There was now nothing but death both before and behind the enemy; their mounted officers, grey-bearded old chieftains, waved their swords high in the air, calling upon their men with shouts and gestures to drive the British from their camp, and thus vindicate their honour and maintain their faith. These brave officers scorned to attempt to save themselves; Sirdars Sham Sing Attariwalla—who had frequently fought under Runjeet Sing—Kishen Sing, Gulab Sing Kupti, Hira Sing, and many other well-known chiefs, conspicuous for bravery, being all killed at the head of their respective commands in attempting to check the British onslaught.

The enemy still endeavoured to rally, but the pressure was too great; many thousands being precipitated headlong into the river; and as our soldiers, flushed with victory, hurled the Khalsa into the rapid stream, our artillery opened a galling fire of grape and shrapnel on the fugitives, rolling over the helpless writhing masses as they struggled in the water. If it be true that Lal Sing and the Lahore Durbar had

---

3. Cunningham's History of the Seiks, p. 328.
4. It was asserted immediately after the battle that this boat had been removed by one of the Khalsa Sirdars, to cut off the retreat of any Seik fugitives from their front.

schemed the destruction of the Khalsa army, they could not have succeeded more completely; for there had been in India no such slaughter since the battle of Buxar, 1764, when the dead of Shuja u'd daulah's army formed a mole, over which the defeated survivors effected their escape. The river Sutlej, after the battle of Sobraon, was the Golgotha of the largest proportion of the Khalsa army.

The Governor-General, in his Notification published four days after this victory, refers to it as being "one of the most daring ever achieved, by which, in open day, a triple line of breastworks, flanked by formidable redoubts, bristling with artillery, manned by 32 regular regiments of infantry was assaulted and carried."

Thus ended the storm and capture of the last Seik stronghold; and thus virtually terminated the Sutlej campaign. The enemy lost between 8000 and 10,000 men, 60 pieces of heavy artillery, and upwards of 200 camel swivel guns (zamburucks); but this grand result was not achieved without an immense sacrifice of life on our side.

During the advance of the 2nd or General Gilbert's Division, 689 men fell within half-an-hour; the 1st European Light Infantry losing 12 officers, 12 sergeants, and 173 of rank and file; their gallant General Gilbert being also wounded at the head of the division, and Brigadier McLaren, who commanded our brigade, and was referred to by the commander-in-chief in his dispatch as "one of the ablest of the senior officers of the force," being mortally wounded whilst leading us to the assault.

This officer was beloved by the 1st European Regiment, having endeared himself by his genial, kindly, fatherly bearing towards those who served under him; and his death was deeply lamented.

It must be borne in mind that our Regiment had suffered so severely at the battle of Ferozeshah as to muster little over 400 when it went into action at Sobraon. Of this number 197 fell in the latter battle; so that nearly one-half of the combatants was either killed or wounded during the three assaults on the enemy's stronghold at Sobroan.

Of all ranks in the British army there were killed at Sobraon 320, and wounded 2063, making a total of 2383.

Before noon the battle was over, and the enemy had been driven from the Company's territories. A strange calm succeeded the furious tumult which had raged since early morning. There came the sad duty of burying our dead and collecting our wounded. Twenty-seven brave men of our regiment were placed in one grave on the bank of the dry bed of the river from which they had made their three gallant assaults.

The enemy were allowed to return to the left bank of the Sutlej for the same purpose, but they contented themselves with carrying away a few only of the bodies of their leaders; amongst which was that of their grand old General Sirdar Sham Sing; those not removed being left as food for the jackal and the vulture.

The scenes in camp that afternoon and during the whole night were sad in the extreme—the watching beside the bed of a dying comrade, the stillness of the night broken only by the groans from the amputating tents—there was no chloroform in those days— these are the realities of war.

The following is a list of the killed and wounded officers of the 1st Bengal European Light Infantry at the battle of Sobraon:—

Killed

Lieutenant F. Shuttleworth.
Ensign F. W. A. Hamilton.

Wounded

Lieutenant J. Lambert (mortally).
Ensign G. H. Davidson (mortally).
Lieutenant G. G. Denniss (severely).
Lieutenant A. Hume (dangerously).
Lieutenant T. Staples (returned slightly wounded, but part of foot amputated)
Lieutenant D. C. T. Beatson (died next day).
Ensign G. O. B. Palmer (slightly).
Ensign P. R. Innes (slightly).
Captain E. Magnay (severely).
Lieutenant J. Pattullo (severely).

When the 1st European Light Infantry left Subathoo on the 10th of December, 1845, there were present 24 officers, and 2 joined afterwards; making a total of 26.

At the battle of Ferozeshah and the storm and capture of Sobraon, 9 officers were killed and 11 less severely wounded; thus a total of 20 out of 26 officers formed the casualty list during the campaign.

The 1st European Light Infantry which had been 640 strong—after having left its sick in hospital, and men on duty with the depôt at Subathoo—lost 406 rank and file killed and wounded; there being left for duty with the headquarters of the Regiment on the 11th February only 6 officers and 230 rank and file.

If the loss of a regiment during a campaign be any indication of its good services, then assuredly the 1st European Light Infantry must be admitted to have fought well indeed; for seldom has a Regiment shown such a casualty list in any single successful campaign.

Would that we could place on record the name of every non-commissioned officer[5] and private soldier who signally distinguished himself and deserves special mention, for many were the individual heroic deeds which can only be known by the general result; but the officers who fell were our intimate friends and companions, their many kindly, brotherly acts bringing their memory more strongly before us.

Of Lieutenant John Lambert, McGregor in his History of the Seiks, says:

> To speak of him as merely a brother officer would be doing injustice to his memory, he was our friend, the friend of the writer of these pages, and never have we known a more zealous, or enthusiastic soldier, or one who more fully sustained the honour of his profession. He had talents of no ordinary kind, and had he been spared, poor Lambert would have been an honour to the fair town of Alnwick which gave him birth; but, he died the death he coveted, fell fighting side by side with his gallant companions before Sobraon, universally lamented by his brother officers.

Captain R. C. Napier, afterwards the hero of Magdala, says, "I saw that fine boy—Lambert—after Sobraon in the Ferozpóre Hospital, with one leg amputated, full of the same spirit that he had displayed at the Battle of Ferozeshah; but he did not recover." The author re-echoes McGregor's words. John Lambert was indeed "an honour to his profession."

Ensign Fred Hamilton was—as has been previously narrated—left on account of ill-health with the depôt of the Regiment when it went on service against the Seiks. It was a sore trial, and he begged with tears to be allowed to accompany his regiment, but the surgeon was inexorable; but no sooner was his health sufficiently restored than he, at considerable risk, hastened to his post, too late to take part in the battle of Ferozeshah; but alas! in time to meet his death at Sobraon, where this handsome, gallant, brave young officer lay a mangled corpse before the outer fortifications. He was shot down

---

5. Sergeant-Major Moore of the 1st European light Infantry was promoted to the rank of Ensign for distinguished services in the field at Ferozeshah and Sobraon.

during the first advance, and in this helpless condition was cut to pieces by the enemy who sallied forth from the embrasures as the Regiment was driven back.

Lieutenant Shuttleworth fell early in the day; he was not, like young Hamilton, hacked and mutilated, but shot dead; and it does not appear that he moved after he fell. Shuttleworth, when our regiment was ordered on service, had obtained leave of absence to visit his home in England, but the rude blast of war cancelled his furlough; and, whilst those near and dear to him were expecting his immediate return, he was lying under the cold earth close to the field of battle at Sobraon.

There was also Gordon Hugh Davidson, the companion and dearest friend of the author. No one knew him so intimately, no one so appreciated his noble, honest nature, his sterling worth. McGregor speaks of him as "uniting the daring courage of a soldier to the meekest, mildest spirit." He was. indeed, brave as he was good. Gordon Davidson was shot by a musket-ball in the right breast, during our first advance, and was conveyed to the field hospital. The bullet was extracted from his spine, and so he was brought to our tent. We had left it together that morning full of hope and joy, but now his face was shrunken and wan and hardly to be recognized. That night fever supervened, with parching-thirst, a weary, helpless look, the last message—the glassy, fixed eye, a deep groan, and all was over. McGregor continues, "Had a brother fallen the grief could not have been more poignant than was that of his young companion in arms who shared the same tent with him, and also watched his departing spirit." McGregor never wrote more truly.

Shuttleworth, Hamilton, and Davidson were buried on the evening succeeding the battle, in a small grove of trees close to our camp. It was almost dark, the moon fitfully shining out, the dead march played by our band being the only sound as the funeral cortege moved along; this was so small that a stranger casually passing might perhaps have thought that the dead officers had but few friends. Alas! they were followed to their graves by all their companions who had survived the bloody campaign—six brother officers.

Early on the morning of the 12th of February our camp was struck, and we advanced towards Ferozpóre, where a double bridge of boats had been constructed; and, on the 13th the whole force, with the exception of our heavy artillery train, crossed the Sutlej; and, making a rapid march, encamped at Kusur, in the Punjab, sixteen miles from Ferozpóre, and about thirty from Lahore.

The remnant of the Khalsa army, after the battle of Sobraon, had encamped at Raebam, about eighteen miles east of Lahore; and with them were their Commanders Tej Sing and Lal Sing; the Citadel of Lahore being guarded by Golab Sing's troops.

On the 15th of February a number of Seik chiefs, escorted by cavalry and bearing a white flag, were seen to approach the British camp; it was the Raja Golab Sing, who arrived with full credentials from the Maharaja of the Punjaub, to beg pardon in the name of the Lahore Durbar, for the offences which had been committed by their army against the British power, and to endeavour to negotiate terms of peace.

The Governor-General assembled his principal officers, and received the Raja in Durbar, but all the usual forms and ceremonies were purposely omitted; the Raja advanced and offered to the Governor-General nuzzurs—complimentary presents—but these were refused.

The following were the principal terms demanded by the British Government; and accepted by Golab Sing on the part of the Lahore Durbar:

1. The surrender of the Seik territory lying between the Bias and Sutlej rivers.

2. Payment of one-and-a-half crores of rupees (1½ million. sterling), as indemnity for the expenses of the war.

3. The disbandment of the present Seik army, and its reorganization on an improved system, to be determined on in. communication with the British Government.

4. The surrender of all the guns which had been employed against us.

5. The British to have complete control of both banks of the river Sutlej.

The Governor-General then directed that the Maharaja Dulip Sing should be brought to the British camp, which advanced the next day to Lulliana; where the young Maharaja, in obedience to the Governor-General's order, arrived with his chiefs, and at once tendered his submission.

The usual salutes and other ceremonies were at first omitted, but on the Maharaja accepting the proffered terms, asking pardon for the offences committed by his army, and begging that he might be restored to the friendship of the Governor-General, the nuzzurs were again presented and this time accepted; and the Durbar broke up under a full salute.

With this treaty terminated what may be called the first chapter of the conquest of the Punjab.

The British army was now informed that as it was the intention of the Indian Council to re-establish the Seik Government at Lahore on friendly terms, that city would be protected from pillage; and our soldiers therefore were ordered to receive one year's extra "batta" in lieu of plunder. The Rani, it was understood, promised a like amount; but it was well known that she had not the means, even if she had the inclination, to fulfil her promise.

The British army encamped on the plain outside the walls of Lahore on the 20th February; and now that the carrying out of the terms of the treaty had been satisfactorily arranged, orders were issued for the breaking up of the "Army of the Sutlej" and the return of the troops to Hindustan.

Lal Sing was appointed to the Vazirship of the Lahore Durbar, and Tej Sing was nominated to the Chief Command of the Khalsa army; both appointments being made with the approval of the Governor-General. But Lal Sing and Tej Sing felt that not only their positions, but. their lives, would be in imminent danger as soon as the Khalsa army should fully realise that they had been betrayed by their leaders—and these leaders the very men now placed in power at the instigation of the British Government. Furthermore, notwithstanding that complete arrangements had been made for the governing power of the Seik Durbar, as well as for the political management and military occupation of our newly-acquired provinces in the Punjaub, the Rani and the members of the Lahore Durbar felt that their own personal safety and that of the young Maharaja could only be assured by the presence of a protecting force at the capital. It was therefore ordered that a; British contingent should remain at Lahore until the end of the year 1846, but no longer. The guns of the fort of Lahore were, at the request of the Durbar, handed over to the charge of our artillery; and, some of our troops having been located in the city, the Rani and her son returned to the Palace, which they had hitherto considered was not a place of safety.

On the 23rd of March the 1st European Light Infantry commenced its return to India; on the 26th recrossed the Sutlej, and on the following day the Regiment was inspected by the Commander-in-Chief, who was overcome with genuine emotion as he realised the reduced condition of the Regiment—truly but a skeleton of its former self. He spoke to the men feelingly and impressively of their gallant conduct during the campaign, and remarked that the number of wounded in the ranks proved how eager they had been to take their share of duty with their more fortunate comrades. To the officers he said that, should Her Majesty be pleased to confer on him her gracious approval for the part he had taken in the late campaign, he should always feel that such approval was due to the officers and men who had gained for him this great success. In conclusion, His Excellency announced to the Regiment that, in reward ;for its distinguished services, he had obtained the permission of the Government of India to create the Bengal European Light Infantry a Fusilier Regiment, and thenceforward it was to be designated "The 1st European Bengal Fusiliers."

The next day the 1st European Bengal Fusiliers continued it's return march to Subathoo, which station it reached early in April.

Orders had previously been issued directing the 2nd Bengal European Regiment[6] to proceed to Subathoo; and, as there was only permanent accommodation for one regiment, the 2nd Europeans were housed in temporary buildings. They reached the station on the 20th of April, when they received a hearty welcome from their sister regiment; and during the time that the 1st and 2nd were quartered together, nothing could have exceeded the good-fellowship which existed between the regiments.

During the autumn of this year Colonel Joseph Orchard, C.B., again commanding the Regiment, met with an accident on parade which unhappily terminated fatally; his horse swerving and throwing his rider violently to the ground. One of the officers ran to his assistance, but, quickly recovering himself, Orchard sprung to his feet, reprimanded the officer for having left the ranks, and ordered the Regiment to "retire by double column of subdivisions from both flanks in rear of the centre." This was the last word of command he ever gave—it was in vain he attempted to remount his horse: the parade was dismissed, and the Colonel was assisted to his house near at hand, where he lingered for a few months, when; he died—February 19th, 1847—and was buried with all military honours in the cemetery at Subathoo.

Nothing could surpass the genuine grief of the fusiliers; for Colonel Orchard was, in every sense, the father of the Regiment, with which he had served over forty years. He was not only respected, he was beloved by all under his command; and his memory has always been held in affectionate veneration by all those who had the privilege of serving under him.

---

6. Now the 2nd Battalion Royal Munster Fusiliers.

The gloom cast over the Regiment was at this time enhanced by the terrible visitation of a very virulent form of Cholera, which created terrible havoc, especially amongst the young soldiers lately joined to fill the many vacancies created during the Sutlej War.

Towards the close of 1847 the 1st Bengal Fusiliers was ordered to Cawnpore, and on arrival the Regiment was placed under the command of Colonel George Huyshe, C. B. In the following autumn the left wing, under command of Major H. IT. Combe, was detached to Agra, where it remained until the close of 1849. In the meantime events of importance had occurred in the Punjab, calling for the interference of the British Government.

As the time approached for the withdrawal of the British troops from Lahore, notwithstanding that the Governor-General had said, "in no case can I consent that the British shall remain in garrison at Lahore, for a longer period than the end of this year,"[7] complications had arisen which rendered the revision of this edict necessary. A treaty was consequently entered into on the 16th December, 1846, between the British Government and the Lahore Durbar, under the provisions of which it was agreed that "a British officer with an efficient establishment shall be appointed by the Governor-General to remain at Lahore, which officer shall have full authority to direct and control all matters in every department of the state."

Colonel Henry Lawrence[8] was the Officer appointed by the Governor-General to this responsible position, and he applied for and obtained the services of some of the ablest officers in the army; amongst those so appointed being Lieutenant Herbert B. Edwardes, of the 1st European Bengal Fusiliers, who was dispatched to the far-distant station of Bunnu, situated in a portion of the Seik territories ceded to the Lahore Durbar by the Afghans. This district had never been conquered, nor had it been, strictly speaking, even occupied by the Punjab troops; it was about thirty marches to the north-west of Lahore, its inhabitants being warlike and independent; so that although the task which Colonel Lawrence imposed upon young Edwardes required sound judgement, courage, and skill, he proved himself fully equal to the responsibility.

Colonel Lawrence's administration of the affairs of the Punjab lasted until the commencement of the year 1848. He inaugurated the principles of Government which he deemed suitable to the circum-

---

7. Proceedings in Durbar held at Lahore, 9th March, 1846.
8. Afterwards Colonel Sir Henry Lawrence, K.C.B.

stances; but he altogether lost sight of the fact that the effect of the treachery of the Seik chiefs on the Khalsa was bearing fruit, which threatened to terminate in mutiny and serious disorder. He believed that the people of the Punjab were in every way satisfied with the regency of the British; and, having received assuring reports from Edwardes, Nicholson, Bowie and others, he anticipated no outbreak or difficulty; so he resigned his charge and accompanied the Governor-General—Lord Hardinge—to England.

Colonel Lawrence was succeeded by Sir F. Currie, Foreign Secretary to the Government of India; who, following his predecessor's policy, elaborated his plans, and trusting to the assurances of the Seik Chiefs by whom he was surrounded that the whole country was in a state of contentment and peace, looked forward to a future rule of tranquillity.

The Khalsa army was now fully convinced that it had been betrayed by its commanders in the last campaign, and it believed that it was in reward for such betrayal that the British had appointed Lal Sing and Tej Sing to responsible posts in the Seik Government. The Khalsa Sirdars believed that the victories gained by the British were the result of treachery; and they concluded that their defeats were due either to gross mismanagement or utter faithlessness; they therefore determined to have another struggle for the mastery.

Dissatisfaction first showed itself at Multan; Mulraj, the Governor of that province, having, since the close of the Sutlej campaign, tried his strength against the Lahore troops and defeated them.

The British were bound to maintain the authority of the Lahore Durbar; but before the day of retribution Mulraj had been brought to reason, terms arranged, and further hostilities avoided; Mulraj agreeing to cede about one-third of his province to the Durbar, and to pay a sum of £20,000 as succession duty. Thus the quarrel was supposed to have been satisfactorily arranged; but Mulraj thought, or pretended to think, that he had been over-reached, and in consequence resigned his governorship; but to his resignation was affixed a condition, *viz.*, that it should be kept a profound secret. Sir Frederick Currie either found this condition irksome or perhaps impossible to maintain; any way it leaked out, and much ill-feeling, in consequence, was engendered. Mulraj, being asked to cancel his resignation, refused; but it was not suspected at Lahore that he was one of the prime movers of an organized revolution in which the remnant of the Khalsa army was deeply implicated. Two Officers, Mr. P. A. Vans Agnew and Lieutenant W. A. Anderson, were appointed by Sir Frederick Currie to proceed to Multan, and make themselves acquainted with the state of affairs in the province, preparatory to its being handed over by Mulraj to the Lahore Durbar.

These officers were accompanied by a body of the Lahore troops, who, on arrival at Multan, mutinied, and throwing off all disguise joined Mulraj's army, which now declared its intention not to surrender the Multan district. Vans Agnew and Anderson were attacked; the former being struck from his horse by one of Mulraj's soldiers and sabred before he could regain his feet, and the latter maltreated by the crowd, and so wounded that he was left for dead; they were, however, extricated by Sirdar Khan Sing, who had accompanied the British officers from Lahore, and who had been appointed by the Lahore Durbar to succeed to the Governorship of the province. The wounded officers, with their escort and six guns, attempted a defence, but were overpowered Agnew's head being severed from his body, and Anderson, who lay helpless on his bed, being hacked to pieces.

This state of affairs at Multan was quickly reported to Edwardes. To have awaited orders from Lahore would have imperilled the status of the British at the Seik capital. Edwardes, therefore, in the absence of regular troops, organized an army from the raw levies at his disposal; and, having made a report of his proceedings to his chief, marched to attack Mulraj. Edwardes' whole force numbered only 1600 men; and was composed for the most part of soldiers of conflicting interests and doubtful allegiance.

The news of the murder of the two officers reached Edwardes whilst he was at Dera Fath Khan, about 90 miles from Multan. He hastily communicated with the British officers at the nearest stations, asking assistance; and one of the murdered officers had, just before his death, sent a message to General Van Courtland, begging that he would come to his assistance with his Patan soldiers. Edwardes, having been reinforced by some of General Van Courtland's troops, attacked and defeated a large body of Mulraj's army; and again, on May 20th, he met and defeated another division of Mulraj's troops at Kineri; and, after nine hours' severe fighting, drove his enemy across the river Chenab, and thus deprived him of a large portion of his territories. Finally, July 1st 1848: having received some further reinforcements, and secured the co-operation of some friendly Seik chiefs, Edwardes advanced on Multan itself. Here he was confronted by Mulraj's main army, under the personal command of that Chief. Nothing daunted, Edwardes gave Mulraj battle; and, after a desperate encounter, forced his antagonist to seek refuge behind his defences.

The 1st Bengal Fusiliers were justly proud of Lieutenant Herbert Edwardes.[9] His courage and forethought, his decision of character and noble bearing exercised a spell on all who were brought within his influence; and it was this power and strength of will which mainly contributed to a success almost unparalleled in Indian history. Had Edwardes been supported by a small British force with a few guns, it is quite possible that he might have averted the impending war—the second chapter in the history of the conquest of the Punjab.

But intrigue in the meantime was rife at Lahore; for in July it was discovered that the Rani—the Queen Regent—was implicated in a plot which threatened to develop into open war. The Rani was sent a state-prisoner to the fortress of Chunar, whilst some other leaders of the rebellion were tried and hanged. But, notwithstanding the sharp measures which had been adopted, the horizon was clouded: and it soon became evident that a second Seik War was imminent.

The Lahore brigade, under General Whish, was ordered to Multan

---

9. The following paragraphs of a military letter, No. 15, to Governor-General of India in Council, dated the 1st November, 1848, was published for general information.

We have the gratification of apprising you that the Queen has been graciously pleased to confer upon Lieutenant Herbert Benjamin Edwardes, of the 1st Bengal European Regiment Fusiliers, the local rank of Major in the Lahore territories. We have further the satisfaction to state that Her Majesty has been graciously pleased, by a special statute of the most Honourable Order of the Bath, to appoint Major Edwardes an extra member of the military division of the Third Class or Companion of that Order. With reference to your dispatches and to those from the Government of Bombay announcing the military operations carried on against the rebel forces of the Dewan of Mooltan by this Officer, we passed on the 13th of September last a resolution, of which the following is a copy:

Resolved unanimously that this Court do present to Major Edwardes a gold medal, in testimony of their high approbation of the important services rendered by him in raising and organizing a large force in a foreign territory under circumstances of the greatest difficulty, in wresting within a very brief period an extensive tract of country from the power of the rebels, in skilfully combining his forces with those of an ally and in signally defeating the troops of the enemy in two pitched battles, thus evincing the possession, in the flower of his youth, of all those qualities which form and ennoble the character of the 'British Officer.'

to support Edwardes; and the Ferozpóre brigade was moved to Lahore, both these brigades being at once pushed on to Multan. On arrival, September 5th, Whish found Edwardes' force, now numbering some 20.000 men, encamped at Suraj Khund, about six miles from Multan.

Whish, with his engineer Officer, Napier,[10] found that the fortress could not judiciously be assaulted without the heavy siege-guns, which had not yet arrived; and it was not until the 7th of September that the siege of Multan commenced. But now an unforeseen difficulty presented itself. The Lahore troops under Sirdar Sher Sing, deserted from the British force; and, declaring their sympathy with the national movement, entered the fortress of Multan and proclaimed their allegiance to Mulraj. The siege was raised; Whish blockading the roads leading into the town, but otherwise remaining inactive. On the 27th of December, reinforcements having joined the British army, the siege operations were resumed; and during the following month[11] Multan was captured by assault, and the Fortress occupied by our troops.

In the meantime events had occurred which left no doubt .as to the intentions of the Khalsa army, and that they had resolved to measure their strength a second time with the British, A General Order was now issued, directing the assembly of an army at Ferozpóre, which was called "The Army of the Punjab" Lord Gough assuming the command in person.

The 1st European Bengal Fusiliers at this time was quartered, the right wing at Cawnpore and the left wing at Agra. The Regiment had been so terribly reduced during the Sutlej War, that its ranks were even now filled by young soldiers and recruits. Under these circumstances the Regiment was left to guard the lower provinces; whilst the 2nd Bengal European Regiment was ordered to take part in the coming campaign.

The 2nd European Regiment marched from Subathoo on the 24th September, 1848, arriving at Ferozpóre on the 14th, of October, when it was appointed to the 4th Brigade of "The Army of the Punjab." This brigade was under Brigadier Godby C.B., the Colonel of the 2nd Bengal Europeans; which regiment was now commanded by Major Steel.

On the 22nd of November, 1848, Godby's brigade joined the army, at this time under the personal command of Lord Gough, at Rámnagar.

The battle of Rámnagar was fought on the day that the 4th Brigade joined the army; the 2nd European Regiment not being actively

---

10. Afterwards Lord Napier of Magdala.
11. January 21st, 1849.

engaged, although they had a few men wounded by stray shots. The battle was precipitated by the impetuosity of our commander-in-chief, who suffered severely for his temerity; the British leaving one gun, which had become embedded in the mud, in the enemy's hands, and some of our best officers were killed and wounded.[12]

After the battle of Rámnagar, the Khalsa army, content with the advantage it had gained, crossed the Chenab and took up its position on the right bank of that river.

Military critics all agree that Lord Gough's policy should now have been to have watched his enemy and quietly awaited the fall of Multan, when he would be reinforced by the troops under Whish. But the commander-in-chief was smarting under his defeat at Rámnagar, and his hot blood induced him to discard this prudent course. He determined to engage his enemy without loss of time; and, on the 1st of December, a division of the British army, consisting of about 8000 men under Sir Joseph Thackwell, taking advantage of the apathy and want of caution of the Seiks, who had neglected to watch the fords, crossed the Chenab; and next day Thackwell marched twelve-miles to the village of Durnwal without meeting any opposition. The day after, Thackwell received orders from the commander-in-chief to attack the Seiks as soon as practicable; and, in obedience to this order, marched the following morning; but, after he had proceeded about six miles, he received instructions to await the arrival of Brigadier Godby's brigade before striking. Godby's brigade, with the 2nd Bengal European Regiment, was at this time crossing the river Chenab at the ford of Ghari. A strange complication followed these contradictory orders. Gough had intended to have made a feint on the enemy's position, and thus attract his attention, whilst Thackwell was making his real attack; but Sher Sing, having heard that Thackwell had crossed the Chenab, formed the idea of catching Gough in his own trap; therefore he left a small portion of his troops to watch Gough whilst he himself marched to give battle to Thackwell. No sooner, however, had Sher Sing started on his march than it appears to have struck him that he was probably placing himself between two fires; for, should Gough convert his feint into a real attack, he might cross the river and assault him in his rear. Nevertheless, Sher Sing continued his advance on Thackwell, who being in ignorance of Sher Sing's intended attack, had, on the morning of the 3rd of December, halted near the village

---

12. Colonels Havelock and Cureton were slain, and upwards of 80 men killed and wounded in this action.

of Sudulapur. The British troops, tired after their march, had piled their arms and were snatching a little rest, when they were unexpectedly alarmed by the roar of artillery. The men rushed to their arms and prepared for action; but Sher Sing contented himself with occupying three villages in Thackwell's front, from which a continuous fire was poured on the British with little result.

It was not till 4 p.m. that Thackwell consented to return the enemy's fire, and at sunset it was discontinued on both sides; Sher Sing returning hastily to his camp on the right bank of the river Chenab.

On the morning of the 4th Godby's brigade, with the 2nd Europeans and two regiments of British cavalry, joined Thackwell's division; and next day Thackwell moved his camp to the village of Helah.

Gough had not left his position at Rámnagar, but was there employed in constructing a pontoon-bridge across the Chenab, which was not completed until the 18th December, when he crossed the river and joined Thackwell's division at Helah.

Soon after this junction, the commander-in-chief received the unwelcome intelligence that our fortress of Atak, on the river Indus, had capitulated, having been beleaguered by Chattar Sing with a strong Seik force; and it was reasonable to suppose that Chattar Sing would now join Sher Sing.

This was the view taken by Lord Dalhousie, the Governor-General, who sent immediate instructions to Lord Gough—"under the altered circumstances"—not to await the fall of Multan, but to strike at his enemy as soon as practicable; and Gough, delighted to have gained the consent of Government, determined to precipitate an action at all risks.

Sher Sing occupied a position of considerable strength at Chillianwalla, with thick jungle in his front and rear, which afforded admirable cover, and on his left the village of Rasul.

Gough's plan of action was to take his enemy in flank and force him back between unfordable rivers, deficient of supplies, and thus prevent the junction of his army with that of Chattar Sing. Gough neared his enemy on the afternoon of the 13th of January, fully intending to bivouac on the field and force Sher Sing to a battle on the following morning; but as soon as he sighted his enemy he could not resist the temptation of engaging him.

Sher Sing opened fire first, and Gough could not brook the insult. He at once hurled his infantry at his enemy, with the simple instructions to his generals that they had to capture the enemy's guns at the point of the bayonet. Gough seems to have forgotten utterly all his carefully digested plans; angry at the temerity of the enemy, he sent his infantry to punish them.

General Gilbert's division—in which was the 2nd Bengal Regiment,—occupied the right of our attacking-line; the left was under Colonel Campbell, and in the centre our heavy guns.

The British line advanced most cheerily; but it had to push its way through dense jungle for a distance of nearly a mile before sighting the enemy; moreover, amongst this jungle were large pools and swamps, necessitating frequent détours and causing some confusion, notwithstanding which the British regiments soon formed up—under a heavy fire—and assumed some kind of order. The command was now given to rapidly advance, and our troops made a decided rush on the enemy with their bayonets, causing him to recoil; but the Seiks, soon recovering themselves, charged down on the left of our line, recapturing some of their own guns which we had previously seized from them. The enemy then made a determined onslaught, surrounding Colonel Campbell's division on three sides.

The Seiks, seeing the right of our line exposed, brought round some guns and infantry, intending to take us in flank; but Brigadier Godby, discerning their object, wheeled back the two companies on the right of the 2nd European Regiment, and fired some volleys on the advancing foe, which caused him to make a détour. The Seiks, however, had completely outflanked our line; and it soon became apparent that they had circled round under cover of the jungle, and were charging down on the rear of the Regiment. There was no time to be lost; Godby could not change his front on account of the dense jungle, so he faced his regiment to the rear, and with his rear rank in front dashed at the Khalsa infantry.

Major Dawes, with his two troops of Bengal Horse artillery, did splendid service on this occasion, by coining to the relief and covering the 2nd Bengal European Regiment, just as it was very hard pressed by the Seik infantry and artillery, fighting the Regiment both in front and rear.

As the enemy approached from the rear they emerged from the jungle, and it was now seen that they were advancing very steadily with drums beating and colours flying; when the Bengal Europeans, still rear rank in front, gave a hearty cheer as they rushed on the Khalsa line. The enemy hesitated as the Europeans approached, some of them retiring, but most held their ground, and, receiving our charge, made a desperate resistance, using their tulwars and knives with terrible effect. After some severe fighting the Seik line fairly gave way; the Europeans, now making a rush at the Seik guns which had been galling them so severely, and capturing two at the point of the bayonet, and Godby, facing to his front, re-advanced to his former position. This exploit of the 2nd Bengal European Regiment proved that in point of steadiness, discipline, and courage, even under the most trying circumstances, it was second to none in our armies.

The tide of battle was now turning in favour of the British. The left of our army had re-formed, and was driving the Seiks back at the point of the bayonet; whilst the right, having cleared the enemy from its rear, had regained the ground which it had lost. Our cavalry—led by General Thackwell—and the Bengal Horse artillery, were doing splendid service on both flanks.

As if it had been pre-concerted, the British army now broke into a hearty English cheer; and with a simultaneous rush forward, the enemy were repulsed along the whole line; and Gough, however justly he may be censured for his rash attack, had the satisfaction of seeing that he had driven the Khalsa from the field, thus winning the battle of Chillianwalla.

Darkness was now setting in. There, were two courses open to the Commander-in-Chief—he might hold the field, which he had just won at so great a cost of life, or he might retire on Chillianwalla where was his depôt of provisions and ammunition. He decided on adopting the latter course, and retired to his former position.

The following is the résumé of this battle by that fearless and just critic, Colonel Malleson, who says:

> The British army then returned from the well-fought field, to win which had cost them, in killed and wounded, 89 officers and 2357 fighting-men, leaving on the field many standards—loot, not captured—six guns, and all their dead. It cannot be said of this battle that 'it was a famous victory.' Indeed, it can only be technically called a victory, and most certainly it was of a Pyrrhœan character.

The following is the casualty list of the 2nd Bengal European 1849. Regiment at the battle of Chillianwalla:—
Lieutenant Nightingale, very severely wounded.
Lieutenant Bleamire, slightly wounded.
Rank-and-file, killed 6, wounded 54.

Eight days after the battle of Chillianwalla[13] Multan fell—January 21st, 1849—and General Whish, with about 9,000 men, hastened to join our Headquarters camp; but this increase would be fully counterbalanced by the army of Chattar Sing joining the Khalsa force. Chattar Sing, who was Sher Sing's father, now assumed the chief command of the Seik army.

Lord Gough, for various strategic reasons, changed his ground several times, and finally, on the 20th of February, having been joined by the Multan force and a Bombay brigade, pitched his camp at Shadiwalla. In the meantime Chattar Sing also had several times changed his ground with the object of again inducing Gough to attack; but this time he was not to be tempted. The Seik army finally took up its position in front of the village of Goozerat, with its right and left resting on two streams, both of which were easily fordable; indeed the stream on the enemy's right was nearly dry, and that on the left formed no serious obstacle. Across and beyond these streams were bodies of the enemy's cavalry.

The two armies, on ,the morning of the 21st February, faced each other; Gough's plan of action being to attack his enemy on his left and centre simultaneously, and drive him back on his Right Wing which he hoped to double up; and, during the confusion, to hurl at him our Left Wing, with which he intended to scatter the Seiks past rallying.

Generals Gilbert's and Whish's divisions, supported by the greater part of the field artillery, were told off to attack the enemy's centre; the 2nd European Regiment being one of those appointed to capture the fortified village of Barrakalra, situated in the enemy's immediate front, and considered to be the key to his position.

The 2nd Europeans advanced in line to the attack; but Barrakalra was defended by some of the best Regiments in the Khalsa army, selected by Chattar Sing for the post of honour, as they had displayed signal bravery at the battle of Chillianwalla. The 2nd European Regiment advanced to within a short distance of the village; when they fired a volley, and the left wing, climbing up the mud walls, sprang on to the roofs of the houses, many of them letting themselves down into the narrow and tortuous streets, and driving the enemy out at the further side. The right wing in the meantime had passed round the village and engaged the enemy's supports; but as soon as the Seik artillery outside the village saw their comrades being overpowered, they elevated their guns so as to clear the tops of the houses, notwithstanding that the British and Seik soldiers were intermixed whilst they struggled for the mastery.

---

13. The decoration, "Chillianwalla," inherited from the 2nd European Bengal Fusiliers, is borne on the colours of the Royal Munster Fusiliers.

Two Seik colours were here captured by the 2nd Europeans; the enemy bravely defended these standards, and every Khalsa falling before they were relinquished.

But the battle was not yet over. The Seik infantry, when they became aware how small was the force which had driven them from the village, returning in masses; so that at this juncture it appeared as if the Regiment must inevitably be doubled up and crushed. Fordyce's horse artillery, which had covered the attacking-party, having retired to obtain a further supply of ammunition, the enemy's artillery, now unopposed, poured showers of grape amongst the Regiment, which was at the same time threatened by the large masses in its front. The 2nd Bengal Europeans were now drawn up in line under a withering fire, but such was their ardour that it was with difficulty Colonel Steele could restrain them from rushing forward at the enemy's guns. Just as the Khalsa troops were approaching the British line, a portion of Fordyce's horse artillery came galloping if up, and in a few seconds unlimbered their guns, and round after round of grape and volleys of musketry tore through the close ranks of the masses of the enemy in front. Under our well-directed fire the Khalsa soldiers faltered, and then slowly and sullenly retired.

From this moment the victory of Goozerat became a certainty. Malleson, in his Decisive Battles in India, p. 391, says of the capture of the position of Barra Kalrá, "The resistance was determined, the bearing of the Seiks heroic. They met the advancing foe face to face, and strove with undaunted courage to drive him back. Vain, however, were their efforts. Step by step did the British troops make good their footing, until at last they forced the enemy, still fronting them, to fall back on his second line. The gallant nature of the defence may be gathered from the loss inflicted by the Seiks on their assailants. In carrying the village of Barra Kalrá, the 3rd Brigade (2nd Europeans, 31st and 70th Native Infantry) lost upwards of 300 killed and wounded. The 2nd European Regiment lost in killed and wounded and missing 143—including 1 Officer, Lieutenant Sprot, killed; and 5—Captain Boyd, Lieutenant Elderton, and Ensigns Toogood, Sandford, and Matheson wounded.

The British cavalry and Bengal Horse artillery followed up the victory of Goozerat,[14] and during the rest of the day the Khalsa army,

---

14. The decoration, "Goozerat," inherited from the 2nd European Bengal Fusiliers, is borne on the colours of the Royal Munster Fusiliers.

now thoroughly disorganized, fled in dismay, throwing away its arms, clothing, and accoutrements; so that the whole line of retreat was thickly strewn with guns, tents, exhausted cattle, standards, and all the débris of war.

Next day two British divisions marched in pursuit; that under General Gilbert—with whom was the 2nd Bengal European Regiment—proceeding towards the river Jhelum, which it crossed, still pressing on the track of the disorganized Khalsa army.

Gilbert followed his enemy with vigour, the British column making one uninterrupted march of forty-seven miles, on which occasion the General expressed his admiration of the spirit and endurance of the 2nd European Regiment.[15]

On the 14th of March the Khalsa army, overtaken prostrate and helpless, surrendered unconditionally; Chattar Sing, the Commander-in-Chief, and Sher Sing, his Lieutenant, together with the principal Seik Sirdars, delivering up their swords to General Gilbert. Forty-one pieces of artillery were surrendered, and the shattered remnant of the conquered army laid down its arms in presence of its conquerors. The Khalsa may have been betrayed at Ferozeshah, but he had again challenged his foe. The battle hail been fought to the bitter end. He had been, this time, worsted in fair fight. Defeated and exhausted, he submitted to his foe.

Thus ended the second chapter of the subjugation of the Punjab, which was now annexed, March 29th, 1849, to the territories of the East India Company, under whose Government that vast province has prospered and improved; and under whose laws all property has been secured from unfair exactions or military plunder. The Khalsa, admitting the inevitable, transferred his allegiance and services to his new rulers, under whom he soon proved himself on an equality with the best troops in the British service.

It was the Seiks who first shook the Indian Empire to its very foundation; and we shall see that, in 1857, it was the Seiks who afterwards saved it.

---

15. For their distinguished services during the Punjab War, the 2nd European Regiment was—18th January, 1850—designated the 2nd European Bengal Fusiliers, "to mark the high sense entertained by the Government of the gallant, exemplary, and praiseworthy conduct of the Regiment during the late operations in the Punjab."—Government Gazette.

CHAPTER 17

The Second Burma War

March, 1850; Immediately after the Punjab War, the right wing of the 1st European Bengal Fusiliers marched from Cawnpore, and, joining the left wing at Agra, the entire Regiment proceeded to Lahore, the capital of our newly-acquired territories in the Punjab; reaching its destination early in 1850.

Lieutenant-Colonel David Birrell, lately returned from furlough, now resumed command of the Regiment.

As there were not sufficient barracks in the newly-built cantonment of Anarkulli for the accommodation of all the European force at Lahore, the 1st Bengal Fusiliers were quartered in the Huzari Bagh, or Royal Garden, a fortified portion of the city in which were the palaces of the Maharajahs. Many of the officers' quarters were constructed of costly materials, the walls being ornamented inside with beautifully-carved marbles; whilst some of the others, above the old gateways, were built of massive masonry.

The Regiment was quartered in the midst of a restless population, not yet habituated to our rule, and consisting of fanatics and discharged Khalsa soldiers, who had so lately been our enemies in the field; yet such was the discipline maintained, that, although our soldiers were frequently insulted and molested in the streets, instances of retaliation on their part were very rare.

In the month of June, 1850, the officer on guard was informed that six Seik fanatics had broken into the square adjoining one of our barracks, which was used as "married men's quarters." Proceeding to the place indicated, he found the dead bodies of the six Seiks lying in the square. They had stealthily entered the enclosure a few minutes before the dinner-hour, and having bound the mystic thread around their wrists and drawn their tulwars, they had attempted to sell their lives as dearly as they could, and to inflict death on all the Europeans who might come across their path. Eleven of the married men of the Regiment had been wounded before the fanatics were killed, but fortunately none of our soldiers were fatally injured, they having defended themselves as best they could with legs of tables, chairs, and footstools, or anything else that came to hand; their wives helping the men by clinging to the Seiks, who, however maddened with *bhang*, or thirsting for blood, never injure either women or children. It was afterwards reported that these Khalsas had said on the previous night that as, owing to the cessation of hostilities, they could no longer live by the sword, they elected to die by the hands of their late enemies, rather than exist in idleness and humiliation.

In the autumn of this year, 1850, the river Ravee so over-flowed its banks during the periodical rains, that the esplanade and surrounding country were placed many feet under water, which also surrounded the fort where our Regiment was quartered, producing malaria, so affecting both officers and men that upwards of eighty per cent, were either on the sick-list or in hospital with fever. The Regiment was now ordered into camp on some rising ground a few miles distant from the City of Lahore; but the sickness was so general and the mortality so great that sepahis were employed on our Regimental guards.

Dr. H. A. Bruce was at this trying time the Surgeon of our Regiment, and nothing could exceed his kindness and attention. Dr. Bruce had at all times been an universal favourite in the Regiment, both with the officers and men, not only professionally, but as the life of the mess-table; and whenever or wherever an act of kindness was needed, his aid was un-ostentatiously ready. The scenes in camp during this severe epidemic were very distressing, the sick in their damp tents suffering much discomfort, and the constantly-occurring deaths throwing si gloom over the camp, which was not relieved until it became known that orders had been received at headquarters for the Regiment to march, as soon as practicable, to Meerut. The conveyance of the sick was a matter of considerable difficulty, no less than three thousand bearers being required to carry the dhoolies containing the invalids. October, 1850; These bearers, who were playfully termed "Bruce's Brigade," were paraded during our march morning and evening. After a week's continual change of air the numbers of the bearers were materially reduced as our soldiers were restored to health. The disease, however, had told disastrously on the constitutions of the men; and on arrival at Meerut a medical board was assembled, February, 1851; under the orders of the commander-in-chief, to report on the health of the Regiment; when it was found that three-fourths of the men were still weakly, and suffering from the effects of the malaria to which they had been exposed at Lahore.

Early in 1852 rumours were rife of a coming war with Burmah; and an intimation was received that in all probability the services of the 1st European Bengal Fusiliers would be called into requisition.

Burmah adjoins the British territories; its northern frontier abutting on Assam: its western coast facing the east of India; the Bay of Bengal intervening.

In 1784 Arracan, on the Burmese coast, which had been exhausted by a succession of internal wars, fell an easy prey to the conqueror Bhodan Phaya, and was permanently annexed to the Avan dominion; and it was this conquest which first brought the Burmese into actual contact with our Bengal frontier, followed by repeated acts of aggression on the part of the Burmese, leading to the war between the East India Company and Burmah in 1824. This war terminated in 1826; and an agreement was entered into between the belligerents, called "the Treaty of Yandabu," under the clauses of which the large provinces of Aracan and Tenasserim were ceded to the Company, and thenceforward became a part of our Indian Empire.

Twenty-six years after the signing of the Treaty of Yandabu, our representatives in Burmah were subjected to constant indignities and repeated insults; the conditions of the above Treaty were ruthlessly violated, and oppressive exactions levied on our traders. Finally, the commander of a British vessel was wrongfully imprisoned by the Governor of Rangoon, heavily ironed, and placed in the public stocks; by which insults discredit and disgrace were brought on the English flag.

The Indian Government at once demanded satisfaction, and the admission of a British resident either at Rangoon or Ava; and it was to enforce these demands that a British squadron was dispatched to Rangoon. Consequent on this prompt action of the Indian Government, the Burmese King ordered the removal of the offending Governor, appointing a successor who it was stated had been instructed to satisfy the British demands. It soon, however, became apparent that the change of Governors was a ruse to tide over the difficulty, for not only was no satisfaction afforded, but the offending Governor was allowed to leave Rangoon with the plunder unjustly extorted from the British traders by his cruel exactions.

The English Commodore (Captain Lambert, R.N.) now sent a representative to the Governor of Rangoon, soliciting an interview; but the request was rejected, and the Commodore's messenger grossly insulted. Still anxious, if possible, to arrive at an amicable settlement, Captains Fishburn, of H.M.S. *Hermes*, and Tatler, the Chief Interpreter, together with other officers, waited on the Governor; but the emissaries returned to the squadron without having succeeded in gaining admission to the inner rooms of the palace; it having been urged in excuse that the Governor was asleep and was not to be disturbed.

It now became necessary to convince the Burmese that reparation would be compelled, as no reply was received to the Commodore's communications demanding satisfaction; and, as this was not otherwise to be obtained, he, on the 7th January, 1852, seized one of the Burmese ships of war, blockaded the town of Rangoon, calling on all British subjects as well as Portuguese, Armenians, and Mussulmans to leave the town and seek protection on board H.M. ships of war.

The property of the refugees who had claimed British protection under the Commodore's orders was immediately confiscated by the Burmese authorities.

During the course of these events the aged Burmese Governor of the town of Dalla, near Rangoon, alone behaved with courtesy; and he, having communicated with the British Commodore, obtained yet another day's grace to enable the Rangoon Governor to come to amicable terms; but, instead of endeavouring to avoid the threatened war, the latter forwarded a notice to the British Commodore, informing him that if he should attempt to pass the stockade which had been erected at the mouth of the river, he would be fired upon by the Burmese guns.

On the 9th of January the Burmese ship which had been captured in the Rangoon harbour was towed down the river towards the sea, under escort of H.M. ships *Hermes*, *Fox*, and *Phlegethon*. On arriving opposite the stockade the Burmese guns opened fire on the convoy, and an artillery fight ensued which resulted in a loss to the enemy of about 300 men. Thus opened the second Burmese War; and on the 10th of February, 1852, the Indian Government decided to send a military expedition to Burmah, to insist upon an apology and compensation being offered.

Military operations were commenced in April, when Rangoon was occupied by our troops, Martaban captured on the 5th of April, Bassain on the 19th of May, and Pegu was temporarily occupied in the early part of June, 1852.

The 1st European Bengal Fusiliers, then under the command of Lieutenant-Colonel Tudor, had received orders to join the army on service in Burmah, proceeding to Allahabad by river boats, and thence to Chinsurah by steamers. Two months were expended in transporting the Regiment to Calcutta, when it embarked on board the Frigates *Sphynx*, *Muzuffar* and *Feroze*, which conveyed it to Rangoon, arriving in the following November.

There was much that was interesting and picturesque to be seen from the decks of the steamers as they made their way up the Rangoon river; the beautiful verdure of the sloping river banks, backed by the adjacent hills and studded with handsome Pagodas—their rich gilding glittering in the sun—formed a series of pictures hardly to be surpassed in tropical brilliancy and beauty. The magnificent and costly pagoda of Syriam only preluded the still grander Shoé Dagon at Rangoon, close to which our vessels cast anchor.

Rangoon was now garrisoned by H.M. 80th and 51st Regiments, the 1st European Bengal and the 1st European Madras Fusiliers, with a detachment of the 18th Royal Irish; and in addition to the above were some batteries of field-artillery and a considerable force of Bengal and Madras infantry.

On the 19th of November an expedition was organized to capture the town and fort of Pegu, which fell into the hands of the British during the previous June, but had been evacuated as we had not at that time sufficient troops at our disposal to garrison it, and had been reoccupied by the Burmese, who had strengthened its defences. It now became necessary for us to recapture and permanently garrison this position, for which purpose the following troops—under Brigadier McNeill—left Rangoon in four river steamers: 300 of the 1st Bengal Europeans, under Colonel Tudor, 300 of the Madras Europeans, 400 5th Madras Native Infantry, with some detachments of artillery and sappers, and two field-guns. General Godwin accompanied the expedition and superintended its operations.

The river being shallow the steamers were not engaged, but the force landed on the 21st, a dense fog prevailing; and having taken up their respective positions, commenced the march through close and difficult jungle towards the town of Pegu. The Bengal and Madras Europeans threw forward their skirmishers, these regiments pushing on steadily, although the thick undergrowth was breast-high, rendering regular movements impossible. Indeed, the soldiers were scattered in single and double files, whilst the enemy, concealed around, were sending amongst them a dropping fire. The heat was so oppressive, and the exertion of pushing through the jungle so great, that several of the Europeans fell from fatigue, and some from sunstroke. Having at last arrived near the gateway of the town, General Godwin formed up his troops for the attack; but the soldiers were so exhausted that it was found impossible to advance until time had been allowed to recruit their strength.

After an hour's rest nearly the whole of the Bengal fusiliers were collected together, and the troops were formed up for action under a fire from the enemy, still concealed on all sides amongst the jungle.

General Godwin now addressed the troops, complimenting them on their almost superhuman exertions under such great difficulties, and explaining to them the work they still had before them. "Now," said he, addressing the fusilier regiments; "you are Bengalies, and you are Madrassies; let's see who are the best men." A hearty cheer was the response, when the Bengal and Madras fusiliers led the assault towards the city gate, which was, after a short struggle, captured; the Burmese soldiers being forced back and seeking shelter under the walls of the Pagoda on the platform above. About noon the whole of the town and fort of Pegu was in our possession; with a total loss in our army of 3 officers wounded, and from 30 to 40 rank and file killed, wounded, and missing.

Sergeant-Major Hopkins,[1] of the 1st Bengal Fusiliers, was promoted to an unattached Ensigncy for his gallant conduct during the storm of Pegu.

On the 22nd November the British troops returned to Rangoon; with the exception of the following, left to garrison Pegu:

200 Madras fusiliers.

200 5th Madras Native Infantry.

A detachment of European artillery, with 2 guns.

This small garrison tempted the Burmese troops to try and recapture the place, and they, having made a vigorous attack on our gunboats, were easily repulsed; but on the evening of the 27th they made a daring attack on the position held by our soldiers, assaulting all sides of the Pagoda, simultaneously. After some hours' smart fighting they were driven back into the jungle, leaving many dead around the fort. On the 3rd December the enemy renewed their attacks, continuing them with but little intermission until the 13th; during which time the little British garrison were closely invested by large numbers; but,

---

1. This Officer, having attained the rank of Lieutenant-Colonel, died at Meerut, in August, 1881.

animated by the hope of speedy relief, our soldiers succeeded in holding the position against the enemy, who, aided by their artillery and cavalry, kept up an incessant fire.

The following description of the Pagoda which was held by the British troops will show how difficult was the task of maintaining their position against an enemy so numerically superior.

The Pegu Pagoda is raised upon three terraces, each side of the upper terrace measuring about 210 yards. Twelve feet below is a second terrace which measures 320 yards along each face, and extends 40 feet from the inner wall; the third terrace is 6 feet lower, the faces being increased to 450 yards, extending also 40 feet from the wall. Outside the stockades high grass impeded the view of the sentries, whilst numerous small pagodas on the east and west sides also gave shelter to the enemy.

On the north and eastern sides the interior of our stockade was commanded by ground higher than the platforms; and to hold this position, as well as to protect the walls of the town, we had but 435 men.

A report of the trying and uncertain position of the Pegu Garrison having reached General Godwin, that Officer immediately organized a relief expedition, which he dispatched in the river steamers, Nerbudda and Mahanuddy; the latter vessel, however, with 250 of the Madras fusiliers on board, becoming disabled, was obliged to return to Rangoon. The steamer Nerbudda proceeded up the river with the boats which conveyed our troops, believing that they were followed by the Mahanuddy. As the Nerbudda approached the village of Lower Seedee, it was found to be occupied in strong force by the enemy, who had planted stakes across the river to impede the progress of our steamers.

Our troops were quickly landed; the enemy during this operation firing from the surrounding thick jungle, which afforded ample cover. The Bengal fusiliers moved up to some houses skirting the village, which they occupied, the enemy retiring on the village Upper Seedee, about a mile distant. Our pickets were now advanced; the troops passing a restless night in the village, whilst volleys and constant dropping shots kept all on the alert, and sometimes inflicted injury on our soldiers.

On the morning of the 7th of December our troops advanced to. the relief of the Pegu Garrison; the detachment of the Bengal fusiliers being now under command of Major Gerrard. On nearing the south-west gate of the city, a party of the enemy supported by cavalry, posted on the plain, prepared to. dispute our advance, but were quickly dispersed; and our force continued its march, soon reaching the gateway, which was protected by a wet-ditch and earthworks. The Burmese advanced from the surrounding jungle, and threatened, the flanks of our column, but a few shots forced them to return to shelter, when our advance-party pushed quickly on to the eastern gateway of the city, which was entered without our progress having been further disputed; and thus the beleaguered garrison was relieved.

During the afternoon the Bengal fusiliers were sent to capture the stockades and defences to the south and west still occupied by the enemy, who, having been expelled, the works were at once demolished, our men returning at dusk to the pagoda.

During the following days the Burmese were employed in throwing up three lines of entrenchments on the plain beyond the jungle to the north of Pegu, and on the 16th December General Godwin advanced his force—with which were 570 of the Bengal fusiliers—to drive the enemy from their newly-formed position. On our column reaching the plain the enemy seemed for the first time aware that we had taken the field, and a judicious and rapid movement might have ensured the capture of a large number of their elephants and cattle, which were feeding unprotected on the plain; but General Godwin, intent on the speedy capture of the position, took ground to the right, and turning the enemy's position, rapidly occupied their first line of entrenchments, when a halt was ordered; during which the enemy, collecting their cattle, moved off in full retreat along the Shoé Gyne road. The whole of the 18 entrenchments were at once occupied by our troops; who, after a few hours' rest, leisurely followed the enemy, reaching the village of Lephandoon before sunset.

It now became evident that General Godwin had been misled by the information received from the Burmese guides; and on the morning of the 18th December he beat across the jungle in the direction of the Shoé Gyne road, along which he proceeded as far as the village of Montsaganu, where the enemy had again entrenched themselves. After some skirmishing—during which the Burmese made merely a show of resistance—the entrenchments were occupied by our troops, and the defences levelled; and, the surrounding country having been completely cleared of the enemy, our troops returned to the Pegu Garrison.

General Godwin has been censured for not having followed up his enemy with greater rapidity and more decision, and perhaps from a military point of view; justly; but may it not have been that the quality of mercy was too strong in him to permit the useless slaughter of these discouraged fugitives?

The exposure to the dews at night, and the fatigue consequent on marching under a tropical sun by day during the 17th and 18th, produced much sickness amongst the Bengal fusiliers, 20 of whom died of cholera alone a few days after their return to Pegu.

About 700 of our soldiers having now been left to garrison the fort of Pegu, General Godwin with the remainder of his troops returned to Rangoon on the 22nd December.

To clear the country of all the Burmese troops, and to drive them from the numerous strong stockades which they had erected on the line of country extending from Martaban to Thonghoo, a column was formed, consisting of 450 of the 1st Bengal Fusiliers under Major Gerrard, 150 of the Madras fusiliers, together with a force of artillery and native infantry, the whole under command of General Steele. The expedition embarked for Martaban in the Honourable East India Company's Steam Frigates *Moozuffur, Zenobia*, and *Bernice*, with three transports, whilst H.M. Steam Frigate *Sphynx* towed another transport carrying ordnance and stores. A brief voyage brought these vessels on the 5th January, 1853, to their destination opposite Martaban; Moulmien, standing on the opposite side of the river, the situation of which is beautiful, showing its numerous white pagodas studded amongst the bungalows forming the town.. A vast difference there was between Martaban, still surrounded by its dense jungles, and Moulmien prosperous, after its 25 years of British rule.

A lovely view of country opened out on both sides of the grand Salween river; many smaller streams dividing the hills covered with beautiful forest trees. It was a busy, as well as a picturesque scene.

January, 1853; The Commissariat Department was transporting stores from Moulmien, or landing them from the fleet. Here were illustrated the difficulties of moving and equipping a column, which was to march for weeks through an almost unknown country; difficulties enhanced by the necessity for transporting across the river about a hundred elephants. These animals, however, swam or waded across the river according to the depth of water, and it was when they sank, leaving in sight only an upraised trunk, that the excitement was at its height. Every Mahout (driver), with earnest prayers to Allah for protection, perched on his animal's shoulders, had to stand up, or hold on as best he could; and with encouraging cries urged him on to reach the opposite shore. After a few mishaps the whole of the elephants reached their destination in safety; but it is a matter of regret that, a few months subsequently, hardly one of these sagacious animals had survived the hardships and dangers of the march through the dense, impenetrable jungles.

Martaban, signifying the "Nose of the Rock," was considered from its strength and position to be the Gibraltar of the Burmese, It was from this place that their armies frequently issued to fight their foes the Siamese; but now it had been formed into a British fortress, containing 14 heavy pieces of ordnance, which were mounted on the North and South batteries and on the Hill stockade.

On the 12th of January the general and his staff surveyed the surrounding country, and on the 14th the column commenced its forward march, leaving Martaban by the Beling gate.

We had before us 240 miles of swamp and dense forest, never before traversed by a European force. The enemy held a strong position at Ky-onk-ye about 4 miles from Martaban; to attack which the advanced portion of our army, with 75 men of the 1st Bengal Europeans moved to the front. On our reaching Ky-onk-ye-the Burmese opened fire from the thick jungle which covered their stockade and village below. The march had been effected through heavy grass and clumps of bamboos, but our troops were by this time inured to their work, and in good marching condition; and, our rockets and howitzers having opened fire, the enemy was driven out of the jungle. Our attacking-party advanced on the stockades, but on our approach they were found vacated. The column now halted for four days; the European soldiers amusing themselves by hunting and killing the huge snakes, large numbers of which were found in the jungles.

An eight-mile march brought us to Gongoh, after having viewed the enemy at some of their outposts, from which a sudden fire was opened on our advancing troops. Gongoh was defended by stockaded breast-works, which were covered by a deep ditch, and numerous-pits with bamboo spikes. The enemy at first showed some confidence, firing round-shot into the head of our column; but our two howitzers and a rocket tube, having been with difficulty dragged to the front through the heavy swamp and long grass and brought into action, the storming-party under Major Seaton of the Bengal fusiliers advanced.

On reaching the stockade it was found that the enemy had retreated, leaving from 80 to 100 dead; many having been thrown into the wells in order to poison the water. At 3 p.m. the troops encamped, having, during their trying march, suffered much from the sun overhead, and the swampy nature of the ground underfoot.

1st EUROPEAN BENGAL FUSILIERS.
(Right Wing.)

"Plassey," "Buxar," "Guzerat," "Deig," "Bhurtpore," "Afghanistan,"
"Ghuznee," "Ferozshah," "Sobraon."

Station, Burmah.   Arrived, 1852.

Season of Appointment.	NAMES.	Rank in the Regiment.	Rank in the Army.	REMARKS.
	COLONEL.			
1800	Sir W. R. Gilbert, Bart., G.C.B.	25 June, '32	L.G. 11 Nov. '51	
—	G. Hunter	7 Jan., '41	do.	On Furlough.
	LIEUT.-COLONELS.			
1818	G. Warren	6 Aug., '43	C. 16 July, '49	*
1819	J. C. Tudor	8 Oct., '50	7 June, '49	
	MAJOR.			
1825	John G. Gerrard	1 March, '50	...	Hissar Stud.
	CAPTAINS.			
1828	Jno. W. Bennett	1 Nov., '44	25 Dec., '43	On Furlo'.
1829	H. T. Combe	1 Nov., '44	M. 1 Dec., '48	
1837	R. W. H. Fanshawe	21 Dec., '45		
1837	Geo. O. Jacob	17 June, '48	...	Comg. 4th Punjab Cavalry
1840	Geo. G. Denniss	29 June, '49		
1839	Edm D. Byng	23 Jan., '50		
1840	South. Greville	1 March, '50		On Furlo'.
1840	H. B. Edwardes, C.B.	do.	M 2 Mch., '50	Civil Emp.
1840	Alex. Hume	16 July, '51		
1842	James Williamson	7 Aug., '52		
	LIEUTENANTS.			
1842	E. Cunliffe	23 July, '44		
1843	F. O. Salusbury	9 March, '45		
1843	C. O. B. Palmer	29 Oct., '45		
1843	P. R. Innes	6 Feb., '46	...	On Furlo'.
1844	C. R. Wriford	10 Feb., '46	...	On Furlo'.
1844	Edw. Brown	10 Feb., '46		

* Commanding Barrackpore, and Hon. A.D.C. to the Governor-General.

1st EUROPEAN BENGAL FUSILIERS (Continued).

Season of Appointment	NAMES.	Rank in the		REMARKS.
		Regiment.	Army.	
	LIEUTS. (continued).			
1845	G. C. Lambert	11 Feb., '46		
1844	Trevor Wheler	4 March, '46		
1845	W. R. H. I. Howell	31 March, '46		
1845	E. St. George	4 May, '46		
1845	H. F. M. Boisragon	13 Oct., '46	...	2nd in command, Kemvan Battn.
1845	R. J. F. Hickey	17 June, '48		
1845	W. S. R. Hodson	1 April, '49	...	Civil Emp.
1845	N. T. Parsons	29 June, '49		
1845	G. M. Battye	23 Jan., '50	...	Revenue Survey
1845	George Price	1 March, '50	...	Dept. Pub. Works
1846	R. C. Birch	do.	...	Gwalior cont. with Regiment
1846	W. Davison	16 July, '51		
1848	Wm. A. Pope	19 July, '51	...	On Furlo'.
1848	H. Maxwell	7 Aug., '52		
	2ND LIEUTENANTS.			
1848	H. M. Wemyss	12 June, '49	9 Dec., '48	
1848	H. Caulfield	18 Aug., '49	27 Dec., '48	
1849	J. Morland	25 May, '50	11 Dec., '49	
1849	J. S. Ingram	do.	12 Dec., '49	
1850	E. E. Ekins	5 March, '51	10 Dec., '50	
1851	C. MacFarlane	24 Sept., '51	20 Jan., '51	
1851	L. B. Magniac	do.	20 Feb., '51	
1851	J. W. Dunnell	17 Feb., '52	16 June, '51	
1851	E. A. C. Lambert	13 Aug., '52	12 Dec., '51	

(Left Wing.)

	MAJOR.			
1818	John P. Ripley	1 March, '50	23 Dec., '42	
	CAPTAINS.			
1827	Jas. Ruth. Pond	1 Nov., '44	M. 3 April, '46	Asst. Adjt.-Genl. Peshawur Divn.
1828	Douglas Seaton	...	M. 19 June, '46	

Adjt. to the Regt., F. O. SALUSBURY, 15 Aug., 1848.
Intr. and Qr.Mr. W. R. H. I. HOWELL, 24 Jan., 1849.
Surgeon   do. H. A. BRUCE, M.D., 5 Oct., 1847.
Asst. to   do.   ,,   ,,   ,,

Uniform, Scarlet ; Lace, Gold ; Facings, Dark Blue.

After this affair at Gongoh the Burmese made no stand whatever; our onward march was unopposed, and our general's difficulties consisted mainly in obtaining information as to the best positions for our camping grounds, near sweet wells or streams. On the 21st January Ouchtada was reached, and so on to Beling, which was occupied on the 28th January; vast quantities of rice falling into the hands of the commissariat. Many of our marches were made through dense forests, infested by wild beasts and reptiles; our track being entirely sheltered from the sun by huge teak-trees, whilst enormous elephant creepers climbed from limb to limb, connecting these kings of the forest by long boughs, laden with highly-coloured and luxuriant orchids, occasionally forming vistas resembling the aisles of a Cathedral. The crossing of the many streams which intersected the country was sometimes arduous, occupying several hours, but all ranks worked cheerfully; and the Bengal sepahis willingly assisted the Europeans, by helping them to carry their arms and accoutrements, as they waded breast-high through the nullahs.

After eight fatiguing, but highly-interesting marches, the column, on the 11th February, reached Shoé Gyne, an important city situated on the left bank of the river Sitanj. Next day the army was refreshed by the sight of the steam-frigate Feroze, which, with three gun-boats, formed the convoy of a welcome supply of provisions for our troops.

At Shoé Gyne the natives seemed well-disposed to the British; and, although at first timid, they soon found they were in no way molested, and flocked to their markets, offering grain, vegetables, cloth, &c, competing eagerly for the custom of the Europeans.

The strong stockade to the north of the town was soon converted into a scientifically-constructed post by our field-engineer, between which stockade and the town our camp was picturesquely situated close by the rivers Shoé Gyne and Sitanj. A "Light Division" of the "Martaban column" was now formed, consisting of about 900 men, with whom were 200 of the 1st Bengal Fusiliers, under Major Gerrard, the remainder of the Regiment being left with the force which garrisoned Shoé Gyne.

After a hearty "God speed" from their comrades, the Flying Column commenced its march to Tonghoo on the 15th February; and the General, using the best information procurable, traversed this country, hitherto unknown to European troops. On the 21st Shandobin, on the banks of the Sitanj river, was reached, a distance of 54 miles from Shoé Gyne. Here the column was halted, and a parley held across the river with a Burmese chief, who appeared on the opposite bank, interrogating the quartermaster-general as to our intentions in invading the country. Invited to visit our camp and be introduced to our general, the chief declined, and, putting spurs to his horse, rode away towards Tonghoo.

The passage of the Sitanj river was accomplished on the 22nd February, the greater part of the column being carried over on elephants. The troops then formed up and marched towards Tonghoo, but they had not proceeded far when they were met by the Authorities of the district, who came to surrender themselves and their ancient walled town of Tonghoo to the British General. The troops were soon housed in the numerous Poonghee or priest's houses; which were airy, well-ventilated buildings, constructed of timber, with side-screens or windows of bamboo. These buildings are usually placed on piles or stakes, and raised about 6 feet from the ground, to allow the water to flow freely during the heavy periodical rains.

A small detachment of Ramghur Horse was sent from Tonghoo in pursuit of the retreating Burmese army, Captains Fanshawe and Maxwell, of the Bengal fusiliers, accompanying this cavalry.

The British soon cleared the whole country of their enemies expelling them from Martaban on the south, to 30 miles north of Tonghoo; and thenceforward the country about this town was as quiet and peaceable as any of our home districts.[2]

On the 11th of April the 1st Bengal Fusiliers left Tonghoo en route for Rangoon, having been relieved by a detachment of the 1st Madras Fusiliers, the headquarters of that Regiment arriving soon after. The return under an April sun was trying, and rendered night marches a necessity.

Before reaching Shoé Gyne our Regiment sustained a great loss by the sudden and unexpected death of Captain Edmund Byng, A.D.C., who died of heat-apoplexy, whilst being carried in a dhooley on the line of march. Captain Byng had lately returned to India from England, and was proceeding to rejoin his staff appointment, when, finding that his regiment was on service, he hastened to join the headquarters; but, as he was not acclimatised, he sunk under the heat, his health rapidly gave way, and he succumbed as described. Byng was one of those jovial characters always popular with his brother officers, who deeply deplored his sad death.

---

2. Major Gerrard, commanding the 1st European Bengal Fusiliers, received the thanks of Brigadier-General Steele for his "ready and untiring aid on all emergencies."

A detachment of the 1st Bengal Europeans, under Major Douglas Seaton, remained at Shoé Gyne, and the headquarters proceeded by boat to Rangoon; about 100 men under Lieutenant Hickey being left at Pegu, to reinforce the stockade garrison at that place.

During the time that the detachment under Major Seaton was stationed at Shoé Gyne, the Burmese soldiers attacked a small garrison of Madras native infantry, who occupied a stockade at Beling, a village to the south-east. The native infantry were forced to retire, the European officer in command having been dangerously wounded. It was now ordered that the Beling Stockade be retaken, and the road between Moulmien and Tonghoo reopened. Major Seaton, commanding the detachment of the 1st European Bengal Fusiliers at Shoé Gyne, was instructed to send one company to join the force for the co-capture of Beling. No. 1 was the Company selected, commanded by Captain G. C. Lambert, Lieutenant Walter Davison being the Subaltern. A small fleet of country boats was collected as quickly as possible, and in these the detachment proceeded down the river Sittang to the town of that name, where they landed. They then marched towards Beling, the Sittang Garrison furnishing as many men as could be spared, in addition to which were the native infantry who had retired from the stockade at Beling. The combined force now advanced to the attack, the company of the 1st Bengal Fusiliers being ordered to assault the front face of the stockade, whilst some of the British troops were sent to cut off the enemy's retreat, should they evacuate their position. Captain Lambert's company advanced, covered by skirmishers, and were received with a sharp fire of small arms; nevertheless, they reserved their fire, and, rushing to the front, succeeded in scaling the Stockade and opening one of the gates from the inside, through which the main portion of the British troops entering, the enemy beat a retreat through a sortie-gate in the rear face of the Stockade. The jungle proved so dense that the retreating Burmese managed to escape the vigilance of our troops, who were waiting in ambush to pounce upon them. The British detachment remained a few days in the neighbourhood, and then, having garrisoned the stockade, returned to their respective stations.

The Governor-General in Council expressed great satisfaction at the manner in which these and other operations had been executed, and at the conduct and gallantry of the troops engaged.

Before the end of 1853 the 1st European Bengal Fusiliers, which had for many months been divided into small commands, was again assembled together, and sent to garrison our newly-acquired frontier towns, Thayetmyo and Meeaday, and, hostilities having completely ceased, the Regiment enjoyed the repose and comfort to which it was fairly entitled, after its exposure to-trying climates and onerous duties performed during the past two-years.

The second Burmese War resulted in the British territories on the east of the Bay of Bengal being vastly increased; these now including the rich province of Pegu in addition to those of Araran and Tenasserim, covering an area of 88,556 square miles, with a population since estimated at 2,942,605.[3]

Towards the end of 1854 the 1st European Bengal Fusiliers was relieved by H.M. 29th Regiment; the former proceeding to Rangoon in flats towed by river steamers; and after a delay of a few weeks the Regiment was conveyed in the Company's transports to Calcutta, where it arrived in February, 1855, having been absent from India two-and-a-half years.

---

3. For annexation of Burmah, Proclamation, 80th June, 1858, see Appendix C.

CHAPTER 18

The Indian Mutiny

Remaining in camp at Calcutta for a few weeks, the 1st European Bengal Fusiliers proceeded upcountry in river steamers to Dinapore, where it occupied the barracks built in 1768; described in those days as being on a "grand scale," but now condemned as unfit for the accommodation of European soldiers.

In January, 1856, the Regiment marched from Dinapore to Cawnpore, the right wing and headquarters proceeding on to Dugshai, a newly-built cantonment on the second range of the Himalayas. The right wing marched from Dugshai in November, and the left wing from Cawnpore in December, to Umballa; where the Regiment joined the camp of exercise, and in March, 1857, the entire Regiment proceeded to Dugshai.

Enemies from without there were none at this time, but for the past few years there had been a growing feeling of discontent in the ranks of the native army, which in some instances had broken into open mutiny, quickly crushed by decided action, but still smouldering. As far back as 1844 some of the native regiments had expressed dissatisfaction, the old batta question having been revived and put forward as the ostensible grievance. Then came the Seik Wars; when the victories gained by the Company's troops for a time silenced the mutterings of the native soldiers. The sepahis hated and dreaded the Khalsa, whose discomfiture was a source of much congratulation, the more so as the Sutlej and Punjab triumphs were partly achieved by the co-operation of our native army.

But, however satisfactory our conquests may have been to the sepahis, they soon experienced, with something approaching to dismay, that the increased extent of our territory entailed harder work and extra responsibility, without a proportionate increase of pay. There was a more galling grievance: the Seiks had been invited to take service in our army, and, the offer having been heartily responded to, the sepahis trembled lest these stalwart northmen should prove so useful to our Government that the services of the old native soldiers would be thrown into the shade, and, possibly, ultimately dispensed with altogether.

These suspicions engendered discontent, the more so as reports were being freely circulated, and believed, to the effect that the British were about to deprive the sepahis of their caste, by surreptitiously mixing bone-dust with their food, tearing down the purdahs from their zenanahs, forcing all widows to remarry, and ruthlessly interfering with all their religious prejudices; finally compelling the Native soldiers to defile themselves by taking between their teeth pig's and bullock's fat, which it was stated was being used in the manufacture of the new cartridges.[1]

---

1. The following extract from a petition presented to a commanding officer of a native infantry regiment shows the true feeling of the sepahis at this time, and sets forth their grievances:

The representation of the whole station is this, that we will not give up our religion. We serve for honour and religion; if we lose our religion, the Hindu and Mahomedan religions will be destroyed. If we live, what shall we do? You are the masters of the country. The Lord Sahib (Governor-General) has given orders, which he has received from the Company, to all commanding officers to destroy the religion of the country. We know this, as all things are being designed by Government. The officers of the salt department mix up bones with the salt. The officer in charge of the Ghee mixes up fat with it; this is well known. These are two matters. The third is this: that the Sahib in charge of the sugar burns up bones and mixes them in the syrup the sugar is made of; this is well known—all know it. The fourth is this: that in the country the Burra .Sahibs (Government-Commissioners) have ordered the Rajas, Thakurs, Zemindars, Mahajuns, and Ryots, all to eat together, and English bread has been sent to them; this is well known. And there is another affair, that throughout the country the wives of respectable men, in fact, all classes of Hindus, on becoming widows are to be married again—this is well known. Therefore we consider ourselves as killed. You all obey the orders of the Company, which we all know. But a King, or any other man, who acts unjustly does not remain. With reference to the sepahis, they are your servants; but to destroy their caste, a council assembled and decided to give them muskets and cartridges made up with greased paper to bite; this is also evident. We wish to represent this to the General that we do not approve of the new musket and cartridge; the sepahis cannot use them. You are the masters of the country; if you will give us all our discharge we will go away.

But whilst dissatisfaction and suspicion had been gaining ground in the native army at the frequent accessions to the Company's territories, the large enlistment of the Seiks, the widely-circulated reports touching interference with caste prejudices, the Governor-General (Lord Dalhousie) in Council, under orders received from the Court of Directors, 2nd January, 1856, was directed to pursue a course of policy which would at once have fanned the embers of discontent into a flame, had the native army been at that time fully prepared for unanimous action.

Sir James Outram, the English resident at the Court at Lucknow, was instructed by the Calcutta Council to inform the King of Oude that our Government had decided that he was to be deposed, and the East India Company to rule in his stead. The King was urged to abdicate, and by treaty to appoint the East India Company to the Government of his kingdom, the King being provided with a maintenance allowance of £120,000 per annum. In the event of a refusal, Sir James Outram was ordered to publish, in alternative, the annexation order which he already held. The King was at first obdurate; then, bursting into tears, prayed for time, promised to reform, and finally refused to sign the proposed abdication. "He uncovered his head, placed his turban in the hands of the Resident, and sorrowfully declared that title, rank, honour, everything were gone, and that now the British Government, which had made his grandfather a King, might reduce him to nothing and consign him to obscurity."[2] But Outram's orders were peremptory; he issued the annexation order, and Oude became British territory.

The Kingdom of Oude had for many years been in a chronic state of misrule and anarchy, its people calling loudly on our Government for reform. Colonel Sleeman, who had for many years been the British representative at the Oude Court, drew a painful picture of the state of the country during his tenure of office: saying—the landowners "take to indiscriminate plunder and murder, no road, town, hamlet, or village is secure from their merciless attacks—robbery and murder become their diversion, their sport; and they think no more of taking the lives of men, women, and children who never offended them than those of deer or wild hogs. They not only rob and murder, but seize, confine, and torture all whom they seize and suppose to have money or credit, till they ransom themselves with all they have or can beg or borrow." No wonder, then, that the people of Oude called loudly for redress and reform.

---
2. Kaye's History of the Sepoy War. Vol. 1., p. 150.

A very large proportion of our Bengal native army was enlisted in Oude, being subjects of the dethroned King. The anarchy and misrule which had existed around their homes did not in any way adversely affect their interests or comfort, for, being soldiers in the Company's army, they had always the right of appeal for redress to the British resident; nay more—the knowledge of this right placed them in an exalted position amongst their brethren, giving them an influence and power otherwise unattainable. Hence, service in the Company's army had always been popular in Oude, and in some families was held to be an hereditary right. The annexation of Oude to the territories of the East India Company placed redress in the hands of all alike, and deprived the sepahis of what they held to be a distinctive right; and this was another fire-brand adding fuel to the smouldering heap of discontent which was being daily developed into a flame.

The annexation of Oude was the last act of Lord Dalhousie's administration. It was reserved for his successor, Lord Canning, to complete the work.

Colonel Sir Henry Lawrence, who had so successfully transformed the Punjab from its previous state of anarchy into prosperity and confidence, was now appointed Chief Commissioner in Oude; the government of the Punjab having been handed over to his brother, Sir John Lawrence. Sir Henry had but a short time assumed office when his serious attention was directed to the mutinous feelings existing, not only in the Regular native regiments, but in those which had been transferred to our service from that of the deposed King. Sir Henry Lawrence had with him at Lucknow H.M. 32nd Foot, some cavalry, and European artillery. On May 3rd it was reported by the Brigadier that the 7th Oude Irregulars had assumed a dangerous, defiant attitude, and were unreservedly talking of bloodshed and murder. Though late in the evening, Lawrence conceived that the time had arrived for action; and, ordering out the troops at his disposal, marched right through the rebellious city in the direction of the lines of the 7th Oude Irregulars. It was a fine, cloudless night, and the moon was shining brightly. After a march of about seven miles the European troops arrived at their destination, taking up ground so as to command the mutineers in front and on both flanks. The 7th Regiment was found already drawn up on parade. Lawrence's decided action had taken them by surprise, and they were paralysed; death was; staring them in the face; they broke their ranks, and some fled in terror, whilst others, assuming a repentant air, gave up their arms and accoutrements. The fugitives were pursued by our cavalry; whilst those who had submitted were marched back under charge of the 32nd Foot; the whole party returning to Lucknow before daybreak.

But this insubordination amongst the Irregulars at Lucknow, was merely the forerunner of the discontent which had been surely spreading throughout the entire Bengal native army.

Meerut, the headquarters of the Bengal artillery, the carabineers and 60th Rifles, was considered comparatively safe; but it was here that the flames first burst forth in all their fury, leaving no doubt that the mutiny of the native soldiers was not confined to one district or cantonment, but that it was national; the whole of the sepahi regiments, well-drilled, well-armed, and full of confidence, were resolved to try issue with the handful of our Europeans, separated by long distances, and spread over a vast tract of country.

At Meerut, on the 10th of May, the native troops rose in, mutiny; breaking open the jail, killing all Europeans within their reach, firing the houses of their officers, and hurrying in the direction of Delhie, where they were joined by the mutineers at that city, who rose and murdered all the Europeans who fell into their hands, without respect to age or sex; and, proclaiming the aged King of Delhie, Emperor of Hindustan, closed the gates of the fortress, and set at defiance the British Government.

The thunder-cloud had burst; but the fury of the storm was. not yet realised at headquarters. Had the action of the sepahis been simultaneous at all the military stations throughout the presidency, the effect might have been fatal; but the intelligence of mutinies, conflagrations, and hideous wholesale murders, arrived at intervals; allowing time for our commanders to issue their orders and complete arrangements for resistance.

All reports received by the commander-in-chief tended to show that the sepahi regiments of the Bengal army were, without exception, more or less implicated; and it was patent to all that the great question on which the maintenance of our power existed was, whether the Seiks would declare for or against us.

Sir John Lawrence was Chief-Commissioner of the Punjab. It was he who had asked the Seiks whether they would be governed by the pen or the sword; they had chosen the former, and now all eyes were anxiously turned towards John Lawrence, hoping that by his influence with the Seiks, India might be saved. The British had governed the Punjab for close on ten years; the people appreciated the blessings of security of property which our rule had ensured; they found that our Judges were just, and our Magistrates listened patiently to their complaints of wrong. This was a state of things to which they had previously been strangers. They had not, like the Hindustanees, forgotten, in the lapse of years, the difference between the undue favouritism of native rule and the impartial justice of the British Government; and, moreover, the Khalsa hated and despised the sepahis, with whom they had no interests in common; but, notwithstanding all these considerations, their decision was trembling in the balance, and it needed a master-mind to turn the scale in our favour. John Lawrence was the man who brought his influence to bear: he turned the scale in our favour.

Then from Lahore came the assuring intelligence that Mr. Robert Montgomery, the Judicial Commissioner, in concert with the military commanders, had, with decision and courage, by a coup-de-main, succeeded in disarming the disaffected sepahis at that station, and transferring the guardianship of the fort from their charge to that of the 81st Foot; and thus, without bloodshed or destruction of property, the capital of the Punjab was secured by a ruse, which gained the respect and ensured the goodwill of the Seiks.

A moveable column of some of our choicest Seik troops was placed under command of General Neville Chamberlain; and, with every demonstration of loyalty, was marching to join the British army already beleaguering the strongly-fortified city of Delhie.

Meanwhile, on the morning of the 13th of May, Major G. O. Jacob, of the 1st Bengal Fusiliers, rode into Dugshai from Simla, with orders from the commander-in-chief for the Regiment to march as soon as arrangements could be completed to Umballa, where further orders would await them. The soldiers of the Regiment were immediately assembled on parade, the weakly men being formed into a depôt for the protection of the sick and station of Dugshai; and, such was the energy displayed by all, that at 4 p.m. on the same day on which the order had been received, the Regiment commenced its march towards Umballa, probably never in finer condition to take the field, both in physique and discipline.[3] The Regiment was 800

---

3. The following Officers were present with the 1st European Bengal Fusiliers when the Regiment marched from Dugshai on May 13th, 1867 (continued on next page):

strong, there was not a recruit in the ranks, and there had for many months preceding been almost a total absence of crime. Orderly room was held but once a week; and more frequently than otherwise there was a clean sheet. The march to Umballa, a distance of 60 miles, was-accomplished in 38 hours; the Regiment arriving at their destination at 7 a.m. on the 15th May. Orders were received on the 17th for four companies of the Regiment to proceed at once to Kurnaul, the remaining companies and headquarters following on the 21st May. It was from this place that Lieutenant W. S. Hodson, 1st Bengal Fusiliers, performed the daring feat of riding by himself with dispatches through a hostile country to Meerut and back, 150 miles. The British force was now assembling at Alipore, one march out of Delhie.

The headquarters and six companies of the 2nd Bengal Fusiliers, under Captain Boyd, had joined the army from Umballa, four companies having remained at that station under Captain Harris to keep open communication with the Punjab.

The 1st Bengal Fusiliers were appointed to the 1st Brigade, under Brigadier Showers; and Colonel Welchman and Captain Brown having joined on 5th June from Dugshai, the former assumed command of the Regiment.

On the 7th June Lieutenant Butler arrived at the headquarters from leave of absence, having, in his anxiety to be at his post, ridden across country on one horse, 110 miles in 40 hours.

All being in readiness, on June 7th, orders were issued for a general advance towards Delhie, the troops, on account of the excessive heat, marching at midnight. As the town of Budlee-ka-Serai, held in great force by the enemy, was on the road between Alipore and Delhie, an immediate attack on it was ordered. For this purpose, on the early

Major G. O. Jacob.	2nd Lieutenant A. G. Owen.
Captain G. G. Denniss.	„ F. D. M. Brown.
„ S. Greville.	„ N. Ellis.
„ C. Wriford.	„ A. R. Chapman.
Lieutenant W. S. R. Hodson.	„ W. H. Warner.
„ J. W. Daniell.	
„ E. A. C. Lambert.	Regimental Staff.
„ J. S. Walters.	Adjutant-Lieut. H. M. Wemyss.
„ J. A. Butler.	Intr. and Qr. Mr. C. MacFarlane.
„‚ W. A. D. Cairnes.	Surgeon Boughton.
„‚ N. H. Wallace.	Assistant-Surgeon Charles.

"East India Register," December 31, 1855.

FIRST EUROPEAN BENGAL FUSILIERS.
(Right Wing.)

"PLASSEY," "BUXAR," "GUZERAT," "DEIG," "BHURTPORE," "AFGHANISTAN," "GHUZNEE," "FEROZSHAH," "SOBRAON."

Season.	NAMES.	Rank in the Regiment.	Rank in the Army.	REMARKS.
	COLONEL.			
1798	J. MacInnes............	13 May, '25 ...	G. 4 July, '36 L. G.	Furlough
1815	George Warren	5 Dec., '53 ...	28 Nov., '54 ...	do.
	LIEUTENANT-COLONEL.			
1809	F. Jenkins	16 Oct., '51 ...	C. 28 Nov.,'54	Civil Employ.
1820	J. Welchman	4 July, '53 ...	C. 14 July, '58	
	MAJOR.			
1837	Geo. O. Jacob	...	5 March, '56	Punjab Cavalry
	CAPTAINS.			
1840	Geo. G. Denniss	29 June, '49 ...		
,,	Southwell Greville...	1 March, '50		
,,	H.B. Edwardes, C.B.	...	Lt.-Col. 28th Nov. '54.	
,,	Alex. Hume............	16 July, '51 ...		
1842	Ellis Cunliffe	18 April, '53	...	On Furlo'.
1843	F. O. Salusbury	1 October	...	do.
,,	C. O'B. Palmer	20 March, '54		
1844	C. R. Wriford	5 April, '55 ...	...	do.
—	Edwd. Brown	14 Jan., '56 ...		
1845	Geo. C. Lambert ...	1 Feb., '56 ...		
1844	Trevor Wheler	5 March		
1845	W. R. H. I. Howell	...	...	Sub.Ast.Com.Gen.
,,	E. St. George			
	LIEUTENANTS.			
,,	H. F. M. Boisragon	13 Oct., '46 ...	...	2nd in comd. Kemvan Battn.
,,	R. J. I. Hickey	17 June, '48 ...	...	2nd in comd. 15th In. Cavalry
,,	W. S. R. Hodson ...	1 April, '49 ...		
,,	N. T. Parsons.........	29 June		

FIRST EUROPEAN BENGAL FUSILIERS (Continued).

Season.	NAMES.	Rank in the Regiment.	Rank in the Army.	REMARKS.
	LIEUTS. (continued).			
1845	G. M. Battye	23 Jan., '50	...	Civil Employ.
,,	Geo. Price	1 March	...	Dep. Pub. Works
1846	R. C. Birch	1 March		
,,	W. Davison	16 July, '51		
1848	H. Maxwell	7 Aug., '52		
,,	H. M. Wemyss	18 April, '58		
1849	J. Morland	5 March, '54		
1849	J. S. Ingram	20 March, '54	...	Dep. Pub. Works
1851	C. MacFarlane	10 May		
,,	L. B. Magniac	17 June, '55	...	Furlo'.
,,	J. W. Daniell	5 Dec.		
,,	E. A. C. Lambert	14 Jan., '56		
1852	Montagu Hall	1 February		
1853	G. N. Money	5 March, '56		
,,	J. S. Walters			
—	W. C. Cox			
1854	T. A. Butler			
,,	W. A. D. Cairnes			
	2ND LIEUTENANTS.			
,,	N. H. Wallace	9 March, '55	9 Dec., '54	
1855	A. G. Owen	18 December	4 Oct., '55	
,,	F. D. M. Brown	7 March, '56	8 December	
1856	N. Ellis	15 April	20 Jan., '56	
,,	A. R. Chapman	27 June	4 January	
	,,			
	,,			
	,,			
	,,			
	,,			

(Left Wing.)

	MAJOR.		L. C.	
1827	Jas. Ruth. Pond	1 Dec., '55	20 Jan., '54	
	CAPTAIN.			
1828	Douglas Seaton	10 Feb., '46	20 Jan., '54	Furlo'.

Facings, Dark Blue.

Adjutant to the Regiment, H. M. WEMYSS, 3 July, '55.
Quartermaster   do.
Surgeon   do.   E. HARE, 24 May, '55.
Asst. Surgeon   do.

morning of the 8th June, Nos. 5 and 6 Companies of the 1st Bengal Fusiliers, under command of Captain Brown, formed the advanced Guard; but when within about 1200 yards of the enemy's position, they found themselves under such a heavy artillery fire that they were ordered to take ground to their right and await the arrival of their headquarters. The whole Regiment now advanced to the attack across the open plain, the enemy's fire perceptibly increasing at every step, so that 20 or 30 of our men were killed or wounded; amongst the latter being Captain Greville and Lieutenant Ellis.

The Regiment was now ordered to take advantage of some rising ground about 400 yards in advance of the enemy's main battery, from which position it attacked a village, defeating a large body of the mutineers, who had kept up a galling fire on our advancing troops. A general assault was next made on the enemy's position at Budlee-ka-Serai, which was completely successful; they being forced to retire from the village on their main army at Delhie, hotly pursued by our troops as far as the Ridge,[4] where the 1st Bengal Fusiliers, after having been fighting and marching for fifteen consecutive hours, joined the British headquarter camp.

The 2nd Bengal Fusiliers also rendered excellent service at the attack on the enemy's position at Budlee-ka-Serai.

On June 9th there was some severe skirmishing, when Drum-Major McGill, of the 1st European Regiment, a man selected for this post on account of his grand stature and splendid figure, was accidentally left wounded on the field, his body being recovered the next morning, terribly mutilated.

On the 11th of June a memorandum was presented to General Barnard, commanding the British army before Delhie, by a committee which had been appointed by him to survey the ground and recommend a plan of attack. Lieutenant W. S. Hodson, of the 1st Bengal European Fusiliers, now attached to the Quartermaster-General's Department, was a member of this committee, which recommended that our troops should storm the city at once by a coup-de-main at the Cabul and Cashmere gates, advancing under existing cover to within 400 to 900 yards respectively, the main assault being made at the Cabul gate "by the channel through which the canal flows from the city."

This scheme, which had been elaborated with great care, and at considerable personal risk, was approved of by the General, and im-

---

4. "The Ridge" is an outcrop of rocks forming a natural defence in front of the ground occupied by the British army.

mediate orders were issued for its execution; but, when the troops assembled in the evening, 300 of the 1st Bengal Fusiliers were absent, being on picket at our outposts, under Brigadier Greaves; who declined the responsibility of withdrawing his men without written orders. He was confirmed in his resolve, as some of our advanced batteries were under charge of native soldiers whose loyalty he doubted. As it was deemed by the General injudicious to attempt the assault without these 300 men, the execution of the scheme was deferred and ultimately abandoned.

The project for a *coup-de-main* which had been recommended by the committee was bold and undoubtedly feasible, and, had it been carried into effect thus early in the siege, there is every reason to believe that the contemplated assault would have been successful. But General Barnard feared that, could he occupy the city, with its extensive fortifications, he had not sufficient troops at his disposal to hold the position; but, on the other hand, had Delhie been captured by our troops in June, and the enemy driven out before they had gained confidence, it is probable that our casualties would have been fewer than in September, when the defences had been strengthened and the numbers of the mutineers vastly increased. It must, however, be borne in mind that had we failed in our attempt on account of the smallness of our force, the effect would have been indeed disastrous.

After the abandonment of the scheme for an immediate assault there were daily skirmishes with the enemy; during one of which, on the 12th June, Lieutenant Thomas Cadell, of the 2nd European Bengal Fusiliers, won the Victoria Cross, for having "brought in from amongst the enemy a wounded bugler belonging to his own regiment;" and a second time proceeded with three men of H.M. 75th Regiment, under a very heavy fire, and "brought in a man of the 75th who was most severely wounded."

On the 17th June 300 of the 1st European Bengal Fusiliers formed part of a force ordered to drive the enemy out of a defended position, called Eed Gar; and the work was performed with courage and decision, one of the enemy's heavy guns being captured by our troops. But here Captain E. Brown[5] was dangerously wounded, the little finger of his right hand being shot off, a bullet passing through his left wrist, striking his chin, smashing his right collar-bone, and from thence lodging in his chest; in addition, he received a flesh wound in his right breast.

---

5. Now in H.M. Body Guard.

On the 19th and 20th June the right wing of the Regiment, under Major G. O. Jacob, was engaged in some severe encounters with the enemy, in rear of our camp; the fighting was chiefly after dark, our men behaving with gallantry and steadiness. Again, on the 23rd June, the whole Regiment was engaged from daybreak till dark.

There was a prophecy, dated immediately after the battle of Plassey—23rd June, 1757—to the effect that the Company's rule would last only one hundred years. This prophecy had often been quoted by those who for the last few years had been inciting the sepahis to mutiny; and no doubt the feelings of the mutineers were worked upon by its repetition when they made their determined attack on the 23rd June, 1857. To the 1st Bengal Europeans it was painfully memorable; for although the enemy failed to make the slightest impression on our defences, they succeeded in severely wounding our Commanding Officer, Colonel Welchman, whilst gallantly leading his regiment to the front. Falling from his horse he was carried to the rear, when it was found that the elbow joint of his right arm was completely shattered.

Private John McGovern, of the 1st European Fusiliers, during the action on the 23rd of June, gained the Victoria Cross for gallant conduct, "he having carried into camp a wounded comrade, under a heavy fire from the enemy's battery, at the risk of his own life."[6]

During this engagement the 1st Bengal Fusiliers lost 40 men, of whom 11 were killed. The 2nd Bengal Fusiliers, who also rendered excellent service, lost Lieutenant Jackson, and 7 men killed and 19 wounded.

The heat during these mid-day encounters was telling adversely on our men, who suffered terribly from exhaustion and thirst, frequently terminating in cholera, sunstroke, and death.

On the 1st July Lieutenant Money joined the Headquarters of the 1st European Bengal Fusiliers, in command of a detachment of about 200 men from the Regimental Depôt at Dugshai. The ranks of the Regiment having been seriously thinned by casualties from the effect of exposure and losses in the field, this addition to its strength was most opportune.

On July 9th an abortive attack was made by the enemy on our camp. There had been heavy firing all the morning from the enemy's batteries, and about 11 a.m., our guns on the "General's Mound" opened fire, when the alarm and assembly were sounded. Whilst the Regiment was "falling-in" a heavy musketry fire was kept up on the

---

6. Extract from The Victoria Gallery, an Official Chronicle.

right, the bullets frequently cutting through the tents; at the same time a frightened mob of our camp-followers, rushing through the camp, crying out that the enemy were following them, and had already captured two of our guns.

There being no time for regular formation, the Regiment went off at the double to the right rear of our camp, where it was met by some of our native artillerymen, who said that our own cavalry had mutinied and were attempting to carry away our guns. For about ten minutes the most complete clamour and confusion prevailed. We had little over 100 men in all, the rest of the Regiment being on picket duty; and we suddenly found ourselves confronted by about 500 cavalry. We soon, however, drove them back, and the affair was over before reinforcements came up.

On Sunday, July 5th, General Barnard's seat at church was vacant, he having that morning been struck down by cholera, and before evening he was dead. He had written to Lord Canning some few months previous, "Cannot you find some tough job for me to do?" The "job" which had been found was too "tough" for him: he, like Henry Lawrence, falling whilst trying to do his duty.

General Reed succeeded, by seniority, to the command of the army; but he soon resigned, his health having completely given way under the anxiety and responsibility of his position; and till command now devolved on Brigadier Archdale Wilson.

It was, perhaps, fortunate that our troops before Delhie were at this time in complete ignorance of what had been taking place at a distance from their scene of action. The reports which had reached our camp were encouraging, and produced a reasonable hope of the speedy arrival of additional troops. It was not known that at Cawnpore the British were beleaguered in their entrenchments, that the city of Lucknow was in the full possession of the rebels, and that nearly all the stations, civil and military, in the Bengal Presidency, were in the hands of the mutineers.

During the afternoon of the 14th July the 1st Bengal Fusiliers were ordered out to clear the Subzi Mundi of the enemy. Marching straight down the road which leads to Delhie, the Regiment received the fire of the enemy on both flanks; No 1 Company being now ordered to skirmish on the right and No 2 on the left. The enemy showed considerable determination—repeatedly charging in masses with fixed bayonets; but they were finally driven back into the gardens and enclosures about 300 yards from the city.

Anticipating an immediate attack on the fortress, the enemy closed the gates, and poured a heavy grape-fire from the Moree Bastion, which, ploughing through our ranks, killed and wounded several of our men, whilst the shot from our own batteries in our rear, passing very close over the Regiment, caused some confusion. The enemy's infantry, now forced back towards the city walls, sought refuge in the passages which lead to the entrance gates, and their cavalry at the same time, hurriedly galloping along the counter-scarp, eager to escape, plunged into the sortie passages—already filled with their infantry—and fell headlong amongst the mass of fugitives, checked by the gates having been closed; when, however, the enemy realised that we had no intention of storming the fortress they threw open the gates, and gradually succeeded in absorbing the quivering mass of horses and men vainly endeavouring to extricate themselves. The objects for which the British detachment had been employed having been attained, and the Subzi Mundi cleared of the enemy, our troops were ordered to return to camp. During these operations, Lieutenant H. M. Wemyss, the Adjutant of the Regiment, was hit by a musket-ball on his side; but he refused to go to the rear, and continued to perform his duties. Lieutenant J. W. Daniell was also wounded; but in his case the injury was so severe that he was obliged to retire, "though the brave young officer was loth to do so, and endeavoured, by attempting to whistle, to hide the agony he suffered."[7] The 1st Bengal Fusiliers during this engagement lost 64 killed and wounded.

As our troops were returning to camp, after their hard day's work, they passed two men of the Seik infantry assisting a wounded comrade, who was unable to walk; but the enemy's fire became so hot that they refused to carry the wounded man further, and left him to the mercy of the pursuers. Captain Greville ordered the Seiks to bring on their comrade; but they, having declined to further risk their lives, left the Seik to his fate; whereupon, Greville ran back a distance of some fifty yards, under a storm of bullets, placed the wounded man on his back, and carried him to a place of safety, for which act he received, the thanks of Brigadier Showers, in command.

The heat in camp at this time was terrific, and it appears marvellous that disease was not more prevalent. The men were exposed during the day to a tropical sun, and all night to malarious dews; the air was tainted with every kind of nauseous smell; there was a total absence of

---

7. 1st Bengal Fusiliers in the Delhie Campaign, by J. P. Brougham.

any attempt at sanitary arrangements; camels and other animals, who had died or been killed, lay in all directions in close proximity to the camp, and dense clouds of flies rendered it unsafe to eat or drink without muslin having been previously placed over the face, the drinking-pot and plate. There thus appeared to be every enticement for disease; but, with the exception of occasional cases of sunstroke and cholera, and the casualties of war, our troops were far more healthy than we had any reason to expect; comparing not unfavourably with the time when our European troops are housed in barracks, with every comfort and luxury about them. Does not this state of things argue that occupation is more necessary to the well-being and health of the European soldier in India than all the punkahs, tatties, and other inventions for inducing the men to remain unoccupied in barracks?

On the 24th July news reached our camp of the treacherous capture and terrible fate of General Wheeler's garrison at Cawnpore, where "a great multitude" of women and children had been fiendishly hacked to pieces by the town butchers, under the orders of the ever-infamous Doondoo Punt, called the Nana. Up to this time the troops before Delhie had been cheered by reports of the rapid advance of a European force; but now the naked truth had been told; Wheeler's brave force, consisting of officers, soldiers, with many women and young children, had been betrayed into a confidence which cost them all, save four,[8] their lives. All communication between Delhie and the lower provinces was closed, and the little British army before Delhie must accomplish, unaided, the stupendous work it had undertaken; our sole hope being in the courage, discipline, and determination of our soldiers.

It became evident, on the morning of the 1st August, that the enemy had arranged an elaborate plan for a vigorous attack on the British position. At 6 a.m. on that day, masses of sepahi regiments were drawn up in battle array in front of our defences, and an attack by successive divisions was continued until the morning of the 3rd, the firing on both sides being during this time uninterrupted. The shouts and yells from the enemy were loud and long; but in the main their attacks lacked earnestness, though the sepahis made some bold rushes at our batteries, in front of which, where three determined charges had been made on the 2nd instant, their dead were now lying in heaps.

---

8. One of the four who escaped from Cawnpore, Lieutenant Delafosse, afterwards joined the 101st Royal Bengal Fusiliers, and commanded the Regiment for several years.

At one point the dead were so numerous that they were heaped up, and used as cover for the attacking-parties, who advanced through the embrasures, in some instances engaging our gunners in a hand-to-hand fight. The noise at this time was almost deafening; the constant roar of the artillery and musketry, the bugles sounding the advance along the whole front, whilst the shouts of the native commanders were distinctly heard, urging their men on to the attack.

This grand effort to push us from our position behind the ridge failed, and, as the British troops had all been acting solely on the defensive, our losses were comparatively trifling.

The 7th of August was rendered memorable by the explosion of the enemy's powder-magazine in the very heart of the city; this was a grand sight, producing, at the instant of explosion, an enormous cloud of dense smoke, which quickly rose, overshadowing the whole city with a heavy black pall, which was slowly swept by the wind across the plain.

The constant outpost-duty, although it was always undertaken with the utmost alacrity and good-humour, was found to be very irksome to the soldiers: those of the 1st Bengal Fusiliers being constantly on duty at "The Metcalf Stables," "The Mosque," and "Flagstaff" pickets; "but the most revolting and unwelcome outpost was commonly called "The Valley of Death".

It was a small old ruined mosque or shrine in the gorge of the valley, in rear of our batteries, and was under a plunging fire from all the enemy's missiles that passed over them. There was no cover, as it was impossible to enter the building, owing to its being literally crowded with cobras, and on the road where two of our sentries were posted, there were dead camels lying in the last stage of decomposition. A night on this picket, in the thick, muggy atmosphere of the rainy season in July and August, under a heavy fire, was almost too much for the best-intentioned soldier to bear."[9]

On the 11th August the 1st European Regiment was attached to the flying column, under General Nicholson, who with his troops from the Punjab, had joined the besieging Army on the 7th.

On the 12th of August the 1st and 2nd Bengal European Regiments were employed with a force under Brigadier-General Showers, ordered to surprise some of the enemy's pickets outside the Cashmere Gate, the detachment quietly moving off at 2.30 a.m. The 1st Fusiliers

---

9. From the diary of an officer of the 1st Bengal Fusiliers.

were to attack the picket at "Ludlow Castle," whilst the 2nd, under Major Coke, advanced against, some pickets in the Koordsia Bagh.

The night was very dark, and the ground difficult. Major Coke was severely wounded soon after his party had started.

Nos. 8, 9, and 10 Companies of the 1st Bengal Fusiliers, under Captain Greville, were now ordered to form the attacking party, and advance in skirmishing order to the front; the remainder of the troops being held in reserve. The ground was open in front, and, under orders previously issued, strict silence was observed. As the advance-party moved along an order was given by their commander in a whisper to fix bayonets, and pass the word on to the next files; and this order was obeyed without a sound. A challenge from one of the enemy's sentries broke the stillness; *"Hookum dar?"* As we closed upon them silence was no longer necessary; and the soldier challenged by the sentry replied, "Take that!" and, firing at the same time, shot him dead. It being still quite dark, there was great difficulty in ascertaining our exact position, or that of the enemy, but, from the direction of the challenge, it was evident that we had overlapped their position. Greville, therefore, closed his troops on their left, and at the same time brought their right shoulders forward, quickly forming his companies in good order opposite "Ludlow Castle." The attacking-party now opened fire, preparatory to their charge. The enemy attempted to bring their batteries to bear on the advancing troops, but there was evidently no order amongst them, for they hesitated; and, after firing two of their guns, the main body of their troops attempted to escape. Our men at once closed on the battery from whence the two shots had been fired; and Private Reagan, rushing upon a 24-pounder howitzer, which was charged with grape, attacked the gunners single-handed, and bayoneted one of them just as he was applying the port-fire. Unhappily, Reagan fell, badly wounded and permanently disabled: but this brave man had the satisfaction of knowing that in risking his own life he saved that of many of his comrades. At this time the day began to dawn, enabling the attacking-party to completely clear the post of the enemy, and carry off four of his guns—2 9-pounders, 1 6-pounder, and 1 24-pounder howitzer—which, with their tumbrils, horses, and appointments, were at once escorted into camp. Captain S. Greville and Lieutenant A. G. Owen were wounded. Lieutenant G. W. Warner, who rendered good service on this occasion, escaped unhurt. Brigadier Showers, in his dispatch to the general commanding at Delhie, makes special reference to "the steadiness, silence, and order with which the 1st Bengal Fusiliers advanced to the attack on the enemy's guns, which was well conceived and gallantly executed by Major Jacob and the officers and men of the Regiment under his command, and Captain S. Greville of the Regiment commanded the skirmishers who made the first attack on the guns."

The total loss of the brigade on this occasion was 19 killed and 93 wounded. The 1st Bengal Fusiliers had 4 killed and 28 wounded; and the 2nd Bengal Fusiliers, who also behaved with great gallantry, lost 1 officer killed (Lieutenant Sherriff) and 7 men wounded.

On the 24th August the flying column, under General Nicholson, was sent from our camp against the enemy, who held a strong position at Nujjufghur. An officer of the 1st Bengal Fusiliers, who was present, gives the following description of the expedition:

> Our column marched out of camp at 11 p.m. on the 24th, taking the route across country, the ground on account of the rains being very heavy, so that we had repeatedly to unharness the horses from the tumbrils and guns and drag them through the morass, putting 100 of our men to each gun. At noon on the 25th we halted for an hour, when grog was served out to our men. At about 4 p.m., whilst the men were wading through a jheel up to their waists in mud and water, the enemy opened fire on our regiment with shrapnel from an old ruined fort, which was concealed by some rising ground at a distance of about 400 yards. Some of our horse artillery and cavalry had made a détour round the morass to our right front. Our regiment was now ordered to form line, taking advantage of the cover afforded by a small ridge directly in front, and at a distance of about 300 yards from the fort. General Nicholson addressed the troops, and turning to the regiment, he said: 'I have nothing to say to the 1st Fusiliers; they will do as they always do.' Major Jacob now gave us the order to advance in line, which was done in magnificent style, the men reserving their fire, although the enemy's artillery and musketry was pouring shot amongst us. When we were at a distance of about 100 yards from the fort, Jacob gave the word to prepare to charge, when the front rank came to the long trail, the whole advancing straight as an arrow, when Jacob, seeing the men were as steady as rocks, gave the word to charge, when, with a wild cheer, the regiment dashed at the fort, and scrambling over the defences came face to face with the mutineers,

who held their ground until our men were close upon them, when the enemy gave way; the fort being quickly cleared of the mutineers, our regiment formed up on the other side, and then rapidly advanced on the enemy's camp, which was to our front; but the capture of their fort had evidently disheartened them, for they fled across the canal, leaving the whole of their camp equipage, baggage, and 13 guns in our possession; we pushing on towards the canal bridge, which we destroyed.

The enemy now returned to the bank of the canal, and bringing with them two 9-pounders, opened a galling fire on our working-parties, but Major Tombs, having brought up his horse artillery, forced them to retire with the loss of one of their tumbrils, which he blew up with one of his shells. About two hours after sunrise next day we commenced our return march, halting at 11 a.m. for breakfast, this being the only meal the soldiers had partaken of since they left our camp at 11 p.m. on the 24th; thus they had been 36 hours without any regular food. Elephants were sent out from camp to bring in our wounded and footsore men, but one only of these useful animals was required to assist 7 of our men who had been injured by an explosion. The regiment reached our camp about 4 p.m. on the 26th August, after an absence of 41 hours, during which time our men had only partaken of one meal.

On the 4th of September, our siege-train having arrived in camp, preparations for the assault of the city were commenced with vigour. On the night of the 7th the 1st Bengal Fusiliers were employed in front of the Cashmere Bastion, breaking ground for the breaching batteries. It was anticipated that our working-parties would be called upon to drive in the enemy's pickets, but it was found that they had all been previously withdrawn. Our first battery was about 300 yards from the Cashmere Gate, and we had run up a breastwork affording sufficient protection to our working-parties before the enemy opened fire, although we were near enough to hear them talking in the Bastion before we commenced our work.

On the night of the 9th September the 1st Fusiliers were employed in making the breaching-batteries in front of the "Water Bastion," the enemy keeping up a heavy fire all night, and shelling us from their batteries in Selim Ghur; but only two men of the regiment were wounded.

On the morning of the 11th our batteries opened fire, but soon afterwards a troop of the enemy's cavalry, consisting of about 100 men (Ghazis)—who had probably sworn to die or drive us from our advanced position—were seen suddenly to emerge from the Subzi Mundi, and make a bold clash at our right breaching-battery; but when within eighty yards they were received with a salvo of grape from our guns which mowed them down like grass. As the smoke cleared off there were but a few who had not fallen, and they quickly turned and fled.

The enemy now appeared to be fully roused to a sense of their impending danger, fighting with increased earnestness and determination; they at this time commenced to make counter-trenches and rifle-pits, repairing during the night the breaches effected by our guns during the day, mounting more wins and constructing; additional batteries between the "Moree" Bastion and the Cashmere Gate; but before these could be completed our assault was to be delivered.

On the 13th of September arrangements for the assault, as recommended by a Council of War, were approved of by General Archdale Wilson, and ordered to be carried into effect.

The 1st Bengal Fusiliers, which had left Dugshai 800 strong, were now reduced to scarcely more than one-half: about 400 only being available for the contemplated assault. A like diminution of strength had taken place in other regiments, so that the force at the disposal of the General consisted only of about 1700 Europeans and 1900 natives, of whom about 1300 were Seiks and the remainder Ghoorkahs. Thus General Wilson had only about 3600 thoroughly reliable troops for the assault, besides 850 of the Maharaja Golab Sing's soldiers, many of whom had not been disciplined or used to war.

The army was divided for the attack into five columns, the first, commanded by Brigadier-General Nicholson, consisted of:

Rank and File

1st Bengal Fusiliers	250
H.M. 75th Regiment	300
2nd Punjab Infantry	450

This column was ordered "to storm the breach near the Cashmere Bastion, and escalade the face of the bastion." General Nicholson, having been appointed to command the advance storming-party, assembled the commandants and seconds in command of his troops, and explained to them in detail how they were to act as soon as they had escaladed the walls; ending his instructions with the following words: "Don't press the enemy too hard; let them have a golden bridge to retire by."

The second Column was placed under the command of Brigadier Jones, C.B., and consisted of:

Rank and File

2nd Bengal Fusiliers	250
H.M. 8th Regiment	250
4th Seik Infantry	350

This column was "to storm the breach in the "Water Bastion."

The third Column, commanded by Colonel Campbell, H.M. 52nd, consisted of:

Rank and File

H.M. 52nd Regiment	200
Kumaon Battalion	250
1st Punjab Infantry	500

This column was to be held in readiness "to assault by the Cashmere Gate after its explosion by the engineers should have taken place."

The fourth Column, commanded by Major Reid of the Sirmoor Battalion, consisted of a detachment of the 1st Bengal Fusiliers (150 men), detachments of H.M. 60th and 61st, together with the "Guides Infantry" and the "Sirmoor Battalion," and about 800 of the Jummoo troops (Golab Sing's). This column was ordered to clear the gardens and blocks of buildings "at Paharunpore and Kishengunge, and to enter the city by the Lahore Gate."

The fifth Column, commanded by Brigadier Longfield, consisted of:

Rank and File

H.M. 60th Rifles	200
H.M. 61st Regiment	250
4th Punjab Infantry	400
Belooch Battalion	300

This column formed "the Reserve."

On the 14th September the Headquarters of the 1st Bengal Fusiliers marched from the camp at 3 a.m., having been selected by Brigadier-General Nicholson to lead the first assaulting-column in the attack on Delhie. It is to be regretted that some unexpected delay took place, the engineers reporting that during the night the breaches must be cleared by our heavy guns before the assault, and it was not until some time after sunrise that the 1st Bengal Fusiliers, under Major Jacob, advanced; his Adjutant, Lieutenant Wemyss, being beside him. On reaching "Ludlow Castle" the scaling-ladders were brought to the front; Nos. 1 and 2 Companies of the Regiment forming the first escalading party, under Lieutenant G. N. Money.[10] Nicholson, before advancing to the assault, had separated his storming column into two divisions; the 1st Bengal Fusiliers forming the first; H.M. 75th, the second.

On emerging into the open, a terrific fire was poured on the escaladers, who, with a cheer, ran forward at the double, followed closely by the rest of the Regiment. On nearing the Cashmere Bastion, it was seen that the ditch was so filled with fallen masonry, that our men were enabled to glide down the incline, and plant the escalading ladders with such rapidity that the top of the ramparts was quickly reached amidst a storm of bullets, and missiles, hurled down from the walls above. Notwithstanding this opposition, the ramparts were gained before the mutineers had collected their forces in sufficient number to make a very determined resistance; and thus a firm footing was obtained on the breach before any attempt had been made to blow open the Cashmere gate. By this time the 75th Regiment had scaled the walls, forced the breach—Nicholson's two divisions having joined—the battle for the mastery on the ramparts raged with fierce fury. Our men, though vastly out-numbered, fought with uncontrolled vehemence, striking down the mutineers with their clubbed muskets where they could not succeed in thrusting home their bayonets. The dense masses of the sepahis now crowding to the front could not withstand the eager onslaught of our men, who for nearly three months had been thirsting for this day of retribution. This was not the usual excitement of battle, it was the individual burning lust of revenge for the atrocities committed by the mutineers, and it is hardly possible to realize the intensity of passion that animated every British heart that day. There were volunteers in our ranks, conductors, and non-commissioned staff who had lost all that had made life most dear; and these men dealt death around at every stroke, crying aloud, above the din of war, "Where is my wife?" "Where are my poor children?"[11] It was a just Almighty retribution, beyond the influence or control of man.

---

10. Now in H.M. Body Guard.
11. An officer of the 1st Bengal Fusiliers writes, "I saw this myself."

Brigadier-General Nicholson now gave instructions to his commanders to push forward, storm, and occupy the Church, as well as the adjacent buildings; all of which were held in strong force; by the enemy. Nicholson led the 1st Division against the Church, which, after a gallant assault, was captured at the point of the bayonet; the 2nd Division at the same time succeeding in possessing itself of many of the buildings in the vicinity of the "Main Guard" and the Church. These important positions having been secured, and small parties left in possession, the 1st Bengal Fusiliers and H.M. 75th assembled at the "Main Guard," when orders were issued for the troops to push on in the direction of the Lahore Gate.

In the meantime Lieutenant G. Money, who, before the assault had received his commanding officer's orders to push along the walls to his right as soon as he got inside, proceeded to execute these instructions. As soon as the Cashmere Battery had been cleared he turned to the right along the lane below the ramparts, accompanied by Sergeant-Major Holford and some of the men of Nos. 1, 2, and 3 Companies. Money supposed that the main column under Jacob was following; but, as just stated, it had gone forward as soon as it escaladed the walls to storm the Church. Money's party, therefore, was unsupported.

After having proceeded a short distance down the lane—between the houses and the ramparts—our detachment came to a slope leading up to the ramparts; which Money, followed by Holford and a number of his men, ascended. The ramparts being defended by the mutineers, there was hard fighting as the party pushed forward, and they, having proceeded about half-way to the Moree Bastion, saw a 12-pounder gun in front worked by the enemy. This gun was quickly turned towards the advancing party, and rapidly loaded with grape; and it now became a race between the gunners and the fusiliers as to whether the latter could reach the gun before the former could load and fire.

When within a few yards of the muzzle, the gunners leapt aside, and the port-fire was applied; the priming flashed, but the gun was dumb. It now appeared that in their panic and confusion the enemy had neglected to prick the cartridge, so that it did not ignite.

Expecting that the attacking party would be blown away, the sepahis had stood their ground; but in a couple of seconds we were upon them, not one escaping. The Moree Bastion was soon reached, and it was found full of men busily working their guns, their whole attention fixed on our breaching batteries outside.

The gunners were all Golundazes, armed with swords only, who, surprised at our sudden entry, jumped in numbers through the embrasures and escaped, whilst others turned and attacked the assailants, sword in hand. One stalwart fellow rushed on Lieutenant Money, slashing at him so fast right and left that he had great difficulty in defending himself with his light regulation sword, when Private Patrick Flynn, No. 3 Company, came to his officer's assistance, rushing at the gunner with his musket at the charge. The mutineer jumped aside and evaded the thrust, and, at the same time, catching the musket under his left arm, aimed a blow at Flynn's head; but the hitter's impetus had been so great that the two men appeared locked in each other's arms, so that the hilt of the mutineer's sword came on Flynn's head; who, half stunned, dropped his musket, and at the same time slightly falling back, gave his enemy a straight hit between the eyes which sent him head over heels; and before he could recover himself Money ran his sword through him. In a short time the bastion was ours; but the artillery working in our No. 1 siege battery on the plain outside, being in ignorance of what had taken place above, still poured salvos of grape on the Moree Bastion, continuing until our signals were understood, when the artillerymen outside mounting the parapets, gave a ringing cheer of recognition. Immediately below the Moree Bastion, on the plain in front of our siege batteries, the enemy had cut trenches and rifle-pits, which were filled with their men, who, startled by the behaviour of our artillerymen to their front, now for the first time realised what had taken place above. For a few seconds they stood stupefied, not knowing how to act, whilst we turned upon them one of their own guns, which caused them to leap from their trenches; and, as they bolted across the open plain, they had to run the gauntlet between their own guns above and ours below.

By this time it became evident that the main column had not followed in support, and Money was hardly pressed; when, fortunately, a party of the 9th Lancers appeared below, the officer in command asking how things were going on. On learning that we had some difficulty in holding our own, he dismounted some dozen of his men who had been instructed in gunnery, and they, clambering up into the battery, took charge of the guns. Fortunately there was a breastwork in rear of the Moree Bastion with one embrasure, in which we placed a brass 6-pounder gun. Two or three determined attacks were made by the enemy to regain their lost position, charging up close to the muzzle of this gun, and wounding two of our lancer gunners. Matters were now looking serious; for the numbers of the enemy in front of our breastwork increased, whilst ours, in defence, diminished.

Colonel Greathead (commanding H.M. 8th Foot) now arrived with some of his own men, part of the 75th, 2nd Bengal Fusiliers, and Punjab Infantry. Almost immediately afterwards, the Headquarters of the 1st Bengal Fusiliers, under Major Jacob, arrived; having been delayed whilst recapturing some of the buildings close inside the Cashmere Gate.

Our Regiment now pushed on towards the Lahore Gate, to reach which we had to force a passage through a narrow defile running parallel with, and immediately below, the rampart. It was whilst the Regiment was advancing towards this defile that Major George Jacob fell mortally wounded.

> He, poor fellow, was shot in the thigh, and died that night. As he lay writhing in his agony on the ground, unable to stand, two or three men went to take him to the rear, but a sense of duty was superior to bodily pain, and he refused their aid, desiring them to go on and take the guns![12]

As soon as Jacob fell, Captain Greville, the next senior officer who was close at hand, assumed command of the Regiment.

In addition to the many guns on the ramparts there were three placed by the enemy to sweep the defile; one of these was on the rampart immediately above, one below at the entrance to the defile, and the third also on the rampart above, but about 100 yards in rear. This last gun was protected by an iron bullet-proof screen, from behind which the enemy fired with impunity on the approaching column, a heavy fire being also kept up from the gun above and that at the entrance of the defile. A portion of the Regiment was above on the ramparts, and a portion below, Greville with the latter.

On pressed the men, driving back the enemy before them; and the guns referred to were soon reached. Greville now called out to the party above to "Spike the guns!" There was a moment's hesitation; when Colour-Sergeant Jordan ran forward, followed by Corporal Keefe (No. 3), Privates Bradley and. L. Murphy. Jordan spiked the gun with Corporal Keefe's ramrod, which he snapped off in the vent, passing the broken portion to Captain Greville, who, rushing forward,

---

12. Extract from a letter written by an officer of the Regiment who witnessed the occurrence.

spiked the gun below. Corporal Keefe, Privates Bradley and L. Murphy, were all killed in assisting Colour-Sergeant Jordan to spike the gun, round which "the bullets fell like hail."

It was now seen that the houses on the city side of the defile-as well as the flat roofs above, were occupied by crowds of men, who poured on our troops a murderous fire from the windows. loopholes, and housetops: whilst the gun behind the iron screen on the ramparts swept the passage with rapid discharges of shrapnel and grape. The defile was at most only about 12 feet-wide, projecting buttresses and towers narrowing it in some places to 3 feet; whilst at the end of the pass was the "Burn Bastion," bristling with heavy guns and filled with the enemy's gunners and infantry. Greville deemed it advisable to break into the houses, and thus attempt to take the enemy in rear and flank; but it was ordered otherwise, Nicholson calling out to the fusiliers to "Charge down the lane! The 75th will charge along the ramparts and carry the position above."

Our officers and men now pushed forward towards the Burn Bastion, which Lieutenants Butler and Speke and about a dozen soldiers attempted to climb; but finding it closed at the gorge, and loopholed inwards, they could not ascend more than a few feet. Butler, being convinced of the fruitlessness of the attempt, ordered his men to drop down and protect themselves, intending to follow; but he found that he was pinned in between two bayonets, which had been thrust at him through the loopholes, on either side. Whilst in this position he received a blow on his head from a stone cast at him from above, felling him to the ground; but, recovering himself, he quickly fired his revolver through the loopholes, and escaped from under the bastion before the enemy could recover himself.

General Nicholson, now in front, shook his sword in defiance at the multitude of the enemy around, who, with shouts and yells, poured grape, bullets, and stones on the party below. Nicholson, "our best and bravest," was struck down mortally wounded; Speke, "gentle everywhere but in the field," also fell mortally wounded; and Greville, in reforming the Regiment, was shot through the right shoulder.

Captain Caulfield (doing duty), Lieutenants Wemyss, Butler, and Woodcock, all fell at this time; as well as a large proportion of the rank and file. Captain Stafford (doing duty) now assumed command. The attempt to force the pass was evidently hopeless; the men were utterly exhausted, having been twelve hours under arms, engaged in a desperate conflict, parched with thirst and faint from want of food. Captain W.

Brooks, of H.M. 75th Regiment, having, by seniority, assumed command of the column, ordered the troops to retire on the Cabul gate. Brooks says, in his dispatch:

> Finding that each effort only caused further loss, without success, I formally drew off my men and retired to the Cabul gate....

In his dispatch of the 7th February, 1858, he says:

> The 1st European Bengal Fusiliers, which had been led to the escalade of the left face of the Cashmere Bastion by the late Brigadier-General Nicholson, after effecting an entrance into the town, stormed the Church and adjacent buildings, and charged the enemy as they retreated from the Water Bastion; we then moved on in pursuit of the enemy, Major Jacob being wounded immediately on our quitting the Cabul gate. The command of that Regiment then devolved upon Captain Greville, a gallant Officer, who has served with it on many a hardly-contested field, and on this occasion was at its head when the Regiment captured two guns. I am most desirous the good and gallant services rendered by Captain Greville should be duly acknowledged.[13]

Considering the fearful loss sustained, and the hopelessness of the attempt to force the passage, which was closed at the further end, Captain Brooke's order for the retirement of the Bengal European fusiliers to the Cabul Gate, before there was further sacrifice of life, was, under the circumstances, not only justifiable, but was well-judged and right. The passage of this lane should never have been attempted.

> And if the operation of turning out the sepahis had been left to the 1st Fusiliers and the 75th, we should have cleared the ramparts and lane without loss; instead of rushing at them, we should have entered the houses and got in the enemy's rear.[14]

During the fighting on the 14th September Sergeant J. M'Guire and Drummer M. Ryan, of the 1st Bengal European Fusiliers, gained Victoria Crosses for conspicuous gallantry; having—

> .... at the assault on Delhie, when the brigade had reached the Cabul Gate, the 1st Fusiliers and 75th Regiment and some Seiks were waiting for orders, and some of the Regiments were getting ammunition served out (three boxes of which exploded from

---
13. Delhie dispatches.
14. Extract from a letter from one of the officers in command.

some cause not clearly known, and two others were in a state of ignition) when Sergeant M'Guire and Drummer Ryan rushed into the burning mass, and seizing the boxes, threw them one after the other over the parapet into the water. The confusion consequent upon the explosion was very great, and the crowd of soldiers and Native followers who did not know where the danger lay were rushing into certain destruction, when Sergeant M'Guire and Drummer Ryan, by their coolness and personal daring, saved the lives of many at the risk of their own.[15]

The second Column, under Brigadier Jones, with which was the 2nd Bengal Fusiliers, under Captain Boyd, were told off to escalade the left breach in the Cashmere curtain close to the Water Bastion, and the supporting party, taking ground to the right, gained the ramparts without, any great opposition; but the ladder-men, principally of the 8th Foot, having to make a slight détour in the open, were exposed to a galling fire from above, which wounded both the engineer officers directing the movements, and struck to the ground twenty-nine of the thirty-nine ladder-party. Notwithstanding this loss the ladders were successfully placed, and the Water-Gate Bastion carried. On reaching the summit, the column tore along the rampart to their right, some joining Money's party at the Moree Bastion, whilst others fought their way as far as the Cabul Gate, on the top of which the column flag was planted.[16] Nicholson, "who had diverged from the intended line of advance, to suppress a brisk fire of musketry from some houses near at hand,"[17] now coming up, joined Jones's column. Jones's orders were to remain at the Cabul Grate until intelligence of the fall of the Jumma Musjid should reach him; he, therefore, had collected his men together, "commanding the approaches, and awaiting the signal to advance;" but as the Jumma Musjid was not captured during the 14th September, Jones' column was principally employed in defending the positions which had been gained.

The third Column was told off to enter the city by the Cashmere Gate, after it should have been blown open by the engineers. In attempting to perform this hazardous duty, Lieutenant Salkeld, of the engineers, commanding, and Sergeants Burgess and Carmichael, gave their lives; the Gate being finally shattered by Sergeant Smith. After-

---

15. The Victoria Cross, an Official Chronicle.
16. Malleson, p. 36, Vol. 2.
17. Kaye, p. 596, Vol. 3.

wards the 3rd Column entered, and rushing forward into the heart of the city, fought its way through the Chandnee Chouk; and, seizing the Kotwallee, attempted to push forward to the Jumma Musjid; but the resistance was so stubborn, and the fire so tremendous, that the column was ordered to return to the Church, where it joined the reserve, which had by this time made its way into the city.

Our attention must now be directed to the 4th Column, under Major Reid, for with it was the left wing (about 150 men) of the 1st Bengal Fusiliers, under Captain C. R. Wriford. Reid had orders to take ground to the right, and, after having cleared the suburbs of Kissengunge, Trevelyangunge, and Paharunpore, to advance on the Lahore Gate, through which he was instructed to push his way into the city. With the 1st Bengal Fusiliers, under Wriford, were the following Officers: Lieutenants E. A. C. Lambert, A. G. Owen and Charles Warner; and Captain McBarnett (55th N.I.) doing duty.

The 4th, or Major Reid's column, was principally formed from, the pickets occupying the "Crow's Nest," "Subzee Mundi," "The Mound," and "Fakir's Tomb" outposts. This was a faulty formation, as detached bodies of men are never so effective as an entire Regiment, and in this case specially so; as Reid's column was called upon to attack a very formidable position, which the enemy had been vigorously strengthening for weeks past, and to reduce which a very much stronger force, with an efficient artillery, was absolutely necessary.

The Cashmere contingent (Golab Sing's), which was attached to the 4th Column, was separated into two divisions: that under Major Lawrence, 800 strong, was employed as a reserve to the 4th Column; that under Captain Dwyer, 400 strong, acted against the village of Eed Gab on the right, where it was early in the morning completely defeated, 4 of its guns being captured by the enemy.

Unfortunately some delay took place in the advance of the 4th Column, on account of the non-arrival of the horse artillery, who had mistaken their orders.

Reid was unwilling to advance without his guns; but heavy firing: to his right—in the direction of the detachment of the Cashmere column—convinced him that they had already engaged the enemy, and might want help; he therefore ordered a general advance, without waiting for his artillery.

The 60th Rifles—second to none in the army—and the Ghoorkahs were sent on in front to clear the ground for our advance; but there was no room to deploy, so they advanced along the road, where they soon found themselves opposed by a breastwork close to a narrow bridge, covered by a second breastwork some distance in front and traversing the road.

As our troops advanced, those leading, were shot down in such numbers that the road became cumbered by the heaps of our dead and wounded. Reid now gave the order, "Fusiliers to the front," and with a wild rush they charged across the bridge, unavoidably treading under-foot the wounded men who lay on the road. Reid led this charge, but soon fell badly wounded, and was carried to the rear; when Captain Muter, of the 60th Rifles, the Senior Officer in front,[18] assumed command. Captain Wriford, and many of the officers in advance, were engaged in single combat with the Mutineers, who pelted our troops from behind their breastworks, with brickbats and other missiles; whilst our ranks were being rapidly thinned by the musketry fire poured upon us by the thousands of the enemy behind their barricades. Here McBarnett was shot dead, and Lieutenant Owen was severely wounded in the head, but was saved from falling under the tulwars of the enemy by Lieutenant E. A. C. Lambert's protection, until the arrival of Corporal Kingon, who carried the wounded officer to the rear. Here also fell Sergeant Dunleary, of the 1st Bengal Fusiliers; whose distinguished bravery was favourably mentioned in the dispatches of the Commander of the Column.

Having carried the bridge and the barricade, the 1st Fusiliers pushed their way through a garden and a mosque; but the fire was still very heavy, and no cover was found under which the broken detachments could be formed up. To advance without artillery was certain death to all; for the road leading to the Lahore Gate was defended by many thousands of cavalry and infantry. It was impossible to do otherwise than retire on our pickets; and although this course was, under the circumstances, judicious, the object for which the 4th Column had advanced had not been attained. Thus terminated this disastrous affair: in which the composite column lost one-half its numbers. The impracticability of the undertaking with so small a force and without artillery is admitted by all; and it would have been far better had the 4th Column been employed in making feint attacks, and attracting the attention of the enemy, whilst the escaladers were employed against the breaches and walls of the city.

---

18. Major Lawrence, serving with the Cashmere contingent, was the next Senior Officer with the column, and took command later on.

The retreat of the 4th Column was conducted with great difficulty, and with many risks. Lieutenant Evans, of the Bengal artillery, who commanded some of our guns at the "Crow's Nest" picket, seeing the dangerous position in which the retreating column was placed, judiciously brought his. guns to bear on the enemy, who were pressing on us; and thus, covering our retreat, prevented what otherwise might have been a terrible disaster.[19]

The positions of the besieging army on the 14th September was as follows: The 1st, 2nd, and 3rd Columns had succeeded in gaining a footing inside the city; but they were with difficulty holding their own, whilst the Engineers were rapidly constructing barricades and loopholing the houses. The 4th Column, terribly reduced in numbers, occupied our outposts in rear of Hindu Rao's house.

General Archdale Wilson, in Chief Command, disappointed and shaken at what he deemed to have been a failure, wished to withdraw from the attack; but, before issuing orders, consulted with Colonel Baird Smith, his Chief-Engineer, and Neville Chamberlain his Adjutant-General.

---

19. A monument, the epitaph on which was written, at Captain Wriford's request, by Dr. O'Callaghan, Surgeon-in-Chief of the besieging artillery, Delhie (now Surgeon-General, retired), was erected at Kissengunge by the 1st Bengal Fusiliers:
Here repose the following officers. non-commissioned officers, and men of the 1st Bengal Fusiliers, killed in the attack on the enemy's fortified position of Kissengunge, on the morning of the successful-assault and storm of Delhie.

Captain G G McBarnett 55th N I (attached)

Sergeant Alfred Webb	Private George W Cook
Sergeant Michael Hutchinson	Private John Dehenny
Sergeant Samuel Pivet	Private John Lavery
Sergeant Austin Dunleary	Private Charles French
Corporal Charles Pogson	Private Walter Hastings
Corporal Thomas Rodgers	Private William Stephenson
Corporal William Fisher	Private John Wood
Private John Tenpenny	Private John McGovern
Private James Stapleton	Private Elijah Taylor
Private Denis Mooney	

Familiar with the aspect of death, whom they had confronted in so many battles from which they always emerged victorious, they met his last inevitable call here with intrepidity, falling on the 14th September. 1857, in the faithful discharge of their duty.
This monument was erected by their officers and fellow-soldiers of the 1st Regiment European Bengal Fusiliers in their remembrance, which is part of its glory. The rest remains with the Lord.'

Baird Smith's reply to his Chief's question "whether he thought we could advance," was characteristic of the man. "We must do so." Neville Chamberlain's opinion was not less firm. "To hold at any cost the positions taken, to fortify them, and to make them the base of a fresh attack at the earliest moment."[20]

The 15th of September was comparatively a day of rest, and towards evening the 1st Bengal Fusiliers were moved into some of the houses, which had been placed in a semi-defensible condition by our engineers, detachments of the Regiment being placed on the ramparts between the Moree Bastion and the Cabul Gate; the former being now held by a party of our men under Lieutenant Money.

About this time a serious casualty occurred, which must here be noticed. Six Sergeants and six orderlies of the 1st European Bengal Fusiliers were in a small brick room, where the daily rations were being served out to the men. There was only one small window, facing towards the enemy, who were at this time firing on the building. Suddenly a shell was seen to lodge on the window-sill, and, falling into the room, it immediately exploded, nine out of the twelve men being killed; Colour and Canteen-Sergeant London, one of the best non-commissioned officers in the Regiment, amongst them.

On the 16th a forward movement was made; when Colonel Burn, who had been appointed to the command of the 1st European Bengal Fusiliers, with whom were Lieutenants Cairnes and Vibart (doing duty), occupied a large house about a quarter of a mile in advance. The headquarters of the Regiment came up next day, leaving only a small party under Lieutenant Money at the Moree Bastion.

During the 18th and 19th there was constant fighting and skirmishing, when some decided advantages were gained. Lieutenant Wallace with 20 men occupied a house further in advance, in the direction of the Burn Bastion, and Lieutenant Vibart with a like number of men succeeded in possessing himself of an important position; and these advantages having been gained by sapping, our loss was small. On the 19th September the Burn Bastion was captured, and on the 20th the Headquarters of the 1st Bengal Fusiliers advanced to the Lahore gate, which the enemy had now deserted.

In the meantime Colonel Brind, with the 8th Foot and 1st Bengal Fusiliers, had occupied the Jumma Musjid, and the enemy was rapidly evacuating the city, which was finally captured on the 20th. On the 23rd the left wing of the Regiment, now only about 80 strong, under

---

20. Malleson's History of the Indian Mutiny. Vol. 2., p. 57.

Lieutenant E. A. C. Lambert, marched through the Lahore gate, and joined the headquarters, which occupied a large house near the Delhie gate. On this day Lieutenant Cairnes, who had taken a foremost part in the siege, and who, by his courage and example, had done admirable service, was seized with cholera, to which he succumbed in a few hours. His death was a sad blow he was popular with the officers and a favourite amongst the men. But an incident full of interest savouring of romance—an incident which materially affected the future—was at this time occurring; the prime mover and instigator being an officer of the 1st Bengal Fusiliers.

Lieutenant W. S. Hodson—called by his brother officers "the Indefatigable"—in addition to his duties as head of the Intelligence Department, commanded a cavalry regiment, commonly known as "Hodson's Horse;" the troopers, Seiks—wild-looking, determined men, clothed in dark-blue with enormous scarlet turbans and sashes—venerated Hodson: who was a Commander after their own hearts, and whose word to them was supreme. Information reached Hodson that the Emperor, with his two sons and grandson, had taken refuge in the Mausoleum of Hoomayon, which, with its surrounding buildings, forms an important suburb of Delhie. This tomb, built of richly-carved pure white marble, covers a vast extent of ground, and is exquisitely and wonderfully truthful in its proportions; its dome and minarets, of the same material, towering above in graceful beauty.

Hodson, without delay, obtained the permission of the general in command to seize the King; the sole condition attached to this permission being that His Majesty was to receive no personal injury or insult.

Delighted with the almost plenary powers conferred upon him, Hodson, having selected a few of his troopers, galloped off in the direction of Hoomayon's tomb. The place was crowded with soldiers, followers of the fallen King; so Hodson, unwilling to suddenly alarm the crowd, concealed his men amongst some buildings close at hand, and sent a message to the King informing him that he must surrender, for our troops were waiting to receive him. Terrified at the aspect of affairs, the King submitted, on the sole condition that Hodson Bahadour would spare his life. Hodson, supported by a few of his troopers, soon appeared before the entrance of the tomb. The Royal Guards on duty at the gate approached; Hodson, too, advanced, and drawing his cigar-box from his pocket, ordered the King's sentry to fetch a light. Half-stupefied and overawed, the man obeyed; the escort watching with pride the sang-froid of their leader. Now the Emperor Bahadour Shah, the last representative "of a dynasty the most magnificent the world had ever seen,"[21] came slowly towards the gate, borne in his palanquin. Hodson, approaching, saluted his Royal prisoner, and again assuring him that his life was secured, the King moved on, guarded by Hodson's men, who, entering the Imperial city by the Lahore Gate, passed along the Chandnee Chouk to the Kotwallee, where the King was handed over to the principal civil officer for safe custody.

No promises of safety had been made to the Royal Princes,[22] who still remained concealed in Hoomayon's tomb, and who, the next, morning. September 21st, were ordered to be unearthed Hodson, this time, with his second in command, Lieutenant MacDowell, and 100 picked troopers, again proceeded to the tomb. The Princes begged the promise of their lives, but Hodson replied that he "had come to seize the Shahzadahs, and he intended to do so, dead or alive." The prisoners, who now surrendered at discretion, were placed in a cart, and the cortege moved on towards the city. There were still some 6000 servants and followers of the Royal household in the enclosure of this marble tomb, but none had had the courage to draw sword to rescue their King from imprisonment, or his sons from death. The crowd pushed rudely forward, when Hodson, with MacDowell by his side, and four troopers only at his back, ordered them to lay down their arms. Instinctively they submitted; there seeming to be a magic in Hodson's commanding figure and address. At his bidding the crowd all laid down their arms; they knew there had been treachery in their camp, and that their only hope of safety lay in submission to the man whose look was proof that he meant to be obeyed.

The collection of the ceded arms was left to Hodson's troopers, he riding after the Princes, who had by this time neared the jail, where the surging crowd, including many escaped convicts, was pressing on the carts and escort. Dashing forward and haranguing his troopers, in a voice which he intended to be heard by all, Hodson exclaimed that the prisoners "were the butchers who had murdered our wives and children," and that they should suffer for their crime. He then ordered the procession to stand still, the Princes to dismount and strip; when, seizing a carbine from the hand of one of his troopers, he shot his Royal prisoners dead with his own hand.

This act of Hodson's has been severely challenged. He was a man who had risen early into power; and there were those who were jeal-

---

21. Kaye, Vol. 3.
22. Mirza Khaza, Sultan Mirza, and Mirza Abu Bhr.

ous of his rapid rise; further, we should not, in times of peace, judge of those who swim in blood; and, lastly, Hodson asserts it to have been his belief that, had he not deprived the Princes of their lives, the rebellious crowd which surged around would have rescued them, and the mutineers would thus still have their leaders to urge them on to further deeds of bloodshed and resistance. Rightly or wrongly, Hodson believed these Princes to have been the instigators of the sickening murders of those helpless wives and daughters who were within the walls of Delhie at the time of the outbreak; the revolting incidents of these massacres causing all brave men's blood to boil with horror and disgust. Hodson deemed it right that the bodies of the perpetrators of such foul crimes should fester on the road in front of the Kotwallee, where, a few months previous, they had gloated over scenes too sickening to contemplate, and too revolting to. detail.

In so prominently referring to the incidents connected with the death of these Princes, it is just that we should, in conclusion, quote Hodson's own words:

> I cannot help being pleased at the warm congratulations I receive on all sides for my success in destroying the enemies of our race. I am too conscious of the rectitude of my own motives to care what the few may say, while my own conscience and the voice of the many pronounce me right.

The following is an extract from a letter dated September 18th, 1857, from an officer of the 1st Bengal Fusiliers before Delhie, to his wounded comrade with the depôt at Dugshai, giving an interesting account of our disabled officers:

> In our regiment, McBarnett, attached (55th Native Infantry), killed. Our poor Major (Jacob), thigh broken, leg amputated, and died about 10 o'clock at night on the 14th, and was buried yesterday evening. All who were in camp followed. It is a great loss to our Regiment, and is much felt by both Officers and men; a better soldier never stepped. Poor Greville is hit again— the third time—through the shoulder; a bad wound, but the doctor thinks he will do well. He is much cut up at Jacob's death. Then Wemyss is hit in the calf of the leg; but it is only a flesh-wound. Speke is wounded in the body—ball not found; a bad wound, but the doctor is in hopes of his doing well (since dead). Owen wounded across the whole of the right side of the head, the skull laid bare; and hit just over the left eye by another

bullet. Lambert is slightly wounded in the leg by splinters. Poor Sergeant London was killed yesterday by a shell bursting in the midst of sixteen men, and it killed and wounded fourteen of the party. I believe there is only six file of your company left. No. 10 Company had 6 killed and 15 wounded at Kissengunge. I really do not think we shall be more than 100 or 150 strong after we come out of Delhie. Our fellows saw lots of women and children in the streets when they went in, and I am happy to say not one of our men fired a shot at them. A great many of them ran up to us.

Immediately after the fall of Delhie, the sick and wounded of the 1st Bengal European Regiment were sent to the regimental depôt at Dugshai. Colour-Sergeant Hardy, No. 4 Company, was promoted to the rank of Ensign, for distinguished gallantry in the field.

But before closing the narrative of the siege of Delhie, a well deserved tribute must be paid to the memory of the dead. The following is from the pen of an officer of the Regiment:

> Captain Speke[23] was devotedly fond of his profession, more particularly that which calls forth the active energies; and for a fight there was no better man than Speke, and his hardy, wiry frame fitted him for the hardships of such a campaign. He entirely gained the hearts of the men of his company, by carrying in one of the wounded men, Private Brock, who had his leg shattered by a round-shot; and the poor fellow, I am told, said to the doctor, after he had been under the knife, 'Oh, doctor, if I die, tell Captain Speke how much I felt his kindness.' Yes, these are indeed the acts which bind men and officers as one, and make them invincible in fight. In all our fights Speke had his share, escaping unhurt till the last. Strange to say, he had almost no pain, and maintained his mental powers, though his wound was very severe. Firmly, yet humbly, did he depart this life, deeply lamented by all who knew him.
>
> Then last, but by no means least, was Major G. O. Jacob, who died commanding his regiment almost in the hour of victory;. and whose kindly, generous, considerate nature was shown in death as in life. He and Greville occupied the same tent, in which they both lay wounded;

---

23. Captain Edward Speke, 65th Regiment N.I., doing duty with the 1st European Bengal Fusiliers.

but Jacob's fear lest his involuntary groans should disturb his wounded comrade and friend, seemed to occupy all his thoughts. "I know you are badly wounded and in pain," said he, "but pray pardon my groaning. I try not to disturb you, but I cannot help it." Greville, utterly exhausted from fatigue and loss of blood, slept for half-an-hour; when, waking suddenly, he saw the sheet drawn over the face of his dead comrade, whose last words had been in perfect harmony with the whole tenor of his life, shown in his never-failing courtesy and consideration for others. George Ogle Jacob was brave and chivalrous in battle, respected by all, and most loved by those who knew him best.

But, having paid a well-deserved tribute to the memory of those who, dying, added lustre to the annals of the Regiment, it is right that prominent reference should be made to the services of Dr. J. P. Brougham—the Surgeon-Major of the 1st Bengal Fusiliers—whose tender care and unremitting attentions conduced so much to alleviate the sufferings of the wounded. Dr. Brougham won the esteem, thanks, and goodwill of his commanders, brother officers, and the rank and file of his Regiment, so many of whom had been under his care in the field hospital before Delhie.[24]

---

24. See Appendix G.

CHAPTER 19
Lucknow

Although the neck of the mutiny had been broken by the capture of Delhie, there was still rough work in store for our troops. Tens of thousands of the rebel sepahis, many of whom had escaped from Delhie, now spread over the country; establishing a complete reign of terror throughout the land. A vast empire had to be reduced to submission, murderers and mutineers to be punished, and the authority of the British, not only vindicated, but restored.

As has been previously pointed out, the ryots—the cultivators of the soil—mechanics, artizans, tradesmen, in short, all who had a stake in the prosperity of the country, all who valued life and protection of property, had not been inimical to our rule; and now these men unceasingly implored that our troops might be sent into their districts to convert the existing chaos into its previous order, and drive out the hordes of the mutinous sepahis, who were perpetrating the vilest crimes unchecked, and inflicting the most odious tortures on the villagers, with the object of extracting money and forcing supplies.

Immediately after the capture of Delhie Colonel Gerrard, who had first joined the Bengal European Regiment in 1825 was appointed to its command; and, as he was an Officer both respected and beloved, his return was a matter of much congratulation and joy.

On the 9th November the Regiment was ordered to encamp outside the Cashmere Gate of the city, and to be in readiness to march the next morning in a westerly direction against several strongholds occupied by the mutineers. The 2nd Bengal Fusiliers had already marched, forming part of a force under Brigadier Showers, who had proceeded towards the Maywatta district, to the south and west of Delhie; where they had been doing good service in reducing some Forts, and relieving many villages which were oppressed by the rebels; and re-establishing order in our provinces.

On the morning of the 10th of November the 1st Bengal Fusiliers left Delhie, our Colonel, Gerrard, having been appointed to command the force, consisting of about 2500 men; the 1st Fusiliers: two squadrons of the carabineers; a troop of Bengal Horse artillery; an Eurasian battery, commanded by Colonel Van Cortlandt; the Seik Guides' corps, cavalry, and infantry; the Mooltanie Horse; and some Seik infantry regiments, forming the brigade.

The only important action fought by this brigade was on the 16th November, near the town of Narnoul. "We left our camp at one a.m. in light marching order, all sickly men and heavy baggage having been placed in the fort at Kanoudj—a somewhat formidable stronghold, protected by three lines of outer defences. The capture of this fort might have given us some trouble, had it not surrendered to Showers' brigade previous to our arrival.

The advance of Gerrard's force was conducted with much difficulty in account of the sandy nature of the soil, some ten hours being occupied in covering twelve miles of road. The sun was very oppressive, and the sand and dust, being blown about by a strong wind, trying. The enemy in considerable force were known to be near at hand; indeed, on the previous day—November 15th—they had held a position of great strength close by, and why they had elected to accept battle on the open plain whilst they had good cover was a marvel to all. The village of Narnoul[1] was soon reached, when heavy clouds of dust indicated the position of the enemy, now seen approaching on our left front. The British troops prepared for action; the centre of the first line being occupied by the 1st European Bengal Fusiliers, immediately in front of which was our brigadier, too conspicuous amongst the staff by his red coat and orders. The fight, as usual, commenced with an artillery duel, succeeded by the rapid advance of our cavalry, the carabineers and guides making a gallant charge; but the enemy, nothing daunted, had also advanced and many hand-to-hand conflicts ensued. A most determined onset was made by the carabineers on the enemy's field artillery; when the gunners, keeping boldly to their posts, were sabred to a man, and the carabineers continuing their onward movement encountered the enemy's cavalry, hastening to the assistance of their gunners.

No sooner had our cavalry ridden through the enemy's batteries

---

1. The fort of Narnoul was reduced during the Maratha War, in 1803.

than their infantry were seen advancing from the left flank; when, retaking their guns, which had not been spiked, they sent a few rounds of grape amongst our infantry, wounding Lieutenant Wallace and 3 of our men, and killing a private soldier named Griffin. The Bengal fusiliers quickly charged the battery, retaking the guns, which they spiked. The whole British force now advanced; and the fight, which had hitherto been principally sustained by the cavalry, became general. Our horse artillery, pushing to the front, poured round-shot, grape, and shrapnel amongst the enemy, forcing him to seek shelter behind the walls of the gardens and broken ground to our left, under cover of which he was attempting to retreat towards his camp. As our force advanced, it was seen that the unevenness of the ground was caused by a stream which cut through the gardens, the banks being covered with brushwood and trees.

Colonel Gerrard, in front, was a conspicuous object, seated on his white charger. His Brigade-Major, Lieutenant G. N. Money, of the 1st Bengal Fusiliers, whose horse had just been shot under him, was by Gerrard's side. At this moment two shots were fired from amongst the brushwood in the nullah, one passing close to Money's head, who, thinking the man who had fired belonged to one of the Seik regiments close by, called out, "Look out where you're firing! you nearly hit us." Almost immediately afterwards two more shots were fired from the same place, and Colonel Gerrard, turning round, said, "I've got it; I'm afraid I'm done for." Both his arms were hanging helpless by his side. Money quickly approaching helped him off his horse to a bank close by; and as he sat down he looked at his side, and said, "It's gone clean through me. I'm afraid I'm done for." Money, mounting Colonel Gerrard's horse, went to fetch Dr. Brougham, who, soon as he had examined the Colonel's wounds, said, "I'm afraid, Colonel, there is no hope." "My poor wife, my poor children," was all he answered, and two hours afterwards he died, whilst the battle was still raging in front.

In the meantime the Regiment, pushing forward, crossed the nullah, and arrived before a small mud fort held by some of the enemy, who were defending it with one brass gun. The fusiliers charged forward, captured the gun at the point of the bayonet, and driving the enemy before them, on to the plain beyond, followed them to their camp, where another gun was captured. But, through some oversight, neither of these guns was spiked; and, as the Regiment pushed further to the front, the enemy returned, and, reoccupying their position, opened a sharp grape fire on our left flank. Lieutenant Warner, who was sent back with two companies, retook the guns, which were this time spiked.

On the fall of Colonel Gerrard, Captain Caulfield (3rd Native Infantry, doing duty with the 1st Fusiliers), being the next senior officer, had assumed command of the brigade; and Lieutenant Macfarlane—an Officer of only six years' service—commanded the Regiment.

It was now seen that a large body of the enemy had taken refuge in a Serai, situated on the outskirts of the town; a square building occupying a large space of ground, with high masonry walls, built for the accommodation of travellers, as a protection against robbers, rather than soldiers. But it possessed some strength, having been partially fortified, and a gun placed in position to protect the entrance gate.

The Regiment soon forced its way inside, but the inmates with few exceptions escaped; one, lagging behind, was shot by Lieutenant Frank Brown with his revolver, whilst three others took refuge in a small turret on the top of the wall.

Orders were given to the sergeant-major to send up some of our men to despatch the sepahis in the turret; when Private McGovern, who was standing near, said, "I'll go, Sir, by myself;" and, suiting the action to the word, ascended a little staircase at the main gate. The officer then told the sergeant-major to send at least half-a-dozen men, but he replied, "Oh, never mind, sir; he'll be no loss." McGovern, it seems, heard this remark, and determined to do the work by himself; so he mounted the narrow staircase, and reached the top of the wall, where the three sepahis were waiting for him. These fired at once, but McGovern, jumping down a couple of the steps, escaped unhurt, and, before the enemy could reload, he, mounting the steps, shot the man in front, and rushing on the other two bayoneted them without giving them time to recover. Private McGovern, who had already won the Victoria Cross for distinguished bravery on June 23rd, 1857, was a well-known character in the Regiment, his reckless, dare-devil acts being the talk of the army; and had he been as abstemious as he was brave, he would have been of sterling worth.

The Serai was the last, position vacated by the enemy, now flying from the field, protected by their cavalry; who throughout the day had behaved with great bravery, repeatedly engaging the British cavalry in single combat.

The enemy's camp, equipage, cattle, and eight guns fell into our hands.

For conspicuous gallantry during the action at Narnoul Lieutenant Francis David Millet Brown, of the 1st European Bengal Fusiliers, was awarded the Victoria Cross, "in having, at the imminent risk of his own life, rushed to the assistance of a wounded soldier of the 1st European Bengal Fusiliers, whom he carried off under a heavy fire from the enemy, whose cavalry were within forty or fifty yards of him at the time."

The objects for which the brigade had been sent out having been fully attained, it now commenced its return march; reaching Delhie on November 29th. But there was a sad gap in the ranks of the 1st Bengal Fusiliers, which had left on the field of battle its gallant and generous-hearted colonel. There was no complaint too trivial, no wrong too slight, to escape the attention, and secure the relief of Colonel Gerrard; known as the soldier's friend, he was ever ready to listen patiently to their injuries, and to redress their wrongs. The melancholy loss of their brave colonel was deeply felt and generally deplored by officers and men alike; there were few amongst them who had not felt the beneficial influence of his noble character, and his memory will be deservedly cherished by those who love to honour and respect the good, the noble, and the brave.

On the return march from Narnoul, Lieutenant-Colonel Thomas Seaton, C.B., having been appointed to succeed Colonel Gerrard, assumed command of the Regiment and brigade.

But there was no rest yet. More arduous duties had to be heartily undertaken and conscientiously performed. The 1st Bengal Fusiliers had returned to Delhie only a few hours when they received orders to hold themselves in readiness to advance towards Lucknow, taking with them a convoy of miscellaneous stores, cattle, &c, for the commander-in-chief's camp. 30th November-8th December; This convoy would, on the line of march, cover over eighteen miles of road; and every soldier knows that this convoy duty must involve much exposure and considerable risk, with little renown.

But the importance attaching to the safe and speedy arrival of this convoy at the commander-in-chief's camp could hardly be over-estimated, he being at this time so crippled for want of carriage, &c, that his movements were retarded and the efficiency of his force impaired.

The brigade told off for this escort duty was placed under command of Colonel Thomas Seaton, and consisted of the 1st Bengal Fusiliers, detachments of the carabineers and 9th Lancers, Hodson's horse, and some regiments of Seik infantry.

The force marched from Delhie at 2 a.m. on the 9th December, and, a few days afterwards, on reaching Allyghur, the strength of the 1st Fusiliers was increased by the addition of 100 men under Major Eld from the 3rd European Regiment.

On the 14th of December the brigade reached Gungehri, where was a small British force of Belochees and some European artillery, beyond whose camp the 1st Fusiliers pitched their tents. The morning meal was being prepared, when suddenly the assembly was sounded from the commander's tent, and all hastened to their posts. The British camp was surrounded by cultivated fields, the high growth of the crops obstructing the view. The brigade was quickly formed in line; the fusiliers being in the centre, flanked by the Seik infantry, and the carabineers and lancers on the extreme right, Hodson's horse on the left. Our horse artillery pushed to the front, whilst our heavy guns, preparing for action, were moving slowly into position in rear of our line.

The enemy was now seen in considerable strength moving on our left, apparently with the intention of taking our brigade in flank; Seaton, therefore, changed his position, advancing along the right side of the high road, our horse artillery opening a pretty heavy grape-fire, which to our surprise was only feebly answered.

It was now seen that the enemy was retiring, his guns merely covering his retreat. Evidently the attack had been intended for the Belooch camp, the enemy having been in ignorance of the arrival of our brigade. The brunt of the skirmish fell on the cavalry, the carabineers and lancers dashing boldly forward at the enemy's guns; but during their advance they encountered a more searching fire than they had anticipated, both of artillery and musketry. The mutineers being concealed amongst the brushwood and sand-hills picked off our troopers as they charged to the front. The enemy's guns were captured, the gunners being sabred at their posts, their infantry taking to flight; but this success was not gained without heavy loss, three of the carabineer officers and six men having been killed and fifteen wounded. Hodson, who had been watching his opportunity, now dashed forward with his cavalry, his course being marked for many miles by killed and wounded, amongst whom were 23 of his own troopers. The captured guns, one 9-and two 6-pounders, were brought into our camp; and it was nearly 3 p.m. before our troops resumed their breakfast.

The next day our brigade marched along the road where the skirmish had taken place. On their arrival in camp at Khass-Gunge, the inhabitants were loud in their praise of the gallantry of our troops, and were grateful to us for having relieved them from the presence of the mutineer army,[2] who had hurried through the town after their defeat.

On the 17th December, whilst on the line of march, Colonel Seaton received trustworthy information that the enemy were encamped near the road about two miles from Puttiallee.

Seaton now concentrated his troops, and rapidly prepared for notion; placing, as previously, the 1st Bengal Fusiliers in the centre, some of our horse artillery, British cavalry, and Hodson's horse on the right; some horse artillery and Seik infantry on our left; our heavy guns bringing up the rear. As our brigade advanced, we reached the summit of a slight eminence, from which was seen the town, surrounded by houses in walled gardens, the country generally being studded with groves of trees.

The enemy were drawn up in front of the town, and appeared determined to make a vigorous stand; so our horse artillery opened fire, which was quickly replied to. It was hazy weather, and, as the grass and crops stood some six feet high, it was difficult to see what was going on in front; where Colonel Seaton and his staff, escorted by a troop of Hodson's horse, saw the enemy limbering up their guns, evidently intent on beating a hasty retreat. Not an instant was to be lost, so Seaton, followed by his staff and escort only, dashed forward at the guns, and sabring the gunners—who were completely taken aback by the suddenness of the movement—the guns were captured, with the loss of only one man. This gallant charge relieved the Infantry of much trouble, whilst Hodson and his men rode quietly forward, keeping to the

---

2. "It must not be at all fancied that during the late émeute the people of Hindustan have united with the simple view of driving the English from their country. Many had a much more pleasant object in view, and it was that of helping themselves to property, to whomsoever it might belong, always provided that such might be obtained without personal risk. Where they could get a good fat buniah (corn-chandler), he was plundered without the slightest hesitation; and, in fact, at this very town, Secunderabad, the following new mode of extracting rupees was practised by the mutineers and parties of armed peasants upon the wealthy, as I was informed by the people of the place:—The persons suspected of being guilty of having money had one or two hooks inserted under the shoulder-blades or other tender part. He was then pitched into a well, and allowed to sink for about half-a-minute, and then drawn up by a rope attached to the hooks. In sober truth, these men have practised greater horrors upon each other than they have upon us."—Blackwood, Delhie Campaign, 1858.

right of the road on which the enemy were retreating, until, reaching the open country, he dashed amongst the mutineers, punishing them severely, and pursuing the flying, disorganized masses for several miles; killing no less, it is said, than 600 men.

Our infantry, in the meantime, had scoured the gardens and town, killing a vast number of the mutineers found hiding.

Seaton's bold dash had so hastened the retreat of the enemy that our loss was insignificant: whilst we captured their camp, cattle, 13 guns, with tumbrils and ammunition.

On the 21st December our brigade approached the old military cantonment of Mynpoorie, adjoining which was the large and important town of that name. Here resided a Rajah named Tej Sing, who was in open rebellion, and announced his determination to make a desperate resistance; but the simple manoeuvre of taking his troops in flank, in place of advancing along the main road, which he had protected by earthworks and guns, so disorganized the enemy that they fled, after having fired only a few badly-directed shots.

In the town a gun foundry was discovered, with moulds probably stolen from our gun factory at Futtehghur; there was also a new 8-inch howitzer of our own make: this gun had never been fired.

Whilst at Mynpoorie, information was received that the commander-in-chief's camp was only distant about 30 miles. Hodson, "eager as usual to be foremost," volunteered to open communication. Permission having been granted, he started off with 100 of his men, but he had only proceeded one march (to Bewar) when he learnt that we had been misinformed as to the position of the chief's camp. Hodson, to execute his design, would have to cover some 20 additional miles; and many of his horses having shown signs of fatigue, he picked out 20 of the most lively, and, leaving 80 of his men at a place called Chibramow, pushed forward with his second in command, MacDowell. In a few hours he succeeded in opening communication with the commander-in-chief, then encamped at Miran-Rederai, who having received Hodson's reports and issued his orders, the little party started to return. They had not proceeded far, when Hodson learnt that the enemy, with about 2000 men, lay in wait to intercept him. A Brahmin, having heard the mutineers discussing their plans. walked along the road, and, meeting Hodson's party, informed their commander of his danger. The man who gave this information had on the previous morning received kindly assistance from Hodson, which was now repaid with interest; for the timely warning probably saved his benefactor's life. Hodson, leaving the main road, passed with his men within earshot of the ambuscade, and reached our camp in safety; having ridden 55 miles in 10 hours without changing horses. Great was the joy of all in camp; for intelligence, apparently reliable, had been received that Hodson and his party had been waylaid and destroyed.

Seaton's column marched into Bewar on the last day of 1857, where it remained until the 4th January, 1858, when it was joined by Brigadier Walpole's brigade; this latter Officer now assuming command of the united forces.

By this junction communication was completely opened from Calcutta to Lahore.

On the 4th January Walpole's force marched into Futtehghur, where was the Headquarters of the Army under Sir Colin Campbell. Colonel Seaton was appointed to command the Futtehghur brigade, and districts to the South and West; a task requiring decision and judgement, he having but a weak force to perform duties full of danger and difficulty.

Captain Ellis Cunliffe and Lieutenant Montague Hall rejoined the Regiment at Futtehghur; and the former, by virtue of his seniority, assumed command.

Before entering on fresh scenes of action, it is necessary that we should briefly note events which had occurred since the outbreak of the mutiny at Lucknow, when on May 3rd, 1857, Sir Henry Lawrence had taken energetic measures to punish the 7th Oude Irregulars for their disaffection. The discontent then openly manifested was but the murmur of the coming storm; and although a few of the native soldiers, who still professed loyalty, continued to serve with our troops, their presence was at first felt to be a source of danger rather than a protection.

The native troops were, with few exceptions, in open mutiny, and the number of our Europeans so small, that measures were speedily taken to occupy the residency and the adjacent buildings, which were now being hurriedly placed in a state of defence.

Soon afterwards the military police broke into open revolt; and as they and their fellow-mutineers now assumed a dangerous and warlike attitude, the residency was at once made "the great point of concentration" and occupied by the European inhabitants and the British soldiers, as well as some loyal detachments of native infantry regiments,[3] and the doubtful native artillery of the ex-King.

---

3. Lieutenant R. H. M. Aitken defended the "Bailie Guard" with his men of 13th Native Infantry, and gained his V.C.

On the 25th of June the rebel army took up its position at Chinhut, eight miles from the residency. Lawrence personally commanded the British force, which he had ordered to proceed against the rebels, intending to drive them from their position and assert British authority. But there were traitors in our camp; the ex-King's artillery purposely disabled our guns, our troops were forced to retire, and the battle of Chinhut terminated in disaster, defeat, and heavy loss.

The rebels now occupied the city in great force, our outposts were withdrawn, and our troops, amounting to only 927 Europeans, and 765 loyal native soldiers, were concentrated within the inner defences of the residency.

On the 4th July Sir Henry Lawrence was killed by a shell, which burst in his room, whilst he was dictating his orders. He was succeeded in the command by Major Banks, who was shot on July 22nd. In the garrison were 68 ladies and 66 children, all suffering terrible hardships, and undergoing acute privations. The garrison, on reduced rations, still defended itself with unflinching valour; the soldiers at the different posts knew no rest, there were no reliefs, each man's order was to defend his post till death if needs be, for succour there was none.

On September 25th, Outram and Havelock, with their brave troops,[4] succeeded in cutting their way through the narrow streets of the city and gaining an entrance into the residency.[5] Their advent was hailed with unbounded joy; but the transports of the defenders were somewhat modified, when they realized that they had been reinforced, but not relieved, and that a greater number of mouths must now be fed from their supplies, already alarmingly insufficient. But the troops returned to their posts and fought on, hoping almost against

---

4. Amongst the troops under Havelock, who so valiantly fought their way into the residency, was an artillery company of veteran soldiers of the "Invalid Battalion," all of whom had volunteered for this dangerous service. Of these brave old soldiers only a very few survived the hardships of the campaign. Four officers of the "Invalid Battalion" also placed their services at the disposal of the commander-in-chief for active service during the mutiny; of these four, three—Captains, W. R. Haslewood, R. W. H. Fanshawe, and P. R. Innes—had been invalided from the 1st European Bengal Fusiliers. They were all promoted, at the conclusion of the mutiny, to majorities, for "Valued services rendered."

5. Lieutenant Montague Hall, of the 1st Bengal Fusiliers, served with General Havelock's Force as Assistant Engineer, rendering valuable service at the actions at Munglewar, 23rd to 25th September, 1857, and the advance of Havelock's force into the residency.

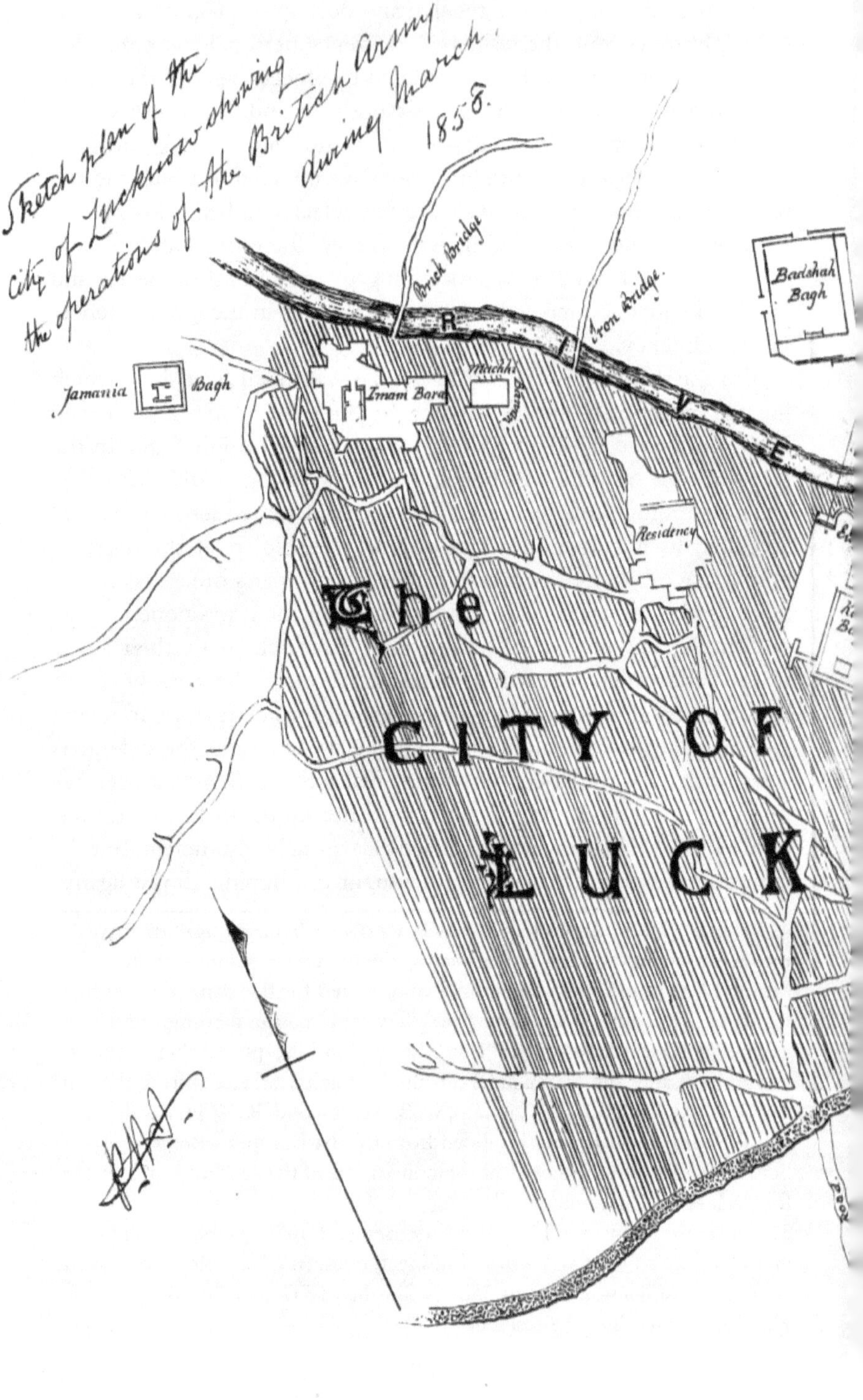
Sketch plan of the
City of Lucknow showing
the operations of the British Army
during March
1858.
Brick Bridge
Iron Bridge
Badshah Bagh
Jamania Bagh
Imam Bara
Machhi Bhawan
R I V E
Residency
The CITY OF LUCK

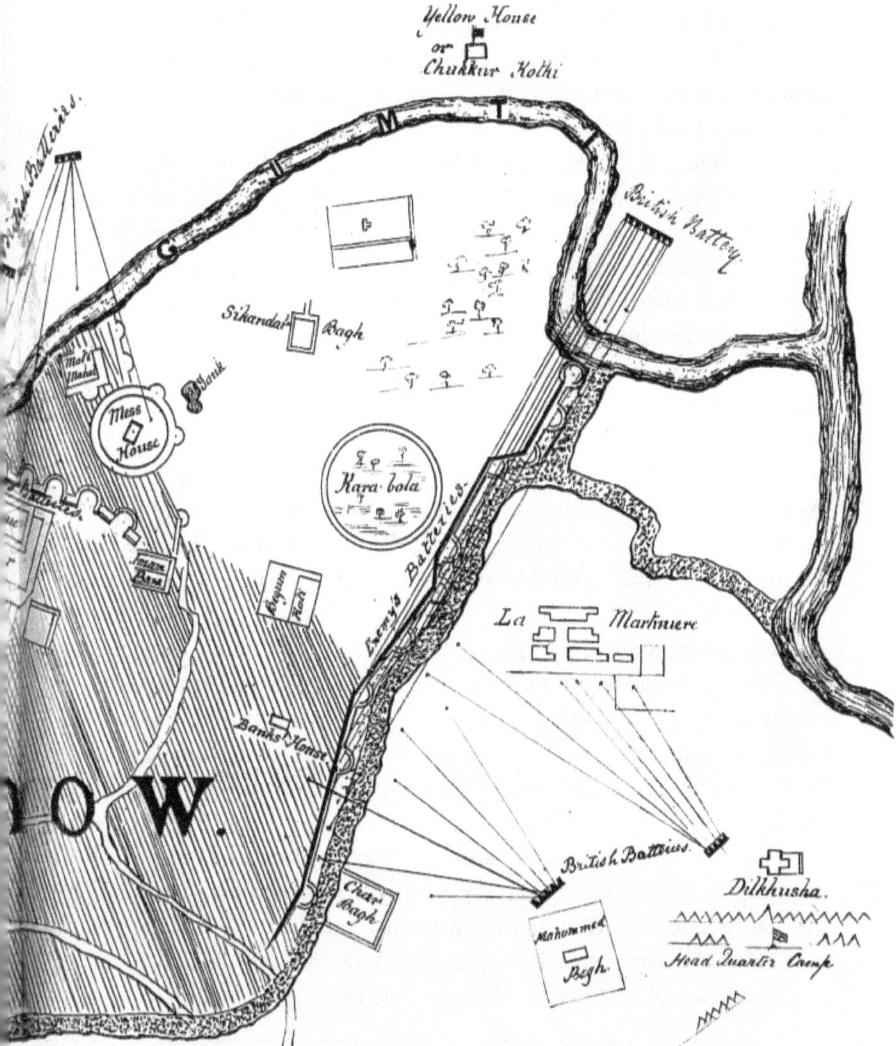
Yellow House
or
Chukkur Kothi
British Batteries
British Battery
Sikandar Bagh
Mess House
Kara·bola
Enemy's Batteries
Begum Kothi
La Martiniere
Banks' House
British Batteries
Dilkhusha.
Mahommed Bagh.
Head Quarter Camp
British Camp.
Alum Bagh

hope, that real relief might come at last. At length Sir Colin Campbell arrived, and on the night of the 22nd November succeeded in creating such an alarm amongst the enemy, by making a feint attack on the Kaisar Bagh—that the beleaguered garrison, including the ladies and children,[6] escaped, through tortuous passages and under ruined buildings, in the dead of night, followed by the garrison, who silently retreated unperceived.

The enemy, in ignorance of the escape of the garrison, continued to pour their accustomed fire into our deserted posts; and it was not until after daybreak that the mutineers discovered that the residency had been evacuated at night and everything of value removed or destroyed. But Havelock only survived the relief a few hours; he had been gradually sinking for weeks; and the insufficient food hastened his decline. At the first halting-ground he passed away.

Sir Colin left 4000 men with 35 guns under General Outram at Alambagh, close to the city, to remind the enemy that though the beleaguered garrison had escaped, Lucknow was ours. He, with 3000 men to guard his convoy of women, children, and wounded, hastened to secure the safety of Cawnpore, where General Windham, "a brave and adventurous soldier,"[7] had been left with an insufficient force to combat the Gwalior contingent, numbering some 15,000 men, cavalry, artillery, and infantry, all drilled and disciplined by us, and led by Tantia Topi, one of the few native leaders admitted to be a General of no mean capacity.

Sir Colin knew that the non-receipt of news from the Cawnpore Garrison boded no good, and therefore left his camp and, followed by his staff, hurried forward to Cawnpore. It was on the evening of the 29th November, 1857, that he crossed the bridge of boats over the Ganges. Firing was heard, and it was evident that a battle was being fought; but Sir Colin had yet to learn that Tantia Topi was so far the victor, and that Windham had been forced to seek the shelter of his entrenchments, after having suffered heavy loss.[8] But the commander-in-chief's arrival at Cawnpore materially changed the aspect

---

6. Of the 68 ladies, 1 had been shot, and 6 had died; of the 66 children, 23 had perished.
7. Malleson.
8. Captain Ellis Cunliffe and Lieutenant N. T. Parsons, who had lately arrived from England, finding communication closed, were unable to join their regiment, were attached to H.M. 64th Regiment, and engaged with that regiment against the Gwalior Contingent under Tantia Topi. Lieutenant Parsons was severely wounded, and invalided to Europe.

of affairs; for, quickly hurrying to Windham's camp, and having gained all necessary information, and instructed Windham to keep close, he returned to his camp across the river, promising to bring relief the next morning. True to his word, daybreak found Sir Colin with his relief troops in the field; confidence was now restored, and a succession of glorious repulses forced Tantia Topi from the positions he had gained—with the loss of camp, guns, cattle, and a large proportion of his army. Nor was this all. Sir Colin, at the head of his cavalry, pursued the defeated foe through the town of Bithoor, where he razed the palace of the infamous Nana to the ground; and, still pressing on, captured the fortress of Futtehghur[9] (January 3rd, 1858); the day following which Walpole's force, with which were the 1st Bengal Fusiliers, marched into Futtehghur; bringing under its escort the much-needed supplies and carriage for the Headquarters army.

On the 27th January the 1st Bengal Fusiliers commenced its march to Cawnpore, reaching its destination on February 3rd.

And was this the Cawnpore that we had only a short time previously known so well?—the assembly rooms and adjacent buildings a heap of ruins, the floors and walls of which had been so lately saturated with blood—the well at the entrance gate, now the tomb of hundreds of murdered women and children, amongst whom were many who had been our friends—the barracks, where our regiment had been so lately quartered, shattered by the missiles of the countless hordes who had assailed Wheeler and his brave garrison—all so treacherously deceived, and, with the exception of four, barbarously murdered. The very trees that remained, sickly with the injuries received, seemed to cry out for retribution, justly claimed. It was such scenes as these that made our soldiers' blood boil, and increased their thirst for vengeance; our wives and little ones—they, at least, had done no wrong. Whilst the Regiment was at Cawnpore, Captain F. O. Salusbury, "a very gallant and capable Officer,"[10] joined; in command of a large draft of recruits, who were the first armed with the Enfield rifle. These recruits had, by the energy of their commander, been so thoroughly disciplined and drilled in the use of the new weapon that, on arrival at Allahabad, the detachment was entrusted with the charge

---

9. It was on this occasion that Lieutenant Frederick Roberts (now Lieutenant-General Sir Frederick Roberts, Bart., G.C.B., of Afghan celebrity), who was born in the Bengal European Regiment whilst his father was its commander, gained his Victoria Cross for distinguished bravery.
10. Malleson.

of a huge convoy, which it escorted to Cawnpore; and, on joining the headquarters of the Regiment, the recruits were handed over efficient soldiers, and at once allowed to take their place in the ranks; an advantage, under the circumstances, hardly to be overestimated.

Lieutenants Maxwell and Magniac also joined from leave of absence; and Lieutenant Hall, who had been employed on the staff with General Havelock's force, with which he entered the residency on September 25th, 1857, had arrived at Cawnpore with Sir Colin's relief army, and returned to regimental duty.

The 1st Bengal Fusiliers was now brought up to a strength of 30 officers and 546 rank and file.

The commander-in-chief's army was at this time being organized for the final assault on the city of Lucknow; the 1st European Bengal Fusiliers, together with H.M. 23rd Royal Welsh and 79th Highlanders, forming the 5th or Brigadier Douglas's Brigade.

On the morning of the 6th of February the brigade commenced its march towards Lucknow, crossing the Ganges by the bridge of boats, and reaching Oonao the same afternoon, where it occupied the admirably-designed defences, constructed by the Rifle Brigade. We halted at Oonao until the 11th February, when we proceeded on our march.

As the British army approached the capital of Oude the desolation of the surrounding country was almost painful. Extensive sandy plains, which had lately been cultivated, were now "sparsely covered with thorns and wiry grass;" the villages, deserted and in ruins, all forming a strong contrast to the appearance of the country through which our Regiment had passed on its march to Futtehghur.

On the 23rd of February we sighted the British camp which had been left by Sir Colin Campbell at the Alambagh,[11] under General Outram; who had, notwithstanding the repeated attempts of the enemy to drive him. from his position, manfully held his ground, and given some severe lessons to those who had the temerity to attack him.

On the 25th February, at 7 a.m., a desperate attack by upwards , of 20,000 men was made on the British position; but Outram's force had been augmented by Walpole's Brigade, as well as by the 7th Hussars, Hodson's horse, and some troops of Bengal Horse artillery.

The battle was hotly contested; and at 10 a.m. the enemy was threatening the British left, whilst a main attack was being made along our whole front and right, the enemy occupying position in rear of our fort of Jellalabad.

---

11. Captain Trevor Wheler joined the Regiment on its arrival at the Alambagh.

Outram now saw his opportunity, and grasped it. Dashing to the enemy's right with a strong force of cavalry, he, at the same time, attacked him vigorously in front; whilst another force of cavalry was sent round to take him in rear, and our horse artillery, under Olpherts and Remmington, attacked him in flank, creating much confusion. Just then Outram completed his plan, by flinging the Queen's Bays and Hodson's horse at him, and seizing two of his guns. This movement caused the enemy to reel back, but not in absolute flight. The mutineers still received our repeated charges with a bold front; and, notwithstanding that they had been forced to give ground, they again brought their masses of Infantry to the attack. Seizing a grove of trees in advance of a village occupied by our pickets, who, from want of ammunition, were forced to fall back, the enemy pushing forward; and were in the act of possessing themselves of the village when they were met by a troop of our cavalry, hastily dispatched to reinforce the picket; and the village was regained.

All night the enemy endeavoured to seize the left of our position; but, towards morning, they realized that their attempts were futile, and drew off towards the city.

General Outram had been ordered, on 24th November, 1857, to firmly retain his hold on the Alambagh. For upwards of three months he had done so in the face of many difficulties; his force of under 4000 men being opposed by an army consisting mostly of trained soldiers, and estimated at 120,000. The trust which the Commander-in-Chief had reposed in Outram had been nobly fulfilled; and on the 1st March Sir Colin Campbell arrived at the Alambagh, and assumed the chief command of the army before Lucknow; now numbering 20,000 men—the choicest in the British service—and 120 guns. With this force, not only was the capture of the city a foregone conclusion; but any lavish expenditure of life would be unnecessary.

The commander-in-chief's plan of action had been arranged in consultation with Brigadier Napier[12] his Commanding Engineer, who had already displayed much ability in counteracting what might have proved a difficulty. In rear of the British camp at Alambagh, where our brigade was placed, was a large jheel or lake, which afforded complete protection to our rear. When this jheel should become dry and passable after the rains, it would have required a very strong picket to have afforded protection to our camp; but this was obviated by the ingenuity of Napier, who, collecting all the spare commissariat elephants,

---

12. Now Field-Marshal Robert Lord Napier of Magdala.

walked them up and down the jheel; so that, baked by the sun, it became a perfectly impassable bed of pitfalls. The jheel now afforded a protection as reliable as if it had been filled with water.

The city of Lucknow may be said to somewhat represent the form of a triangle; the apex pointing towards the east, the north side of the triangle formed by the river Goomti, the south by a canal, and the base, facing west, about 3½ miles in length, by fortified houses and works. In the centre of this triangle is the city of Lucknow, consisting of noble palaces, mosques, houses with gardens, and close, narrow, winding streets.

The Alambagh, or Garden of the World, is situated south of the apex of the triangle, and on the plain near at hand is a palace called the Dilkusha, or the Heart's Delight, and La Martinière, a handsome building erected by Captain Claude Martine; who, with his company of Frenchmen, joined the Bengal European Regiment in 1763. The Alambagh was the point from which Havelock and Outram had attempted the relief of the residency on September 25th, 1857; and it was from this place, also, that Sir Colin Campbell had effected the relief on the 22nd of November following. As the previous advances had been made from the direction of the Alambagh, the enemy evidently anticipated that the capture of the city would on this occasion be attempted from the same base: and they had planned their defences accordingly. The canal on the south face of the city was defended by a triple line of works of enormous strength, erected, at a great expenditure of labour, by trained engineers; but the river face, east and north, was comparatively undefended; and, as the left or north bank was higher than that on the city side, our guns could be worked with great effect.

The commander-in-chief was fully alive to the want of judgement displayed by the enemy; and formed his plan of attack so as to profit by it. He ordered a strong force under Outram to gain possession of the left bank of the river Gumti, east and north. The apex of our supposed triangle towards the east is irregular, and connected with the south or canal face of the defences by a wet, sandy channel.

Sir Colin Campbell fixed his Headquarters at the Dilkusha, where he would remain with the main Army until assured of the success of Outram's movement; which was to be made known by raising colours on the roof of a tall building, called the "Yellow House" or Chukkur Kothi, easily visible; from the top of the Dilkusha, and the occupation of which would be a sure indication that Outram's force had succeeded in taking the enemy in reverse.

The Martinière, situated on a plain between the Dilkusha, and the enemy's line of works on the canal, was still held in strong force by the rebel army. The commander-in-chief had no intention of disturbing him until, finding that Outram had succeeded, he could advance with his main army to attack the city from the south and west, when a brigade, under Adrian Hope, would be sent forward to clear the Martinière.

The British army was now of sufficient strength to warrant Sir Colin Campbell in dividing it into separate *corps d'Armée*; and he would thus be enabled to enfilade the enemy's batteries on the canal, and also effect his entry into the city without any great sacrifice of life.

The plan of attack having been arranged in its minutest details, the movements of our troops commenced on March 2nd at 2 a.m.; when the 1st Bengal Fusiliers struck camp, and, with a heavy battery of siege-guns under their escort, proceeded to occupy a position somewhat in rear of the Dilkusha.

But next day orders were received to leave our camp standing, and proceed to the protection of one of our heavy batteries close March 3rd, to the Mahummed Bagh, a garden to the left of the Dilkusha, in the centre of which was a large masonry house surrounded by well-constructed walls. The Mahummed Bagh was within 700 yards of the enemy's batteries, from which a heavy fire was being maintained; but no damage was done, as the Regiment was well under cover.

At night the movements of the enemy could be distinctly heard; indeed, our guards were relieved by the sound of the enemy's gongs.

Our heavy guns, which had now opened fire from the Dilkusha, and Mahummed Bagh batteries, soon succeeded in silencing those of the enemy; and on the morning of the 5th our Regiment returned to the Dilkusha, camp to find that the whole of the 3rd, 5th, and 6th Brigades of the British army, and a large portion of our siege-train, had pitched their camp close at hand. It now became known that our brigade was to proceed with the division under General Outram, to carry out the first part of Sir Colin Campbell's operations. The right flank of our division nearly reached the bank of the river Gumti, which, after leaving the city, makes a sudden bend to the south. Our left flank stretched out towards the Alambagh, whilst between the right and left flanks there was an interval, at this time occupied by Hodson's horse, 1600 strong.

On the morning of the 6th of March our division struck camp and took ground to the right; and thus, circling round the apex of the triangle, it would gain the east and north banks of the Gumti, which were destined to be the scene of our operations. In the early morning our regiment crossed the river by one of the bridges which had been constructed by our engineers. The day broke bright and clear, and the goodly array of British troops was a grand sight—the Queen's Bays, the 9th Lancers, and the wild troopers of the Punjab cavalry, with our splendid horse artillery and light field batteries. Then on our right and left were the 23rd Royal Welsh and the 79th Highlanders, with two battalions of the rifle brigade close by; all looking ready for the work in hand.

The ground was undulating, and in some places heavy; water was scarce, and the sun soon shone out in great power; but the troops, making a joke of their discomforts, were all cheerful and full of excitement.

Just as the Regiment, after having been marching several hours, emerged from a grove of trees, through which it had passed, on to an open plain, the sound of heavy firing was heard ahead. Our horse artillery galloped to the front, and, quickly replying with shot, grape, and shell, prevented the enemy from approaching our line. But the fusiliers now changed position: halting, sent pickets to the front, whilst the rest of the force, reposing under the cool shade of a grove of trees, partook of a kind of picnic meal; and soon proceeding on, encamped that night near Chinhut, where Sir Henry Lawrence had met with his reverse.

Early on the morning of March 7th our men were aroused by an artillery fire from the enemy close by, some of their shots passing through our camp and wounding a few of our soldiers. Our regiment was quickly under arms; and none too soon, for the enemy in force were seen approaching our camp. Our troops, moving to the front, caused them to halt; and the rifle brigade, skirmishing very effectively, made them keep their distance, and prevented them from observing our movements, which was evidently the object they had in view. Having failed in effecting their reconnaissance, they retired; and the villages in front were occupied by two companies of our regiment under Captain Salusbury. The headquarters now returned to camp.

On this day Captain Hume joined the Bengal fusiliers; and in virtue of seniority assumed command. The 8th of March was comparatively a day of rest, but early on the morning of the 9th the serious work commenced.

Soon after midnight the 1st Bengal Fusiliers were on parade being under orders to escort our heavy siege-guns into our most forward batteries, which had been prepared for their reception on the previous day, and which were within 600 yards of the enemy's nearest works.

Our elephants being harnessed to the guns, the convoy slowly and silently moved along, aided by a bright, clear moon. Having advanced about a mile, our forward pickets were reached, and here the main body of our troops halted, whilst two companies of the 1st Bengal Fusiliers proceeded with the guns up to the batteries. It had been anticipated that some resistance would be offered; but notwithstanding that the elephants, in disobedience to the orders of their Mahouts, occasionally trumpeted, and the noise consequent on getting the guns into position was considerable, the enemy did not interfere. The guns were placed in array before daybreak; when they soon announced their presence by raking through the enemy's position in front. Leaving a small force to protect the guns, our Regiment now advanced.

In the meantime the skirmishers of our division had cleared the ground in front, when the 1st Bengal Fusiliers and two Companies of the 79th pushed forward. Advancing steadily, a small stream was crossed, and moving up a slight incline, a sandy plain was seen at our feet, on the further side of which was a trench or outer defence; and beyond stood the "Yellow House." The trench was quickly passed, the enemy driven back, and the "Yellow House" was captured.

Lieutenant Money led the advanced party, consisting of 2 of our companies; and, believing that the house had been cleared of the enemy, he halted outside, but soon some shots from the basement of the house wounded some of our men.

In the meantime the colours of the 1st European Bengal Fusiliers had been planted on the roof of the "Yellow House;" but it was discovered that, although the upper stories of the building had been cleared of the enemy, the large arched basement was held by a few determined rebels, who intended to sell their lives as dearly as possible. It was no easy matter to dislodge these men; for it was quite dark inside, and the basement was intersected by numerous walls. Our men advanced, and three times rushed into the building; but they could see nothing, though they knew the enemy must be concealed inside. Captain E. St. George, followed by Lieutenant Magniac, entered one of the passages, and shot some of the enemy with their revolvers; but here St. George fell, a musket-ball having passed through his body. An attempt was now made to burn the rebels out; some of the thatch of the old cavalry lines close at hand being placed to windward and fired, but without effect. Holes were also made in the floor above; and live shells dropped into the passages below, which, exploding, startled the occupants, who, nine in number dashed out, and ran the gauntlet towards the river. All fell save one, who, plunging into the stream, swam for his life, and probably might have escaped, had not Hospital-Sergeant Wilson, who was bringing in some wounded men, taken a steady aim at the fugitive just as he reached a shallow in the centre of the stream, and he, too, rolled over, mortally wounded.

We were now complete masters of the "Yellow House" and the ground some distance in advance; and the signal of our success had been shown aloft to the commander-in-chief. Our loss had been small, the enemy having been taken in reverse; and whilst the companies under Money had been employed as just described, our troops had cleared the jungle and villages covering the position to the north and west. So confident was Outram now of success that he would have pushed further on; but orders were received from the chief telling him to hold his ground, but nothing more.

Sir James Outram in his dispatch says "the left column of attack, composed of the 1st Bengal Fusiliers supported by two Companies of the 79th Highlanders, carried the Chukkur Kothi, (or Yellow House), the key of the rebel position, in gallant style, and thereby turned the strong line of entrenchments which had been constructed by the enemy on the right bank of the Goomtee."

General Outram now gave orders for a party of the 1st Bengal Fusiliers to retrograde along the river bank with some heavy guns; and, having reached the junction of the Gumti and the canal, to enfilade the enemy's batteries, which formed their first defence on the city side of the canal. The expedition was commanded by Major Nicholson of the engineers. The infantry was under Captain F. O. Salusbury.

Arrived at their destination, the enemy's works were seen to be of enormous strength; but no reply was made to our enfilading fire, which raked through and through their batteries in flank. Nicholson now formed the opinion that these batteries must be deserted; and Salusbury, anxious to test the accuracy of the surmise, offered to get some boats and cross the river with his men; Nicholson refusing to sanction the proposal, as he was loth to let his guns be left without support.

Lieutenant Thomas Butler, one of Salusbury's subalterns, now came forward to solve the difficulty; volunteering to personally ascertain whether the fortifications on the opposite bank of the river were occupied by the enemy or not. It should be borne in mind that, though it appeared that no great numbers were inside the fortifications, the chances were that there would be many of the mutineers in or about the place; and those acquainted with the habits of the natives of India will fully realize the danger of the task which Butler had proposed to undertake.

Nicholson, whilst warning Butler of the risks he ran, gave his consent; and Butler, throwing off his coat, took to the stream, which was here some sixty yards across, with a strong current flowing at the time. Arrived on the inner bank, Butler looked round; the inside of the enemy's works was still as silent as the grave; but, even so, it needs some nerve to storm a fort alone. Passing to the rear, Butler gained an entrance unopposed; and, mounting on the parapet, signalled with a white flag which he had improvised, to a staff officer of Adrian Hope's brigade. This officer came near, but sent no aid; and so Butler was left unarmed, and cold and wet, to garrison the fort alone. Gesticulating for help, Butler was seen by an officer of a Highland regiment on the plain in front of the Martinière, who, rapidly advancing with his men, occupied the fort. The Seiks soon followed, when Butler, relieved, swam back; having performed an act of cool and dauntless courage, which won for him the Victoria Cross, and his Regiment the honour of adding one more to the long list of heroes who have adorned its ranks.[13]

On the evening of the 9th March the companies under Salusbury rejoined the Headquarters of the Regiment, and bivouacked near the "Yellow House."

The success of Outram's division was complete. He had possessed himself of the left bank of the river, occupied the Badshah Bagh and its surroundings, silenced the enemy's batteries on the right bank of the river, and finally enfiladed those on the south face of the triangle, forcing him to vacate his defences.

It was now time for Sir Colin Campbell to act.

On the morning of the 9th the commander-in-chief, seeing through his telescope the colours of the 1st Bengal Fusiliers floating on the top of the "Yellow House," sent Brigadier Adrian Hope with

---

13. Extract from The Victoria Cross, an Official Chronicle: Lieutenant Thomas Adair Butler—Date of act of bravery 9th March, 1858. Of which success the skirmishers on the other side of the river were subsequently apprised by Lieutenant Butler of the Bengal fusiliers, who swam across the Goomtee, and, climbing the parapet, remained in that position for a considerable time under a heavy fire of musketry until the work was completed.—Extract from Lieutenant-General Sir James Outram's *Memorandum of Operations at the Siege of Lucknow.*

his Brigade to seize the Martinière. This was quickly done, the enemy having withdrawn their guns across the canal. The 42nd Highlanders, forming part of this brigade, had relieved Lieutenant Butler of his charge, and then swept down the line of works, penetrating as far as Banks' house.

Next day, the 10th, there was some skirmishing, but our regiment was not engaged. Our camp changed ground, but was still in rear of the "Yellow House;" which was not occupied, as the Regiment bivouacked out until the morning of the 11th, when it took possession without opposition of a Mosque which commanded the iron bridge, nearly opposite to the Machi Bawn. But, during this day, vast progress had been made by the main army under Campbell. The two sides of our triangle had been completely gained; and the base had been assaulted with such success that Banks' House and the Begum Koti were occupied before nightfall, and the Kaisar Bagh or King's Palace was almost within our grasp. It was at the storm of the Begum Koti that Major W. S. Hodson,[14] of the 1st Bengal European Regiment and Commandant of "Hodson's Horse," was mortally wounded.

Major Hodson, who had ordered his regiment to parade, preparatory to crossing the canal, rode to the front to select a fitting spot; but seeing Brigadier Napier advancing on the Begum Koti, Hodson joined his force; and after passing through the breach he pressed forward to see what was going on inside, when a shot fired by a mutineer from a window entered his side, giving him his death-wound.

Hodson's short career was one of marvellous brilliancy; and, had he not succumbed to his wound, it is more than likely that he would have lived to be one of England's greatest soldiers. But it was otherwise decreed. Hodson had many friends, but he had some enemies; and we ask these latter to say of his memory as of his soul—Requiescat in pace.

On the 11th, 12th, 13th, and 14th of March, although the main army, under Sir Colin Campbell, was making vast progress, pushing its way into the very heart of Lucknow, our division was comparatively inactive. Outram, burning with anxiety to take a leading part in the fray, sent to the commander-in-chief, to ask permission to be allowed to cross the iron bridge, but Sir Colin's policy was irrevocable; India was reeking with British blood, and the capture of the City of Lucknow must be accomplished without needless loss of life.

Awaiting the chief's reply, Outram drew up his troops opposite the

---

14. Captain Hodson had received his Brevet-Majority for distinguished services before Delhie.

bridge, the tête-du-pont of which was occupied in great force by the enemy, who, with some guns, which they were serving well, prepared to dispute our passage across; these occasionally firing at our troops, and doing some injury; one of the bullets, passing-through Lieutenant Ellis's padded coat, and slightly wounding Captain Salusbury in the left leg.

An aide-de-camp now arrived with the chief's reply, which only gave permission to Outram to cross the iron bridge, if he could do so without the loss of a single man. This condition rendered the assault impossible, without disobeying orders; so Outram unwillingly withdrew his troops.

Before the 15th the main army had stormed the Imam Bara, the second line of the enemy's works being thus turned. On the 14th the chief penetrated to the China Bazaar; and thus the third line of the enemy's defences was gained. The Moti Mahal, the Chattar Munzil Palace, the Tara Koti, all fell into our hands; and, before the day was over, the Kaisar Bagh was captured. Its cellars, containing embroidered cloths of priceless worth, gold and silver ornaments, jewels of every description, diamond tiaras, and gorgeous Royal standards, banners, china, jade, and every kind of valuable, all fell into our hands. The captors, "drunk with plunder," revelled in the spoil, heaping on a bonfire in the centre court the rich brocades and gold embroidered shawls, in order that they might collect the melted gold.

By this time the mutineers were streaming out from the captured city; and Outram's Brigade returned to camp behind the "Yellow House," where, for the first time for five days and nights, the men were un-accoutred.

On the 16th of March our brigadier received permission to cross the river near Secundra Bagh, over a hastily-constructed pontoon bridge, floating on casks; so, marching past the 32nd mess-house—or, rather, where the house had stood—we reached the Kaisar Bagh, when an attack was ordered to be made on the residency, which still contained some of the rebel troops. A rush in the face of a few wild shots, and the residency was in our hands; the defence of which now formed a feeble contrast to the occasion on which Outram and Havelock, with their brave residency force, held the position for months, in the very teeth of countless multitudes. Our troops, still pushing on, seized the ruined fortress of Machhi Bawn, from which Captain Salusbury, with his company, pushed on up to the gateway overlooking the Husanee Bagh, capturing three guns upon the riverbank, and one at the gateway of the garden.

Lieutenant Charles Macgregor,[15] attached to our regiment, was, as usual, to the front, and greatly distinguished himself by engaging in single combat with "one of the bravest of the rebels," whom he reduced to eternal submission by sending his sword through his body up to its hilt. Brougham says, "Mac returned looking very warm and exceedingly wild and happy."

The detached duties upon which our regiment was now employed were not unattended with danger, for Lieutenants Maxwell and Ellis nearly came to an untimely end. One of our soldiers, having misunderstood his orders, set fire to a powder factory; which, exploding, seriously injured four of our men; but, happily, there was no loss of life. Lieutenant Ellis, who was near at hand at the time of the explosion, escaped minus his eyebrows, whiskers, and moustache, and was fortunate enough not to lose his sight.

By the 21st of March the city of Lucknow had been completely cleared of the mutineers; and a few days after the townspeople commenced to return to their homes. Gradually the shops were opened, buildings repaired, and the streets were again crowded with citizens eager to trade. The fields around became green with cultivation, the dead lay silent in their graves, and all was peace again.

During the operations against Lucknow the following officers of the 1st Bengal Fusiliers were wounded:—

Captain Salusbury (slightly).

Captain St. George (dangerously).

Lieutenant Ellis (slightly).

8 rank and file being killed and 21 wounded. The total loss of the British army was 127 killed and 595 wounded.

During the following April a flying column under Major-General Sir Hope Grant was organized to restore confidence in the Fyzabad district, and rid the country of some powerful bands of mutineers, who were looting the villages and destroying the peace of the inhabitants. The 1st European Bengal Fusiliers served with Sir Hope Grant's force.

On the 13th of April an engagement took place against some thousands of the rebels near Baree ; when an attempt was made to seize our baggage, which straggled over 3 miles. The 1st Bengal Fusiliers were ordered to assist the rear-guard in repelling the attacks of the enemy's cavalry, who had succeeded in rounding the village, the point of our assault. They were charging down on the baggage when

---

15. Now Major-General Sir Charles Macgregor, K.C.B., C.S.I., C.I.E., Quartermaster-General of the army in Bengal.

they encountered Nos. 5. and 6 Companies of the Regiment under Captain Cunliffe, who, allowing the cavalry to come within 30 yards at the charge, said, "Steady, men, and give them a volley." The order was carried out so efficiently, and the aim of our soldiers was so true, that a vast number of the enemy fell and the remainder fled.

The rebel cavalry was said, on this occasion, to have been commanded in person by "The Moolvie," one of the principal leaders of the Lucknow rebellion. This man had been formerly placed in irons by our commissioner for sedition; but, having escaped, became our bitterest enemy.

During September the 1st Bengal European Regiment was employed in driving a large force of mutineers from an island in the river Gogra, not far from Durriabad, where the Regiment was quartered. The expedition was completely successful, the enemy being defeated with heavy loss. In this engagement the Regiment had one man killed, and four wounded; again on the 6th October the mutineers were attacked, and this time dispersed with the loss of many men and one gun; finally, on the 30th, October, Captain Trevor Wheler,[16] of the 1st Bengal Fusiliers, commanded a force, with which were about 200 rank and file of his Regiment under Lieutenant W. Warner, a troop of Hodson's horse under Lieutenant F. Brown of the 1st Bengal Fusiliers,. and about 600 artillery, native cavalry and infantry. Wheler's force left Durriabad on the early morning of 30th October, and, having marched rapidly for about 15 miles, came on the track of a large body of the mutineers near Nawab-Gunge. Pursuit was ordered, and the detachment—

.... after marching for miles through a country much intersected by ravines, came upon the enemy's pickets. These were speedily dislodged, and the movement for attacking the main body was at once commenced although somewhat impeded by our having to cross a nullah, which required to be partially bridged before our guns could cross over. This difficulty overcome our advance became a rapid one, and having come upon the main body a running fight was kept up for more than two hours and over more than five miles of country. In this advance the enemy was driven from village to village and eventually discomfited at Sahadit-Gunge, where we captured 5 guns, complete, with bullocks and munitions of war, one elephant and much baggage."[17]

---

16. Now Colonel Sir Trevor Wheler, Bart.
17. Extract from dispatch dated Durriabad, 31st October, 1858.

This skirmish is specially worthy of notice on two accounts. It was the last occasion on which the Regiment, under its time-honoured designation of 1st European Bengal Fusiliers, was engaged against the enemy; and, secondly, it was the first engagement in which Ensign Cavagnari—who had lately been gazetted to the Regiment—had been engaged; his commanding officer specially recording "with satisfaction the cool courage" of this promising young officer, who, as Major Sir Louis Napoleon Pierre Cavagnari, K.C.S.I., nobly sustained at Cabul in 1879 the character he had established thus early in his career, and added one more to the long list of heroes who have shed lustre on the annals of the "Bengal European Regiment."

In March, 1859, the 1st European Bengal Fusiliers returned to their station at Dugshai, arriving April 18th, after two years as severe and campaigning as perhaps was ever experienced by any regiment; and during which it's officers and rank and file had gained no less than five Victoria Crosses:

Lieutenant T. A. Butler, V.C.
Lieutenant Frank D. M. Brown, V.C.
Sergeant J. M. Guire, V.C.
Private J. McGovern, V.C.
Drummer M. Ryan, V.C.

The sepahi mutiny war was now over. The neck of the rebel mutiny had been broken at Delhi, its heart had been plucked out at Lucknow, and its limbs had been severed from its carcase far and wide. The rebellion which had assumed such gigantic proportions, and caused British supremacy in India to tremble in the balance, had been fought out; and it will ever be remembered with pride that it was the 1st Bengal Fusiliers who led the main storming-party at the Siege of Delhi, fulfilling the confidence placed in them with courage and determination unsurpassed in British history.

All honour, then, to the multitude of brave soldiers who gave their lives and blood to uphold and extend the glory of England; and all honour to the Regiments who fought so well to retain under British rule those Indian possessions of which England is so justly proud, and which form the brightest jewel in her Imperial Crown.

CHAPTER 20

Company to Crown

Whilst the 1st European Bengal Fusiliers was quartered at Durriabad—1858—a Proclamation[1] was issued by the Queen of England intimating that Her Majesty had assumed the Government of India from the East India Company; that the troops in the Indian service would be transferred to that of the Crown; and, in 1861, a Royal warrant[2] directed the amalgamation of the European troops lately in the service of the Company with those of the Royal army.

In 1857 the Regular army of the East India Company numbered 237,476 soldiers; of whom 15,207[3] were enlisted in Great Britain.

The Company, which may aptly be described as having been a republic under the suzerainty of the Crown of England, had ruled with liberality and consideration for the feelings and interests of its servants for upwards of 250 years; engendering feelings of regard and gratitude towards a highly-popular form of government. The conditions of its service suited the requirements of those younger sons who sought to be the fathers of their own fortunes; and to whom a commission in the Indian service was not only a provision for life, but promised a career to the deserving of honour and distinction.

Service in the ranks of the Company's European army suited, in many instances, not only the class from amongst which our recruits are usually obtained, but was adapted to those of all grades of life, who, for various reasons, wished to lose their identity, to disconnect the new from the old life, and to obtain employment in a land from which return to their native country was, in exceptional cases only, at-

---

1. See Appendix D.
2. See Appendix E.
3. In addition to these troops in the Company's service, there were 24,263 soldiers of the Royal army in receipt of pay from the East India Company.

tainable. Of the many such who found their way into the ranks of the Company's European Regiments, by far the larger proportion became an honour instead of a disgrace to their country.

Rightly or wrongly, it was with feelings of apprehension that it was realized by a large number of the Company's servants that the time had arrived for a change which would uproot old associations, and possibly deprive them of privileges hitherto exclusively their own; and, further, there were far-seeing men who, as in Fox's time, dreaded that India, under the immediate control of the Home Government, might be sacrificed to party ambition; and even the safety of our Indian Empire jeopardized, to create a babble popularity in the see-saw of public opinion at home. Finally, there were many who thought that the nomination of the Governor-General of India by a non-political body had been a guarantee that our Eastern possessions would be protected from the danger of falling a prey to party politics in England, tending to lower the Governors of India and their officials in the estimation of its people.

The Company's army had at all times been conspicuous for its loyalty and devotion to the Crown; having for centuries fought under the British flag, its soldiers ever foremost in the fight for England's honour; and it was no lack of loyalty that caused some of its servants to view with apprehension and dismay the change which had become inevitable.

It tells well for the internal discipline of the 1st European Bengal Fusiliers that, although after the annexation proclamation there followed an interregnum of years, during which the officers of the European Regiments were removed to a general list, and directed to "do duty" only with their former regiments, and although a large proportion of the Company's European army was in a dissatisfied state, closely bordering on mutiny, there was no single instance of insubordination in the ranks of this Regiment.

Under the Royal Warrant the amalgamation of the Indian with the British armies was effected; the officers and men of the Indian European Regiments being invited to volunteer for general service. The commissioned officers were guaranteed, under act of British Parliament, all the retiring and other privileges which they had held under the East India Company; the rank and file being offered a bounty for volunteering, and to count their former service for pension.

It was further announced that Her Majesty had been pleased to confer upon the 1st European Bengal Fusiliers the honourable designation of the "101st Royal Bengal Fusiliers;" the 2nd European Bengal Fusiliers being nominated the "104th Bengal Fusiliers."'

The volunteering of the 1st Bengal European Regiment took place on May 2nd, 1861, when the following 17 out of 89 officers with 588 rank and file volunteered for the 101st Royal Bengal Fusiliers:

Major A. Hume
Captain F. O. Salusbury
Captain E. Brown
Captain G. C. Lambert
Captain R. G. F. Hickey
Captain N. T, Parsons
Lieutenant L. B. Magniac
Lieutenant J. W. Daniell
Lieutenant M. Hall
Lieutenant T. A. Butler, V.C.
Lieutenant N. H. Wallace
Lieutenant F. D. M. Brown. V.C
Lieutenant W. S. Jervis
Lieutenant W. H. Warner
Lieutenant J. C. Partridge
Lieutenant G. H. Holley
T. E. Harden

The following 15 out of 41 officers of the 2nd Bengal European Regiment volunteered for H.M. 104th Bengal Fusiliers:

Captain G. Gaynor
Captain J. Bleaymire
Captain W. D. Harris
Captain C. Clark
Captain D. W. Becher
Captain L. J. Trotter
Lieutenant A. Willes
Lieutenant G. A. Bishop
Lieutenant Sir A. K. Lake, Bart.
Lieutenant A. L. Douglas
Lieutenant T. A. Hunter
Lieutenant H. Spalding
Lieutenant H. Carter
Lieutenant W. H. Brind
Lieutenant H. P. Evans

Distinct reference has not been made to those European Regiments in the East India Company's service—both cavalry and infantry—which were hastily raised in England for service in Bengal in consequence of the Indian mutiny; for these regiments were in no way connected with the services of the Bengal European Regiment.

Owing to the immense interests at stake, and the vast numbers of individuals who were concerned, the process of amalgamation, commencing with the Royal Proclamation, November 1st, 1858, was not finally carried out until after a lapse of upwards of two years. During this interval serious complications arose, which, at one time, threatened to assume the form of a European mutiny.

The troops, with some show of justice, put forward a. claim to a "bounty" on transferring their services from the Company to the Crown; but on its having been announced that the "bounty" claimed was granted, all discontent disappeared, and the process of amalgama-

LIST OF THE FIRST OFFICERS OF H.M. 101st REGIMENT (ROYAL BENGAL FUSILIERS).

"PLASSEY," "BUXAR," "GUZERAT," "DEIG," "BHURTPORE,"
"AFGHANISTAN," "GHUZNEE," "FEROZSHAH," "SOBRAON,"
"PEGU," "DELHIE," "LUCKNOW."

RANK.	NAMES.	RANK.	NAMES.
Colonel	—	Lieutenant	Nelson Ellis.
Lieut.-Colonel	—	,,	G. S. Goad.
Major	A. Hume.	,,	H. H. Chapman.
,,	F. O. Salusbury.	,,	W. S. Jervis.
Captain	E. Brown (Bt. Mjr.)	,,	W. H. Warner.
,,	G. C. Lambert.	,,	J. C. Partridge.
,,	R. G. F. Hickey.	,,	M. C. Smith.
,,	N. T. Parsons.	,,	J. S. Bagshaw.
,,	C. M. L. Clark.	,,	A. Harrison.
,,	H. G. Delafosse (Bt. Major).	,,	C. W. Riggs.
,,	H. C. Moller.	,,	G. H. Holley.
,,	S. A. Hunter.	,,	J. E. Harden.
,,	L. B. Magniac.	Ensigns	C. Pakenham.
,,	J. W. Daniell.	,,	H. P. Airey.
,,	M. Hall.	,,	A. Peel.
,,	W. L. Louis.	,,	F. O. Fuller.
Lieutenant	T. A. Butler, V.C.	,,	R. H. A. Quinet.
,,	N. H. Wallace	,,	C. M. Stockley.
,,	F. D. M. Brown, V.C.	Quartermaster	E. Farrant.

Uniform, Scarlet. Facings, Blue.

LIST OF THE FIRST OFFICERS OF
H.M. 104TH REGIMENT (BENGAL FUSILIERS).

"Punjaub," "Chillianwallah," "Goozerat," "Pegu,"
"Delhie."

RANK.	NAMES.	RANK.	NAMES.
Colonel	—	Lieutenant	L. Smith.
Lieut.-Colonel	W. Birch.	,,	T. A. Hunter.
Major	G. Gaynor.	,,	C. Pigou.
,,	J. Bleaymire.	,,	T. H. Lewin.
Captain	W. D. Harris (Bt. Mj.)	,,	C. M. Boswell.
,,	J. J. Hockley.	,,	W. R. Birney.
,,	C. H. E. Græme.	,,	H. M. Evans.
,,	C. Clark.	,,	M. G. Taylor
,,	D. W. Becher.	,,	H. Spalding.
,,	J. Hind.	,,	T. J. Quin.
,,	L. J. Trotter.	,,	H. Carter.
,,	A. Willes.	,,	W. H. Brind.
,,	J. G. Campbell.	,,	H. P. Evans.
,,	G. A. Bishop.	Ensigns	H. F. Showers.
,,	F. J. Conway-Gordon	,,	R. C. Richardson.
,,	C. K. Mylne.	,,	M. F. Stokes.
Lieutenant	Sir. A. K. Lake, Bt.	,,	H. J. Woodward.
,,	A. L. Douglas.		

Uniform, Scarlet. Facings, Blue.

tion was peaceably effected. His Royal Highness the Field-Marshal Commanding-in-Chief then issued the following General Order:

> The General Commanding-in-Chief has received Her Majesty's commands to make known to the British army serving in India that the arrangements for consolidating the European forces of the Crown in that country have now been completed.
>
> His Royal Highness hails with satisfaction an event which he trusts may be conducive to the best interests of the Empire, whilst it will be of advantage to the troops whom it may concern.
>
> He feels persuaded that the glorious deeds of arms for which the line and local troops have been ever conspicuous will not be forgotten by them now that they are about to join one united army, and that the only feeling of rivalry which will henceforth exist between the various corps will be a high spirit of emulation as regards discipline and good conduct during peace, and of gallant bearing and devotion, should their services be hereafter called for in the field.
>
> In the name of the army, the Commander-in-Chief most heartily and cordially welcomes to the ranks of the general service of the Crown, the officers, non-commissioned officers, and soldiers of the local services of the three Presidencies in India.
>
> *George*
> General Commanding-in-Chief

Lieutenant-General A. B. Roberts, C.B., who had for many years commanded the Bengal European Regiment, was appointed its Colonel; and Lieutenant-Colonel (now Major-General) F. O. Salusbury, C.B., who had served in the Regiment since 1842, shortly afterwards assumed command of H.M. 101st Royal Bengal Fusiliers; and under this latter Officer the Regiment took a prominent part in the Umbeyla campaign, specially distinguishing itself on the 13th November, 1863, when, led by Colonel Salusbury, it carried at the point of the bayonet the "Craig's picket," a difficult position in the upper heights, which had fallen into the enemy's hands.[1] H.M. 101st Foot evinced throughout this campaign, the same courage, discipline, and efficiency for which, as the "Bengal European Regiment," it had ever been prominently distinguished.

On the 25th of February, 1862, new colours were presented to the Royal Bengal Fusiliers in substitution of the last colours of the

---

1. For a move detailed account of the Umbeyla campaign see Appendix F.

1st Bengal European Regiment (Light Infantry); which were handed over to the custody of the 101st Foot, by whom they were, on the 18th July, 1871, with all ceremony and reverence, deposited in Winchester Cathedral, where they now rest.

In July, 1881, a general change in the nomenclature of the regiments of the line took place; the 101st Royal Bengal Fusiliers becoming the 1st, and the 104th Bengal Fusiliers the 2nd, Battalion of "The Royal Minister Fusiliers." Thus history repeats itself; the 1st and 2nd Bengal European Regiments are again united under one designation, and although its new title bears no reference to the country or service in which these battalions gained such signal distinctions, we may rest assured that the "Royal Munster Fusiliers" will ever maintain the character for loyalty, discipline, and courage, inherited from its predecessor, the Bengal European Regiment.

Recapitulation

The History of the Bengal European Regiment; and How it Helped to Win India has been told; its triumphs and it's glories, its reverses and its failings, have all been faithfully recorded; its birth, infancy, and military maturity forming perhaps the most varied and extraordinary narrative of the career of any military body to be found in ancient or modern history.

The officers and soldiers composing the "Bengal European Battalion" entered upon their military duties far from their native land, and on arrival in India they found themselves embodied in the service of the East India Company, without the prestige, patronage, or support of their parental Government; their career embracing as varied records of military adventure, hardships, daring, and victory as can be found in Greek or Roman history. Embarked in their profession, they had to advance into and subdue vast provinces, and even kingdoms, supported by trained armies, enormous wealth, and unknown resources. Engaged in these campaigns, they had to endure heat greater than that of Parthia or Persia; to traverse swamps and forests at least equal to those described by Tacitus in Germania or Holland; it may safely be said that in the early part of their history they had scarce a better or safer base of operations than Cortes or Pizarro; and that, in fact, they carried this base with them, in their own self-reliance, fortitude, and courage; and had these attributes failed, then there was nothing left but night, dispersion, and death.

For many years of the East India Company's wars and conquests, the Bengal European Regiment, expanding at times into several battalions, formed the main strength of the small armies which conquered and annexed the vast provinces and kingdoms now forming the Presidency of Bengal; in whose fortunes, it may be said, rested the supremacy of British power and the foundation and consolidation of our Indian Empire, in Bengal. The achievements which led to this crowning result have been detailed in the preceding pages; but, in addition, we will take a panoramic view of the signal and glorious exploits of this Regiment.

Commencing with the defeat of native armies in Lower Bengal, they soon afterwards carried the British flag into the North-Western provinces of India; deposed and appointed the Nawabs of Bengal, brought the Nawab Vazir of Oude, and even the Mogul Emperor of Hindustan, as allies or suppliants into the British camp. In this career they confronted, defeated, and pursued the Marathas and the Rohillas; dictated the Government of the kingdom of Oude; and replaced upon his apparently lost throne the blind and persecuted Mogul Emperor. Thus far we have glanced at the services and conquests in which the Bengal European Regiment took part in the early days of its career as against the native powers; but, serious as were the dangers encountered and obstacles overcome, more serious and more dangerous were the wars in which the Regiment took part, against the French and the Dutch for the possession of Hindustan; skilled commanders, with well-disciplined armies, took the field against the British, either as opponents with native allies, or as subsidiary forces with native monarchs or pretenders.

These campaigns, in which the Bengal European Regiment took so prominent a part, finally swept away the fleur-de-lys of France and the tricolour of the Dutch from the plains and fortresses of India; and left England further unmolested by foreign interference, to pursue her career of dominion and civilization up to our own time.

But their victories were not confined to Bengal alone. Twice. under most critical circumstances, the Regiment went to the aid of the sister Presidency of Madras; and there, in two separate campaigns, vindicated the power and honour of the British arms against vastly superior numbers.

Then followed the battle and the storm of Deig, the disastrous first sieges of Bhurtpore, and the second Maratha and Pindarie Wars.

To these wars succeeded a comparatively long period of peace, during which were effected in the Regiment many improvements, in internal economy, impracticable during the turmoil of war and camp life.

At the second siege of Bhurtpore the 1st Bengal European Regiment, in this state of efficiency, took a prominent part in the operations under Combermere; the final siege and capture of this Fortress, which in 1805 had resisted our repeated assaults.

After this memorable campaign there again followed a period of cantonment life of thirteen years, until the outbreak of the Afghan War in 1839, when the Bengal European Regiment formed part of the British army of invasion under Sir John Keane; whose marches through deserts and passes, with the hardships endured, the assault and capture of the fortress of Ghuznee, and subjection of Cabul, have been fully detailed.

But a short interval of peace intervened for the 1st Bengal European Light Infantry up to the sudden invasion of our territory by the Seiks in 1845; the battles of Ferozeshah and Sobraon, with the details of exploits and terrible sacrifice of life, have been recorded, as well as the expressions of gratitude received from H.M. the Queen, the Parliament of England, the Commander-in-Chief, and the Government of India.

In 1852, the 1st European Bengal Fusiliers and the 2nd European Regiment traversed India from Meerut to Calcutta, to embark for Burmah, where they took prominent part in the operations which led to the defeat of the Burmese:, the capture of Rangoon, and the annexation of Pegu.

But four years of tranquillity until the outbreak of the great Indian mutiny—1857—in withstanding and subduing the storm of which both the 1st and 2nd Bengal Fusiliers took such distinguished parts, from Budlee-ka-Serai, on the 8th June, through the investment, storm, and capture of Delhie, up to the termination of the war, October, 1858; including many minor, and difficult operations.

The reader may probably have surmised that a regiment born under such rude circumstances, and amidst such untutored surroundings, brought up in the distraction of campaigns, battles, and sieges, and scarcely in communication with Europe, might have been defective in the performance of military duties, and careless in many of the requisite accessories of regimental training. Such, however, was by no means the case; for when these European Regiments were relegated to the British Crown, they were not in any military attribute or social organization, a whit inferior to any regiment in the British line, past or present.

Into that Line, on the 2nd May, 1861, passed the Bengal European Regiment, with its decorations and its services richly emblazoned, gloriously renowned, and brightly coloured with that impalpable halo called Glory—the glory of duty well performed.

Appendix A
Decorations

In the year 1828, the 1st Bengal European Regiment bore upon its colours the following decorations: "Plassey," "Rohilcund," "Mysore," "Deig," "Bhurtpore." The 2nd Bengal European Regiment bore upon its colours the same decorations, with the exception of "Bhurtpore," at the siege of which it was not present.

In the year 1830, these Regiments appear in the East India Register as bearing the decoration "Guzerat" in substitution for "Mysore," and in 1831 "Buxar" was substituted for "Rohilcund." At this time the 2nd Bengal European Regiment had become the left wing of the Bengal European Regiment.

Rohilcund.—The decoration "Rohilcund," was borne upon the colours of the Regiment in commemoration of the two Rohilla campaigns, 1774 and 1794, in both of which the old 2nd Bengal European Regiment served before it was absorbed into the 1st in 1803, when the latter inherited the decoration; and it is unaccountable why "Rohilcund" should subsequently have been withdrawn.

Mysore.—Although the Bengal European Regiment was not present at any action fought in "Mysore," it had rendered singularly distinguished services against Haidar Ali, the ruler of Mysore, when he invaded the Carnatic. Full details of this campaign have been recorded in chapter 11, and it appears highly probable that as no decoration—independent of medals—was, at the time, granted for the four years' campaign against Haidar Ali, that the word "Mysore" was subsequently placed on the colours of the Regiment for the same service; some of the Regiments of the Bengal native infantry bore the word "Carnatic" on their colours, but the decoration was not granted to H. M. 73rd,[1] the Bengal, or the Madras European Regiments, although

---
1. Afterwards the 71st Foot; now 1st Battalion Highland Light Infantry.

the last was allowed to wear the decoration "Sholingur." It is clear, then, that if the Bengal European Regiment did not bear either "Mysore" or "Carnatic" on its colours, it was entitled to "Sholingur," which was granted to the sister regiment of Madras for the same service, and inherited by the Royal Dublin Fusiliers.

Guzerat.—The decoration, "Guzerat," which is borne on the colours of the Royal Munster Fusiliers, and which was granted to the Bengal European Regiment in substitution of one of the decorations withdrawn, is in commemoration of the campaign in Guzerat in the Bombay Presidency, 1804-5. in the first Guzerat war, 1780, under General Goddard, no Bengal European soldiers were employed, and even had they served during that war no decoration was granted. In the second Guzerat campaign, 1804-5, under Colonel Murray, some of the Bengal native infantry regiments served; and the decoration "Guzerat" was granted to such regiments, but the Bengal European Regiment. was at this time fighting, under General Lake, at the battle and siege of Deig, and the unsuccessful assaults on Bhurtpore. The Regiment, not having been present during either of the campaigns in Guzerat, was not entitled to the decoration.

Whilst reviewing the subject of "Decorations," prominent reference must be made to "Condore" having been placed on the colours of the Madras European Regiment, and inherited by the Royal Dublin Fusiliers, in place of on those of the Bengal European Regiment, which was the only British regiment employed in the campaign in the Northern Circars, under Colonel Forde, during which the memorable battle of Condore and the celebrated siege of Mussulipatam were fought. It is a crying injustice to the Royal Munster Fusiliers that it should be denied the decoration, "Condore," to which it is clearly entitled.

The subject of the decorations to which the Royal Bengal Fusiliers are entitled was referred, in April, 1883, by Colonel Montagu Hall (then commanding the Regiment) to the horse guards. The correspondence was forwarded to the India Office for report. Lord Kimberley states that The Bengal European Regiment was present at the action of Condore, but the Madras European Regiment was not; and that, in his opinion, "Condore" should be placed on the colours of the Royal Munster Fusiliers. See Appendix B, and G.O., Commander-in-Chief in India, November 22nd, 1868; also Military Department, Fort St. George, September, 1877, &c.

The decorations to which The Royal Munster Fusiliers, as successor to the 1st and 2nd Bengal European Regiments, is entitled, are as follows: "Plassey," "Condore," "Buxar," "Rohilcund," "Sholingur," "Deig," "Bhurtpore," "Afghanistan," "Ghuznee," "Ferozeshah," "Sobraon," "Punjaub," "Chillianwallah," "Goozerat," "Pegu," "Delhi," "Lucknow."

APPENDIX B

Governor-General's Tribute to H.M. 101st Royal Bengal Fusiliers

Headquarters
November 2nd. 1868
The Commander-in-Chief in India has great satisfaction in publishing the Right Honourable the Governor-General's order, No. 1010, of October 30th, 1868, in favour of the 101st Royal Bengal Fusiliers.

As shown by this order, the record of this Regiment contains the history of the advance of the British arms from Calcutta to the Indus, and includes many campaigns beyond the limit of India.

It is with a feeling of no ordinary gratification that His Excellency is able to assure the 101st Foot, when bidding the corps farewell, that in point of order, discipline, and efficiency the Regiment, as now organized, is well worthy of its glorious history.

No. 1010, dated October 30th, 1868. The 101st Royal Bengal Fusiliers being about to proceed to England, His Excellency the Viceroy and Governor-General in Council cannot allow this Regiment, the nucleus of which has existed in this Presidency, in some shape or another, for more than 200 years, and which has been formed as a Regiment, expanding at times into several battalions, for 112 years, to take its departure without expressing in the strongest terms the appreciation of the Government of India of its most valuable and distinguished services.

Successively as the Bengal European Regiment, the 1st European Regiment, the 1st European Light Infantry, and the 1st Bengal European Fusiliers, the Regiment served the Honourable the East India Company for more than 100 years; and besides being actively engaged in nearly every part of its own Presidency, was detached to the Northern Circars of the Madras Presidency in 1758, and has subsequently served out of Bengal, in the Carnatic, in Java, in the Island of Celebes, in Afghanistan from Ghuznee in one direction to Pushoot on the borders of Koonur in another, and in Burmah.

The distinguished conduct of the Regiment in the field as the senior battalion of infantry of the Bengal army was proverbial; and its colours are covered with the names of operations in which it bore a prominent part. Some are not thus recorded, but the following list includes the more important of the campaigns, battles and sieges in which the Regiment has been engaged:—

Defence of fort William, against Suraj-o'-daulah in 1756, when four companies, of which the corps was composed, were almost annihilated,

Capture of the fort of Budge Budge, recapture of Calcutta, battle of Chitpore, siege and capture of Chandernagore, capture of the fort of Kutwah, and battle of Plassey, 1756-1757.

Campaign against the French in the Northern Circars, in 1759, including the battle of Condore, and the siege and capture of Musulipatam.

Defeat of the Dutch force at Bedarrah, 1759.

Campaign against the Emperor of Delhie 1760-61, including the battles of Seerpore, Beerpore, and Suan, in which latter the French mercenaries were defeated, and their leader, the celebrated M. Law, taken prisoner.

War against the Meer Kassim, ex-Nawab of Murshedabad, 1768-66, and present at the battle of Manjee, near Patna, where four Companies were overwhelmed and destroyed after a gallant resistance, battle of Kutwah, capture of Murshedabad, battle of Gheriah, storm of the lines of Oodwah nullah, capture of Monghyr, siege and storm of Patna, action near Patna, May 3rd, 1764, battle of Buxar, assault of Chunar, and battle of Kalpee.

In 1774, in the 1st Rohilla campaign, under Colonel Champion, including the decisive action on St. George's Day of that year, when Hafiz Kehmut was killed; four Companies employed against Hyder Alice in the Carnatic from 1780-83, and present at the relief of Wandiwash, battles of Porto Novo, Polilore, Solinghur, Veracundalore, relief of Vellore, battle of Arnee, and siege of Cuddalore.

Again employed in the second Rohilla war, under Major-General Sir Robert Abercrombie, and suffered severely at the battle of Bittoorah, on the 26th October, 1794.

In Lord Lake's campaign against the Maharattas in 1804-5, at the battle of Deig, siege and storm of Deig, and the first siege of Bhurtpore.

In Java, from 1812-15, and in the Island of Celebes in 1816, a detachment employed in the Terai during part of the Nepaul war, and two companies employed against the Pindaries, in 1817-18.

The right wing of the Regiment at the siege and capture of Bhurtpore, 1826, and engaged in the assault.

Joined the army of the Indus in November, 1838, and served during the first campaign in Afghanistan, 1839-44, and prominently engaged in the storm of Ghuznie, a detachment was employed at the attack on the fort of Pushoot, in January, 1840.

On the Seiks crossing the Sutledge, in December, 1845, the Regiment moved from the hills by rapid forced marches, and was engaged at the battles of Ferozeshah and Sobraon, losing 20 officers and 392 men, killed and wounded.

Engaged in the Burmese war, 1852, 53, and present at the recapture of Pegu, relief of the Pegu garrison, and subsequent operations in the vicinity of that place.

In May, 1857, on the outbreak of the Indian mutiny, moved with great rapidity, notwithstanding the great heat, to Umballa, and thence marched to Delhie, was one of the four regiments of British infantry that served throughout the siege of that place, from the action of Budlee ka. Serai, on the 8th June, 1857, to the final capture of the city on the 20th September, and was repeatedly distinguished specially in the assault, where it formed part of the column led by Brigadier-General John Nicholson. The Regiment lost 14 officers and 305 men, killed and wounded, at Delhie. Served subsequently during the latter part of 1857 and in 1858, at the action of Narnoul, Gungeree, Pattiallee and Mynporie, at the siege and capture of Lucknow, and in various minor affairs in Oude

These services, which can hardly be surpassed by those of any regiment in existence, were rendered when the corps belonged to the army of the Honourable East India Company.

In 1861, the Regiment became H.M. 101st Royal Bengal Fusiliers. and since then as one of H.M. Regiments of the line was employed in the operations at Umbeyla in October, November, and December, 1863, and well maintained its precious reputation in the various struggles with a brave foe throughout that arduous service.

The 101st Regiment now proceeds to England for the first time of home service, and it leaves India full of honour, and with a reputation for discipline and efficiency, as the Governor-General in Council is assured by H.E. the Commander-in-Chief, quite worthy of its character for gallantry and endurance.

The Governor-General in Council is convinced that, wherever the 101st Regiment goes, it will maintain its ancient renown, and H.E. in Council desires to assure the Regiment that the Government in India is proud to send such a corps to take its place in England with the battalions of Her Most Gracious Majesty there stationed.

By order of H.E. the Commander-in-Chief,

H. E. Longden
Colonel
Adjutant-General

Appendix C
Notification

Fort William
Foreign Department
30th June, 1853

In the proclamation by which the province of Pegu was annexed to the British dominions in the East, the Governor-General in Council declared that he desired no further conquest in Burmah, and was willing to consent that hostilities should cease. Thereafter the Burman troops were everywhere withdrawn. The King was dethroned by his brother, the Mengdoon Prince, and an envoy was sent from Aven to sue for peace. The Burman envoy, confessing their inability to resist the power of the British Government and submissively soliciting its forbearance, announced its willingness to sign a treaty in accordance with the proclamation, objecting only to the frontier being placed at Meaday. The Government of India, while it maintained its un-doubtful right to fix the frontier where it had been placed, at the same time gave signal proof of the sincerity of its desire for the renewal of friendly relations between the states; for, in the hope of at once concluding a treaty of peace, the Governor-General in Council consented to withdraw the frontier from Meaday, and to place it in strict conformity to the most liberal wording of the proclamation, immediately to the northward of Prome and Toungoo cities, which have been described at all times as within the northern limits of Pegu, in the official records of transactions between the two states.

But when this concession was offered, the Burman envoy, wholly receding from his previous declarations, refused to assent to any treaty by which a cession of territory should be made. Thereupon the negotiations were at once broken off, the frontier of the British territories was finally fixed to the northward of Meaday and Toungoo, and the envoy was directed to quit the camp.

The envoy proceeded to the capital, whence he has now conveyed to the Government of India the sentiments and proposals of the Court of Ava.

The King expresses his desire for the cessation of war. The King announces that orders have been issued to the Governors of the districts not to allow the Burmese troops to attack the territories of Meaday and Toungoo, in which the British Government have placed their garrisons. Furthermore, the King has set at liberty the British subjects who had been carried prisoners to Aven; and he has expressed his wish that the merchants and people of both countries should be allowed, in accordance with former friendship, to pass up and down the river for the purpose of trading. Mindful of the assurance he gave that hostilities would not be resumed so long as the Court of Ava refrained from disputing our quiet possession of the province of Pegu, the Governor-General in Council is willing to accept the pacific declarations and acts of the King as a substantial proof of his acquiescence in the proposed conditions of peace, although a formal treaty has not been concluded. Wherefore the Governor-General in Council permits the raising of the river blockade, consenting to the renewal of former intercourse with Ava, and now proclaims the restoration of peace. The army of Ava will no longer be maintained on a war establishment. At the same time, a force will be permanently retained in Pegu, adequate for its defence and fully prepared for the event of war. The Governor-General in Council, while he announced the successive events of the war has gladly seized each fitting occasion for bestowing promptly on the several officers whose services were mentioned with distinction, the cordial thanks and approbation of the Government of India. His Lordship in Council deems it unnecessary now to repeat in detail acknowledgements of individual merit that are still so recent; but he cannot close the record of this war without again conveying to the services generally an assurance of the admiration with which he has viewed the combined exertions, which under God's good providence, the supremacy of our power in the east has once more been asserted and upheld, (here follows the thanks of the Government to individual officers).

In testimony of the sense that is entertained of the services and conduct of the combined force, the Governor-General in Council is pleased to direct that a donation of six months batta shall be issued to all the officers, non-commissioned officers and men of the several naval and military forces that have been employed during the progress of the war with Burma. And it shall be the further care of the Governor-General in Council to bring their services and conduct under the special notice, and to commend them to the most favourable consideration of Her Majesty's Government, and of the Honourable Court of Directors.

By Order,
(Signed) *J. P. Grant*
Official Secretary to the Government of India

Appendix D
Proclamation

Victoria, by the Grace of God, of the United Kingdom of Great Britain and Ireland, and of the colonies and dependencies thereof in Europe, Asia, Africa, America, and Australia, Queen, Defender of the Faith.

Whereas, for diverse weighty reasons, we have resolved, by and with the advice and consent of the Lords Spiritual and Temporal, and Commons in Parliament assembled, to take upon ourselves the Government of the territories of India, heretofore administered in trust for us by the Honourable East India Company. Now, therefore, we do by these presents notify and declare that by the advice and consent aforesaid, we have taken upon ourselves the said Government, and we hereby call upon all our subjects within the said territories to be faithful, and to bear true allegiance to us, our heirs, and successors, and to submit themselves to the authority of those whom we may hereafter from time to time see fit to appoint to administer the Government of our said territories in our name and on our behalf.'

And we, reposing especial trust and confidence in the loyalty, ability, and judgement of our right trusty and well-beloved cousin and councillor Charles John Viscount Canning, do hereby constitute and appoint him, the said Viscount Canning to be our First Viceroy and Governor-General in and over our said territories, and to administer the Government thereof in our name, and generally to act in our name and on our behalf, subject to such orders and regulations as he shall, from time to time, receive from us through one of our principal Secretaries of State.

And, we hereby confirm in their several offices, civil and military, all persons now employed in the service of the Honourable East India Company, subject to our future pleasure, and to such laws and regulations as may hereafter be enacted.

We hereby announce to the native Princes of India that all treaties and engagements made with them by, or under the authority of, the Honourable East India Company are by us accepted and will be scrupulously maintained; and we look for the like observance on their part.

We desire no extension of our present territorial possessions; and while we will permit no aggression upon our dominions or our rights to be attempted with impunity, we shall sanction no encroachment on those of others. We shall respect the rights, dignity, and honour of the native princes as our own, and we desire that they, as well as our own subjects, should enjoy that prosperity and that social advancement which can only be secured by internal peace and good Government.

We hold ourselves bound to the natives of our Indian territories by the same obligations of duty which bind us to all our other subjects; and those obligations, by the blessing of Almighty God, we shall faithfully and conscientiously fulfil.

Firmly relying ourselves on the truth of Christianity, and acknowledging with gratitude the solace of religion, we disclaim alike the right and the desire to impose our convictions on any of our subjects. We declare it to be our Royal will and pleasure that none be in any wise favoured, none molested or disquieted, by reason of their religious faith or observances, but that all shall alike enjoy the equal and impartial protection of the law; and we do strictly charge and enjoin all those who may be in authority under us that they abstain from all interference with the religious belief or worship of any of our subjects on pain of our highest displeasure.

And it is further our will that, so far as may be, our subjects, of whatever race or creed, be freely and impartially admitted to offices in our service, the duties of which they may be qualified, by their education, ability, and integrity, duly to discharge.

We know and respect the feelings of attachment with which the natives of India regard the lands inherited by them from their ancestors, and we desire to protect them in all rights connected therewith, subject to the equitable demands of the state; and we will that, generally, in framing and administering the law. due regard be paid to the ancient rights, usages and customs of India.

We deeply lament the evils and misery which have been brought upon India by the acts of ambitious men, who have deceived their countrymen by false reports, and led them into open rebellion. Our power has been shown by the suppression of that rebellion in the field;

we desire to show our mercy by pardoning the offences of those who have been thus misled, but who desire to return to the path of duty.

Already, in one province, with the view to stop the further effusion of blood, and to hasten the pacification of our Indian dominions, our Viceroy and Governor-General has held out the expectation of pardon, on certain terms, to the great majority of those who, in the late unhappy disturbances, have been guilty of offences against our Government, and has declared the punishment which will be inflicted on those whose crimes place them beyond the reach of forgiveness. We approve and confirm the said act of our Viceroy and Governor-General, and do further announce and proclaim as follows:—

Our clemency will be extended to all offenders, save and except those who have been or shall be convicted of having directly taken part in the murder of British subjects.

With regard to such, the demands of justice forbid the exercise of mercy. To those who have willingly given asylum to murderers, knowing them to be such, or who may have acted as leaders or instigators in revolt, their lives alone can be guaranteed; but in appointing the penalty due to such persons, full consideration will be given to the circumstances under which they have been induced to throw off their allegiance, and large indulgence will be shown to those whose crimes may appear to have originated in a too credulous acceptance of the false reports circulated by designing men. To all others in arms against the Government, we hereby promise unconditional pardon, amnesty, and oblivion of all offences against ourselves, our Crown and dignity, on their return to their homes and peaceful pursuits. It is our Royal pleasure that these terms of grace and amnesty should be extended to all those who comply with these conditions before the first day of January next.

When, by the blessing of providence, internal tranquillity shall be restored, it is our earnest desire to stimulate the peaceful industry of India, to promote works of public utility and improvement, and to administer it's Government for the benefit of all our subjects resident therein. In their prosperity will be our strength: in their contentment, our security; and in their gratitude, our best reward. And may the God of all power grant unto us, and to those in authority under us, strength to carry out these our wishes for the good of our people.

Proclamation dated November 1st, 1858.

Appendix E
Extract Official Papers

Fort William Military Depot
April 10th, 1861

11—Despatch 28. paras. 10,11, 17, 23, 26. It is desired by H.M.'s Government to maintain as integral Regiments, the three oldest European Regiments of the Bengal presidency, and all of the three regiments of the Madras and Bombay presidencies are to keep the men who are in each of these corps, and who may volunteer for H.M.'s general service in the regiments, which, when transferred to the line, will represent those to which they now respectively belong.

13—H.M. having graciously determined to mark her estimation of the services of her Indian Armies, by conferring the distinction of 'Royal' upon three of the European Regiments, and by selecting for this honour one regiment from each presidency, the selection of which has been left by H.M. to the judgement and discretion of the Governor-General of India, the Viceroy and Governor-General in Council has much gratification in announcing that the following regiments will henceforward bear the honourable designation of 'Royal Regiments':—

The 1st Bengal Fusiliers,
The 1st Madras Fusiliers,
The 1st Bombay Fusiliers.

14—The three older regiments in the several presidencies will thus be converted into regiments in H.M. general army, and will be renumbered and designated as follows:—

The 101st Regiment of Foot (Royal Bengal Fusiliers),
The 102nd Regiment of Foot (Royal Madras Fusiliers),
The 103rd Regiment of Foot (Royal Bombay Fusiliers),
The 104th Regiment of Foot (Bengal Fusiliers),

The 105th Regiment of Foot (Madras Light Infantry),
The 106th Regiment of Foot (Bombay Light Infantry),
The 107th Regiment of Foot (Bengal Infantry),
The 108th Regiment of Foot (Madras Infantry),
The 109th Regiment of Foot (Bombay Infantry).

15—Despatch 28, paras. 17, 23-26. The corps transferred to H.M. service will retain all honorary distinctions which they have won. These will be borne on appointments and colours, or in the army list, in such manner as H.M. Government may think best suited to the arm of the service to which the corps belong.

21—The immediate issue of bounty to men volunteering is hereby authorized on their making the declaration appended to this G.O. before a justice of the peace or magistrate.

Appendix F

The Umbeyla Campaign

The following is an account of the services of H.M. 101st Royal Bengal Fusiliers whilst employed in the Umbeyla campaign, 1863:—

In August, 1863, rumours were current of the disturbed state of our relations with some of the frontier hill tribes in connection with the colony of fanatics at Litana and Mulkol. and also of the uneasy feeling existing amongst the hill tribes in Hayara; it was therefore determined to send the 101st Regiment into the Hayara hills, partly as a demonstration, and partly for the recovery of the men's health, which, though it had gradually improved since their arrival at Rawul Pinder, was still very unsatisfactory. The regiment took up quarters at Abbottaba, and on the 4th October orders were received from Sir Neville Chamberlain, K.C.B., commanding in Hayara, for the regiment to move across the Indus to a place in Ensufyze called Swabage, and it was further directed that the regiment must be at that place by the 14th of October, which was effected, although the marches were very difficult. It was well known that whatever service was to be performed the 101st would share in it, and the young soldiers, for with very few exceptions the whole of the regiment was comprised of very young soldiers, and had never seen service, burned with ardour for their maiden fight, and remembering the gallant deeds of the old regiment were eager to have their first brush with the enemy under the new colours of the 101st. After a halt of a few days the camp was broken up, and the force destined to enter the hills assembled on the 18th of October, In addition to the 101st there were the splendid 71st Highlanders, under the command of Colonel Hope, C.B., some Royal artillery, and numerous (though weak) native corps. On the 20th of October the Ensufyze field Force (as it was now designated) entered the hills under the personal command of Sir Neville Chamberlain by the Umbeyla Pass, leading from Ensufyze into the Chumla valley. The force arrived at the fort of the pass after a most fatiguing march. The enemy were quite taken by surprise, or otherwise the pass could not have been forced without much labour and very severe loss, in consequence of the natural difficulties and many splendid opportunities offered for defence, there being on each side, within gunshot, hills which were almost inaccessible. The pass itself was filled with dense jungle and enormous stones, an immense water-course running down the centre. The troops could only move in single file. At first there were no signs of the enemy, but after the first three days they appeared in vast numbers and lost no opportunity of attacking the position of the British troops. The duties imposed on our troops were very severe indeed, far harder than usually fall to the lot of soldiers; for nearly four weeks the men never had their accoutrements off, save for the purpose of washing, and for five weeks no tents were pitched, the men lying on the bare ground without a covering of any kind. On the 18th of November, the 101st, led by Lieutenant-Colonel Salusbury, carried a position in the upper heights on the right defence called the Crag picquet, which had fallen into the hands of the enemy, and which so long as they held it commanded our upper camp entirely. The loss to the 101st was 5 killed and 26 wounded, and the Regiment received the thanks of the General Commanding for this exploit. On the 18th of November the General changed his position on the left heights and established himself on the right heights. The enemy then made several attacks, and inflicted considerable loss on the British forces. Amongst those killed was Lieutenant Chapman, Adjutant of the 101st. Lieutenant Chapman was as gallant and noble a soldier as ever wore the British uniform, and although he was mortally wounded, he knelt down beside Captain .Smith, of the 71st, who had been badly shot, and began to dress his wounds. He refused to be carried away, as he said it was useless, he being mortally wounded, but he urged the removal of Captain Smith. In the meantime the enemy made a desperate rush, and both these officers fell into their hands and were hacked to pieces, their heads being cut off and their bodies shockingly mangled. In Lieutenant Chapman the 101st lost an officer of rare ability, of untiring energy, the perfect type of an English gentleman and a British officer. On the 20th of November the enemy made a most vigorous assault on the British position, particularly against the Crag picquet, which was partly comprised of men from the 101st Regiment. This was attacked by overwhelming numbers and finally overpowered; the

101st lost two officers and eleven men killed and 25 wounded. The two Officers killed were Ensign Algernon Sanderson and Assistant-Surgeon Pill, both of whom behaved with marked gallantry. On this day General Chamberlain was wounded, and the 71st (led by Colonel Hope, C.B., who was also wounded) lost several men. About the 6th of November the British forces received some reinforcements, amongst them the 7th Royal Fusiliers and the 93rd Highlanders, half a battery of Royal artillery, with two or three native regiments, bringing the strength up to nearly 9,000 men. General Garvock, commanding the Peshawur division also arrived to relieve General Chamberlain of the command. On the 15th the enemy's position was attacked, and the forces were divided into two divisions of 2,500 each, the remaining 4,000 being left in charge of the camp. The 101st behaved with great gallantry. Nothing could resist the daring advance of the Regiment, and the men did not stop until the prize was theirs. In the assault only one was killed and 13 wounded. Other engagements took place, the 101st rendering valuable service. The men experienced great hardships, having to lie on the bare ground with only a blanket to protect them from the rain. After a treaty had been concluded, the brigade to which the 101st was attached destroyed several villages occupied by the fanatics, the brigade encamping again at Ensufyze on the 1st of January, 1864. The brigade was then broken up, and the 101st left on its way back to quarters at Rawul Pinder, having in the campaign lost 87 officers and men, killed and wounded. The Officers wounded were Lieutenant C. Rigge and Ensign C. Stockley. Brigadier Wilde, C.B., who commanded the brigade of which the 101st formed part, conveyed to Lieutenant-Colonel Salusbury and the officers and men by general order the high appreciation he entertained of the cheerful, high-spirited, willing, and soldier-like manner in which all duties had been performed and all hardships borne by the Regiment. Twice the Regiment did good service under his command, first in retaking the Crag picquet on the 13th of November, and secondly in storming the conical hill on the 15th of December, 1863. Colonel Wilde testified to both officers and men having faithfully done their duty with credit to themselves and honour to their Regiment. The 101st marched into Rawul Pinder on the 11th of January, 1864, and left on the 20th of December for Dugshai. On their departure a general order was issued by Brigadier-General A. Tucker, C.B., expressing the high estimation in which he held this distinguished Regiment, and his deep regret at its departure from under his command. He also spoke of the exemplary conduct of the men, which he said reflected the highest credit on Lieutenant-Colonel Salusbury and the officers. The Brigadier went on to say that when detached from his brigade to join the force assembling on the frontiers, their cheerful alacrity in meeting and overcoming all difficulties, their gallant bearing and their indomitable pluck when brought hand to hand with the enemy was notorious, and it was with peculiar gratification that he (the Brigadier-General) had placed on the breasts of so many soldiers of this gallant Regiment the medal bestowed on them by Her Majesty for 'distinguished service in the field.' Gallantly had the 101st, in the recent campaign, maintained the fame of the old 1st Bengal Fusiliers, whose various victories they bear inscribed upon their present colours.

Appendix G
Letter

Extract of letter from Lieutenant-Colonel Douglas Seaton to Captain Biddulph, regarding the services of Surgeon-Major J. P. Brougham.

There is one officer who has been recently moved from the Regiment to superior employ, whose great services I desire to bring prominently to notice. Surgeon J. P. Brougham, M.D., is the Officer I allude to; it is impossible to speak too highly of the professional services of Dr. Brougham, no praise of mine can be too great for all he has done for the officers and soldiers of this Regiment as its Surgeon to Delhi, and from the day of its march from Dugshai until he was appointed Field Surgeon in September last, his exertions have been unwearied, unremitting, and invaluable, the large number of wounded men, the numerous cases of amputation, the remarkable success which attended all his operations, are well-known. I only allude to them to recall them to notice. Let me mention that most unfortunate circumstances have alone prevented the eminent services of Surgeon Brougham being brought forward to notice, indeed, he with others have suffered much by the following contingencies:

Colonel Welshman, severely wounded at Delhi, sent away invalided, unable to write a despatch.

Major Jacob, killed at Delhi, no despatch from him.

Colonel H. P Burn, Lieutenant-Colonel Dunsford, Captain Caulfield, held command for too short a period to warrant their bringing officers' services to notice.

Colonel Gerrard, killed at Narroul, no despatch.

Brigadier Sir F. Seaton, in command for six weeks, too actively employed to be able to review the services of the Regiment.

Captains Cunliffe and Hume and Major Denniss, all on command for short periods, and as temporary Commandants, did not feel themselves justified in noticing the past conduct of their officers without being especially called upon to do so.

May I, therefore, avail myself of the opening now offered me, and solicit General Sir Hope Grant's recommendation of this most excellent and highly-deserving Officer. I believe that the whole Regiment would be greatly gratified to see that much-respected medical adviser and friend awarded. So impressed am I from all I have been told of the value of Dr. Brougham's services, I believe I am only doing him simply justice in bringing his services to notice at this particular time. I believe the General knows quite sufficient of Dr. Brougham to accept with kindly consideration this appeal on his behalf.

ALSO FROM LEONAUR
AVAILABLE IN SOFTCOVER OR HARDCOVER WITH DUST JACKET

WAR BEYOND THE DRAGON PAGODA by *J. J. Snodgrass*—A Personal Narrative of the First Anglo-Burmese War 1824 - 1826.

ALL FOR A SHILLING A DAY by *Donald F. Featherstone*—The story of H.M. 16th, the Queen's Lancers During the first Sikh War 1845-1846.

AT THEM WITH THE BAYONET by *Donald F. Featherstone*—The first Anglo-Sikh War 1845-1846.

A LEONAUR ORIGINAL

THE HERO OF ALIWAL by *James Humphries*—The days when young Harry Smith wore the green jacket of the 95th-Wellington's famous riflemen-campaigning in Spain against Napoleon's French with his beautiful young bride Juana have long gone. Now, Sir Harry Smith is in his fifties approaching the end of a long career. His position in the Cape colony ends with an appointment as Deputy Adjutant-General to the army in India. There he joins the staff of Sir Hugh Gough to experience an Indian battlefield in the Gwalior War of 1843 as the power of the Marathas is finally crushed. Smith has little time for his superior's 'bull at a gate' style of battlefield tactics, but independent command is denied him. Little does he realise that the greatest opportunity of his military life is close at hand.

THE GURKHA WAR by *H. T. Prinsep*—The Anglo-Nepalese Conflict in North East India 1814-1816.

SOUND ADVANCE! by *Joseph Anderson*—Experiences of an officer of HM 50th regiment in Australia, Burma & the Gwalior war.

THE CAMPAIGN OF THE INDUS by *Thomas Holdsworth*—Experiences of a British Officer of the 2nd (Queen's Royal) Regiment in the Campaign to Place Shah Shuja on the Throne of Afghanistan 1838 - 1840.

WITH THE MADRAS EUROPEAN REGIMENT IN BURMA by *John Butler*—The Experiences of an Officer of the Honourable East India Company's Army During the First Anglo-Burmese War 1824 - 1826.

BESIEGED IN LUCKNOW by *Martin Richard Gubbins*—The Experiences of the Defender of 'Gubbins Post' before & during the sige of the residency at Lucknow, Indian Mutiny, 1857.

THE STORY OF THE GUIDES by *G.J. Younghusband*—The Exploits of the famous Indian Army Regiment from the northwest frontier 1847 - 1900.

AVAILABLE ONLINE AT
www.leonaur.com
AND OTHER GOOD BOOK STORES

www.ingramcontent.com/pod-product-compliance
Lightning Source LLC
Chambersburg PA
CBHW020939230426
43666CB00005B/81